THE HUMAN FACTOR

T0055089

THE HUMAN FACTOR

Gorbachev, Reagan, and Thatcher, and the end of the Cold War

ARCHIE BROWN

OXFORD
UNIVERSITY PRESS

OXFORD
UNIVERSITY PRESS

Oxford University Press is a department of the University of Oxford.
It furthers the University's objective of excellence in research, scholarship,
and education by publishing worldwide. Oxford is a registered trade mark of
Oxford University Press in the UK and in certain other countries

Published in the United States of America by Oxford University Press
198 Madison Avenue, New York, NY 10016, United States of America.

A copy of this book's Cataloging-in-Publication
Data is on file with the Library of Congress.

ISBN 978–0–19–061489–8 (Hbk.)
ISBN 978–0–19–763509–4 (Pbk.)

1 3 5 7 9 8 6 4 2
Printed by Lakeside Book Company, United States of America

CONTENTS

Illustrations   vii
Abbreviations and Glossary   ix
Note on Terms and Transliteration   xi

Introduction   1

PART I

1. The Cold War and Its Dangers   9

2. The Making of Mikhail Gorbachev   31

3. Gorbachev's Widening Horizons   43

4. The Rise of Ronald Reagan   58

5. Reagan's First Term   70

6. Margaret Thatcher: The Moulding of the 'Iron Lady'   90

7. Thatcher and the Turn to Engagement with Communist Europe 113

PART II

8. Breaking the Ice (1985)   131

9. Nuclear Fallout: Chernobyl and Reykjavik (1986)   154

10. Building Trust (1987)   187

11. The End of the Ideological Divide (1988)   218

12. The End of the Cold War (1989)   247

13. Why the Cold War Ended When It Did   289

PART III

14. Unintended Consequences (1990)   313

15. Final Year—of the USSR and of Gorbachev's Power (1991)   343

16. Political Leadership and the End of the Cold War:
Concluding Reflections   378

Notes   403
Acknowledgements   475
Picture Credits   479
Index   480

ILLUSTRATIONS

1. Secretary for Defense Caspar Weinberger, President Reagan, and
   Secretary of State Alexander Haig, August 1981.   52
2. Ronald Reagan and Margaret Thatcher at White House welcoming
   ceremony for Prime Minister Thatcher, February 1981.   77
3. Mikhail Gorbachev's first meeting with Margaret Thatcher, Chequers,
   December 1984.   89
4. Geoffrey Howe, Margaret Thatcher, Michael Heseltine, and Robin
   Butler (private secretary to the prime minister).   99
5. An early meeting between Eduard Shevardnadze and George Shultz,
   with Pavel Palazchenko interpreting and Ronald Reagan observing.   139
6. Reagan with National Security Adviser Robert (Bud) McFarlane and
   White House Chief of Staff Donald Regan aboard Air Force One, July 1985.   144
7. Reagan makes clear to Gorbachev his disappointment at the end of the
   October 1986 Reykjavik summit.   174
8. Margaret Thatcher, who made a big impression during her 1987 visit to
   the Soviet Union, being greeted warmly in Soviet Georgia.   196
9. Gorbachev with his two most influential aides, Anatoly Chernyaev
   and Georgy Shakhnazarov.   199
10. Gorbachev and Reagan, each holding copies of the INF Treaty, at the
    December 1987 Washington summit.   215
11. In Moscow's Red Square during the American president's 1988 visit,
    Gorbachev lifts a small child from his mother's arms and asks him to
    'shake hands with Grandpa (*dedushka*) Reagan'.   227
12. Gorbachev making his ground-breaking speech to the United Nations
    in New York, 7 December 1988.   242
13. Vladimir Kryuchkov in conversation with Aleksandr Yakovlev.   244
14. Eduard Shevardnadze with new US Secretary of State James Baker,
    10 May 1989 (Baker's first visit to Russia).   254
15. Soviet Defence Minister Marshal Dmitry Yazov, US Secretary of
    Defense Frank Carlucci, and Soviet Chief of the General Staff Marshal
    Sergey Akhromeyev: Moscow, May 1988.   268
16. Mikhail Gorbachev with his favourite foreign leader, Spanish Prime
    Minister Felipe González: Madrid, October 1990.   274

17. Raisa Gorbachev, Polish President Wojciech Jaruzelski, Mikhail
Gorbachev, and Barbara Jaruzelski in Kremlin, April 1990.   277
18. Young people from East and West Berlin clambering on to the Berlin
Wall after it was breached with impunity in November 1989.   279
19. Gorbachev with French President François Mitterrand during
Gorbachev's visit to Paris, October 1985.   323
20. A break in the Gorbachev–Kohl discussions on German unification in
the southern Russian village, Arkhyz, July 1990.   329
21. Margaret Thatcher and President George H. W. Bush at 10 Downing
Street, July 1990.   334
22. Gorbachev in conversation with Bush at 1991 summit at Novo-
Ogarevo (near Moscow), July 1991.   355
23. Margaret Thatcher and Mikhail Gorbachev in 1989.   358

ABBREVIATIONS AND GLOSSARY

ABM Treaty	Anti-Ballistic Missile Treaty
ANC	African National Congress
BBC SWB	British Broadcasting Corporation Summary of World Broadcasts
CC	Central Committee [of Communist Party]
CFE	Conventional Forces in Europe
CIA	Central Intelligence Agency (US foreign intelligence service)
CIS	Commonwealth of Independent States
CMEA	Council for Mutual Economic Assistance (of USSR and Eastern Europe, known in the West as Comecon)
COCOM	Coordinating Committee for Multilateral Export Controls
CPS	Centre for Policy Studies (UK)
CPSU	Communist Party of the Soviet Union
CSCE	Conference on Security and Co-operation in Europe
FBI	Federal Bureau of Investigation (US domestic intelligence and security organization)
FBIS	Foreign Broadcast Information Service (USA)
FCO	Foreign and Commonwealth Office (UK) [also FO, Foreign Office]
FOI	Freedom of Information (Act, UK)
FRG	Federal German Republic (West Germany, prior to German unification, and united Germany today)
GCHQ	Government Communications Headquarters (UK government intelligence-gathering organization)
GDR	German Democratic Republic (East Germany when under Communist rule)
glasnost	transparency, openness
Gosplan	State Planning Committee of USSR
HIA	Hoover Institution Archives (Stanford, California)
ICBM	intercontinental ballistic missile
ID	International Department (of the Central Committee of the CPSU)
IMEMO	Institute of World Economy and International Relations
INF	intermediate-range nuclear forces
institutchiki	researchers in academic, especially policy-related, institutes
KGB	*Komitet gusudarstvennoy bezopastnosti* (Committee of State Security)
MAD	Mutually Assured Destruction

memcom	memorandum of conversation
mezhdunarodniki	Soviet specialists on international affairs
MFA	Ministry of Foreign Affairs (USSR)
MI6	common name for UK Secret Intelligence Service (SIS)
MIRV	Multiple Independently Targeted Re-Entry Vehicle
NKVD	*Narodnyy komissariat vnutrennikh del* (People's Commissariat of Internal Affairs, a forerunner of the KGB)
NATO	North Atlantic Treaty Organization
NIE	National Intelligence Estimate (USA)
NSA	National Security Agency (US Department of Defense)
NSA (GWU)	National Security Archive (George Washington University)
NSC	National Security Council (USA)
OSCE	Organization for Security and Co-operation in Europe (formerly CSCE)
perestroika	reconstruction; and the name for the period (1985–91) when Mikhail Gorbachev was Soviet leader
PCI	*Partito Comunista Italiano* (Italian Communist Party)
RUSI	Royal United Services Institute (UK)
SAG	Screen Actors Guild
SALT	Strategic Arms Limitation Talks
SDI	Strategic Defense Initiative (Reagan's anti-ballistic missile project)
siloviki	Russian term for those who work in agencies with coercive force at their disposal (internal security forces and the military), also known as the power ministries
SLBM	submarine-launched ballistic missile
START	Strategic Arms Reduction Talks
UK	United Kingdom of Great Britain and Northern Ireland
USSR	Union of Soviet Socialist Republics (Soviet Union)
Warsaw Pact	Collective defence treaty of Soviet and East European Communist states

NOTE ON TERMS AND
TRANSLITERATION

I use 'East Europe', with capital letters, to refer to that part of Europe under Communist rule. This term was in use throughout the Cold War to describe what was a political, rather than geographical, entity. 'East (or Eastern) Europe' contained both east and central European states, but the longer and geographically more precise wording is used only occasionally in the book, for its repetition would be a cumbersome substitute for the easily understood politically defined term. For the post-Communist period, in contrast, it would be nonsensical to refer to the Czech Republic (for example) as part of east (or East) Europe.

There is always a tension between consistency and familiarity in transliteration from Russian, especially where people's names are concerned. In the bibliographical references in the endnotes and, for the most part, in the main text, I have used *y* for й and also for ы, *yu* for ю, *ya* for я, and 'iy' for ий. I have made exceptions, however. Thus, Andrei Gromyko and Andrei Sakharov were better known in the West as Andrei than as Andrey and they remain 'Andrei' in this book. With names such as 'Georgiy' and 'Anatoliy', I have preferred familiarity to precise transliteration: thus, Georgy and Anatoly. Use of the Russian soft sign has been avoided, other than in the endnote references—thus, Yeltsin rather than Yel'tsin and glasnost rather than *glasnost'*. In the bibliographical references, however, transliteration is precise. There are exceptions to its consistency only in those cases where a different transliteration of Russian authors' names is to be found in a book they published in English, where I have followed the spelling used by their publisher.

Winner of the Pushkin House Book Prize

"*The Human* Factor makes a major contribution to scholarship and policy analysis. Brown is the leading Western authority on Soviet politics in the late Soviet era...a shrewd analyst and indefatigable researcher....Archie Brown's outstanding book shows how the unanticipated end of the Cold War came to pass."

Bruce Parrott, *Journal of Cold War Studies*

"A superb piece of scholarship...meticulously detailed without being overweighted, calmly authoritative without declamation, and judiciously argued."

Christopher Read, *Diplomacy and Statecraft*

"Archie Brown, who might be considered the dean of Western Soviet experts, comes out with a novel and yet nuanced argument for understanding the role of political leaders in historical processes. [*The Human Factor*] is a richly researched and originally-framed contribution to a period of history that is still unaccountably poorly understood."

Felix Light, *Moscow Times*

"Archie Brown's new book, lucidly written and scholarly, carries the argument [on Gorbachev] further. Always interested in big ideas (he has written on the history of world communism and the myth of the strong leader), he is fascinated by the evolving interplay between three remarkable but very different people who presided over the ending of the Cold War."

Rodric Braithwaite, *The Spectator*

"A masterly survey of the end of the cold war and the roles played in it by Gorbachev, Ronald Reagan and Margaret Thatcher."

Tony Barber, *Financial Times*

"Archie Brown, arguably the world's greatest authority on late-Soviet Russia, mounts a scrupulously detailed account of the three major players, their key roles, and those of senior advisors around them. However, "Mutual trust, painstakingly gained, and then lost, is especially difficult to re-establish". Brown's judgment should be a motto on every Western leader's desk."

Gary Hart, United States Senator (ret.)

"A fascinating and instructive read...everybody will learn something from this first-class book."

Dominic Sandbrook, *Sunday Times*

"A magisterial work...based on a wealth of sources in Russian and English...*The Human Factor* is as much a fine work of foreign policy analysis as it is Cold War history...a fascinating, close-structured narrative."

Christopher Hill, *Cold War History*

"Another tour de force from Archie Brown: detailed scholarship, elegant prose, and a clear argument. Read this book to find why we should not ignore the "human factor" underpinning great historical shifts. A fascinating account of how the Cold War ended, explored through the personal interactions between three world leaders—Gorbachev, Reagan, and Thatcher."
Bridget Kendall, Master of Peterhouse, Cambridge; former BBC Diplomatic, Moscow, and Washington Correspondent

"It is often a challenge for historians to find the right balance between the human factor and the historical forces at play. The value of Archie Brown's study of the three extraordinary politicians who brought the Cold War to a peaceful end is that it does precisely this."
Christopher Coker, *Literary Review*

"Here and elsewhere, as he once did for the leaders about whom he now writes, Archie Brown's scholarship can provide wisdom and hope."
James Graham Wilson, State Department Historian, *H-DIPLO*

"What *The Human Factor* does do, and does so well, is provide a fascinating new perspective on already well-trodden ground."
All About History

"Thanks to Archie Brown, world-renowned author of several outstanding books on Mikhail Gorbachev, we now have his meticulous, definitive account of how Gorbachev, Ronald Reagan and Margaret Thatcher all contributed mightily to ending the Cold War."
William Taubman, Pulitzer Prize-winning author of *Khrushchev: The Man and His Era* and of *Gorbachev: His Life and Times*

"The book is crammed with information, is well-written, and shows that Brown has a dry sense of humour."
Society for Co-operation in Russian and Soviet Studies Newsletter

"Brown's narrative is peppered with anecdotes that add texture to our knowledge of this period. At times…he injects great humour. At others, as in his retelling of the failed coup against Gorbachev and the eventual collapse of the Soviet Union, he infuses the narrative with drama and gripping suspense…."
English Historical Review

"*The Human Factor* is certain to become an indispensable book on late 20th century history."
Douglas Smith, winner of the inaugural Pushkin House Book Prize

INTRODUCTION

In a speech to American evangelicals in March 1983 President Ronald Reagan famously denounced the Soviet Union as 'an evil empire'. Just five years later he stood in Moscow State University, in front of a bust of Lenin, extolling political, intellectual, and religious freedom. Addressing a Russian student audience, who gave his speech a standing ovation, he told them, 'Your generation is living in one of the most exciting, hopeful times in Soviet history.'[1] Strolling amicably in Red Square with the Communist Party leader, Mikhail Gorbachev during that same Moscow visit, Reagan was asked whether he still thought the country he was in was an evil empire. 'No', he replied. 'That was another time, another era.'[2]

Margaret Thatcher took pride in the name 'The Iron Lady', bestowed on her in the mid-1970s (when she was leader of the Conservative Party but not yet prime minister) by the Soviet army newspaper. They were mocking her hard-line stance towards the Communist world and her view that the Russians were 'bent on world dominance'.[3] Just over a decade later at a Kremlin banquet in March 1987, addressing Gorbachev as 'Mr General Secretary', Mrs Thatcher declared that 'you have certainly embarked upon a great endeavour and we most earnestly wish you and your people well.'[4]

Mikhail Gorbachev proclaimed in April 1983, 'The Communist idea and the triumphant theory of Marxism-Leninism illuminate our path to the future.'[5] Two years later he succeeded Konstantin Chernenko in the highest office of the Communist Party, which at that time conferred leadership of his country, and embarked on a process of increasingly fundamental reform and jettisoning of past dogma. By 1988 he was insisting that 'We, of course, are far from laying claim to indisputable truth.' What matters is 'freedom of choice, a universal principle to which there must be no exception'.[6]

It was not only the rhetoric and the perceptions of these three leaders that changed so dramatically during the 1980s. The geopolitical world was transformed. The Soviet system's shift from extreme authoritarianism to political pluralism was matched by a transformation of the country's foreign policy. Soviet troops remained in their barracks while the countries belonging to the Warsaw Pact became independent and non-Communist in the course of 1989. The Cold War, as I shall argue later in this book, ended in its ideological dimension with Gorbachev's speech to the United Nations in December 1988. It ended on the ground the following year, when the Soviet leadership refused to use force to prevent Poles, Hungarians, Czechs, and other central and eastern Europeans from exercising that freedom of choice of which Gorbachev had spoken, and when they allowed the Berlin Wall to be breached without a shot being fired.[7]

It is beyond dispute that the political map of Europe changed more profoundly during the years in which Gorbachev occupied the Kremlin than at any time since the 1940s. Far from comparable agreement, though, exists on how this change should be explained. Many believe, especially in the United States, that the transformation came about as a result of the Soviet Union admitting defeat in the face of the economic and military pressure applied by the Reagan administration.[8] Such an explanation sits oddly with the fact that the first three decades of the post-war era were a period of Communist expansion, though the military gap between the two sides was at the time unquestionably to the advantage of the USA. By the mid-1980s, in contrast, a rough parity in military strength had existed between the two most powerful countries on earth for more than a decade. Each had more than enough deliverable nuclear weapons to destroy the other several times over.

President Reagan overlapped with four Soviet leaders. His occupancy of the White House coincided with the last two of Leonid Brezhnev's eighteen years at the top, the fifteen months of Yury Andropov, and the thirteen months of Konstantin Chernenko. Throughout Reagan's first term, death took its toll of Soviet leaders, but continuity was provided by the long-serving Andrei Gromyko and Dmitry Ustinov who wielded great influence in their respective posts of Minister of Foreign Affairs and Minister of Defence. In another example, however, of the years catching up with the aging Soviet oligarchy, Ustinov died in December 1984, shortly after Reagan was re-elected to a second term. Throughout his first term, the Cold War, far from being ameliorated, got colder. We now know from Russian archives that none of the leaders just mentioned saw a need for far-reaching domestic reform, for any concessions on defence policy, or for any softening of Soviet foreign policy towards the United States and NATO. The notion that the Reagan administration left the Kremlin leaders no option but to change the system and seek accommodation with the US and its allies is as questionable as it is popular.

The relative significance of each of the three leaders on whom this book focuses remains a matter of contention, and different interpretations of the Cold War's ending have not only scholarly significance. What people believe brought about the end of the Cold War also has practical implications for international relations up to the present day. The major concerns of the pages that follow are with the leadership, the foreign policy roles, and the interaction of Gorbachev, Reagan, and Thatcher, accompanied by attention to a variety of big questions. What exactly *was* the Cold War and *why* did it end in the way it did *when* it did? How can we explain the shift from dangerous rivalry and the threat of military confrontation—which lasted from the second half of the 1940s to the first half of the 1980s—to the constructive and even amicable relations so readily discernible by the end of the eighties?

There is a school of thought, not least in Russia, which holds that the Cold War never did end. That misinterprets the nature and significance of the dramatic change that occurred at the end of the 1980s. It does, though, raise the question of why there has been a failure to build on the achievements of the late eighties. That is a subject of great importance which is briefly touched upon at the end of this volume, but is essentially one for other books.[9]

To understand the significance of the parts played by Mikhail Gorbachev, Ronald Reagan, and Margaret Thatcher in the Cold War's ending, we need to move to more specific questions. What were the mindsets they brought to East–West relations? How did their perceptions evolve? What were the major influences on them? To what extent were these leaders reflecting the views of their own political establishment or challenging them? What pressures and constraints did they encounter in their domestic political environments? How important were the relations between them when they met one-to-one? Would any of the realistically alternative leaders of their countries in the 1980s have pursued approximately the same policies?

This book will not offer a blow-by-blow—or even concession-by-concession—account of the Cold War's ending. Nor will it provide a comprehensive history of international relations in those years, for it pays more attention to Ronald Reagan than to George H. W. Bush, and far more to Margaret Thatcher than to French President François Mitterrand or German Chancellor Helmut Kohl, although they also come into the story. The focus is, moreover, by no means exclusively on the individuals at the top of the hierarchies, no matter how vivid the personalities and however different their leadership styles. Influential members of the top leadership teams in the Soviet Union, the United States, and Great Britain are given their due.

Since the USA and the Soviet Union were the main and most powerful antagonists during the Cold War, it follows that American presidents and Soviet leaders mattered more than did British prime ministers. Margaret Thatcher's inclusion in the trio may even seem anomalous. Yet, she was the foreign leader to whom Ronald Reagan felt closest, and she established an intriguingly strong connection to Mikhail Gorbachev. Indeed, Mrs Thatcher immersed herself in relations with the Soviet Union and Eastern Europe to an unusual degree for a British prime minister and had more meetings with Gorbachev than any previous UK premier did with *any* earlier leader of the Soviet Union. Only Winston Churchill even approached that level of engagement with a Soviet leader, and he did so at a time when the Moscow, Washington, and London governments were allies. During the Second World War Churchill met Josif Stalin five times (including the 1943 Teheran and 1945 Yalta conferences, when the American president, Franklin D. Roosevelt, was also present). Not everyone in Mrs Thatcher's team wholly approved of the intensity and content of her engagement in East–West relations. Her foreign policy adviser in 10 Downing Street, Sir Percy Cradock, wrote, 'Mrs Thatcher came close to claiming that she had discovered, even invented, Gorbachev; her meetings and debates with him were deliberately high profile and added to her, and Britain's, international standing. More seriously, she acted as a conduit from Gorbachev to Reagan, selling him to Washington as a man to do business with, and operating as an agent of influence in both directions.'[10]

In central Europe, especially in the Czech Republic, there are many who rank Thatcher second only to Reagan for the role she played in the demise of Communism. The abandonment of Marxist-Leninist doctrine and the rejection of Communist rule in Europe were, understandably enough, seen as intimately linked to the end of the Cold War. In Poland pride of place tends to be given to their native son, Pope John Paul II, with Reagan revered and Mrs Thatcher held in high regard. John O'Sullivan, a journalist who was at one time a speech-writer for Thatcher, argues that 'without Reagan, no *perestroika* or *glasnost* either' (a view he also attributes to Thatcher).[11] Whether that contention stands up to scrutiny will emerge in the pages that follow.

This is a book on political leadership as well as on the making of foreign policy and the conduct of international relations at a time of enormous change. A study of leadership is of limited use if it ignores the domestic political context and the influences and pressures, including economic and interest-based constraints, on leaders. Some writing on the Cold War's ending, however, goes to an economic determinist extreme, holding that it is wrong to see particular leaders, especially Soviet, as having been in any way decisively important. What brought about the end of the Cold War, according to this school of thought, was the economic backwardness of the Communist world in comparison with the West. A long-term decline in the Soviet rate of economic growth, together with technological lag, was, indeed, a stimulus to reform. If, however, it was the overwhelming driving force for change, it is odd that Gorbachev gave a much higher priority to political than to economic reform. Only late in his leadership did he accept that the country had to move from an essentially command economy to a form of market economy.

There are, therefore, grounds for seriously questioning the conventional wisdom on the way political change was brought about in the Soviet Union and on the determinants of the Cold War's ending. I have written at length elsewhere on what caused the transformation and, subsequently, the demise of the Soviet political system.[12] On the end of the Cold War, there remains much to be learned from examining the evolving views and interactions of Gorbachev, Reagan, and Thatcher. This book pays particular attention to 'the human factor', a phrase much used by Gorbachev,[13] as political leaders responded to events that developed in ways they had not expected and that they could only partially control.

Margaret Thatcher became British prime minister in 1979 and Ronald Reagan won the American presidency in 1980, but it was not until March 1985 that Mikhail Gorbachev succeeded to the Soviet leadership. This meant that the greater part of Thatcher's premiership and of Reagan's presidency had already occurred before Gorbachev was chosen to be General Secretary of the Communist Party of the Soviet Union. The way their thinking on East–West relations developed during those years is examined in Part I of the book with special attention given to the interaction among these leaders—between Reagan and Thatcher during Reagan's first term and between Thatcher and Gorbachev in 1984.

The fact that Thatcher met Gorbachev in Britain three months before he attained the highest position of power in Moscow was all the more important because of her existing connection with Reagan and his respect for her judgement. Reagan met Gorbachev for the first time almost a year later, in Geneva in November 1985. The most decisive meetings and communications from that point onwards were those between these two leaders. It was during the first five years of Gorbachev's occupancy of the Kremlin that the great divide between Communist Europe and the Western world was consigned to the history books. The manner in which the Cold War ended, and the forces and personalities driving the process, constitute the main themes of Part II. Although they cover a lot of ground in fairly brief compass, the chapters in that second part make up the longest section of the book, for they pay attention not only to international relations but also to their domestic political contexts. Part III is concerned with the immediate consequences—in 1990–1—of the end of the Cold War and of the pluralization of the Soviet political system.

The major concern of the book as a whole, however, is with the nature and significance of the parts played in the Cold War's ending by three individuals, Mikhail Gorbachev, Ronald Reagan, and Margaret Thatcher and in examining how they related to each other. The story of their interconnections is a contribution not only to an explanation of the end of the Cold War but also to a much older debate on the role an individual may play in the making of history.

PART I

1

THE COLD WAR AND
ITS DANGERS

Twenty-first-century turmoil and terrorism can generate a misplaced nostalgia for the years of the Cold War. It may appear that once upon a time two superpowers maintained world peace, while underpinning order of a kind in countries that, more recently, have experienced foreign intervention or civil war and sometimes both. Even a brief account of the realities of the East–West stand-off shows how fanciful is that rosy perspective on the Cold War, for it glosses over a much grimmer and more dangerous historical reality.

The Cold War exacerbated a series of regional hot wars which at various times involved large numbers of American and Soviet troops in armed conflict (although never in direct confrontation with each other). There were moments when humanity teetered on the edge of still greater catastrophe, with the world only one false step away from all-out nuclear conflagration. So, before looking at the last years of the Cold War, especially the period from Ronald Reagan's assumption of the American presidency in January 1981, we should remind ourselves of just what the Cold War entailed in the years before it was wound down and concluded peacefully.

There is no definitive answer to the question: when did the Cold War start and when did it end? In Europe and North America, as distinct from parts of Asia and Africa, it was not a 'real' war in the sense that one side was bombing or shelling the other. That would have enabled us to name the date when battle commenced and to specify when the bombs stopped falling and the guns fell silent. Yet, the Cold War's potential to become an all-encompassing hot war meant that the stakes could not have been higher. A conflict in which each side had the means utterly to annihilate the other would have put all human life on the planet in extreme jeopardy. Even short of such a calamitous outcome, the antagonism was fateful enough. This was a struggle not only between two hostile blocs for military supremacy in an arms race, but also between incompatible ideologies and between rival political and economic systems. The dominant power in each of the blocs, the USA and the USSR, espoused a set of principles which they held to be of universal application and the leadership in each of these countries felt a need to show that 'their' system was making progress. This meant that 'defection' from the sphere of influence of each, or even the prospect of it, was liable to lead to retaliation from the patron superpower of varying degrees of severity.[1]

One view has it that the Cold War began with the Bolshevik Revolution in 1917, but that interpretation is unconvincing. Soviet Communism in the 1920s and 1930s was seen by many in the West as a source of inspiration (even 'a new civilization').[2] Most Western governments, in contrast, saw it as a wellspring of ideological contagion, but even conservative political leaders did not in those years view Moscow as a military threat. Moreover, in the Second World War, the Soviet Union became the USA's and UK's key ally. The Red Army played the most decisive part in the Allied response to Nazi aggression, bearing the brunt of the land war in Europe. Three-quarters of the German soldiers who lost their lives did so at the hands of their Soviet adversary. The total of Soviet war deaths, military and civilian, was between 26 and 27 million, the highest of any country, and more than five times greater than that suffered by Germany.[3] Approximately 400,000 members of the armed forces of the United States lost their lives in the Second World War as compared with almost 9 million of their Soviet military counterparts.[4]

Given the extent of their people's suffering in the war and the magnitude of their contribution to the Allied victory, Soviet security demands initially met with a sympathetic response from their Western partners. In the Teheran conference of 1943, at which President Franklin D. Roosevelt, British Prime Minister Winston Churchill, and Soviet leader Josif Stalin discussed the progress of the war and how frontiers should be redrawn after it was over, the fate of post-war Poland was broached. The Soviet Union appeared to be the prime beneficiary, with Poland losing territory in the east that became part of Soviet Ukraine. The Poles, however, gained territory in the West at the expense of Germany. Churchill, in his memoirs, claimed credit for the idea: 'I then demonstrated with the help of three matches my idea of moving Poland westwards. This pleased Stalin...'.[5]

On a ten-day visit to Moscow in October 1944, Churchill discussed with Stalin spheres of influence in post-war Europe in a way that would have seemed less extraordinary in the nineteenth century than it does in the twenty-first. Churchill's proposal of 90 per cent Russian 'predominance' in Romania and 75 per cent in Bulgaria, but 90 per cent British influence over Greece was accepted by Stalin, as was, initially, his suggestion of a 50–50 supervisory share for Yugoslavia and Hungary.[6] While his proposals were being translated, Churchill wrote them down on a piece of paper to which Stalin, using a blue pencil, added a tick. A silence followed which Churchill broke by saying, 'Might it not be thought rather cynical if it seemed we had disposed of these issues, so fateful to millions of people, in such an offhand manner? Let us burn the paper.' 'No, you keep it', Stalin replied.[7] Churchill and Roosevelt, whose health did not permit him to come to Moscow to join in the talks, accepted that there should be governments in the Soviet neighbourhood that did not pose a threat to 'Russia'. (Churchill always called the Soviet Union, which was larger than Russia and contained a great many other nationalities, 'Russia'. More surprisingly, Stalin, who was not a Russian but a Georgian, often did so, too.) Neither Churchill nor Roosevelt intended, however, to give 'Uncle Joe' (as they called Stalin in their correspondence, often abbreviated to 'U.J.') their imprimatur for the establishment of Communist regimes in Eastern Europe and the Balkans.[8]

The international organization of the Communist movement, the Comintern—which had been dominated by the Soviet Union and served, principally, as an instrument of that country's foreign policy—had been wound up in 1943, creating the impression, and one that Stalin intended to convey, that Communism's proselytizing zeal and international ambitions had abated. Eager to believe that this was so, Churchill wrote to Stalin in October 1944, 'We feel we were right in interpreting your dissolution of the Comintern as a decision by the Soviet Government not to interfere in the internal political affairs of other countries. The more this can be established in people's minds the smoother everything will go.'[9]

Not every Communist state was simply a creature of Moscow. The Yugoslav Communists were sufficiently strong to take over their country themselves and later were independent enough not only to ignore the 50 per cent supervisory role that Britain was supposedly to exercise over them but also, from 1948, to break with the Soviet Union.[10] In other cases, the informal agreements on spheres of influence did count for something. Those countries deemed to be in the Soviet sphere, such as Poland and Hungary, where Communist parties did not have enough domestic strength either to win free and fair elections or to make their own revolutions, not merely became Soviet allies but also acquired Communist systems. They achieved this through a combination of rigged elections and 'salami tactics' whereby anti-Communist groups and non-Communist political parties were sliced off one by one. Soviet security police 'advisers' were on hand to supervise the process of Communization, their counsel underpinned in most cases by the continued presence of Soviet troops who had liberated the countries from the Nazis.

Greece, in contrast, endured a bitter civil war in which Stalin withheld the kind of support for Greek revolutionaries that he gave to Communists in countries agreed to fall within the Soviet sphere of influence. Urged by the Yugoslav Communists to do more to assist their Greek comrades, Stalin made clear to a delegation from Belgrade in early 1948 that there would be no Soviet intervention on the side of the Greek insurgents. Although he omitted to mention to the Yugoslavs the 'Big Three' conclusions on spheres of influence, he stressed the need to avoid antagonizing the United States (in particular) and Britain, thereby putting at risk the Soviet Union's gains elsewhere in Eastern and Central Europe. When one of the Yugoslavs mentioned that the Chinese Communists had been victorious, and implied that their Greek counterparts could be equally successful, Stalin responded, 'Yes, the Chinese comrades have succeeded, but in Greece there is an entirely different situation. The United States is directly engaged there—the strongest state in the world.'[11]

It was far easier for the Big Three to find agreement concerning the boundaries of post-war Poland than to reach accord on the composition of the country's provisional government. In Churchill's view 'a strong, free, and independent Poland was much more important than particular territorial boundaries'.[12] For their part, Poles had ample reasons for apprehension about coming under Soviet tutelage. They were well aware that Soviet security forces had carried out the killings in cold blood of more than 20,000 Polish prisoners, the majority of them army officers, in Katyn forest, near Smolensk, in 1940, although Soviet propaganda attributed the massacre to the Nazis.[13] It was not only Poles opposed both to Russia and to Communism who had been slaughtered by the NKVD. Even many Polish Communists had disappeared during Stalin's pre-war purges; those who survived in the USSR did so by slavishly following the line laid down by their Soviet patrons. Stalin told Roosevelt in December 1944 that the group known in Moscow as the Polish Committee of National Liberation would transform itself into a Provisional Polish Government and that it should be recognized as such. Justifying this, Stalin argued that the fate of Poland mattered more to the Soviet Union than to any other major power, not only because Russia was bearing 'the main brunt of the battle' for its 'liberation', but also because Poland bordered the Soviet state. Thus, the Polish problem was 'inseparable from the problem of security of the Soviet Union'.[14]

The Cold War began in 1945–6. Soviet troops liberated and subsequently occupied much of Eastern and Central Europe and the territories they had conquered remained under their control, to a greater or lesser degree, until the Cold War ended more than four decades later. In the Yalta and Potsdam conferences of 1945 new boundaries for a number of European states—in particular, Poland and Germany—were discussed, and the Soviet Union got most of what it wanted. That was notwithstanding the fact that the United States emerged from the war wealthier and stronger than ever before, whereas every European country, including Russia, had been impoverished by the conflict.

At the February 1945 Yalta conference, when President Roosevelt headed the American delegation and Winston Churchill the British, Poland was discussed in seven of the eight plenary sessions. Although Stalin was insistent on the Soviet-backed Polish Communist group forming the nucleus of an enlarged provisional government, he appeared to make concessions, welcomed by the Americans and British, on early elections and Polish sovereignty. The problem, as Churchill discovered, was the difference 'between us and the Russians on the meaning of such terms as democracy, sovereignty, independence, representative Government, and free and unfettered elections'.[15] With President Roosevelt's health failing, Churchill took it upon himself to stand up for the Poles' right to self-determination, pointing out to Stalin that it was the Nazi invasion of Poland that had led Britain to enter the war against Germany.

Roosevelt died in April 1945 and his successor as president, Harry Truman, initially was quite taken with Stalin and suspicious of Churchill. In May 1945, Truman told Eleanor Roosevelt that 'the difficulties with Churchill are very nearly as exasperating as they are with the Russians'.[16] When he met Stalin for the first time, at the

Potsdam conference a little over two months later, Truman's initial impression was positive. 'I can deal with Stalin', he wrote in his diary on 17 July. 'He is honest—but smart as hell.' A fortnight later, he was worrying about 'what would happen to Russia and Central Europe if Joe suddenly passed out'. Truman thought that others in the Soviet leader's entourage—Vyacheslav Molotov, Andrei Vyshinsky and Ivan Maisky—lacked the 'sincerity' and 'honesty' he attributed to Stalin.[17] Even Winston Churchill at times expressed trust in Stalin. In the immediate aftermath of Yalta, he told a ministerial meeting that, whereas Neville Chamberlain had been wrong in believing that he could trust Hitler, 'I don't think I'm wrong about Stalin.'[18] And he wrote to Stalin, 'I pray that you will long be spared to preside over the destinies of your country which has shown its full greatness under your leadership...'.[19]

Once it became clear that for Stalin it was not enough for a country in the Soviet sphere of influence to pursue an unthreatening foreign policy, they had also to adopt a Soviet-style system and be under Moscow's tutelage, attitudes toward the Soviet Union hardened. Churchill, in the last months of his premiership, had deeper concerns than Truman harboured about Soviet intentions, and he tried in the days after the war in Europe ended to place the Soviet Union's future role in the continent at the top of Truman's foreign policy agenda. On 12 May 1945, Churchill warned the American president of Russian 'misinterpretation' of the Yalta decisions. He expressed particular concern about the combination of 'Russian power' with Communist techniques of control in territories they occupied and with the Soviet ability 'to maintain very large armies in the field for a long time'. An 'iron curtain is drawn down upon their front', he told Truman, and 'We do not know what is going on behind.' This made a new meeting with the Soviet leadership imperative.[20]

By the time that summer meeting—at Potsdam—ended, Stalin was the only member of the original 'Big Three' still in place. The British general election had been held on 5 July, but the result remained unknown until all the ballots from servicemen had been counted almost three weeks later. Churchill attended the morning session on 25 July and flew home that afternoon. He had expected to return as UK prime minister, and Stalin assured him, on the basis of his 'information from Communist and other sources', that he and his Conservative Party would be returned to power with 'a majority of about eighty'.[21] In fact, the result was a landslide victory for the Labour Party. Churchill resigned and Clement Attlee became prime minister. Attlee, who had already been attending the Potsdam conference at Churchill's invitation, although not part of the innermost circle meetings of the 'Big Three' and their interpreters, now found himself taking Churchill's place as head of the British delegation. The Potsdam conference agreed that the new Polish Western border would be on a line from the Oder to the Neisse rivers and recognized the Polish government led by the Moscow-backed Communist Bolesław Bierut, but on the understanding that free elections would follow. The conference also formulated plans for the administration of Germany and, in effect, granted the Soviet Union control of East Germany.

While the conference was underway the Americans had successfully tested an atomic bomb in the Nevada desert. Churchill had known that this was in the offing, but when Truman informed Stalin, without going into details, that they had a new weapon of great destructive power, he was surprised that Stalin received the news placidly and asked no questions. Both Truman and Churchill assumed that Stalin had no previous inkling of the bomb's development and that he had failed to take on board its significance. In fact, the Soviet Union had its own informants inside the Manhattan Project and Stalin knew that atomic weapons were being developed. With the Potsdam Conference still underway, an ultimatum was delivered to Japan, calling for its unconditional surrender and threatening 'utter devastation of the Japanese homeland' should the surrender not be forthcoming. The terms were rejected by Japan's rulers and on 6 August an atomic bomb was dropped on Hiroshima, followed three days later by the dropping of a second nuclear bomb, this time on Nagasaki. A few days later Emperor Hirohito announced Japan's surrender.

The use of atomic weapons added to the unprecedented character of the Cold War, especially after the Soviet Union acquired nuclear arms of its own from 1949. For the first time in history, underlying the tension between nations and military blocs, was the knowledge that a descent into armed conflict between them would bring death and destruction qualitatively more horrendous than anything seen before.[22] The longer-term implications were later spelled out by former US Defense Secretary William J. (Bill) Perry: 'The atomic bomb, whose horrors we had first seen in Hiroshima, was 1,000 times as destructive as the largest conventional bomb. The new hydrogen bombs we were testing [in the 1950s] had the destructive power of 1,000 times the Hiroshima bomb. So, in a brief ten years mankind had increased its destructive power by 1,000 times 1,000—by 1 million times—a magnitude of destruction nearly impossible to comprehend.'[23]

Truman later wrote that he had gone to Potsdam not only with a positive view of Stalin but with 'the kindliest feeling for Russia and the Russian people'.[24] Reflecting on Potsdam during his retirement, Truman wrote: 'What a show that was! But a large number of agreements were reached in spite of the setup—only to be broken as soon as the unconscionable Russian dictator returned to Moscow! And I liked the little son of a bitch.'[25] Aware of his inexperience of international affairs and of top-level negotiation, Truman, who was meeting Churchill (as well as Stalin) for the first time at Potsdam, had prepared himself far more thoroughly for the conference than had the British prime minister who had been involved in the general election campaign at home and who believed that his vast experience left him in little need of foreign policy briefings. The British Foreign Secretary, Anthony Eden, observed that Churchill had been 'woolly and verbose', and the head of the diplomatic service, Alexander Cadogan, concurred, saying in a letter to his wife that whereas Churchill had talked too much, Truman had been admirably businesslike.[26]

The Communist Takeover of Eastern Europe

America's economic and military strength was much greater at the end of the Second World War than that of the Soviet Union, and for several years thereafter only the US had nuclear weapons. Nevertheless, the Soviet side was able to keep large numbers of soldiers in uniform, whereas American demobilization had been carried through quickly. Communist regimes, under Soviet overlordship, were established and consolidated in eastern and central Europe. Czechoslovakia was initially an exception inasmuch as its Communist Party was genuinely popular and emerged as the largest single party in free elections in 1946, yet the country remained recognizably democratic. This changed when the Communists seized full power in February 1948, putting an end to political pluralism, and establishing an orthodox Communist party-state. They achieved this without drawing on Soviet military support, but with the blessing of Moscow. The Czech Communists' belief that they had made their 'own revolution' led them to suppose they enjoyed more autonomy than they did. (They were made painfully aware of its limits two decades later when a Soviet-led invasion by half a million troops put an end to the 'Prague Spring' in 1968.)

The dividing lines between East and West Europe hardened during 1946. Churchill had used the term 'iron curtain' on several occasions in his correspondence with American presidents. In a widely publicized speech at Fulton, Missouri, on 5 March 1946, he employed it publicly, declaring that 'an iron curtain has descended across the continent' of Europe. Churchill was merely Leader of the Opposition at this point, but his wartime fame, the fact that the speech was made in the presence of President Truman, and its timing gave it great resonance. Truman by now agreed with Churchill's gloomy assessment of the way relations with the Soviet Union were going, as did Ernest Bevin, the former trade union leader who was Foreign Secretary in Britain's Labour government. Bevin and Prime Minister Attlee made clear that their brand of democratic socialism had nothing in common with Communism and that it was compatible with a continuing alliance with the United States in resistance to the expansion of Soviet power and influence in Europe. Bevin was far more sceptical of the chances of progress in discussions with Stalin and Soviet Foreign Minister Vyacheslav Molotov than was the first of the American Secretaries of State with whom he overlapped, James F. Byrnes. George Kennan, who was number two in the US Embassy in Moscow and temporarily in charge during one of Ambassador Averell Harriman's frequent absences, attended a meeting of the 'Big Three' foreign ministers chaired by Molotov at which he found himself much more in sympathy with Bevin than with Byrnes. 'Bevin', Kennan noted, 'looked highly disgusted by the whole procedure' and was 'well aware that nothing good could come out of the meeting'.[27]

Just a fortnight before Churchill's 'iron curtain' speech in Missouri, an even more important text was distributed among senior officials in Washington, although it was not known to the general public at the time. This was Kennan's 'long telegram' (and it *was* long—8,000 words), sent from the American Embassy in Moscow to the State Department. Kennan, who was both a serious student of Russia and the Soviet Union and a discerning foreign policy analyst, believed that Washington had become too sanguine about the prospect of reaching agreements with the Soviet state in its Stalinist incarnation. He viewed the drive by the regime to isolate the Russian population from the outside world and to extend the limits of 'Russian police power' as 'the natural and instinctive urges of Russian rulers'. The Russian nationalism that appeared in the 'new guise of international Marxism' was, 'with its honeyed promises to a desperate and wartorn outside world' even 'more dangerous and insidious' than before.[28] Analysing Soviet strengths and weaknesses, Kennan advocated a long-term policy of containment, based on 'cohesion, firmness and vigor' in dealing with the USSR, while warning at the same time against 'hysterical anti-Sovietism'. He made a distinction between Soviet ambitions and those of Hitler's Germany, arguing that Soviet policy was not prone to take unnecessary risks and that it was 'highly sensitive to the logic of force', although 'impervious to the logic of reason'. Yet it was a problem the US could solve and 'without recourse to any general military conflict'.[29]

On 12 March 1947, less than a month after Kennan's telegram reached Washington and one week after Churchill's Fulton speech, President Truman addressed a joint session of Congress, calling for support for democracy in Greece and Turkey. His emphasis was on financial and economic aid, but when he said that 'it must be the policy of the United States to support free peoples who are resisting attempted subjugation by armed minorities or by outside pressures', the implication was that military force would be used, if required, to prevent those countries succumbing to Communist rule. This declaration that the US would not permit Communist expansion in Europe outside the sphere of influence it had already tacitly ceded to the Soviet Union became known as the 'Truman Doctrine'.[30] It was a continuation of a firmer line against Communist expansion that had been gradually evolving, and very much in line with Kennan's thinking.[31] At the same time, Truman was dismissive, both then and later, of those who claimed that the United States itself was at serious risk of Communist subversion. When the demagogic Senator Joseph McCarthy began in 1950 a witch hunt that continued until 1954, with accusations of reds under and in Washington beds, the president was scornful. Reacting in 1950 to McCarthy in full cry, Truman described him as 'the greatest asset the Kremlin has'. When a reporter asked for his reaction to Senator Robert A. Taft's accusation that the president had libelled McCarthy, Truman's response was, 'Do you think that's possible?'[32]

If the Truman Doctrine made the developing Cold War still colder, the political and economic gulf between Western and Eastern Europe was further widened by the Marshall Plan, introduced in June 1947. General George Marshall had succeeded Byrnes in January as US Secretary of State and, in that role, he led the Truman administration's campaign for financial support of European countries in dire straits as a result of the physical and economic destruction caused by the war. The offer was, in principle, open to East European countries, even to the Soviet Union, although the State Department was sure that Moscow would decline the offer of help. Those Eastern European countries that were already controlled by the Soviet Union were, indeed, forbidden by their Kremlin overseers from accepting Marshall aid. Czechoslovakia initially accepted the American offer, but, following pressure from Stalin, that decision was reversed. In 1947 the Prague government was still a coalition in which Communists predominated, though both the presidency and the Foreign Ministry were in the hands of respected non-Communists—Eduard Beneš and Jan Masaryk. While, in principle, Czechoslovakia was free to accept American assistance, doing so against the strong opposition of the Soviet Union was for Czech Communists unthinkable. In Washington there had been fears that economic hardship would drive more and more people elsewhere in Europe into the hands of the Communists. Not only was any such outcome avoided, the Marshall Plan played an important part in winning acceptance in Western Europe of American international leadership in the Cold War.

The Communist takeover of Czechoslovakia in February 1948 further chilled Cold War relations, for this was a country which, uniquely in Central Europe, had remained democratic between the two world wars and had preserved its democracy in the post-war period until the Communist Party ended political pluralism. The most strategically sensitive country in Central Europe was, however, not Czechoslovakia but Germany and it was there that a more overt East–West clash began just a few months later. Berlin had been divided by agreement at the Yalta conference into four sectors—Soviet, American, British, and French—but, in an attempt to seize control over the whole city Soviet forces closed all rail and road links to those parts of Berlin under Western supervision. They had hoped to starve or freeze West Berlin into submission. The Western response combined prudence with resolution. They took the bold decision to airlift supplies of food, clothes, and fuel to the population of the Western sectors in non-stop flights by American, British, and French aircraft and kept this up from June 1948 until May 1949, when the Soviet side relaxed their blockade. The circumvention of Moscow's aims was as shrewd as it was unwavering, for it avoided direct military engagement with the Soviet occupying forces in Germany.

The Asian Battleground

Although Europe remained a central preoccupation for both Soviet and American leaders over four decades, the Cold War became a worldwide phenomenon, with Asia an important battleground. Civil war raged in China, the world's most populous state, between 1945 and 1949, with the Communists under the leadership of Mao Zedong gradually winning more and more territory from the Kuomintang government led by Chiang Kai-shek. While the Americans backed Chiang, they tried to broker a peace as well, and though the Soviet Union gave support to the Chinese Communists, Stalin urged caution. Mao pressed on, however, and the Communists took control of Beijing in February 1949 and of the whole country by October. Their success was essentially an indigenous achievement, not dependent on Soviet support. Massive corruption and hyperinflation under the Kuomintang had led to a haemorrhaging of support for the non-Communist government. Chiang Kai-shek's appeal for more aid from the United States went unheeded, and he retreated with what was left of his government and army to the island of Taiwan. Mainland China became in 1949 a Communist state and politically, although not economically, it still is.

The Cold War conflicts that most directly involved Western troops with Communist adversaries were in Asia. In two major wars—Korea between 1950 and 1953 and Vietnam between 1965 and 1975—American troops were by far the largest outside contingent on the anti-Communist side. The first of these wars began when the North Korean Communist leader, Kim Il-sung, succeeded in 1950 in persuading Stalin that an invasion of the South would bring speedy success and lead to the unification of Korea under Communist rule. This was a serious miscalculation, the more so because the Soviet Union was boycotting the United Nations at that time, and the US and its allies were, therefore, able to get UN approval for an international coalition force to drive the North Koreans back. After they had made progress in doing so, Stalin put pressure on Mao Zedong to send Chinese 'volunteers' to help their Korean comrades, although he kept Soviet troops out of the fight. After some hesitation, the Chinese Communist leader authorized such an intervention. Mao's son was among those who died in the conflict. In three years of bitter fighting, more than 2 million people were killed, mainly Koreans and Chinese. Of the 35,000 UN troops killed, 33,000 were American. Stalin died in March 1953 and this provided an opportunity for armistice talks to make headway. A ceasefire took effect in July 1953 with Korea still divided between a Communist North and non-Communist South. The demarcation line was not very different from where it had been before so many lives were lost.

Communism in Asia gained popular support through its opposition to Western colonialism, with anti-imperialism and anti-capitalism closely interlinked in the minds of many. At the end of the Second World War the Vietnamese Communist leader Ho Chi Minh chose to emphasize the former rather than the latter. He quoted both from the American Declaration of Independence and the French Revolution's Declaration of the Rights of Man, focusing on national liberation and democracy, partly in the hope of gaining the sympathy of the United States for Vietnam's struggle against French colonial hegemony. In the light of rising tensions with Moscow, however, both Truman and the State Department were more concerned with what was happening in Europe and loath to alienate the French government.[33] The Vietnamese succeeded in liberating themselves from French jurisdiction by 1954, but their country was left divided between the North, controlled by Communists, and the South with an anti-Communist government in Saigon. When civil war between them ensued, President Kennedy authorized the sending of American military advisers to support the South Vietnamese regime, and their numbers were creeping up significantly by the time of his assassination in 1963. By 1967 there were more than half a million American troops in Vietnam. They encountered highly motivated Communist fighters in the South, many of whom had infiltrated from the North.

By the time Vietnam was united under Communist rule in 1975, the US having retired from the fray in 1973, some 3 million Vietnamese soldiers and civilians had been killed and the country was devastated. Toxic chemicals that American planes had sprayed to defoliate forests and expose enemy soldiers caused birth defects and cancers long after the war ended.[34] Close to 60,000 American servicemen lost their lives in Vietnam and more than 300,000 were wounded. The growing unpopularity of the war led President Johnson in 1968 not to seek a second presidential term. His considerable domestic achievements had become overshadowed by hostility to the apparently endless conflict in Asia and to the draft of young Americans. A quarter of the American troops who served in Vietnam were not professional soldiers but conscripts.

Laos and Cambodia also became Communist states and suffered both from American attacks and Communist retaliation against those in the indigenous population who had sided with the US. The American withdrawal from the area left most of the latter defenceless. Around 100,000 of the Hmong people of Laos were killed by the Laotian and Vietnamese Communists. Another 100,000 eventually made their way to a new life in the United States.[35] The most vicious of all Communist regimes was established in Cambodia under the Khmer Rouge, who renamed the country Kampuchea. About 2 million people out of a population of 7 million died at the hands of the country's Communist rulers, mostly by assassination but also through hunger. By 1979, 42 per cent of Cambodian children had lost at least one parent.[36]

Although there was debate in the United States about 'who lost China' (hardly America's to 'lose'), the Soviet Union was seen as the principal threat and US policy toward China was generally pursued with Russia in mind. Many Americans, Ronald Reagan among them, for long refused to believe that the Sino-Soviet split, which developed in the late 1950s, was anything other than a ruse. In the 1960s the differences between the two Communist giants became so obvious that even many sceptics had to accept that there was real hostility between Moscow and Beijing, all the more so when at the end of that decade the conflict moved beyond polemics to skirmishes between Soviet and Chinese troops on the border between the two countries.

The China card against the Soviet Union was first played by President Richard Nixon, with groundwork laid by his National Security Adviser, Henry Kissinger, who had first broached the subject of a change of America's China policy with Nixon in the autumn of 1969. Kissinger's own visits to China prepared the ground for the president's meetings with Mao Zedong in 1972. The Nixon–Kissinger view was that turning the bilateral US–Soviet relationship into a triangular one in which the Americans would have closer relations with both China and the Soviet Union than either of the Communist giants had with each other would work to the advantage of the United States.[37] Neither Nixon nor Kissinger were inhibited by the fact that Mao was presiding over the Cultural Revolution, involving persecution of millions of Chinese citizens on a scale far surpassing human rights abuses in Leonid Brezhnev's Soviet Union.

When President Jimmy Carter and his National Security Adviser, Zbigniew Brzezinski, picked up the China card later in the decade, thwarting the Soviet Union again outweighed China's record on human rights. That made the initiative in some ways more surprising, since Carter and Brzezinski both placed a strong emphasis on rights and freedoms, applying those principles to Latin America as well as, first and foremost, to the Soviet Union and Eastern Europe. In contrast, Nixon and Kissinger had downplayed such concerns and held that they should not get in the way of interest-based relations between states. Kissinger, for example, evinced little enthusiasm for the Helsinki Final Act of 1975, an agreement that followed three years of negotiations involving all the states of Europe—including the Soviet Union—other than Albania, with the addition of the United States and Canada. Not only did the agreement specify that the borders of the signatory-countries could not be altered by force (widely, and mistakenly, interpreted as legitimating the Communist status quo in Eastern Europe), it also stipulated respect for human rights and freedoms. Failure to adhere to that commitment was monitored in subsequent years and used to good effect by dissidents in Eastern Europe, including Russia. At the very time the agreement was being criticized as a sell-out by many in the West, Ronald Reagan and Margaret Thatcher among them, senior members of the Soviet Politburo were far from sanguine about the USSR 'assuming international commitments that could open the way to foreign interference in our political life'.[38]

When US relations with China were qualitatively improved during the Carter administration, the triangular relationship with the Soviet Union was a prime factor for Brzezinski in particular. He espoused a policy of greatly expanding relations with China, which met opposition from Secretary of State Cyrus Vance, who was concerned both about its effect on US–Soviet contacts and on the chances of improving relations with Vietnam. Brzezinski's view prevailed. In economic matters, he was in favour of 'China being treated quite explicitly on a more favored basis than the Soviet Union' and he also supported an expansion of US–Chinese security relations, since he believed that it would enhance American leverage over the Soviet Union.[39]

Change and Unrest in Eastern and Central Europe

Between 1947 and 1956 a successor body to the Comintern called the Cominform (the Communist Information Bureau) attempted to coordinate the international Communist movement. Both its membership and its functions were more limited than those of its predecessor. In January 1949 the European Communist bloc countries, led by the Soviet Union, formed an economic organization called the Council for Mutual Economic Assistance, usually abbreviated to Comecon. It aimed, never wholly successfully, to coordinate economic policy and oversee a division of labour in their planned economies. Partly a counter to the Marshall Plan, Comecon was later joined by Mongolia, Cuba, and Vietnam.

More consequential on both sides of the Cold War divide were the multinational military institutions that were created. NATO was established in April 1949 in response to the perceived threat of Soviet expansion. From the outset, the United States played the leading role within it, though NATO brought together North American and European democracies and obliged them to come to the defence of any member state that was attacked. A formal military alliance on the other side, known as the Warsaw Pact, did not come into being until 1955. Its creation was partly in response to the entry that year of West Germany (the Federal Republic of Germany) into NATO. The supreme commander of the Warsaw Pact was invariably a Soviet general, and Soviet dominance of this military organization was much more absolute than was American leadership of NATO. The existence of these two military alliances may have made attacks from outside them on any member-country less likely. It also meant, however, that if such an attack did take place, the consequences were liable to be more horrendous.

In fact, no Warsaw Pact country attacked a member of NATO and no member of NATO encroached upon a state belonging to the Warsaw Pact. This did not, though, prevent military action by one or more members of the Warsaw Pact against a fellow-member. A modest political thaw occurred inside the Soviet Union following Stalin's death in 1953 and it led also to a partial and temporary relaxation of international tensions. When party leader Nikita Khrushchev launched an attack on Stalin at the party's Twentieth Congress in February 1956, the reaction was more than he and his colleagues had bargained for. In particular, it gave encouragement both to Communist reformers and to outright opponents of Communism in Eastern Europe.

The impact was especially great in Poland and Hungary. In both countries Communist leaders who had earlier been expelled from the party, Imre Nagy and János Kádár in Hungary and Władysław Gomułka in Poland (in Kádár's and Gomułka's cases, they had been imprisoned as well), were returned to high office in the hope that this would alleviate popular unrest. The return of Gomułka, together with significant policy change in Warsaw, was enough to allow the authorities in Poland to regain control and stave off the threat of Soviet military intervention. Prior to Gomułka's return, demonstrations in several Polish cities had involved as many as 100,000 people, rising in Warsaw to around half a million. Khrushchev told the Presidium of the Central Committee of the Soviet Communist Party that there was no shortage of reasons for them to intervene directly in Poland, but he recognized that 'finding a way to end such a conflict later on would be very hard'.[40] His toleration of the return of Gomułka bought time for the Soviet Union, for he remained Polish Communist leader until 1970, notwithstanding growing disillusionment with him in his own country. Although Gomułka was never a mere puppet of the Soviet Union, he kept Poland in close alliance with Moscow, as Khrushchev, who had accepted his return to power only very reluctantly, came to appreciate.[41]

In Hungary tensions came to a head in October 1956, but took a different turn. They involved the toppling of a giant statue of Stalin in Budapest, the assassination of the first secretary of the party of the Budapest city committee, and the lynching of Communist secret policemen. Nagy, who had been readmitted to membership of the Hungarian party only in mid-October, became prime minister for a second time within a fortnight of getting back his party card. Even though he had spent years in the Soviet Union and had collaborated with the Soviet secret police, Nagy emerged as a 'national Communist' and a focus of identification for those who wished to assert Hungarian independence. Nagy went so far on 31 October as to raise the possibility of Hungary leaving the Warsaw Pact. By then the Soviet leadership had already decided to intervene militarily with overwhelming force to crush the popular rising and to remove Nagy from power. (He took refuge in the Yugoslav Embassy; when he left it, he was arrested, deported to Romania, where he was kept under house arrest before being returned to Budapest. In 1958 he was sentenced to death and hanged.) As Khrushchev told the Yugoslav leader, Josip Broz Tito, an opportune moment to send tanks and troops into Hungary had been provided by Britain, France, and Israel. The Israelis, in secret collusion with the British and the French, had attacked Egypt in late October 1956 with the aim both of reversing the nationalization of the Suez Canal and of removing from power the Egyptian president, Gamal Abdel Nasser.[42] At the beginning of November Soviet troops began their suppression of the Hungarian revolution.

Khrushchev was correct in his assessment of the timing. The attack on Egypt took precedence in the deliberations and condemnation of the United Nations over repression in Hungary. The attention of President Eisenhower was torn between events in Hungary and those in the Middle East, but his response to the Anglo-French connivance with Israel to invade Egypt had priority. The Eisenhower administration was able, through financial pressure, to get the British and French to call a halt to their Suez war, whereas the president felt powerless to stop the Soviet crackdown in Hungary.[43] For all the brinksmanship of Secretary of State John Foster Dulles, and talk in Washington circles of a rollback of Communism in Europe and of liberation of the 'Captive Nations', this remained at the level of rhetoric.[44] The division of Europe that had been accepted at the end of the Second World War was still in place. The more evident purpose of this language was to sound tough enough to mollify Senator Joseph McCarthy and his supporters and to 'roll back the Democrats from Capitol Hill', but not to risk war by trying to reverse the Soviet takeover of Eastern Europe.[45]

Western governments were slow to understand the evolutionary change that could take place within ruling Communist parties and to appreciate that behind their monolithic façade such parties in the post-Stalin era contained people of very different political beliefs and mindsets. Although the revolt in Hungary developed into an anti-Soviet movement, it was not especially anti-socialist and it was led by long-standing members of the Communist Party. That was still more clearly true of Czechoslovakia's 'Prague Spring', which resulted in another major Soviet military intervention. The Prague Spring was the culmination of a reform movement within the Communist Party of Czechoslovakia that had been gathering strength for five years prior to 1968 and which got its crucial breakthrough in January of that year when the long-standing party leader (who was also president of the country), Antonín Novotný, was replaced as first secretary of the party by Alexander Dubček. Political and economic reform was promptly initiated from within the party, with Dubček playing a facilitating role rather than that of prime mover.

The system was such that it was difficult for radical change to be launched from anywhere other than the top echelons of the party, but as the months went by, Czech and Slovak society as a whole became more active and politicized. Soviet efforts to cajole or intimidate the reformist grouping within the leadership of the Czechoslovak Communist Party into implementing their own crackdown failed. In August 1968 the Soviet leadership resorted to invasion, with contingents from all the other European members of the Warsaw Pact (apart from Romania) participating. Reformers were removed from office in Czechoslovakia and replaced by conformists who would uncritically follow Moscow's guidance. The process was, however, more gradual than the Soviet Politburo had initially intended because of the sheer scale of the non-violent resistance to the invasion. In Washington, the reaction of the Johnson administration to the invasion was muted even at a rhetorical level. They saw the Soviet military intervention as action by the major Communist power against a government within its acknowledged sphere of influence. The administration was also far more preoccupied with the Vietnam War and hoping that the Soviet Union might use its leverage to restrain its North Vietnamese allies.

Unrest in East and Central European Communist states occurred at frequent intervals from the 1950s to the 1980s. Among the first to take direct action in the early months after Stalin's death were East German workers who in June 1953 went on strike against higher work norms being demanded. Dozens of demonstrators were killed, others arrested, and later there were executions. The usual response of Communist authorities to serious unrest was to make economic concessions and take drastic action against those in the forefront of protest. Poland, the most obstreperous barracks in the camp, saw major conflicts between citizens and the authorities in 1956, 1968, 1970, and 1976 before the greatest challenge of all to Poland's Communist rulers arrived with the emergence of Solidarity, the unofficial trade union that became a mass movement, in 1980–1.

Once again, the Soviet leadership reacted cautiously where Poland was concerned. This most populous of East European countries had a tradition of resistance.

Moreover, the Polish diaspora had influence in the United States and an invasion of Poland could have had more serious international consequences for Moscow than interventions in Hungary and Czechoslovakia. Soviet relations with the United States, Western Europe, and China had already deteriorated after Soviet troops were sent into Afghanistan in December 1979 to remove (by killing) a supposedly pro-Soviet Afghan leader they had come to distrust and to support the ostensibly Marxist-Leninist Afghan government in a civil war with Islamic tribesmen. The war in Afghanistan was also a factor making armed intervention in Poland less likely. The director of the Institute of the USA and Canada in Moscow, Georgy Arbatov, an adviser to the Soviet political leadership, noted that Soviet troops being bogged down in Afghanistan 'may have helped us avoid an even more dangerous adventure: intervention in Poland during the political crisis in 1980'.[46]

The Soviet Politburo did, briefly, contemplate military intervention in Poland in August 1980,[47] but soon reverted to a more cautious line (which even the frequently impulsive Khrushchev had taken in 1956 in response to Polish unrest). Their policy in 1980–1 was to put intense pressure on the Polish Communist authorities to stop compromising with Solidarity (as they had done in the face of massive popular support for the movement) and to crack down on it. The Polish Communist leadership, in which General Wojciech Jaruzelski became first secretary of the party in October 1981, finally succumbed to this pressure from Moscow and declared martial law in December of that year. Solidarity leaders were imprisoned and the movement was reduced to a muted, underground resistance until, following radical change in Moscow, it was able to re-emerge in the later 1980s as a major political force.

On the Verge of Catastrophe

Some of the most dangerous moments in the Cold War occurred during the first Reagan administration, but there were times of great peril that were survived, partly by luck and partly through good judgement, in the years between Stalin's death in 1953 and the start of Reagan's presidency in 1980. They are touched on only sparingly here, for the main focus of this book is on the 1980s, especially the second half of that decade. But the enormous significance of what happened later emerges more clearly when it is appreciated how close the world came to catastrophe during the earlier Cold War years.

The Cuban missile crisis of October 1962 is, with good reason, regarded as the moment when the world came closest to nuclear war between the United States and the Soviet Union. By this time Nikita Khrushchev had increased his power in the Soviet leadership and was pushing through policies whose wisdom was doubted by some of those around him—and on the Cuban question specifically, by the longest-serving Politburo member, Anastas Mikoyan. His colleagues were generally too intimidated, however, by the force of Khrushchev's personality and the institutional power he wielded as head both of the Communist Party and of the Soviet government to withstand for long his determination to act. For Khrushchev, the surreptitious dispatch of nuclear missiles to Cuba had more than one advantage. At a time when the military balance of power still favoured the United States (the US had a 17–1 advantage over the Soviet Union in deliverable nuclear missiles), it was a way of reminding the American leadership that they could be placed in as imminent danger of destruction, and of preventing them from making any further attempt to overthrow Fidel Castro's government. Khrushchev was not looking to get into a war with the United States, although no-one in Washington could be sure of that at the time. He intended, rather, to use nuclear-armed missiles in Cuba as a bargaining chip. His intention was to keep their installation secret until after the US congressional elections were held in November 1962, then inform Kennedy of this fait accompli in a face-to-face meeting, before travelling on to Cuba to sign a defence agreement with Castro. The missiles, he told a Soviet delegation departing for Havana, were 'the only way to save Cuba' and 'to scare' the Americans. It would 'restrain them' and 'give them back some of their medicine'.[48]

The United States had better technical intelligence expertise than Khrushchev had reckoned with. One of the experts in electronic surveillance of Soviet nuclear weapons systems was the 35-year-old scientist, Bill Perry, later in his career a senior Defense Department official in the Carter administration and Bill Clinton's Secretary for Defense from 1994 to 1997. Perry was summoned from California in mid-October 1962 to join the Washington team analysing high-resolution photographs being taken by US reconnaissance aircraft flying low over Cuba. He and the others were able to identify the missiles as those with a range that would enable them to hit much of the United States. They believed that the weapons were, however, still several weeks away from being fully operational and equipped with nuclear warheads.[49]

President Kennedy was determined to keep American options open for as long as possible. He set up an informal body, rather misleadingly known as the Executive Committee (or ExComm), which sometimes met without the president and had a fluctuating membership. It became a forum for wide-ranging and uninhibited discussion of the pluses and minuses of the various responses. The idea that gradually came to dominate, and which appealed to Kennedy, was that of a naval blockade around Cuba, which was given the less belligerent name of a 'quarantine'. The purpose was to give the Soviet leadership time for second thoughts, time for their ships to change course, time also for secret diplomacy to take effect. The military chiefs, in contrast, advocated 'a surprise attack on comprehensive targets, leading to complete blockade and invasion' of Cuba. They believed that the crisis would end in war with the Soviet Union and that it should be fought on the terms least disadvantageous for the United States.[50] General Curtis E. Le May told the president that a naval blockade would not solve the problem, for it would allow the missiles to be concealed, and that the policy being proposed 'is almost as bad as the appeasement at Munich'.[51] The military chiefs admitted, however, that an air strike would not instantly destroy all the known missiles and that those they knew of might comprise only some 60 per cent of the total.[52] Thus, it was clear enough that, far from 'solving the problem', air strikes as a first resort would be likely to lead to retaliatory attacks on the United States.

Kennedy also consulted foreign leaders, especially British Prime Minister Harold Macmillan, with whom he spoke daily by telephone. In a meeting Kennedy held with the Congressional leadership, in which they urged air strikes on Cuba and criticized the naval quarantine as too weak a reaction, the president read out a letter he had received from Macmillan. 'Many of us in Europe', wrote the prime minister, 'have lived so long in close proximity to the enemy's nuclear weapons of the most devastating kind that we have got accustomed to it.' Kennedy informed Macmillan of the planned blockade, whereby Soviet ships would not be allowed to come closer to Cuba than 800 miles. Macmillan supported the suggestion of the UK ambassador to Washington, David Ormsby-Gore, who enjoyed good relations both with the president and with the prime minister, that the radius be reduced to 500 miles from Cuba to give the Soviet leadership more time for a change of maritime and political course. This was informally agreed by Kennedy, although the line was deliberately kept flexible.[53]

The policy of seeking a breathing space for both sides worked. Diplomacy, including not only correspondence between the president and Khrushchev but secret negotiations conducted by Robert Kennedy with the Soviet ambassador, Anatoly Dobrynin, succeeded in establishing some common ground.[54] Soviet missiles already in Cuba were removed and the ships carrying missiles that were on their way to the island returned to Soviet ports with their cargoes. To the world at large it seemed like an American victory, and Kennedy's skill in the handling of the crisis, given the peaceful outcome, was widely admired both at home and abroad. Nevertheless, in the United States, in particular, there were influential figures both in the ranks of military and among civilian advisers who felt that Kennedy had conceded too much and that the US should have taken a tougher line. Thus, even a quarter of a century after the Cuban missile crisis, the American arms negotiator Paul Nitze, could write: 'With the nuclear balance heavily in our favour, I believed we could have pushed the Kremlin in 1962 to give up its efforts to establish Soviet influence in this hemisphere.'[55]

In spite of the fact that the Soviet Union achieved some of its objectives, the crisis did Khrushchev little good domestically. When his colleagues got together to remove him from power while he was holidaying on the Black Sea coast two years later, part of the indictment was his reckless foisting of nuclear missiles on Cuba. Fidel Castro had, in fact, been reluctant to receive them in the first place and was even angrier when the Soviet leader agreed to their removal without consulting him. He felt that Khrushchev could have exacted a higher price for their withdrawal, including the closing of the American naval base at Guantánamo Bay.[56]

The deal that was agreed behind the scenes involved two major concessions by the Americans. The first, which was made public, was that the US would not to try to overthrow by force the Castro regime.* The second was to agree that, after a decent interval (to obscure the connection with the settlement of the Cuban crisis), they would remove NATO missiles from Turkey. Khrushchev was denied credit in his own country for that compromise on the part of the US because it was part of the deal that the link would not be publicized. In one respect, it was, nevertheless, a bonus for the Soviet Union. Khrushchev had already dictated a speech that, in essence, accepted America's demands for ending the crisis before he learned of the extra US concession over Turkey.[57]

What Americans did not know at the time they were trying to formulate their response to the missiles was that, as Perry noted in his memoir years later, a lot of the nuclear warheads to be carried by the 162 missiles were already in Cuba.[58] A more belligerent US response could have led to direct nuclear attack from Cuba on American cities and military sites. Although the crisis ended without war, Perry, after a lifetime in the American defence establishment, wrote in 2015 that he believed in 1962, and still believed, that 'the world avoided a nuclear holocaust as much by good luck as by good management'.[59] Mikoyan, who had been a voice of moderation on the Soviet side throughout the crisis, was in no doubt that the two sides had been 'on the verge of a Third World War'.[60]

The Cuban Missile Crisis was just one among a number of occasions when nuclear war could have been started by accident—as a result either of technical malfunction or of human error. There was a real possibility of war being triggered without the imprimatur of those in the highest positions of political authority. The Soviet ships bound for Cuba were escorted by nuclear-armed submarines. 'Only years after the crisis', noted Perry, 'did we learn that one of the Soviet commanders had seriously considered firing one of his nuclear torpedoes at an American destroyer that was trying to force him to surface. He was dissuaded from doing so only by the other officers on the submarine.'[61]

Soviet commanders in Cuba had the authority to fire their medium-range nuclear missiles if they believed that they were about to be attacked. There were, moreover, circumstances in which the decision to launch nuclear weapons could be taken by American generals rather than by the president. Some US actions might have been construed as presaging an attack, leading to pre-emptive action from the Soviet side.

---

* It had been tried before, especially when Cuban exiles were landed at the Bay of Pigs in Cuba in 1961, quickly rounded up, and comprehensively defeated. So, in agreeing not to repeat such follies, the administration was doing itself a favour as well as the Russians and Cubans. This did not prevent the continuation by successive administrations of economic sanctions against Cuba and the attempted isolation of its regime, even many years after the Soviet Union—and the international Communist movement—had ceased to exist. It was not until the presidency of Barack Obama that was this self-defeating policy was belatedly abandoned.

When an American U-2 spy plane ventured into Soviet Siberian airspace, Khrushchev warned that it could have been mistaken for a bomber. In fact, American bombers, at the height of the Cuban crisis, flew further than their normal turnaround points toward Soviet airspace. This could have led Soviet radar operators to believe that war had begun.[62] General Tommy Power, who was in charge of America's bomber aircraft, was granted authority to order retaliatory attacks on the Soviet Union 'if time or circumstances would not permit a decision by the President'.[63] As the historian of nuclear weapons Gerard DeGroot notes, Power had the planes under his command in the air, flying over the Mediterranean and Northern Canada, ready to attack the Soviet Union at any moment. 'One mistake, one tiny miscalculation, one minuscule misreading of signals and the world might have been destroyed.'[64]

In November 1979, when Perry was Undersecretary of Defense, he was woken up in the middle of the night by an American general to tell him that his warning computer was showing 200 Intercontinental Ballistic Missiles in flight from the Soviet Union to the United States. The officer said he would have to report the incident to the president in the morning, but he had concluded that this must be a false alarm and he wanted help to determine what could have gone wrong. It turned out that a training tape had accidentally been installed in the computer—another instance when 'catastrophic nuclear war could have started by accident'.[65]

Four years later, on the night of 31 August/1 September 1983, a Korean passenger airliner (KAL 007) was shot down after it had gone comprehensively off course and strayed deep into Soviet airspace. An American spy plane had been in the vicinity when the civilian plane first flew in the direction of Sakhalin and Soviet ground controllers confused the two. The recorded conversations among those who took the decision to shoot down the airliner included the airing of doubts about what kind of plane this was, for the airliner was not on a route permitted to any passenger aircraft and had ventured further than any US spy plane normally did. The local commanders, who took the decision (no politicians were involved), concluded it must be a military aircraft and the order was given to destroy it. All 269 people on board were killed. The international outrage was all the greater because almost a week elapsed before the Soviet authorities even admitted to having shot down the plane. Moscow's dissimulation was compounded by unwarranted Western accusations that the Soviet forces had deliberately and knowingly shot down a civilian aircraft. In reality, this was an example of human error with tragic consequences. It further embittered an already febrile international atmosphere.[66]

Neither hot-headedness nor prudence were the exclusive properties of just one side in the Cold War. Less than four weeks after the KAL 007 tragedy, a disaster on a much vaster scale was avoided when a Soviet officer refused to be panicked by the most alarming information he had ever encountered. Stanislav Petrov, a lieutenant-colonel with mathematical and engineering qualifications, was manning an early-warning station south of Moscow on the night of 26 September 1983, when his electronic control panel indicated that an American attack had been launched. He was aware that Minutemen bases in the United States, whose location was marked on the map in front of him, contained 1,000 intercontinental ballistic missiles, armed with nuclear warheads. They would take just thirty-five minutes to reach the Soviet Union. A light on the map at one of the American missile bases had come on and a siren had sounded.

Initially, the data appeared to indicate that one missile had been fired, and Petrov's training had led him to expect a nuclear war would begin with a massive attack. But then the panel told him that a number of missiles had been fired, as the system went into overdrive and 'the red letters on the panel began to flash MISSILE ATTACK'. This information was automatically being conveyed to higher levels of the military. However, as the commander in charge at the early-warning station (whose alternative sources of information included data from an optical telescope which did not yet show any sign of incoming missiles), Petrov had to give his assessment to higher authority. If he confirmed that intercontinental missiles were on their way, this would leave the General Staff and the Soviet political leadership several minutes to come to a decision on their response. With no visual sighting of missiles or any data on them from radar, Petrov decided that the emergency must have been caused by a computer malfunction. Throughout the crisis, he had a phone in one hand as he appraised the scant data, weighed up the probabilities, and then reported his assessment to the senior officer at the other end of the line: 'this is a false alarm'.[67]

During the Cold War, many of those who thought of themselves as 'realists', whether in politics or as academic specialists on international relations, believed that the leaders of the superpowers were rational actors and could, therefore, be relied upon to avoid nuclear war. Yet, so long as Stalin was alive, official doctrine stuck with the Leninist postulate that while capitalism existed, war was inevitable. A significant shift occurred in the mid-1950s when Soviet leaders, beginning with Nikita Khrushchev, espoused a doctrine of 'peaceful coexistence'. The Soviet side emphasized that this did not mean ideological coexistence. There would still be a fierce and unrelenting struggle of ideas, and in the Communist world everyone needed to be on their guard against infiltration of 'bourgeois' ideology. Nevertheless, there was no necessity for this ideological struggle to lead to war between the super-powers. Whatever military men on both sides might say from time to time, the top political leaders in Washington and Moscow were agreed that in a nuclear war between the United States and the Soviet Union, there could be no winners.

That was a big step forward. To assume, nevertheless, that there would always be rational actors, with enough time during a crisis to reach a prudent decision, was more Panglossian than realistic. We now know how close the world came to nuclear war by accident and how, on a number of occasions, this could have happened without the top leaders consciously deciding to wage war. Moreover, as Daniel Kahneman has put it, 'the only test of rationality is not whether a person's beliefs and preferences are reasonable, but whether they are internally consistent'.[68] Unreasonable and inhumane beliefs can be held with a degree of logical consistency, as they were both by Stalin and by Hitler. Stalin, convinced that war against the Western powers would take place sooner or later, was in the late 1940s preparing for such a future military confrontation.[69] There were periods even in the post-Stalin era when one side believed that the other was intent on war. This led in such times of high tension to the fear of a pre-emptive strike and the temptation, accordingly, for the more alarmed side to get *its* pre-emptive strike in first. Thus, the Cold War, which encompassed not only the all-too-real Korean and Vietnam wars in Asia but also proxy wars in Africa, when the superpowers backed and supplied opposing sides, always contained the very real possibility of cataclysm on a far vaster scale.[70] The magnitude of the looming disaster was such that even some of those involved in the policy process found it hard to grasp. As President Kennedy said to his press secretary, Pierre Salinger, after one ExComm meeting during the Cuban missile crisis, 'Do you think the people in that room realize that if we make a mistake, there may be 200 million dead?'[71]

2

THE MAKING OF MIKHAIL GORBACHEV

Eamast–West tensions remained dangerously high when Mikhail Gorbachev became Soviet leader in March 1985. More than anyone else in the Politburo at that time, he was acutely conscious of the Cold War's potential to escalate out of the control of politicians with disastrous consequences for humanity. Gorbachev had a different mindset from that of any other member of Konstantin Chernenko's Politburo, and his political thinking continued to evolve significantly while he held the post of General Secretary of the Central Committee of the Communist Party of the Soviet Union between 1985 and 1991. This chapter, however, is concerned with Gorbachev's formative experiences and the influences on his thinking before he attained the position of greatest power in the Soviet system.

Gorbachev was born into a peasant family on 2 March 1931 in the village of Privolnoe, in the Stavropol region of southern Russia. Ethnically Russian on his father's side (and identified as Russian on his Soviet passport), his mother's parents were of Ukrainian descent. The collectivization of agriculture was underway at the time of Mikhail's birth and his grandparents reacted to it very differently. His Russian grandfather, Andrey Gorbachev, kept his individual peasant holding for as long as was possible and became a collective farmer only when there was absolutely no alternative. In contrast, Mikhail's Ukrainian grandfather, Panteley Gopkalo, enthusiastically embraced the Bolshevik cause, joined the Communist Party in 1928, and in the 1930s was chairman of a collective farm about 20 kilometres from Privolnoe. By virtue of that position, Gopkalo's living accommodation, although primitive, was not quite as cramped as that of Mikhail's parents. Until he went to school, Mikhail lived mainly in the home of these maternal grandparents, to whom he felt especially close. Neither grandfather was a religious believer, any more than was Gorbachev's father or Gorbachev himself, but his grandmothers and his mother were, and they had him baptized as a baby. There was a tolerance within the family that contrasted with the intensive anti-religious propaganda of the regime (which was relaxed, however, during the Second World War). Grandfather Gopkalo, his Communist beliefs notwithstanding, did not belittle his wife's religiosity, and an icon and an icon lamp stood in a corner of the room in 'peaceful coexistence', as Gorbachev put it, with the portraits of Lenin and Stalin that rested on a small homemade table.[1] Gorbachev was effectively an only child, for his one sibling—also a boy, Aleksandr—was not born until 1947, when Mikhail was 16.

Gorbachev's mother, Maria (Gopkalo) Gorbacheva, was a determined and hard-working woman, a strict disciplinarian at home—and illiterate. His father, Sergey Gorbachev, although he had only a rudimentary education, was fully literate, an intelligent and considerate man of broad interests and an exemplary farm worker. Although Mikhail was devoted to both of his parents, he felt the greater affinity with his father. Sergey's affection and encouragement for his son, combined with the unconditional love of his grandparents and the tough love of his mother, meant that Gorbachev remembered the first ten years of his life as a happy childhood. That was in spite of the fact that they were a time of hardship, tragedy and trauma for his country, for his village, and for his own family. His view of the first decade of his life may also be coloured by his vivid memories of what was immediately to follow.

Severe famine hit southern Russia, including the Stavropol region, in 1933, caused by a combination of the harsh procurement policies imposed from Moscow, the regime's prioritizing of the needs of workers in the city over peasants in the country-side, inefficiencies in the supply chain, collectivization, and drought. Gorbachev's father, one of six children, lost three of his siblings in that famine, and between a third and a half of the population of Privolnoe died. These tragedies were compounded by the arrests of both of Mikhail's grandfathers in the course of the same decade. Grandfather Andrey was arrested in the spring of 1934 for not having fulfilled the sowing plan, although there had been no seeds supplied for him to sow. He spent the next year and a half felling trees in a forced labour camp in Siberia. He was then released, and given a written commendation for his hard work. Maternal grandfather and party member Panteley Gopkalo was arrested in 1937, the peak year of Stalin's purges. He was accused of being a member of a 'counter-revolutionary right-wing Trotskyist organization' and of having agitated against the Soviet system and against collectivization. None of this was even remotely true, but the security agencies had to find real or imaginary enemies, subversives and saboteurs in order to meet the quotas of arrests imposed from Moscow. Gopkalo was subjected to a variety of tortures, but he endured these without, apparently, confessing to the fictitious charges. He was eventually released in December 1938 after fourteen months of internment. His health was undermined by the experience and he died at the age of 59.

Whether such cases ended with the prisoner's execution or release from captivity depended quite largely on chance. Petr Parada, the maternal grandfather of Gorbachev's future wife, Raisa Titarenko, was arrested—also in 1937—in the Altai region of Russia, thousands of kilometres from Stavropol, and charged with the same spurious offences. He was found guilty by the troika of three officials who wielded the power of life or death over the accused, and was shot. The families of those arrested suffered the loss not only of their loved ones but also social exclusion. They were shunned by friends and neighbours who feared that contact with them would be seen as evidence of guilt by association. Writing about the experience of his own family, Gorbachev noted that when his maternal grandmother, Vasilisa Gopkalo, came to live with them in Privolnoe after the arrest of her husband, this immediately had the effect of putting them in a kind of quarantine—'the home of an enemy of the people'. If anyone dared to visit them, it was only at night. 'This', he wrote when he was already over 80, 'has remained in my memory'.[2]

Like a majority of Soviet families at the time, the Gorbachevs and Gopkalos did not in the 1930s hold Stalin or the Soviet system responsible for the injustices they had experienced. It was assumed that Stalin would have intervened to prevent these false accusations if only he had known about them. The fault, it was believed, lay with malicious or misinformed members of the security police, the NKVD. When Stalin's purge extended to leaders and members of the NKVD as well, this was seen as a restoration of some kind of justice—corroboration of the validity of the innocent victims' faith in Stalin who was now giving the persecutors their due deserts. Not until Nikita Khrushchev first revealed the role of Stalin as chief orchestrator of the purges at the Twentieth Congress of the Soviet Communist Party in 1956 did many of the survivors, and the families of those who did not survive, come to understand the extent of Stalin's guilt. A very few of them went a step further and raised, in the company of trusted friends, the question of what was wrong with the system that had enabled Stalin to preside over mass murder. Reformers and anti-Stalinists in the post-Stalin epoch were disproportionately to be found among those whose families had been directly affected by Stalin's purges. It is clearly relevant to an understanding of the reformism and anti-Stalinism of the future Soviet leader, Mikhail Gorbachev, that both of his grandfathers, neither of whom had committed any crime, were among the victims of such blatant injustice.[3]

The 1940s

The German attack on the Soviet Union launched on 22 June 1941 meant that, aged 10, Mikhail had to start shouldering responsibilities more onerous than those that fall to most adults in normal times. His father was conscripted into the army and at one point reported to have been killed in action. The information turned out to be wrong, although he was on two separate occasions wounded and ended the war in hospital in Czechoslovakia. From the time his father left for the front, Mikhail Gorbachev (between the ages of 10 and 14) had to work the vegetable patch beside the family home which provided the food that kept his mother and him alive. It was the boy's task also to find fodder for their one cow and firewood to heat the small wooden house, while his mother worked all day on the collective farm.

For two years Mikhail did not go to school, for there was no longer a school to attend. From August 1942 until January 1943 Privolnoe was under German occupation. Communist Party members and their families came a very close second to Jews as prime candidates for extermination. Following rumours of executions and the reality of them in neighbouring towns, Gorbachev's grandmother and mother hid 11-year-old Mikhail on a farm some kilometres from the village for fear that he would be targeted as the grandson of the collective farm chairman and the son of a soldier in the Red Army. Soviet troops liberated the area in late January 1943, less than a week before a massacre by the Nazis, abetted by local collaborators, was due to take place.[4] When the snow cleared in March 1943, Gorbachev roamed some way beyond the village with other children in the pursuit of war trophies. They came across a mass of rotting corpses: Soviet soldiers who had been killed in battle the previous summer and whose bodies were visible only now with the arrival of the thaw.[5]

Mikhail Gorbachev's war years were incomparably grimmer than those of his future adversary and partner, Ronald Reagan, or, for that matter, of Margaret Thatcher. President George H. W. Bush, in contrast with his predecessor in the White House, had extensive first-hand experience of war as a naval aviator who flew almost sixty combat missions and who was rescued from the Pacific Ocean after his plane was hit by Japanese anti-aircraft fire. Among Gorbachev's later counterparts, the person who experienced devastation and suffering in his own homeland and shared with him a full understanding of the horrors of war was German Chancellor Helmut Kohl. He was a schoolboy in Germany during the war years, but his elder brother was killed on active service while still in his teens. Gorbachev's wartime experiences remained vivid to him throughout his life. Looking back in 2012, at the age of 81, he wrote that he could still see in his mind's eye the ravaged post-war countryside. 'Our generation', he wrote, 'is the generation of children of the war. It scorched us, it put its imprint on our character and on our perception of the world. What we lived through in childhood most likely explains why precisely we, wartime children, resolved to change the existing way of life.'[6]

In November 1944 Gorbachev returned to school—housed in a collection of makeshift buildings, and lacking the most basic resources. At first, it seemed unreal and irrelevant following the day-to-day struggle for survival that had preceded it, and after his first day the 13-year-old Mikhail told his mother he had had enough of it and would not be going back. His grandfather Gopkalo and his father, in a letter from the front, impressed upon him the value of schooling, and his mother, though she could not read herself, disappeared for a day and came back with a pile of books for him. He spent the night reading them and returned to school the next day. He flourished there and in every academic year after 1944–5 he was given an 'excellent' grade, receiving a silver medal in his final year.* The local school did not go beyond the

---

* Far away, in Siberia, his future wife, Raisa Titarenko, went one better—she was presented with a gold medal. That award enabled her to go to any Soviet university of her choice. She chose Moscow State University which was where, in 1951, she met her future husband.

eighth grade. For those who wished to continue to the ninth and tenth grades, the nearest secondary school providing such education was 20 kilometres away in Krasnogvardeysk, called Molotovskoe at the time Gorbachev studied there, in honour of Stalin's right-hand man, Vyacheslav Molotov.[7] He shared a room with another pupil and returned to Privolnoe once a week to visit his family and stock up with food.

Gorbachev became secretary of the Komsomol (Young Communist League) at the school and took an active part in amateur dramatics, touring the villages with a group of young performers. He said later that he took to acting both from a wish to mix with his peers and also from 'the desire to express myself'.[8] Another incentive, as noted by Gorbachev's most recent and most comprehensive biographer, William Taubman, was that 'Yulia Karagodina, a girl in whom he had more than a passing interest, was his leading lady.'[9] They performed classic Russian plays, including those of Chekhov and Lermontov's *Masquerade*. In Karagodina's recollection, Gorbachev was 'a very good actor' who even talked with her about the possibility of 'trying for a theatrical institute'.[10] Both the Komsomol and the amateur theatricals provided an early introduction to the art of public speaking.

Gorbachev made his first public speech, however, when, aged 17 in 1948, he received a notable state award for his labour feats. As a teenager, Mikhail combined school with hard physical labour. In the summer months, he worked alongside his father, now recovered from his war wounds, in the fields around Privolnoe. Gorbachev received the Order of Red Banner of Labour and his father was given the Order of Lenin. This was for their harvesting heroics in which they exceeded the high state prize target for grain.[11] When Mikhail entered Moscow University, there were some older students who had served in the war who wore the Red Banner insignia, but it was highly unusual for a young student who had come straight from school to have earned the right to do so.[12]

Like many others in the immediate post-war years, Gorbachev was inspired by patriotic zeal to rebuild a shattered country and to help feed an impoverished population. Establishing his credentials as an exceptionally meritorious worker was also, however, of particular political significance for Gorbachev because it overrode two negative features in his biography. The fact that both his grandfathers had been arrested at different times in the 1930s and the circumstance that he had lived, albeit as an 11-year-old, under German occupation would have been held against him, especially in Stalin's time, and would have blighted his prospects. The odds against a peasant boy being accepted by Moscow University in 1950 were very high. That Gorbachev was admitted to the Law Faculty of that university was thanks to a combination of getting the maximum grade of 5 in all subjects except German (in which he got a 4—hence a silver, rather than gold, medal), his Komsomol leadership at school, and, above all, the award of the Red Banner.[13]

Moscow University

Gorbachev's train journey to Moscow to begin his university studies took him to the Soviet Union's capital city for the first time. His nineteen years had been full of drama, but far from the centre of Russian political and cultural life. The next five were to leave a different, but no less profound, mark on him. His own experience, and that of his family, had already made Gorbachev aware at one level of the gulf between propaganda and reality in everyday Soviet life. Moreover, through his wide reading as a teenager he already had access to values and ideas other than those to be found in Soviet Marxism-Leninism. The modest holdings of the Privolnoe library included a new one-volume collection of the writings of the radical nineteenth-century Russian critic and Westernizer, Vissarion Belinsky, which Gorbachev read and then reread. When he came to Moscow it was the first book he bought for himself.[14] By this time he had already devoured many classics of Russian literature, including works of Pushkin, Lermontov, Gogol, Tolstoy, Dostoevsky (a writer only infrequently published during the Soviet period) and Turgenev.[15] The limitations of his rural schooling meant that, in spite of all the reading he had undertaken on his own initiative, he was less well-informed than many other new students in Moscow University. He quickly caught up, for as his good friend in the Law Faculty, Zdeněk Mlynář, a young Czech Communist who was later to become one of the most important reformers of the 'Prague Spring', observed, Gorbachev was 'very intelligent and gifted'.[16]

Mlynář was not only Gorbachev's first foreign friend but the person—his wife Raisa always excepted—to whom even years later he felt closest. He is the best-informed source on Gorbachev's university years.[17] As a student, Mlynář noted, Gorbachev was a good listener, and that was a quality he preserved, even though it went alongside a tendency to speak at often excessive length. Writing at the very outset of Gorbachev's leadership in 1985, Mlynář described him as both 'loyal and personally honest', and said that, as a student, he had 'an informal and spontaneous authority'.[18] Thirty years after graduating from Moscow University, Mlynář had no reason to be sympathetic to high-ranking Soviet Communists, for he was by then a political exile from his own country.[19]

When he entered the university Law Faculty in 1950 and for many years thereafter, Gorbachev was a true believer in the achievements and potential of the Soviet system and of the role played by the Communist Party. He was also an avid reader of the writings of its principal founder, Vladimir Lenin. Whereas many students relied on rote learning of passages from Marx and Lenin in order to pass the ideological examinations that had to be taken each year, he approached Marxist literature as 'an instrument for understanding the world'.[20] But he had a favourite quotation, 'truth is always concrete', that was taken, somewhat paradoxically, from Hegel (who was hardly the most down-to-earth of philosophers). This phrase he deployed when university teachers came out with stereotypes far removed from real life. Thus, it was from Gorbachev that Mlynář learned how remote from rural reality were the lectures they heard on collective farm law. When they saw the film, 'Cossacks of Kuban', an absurdly idealized account of life in southern Russia, with tables bending under the weight of food piled up on them, Gorbachev taught him what those tables were really like.[21] Yet an ability to separate starry-eyed illusions from reality had nothing in common with disaffection. The Soviet system had enabled a young person from a peasant background to be admitted to Russia's top university and subsequently to rise through the political hierarchy.

The five years Gorbachev spent at Moscow State University were life-enhancing. He met his future wife, Raisa Titarenko, a student in the Philosophy Faculty who was a year ahead of him at the university but a year younger, in 1951. They married in 1953 and remained devoted to each other and inseparable until her death in 1999. Together, they took advantage of the cultural riches of Moscow—art galleries, theatre, ballet, and opera. Soviet theatres were heavily subsidized and inexpensive and Mikhail's and Raisa's student grants just about stretched to the cheapest tickets, although they ran out of money for food by the end of each month. Of greater immediate relevance to his future career, Gorbachev became the head of the Komsomol for his particular year in the Law Faculty (*komsorg kursa*) and was accepted as a full member of the Communist Party in 1952. The early 1950s were years of renewed repression in Stalin's Soviet Union and much of the teaching in the Law Faculty involved incantation of Stalinist nostrums and lectures on legal doctrine that had little or nothing in common with the reality of judicial practice. Yet there were several erudite scholars and stimulating teachers even in the Law Faculty. One such teacher was Professor Stepan Kechekyan, whose own pre-revolutionary education had involved study in France. His lectures on the history of legal and political thought, including the ideas of the Enlightenment, fascinated Gorbachev and Mlynář.*

In a recorded conversation with Mlynář four decades later, Gorbachev recalled that Moscow University had been for him 'a different world, a different atmosphere from the one I had lived in before'. Probably the most important thing, he said, 'came as a result of contact with outstanding university professors', to which Mlynář added 'especially with professors of the old school'. 'Like Kechekyan', Gorbachev interjected. He 'opened up an entire world of ideas for us: the Vedas of India, Confucianism, Plato and Aristotle, Machiavelli and Rousseau. The history of human thought, a world we had not known, excited our minds.' Before entering university, he said,

---

* I also retain a high regard for Stepan Fedorovich Kechekyan. On my first visit to Russia, for three months in early 1966 on a British Council–Soviet Ministry of Higher Education exchange scholarship, he was my official academic adviser.

'I was trapped in my belief system in the sense that I accepted a great deal as given, as assumptions not to be questioned. At the university I began to think and reflect and to look at things differently. But of course that was only the beginning of a prolonged process.'[22]

If by far the most important event in Gorbachev's personal life during his time at Moscow University was his meeting with his future wife, the most important event politically during his university days was the death of Stalin, which happened just beyond the mid-way point of his five-year course. Following Stalin's death, conversation among the students became notably freer in the atmosphere of what became known as 'the thaw'.[23] Gorbachev got to know some of Raisa's fellow-students in the Philosophical Faculty, among them a Georgian and future dissident philosopher named Merab Mamardashvili and a young man who was to become in later years one of Russia's leading sociological researchers, Yury Levada.[24] Gorbachev finished his university studies with a much better-informed and more open mind than he had when he embarked upon them. The evolution of his thinking, though, still had a long way to go.

Back to Stavropol

With Raisa already embarked on a further degree at Moscow University, Gorbachev had hoped to stay in Moscow after graduating and to work in the central Procuracy, the body that oversaw the legal system. His failure to obtain such a post was a blessing in disguise, for the Procuracy would not have provided a path to a high-flying political career. The established route to political power and influence was through the apparatus of the Communist Party. Gorbachev returned to his native Stavropol region and was soon joined there by Raisa, who later took up a teaching post in the Stavropol Agricultural Institute and completed sociological research for the Soviet equivalent of a PhD on the way of life of the peasantry in the Stavropol region.[25] After a few weeks in the Stavropol Procuracy, Gorbachev decided that a life in the Soviet legal profession was not for him and, thanks to his Komsomol background, secured a post as deputy head of the Department of Propaganda and Agitation of the Stavropol Komsomol regional committee. Thereafter, he enjoyed speedy promotion through the ranks—first of the Komsomol, and then of the Communist Party organization in his native province. After he became party first secretary for the Stavropol region in 1970, a post he held until 1978 when he joined the top leadership team in Moscow, he enjoyed far more autonomy as the party boss for a vast territory than he would have been able to exercise in a subordinate position in the capital.

In addition to being far from Moscow, and exercising great authority within his own domain—true for other Soviet regional party secretaries, people sometimes referred to as 'the barons' or as 'the Soviet prefects'[26]—Gorbachev benefited from a particular feature of his southern Russian region. The Stavropol territory contained a number of spas and was a favourite holiday resort for some of the leading members of the Politburo. In particular, it was a regular destination for Mikhail Suslov (the second secretary of the party in the years when Leonid Brezhnev was general secretary) who had at an earlier stage of his career been the Stavropol first secretary. It was also a destination for Yury Andropov, the Chairman of the KGB (and future General Secretary of the Communist Party), himself a native of the Stavropol region; and for the Chairman of the Council of Ministers, Aleksey Kosygin. The regional first secretary was obliged to meet and greet leading politicians visiting from Moscow, and Gorbachev took full advantage of the opportunities this afforded him, making a good impression on these senior members of the Soviet political elite.

While the death of Stalin produced some relaxation of the oppressive atmosphere in the Soviet Union, the Twentieth Congress of the Communist Party in February 1956 had an even greater political impact. This was the forum at which Khrushchev made his famous 'Secret Speech'—in a closed session of the Congress—when he divulged many of the crimes of Stalin, especially those committed against people such as the Congress delegates. (Persecution of non-party intellectuals and of the Orthodox Church and other religious groups was passed over in silence.) Since these Communist officials and activists had been socialized into believing in the infallibility of the party and of its leader, the great Stalin, the revelations came as a profound shock. The exposure of at least some of the crimes of Stalin had huge repercussions also within the international Communist movement and it was, as we have seen, a stimulus to massive demonstrations in Poland and to revolution in Hungary.

Already a member of the regional committee of the Communist Party, by virtue of his high office in the Stavropol Komsomol, Gorbachev was one of the small minority of Soviet citizens allowed to read a near-verbatim report of Khrushchev's speech. The new policy of condemnation of Stalin's personality cult had to be explained to citizens at large and Gorbachev travelled around the Stavropol region doing so. Many people he met resented the attacks on the leader whom they had revered and resisted the idea of owning up to historic wrongs. At the Twenty-Second Party Congress in 1961, however, Khrushchev returned to the attack on Stalin, and this time in public session. Younger and better-educated citizens and those whose families had suffered directly from Stalinist repression were the most receptive to denunciation of the man who had led the Soviet Union through collectivization, industrialization, the purges, and the Second World War.[27] Within the party leadership, however, both at the local and at the national level, there remained deep misgivings about Khrushchev's revelations, for they gave rise to the question, 'Where were you when all this was happening?'[28]

With his Moscow University education and having lived in the household of an 'enemy of the people', Gorbachev fitted perfectly into the category of those receptive to Khrushchev's bold initiative. He could relate what he learned to the experience of his grandparents in the 1930s. As he later put it, Gorbachev saw the 1956 Congress 'as the beginning of something new, as providing tremendous new opportunities for the future', bringing hope even of 'greater openness and democracy'.[29] In the Soviet Union in the 1970s and 1980s, 'Children of the Twentieth Congress' was a term applied to people old enough in 1956 for the denunciation of Stalin to have had an impact on them, young enough to cast off many of their previous beliefs—including, naturally, veneration for Stalin*—and inspired to work for reform of the system.[30] While they believed that there was much that needed to change in the Soviet Union, that did not mean they considered the system was fundamentally flawed and beyond repair. As Gorbachev later put it, referring to his optimism in the immediate aftermath of the Twentieth Congress, 'the thought that we were traveling on the wrong road, that it was necessary to change the whole system of economic and political relations down to their foundations—there was no such concept'.[31] Gorbachev's thinking continued to evolve, but that radical conclusion—that the system needed to be utterly transformed, replaced rather than merely reformed—was one he reached only much later: thirty-two years later, in 1988.

In September 1956 Gorbachev was appointed first secretary of the Komsomol of Stavropol city. By 1961 he was first secretary of the regional Komsomol organization, and in 1962 he moved from that post into the Communist Party apparatus. His subsequent promotion within the ruling party was rapid. He was only 39 (young for a regional boss in the Brezhnev era) when he was chosen as party first secretary for the Stavropol province in 1970. That was followed by his election to the Central Committee of the Communist Party in 1971.

Central Committee membership came with a number of privileges, including the opportunity to order books from Moscow that were available only to a narrow segment of the political elite. They included the memoirs and other writings of Western politicians in Russian translation, among them the works of prominent social democrats, most notably former West German Chancellor Willy Brandt. Also published in these restricted editions were books by 'Eurocommunists'—leading representatives of the reformist strand that, much to the consternation of the Brezhnev leadership in the Soviet Union, had arisen in several European Communist parties, particularly in Italy and Spain. Gorbachev was an unusual regional party secretary in making assiduous use of these materials to broaden and deepen his political knowledge. His wide reading embraced the works of Georgy Shakhnazarov, a party intellectual and future Gorbachev aide who was flattered to discover that this rising official in the

---

* During his years in power, Gorbachev spoke bluntly about the crimes of Stalin with foreign Communists as well as with members of his own party. In a conversation with the General Secretary of the Italian Communist Party (PCI), Ochille Occhetto on 28 February 1989, Gorbachev said that in the 1930s the Communist Party of the Soviet Union (CPSU) had become 'prisoners of the Stalinshchina' and that the latter had constituted 'a definite group who usurped power and brought about calamities' ('Iz besedy s general'nym sekretarem Ital'yanskoy kompartii A. Okketto, 28 fevralya 1989 goda', in Gorbachev, *Sobranie sochineniy*, Vol. XIII (Ves' mir, Moscow, 2009), pp. 292–311, at p. 293).

party secretariat had read some of his books.[32] Gorbachev surprised his London hosts on his first visit to Britain in December 1984 by citing C. P. Snow's *Corridors of Power* and C. Northcote Parkinson's satirical *Parkinson's Law*, both of which he had read in the 1970s when they were published in Russian translation.[33] He and Raisa subscribed also to the major literary monthlies, including *Novy mir*, the most anti-Stalinist of the journals and the publisher in the 1960s of early works by Aleksandr Solzhenitsyn. (That was before Solzhenitsyn's root-and-branch rejection of the system became increasingly clear and resulted in his forcible ejection from the country in 1974.)

A regional party boss had a vast amount of authority within his own domain, even though the main lines of policy were determined by Moscow. The Stavropol territory was a major agricultural producer, and so raising the efficiency of agriculture was one of Gorbachev's biggest concerns. To his practical experience he sought to add scientific knowledge and found a valuable mentor in Aleksandr Nikonov, who became director of the Stavropol Agricultural Institute in 1963. Nikonov, the son of a Latvian mother and Russian father, grew up bilingual in independent Latvia between the world wars. Minister of Agriculture in Latvia from 1951 to 1961, Nikonov was critical of Khrushchev's agricultural policies and he also made an enemy of the hardline Latvian Communist Arvid Pelshe, who became party first secretary of that Baltic republic in 1959. Pelshe threatened to bring Nikonov to trial for his opposition to excessively large collective farms and accused him of belonging to an 'anti-party group'.[34] Nikonov's transfer to an academic post in Stavropol was a clear demotion and mild political punishment.

Gorbachev decided to add a degree in agriculture to his law diploma. He worked on this in his spare time, with Nikonov as his supervisor. Whereas some party officials embellished their curricula vitae by acquiring higher degrees through the simple expedient of getting someone else to write their dissertation, Gorbachev acquired his second diploma entirely through his own efforts.[35] Gorbachev's respect for the knowledge and character of Nikonov was such that, once he moved to Moscow in 1978 as secretary of the Central Committee responsible for agriculture, he appointed him to a series of senior posts in agricultural education and administration. He also worked with Nikonov to secure the posthumous rehabilitation of outstanding Soviet economists of the 1920s, among them Aleksandr Chayanov and Nikolay Kondratev (better known to Western economists as Kondratieff of 'long wave' theory), who had perished in Stalin's purges of the late 1930s.

During Gorbachev's Stavropol years, he was far removed from the Soviet foreign policy-making process and found it hard enough even to influence agricultural policy at the national level. His interest in the outside world was, however, enormously stimulated by a series of foreign trips he was able to make—more than were usual for a regional party official. He went with a Soviet delegation to Communist Czechoslovakia in 1969 and got a first-hand lesson on what Czechs thought of the 'fraternal help' (as Soviet propaganda had termed their invasion of Czechoslovakia the previous August) when the workers at a factory they visited literally turned their backs on them. In the 1970s Gorbachev went to a number of West European countries, beginning with Italy in 1971 and followed by Belgium, the Netherlands, France, and West Germany—in some cases as a tourist at the invitation of the local Communist parties and in others as part of a Soviet delegation.[36] As Gorbachev himself has noted, and some of his closest aides have confirmed, these visits broadened his political understanding as well as his geographical horizons. He was surprised to find in chance conversations with ordinary folk in Western Europe no hostility to Soviet citizens as people, and he could hardly fail to note the higher standard of living the West Europeans enjoyed. What struck Gorbachev most was the freedom with which people discussed politics, not hesitating in his company to disagree with each other, whereas those in the Soviet group felt obliged to stick to the same official line. Seeing what he later called a 'functioning civil society' and Western political systems at first hand, Gorbachev began to question his a priori assumption of the advantages of 'socialist democracy' over West European variants of 'bourgeois' democracy.[37]

3

GORBACHEV'S WIDENING HORIZONS

In Stavropol, Gorbachev was often frustrated by the restrictions placed upon his freedom of action by Moscow, and yet he was more his own boss in his home territory than he was at the end of the 1970s in Moscow, though that move was a big promotion. Earlier there had been a time when Gorbachev had even thought of giving up his career in the party in favour of further study with a view to becoming an academic, the reason being that 'I didn't like being bossed around. My nature is to be independent.' He added that 'I'm the sort of person who can do ten times more when I'm not pushed and pestered, but rather given the chance to think.'[1] Yet, it was only through rising still higher in the party hierarchy that he could give himself the opportunity to do this in the political sphere. During the Brezhnev era, when the general secretary took pride in what was known as the 'stability of cadres', promotion was generally slow. Many senior officials served in their posts until they dropped dead. In Gorbachev's case, an opportune death provided him with the chance to rise faster than his contemporaries.

Fedor Kulakov, the party first secretary of the Stavropol region from 1960 to 1964, had given Gorbachev some of his early promotions. Kulakov's death at the age of 60 in 1978 paved the way for Gorbachev to become the youngest member of the top leadership team in Moscow. Kulakov had been both a secretary of the Central Committee, overseeing agriculture, and a full member of the Politburo. Gorbachev was appointed his successor as secretary of the Central Committee for agriculture. In addition to gaining the support of several senior members of the Politburo, especially Suslov and Andropov, Gorbachev had brief interviews with Brezhnev and with his right-hand man, Konstantin Chernenko, who wanted to be sure that any newcomer would be loyal to Brezhnev.

Once in Moscow, Gorbachev's rise was rapid. While retaining his Central Committee secretaryship, he became a candidate member of the Politburo in 1979 and a full member in 1980. At the end of 1978 the Soviet top leadership team of Politburo members, candidate members, and Secretaries of the Central Committee comprised twenty-seven people (all men), with Gorbachev twenty-seventh in the ranking. By the end of 1980 he was in the top ten, and when Yury Andropov succeeded Brezhnev as general secretary on the latter's death in November 1982, he expanded Gorbachev's responsibilities to include oversight of the economy as a whole, not only agriculture, within the Central Committee Secretariat. By the time Andropov died in February 1984, Gorbachev was in the top five of the leadership team and he had been Andropov's favoured candidate to succeed him as general secretary. Andropov was, however, too ill to attend Politburo meetings during the last months of his life and unable to implement his wish that Gorbachev become acting party leader during his illness, which would have put him in pole position to be Andropov's immediate successor.[2]

Chernenko continued as second secretary to Andropov until the latter's death, and then was chosen to succeed him, though he himself was in failing health. The veteran Defence and Foreign Ministers, Dmitry Ustinov and Andrei Gromyko, backed Chernenko because he posed no threat to them. The even older Chairman of the Council of Ministers, Nikolay Tikhonov, supported him enthusiastically. It was an arrangement that suited all three, for it enabled them to continue as masters of their own political realms. Gorbachev—after some resistance, not least from Tikhonov—in due course acquired the position of second secretary to General Secretary Chernenko, making him thereby the heir apparent. The succession was far from being assured. There were colleagues who were jealous of the youngest of their number having been promoted so fast. The rivalries were more personal than political. If Politburo members had thought that Gorbachev was insufficiently committed to preserving the pillars of the system, or to maintaining the shared hegemony of those who sat alongside him at the top of the party hierarchy, his chances of becoming general secretary would have been zero.

Although he had a seat at the Politburo table, whose meetings became briefer and more perfunctory during Brezhnev's last years, Gorbachev had no influence on the making of Soviet foreign policy at that time. Any major decision required the ultimate imprimatur of Brezhnev, who was in declining health for several years before his death in November 1982. More often than not, he simply acquiesced in decisions that had, in essence, been taken by his senior associates. The form of government was more oligarchic than autocratic, but within the larger oligarchy of the Politburo and Central Committee Secretariat, there was a smaller group responsible for foreign and defence policy, consisting of Brezhnev, second secretary of the party Suslov, Defence Minister Ustinov, Gromyko (who had been Foreign Minister since 1957), and KGB Chairman Andropov. Boris Ponomarev, who had been head of the International Department of the party's Central Committee since 1955, also participated in high-level foreign policy discussions but, as a candidate rather than full member of the Politburo, he wielded less authority than Suslov, Gromyko, Ustinov, and Andropov. In domestic policy, an overlapping but not completely identical ruling group was comprised of Brezhnev, Suslov, Andropov, Chernenko (a Brezhnev protégé of long standing and particularly loyal ally), and Tikhonov (whose ties to Brezhnev also went back a long way and who, though he was already in his mid-seventies, succeeded Kosygin as Chairman of the Council of Ministers in 1980).

The major foreign policy decision of the later Brezhnev years, the Soviet invasion of Afghanistan, illustrates how policy was made by an inner circle of the Politburo and the remaining members presented with a fait accompli. Brezhnev's concurrence with the decision was required and it was eventually (albeit hesitatingly) forthcoming, but he was simply endorsing the recommendation reached by Andropov, Ustinov, and Gromyko. They had gradually come to the conclusion that armed intervention by the Soviet Union was needed to bolster the position of the Afghan Communists and also to effect change in their top leadership. The intervention was widely misinterpreted in the West as betokening a new stage of Soviet expansion. President Carter's National Security Adviser, Zbigniew Brzezinski, saw it as part of a 'drive toward the Persian Gulf', which had been 'a historic element of Soviet foreign policy'.[3]

Viewed from Moscow, the intervention was a defensive measure to prevent neighbouring Afghanistan from falling into hostile hands, though the introduction of Soviet troops made what was, from a Kremlin standpoint, already a bad situation ultimately much worse. The Afghan Communists, who lacked any sizeable social base in their Islamic country, had bloodily overthrown the country's president in what they called a 'revolution' in April 1978. They proceeded to engage in personal and factional feuds within their own ranks and rejected advice from Moscow to widen the political and social composition of their government. Their seizure of power had taken the Soviet leadership by surprise, and in the small but faction-ridden band of Afghan Communists, it was not the part supported by the party's International Department and by the KGB, but its rival faction, which carried out the coup. Rather than being an asset for the Soviet Union, 'the Afghan Communists were a growing nightmare for the Russians almost from the beginning', observed Sir Rodric Braithwaite, the last British ambassador to the Soviet Union.[4]

Not content with making enemies of deeply conservative Islamic traditionalists in the countryside, the Afghan Communists put almost as much energy into imprisoning and killing each other. Soviet leaders continued to urge them to adopt more conciliatory, moderate, and inclusive policies, but they ignored the advice. Within the Soviet leadership, Chairman of the Council of Ministers Aleksey Kosygin was a notable voice of caution and he remained to the end an opponent of armed intervention. In March 1979 he told the leader of the radical Afghan Communist faction which had seized power, Nur Mohammad Taraki, that the USSR could not consent to his request for Soviet fighting personnel to help them in their struggle. He drew their attention to the example of the Vietnamese, who had managed, without such help, to see off both the Americans and the Chinese. 'Our common enemies', he added, 'are just waiting for the moment when Soviet troops appear in Afghanistan.'[5] The Soviet system was such that a formal decision on major policy had to be unanimous.

When the inner circle had finally settled on direct military intervention in Afghanistan, Kosygin contrived to be absent from the Politburo meeting at which it was rubber-stamped.

Andropov and Ustinov, who were initially almost as wary as Kosygin of any direct military intervention in Afghanistan, had come round to the view that there was no other way of safeguarding Soviet security interests on their Central Asian border. Of the two leaders of the particular Communist faction that held sway, Taraki and Hafizullah Amin, the Soviet leadership found the former exasperating but the latter more dangerously unpredictable. They encouraged Taraki to arrest Amin, and in September 1979 Taraki's presidential guards opened fire on Amin, killing two of his assistants but missing their principal target. The initiation and organization of that episode remains debated, but following his narrow escape Amin had enough support in the Afghan military to have Taraki removed from power and arrested.[6] Taraki was subsequently executed in prison, in defiance of appeals from Moscow for clemency.[7] The KGB, headed by Andropov, became worried that Amin would 'do a Sadat' and abandon alliance with the Soviet Union in favour of closer relations with the United States, as Anwar Sadat had done in Egypt.[8] Amin himself did not realize how disillusioned with him Moscow had become. Right up to the time Soviet troops moved into Afghanistan on 25 December 1979, he was eagerly requesting direct military assistance from his powerful neighbour. The Soviet troops who arrived were accompanied by more than 700 members of the KGB special forces. The latter attacked Amin's residence and killed him along with a number of his relatives and aides. The following day, Babrak Karmal, who was from the faction of the Afghan Communists favoured by Moscow and who had long been Moscow's preferred leader, announced that he was now both prime minister and General Secretary of the People's Democratic Party of Afghanistan (as the Communists styled themselves).[9]

Gorbachev, a candidate member of the Politburo at the time, was not involved in the decision-making process, nor was his fellow candidate member (and future Foreign Minister), Eduard Shevardnadze, then the first secretary of the Georgian party organization. The two men met shortly after the invasion had taken place and, as Shevardnadze later wrote, 'agreed it was a fatal error that would cost the country dearly'.[10] Needless to say, neither man aired such views in Politburo meetings, far less publicly. To have done so would have led to their very rapid removal from power. Ascending the party ladder meant observing the rules of the game. At the end of the 1970s and early 1980s, Gorbachev could express only moderately reformist ideas even on agricultural policy, for which he bore responsibility. Criticism of Soviet foreign policy was utterly off-limits. With Andropov's accession to the general secretaryship in November 1982, Gorbachev's authority was enhanced, but it was only after Andropov's death in February 1984, when Gorbachev became the de facto second secretary of the party, that he also became the overseer within the party secretariat of foreign policy. Even then, with the vastly experienced Gromyko as Foreign

Minister and Ustinov (a key figure in the Soviet military-industrial complex since the Second World War) as Defence Minister, Gorbachev could not yet be the dominant influence on Soviet foreign and security policy.

New Vistas

Nevertheless, of all members of the Soviet top leadership team, Gorbachev showed the most interest in learning from others, whether on international affairs or domestic policy. His sources of information included specialists from outside the party bureaucracy and the governmental machine, as well as what he saw and heard for himself on visits abroad. He made three especially significant foreign trips in 1983 and 1984 which attracted far more attention than his overseas forays as the party boss of Stavropol. International scrutiny was particularly great when Gorbachev paid his first visit to Britain in December 1984. Chernenko was looking increasingly frail, and so there was keen interest in the West in the man who appeared to have a good chance of succeeding him.

Before that British trip, however, Gorbachev had headed a Soviet delegation to Canada in 1983 and to Italy a little over a year later. The Canadian Minister of Agriculture in Pierre Trudeau's Liberal government, Eugene Whelan, had visited the Soviet Union in 1981 and met with Gorbachev, as the party overseer of Soviet agriculture. Whelan invited Gorbachev to pay a return visit to Canada in mid-May 1983. By then Andropov was general secretary and he relied more on Gorbachev than on anyone else within the Soviet leadership. Chernenko had become the second secretary—he and Andropov had been rivals to succeed Brezhnev—and Andropov was already planning to put Gorbachev in that number two position in the party. Unfortunately for him, and for Gorbachev in the short term, his health gave out before Chernenko's did.[11] When Gorbachev told Andropov about the Canadian invitation and his wish to accept it, the general secretary was taken aback. 'To Canada?' he said, 'You're out of your mind.'[12] Yet Gorbachev persisted, arguing that it was important to look at Canadian agriculture because of the similarities of climate and terrain between Canada and Russia. Moreover, he needed a ten-day break. Andropov softened his resistance and conceded the principle of Gorbachev's trip, adding, however, that ten days was too long and he could be away for a maximum of seven.[13]

The visit was exceptionally important in the development of Gorbachev's thinking, not so much for his scrutiny of Canadian farms and agricultural policy, impressed by them though he was, or for his amicable conversations with Whelan or even his meetings with Prime Minister Trudeau, but because of a long and frank discussion he had with the Soviet ambassador to Canada, Aleksandr Yakovlev, who was subsequently to become a key reformist ally of Gorbachev during the Soviet perestroika and a foreign policy adviser. Yakovlev had been acting head of the Department of Propaganda of the Central Committee of the Communist Party—a politically more important post than an ambassadorship—but had fallen out of favour after publishing an attack on Russian nationalism. This caused offence in some quarters within the party apparatus as well as in certain intellectual circles. Party leader Brezhnev could not understand how Yakovlev could have published the piece without first seeking and securing permission for it.[14] For Brezhnev this was merely confirmation of a more general suspicion he had of Yakovlev. He looked for 'personal devotion', and was not mistaken in believing that Yakovlev was no devotee.[15]

Seeing that his party career was now hitting the buffers, Yakovlev asked if he might be sent as ambassador to an English-speaking country. He got his wish, and much though he came to like Canada, he had not expected to spend the next ten years (1973–83) there. Yet this lengthy experience of a pluralistic political system, a successful market economy and freedom of speech and publication made a deeper impression on him than did his year in New York as a mature Soviet exchange student at Columbia University in 1959. A decade in Canada made Yakovlev much more critical of what he had come to regard as Soviet political and economic backwardness. He claims in his memoirs that he told Canadian Prime Minister Pierre Trudeau that he was certain that Gorbachev would become leader of the Soviet Union—a surprisingly bold prediction for a Soviet ambassador to make to a Western head of government—and that it was on the strength of this that Trudeau met three times with Gorbachev. Trudeau and Gorbachev got on well, and when Trudeau was no longer in office, Gorbachev arranged a trip for him and his sons, including future Canadian Prime Minister Justin Trudeau, around Siberia.[16]

Of still greater import, though, for future Soviet policy was the rapport Gorbachev established with Yakovlev, who was a decade older but, in the hierarchical Soviet system, very much his junior in rank. Gorbachev spoke of the 'necessity for cardinal reforms' and complained about Soviet 'dogmatism'. The Ottawa-based Yakovlev, for his part, told Gorbachev how 'primitive and shameful Soviet policy looked from here, from the other side of the planet'.[17] His ten years of dignified exile in Canada had provided the great advantage of 'time to think'. It had also given him the opportunity to study Canadian life which he had found to be 'very simple, pragmatic, and permeated by common sense'.[18]

Yakovlev made clear that he wanted to return to Moscow and Gorbachev was able to facilitate his wish. He paved the way for Yakovlev to be offered the directorship of the Institute of World Economy and International Relations (IMEMO), the major policy-oriented institution in Moscow for the study of international affairs.[19] During the two years he headed IMEMO, Yakovlev was an important informal adviser of Gorbachev and a useful channel of information emanating from the research and reflections of IMEMO scholars. When Gorbachev became general secretary in 1985, he promoted Yakovlev, at a speed that was extraordinary by post-Stalin Soviet standards, to his inner circle. Yakovlev's role in the change that took place in Soviet domestic and foreign policy in the second half of the 1980s is sometimes exaggerated—the 'father of perestroika' was not Yakovlev but Gorbachev—but it was unquestionably significant. It was particularly helpful for Gorbachev to have an intellectually formidable counterweight to the conservative forces within the Soviet establishment who had experience both of the outside world and of the Soviet corridors of power. And though a veteran of the Second World War, Yakovlev was willing to stand up to the military-industrial complex.

The second of three especially important visits Gorbachev made during the two years immediately before he became the Soviet top leader was to Italy for the funeral of the leader of the most vibrant Communist Party in Western Europe, Enrico Berlinguer, who had died suddenly on 12 June 1984. Although it was obvious that the Soviet Communist Party would send an important delegation to his funeral, it was less clear who should lead it. Boris Ponomarev, the head of the International Department of the Central Committee which conducted relations with non-ruling Communist parties and other parties of the Left, assumed that he was the obvious choice. Ponomarev saw himself as a guardian of Marxist-Leninist orthodoxy, and was a veteran ideologue who had long been at odds with Italian 'revisionists' and 'Eurocommunists'. Chernenko's foreign policy adviser Andrey Aleksandrov-Agentov and First Deputy Head of the International Department Vadim Zagladin told the Politburo that it would cause a 'scandal' to send Ponomarev. The Italian Communists themselves were consulted and they made clear their hope that the Soviet delegation would be led by Gorbachev. The Politburo duly nominated him.[20]

In the course of his conversations in Rome, Gorbachev established a close rapport with those in the leadership group of the Italian party who were following in the footsteps of Berlinguer. Under Berlinguer's leadership, the Italian Communist Party (PCI) had preserved its links with Moscow and with the international Communist movement, but had criticized a number of Soviet actions—from the invasion of Czechoslovakia in 1968 to the intervention in Afghanistan in 1979. They had also made overtures to social democratic parties and replaced unremitting hostility to religion with advocacy of a 'historic compromise' between Communism and Catholicism in Italy.

Gorbachev was privately sympathetic to much of the PCI's fresh thinking, although, unlike them, he was not free publicly to criticize the official line of the Communist Party of the Soviet Union (CPSU).[21] He was already in touching distance of the top post which, if he attained it, would radically widen his opportunities to set the political agenda. One conversation that began between Gorbachev and the Italian Communists in the Soviet Embassy on the evening of 13 June continued through the night, at the end of which there was, as he later put it, 'mutual understanding'.[22] Although the Italian Communists had frequently been chastised by Moscow for their deviations from the approved line of the International Communist Movement, Gorbachev told them that he had no problems with their refusal to recognize Moscow as a 'centre' that could issue them with commands. He favoured their getting together to exchange ideas. Over and above this meeting of minds, Gorbachev was impressed by the vastness of the crowd who had turned out spontaneously to mourn a genuinely popular Communist leader and by the fact that the Italian president, Alessandro Pertini, bowed before Berlinguer's coffin, as did the leaders of Italy's various political parties. 'All this', Gorbachev later wrote, represented 'a way of thinking uncharacteristic for us and was a manifestation of a different political culture'.[23]

Five Hours with 'the Iron Lady'

Experiences such as his discussions with the Italian Communists had an impact on the evolution of Gorbachev's political thinking, as—to a still greater extent—did his last major visit to a foreign country while he was still number two within the Soviet hierarchy. That was the week he spent in Great Britain in December 1984. It was not a foregone conclusion that Gorbachev would be allowed to accept the British invitation. The final decision was Chernenko's, but Gromyko was opposed. Deputy Foreign Minister Anatoly Kovalev, although normally 'extremely cautious', came out firmly in favour of Gorbachev being allowed to accept the invitation, thereby incurring Gromyko's disfavour. Once Gorbachev was in the Kremlin and Eduard Shevardnadze in charge of the Foreign Ministry, Kovalev was promoted to First Deputy Foreign Minister.[24] Gorbachev's own desire to accept the invitation must also have been weighed in the balance by Chernenko. To lead the Soviet 'parliamentary' delegation offered an opportunity for Gorbachev to get to know Margaret Thatcher, who had already made her mark on British domestic and foreign policy and was the European leader closest to American President Ronald Reagan. Gorbachev prepared for the visit very thoroughly, consulting Soviet specialists on foreign policy and on the United States as well as the UK. The delegation he led included IMEMO director Yakovlev; Vadim Zagladin, a far more knowledgeable and enlightened official than his International Department head, Ponomarev; the opportunistic head of the International Information Department of the Central Committee, Leonid Zamyatin, who later became Soviet ambassador to the UK; and the prominent nuclear physicist Yevgeny Velikhov, who was also vice-president of the Academy of Sciences.

Although the invitation Gorbachev accepted had formally come from the British Parliament under the aegis of the Inter-Parliamentary Union, Gorbachev knew in advance of his visit that he would be having discussions not only with UK parliamentarians and business leaders but with the Foreign Secretary, Sir Geoffrey Howe, and Thatcher. The Thatcher–Gorbachev meeting at the prime minister's country residence, Chequers, lasted for more than five hours, exceeding the time that had been allotted for it in the official programme. Ahead of his visit, Gorbachev had told the British ambassador to Moscow, Sir Iain Sutherland, that he wanted 'frank political discussion with the Prime Minister, with no diplomatic niceties, on the current world situation'.[25] Such sentiments fitted perfectly with Mrs Thatcher's style and preferences, though a high-level guest less intellectually agile than Gorbachev might have concluded that he got rather more than he had asked for.

The Chequers meeting began with lunch and the prime minister almost immediately launched into a critique of Soviet policy and of the Soviet system, to which Gorbachev responded robustly but good-temperedly. He ate practically nothing, giving all his attention to what the prime minister was saying and to formulating his own response.* When Mrs Thatcher remonstrated with him for neglecting the food, he replied that 'man eats to live and does not live to eat'.[26] Thatcher held forth about the inefficiency of Soviet central planning, the merits of a market economy, Soviet financial support for the National Union of Mineworkers in Britain (the meeting took place during a prolonged miners' strike), and Soviet unwillingness to let Jewish and other would-be emigrants leave the Soviet Union. On the last point Gorbachev told Thatcher that the percentage of those allowed to emigrate was greater than she thought, but he did not go out of his way to defend the lack of freedom of movement. Mrs Thatcher said the press would have to be told that she had raised the issue of Soviet 'refuseniks' and asked him what they should be told. He replied that she should say that he 'had added nothing new to the known Soviet position and had referred to existing Soviet laws'.[27] This had the dual advantage of being true and of providing no ammunition for those ill-disposed to him in Moscow.

At the official talks between Gorbachev and Thatcher at Chequers that followed the lunch, Gorbachev was accompanied by Yakovlev and Zamyatin and by his interpreter at that time, Nikolay Uspensky, while Mrs Thatcher had alongside her Sir Geoffrey Howe, her private secretary Charles Powell, and interpreter Tony Bishop. The main subjects of the conversation were international relations and the arms build-up, the policies of the Reagan administration, including the Strategic Defense Initiative (SDI), which could lead, said Gorbachev, to an arms race in outer space whose 'consequences would be unpredictable and control virtually impossible'.[28]

---

* In a conversation I had with the Soviet ambassador to the UK, Viktor Popov, when he and his wife came to dinner at St Antony's College, Oxford, on 1 February 1985, less than six weeks after he had accompanied Mikhail Gorbachev to his engagements in Britain (and almost thirty years after Popov had spent an academic year as a mature student at St Antony's in the 1950s), we discussed Gorbachev's UK visit. Popov said that Gorbachev ate practically nothing at any of the lunches and dinners held for him, not only at Chequers where Mrs Thatcher had said that they must not let the press know he hadn't eaten. The result of Gorbachev's complete focus on the conversation, at the expense of eating, said Popov, was that when he returned to the embassy, where he and his wife were staying in the ambassador's apartment, he was always hungry and would have a meal prepared for him at 1 o'clock in the morning. Each day he went to bed at 2 a.m. and rose at 7 a.m. An ability to work long hours and to operate efficiently after little sleep was a characteristic Gorbachev shared with Thatcher.

Figure 1 (L to R) Secretary for Defense Caspar Weinberger, President Reagan, and Secretary of State Alexander Haig, August 1981.

Powell reported him as saying that the United States also 'seemed to claim the right to use force even where they had no specific interests' and that the Soviet Union was especially concerned by the activities of Secretary of Defense Caspar Weinberger and Richard Perle.[29] Mrs Thatcher defended Reagan's SDI motives, arguing that the intent was defensive, not aggressive, though she made clear that she did not think the project was realistic. Gorbachev added that if SDI was simply a bargaining chip, there was no problem. The Soviet Union could bargain and compromises could be found on the basis of equality of security. But if talks on space were held 'without a proper sense of responsibility and without the interests of both sides being taken into account, then it would be another matter'.[30] Earlier in the conversation Gorbachev quoted nineteenth-century British Prime Minister Lord Palmerston's remark that Britain had no eternal friends or enemies but only eternal interests. He agreed with the philosophy behind this, but it 'carried the corollary that other countries had their own interests as well'.[31]

Two days later, Gorbachev gave a speech at the Houses of Parliament. Although it was the freshness of his style, rather than the language and concepts he deployed that got noted, Gorbachev introduced a number of ideas which were to become part of the Soviet 'new thinking' once he was his country's leader. To overcome the Cold War and to have fruitful negotiations and cooperation, he said 'not only words are necessary', although, he added, 'in politics they are also important'.[32] War in the past had been a great calamity, but nuclear war would mean much more—the 'death of humanity'. That was why 'the nuclear age ineluctably dictates new political think-ing'.[33] The Cold War was an abnormal state of affairs because it carried within it a military threat.[34] Writing almost a generation after his first visit to the UK, Gorbachev stressed the significance of that experience in 1984: 'It was precisely here, in the British parliament, that my observations and thoughts on foreign policy and world order, developed over several years, were first expressed.'[35]

A novel feature of Gorbachev's visit to Britain was that he was accompanied by his wife, Raisa, although that was to become a regular occurrence during his years as Soviet leader. Both of the Gorbachevs made a favourable impression on the British public, with the mass-circulation newspapers paying at least as much attention to Raisa as to her husband. Foreign Office Minister of State Malcolm Rifkind observed that 'Gorbachev's decision to have his wife, Raisa, accompany him to Chequers made the meeting with Margaret Thatcher warmer and more convivial from the start.'[36] Nevertheless, at the Chequers lunch, Mikhail and Raisa Gorbachev were placed at separate tables (Raisa in the company of Denis Thatcher), which enabled Mrs Thatcher to be more uninhibited in attacking the fundamentals of Communism as she saw them.

For someone who was not a head of government, Gorbachev was given a very high-level reception in Britain. The Chequers meeting with the prime minister and his speech in Parliament were highlights, but he also had a significant separate meet-ing with Foreign Secretary Howe, met Opposition political leaders and business people, visited several industrial enterprises, including a car factory in Oxford, and flew to Edinburgh. The Scottish part of his itinerary was shorter than planned, for the death of Dmitry Ustinov led Gorbachev to decide to return to Moscow immediately. The demise of a senior member of the Politburo was a serious matter and Gorbachev needed to be involved in the discussions on Ustinov's successor.

Gorbachev's ability to argue a case spontaneously and persuasively, relying nei-ther on dogma nor on a script, impressed his interlocutors. Labour's Shadow Foreign Secretary, Denis Healey, an outstanding Defence Secretary in the 1960s and formidably knowledgeable on international affairs, described Gorbachev as 'a man of exceptional charm' who was 'frank and flexible with a composure full of inner strength'. Healey's meetings with Soviet leaders went back as far as Khrushchev, but he had never before met one like this. The only 'puzzling ques-tion' he was left with was: 'how can a man who seems so genuinely nice and human run the Soviet system?'[37] The person who had the most sustained opportunity to observe Gorbachev during his UK visit, and who possessed the advantage of speak-ing superb Russian, was the official interpreter on the British side, Tony Bishop. He wrote an interesting four-page memorandum, giving his impressions of Gorbachev, for the Foreign Office and 10 Downing Street. The document is worth quoting from at length:

There was about [Gorbachev's] movements and his utterances an unaffected, self-assured and un-self-conscious air of competence and confidence. One was conscious of great resources of energy in him, well-harnessed. Although he joked about his heavy programme—'we'll fulfil it if it kills us'—he never flagged nor faltered...He would listen, immobile, with concentration and great attentiveness, and would almost invariably answer all questions put to him—in his own time, of course, and only in the degree of detail which suited him. He had a knack of doing so in a disarmingly straightforward, unpolemical manner and of finding apt, often humorous turns of phrase to register his point or defuse unwanted tension. He was aided in this by a ready smile and occasional laughter. A roguish twinkle was never far from his eye (he even once winked at me over his shoulder as I interpreted a neat parry of his to one of the Prime Minister's verbal thrusts).[38]

One feature Bishop misleadingly attributed to Gorbachev was 'Slav nationalism'. Steeped though he was in Russian literature, this did not mean that he was a Slavophile of a Russian nationalist type. On the contrary, he was far more of an internationalist than nationalist in outlook. The British government interpreter doubtless did not wish to appear entirely uncritical in his evaluation of the man who was likely to be the next leader of the Communist Party of the Soviet Union, and he concluded his generally perceptive assessment with these cautionary words: 'The combination of cleverness, modern-mindedness, Slav nationalism, energy, charm, self-assurance and single-mindedness would make him at worst a formidable adversary and at best an interlocutor to be treated with the utmost respect and circumspection.'[39] Bishop noted that Gorbachev's style of leadership of the delegation was not in the least overbearing, for he did not 'give himself airs' or 'pull rank' and 'not infrequently gave members of his team the floor to speak on subjects close to themselves'.[40] Summing up the man whose every word and gesture he had spent a week interpreting, Bishop highlighted Gorbachev's personal magnetism and Western-style political skills: 'He handled the British media like a "natural"—with patience, decisiveness and winning touches of humour.'[41] The positive reporting around the world of Gorbachev's visit to the UK alarmed some Western hard-liners. Later critics of any improvement in relations with Moscow asserted that precisely because of his charm and intelligence Gorbachev was an especially dangerous adversary.[42]

Back in the Soviet Union, not everyone was enthusiastic about the good impression Gorbachev had made in the UK. Although just a few months later Foreign Minister Gromyko was to be the person who proposed Gorbachev as next Soviet leader to the Politburo and, subsequently, to the Central Committee of the Communist Party, his reaction to Gorbachev's warm reception in London was reserved, to put it mildly. He criticized Anatoly Dobrynin, the Soviet ambassador to the US, for reporting too fulsomely the positive assessments of Gorbachev's performance in London that had appeared in the American press. On Dobrynin's next visit to Moscow, Gromyko demanded to know why he had been sending telegrams from Washington about what was only a parliamentary delegation. What significance did it have?[43] Nevertheless, the fact that Gorbachev had handled himself so adeptly in discussion with experienced Western politicians, and had flourished rather than wilted under the scrutiny of the world's mass media, did him far more good than harm domestically. It was further evidence that he was not only best placed but best qualified to be Chernenko's successor as General Secretary of the Communist Party. Speaking off the record less than six weeks after Gorbachev's visit, the Soviet ambassador to the UK, Viktor Popov, said it had been 'a visit by the right man at the right time' and had been 'successful and useful in many different ways'. The ambassador's wife added that one of the reasons the visit had been such a success was that the Gorbachevs 'did not look like people from Madame Tussauds'.[44] The allusion to the waxwork appearance of some of their recent guest's Politburo colleagues needed no elaboration.

Before American Secretary of State George Shultz went to Camp David to get Margaret Thatcher's first-hand account of her talks with Gorbachev, he had a meeting with Soviet Ambassador Dobrynin, who later described Shultz's bewildered reaction to the news coming out of London: '"What on earth did he do to fascinate the Iron Lady?" Shultz wondered out loud, and with a smile.' Dobrynin added: 'Perhaps I should have told him. I had first met Gorbachev the previous summer during my visit to Moscow. I did my usual rounds among the Politburo and virtually no one asked me anything beyond the usual: How are things going? But Gorbachev plied me with questions—twenty or thirty of them. He had been reading everything he could find about the United States and there was plenty that he wanted to know.'[45] Dobrynin was far from alone among well-informed specialists in finding Gorbachev eager to learn. Georgy Arbatov, the director of the Institute of the United States and Canada in Moscow, noted that during the period of Chernenko's leadership, he met with Gorbachev fairly regularly, 'when I had questions or things to discuss with him regarding foreign policy, for he was the only one who still made the machine go on working'.[46]

Gorbachev's Thinking on the Eve of Perestroika

A few days before flying to London in December 1984 Gorbachev delivered a major speech to a conference on ideology in Moscow at which, for the cognoscenti, he outed himself as a reformer. The very word *reforma* was still taboo in the Soviet Union—it had become suspect ever since being embraced wholeheartedly by Czech Communists during the 1968 Prague Spring—but Gorbachev attacked stereotypical thinking, criticized excessive centralization in the Soviet system, and hinted broadly at the need for an overhaul of the economic system. He used the term, 'commodity-money relations', which was essentially a euphemism for marketizing reform, although he was still several years away from accepting that the market should be the mainspring of the economic system, superseding the command economy and central planning. At the time of the conference and when he came to power three months later, Gorbachev was nonetheless supportive of introducing market elements into the existing system, as had happened in Hungary where improvements to agriculture and in the supply of foodstuffs had resulted. He called on social scientists to come up with 'serious scientific recommendations on the application in contemporary conditions of such economic levers as price, cost, profit, credit and certain others' and to stop trying to fit their investigations into 'preconceived schemes' which led them to 'revolve in a circle of scholastic reasoning'.[47]

A significant part of the vocabulary with which we now associate Gorbachev and the perestroika years was taking shape in that speech. Some of the concepts that figured in it, such as *samoupravlenie* (self-management) and *uskorenie* (acceleration) were used mainly in the earliest years of Gorbachev's time in power; others, such as *glasnost* (transparency, openness), *demokratizatsiya* (democratization), and *chelovecheskiy faktor* (the human factor) were employed throughout the period. Over time they came to connote significantly more radical change than Gorbachev had in mind in 1984. Nevertheless, to speak of the need to take 'fuller account of the *diverse interests* of Soviet people' (italics added) and to give 'a new impetus to the democratization of our social and economic life', and to maintain that 'glasnost is an inalienable aspect of socialist democracy and of all public life' was heady stuff for 1984.[48] It was, as Vadim Medvedev (a member of the group Gorbachev gathered round him to work on the text) observed, as realistic and as critical an evaluation of the state of affairs as was possible at that time.[49] *Pravda* published a shortened version of the long speech, omitting the passages that were most at odds with standard Soviet discourse.

In preparing his speech for the December 1984 conference, Gorbachev was influenced by his discussions with reform-minded social scientists, such as sociologist Tatiana Zaslavskaya and economist Abel Aganbegyan. Aleksandr Yakovlev was much involved in its drafting, as were a number of other party intellectuals of reformist disposition. Although the speech mixed the old and the new, there was enough that was critical of the status quo to set alarm bells ringing in the most conservative party circles. In keeping with Soviet custom, Gorbachev had circulated his speech in advance of its delivery to Politburo members and to the office of the general secretary in the first instance. Several of Chernenko's aides objected to the speech, as did an influential adviser of the Kremlin, Richard Kosolapov (chief editor of the journal, *Kommunist*), whom Chernenko chose to regard as 'the leading ideologist and theoretician' in the country.[50] Urged on by Kosolapov and by his aides, Chernenko phoned Gorbachev on the very eve of the conference and told him to cancel the event or, failing that, to cut out those passages which the general secretary and his advisers found objectionable. Gorbachev flatly refused, which was, in the pre-perestroika Soviet system, virtually unheard of. Yakovlev happened to be in Gorbachev's office when the call from Chernenko came through. He later wrote that Gorbachev not only contradicted the general secretary but did so in 'what was for me an unexpectedly severe tone'. Gorbachev was furious when he put the phone down. and said to Yakovlev 'To hell with him!', adding 'Everything in the text will stay as it is.'[51]

In 1984 Gorbachev believed that the Soviet Union was badly in need of reform, but that it was, nevertheless, reformable. He viewed the country's economic slow-down and political stagnation through more critical eyes than any of his Politburo colleagues. His different perspective on the need for change had many roots. His five years at Moscow University had made him the best-educated member of the Politburo. He had spent most of his adult life far from Moscow and was well acquainted with the stultifying effects throughout the country of the centralized bureaucracy. Both in Stavropol and, still more, after he had joined the top leadership team in Moscow in 1978, he listened to those with real expertise both on Soviet problems and on how things were done elsewhere. He had seen Western countries first-hand and had conversed and argued with their leaders. The December meetings in the United Kingdom made almost as big an impact on Gorbachev as on his hosts. Several of those who worked most closely with him during his years as general secretary have said that Gorbachev often referred to that visit as eye-opening for him.[52] Endowed with an inquiring mind, Gorbachev went through a prolonged process of political learning that meant his way of looking at the Soviet system and the world was already different from that of any other member of Chernenko's Politburo, and it was to become more different still once he had become Soviet leader.

As overseer within the party apparatus of Soviet foreign policy during Chernenko's final year, Gorbachev had become increasingly concerned with the impasse in which East–West relations found themselves and with the dangers inherent in the Cold War. When he spoke of the need for a radical reduction in weaponry on both sides and the need to build trust, as he had done in his conversation with Margaret Thatcher, this was not just propaganda, as many in the West had assumed. Gorbachev had no personal ties to the Soviet military-industrial complex and believed that they wielded too much influence over Soviet decisions. He was well aware, however, that precisely because they were such a formidable institutional interest within the system, he must take pains to keep them on board. When Gorbachev succeeded Chernenko as general secretary one day after the latter's death on 10 March 1985, there was widespread relief in the Soviet Union. Here was a leader who might inject new life into the sclerotic Soviet system. Almost everyone could—for a time, at least—rally behind a man who looked as if he would get the country moving again.

4

THE RISE OF RONALD REAGAN

When Mikhail Gorbachev became Soviet leader, Ronald Reagan was two months into his second term as American president. The first term had been marked by a worsening of US–Soviet relations, dangerously so in 1983. Reagan had come to power with a deep suspicion of Soviet intentions and the determination to pursue peace through strength. Although he was serious about both parts of that policy, it was far from clear to the Soviet leadership that the peace component was anything more than window-dressing for the military build-up, especially since the latter was accompanied by sharpened anti-Communist rhetoric.

Opinion on Reagan in the United States in 1985 remained deeply divided, while in Western Europe opposition to his foreign and defence policy was on a scale sufficient to alarm even the most the pro-American governments. In several of the East European countries, Reagan's hard line was welcomed by significant sections of the population who were no less critical of Communist rule but could vent disenchantment or anger with their rulers only in the company of trusted friends. In the Soviet Union itself, however, the view that Reagan was a dangerous warmonger was widely shared. The belief that this American administration was unremittingly hostile and making war more likely had great resonance in a country in which there was scarcely a family that had not suffered losses during the Second World War.

Before we come to consider Reagan's first term as president in the next chapter, it is important to look at where he came from, to understand how his political views developed, to examine what were the major influences on him at different stages of his career, and to discern how he saw the Cold War and US–Soviet relations when he was on the verge of entering the White House in 1980.

Reagan's childhood was not scarred by war as was Gorbachev's, but it was far from idyllic. Born in 1911, he was twenty years older than Gorbachev, and though the First World War did not affect his life, the Depression of the early 1930s did. His childhood was marred still more by his father's alcohol problem. There were frequent house moves, sometimes brought about by Jack Reagan's ambition to come closer to owning his own shoe shop, but on other occasions a result of being fired by his employer. The family lived in various Midwestern towns, and always in rented accommodation. (Reagan's parents never owned their own home until their son had done well enough in Hollywood to buy them a house there. They then moved to California, where Jack was happy to find a role sifting through his son's fan mail.) The longest they lived in any one town was in Dixon, Illinois, where they arrived when Ronald was aged 9. Even in Dixon, they moved house five times. Forming warm friendships was difficult because of the frequent changes of location.[1] As Nancy Reagan later observed, the constant moves, and coping with the fact that it was common knowledge that his father was an alcoholic, explained 'why Ronnie became a loner'. He didn't let anyone come too close: 'There's a wall around him. He lets me come closer than anyone else, but there are times when even I feel that barrier.'[2] In the Reagan Presidential Library archives in Simi Valley, California, there are numerous replies Reagan handwrote to some of the people who had written to him, as thousands did every week during his presidency. A selection of the incoming letters was regularly drawn to his attention by his staff, and to quite a number of them he felt moved to respond. He kept all his drafts of these letters which usually were, as Nancy Reagan observed, 'warm and personal'. She added that sometimes this was 'easier with people you don't know'.[3]

One Illinois winter day, in 1922, when Reagan was 11, he came home to find his father drunk and unconscious on the porch of their house. He dragged him inside and managed to get him to bed.[4] It was something he never forgot, and often mentioned. While the future president had reason to admire his mother more than he did Jack, his mother taught him to regard alcoholism as an illness, even though it was a source of discord within the home. Reagan remained fond of his father and admired his gift as a raconteur. He also credited him with a lack of religious and racial prejudice which was far from typical in the American Midwest (or in most other places, for that matter) between the world wars. On one occasion, when Jack was a travelling shoe salesman, he checked into a small-town hotel and was told by the counter clerk, 'You'll like it here, Mr Reagan. We don't permit a Jew in the place.' Jack Reagan's reaction was not what he expected. 'I'm a Catholic', he replied, 'and if you don't take Jews, I guess you don't want Catholics either.' He left the hotel and spent the night sleeping, and freezing, in his car.[5] With the exception of a few months when he was aged 3 and living in Chicago, when his father had a job in a city department store, Ronald Reagan's boyhood was spent entirely in rural Illinois.[6]

Neither Ronald nor his brother Neil knew any of their grandparents, all four having died before they were born.[7] Their father's paternal grandparents left Ireland in the mid-nineteenth century. Reagan's great-grandfather, Michael O'Regan, eloped, in the first instance to England, from County Tipperary in 1852 with his girlfriend, Catherine Mulcahy, and when he signed the marriage register in London, his name was anglicized to Reagan, and so it remained. They came to the United States via Canada, with their three children in 1856, and settled in Illinois.[8] It was from his mother, in particular, that Reagan imbibed many of his values. Nelle Wilson, as she was before her marriage to Jack Reagan, was the daughter of an Englishwoman who arrived in the United States aged 16. Her father was an American of Scots descent. Nelle was by far the more religious of the two parents. Whereas Jack was an unobservant Catholic, Nelle was a committed member of the 'liberal fundamentalist' Disciples of Christ Church, a regular church attender, Sunday School teacher, and visitor of those in need.[9] Reagan, in his memoirs, said of his mother: 'She always expected to find the best in people and often did, even among the prisoners at our local jail to whom she frequently brought hot meals.'[10] He added: 'From my mother, I learned the value of prayer, how to have dreams and believe I could make them come true.'[11] Reagan himself was a regular churchgoer as a boy (a habit he later lost) and also taught in Sunday School up until the time he left home to study at Eureka College, a small liberal arts institution in Illinois affiliated to the Disciples of Christ Church. Reagan inherited much of his mother's optimism. His father's outlook was different. He was, said Reagan, 'a cynic' who 'tended to suspect the worst of people'. Yet, in the lengthy periods between his drinking benders (when he would disappear for days at a time), he was hard-working. Reagan believed that 'I learned from my father the value of hard work and ambition, and maybe a little something about telling a story.'[12]

From the time his father described the baby Ronald Reagan as looking like 'a Dutchman', he became known as 'Dutch'. Throughout his boyhood, he preferred that nickname to Ronald, Ron, or Ronnie. Even when he was president, the letters of some of his older friends address him as 'Dear Dutch'. He enjoyed cowboy movies and was keen on sport but avoided baseball because he could not see the ball coming. His parents had not spotted how short-sighted he was until he was aged 9 when, on a car journey with them (his father driving the borrowed vehicle), he tried on his mother's glasses. Until that moment he himself had not realized how much he was missing that others could see clearly. For the first time he was able to read the road signs and see faces outside that were no longer a mere blur. Following this revelation, he was fitted with thick-rimmed glasses, which he disliked because he felt they made him look 'bookish', but which he mostly put up with. When contact lenses became available from the early 1940s, Reagan immediately switched to them and wore them for the rest of his life.[13] Even though he was anxious not to be seen as a bookworm, Reagan did read a lot as a boy, acquiring a liking for science fiction, which never left him. Many years later he surprised Gorbachev by saying that if the Soviet Union and the United States were threatened by another planet, they would surely band together.[14]

In his teens, when he attended North Dixon High School, Reagan took on a variety of spare-time and vacation jobs, for money was scarce at home. His aim was to acquire enough savings to enable him to go on to college. His main job, as a result of his swimming prowess, was as a beach lifeguard, though he also worked on a construction site, and did golf caddying. He had set his sights on Eureka College, partly because it was a Disciples of Christ Church institution and partly because his girlfriend, Margaret Cleaver, the daughter of the minister of the Dixon church Reagan and his mother attended, was going there.[15] He had begun acting in plays while still at school and joined the Dramatic Club at college, having the additional incentive that Margaret was eager to join.[16] At Eureka he received a sports scholarship—on the basis of his swimming ability and a more modest talent for football—which covered part of his fees, and found employment on the campus to help pay for the remainder. One stint was as a dish-washer in the female students' dormitory, which Reagan later described as 'the best job I ever had'.[17] He passed his exams, relying on an excellent memory rather than on diligent study, and his grades were modest. Speaking in Moscow in 1988, Reagan self-deprecatingly remarked, 'Twenty-five years after I graduated, my alma mater brought me back to the school and gave me an honorary degree. And I had to tell them they compounded a sense of guilt I had nursed for 25 years because I always felt the first degree they gave me was honorary.'[18]

His extensive extra-curricular activities at Eureka were useful for both his acting and his political careers. When the unpopular president of the cash-strapped college tried to abolish a number of courses and lay off some of the teachers, Reagan was the spokesperson for the students who went on strike in support of the threatened faculty and of students who would be deprived of courses on which they were already embarked. He edited the student newspaper, was a member of the student senate, and treasurer of the dramatic society. In his senior year he won an acting award when Eureka came second in an inter-collegiate competition for performance of one-act plays. The head of the department hosting that event—at Northwestern University—was sufficiently impressed to suggest that Reagan consider an acting career.[19] Looking back on his Eureka College years, Reagan saw them as among the happiest of his life, and he frequently returned to the campus in later years, making several of his major speeches there.

Hollywood

One of Reagan's assets was a warm and pleasant speaking voice. This, combined with his knowledge of sport and good memory, enabled him to get a job as a radio sports announcer in Iowa, first in Davenport and, then, with a larger audience and higher salary, in Des Moines. His real ambition already was to be an actor, but Hollywood seemed so remote a possibility that he kept quiet about it. His radio work in Des Moines, however, was extended to include interviews of well-known sports figures and film stars who happened to be in town. One of them was Joy Hodges, a native of Des Moines who had made a successful career as a singer in Hollywood. When he interviewed her in 1937 Reagan took the opportunity to ask how he could make film industry contacts. She put him in touch with a friend who was an agent, and Reagan made a brief visit to Hollywood. He saw the agent on his first day, had a screen test at Warner Brothers the next day, and when he got back to Des Moines found a telegram from the agent saying that Warner were offering him a year's contract, starting at $200 a week. Reagan wired back that he should sign immediately 'before they change their minds'.[20]

Reagan went on to act in fifty-four full-length films, a majority of which were B movies though some were the main features. Among the latter, one of his most notable was the 1940 film *Knute Rockne, All American*, named after the Norwegian-born coach of the University of Notre Dame football team. Reagan played the part of George Gipp ('the Gipper'), their star player who died two weeks before he was due to play his final game. 'The Gipper' was later used of Reagan himself and, indeed, as president he would urge Congress to pass legislation he wanted by saying 'Win one for the Gipper'.[21] Another success was *Kings Row* (made in 1941 and released in 1942) which Reagan described as 'the finest picture I ever appeared in', and which 'elevated me to the degree of stardom I had dreamed of when I arrived in Hollywood four years earlier'.[22] His career was flourishing in the last years before the United States entered the Second World War. In 1940 he married Jane Wyman who went on to become a bigger film star (and Oscar-winner for her role as a deaf mute in *Johnny Belinda*). They divorced in 1948.

Reagan's poor eyesight meant that he could not serve in any operational role during the war, and he remained in the United States. He was assigned to what was called the First Motion Picture Unit and became one of a number of Hollywood professionals who took part in scores of military training films. He returned to regular movies after the war, but it was in the early post-war years that his political career took off. Throughout his life thus far Reagan had identified as a Democrat. An admirer of Franklin D. Roosevelt, Reagan was following also in the footsteps of his father who, scarred by the Depression, was a firm Democrat. It was not until the early 1960s that Ronald Reagan registered as a Republican (and spoke in support of Barry Goldwater's presidential candidacy in 1964), but his position had been shifting over the previous decade and a half. By the early 1950s he was already a 'Democrat for Eisenhower'.[23] This partly resulted from his predicaments as president of the Screen Actors Guild (SAG), which he led from 1947 until 1952, having been regularly re-elected by a majority of its members. It was a role that gave him experience of negotiation and deal-making with the studios as well as confrontations with Communists and their sympathizers who had a significant presence in Hollywood.

Reagan became increasingly anti-Communist in the late 1940s and early 1950s, reflecting the mood of the country as well as his own vexation over the opposition he encountered from those in the SAG whom he regarded as Communists or fellow-travellers. He was a cooperative witness before the House of Representatives Un-American Activities Committee in 1947. At that time, however, Reagan made an attempt to steer a middle way between the Hollywood Communists and anti-Communist hysteria. Appearing before the Committee, he declined to identify people he suspected of being Communists, though he had already privately supplied names to the FBI. He argued at the Committee against outlawing the Communist Party, saying that democratic procedures should prevail, but he did not share the view of Humphrey Bogart, Lauren Bacall, Danny Kaye, and other Hollywood liberals that the Un-American Activities Committee was doing more damage to American democracy than Communists were capable of inflicting.[24] It was for being uncooperative witnesses at these same hearings that the 'Hollywood Ten' (screenwriters Ring Lardner, Jr and Dalton Trumbo among them) were jailed for contempt. In the late 1940s and early 1950s Reagan's political trajectory was from New Deal liberal to liberal anti-Communist and, finally, to anti-Communist conservative.[25]

There were other influences on Reagan's growing conservatism. Not long after his divorce from Jane Wyman, he spent a winter in Britain, making the 1949 film *The Hasty Heart*. He did not like what he saw of post-war austerity under a Labour government that retained rationing and other wartime necessities and pursued egalitarian policies, backed by high taxation. This was in a country which was undergoing the rebuilding not only of its economy but of its physical infrastructure, which had suffered severe damage during the war and faced a task of reconstruction that was incomparably greater than America's, a difference for which Reagan failed to make any allowance.[26] He decided that he did not like socialism in any form, even when it was British, democratic, and (with Ernest Bevin as Foreign Secretary and Clement Attlee as prime minister) firmly anti-Communist. Now that he was a high Hollywood earner, Reagan also felt he was paying too much tax at home. In a 1951 speech, he said that 'no industry has been picked for such discriminatory taxes as have the individuals in the industry of motion pictures'.[27]

Reagan's second marriage further underpinned his developing conservatism. He met Nancy Davis when the Hollywood starlet was agitated to find her name on a list of 208 signatories of a petition in support of the 'Hollywood Ten,' a document which she had not signed and had no intention of signing. It turned out that there was another Nancy Davis who had put her name to the petition. Although the confusion could have been cleared up without a meeting with the head of the Screen Actors Guild, Nancy was keen to meet and discuss her problem with Reagan personally. Their first get-together over dinner in November 1949 went well, for as one of Reagan's most recent biographers put it, 'Nancy was an interested listener of Reagan's tales of his SAG battles with communists and laughed at his jokes, both a turn-off for Jane Wyman.'[28] In October 1952, when Nancy was already pregnant with their first child, Patti, she and Ronald Reagan got married.[29] Nancy's comfortably-off parents were themselves highly conservative, especially her stepfather, Loyal Davis, a Chicago neurosurgeon, who is often credited with strengthening Reagan's rightward ideological leanings. He has been described as a man of 'hidebound views on issues medical and nonmedical' who 'detested socialized medicine and any other form of government intervention in medicine'.[30]

Politics Beckons

As Reagan's Hollywood career wound down in the early 1950s, a new opportunity opened up. In 1954 he was appointed host of half-hour episodes of *General Electric Theater* which was televised by CBS on Sunday evenings. Reagan not only presented the programmes, he acted in some of them, and signed off every week with a tribute to the company that ended with the words, 'at General Electric, progress is our most important product'.[31] The programme had high ratings and kept Reagan in the public eye. Reagan's well-paid employment by GE included a role as goodwill envoy for the company. He spent up to twelve weeks a year touring the company's enterprises throughout the United States, visiting all 139 of them and addressing most of the quarter of a million employees. This activity has been aptly described as 'a dry run for politics', for Reagan developed the art of interacting with a live audience and refining the stories he told them.[32]

Because he had in those days a fear of flying, Reagan's contract stipulated that he would travel by train. He used the long train journeys to read and to write, and his reading included Hayek's *The Road to Serfdom*, a book which provided ammunition for those who were opposed even to social democratic versions of socialism, and *Witness*, a memoir written by Whittaker Chambers, a former Communist who had also been a Soviet agent before he turned anti-Communist.[33] Reagan concluded that America was traversing Hayek's road to serfdom by 'piling one federal program on top of another'.[34] And he came to revere Chambers—so much so that in 1984 he awarded him the Presidential Medal of Freedom, almost a quarter of a century after Chambers's death. Reagan also read the *National Review*, founded by William F. Buckley in 1955, which inveighed against big government and advocated a more militant anti-Communism, not merely 'containment'.[35]

In 1959 Reagan endorsed Richard Nixon for the presidency when he was John F. Kennedy's Republican opponent. A year earlier, in a speech to General Electric executives, he had linked the perils of Communism with the expansion of government activity in the United States. In his speeches, at every stage of his career, he used stories and 'quotations' that came from very unreliable sources or from the recesses of his own mind, often drawing on films he had acted in or seen. They were popular ways of illustrating what he wished to argue and were effective tools of persuasion. For Reagan, whether they were actually true or not appeared less important than the part they played in his narrative. Over time, with constant repetition, he almost certainly came to believe them. A favourite tale he told that could bring an audience to tears, and left the speaker himself visibly moved, was of an American aircraft hit by German fire when returning from a bombing raid in the Second World War. The young gunner was wounded, trapped, and scared. The last person to bail out heard the pilot say, 'Never mind, son, we'll ride it down together', while he held the wounded boy's hand. 'Congressional Medal of Honor posthumously awarded', Reagan would usually conclude. No such honour was conferred, since the entire episode was no more than Reagan's imaginative reconstruction of scenes from more than one movie.[36]

If such tales were meant to inspire, other parts of the speeches were intended to alarm. Reagan had a quotation from Marx that the best way to impose socialism was 'to tax the middle class out of existence', and from Nikita Khrushchev (supposedly with the US in mind) that 'your country is becoming so socialistic that in fifteen years the causes of conflict between our two countries will have disappeared'.[37] Not only are such statements unknown to serious students of Marx and Khrushchev, but any such student could hardly be unaware that neither the one nor the other could ever have expressed such sentiments. They were both, in their very different ways, revolutionaries, not gradualist Fabian socialists. But Reagan's way of making sense of the world and of promoting his beliefs was by telling stories.[38] His skill in doing so made him, indeed, a much more effective communicator than political rivals of greater analytical sharpness who were unable to evoke comparable emotional associations or construct a compelling political narrative.[39]

Reagan established himself as an eloquent advocate of the conservative cause, and increasingly he was being encouraged to enter directly into the political fray. In discussions with the Nixon team in 1960, he was persuaded to delay his formal switch to Republican on the grounds that his attacks on Democratic candidate Kennedy would have a greater impact if he officially remained a Democrat. He duly obliged and portrayed Kennedy as a dangerous, leftist authoritarian ruler in waiting, saying 'Under the tousled boyish haircut it is still old Karl Marx—first launched a century ago.'[40]

General Electric ended its contract with Reagan in 1962, and for a time he relied on roles as a guest star, on fees for speeches, and on paid advocacy. He became a well-remunerated spokesman in the early 1960s for the American Medical Association, warning of the dangers of subsidized medical care and of 'creeping socialism'.[41] Business and politics were coming together, with increasing emphasis on the latter. Having strongly supported Senator Barry Goldwater's quest for the Republican presidential nomination in the 1964 primaries, he was critical of the party's moderate wing and its favoured candidate, Governor Nelson Rockefeller of New York. He gave such a stirring, televised and well-received speech at a Goldwater fundraiser in Los Angeles that wealthy backers realized that Reagan could make a better pitch for their cause than could Goldwater himself.[42] When Goldwater was comprehensively defeated by Lyndon Johnson in the presidential election, a group of Californian businessmen formed a Friends of Ronald Reagan committee to promote him as a candidate for the governorship of their state in 1966. His mastery of television and ability to deliver a well-rehearsed script in folksy style served him well. He also benefited from his evident sincerity. It was not just that, as a good actor, he could deliver his lines, but that he firmly believed what he said.[43]

This was a time of student revolts and growing opposition to the Vietnam War, of racial conflict (rioting, and its repression, in the Watts district of Los Angeles in August 1965 left 34 dead, over 1,000 people injured, and caused $40 million of damage),[44] and of higher taxes to pay for social programmes, and Reagan's response to all this resonated with many voters. He drew on his film background for images that his listeners could instantly recognize, even when they were caricatures. The Californian hippies, Reagan declared, 'had hair like Tarzan, look like Jane, and smell like Cheetah'.[45] Although his lack of political experience was used against him by the Democrats, Reagan's response, referring to Governor Edmond G. (Pat) Brown, was to say, 'The man who has the job has more experience than anybody. That's why I'm running.'[46] Brown initially welcomed Reagan's winning the Republican nomination to run against him, believing that he would be easier to beat than a more experienced and more liberal Republican opponent, but he was warned by the Democratic fund-raiser Manning Post that this would not be so. 'He's the guy with the white hat', said Post. He has 'the image of a good guy' and you 'just can't make him a bad guy'.[47] In the election, Reagan was a convincing winner, taking 58 per cent of the votes cast. The value of his instant name recognition and ease in front of a camera or microphone had been major assets. The national mood was also changing, and Republicans generally did well in the 1966 elections.

Reagan got off to an awkward start as governor. When asked by a journalist what his political priorities were, he could not think of an answer. He turned to an aide and said, 'I could take some coaching from the sidelines, if anyone can recall my legislative program.'[48] He turned out to be a more pragmatic governor than his campaign rhetoric appeared to predict. He signed a bill in 1967 which, in effect, legalized abortion, compromised over budget cuts in the state universities (state spending on higher education actually doubled during his governorship), and signed stricter environmental protection laws than were to be found elsewhere in the country. This included adding 145,000 acres to the state park system.[49] In 1967, Reagan, the ideologically convinced tax-cutter, introduced the biggest tax increase of any governor of any American state, four times larger than the tax hike of his predecessor, Pat Brown, in 1959. By doing this so early in his incumbency, he successfully put the blame for the increase on the Democrats, saying that Brown had 'looted' the state treasury 'in a manner unique in our history'. Reagan's approval ratings remained high.[50] He did enough both to reassure his conservative supporters and to provide liberal opponents with ample grounds for continuing opposition to him. These included his vigorous support for the Vietnam War and strong backing for the principle of low taxation (even though his practice was more flexible).

Elected to a second term as governor in 1971, Reagan served until 1975 and chose not to seek a third. During his second term, he cut the state's welfare bill and tried to curb taxation through constitutional reform. Proposition 1, which was put to a ballot of the Californian electorate, would have kept down the percentage of a person's income that could be collected in taxation in the absence of a special vote to endorse a higher increase. Reagan lost the vote by 54 to 46 per cent, but the campaign 'captured the conservative imagination nationwide'.[51] He also took a hard line against student unrest. In a remark that went down well with conservative audiences, Reagan quipped that 'their signs said, make love, not war, but they didn't look like they could do either'.[52] With his backing, the California National Guard used tear gas against protesting students at Berkeley. Many years later, answering questions from students at Moscow State University, Reagan remarked, 'When I was Governor of California, I could start a riot just by going to a campus.'[53]

As governor—and, later, as president—Reagan was very ready to delegate responsibility to members of his team. Among those he brought into it during his first term as Californian governor, several were to play significant roles in the Reagan White House—Caspar Weinberger, William Clark, Edwin Meese III, and Michael Deaver, among them. Some of Reagan's wealthy backers, who had seen him as a more attractive face of conservatism than Barry Goldwater had presented, were keen for Reagan to seek the Republican presidential nomination as early as 1968, and they raised seed money for that purpose. Reagan was convinced that the bid was premature and insists in his memoirs that he was never tempted. He had been governor for only two years at that time, and 'knew I wasn't ready to be president'.[54] The way was clear for Nixon to receive the nomination and to win the presidential election. Reagan had disapproved of Nixon in the 1950s, when he was Eisenhower's vice-president, but was loyal to him throughout his presidency and retained good relations with him thereafter. He had little respect, however, for Nixon's successor, Gerald Ford, who chose Nelson Rockefeller, the Republican conservatives loved to hate, as his vice-president and offered Reagan (by this time no longer California governor) only lowly Cabinet positions, which he refused.

Reagan challenged Ford for the Republican nomination in 1976 and came close to succeeding, Ford gaining 1,187 votes of delegates at the convention to Reagan's 1,070. After delivering his acceptance speech, Ford called Reagan to the stage while delegates shouted 'Speech! Speech!' Often less than convincing without a script, Reagan on this occasion touched on many of his favourite themes and received rapturous applause for a six-minute speech in which he spoke of two powers with the military ability to destroy each other within minutes and stressed the urgency of saving the world from nuclear destruction. Earlier in the same day he told his supporters that there were millions of Americans who wanted 'what you want', that their country should be 'a shining city on a hill'.[55]

Reagan had laid down a strong marker to be the Republican presidential candidate in 1980, and he spent much of the next four years consolidating his support among groups that could make that happen. He established a firm rapport with the critics of détente who wished to take a tougher anti-Soviet line, notably the influential group who constituted the Committee on the Present Danger, established in 1976. It contained Democrats as well as Republicans, but had a strong neo-conservative flavour. Among the more influential members were Paul Nitze, who served as a senior arms control negotiator in the Reagan administration, and Harvard history professor Richard Pipes who later became the Soviet expert on Reagan's National Security Council. In language that chimed with Reagan's beliefs, the Committee argued that the Soviet Union was still striving for a 'Communist world order', that within a few years it was on course to 'achieve strategic superiority over the United States', and that the Soviet side did 'not subscribe to American notions of nuclear sufficiency and mutually assured deterrence'.[56]

Reagan was also able to appeal to the business community, who were attracted by his views on tax-reduction, and to the Christian Right. After Jimmy Carter had defeated Ford in the 1976 election, his administration antagonized the evangelicals who disagreed with Carter on, for example, abortion and gay rights and who deeply resented his unwillingness to overrule the Inland Revenue Service's revocation of the tax-exempt status of private schools who had admitted an 'insignificant number of minority students'. This particularly affected the evangelical schools, almost exclusively white, which were to be found particularly in the south.[57] Reagan had no difficulty in winning the support of that constituency, especially since his main rival for the nomination was the Republican moderate George H. W. Bush, former director of the CIA. Once the nomination was secured, however, Reagan lost no time in broadening his appeal by bringing Bush in as his running mate.

In the 1980 presidential election campaign, Carter was given a very hard time by conservative religious and political groups. Apart from saying that he was encouraging abortion and homosexuality, they accused him of being soft on Communism and of weakening the country's defence by negotiating the Strategic Arms Limitation Treaty (SALT 2) of 1979, which put ceilings on the strategic nuclear arsenals of both sides.[58] Reagan received the warm support of these groups, yet survey research suggested that the economy bulked larger in voters' minds than either social or foreign policy, and 63 per cent of respondents to a *Time* poll saw the election as 'mostly a rejection of President Carter', compared with only 25 per cent viewing it as a 'mandate for more conservative policies'.[59] Carter had expected his superior knowledge of the issues to be decisively important when he debated on television with Reagan. The Republicans did not agree to the Democrats' wish to have a series of Carter–Reagan debates. The one televised debate between the two main candidates was held just a week before the election and, as Carter himself admitted, Reagan made a 'better impression'. Explaining this to himself in notes he made the following evening, Carter wrote that Reagan 'has his memorized lines, and he pushes a button and they come out'.[60] Reagan won the 1980 election convincingly, capturing 489 against 49 of the electoral college votes and over 50 per cent of the popular vote, even though there was a serious third candidate, John Anderson, who took 6.6 per cent of the total vote.[61]

One politician who applauded Reagan's election—and, in turn, impressed him— was Margaret Thatcher. Just as she benefited from making the acquaintance of Mikhail Gorbachev before he became Soviet leader, her friendship with Reagan was enhanced by the fact that they first met in London in 1975 while he was still governor of California and she had just been elected Leader of the Conservative Party. As early as the late 1960s, she had read the text of a speech Reagan made to the Institute of

Directors in London about which her husband, Denis, had come home enthusing. She wholeheartedly agreed both with the economic policies Reagan was espousing and with his emphasis on strong defence and suspicion of détente.[62] Of the 1975 meeting between the future president and the future prime minister, Reagan wrote in his memoirs, 'I'd planned on spending only a few minutes with Margaret Thatcher but we ended up talking for almost two hours...and it was evident from our first words that we were soul mates when it came to reducing government and expanding economic freedom.'[63]

5

REAGAN'S FIRST TERM

Unsurprisingly, Ronald Reagan's election in 1980 was greeted warmly by Margaret Thatcher. She noted that his 'style of work and decision-making was apparently detached and broad-brush—very different from my own'.[1] Nonetheless, he embodied 'the American dream in action'. She thoroughly approved of his defence build-up and was naturally 'delighted to learn that the new president wished me to be the first foreign head of government to visit the United States after he took office'.[2] When Thatcher telephoned Reagan the day after his inauguration, the president told her that they would 'lend strength to each other'.[3] Reagan instructed his staff to make Thatcher's visit 'special' and, in a memorandum to the president, Secretary of State Alexander Haig underlined that the aim of the visit was to demonstrate that 'Thatcher is the major Western leader most attuned to your views on East-West and security issues.' She wanted to build on their personal relationship with the president and have her visit seen as 'a very strong reaffirmation of the "Special Relationship"' between Great Britain and the United States.[4] In general, that relationship has appeared more special to the British than to the American side, but it was lodged in the institutional memory of the State Department that these were words visiting British politicians liked to hear. When he was West German Chancellor, Helmut Schmidt quipped that the relationship was 'so special that only one side knows it exists'. Sir Rodric Braithwaite, the former British Ambassador to Moscow, who later advised Mrs Thatcher's successor, John Major, on foreign policy and chaired the Joint Intelligence Committee in the Cabinet Office, observed that Downing Street's emphasis on the specialness of the relationship has served mainly to bolster the egos of British prime ministers and their entourages.[5]

The closeness, politically and personally, of Reagan and Thatcher was, however, a reality. A characteristic entry in Reagan's diary (on 21 July 1981, following discussions at a G7 summit meeting in Canada) noted that 'Margaret Thatcher is a tower of strength and a solid friend of the U.S.'[6] There were American policies on which the two leaders disagreed and Mrs Thatcher had no inhibition, in those circumstances, from sharply expressing her disapproval. Yet, on most of the big issues in domestic and foreign policy Reagan and Thatcher saw eye to eye. These included their commitment to a less state-regulated economy, vigorous support for private enterprise and the market, backing for increased defence spending, and the suspicion that their predecessors had been insufficiently vigilant in the struggle against Communism. In their desire to seize the ideological initiative from the Soviet Union in the Cold War, they were as one. More surprisingly, since both of them earned their reputation as hard-liners vis-à-vis the Soviet Union, Reagan was later to be attacked in 1987 by Washington conservatives for having gone soft on Moscow and conceding too much to Mikhail Gorbachev in arms reduction negotiations, while no conservative political leader in Western Europe took a more intense and friendly interest in the ever more radical Soviet reforms of the second half of the 1980s, under the umbrella of perestroika, than did Margaret Thatcher.

Reagan's softer second-term policy toward the Soviet Union is often sharply contrasted with his first four years in the White House. Real headway in East–West relations did, indeed, only start to be made after Gorbachev became Soviet leader in 1985, but the pacific component of Reagan's 'peace through strength' foreign policy was also present during his first term, albeit barely visible in 1981–2 when the emphasis was very much on building up American military might.[7] Although, in principle, Reagan wished to have a face-to-face meeting with the Soviet top leader— they were four different people during the eight years Reagan occupied the White House—he was in no rush to do so, and it was hardly a practical proposition during the first two years of his presidency. His Soviet counterpart, Leonid Brezhnev, was declining both mentally and physically and in no shape to conduct negotiations.

Reagan himself was more seriously wounded than was made fully public at the time when he was shot by John Hinckley as he left a lunchtime meeting he had addressed at the Washington Hilton on 30 March 1981. He lost a dangerous amount of blood and the bullet that struck him lodged less than an inch from his heart. The United States came alarmingly close to losing a president to a lone gunman for the second time within two decades. The injury and the operation may have had an effect on his formerly excellent memory. Not long after the assassination attempt, Reagan failed to recognize the only black member of his Cabinet, Samuel Pierce, who was Secretary for Housing and Urban Development, greeting him with 'How are you, Mr Mayor? How are things in your city?'[8] Yet Reagan lost little time in resuming his duties, for his outdoor lifestyle had made him a resilient septuagenarian. The popular reaction to the assassination attempt did the president enough political good to go some way toward balancing the physical harm, for his grace and humour during this dire emergency evoked widespread admiration. 'Honey, I forgot to duck', Reagan told his wife who had rushed to be with him, and as he was wheeled into the operating theatre, he quipped to the medical team, 'I hope you're all Republicans.'[9]

Reagan had a few big issues he cared deeply about and combating Communism was clearly one of them. He frequently referred to a Soviet goal of creating a single Communist state encompassing the world, although that was far from the agenda of the aged oligarchy headed by Brezhnev. While the Soviet Union competed with the United States for influence in the 'Third World', their leaders' most basic concern was to preserve the power bloc they already dominated and to uphold their own domestic power structure. Keeping their East European client states in line was challenging enough, as were managing relations with Communist China which varied between uneasy and distinctly hostile. To try to swallow Western Europe or the United States would have been vastly more than the Soviet Union was capable of digesting, even in the absence of nuclear deterrence. Reagan was on somewhat surer ground in believing that the Soviet Union had seized a potential military advantage by deploying their SS-20s. These were mobile nuclear missiles with three independently targeted nuclear warheads that had a greater range and accuracy than the missiles with single nuclear warheads they replaced in 1977. They could hit the capitals of NATO countries in Europe in less than five minutes from their launch.[10] From a Soviet point of view, they strengthened deterrence, making any attack on the USSR from Western Europe more certainly suicidal for the aggressor.

Plans to combat this enhanced Soviet weaponry predated Reagan's presidency. In December 1979, more than a year before Reagan entered the White House, NATO agreed that two new weapons should be developed by the United States and that they would be deployed in the absence of a deal with the Soviet Union for removal of the SS-20s. The weapons were the Pershing II, a ballistic missile, and the Tomahawk cruise missile. Hundreds were to be placed in Europe in 1983 in the event of failure of the 'dual-track' approach (the term used to denote the policy whereby the weapon development would proceed concurrently with diplomacy that might render their deployment unnecessary). The removal of the Soviet SS-20s and the abandoning of deployment of the Pershing and Cruise missiles became known as the 'zero option'. Within the Reagan administration there was a division between those who hoped that a compromise could be reached with the Soviet Union on this matter and those whose support for the zero option was predicated on their conviction that it would be totally unacceptable to the Kremlin.[11]

Ironically, whereas Secretary of Defense Weinberger supported the zero option because of his certainty that the Soviet Union would reject it, it was because he was equally sure that it was a non-starter for the Soviet leadership that Secretary of State Haig opposed it. As Haig put it, 'The fatal flaw in the Zero Option as a basis for negotiations was that it was not negotiable.' He thought it was 'absurd to expect the Soviets to dismantle an existing force of 1,100 warheads', in exchange for a mere promise from the United States not to deploy a missile force not yet built and which was encountering resistance in Western Europe.[12] The eventual outcome does not mean that Haig's assumption was wrong, for when Gorbachev, on behalf of the Soviet Union, did eventually accept the zero option, it was after very real American missiles had been put in place that needed to be removed. Reagan himself glossed over possible policy differences between the Secretary of State and himself. In his diary entry of 25 June 1982, he said that the only difference between him and Haig was over which of them made policy.[13]

Particularly in the early years of the Reagan administration, somewhat different foreign policies were being pursued in the National Security Council (NSC), in the State Department and in the Defense Department. Another contributor to the foreign policy process, the CIA, was itself far from monolithically united in its assessments. It was usually supportive of the position of the civilian heads of the Defense Department, though its Soviet analysts included not only hard-liners—most notably, Fritz Ermath and, at a still higher level of the agency, Robert Gates—but also specialists whose more nuanced views of Soviet policy were closer to those of the State Department. When in January 1982 William Clark, a close ally of Reagan who had worked with him in California, moved from being number two to Haig in the State Department to become National Security Adviser, in succession to Richard Allen, the authority of the NSC was greatly enhanced. Clark took an intransigent line vis-à-vis the Soviet Union, and the influence he wielded with Reagan was resented by the Secretary of State. Haig complained in his memoirs that Clark, who 'had been such an agreeable deputy to me in my early days at the State Department' had turned against him, and at the NSC he 'seemed to be conducting a second foreign policy, using separate channels of communication'.[14] For his part, Clark was reflecting Reagan's growing dissatisfaction with what he perceived to be Haig's assumption that he, rather than the president, was the principal foreign-policy maker.[15]

There were reasons on both sides why the zero option was a non-starter before 1983 when the Pershing and Cruise missiles were deployed on schedule in Western Europe. Concerned as Soviet leaders were about the projected deployment in West Europe, and especially about the missiles in West Germany (the first time in history that nuclear weapons would be stationed on German territory), they were unwilling to accept that the introduction of the SS-20s had been a mistake or that Pershing and Cruise deployment could be regarded as a logical consequence of that policy. They had reason to hope that deployment might still be averted by a sustained campaign aimed at West European public opinion. Opposition to what seemed like a dangerous escalation of the arms race was already widespread in the countries concerned, and Soviet policy was aimed at forcing Western European governments to backtrack on agreeing to nuclear missile deployment or risk losing elections to opponents more responsive to public protests. In a summary of the key points that had emerged in a meeting between Reagan and the US ambassador to Britain in November 1981, National Security Adviser Richard Allen wrote, 'There is little anti-Americanism per se in the UK, but the anti-nuclear demonstrators must be taken seriously (i.e. we must make a greater effort to appeal to British and European public opinion).'[16] In the United States itself, there was some opposition to yet more nuclear weapons being manufactured and deployed. Misgivings were expressed by religious leaders, especially the Catholic bishops. The Protestant evangelist Billy Graham and Father Theodore Hesburgh, the influential president of the University of Notre Dame, were also among those warning of the danger of drift toward nuclear war.[17]

Those senior officials in the Defense Department and the NSC, who paid lip service to the zero option only because they were confident that it would be rejected by the Soviet leadership, were correct in the latter assumption (until, at least, well into Reagan's second term). Defense Secretary Weinberger and his deputy Richard Perle were so suspicious of the Kremlin's intentions and so intent on completing a massive build-up of American military strength that they had no desire to reach agreements with the Soviet Union or indeed any interest in reducing tensions between the nuclear superpowers. Perle made clear the reasoning behind that stance when, in February 1983, he said 'Democracies will not sacrifice to protect their security in the absence of a sense of danger, and every time we create the impression that we and the Soviets are cooperating and moderating the competition, we diminish the sense of apprehension.'[18] Defence expenditure was a huge exception to Reagan's belief in smaller government and balanced budgets. The president also did not see any incompatibility between the pursuit of peace and improved US–Soviet relations, on the one hand, and a huge hike in the military budget, on the other. For Perle and other hardliners, the former was a threat to the latter which was the higher priority.

The top specialist on the Soviet Union within the NSC, Richard Pipes, was at least as sceptical about the possibility of improved relations with the Soviet Union as were Weinberger and Perle. In a 1981 interview, he claimed that war with the USSR was inevitable 'unless Moscow changed its political system'. In the same year, the senior military adviser on the National Security Council, Major-General Robert L. Schweitzer, said that the Soviet military build-up was producing a 'drift toward war', adding that the Soviet Union had 'achieved superiority in the strategic triad of land and sea-based missiles and in air power'. Schweitzer was dismissed from the NSC by National Security Adviser Richard Allen for his unauthorized remarks in which, said Allen, he had 'overstated his case'. The general was reassigned to a post in the Pentagon. Reagan took issue with Schweitzer's analysis, arguing that, while what the general had said might have been true 'when we were unilaterally disarming', the strengthening of the American military by his administration was preventing a move toward war.[19]

The Defense Department was determined to go ahead with deployment of medium-range nuclear missiles, come what may, and there was strong support for their position from within the NSC. Reagan's first National Security Adviser, Richard Allen, lasted only a year in the post and did not report directly to Reagan but to the president's Counsellor, Ed Meese. An exceptionally well-informed observer of the Reagan administration, Lou Cannon, noted Allen's 'lone-wolf approach to a job in which collegiality is an essential asset' and reported a widespread perception that he was 'in over his head'.[20] When the arch-conservative Clark succeeded Allen, he was also such an old friend and ally of Reagan's from California that he had no difficulty in getting direct access to the president written into his job specification. That was in spite of the fact that, in general, Reagan liked his senior aides—Chief of White House

Staff James Baker, his deputy Mike Deaver, and Counsellor Ed Meese—to act as his intermediaries, summarizing the views of senior Cabinet members for him. Even Haig did not have regular direct access to Reagan, much to his annoyance.

Haig at times pushed for policies that seemed dangerously rash to Reagan's inner triumvirate, especially to Deaver, who was the least attracted by foreign interventionism. The Secretary of State was among those acutely exercised by what he saw as Communist subversion in Latin America, for which he placed much of the blame on Cuba. In one meeting with Reagan and a small group of his staff, Haig said, 'Give me the word and I'll make that island a fucking parking lot.' After Haig had departed, Deaver said to William Clark, still at the time number two to Haig in the State Department and shortly to become National Security Adviser in place of Allen, 'Good God, I cannot believe that I'm in the room with the president of the United States and the secretary of state's talking about bombing Cuba.' To Clark's observation that it was done for effect, Deaver responded that it had certainly had an effect on him: 'It scared the shit out of me'—to which he later added that it also 'scared the shit out of Ronald Reagan'.[21] Deaver was Nancy Reagan's main informant on what was going on in the West Wing and, in turn, the person who made sure that her views, especially on the president's diary, were taken fully into account by the senior White House staff. In her memoirs, Mrs Reagan wrote that 'If Ronnie had given him the green light, Haig would have bombed everybody and everything' and that there was relief when he left in the summer of 1982.

That view of Haig as excessively gung-ho was partly based on his belligerent attitude to Cuba,[22] although somewhat at odds with the fact that in appointing him, Reagan had taken the advice of Richard Nixon, whose espousal of détente with the Soviet Union had been viewed with suspicion by Reagan's neo-conservative supporters. Appointing Haig went against the counsel of the president's main advisers—the inner-sanctum troika of Ed Meese and Mike Deaver, who had played important parts in Reagan's administration when he was Governor of California, and James Baker. Although junior to Baker and Meese (and to Haig and Weinberger), Deaver was trusted by Reagan and earned a reputation as his adroit image-maker, while his excellent relations with Nancy Reagan reflected his skills as a courtier.[23]

If a strong leader is defined as one who seeks to gather and to hoard as much power as possible in his or her own hands and who takes all the big decisions, Reagan was not a strong leader. That does not mean he was an ineffective president. Maximization of power in the office of head of government is not the same as political efficacy. Since there is a limit to how much any individual leader can or, indeed, should do, the more important question is whether that person can keep a strong team together—people who, collectively, are capable of attracting support and achieving results.[24] The Reagan administration presented a mixed picture in those respects. The president made both bad and good appointments, yet his relative remoteness from the policy process and especially from policy detail made the political judgement, values, and skills of department heads within his administration even more conse-quential. Their ability or failure to get along with each other mattered hugely, and throughout all of Reagan's first term and for much of the second, senior members of his team were at loggerheads.

Robert McFarlane, who served in both the State Department and the NSC of the Reagan administration (from 1983 to 1985 as the president's National Security Adviser) noted that tensions between the State and Defense departments had existed to some extent in all American administrations, but that under Reagan they were even more 'corrosive'.[25] Referring to Reagan's first-term experience in particular, George Shultz wrote of 'the tension and frustration' he felt working in the administration. He noted that, given the division within the White House—'with Deaver and Baker contending with Clark and Meese'—whatever he did was perceived as a point scored for one side or the other.[26] Reagan was averse to getting involved in these conflicts, especially if they were between people he liked and had personally appointed, and so was slow to intervene. The White House press corps were enlisted by the warring parties in the administration, so much so that Donald Regan, a man with an autocratic leadership style and, according to McFarlane, 'a fiery temper',[27] predicted that when the archives were opened, there would be few revelations. In Regan's words, this was an adminis-tration in which 'the leak was raised to the status of an art form. Everything, or nearly everything, the president or his close associates did or knew appeared in the news-papers and on the networks with the least possible delay.'[28] Regan was successively Treasury Secretary and then Chief of Staff in the White House, following James Baker. The two men themselves simply agreed that they would exchange jobs and then sought and received presidential blessing for the swap.[29]

New Broom at the State Department

The conduct of foreign policy by the Reagan administration improved over time as a result of key personnel changes. Of particular importance was the appointment of Shultz as Secretary of State in mid-1982, following the resignation of Haig. A former Supreme Allied Commander of NATO Forces in Europe who was accustomed to being the ultimate authority, Haig had clashed with others in the administration and threatened on several occasions to resign. He hinted at it once too often, and was taken by surprise when Reagan handed him an unsealed envelope. In his memoirs, Haig recorded: 'I opened it and read the single typed page it contained. "Dear Al", it began. "It is with the most profound regret that I accept your letter of resignation."' The presi-dent, Haig continued, 'was accepting a letter of resignation that I had not submit-ted'.[30] Reagan got Shultz's agreement the same day that he would be willing to step in at the State Department.

Shultz was to clash frequently with Defense Secretary Caspar Weinberger and also with Robert Gates of the CIA, but not with Reagan. The new Secretary of State was a

Figure 2 Ronald Reagan and Margaret Thatcher at White House welcoming ceremony for Prime Minister Thatcher, February 1981.

more talented politician than was his predecessor and more skilful at building necessary alliances within the administration. Significantly also, he established good relations with Nancy Reagan, whose judgement, especially of people, counted for a lot with her husband. Mrs Reagan noted that 'Ronnie and I both respected and admired' Shultz, who served as Secretary of State for the whole of the remainder of Reagan's presidency.[31]

Shultz's internal as well as external diplomacy eventually led Reagan to side with State rather than Defense on most issues involving the Soviet Union. Even Haig, notwithstanding Deaver's and Nancy Reagan's view of him as excessively belligerent, had been more flexible in his approach to the Soviet Union and to arms control than Weinberger and Richard Perle, although that was not a high hurdle to surmount.[32] General Colin Powell, who worked with Weinberger and admired him, observed that he was 'a man of stubborn principle. His critics would have said "stubborn" period.' He added that Weinberger was constantly ready to do battle with other Cabinet members or critical Congressmen, but could not bring himself to cross the president, even though Reagan was 'probably the most pliable man in the administration' and someone Weinberger 'idolized' and to whom his loyalty was total.[33] That does not mean that Weinberger was always of like mind with the president. He was very far from sharing Reagan's desire for dialogue with Soviet leaders, although he did accurately convey to the president in December 1981 Margaret Thatcher's view that 'a summit meeting with Brezhnev could be very useful'.[34] Weinberger surprised even the Pentagon staff with the size of the increases in the defence budget he sought, taking full advantage of the president's commitment to enhancing still further America's military strength. When, early in Reagan's first term, the Chiefs of the Armed Services put in requests for a 9 per cent increase of defence spending in real terms, the Defense Secretary told them they were asking for too little. According to Powell, they went 'from their wish lists to their dream lists', and Weinberger upped 'the inherited Carter budget by 11 per cent, or $25.8 billion, the pattern for the foreseeable future'.[35]

Though it turned out to be the year in which the Cold War became distinctly colder, 1983 began with a change of emphasis in American policy toward the Soviet Union, reflecting the influence now being exerted by Shultz. On 17 January a major new statement on America's Soviet policy was produced for internal use within the government, providing the first clear outline of what the administration did and did not seek in the relationship with the Soviet Union.[36] This was National Security Decision Directive No. 75 (NSDD-75) on 'U.S. Relations with the Soviet Union'. It noted that the administration should 'attempt to reach agreements which protect and enhance US interests and which are consistent with the principle of *strict reciprocity and mutual interest*' (italics added). The primary focus was to 'contain and over time reverse Soviet expansionism', and to compete effectively with the USSR 'in the overall military balance and in geographical regions of primary concern to the United States'. The policy document did not at any point seek the break-up of the Soviet Union. And the nearest it came to calling for regime change was the aim of promoting, '*within the narrow limits available to us*, the process of change in the Soviet Union toward a more pluralistic political and economic system in which the power of the privileged ruling elite is *gradually reduced*' (italics added).[37] The directive also stated that the United States must make clear to the Soviet leadership that 'genuine restraint in their behavior' would create the conditions for mutually beneficial East–West relations.[38]

'Evil Empire' and SDI

Reagan endorsed this moderate statement of policy, but his rhetoric gave out mixed signals. Two speeches he made in March 1983—in the first of which he described the Soviet Union as an 'evil empire' and, in the second announced his Strategic Defense Initiative (SDI)—alarmed not only the Soviet leadership but also America's European allies. The first speech was delivered on 8 March at the annual convention of the National Association of Evangelicals and was mostly devoted to domestic policy. Reagan spoke of his attempt to put prayer back into public schools and his desire to reverse legislation that legalized abortion. Near the end of his speech, however, he referred to 'the aggressive impulses of an evil empire' and said that the arms race was not 'a giant misunderstanding' but a 'struggle between right and wrong and good and evil'.[39] Although he spoke also of his administration's efforts to 'negotiate real and verifiable reductions in the world's nuclear arsenals, and one day, with God's help, their total elimination',[40] the 'evil empire' rhetoric made by far the bigger impression in Moscow, along with Reagan's prediction (which within a decade was to seem surprisingly prescient) that communism was another 'sad, bizarre chapter in human history whose last pages even now are being written'.[41] To the Soviet leadership, this sounded like an intensification of the US ideological offensive.

That the same month of sharpened anti-Communist rhetoric saw the announcement of a major new defence initiative—SDI—greatly alarmed the Soviet leadership. Reagan had long been dissatisfied with Mutually Assured Destruction (MAD) as the only strategy for preventing war, since if it failed to deter, there would be no way of preventing utter devastation. He was a firm believer in the biblical Armageddon,[42] and for a president to be convinced that Armageddon was going to happen and to regard it as impervious to human agency would have been a dangerous combination. The issue surfaced in the 1984 television debate between Reagan and Democratic presidential candidate Walter Mondale when Reagan said that no-one knew whether 'Armageddon is a thousand years away or the day after tomorrow'.[43] Reagan believed both in the inevitability of Armageddon, which he linked with nuclear catastrophe, and yet in the providential role he could play in preventing it, as his former National Security Adviser, Robert (Bud) McFarlane, noted shortly after Reagan demitted office.[44] Even a preordained catastrophe could, apparently, be avoided or at least mitigated, and Reagan saw his mission being 'to protect Americans from the risk of nuclear annihilation'.[45] That underlay his determination to build up American military strength, his desire to rid the world of nuclear weapons, and his wish to believe in the efficacy of SDI.

The president was receptive to any suggestion that there was a way of defending the United States from nuclear attack. The idea that anti-ballistic missiles could be developed that would destroy incoming missiles—the equivalent of firing a bullet to hit an approaching bullet—hugely appealed to Reagan. A number of people had persuaded him that the SDI anti-missile defence—soon to be labelled 'Star Wars' (though not by the president)—was feasible if enough resources were poured into it. The physicist Edward Teller wrote to Reagan on 23 July 1982, about 'an important new class of defensive nuclear weapons' that could be 'employed in space to defend against both nuclear and conventional attacks'. In a note to National Security Adviser Clark, Reagan said 'We should take this seriously & have a real look'.[46] Other scientists warned that it was both impractical (inconceivable that every incoming missile could be stopped in its tracks) and imprudent, for it would intensify Soviet concerns and threaten international stability. Those who hoped to benefit from the massive new investment prevailed, however, and SDI became official American policy. Teller, who met with Reagan in September 1982, again talked up its potential, and a member of

Teller's team alleged that the Russians would have their own space-based anti-ballistic missile system by 1985.[47] SDI had some support within the administration, not least from Bud McFarlane, deputy to National Security Adviser at the time and later his successor. McFarlane, however, saw the SDI project as a potential bargaining chip with the Soviet Union, rather than as something that would ever be deployed and really work.[48]

Reagan, in contrast, became increasingly committed to the idea, partly for political reasons, seeing it as a bold and surprising initiative, but also, and much more fancifully, as a way of countering the threat to humanity of nuclear weapons. McFarlane was instructed by Reagan and Clark to insert a passage about SDI into a speech on national security that the president was to deliver from the Oval Office on 23 March 1983 which would go out on all the major television networks.[49] The wording of the speech underwent change up until shortly before its delivery. George Shultz saw various versions of it and was able to have some minor influence in toning it down but he was far from satisfied with the final version. However, he accepted that a decision in principle on SDI had been made and that the president had a right to make it.[50] To mitigate the damage to US–Soviet relations, Shultz gave a copy of the speech to Soviet ambassador Anatoly Dobrynin a few hours before Reagan delivered it and stressed that what was being proposed was 'a research and development effort' that would be consistent with the Anti-Ballistic Missiles (ABM) Treaty. Dobrynin responded, 'You will be opening a new phase in the arms race.'[51]

In the speech, Reagan called upon the scientific community who had provided the United States with nuclear weapons to 'turn their great talents now...to the means of rendering these nuclear weapons impotent and obsolete'. He declared that the US was seeking 'neither military superiority nor political advantage' but searching for 'ways to reduce the danger of nuclear war'.[52] In his diary entry of the same day, Reagan wrote that giving the speech 'felt good'. He acknowledged that the task was one which might take twenty years but 'we had to do it'.[53] Following the televised speech, Reagan joined the party of past and present Secretaries of State and National Security Advisers, scientists, and military chiefs who had been invited for dinner that evening in the White House. The group, wrote Reagan in his diary, praised his speech 'to the sky' and 'seemed to think it would be a source of debate for some time to come'.[54]

The forecast was certainly correct. After billions have been poured into SDI, it remains some thirty-five years later as much of a delusion—and job-creation scheme for the military-industrial complex—as it was in 1983. Yet argument continues as to whether it hastened or hindered the end of the Cold War. One prominent international relations specialist, Adam Roberts, provocatively suggested 'a worrying possibility' that 'the Cold War would not have ended but for two myths: that Soviet-style communism could be reformed, and that Star Wars could work'.[55]

Soviet national security policy did not, however, change fundamentally in the first half of the 1980s when Dmitry Ustinov and Andrei Gromyko remained powerful political actors and Yury Andropov and Konstantin Chernenko were, in quick succession, general secretaries of the Communist Party.* The Soviet leaders' collective reaction to the harder line from Washington was a toughening of their own position vis-à-vis the United States, accompanied by a desire to exercise greater diplomatic flexibility elsewhere in order to win over international opinion. Thus, the response of the Soviet Politburo to the apparent hardening in the US position had several different aspects. The most basic element was to maintain to the full the Soviet Union's armaments programme. As Ustinov put it, 'Everything that we are doing in relation to defence we should continue doing' and all the planned missiles should be delivered.[56] The Politburo on 31 May 1983 also agreed that a meeting should be convened of the Soviet Union's East European allies to establish a common line and maintain a united front, that they would undertake diplomatic initiatives with the aim of improving their relations with China and Japan, and that they must intensify both international and domestic propaganda against Reagan's 'anti-Soviet fabrications'.[57]

Writing several years after the USSR had ceased to exist, the long-serving Soviet ambassador to Washington, Anatoly Dobrynin, observed that Reagan's policy had the opposite effect on Kremlin debates from that intended, for it 'strengthened those in the Politburo, the Central Committee, and the security apparatus who had been pressing for a mirror-image of Reagan's own policy'. The American president had succeeded in creating a 'solid front of hostility' among Soviet leaders. Any proposal he made was automatically greeted with suspicion and nobody in Moscow trusted him. This resulted, wrote Dobrynin, in a 'unique situation' in US–Soviet relations which 'threatened dangerous consequences'.[58]

A Shift of Personnel and of Priorities

Two extremely important personnel changes in 1983 in Reagan's National Security Council helped to tilt the balance of opinion within the highest echelons of the White House more in the direction of Shultz and the State Department and away from the Defense Department, where relations with the Soviet Union were concerned. The first came in June when Jack Matlock was appointed to succeed the hard-line Richard Pipes as the leading Soviet and Russian specialist on the NSC, Pipes having returned

---

* Ustinov, who was appointed People's Commissar of Armaments in June 1941 at the age of only 32 and went on to play an important organizational role in the Soviet war effort, was Minister of Defence from 1976 until his death in December 1984. Gromyko was Minister of Foreign Affairs from 1957 until June 1985 when Gorbachev moved him to the prestigious but largely honorific post of Chairman of the Presidium of the Supreme Soviet. Andropov became general secretary on the death of Leonid Brezhnev in November 1982, but he himself died in February 1984 after just fifteen months as Soviet leader. Konstantin Chernenko's tenure as general secretary was even shorter—thirteen months between his succeeding Andropov and his death in March 1985 when Gorbachev was speedily chosen as party leader.

to his Harvard professorship. Matlock, an experienced diplomat, was to become closely involved in the dramatically changing US–Soviet relationship, first as Special Assistant to the President and Senior Director for European and Soviet Affairs in the NSC from 1983 until the end of 1986 and then, from 1987 to 1991, as American Ambassador to the Soviet Union. Immediately prior to joining the NSC, Matlock had been ambassador to Czechoslovakia and he had earlier spent eleven years in the Soviet Union in three separate stints in the US's Moscow Embassy, latterly as deputy head of mission and, for a time, acting head of mission.

The second consequential change in 1983 was the departure from the NSC of William Clark and his replacement as National Security Adviser by his deputy, Bud McFarlane. Baker and Deaver had for some time wanted to see the back of Clark, and they were to be joined by Shultz (and Nancy Reagan) who had come to view him as an impediment to improving relations with the Soviet Union. Clark moved to the post of Secretary of the Interior, succeeding one of the most disastrous of Reagan's Cabinet appointments (especially for the environment), James G. Watt.[59] Clark himself mooted the move, and White House Chief of Staff Baker was an enthusiastic supporter, since it simultaneously got rid of Watt* and dislodged Clark from the White House.[60] Baker and Deaver moved quickly and quietly to persuade the president that Baker should be National Security Adviser and that Deaver should succeed him as White House Chief of Staff. Reagan readily agreed, but before this could be a done deed, Meese and Clark got wind of the manoeuvre and dissuaded the president from going ahead with those appointments, even though they had already secured the approval of Nancy Reagan and of George Shultz. Meese, Clark, CIA director William Casey, and Defense Secretary Weinberger were all opposed to such an alliance of pragmatists holding sway as Reagan's principal White House advisers and the intermediaries between him and members of his Cabinet.[61]

The candidate for the post of National Security Adviser most favoured by the conservative members of the administration was Jeane Kirkpatrick, whose 1979 article in the magazine, *Commentary*, distinguishing totalitarian regimes from authoritarian had made a big impression on Reagan.[62] It had provided a rationalization for treating right-wing, but pro-American, authoritarian regimes in Latin America leniently and dealing implacably with totalitarian regimes, a category to which Communist states were indiscriminatingly assigned.[63] Kirkpatrick, although her earlier political allegiance had been to the Democrats, attacked the policies of the Carter administration. From the outset of the Reagan administration she was a forceful and uncompromising United States ambassador to the United Nations, an organization she greatly dis-

---

* The contrast between Reagan's environmentalist record as governor of California and as president is testimony to his remoteness from day-to-day decision-making and to the vast difference that could be made by particular office-holders in his administrations.

liked. Reagan was usually ready to compromise for the sake of peace on personnel issues, and that applied even to an appointment as important as his National Security Adviser. Having allowed the conservatives to veto Baker and Deaver, he let the pragmatists (Shultz in particular) block Kirkpatrick.[64]

This left McFarlane as the compromise candidate, albeit 'everyone's distant second choice',[65] as Lou Cannon put it. True though that was of the major players, the NSC staff, in Matlock's recollection, 'virtually without exception' favoured the choice of McFarlane.[66] While he was less hard-line than Kirkpatrick, his selection was seen as continuation of a conservative trajectory rather than a tilt toward those who wished for more diplomatic engagement with the Soviet Union. Initially true, that did not remain the case for long. It was, at most, a very temporary success for Weinberger, as he and McFarlane 'found each other impossible'.[67] McFarlane's approach to Soviet matters, Matlock believed, was 'close to Secretary Shultz's', although Shultz at times failed to appreciate that.[68]

The commitment to engagement with the Soviet Union was already part of the Reagan administration's policy, even while Clark was National Security Adviser. The president's view, as well as that of Shultz, was encapsulated in a particular sentence of Shultz's 15 June (1983) statement to the Senate Foreign Relations Committee: 'Strength and realism can deter war, but only direct dialogue and negotiation can open the path toward lasting peace.'[69] Matlock is less critical of Clark than were Baker and Shultz, but he noted the deficiencies of the NSC staff that Clark had inherited from Allen. Most had come from the military, the CIA, the FBI, or Reagan's political campaign, and there was a conspicuous absence of professional diplomats. No-one on the NSC, until Matlock arrived, had 'lived in the Soviet Union for a significant amount of time', and some, said Matlock, 'acted simply as mouthpieces for the agencies they came from, never willing to question their agency's preferences'.[70]

Already in 1983 Reagan was looking for an opportunity to have a summit meeting with his Soviet counterpart, though the reaction in Moscow to his public pronouncements, taken in conjunction with Andropov's deteriorating health, made an enthusiastic Soviet response unlikely. The shooting-down of the Korean airliner which had strayed far into Soviet airspace at the end of August made a meeting politically impossible. The official Soviet line that it had been on a spying mission added to the damage done by the ruthless action. What was also clear, however, was that trigger-happy responses were more likely to occur, to the danger of world peace, in times of high tension between the military superpowers.[71]

This nervousness was illustrated in October 1983 when some Soviet intelligence reports speculated that a NATO exercise simulating the release of nuclear weapons in a full-scale rehearsal for a European military conflict might be a possible cover for a real surprise attack on the Soviet Union. Known as 'Able Archer', the exercise was scheduled to take place in early November. The information about Moscow's concerns came from Oleg Gordievsky, a KGB colonel in the Soviet Embassy in London who was a double-agent, working for the British foreign intelligence service, MI6.[72] The UK government conveyed Gordievsky's information to Washington and the upshot was that the exercise was altered to make more abundantly clear that this was only an exercise.[73] A secret 1990 American study of the Able Archer episode, carried out by President George H. W. Bush's Foreign Intelligence Advisory Board (PFIAB)— declassified in 2015—concluded that 'In 1983 we may have inadvertently placed our relations with the Soviet Union on a hair trigger' and that there had been a real danger of 'a pre-emptive strike against the U.S. in response to a perceived but non-existent threat'.[74]

Recent research has shown that, though there were different views in Moscow of the extent of the danger, at the highest political and military levels the fear that the world might be on the brink of nuclear catastrophe was nothing like as great as it was (with some justification) during the Cuban missile crisis of 1962.[75] Nevertheless, the episode illustrated the significance of one side's perceptions of the other's intentions. What is beyond doubt is that the Soviet Union put a lot of resources in the early 1980s into an operation, involving worldwide cooperation between the KGB and the GRU (Soviet military intelligence), codenamed RYAN (the Russian acronym for Nuclear Missile Attack), to discover whether the West might be planning a nuclear first strike. Instructed to be alert for any signs that such an attack might be approaching, GRU and KGB officers were perturbed when they observed American forces having apparently been put on higher alert. This, however, had nothing to do with a hypothetical nuclear strike, but was a tightening of US security overseas in response to the terrorist bombing, which killed 241 American marines, at a US military base in Lebanon in October 1983.[76]

Mixed Signals

Concerned that Reagan, in spite of his desire for a more constructive relationship with the Soviet Union, 'did not seem to be focusing on the substantive issues', and frustrated by the incessant squabbling among various government agencies that delayed decisions, Shultz in late 1983 initiated a series of secret Saturday breakfast meetings of senior members of the administration. The main participants were Weinberger, CIA chief Casey, McFarlane, Meese, and Vice-President George H. W. Bush, with Matlock present as both Soviet expert and notetaker. General agreement was reached on American goals, although there were sharp disagreements on the means of achieving them. Matlock records that 'nobody argued that the United States should try to bring the Soviet Union down', later describing suggestions by some Reagan administration officials that this had been American policy as 'products of rationalization after the fact'.[77]

US aims, as established by this high-powered group, were to negotiate with the Soviet Union from a position of strength and to seek 'a real reduction of tension, not agreements which simply cover up real problems and thus mislead the public'. What were *not* American goals, Matlock observes, were challenging the legitimacy of the Soviet system, achievement of military superiority, or forcing 'the collapse of the Soviet system'. The aim, rather, was to reach agreements with the Soviet Union, exerting pressure to ensure that they abided by them.[78] Throwing further light recently on the meetings, Matlock observed that when he proposed that the president should instruct the bureaucracy 'not to question the legitimacy of the Soviet government (in current parlance, no "regime change")', Meese responded that some of the president's supporters 'won't like this'. Yet Meese went along with the policy because he was 'extremely loyal to the president and knew that Reagan was determined to try to deal with the Soviet leaders'.[79]

Reagan himself could still send out mixed signals, but his fear of nuclear war and desire for better relations with the Soviet Union were given more than one impetus during the later stages of his presidential first term. Films were always liable to make a greater impact on him than books, and when he saw *The Day After*, about the aftermath of a US–Soviet nuclear exchange which wiped out the city of Lawrence, Kansas, more than a month before it was shown on television on 20 November (and viewed then by over 100 million people), it left him 'greatly depressed'. 'My own reaction', he wrote in his diary that same evening, 'was one of our having to do all we can to have a deterrent & to see there is never a nuclear war.'[80] The pacific component of Reagan's belief in peace through strength had always been present (although it was far from salient in popular American assumptions about his beliefs, still less in Soviet perceptions of him). Thus, when Reagan decided to give a speech on relations with the Soviet Union, he felt there was nothing new in the first draft prepared for him. Yet others in the White House recognized that it was highlighting elements in Reagan's thinking that had not come across clearly hitherto, such as the desire to intensify Soviet–US dialogue, a preference for cooperation over confrontation, the need to find practical solutions to real problems, and, above all, a shared interest in avoiding war.[81] Reagan noted that greater respect for human rights would facilitate progress in other areas of the Soviet–US relationship. He also introduced a folksy element of his own that was not in the first draft by stressing the common interests and concerns of two hypothetical couples, Russians Ivan and Anya and the Americans Jim and Sally. Reagan concluded the speech, 'If the Soviet Government wants peace, then there will be peace. Together we can strengthen peace, reduce the level of arms, and know in doing so we have helped fulfill the hopes and dreams of those we represent and, indeed, of people everywhere. Let us begin now.'[82]

The speech was meant to be delivered in late December 1983, but was delayed until mid-January. This, it transpired, was on the advice of Nancy Reagan's Californian astrologer. To a remarkable degree, the president's schedule—decisions on which days he would fulfil particular public engagements—was determined by

Mrs Reagan, after consultations with her astrological friend, as Donald Regan first revealed in some detail to an astonished world in his 1988 memoirs.[83] The hold-up did not appear to do any harm to the reception of the speech, other than lead some to interpret it as mere electioneering, since it had been delayed until the country was entering a presidential election year. The speech went down well with West European governments, for whom Reagan had at last struck 'the right balance between firmness and negotiability'.[84] It made, however, little impact in the Soviet Union where the country's leadership was preoccupied with the looming succession. Andropov's health was in rapid decline and he died the following month without ever having set foot in a Western democracy. He was succeeded as party general secretary by Konstantin Chernenko, who knew far less about foreign and defence policy than did Andropov, and was more completely dependent on Gromyko and Ustinov.

Reagan noted in his memoirs that his attitudes toward the Soviet Union were 'changing a little' throughout 1984. One influence on him was Yugoslav President Mika Spiljak, whom Reagan found 'personable and reasonable' when he came to the White House for lunch. Spiljak's advice was that the US should be trying to 'open up' the Soviet Union, and he helped Reagan to realize that people in the Soviet Union were 'genuinely frightened' about their security and concerned about the possible actions of the United States.[85] Attempting to reach out to the new Soviet leader, Reagan sent Chernenko a handwritten letter expressing interest in meeting him face-to-face. The response, however, was that a summit meeting was out of the question. Shultz likewise got nowhere with the Soviet leadership when he told Dobrynin that the United States was willing to negotiate on large issues or, if they preferred, see what small steps could be taken to improve relations.[86] A more unusual initiative, the main importance of which was in strengthening Reagan's understanding of the Russians as people, was the president's response to an enterprising ('pushy' was Nancy Reagan's adjective)[87] private scholar, Suzanne Massie. Her influence on Reagan was of some significance, for it reinforced the priorities of Shultz and Matlock rather than those of Weinberger and Casey. A quite frequent visitor to the Soviet Union, Massie was concerned with the gloomy Cold War atmosphere prevailing in 1983 and tried hard to get in direct contact with President Reagan. She managed to meet with McFarlane in October of that year, and he sensed both that her jargon-free way of speaking about Russians as people would appeal to the president and that she would reinforce the pacific side of Reagan's peace through strength policy, rather than the military and confrontational component. McFarlane arranged a meeting for Massie with the president on 17 January 1984, the day after Reagan's speech indicating US government readiness to engage with its Soviet counterparts.

Massie took credit for persuading Reagan not to view the Russian people as 'faceless communists', but since she first met him the very day after he had made his

'Ivan and Anya' speech, that was a bit of an overstatement. She did, though, deepen Reagan's understanding of the distinction between regime and society in the Soviet Union and of a desire within that society for peaceful relations with the United States. Massie also claims to have been the person who taught Reagan the Russian proverb, *doverai no proverai*—Trust but Verify—which he later liked to quote whenever he met Gorbachev.[88] Another informal envoy used by the NSC was Senator Edward Kennedy's assistant, Lawrence Horowitz, who had contacts with much more senior officials than Massie saw—among them, Vadim Zagladin, the First Deputy Head of the CPSU's International Department. Horowitz, as an associate of a leading Democrat, made at least some limited headway in persuading his Soviet interlocutors that Reagan was serious about negotiation.[89]

A Soviet attempt to curtail SDI, and an ostensible desire to get talks started again, was conveyed in an invitation at the end of June 1984 for the United States to send a delegation to Vienna to discuss preventing 'the militarization of outer space' and to agree on a moratorium on the testing and deployment of space weapons.[90] Reagan was not going to agree to an abandonment of his cherished SDI project, and so the American assumption was that the Soviet proposal was made for propaganda purposes in the expectation that it would be rejected. An initial inclination to do just that changed following a discussion, in which McFarlane was an influential voice, to acceptance, provided that the meeting would also discuss ways to resume negotiations on INF (intermediate-range nuclear forces) and START (Strategic Arms Reduction Talks). Since the Soviet proposal had, indeed, been designed to be rejected, for at that stage their leaders still had hopes that Reagan would lose the November election, the Soviet leadership decided they would not send a delegation to Vienna.[91]

The Soviet Union boycotted the Los Angeles Olympic Games in July, just as the United States had boycotted the Moscow Olympics in 1980 (following the Soviet invasion of Afghanistan). Reagan's capacity to send out contradictory signals was illustrated, however, when, simply to establish the sound level for an interview on National Public Radio in August 1984, Reagan 'joked', 'My fellow Americans, I'm pleased to tell you today that I've signed legislation that will outlaw Russia forever. We begin bombing in five minutes.' As American Soviet specialists observed, nobody in Russia got 'the joke'.[92] Nevertheless, as it appeared increasingly likely that Reagan would be re-elected, Gromyko accepted an invitation to come to the White House in September when he was going to be in the US, attending the General Assembly of the United Nations. This was the first time that Reagan had met the Soviet Foreign Minister during his presidency, although they had once encountered each other while Reagan was governor of California.[93]

The meeting ended with predictable deadlock on the issues, but with civilities preserved. In the November 1984 presidential election, Reagan decisively defeated

Walter Mondale, winning forty-nine of the fifty states and almost 59 per cent of the popular vote. He was thus in a strong position to assert his authority, and soon found a need to do so. The last weeks of his first term and the early weeks of his second saw an escalation of tensions within the administration, as conservative opponents of the policy of seeking better relations with the Soviet Union made a concerted attack on Secretary of State George Shultz. Weinberger and some of his advisers at the Pentagon were, said Reagan, 'strongly opposed' to 'some of my ideas on arms control that George supported, including my hope for eventually eliminating all nuclear weapons from the world'. Weinberger's allies, wrote Reagan, thought Shultz had 'gone soft on the Russians and they wanted me to fire him—an idea, I told them, that was utter nonsense'.[94] In his diary entry for 14 November, Reagan noted that things had become so bad that Shultz 'wants out'. He was determined not to let that happen: 'Actually George is carrying out my policy. I'm going to meet with Cap [Weinberger] & Bill [Casey] & lay it out to them. Wont [sic] be fun but has to be done.'[95]

Even within the National Security Council, however, there were attempts to push Reagan in the opposite direction. An NSC staffer named John Lenczowski sent a paper in mid-December 1984 to McFarlane who, in turn, decided it was worth forwarding to the president. Lenczowski wrote that it was an illusion to think that the Soviet people shared the fears of Americans. Indeed, the 'very act of sitting at a negotiating table' with the Soviet side fostered the illusion that a 'live-and-let-live policy' was 'acceptable to the Soviets, when in fact it is not acceptable whatsoever', since their objective remained 'the political transformation of the U.S.'[96] In his annotation of the document for the president, McFarlane, who was hedging his bets, wrote that 'we must not dismiss the possibility that this analysis is correct'.[97]

Just a few days later, after that paper was passed to Reagan, a powerful argument on the side of engagement was made by Margaret Thatcher when she played a leading role in a foreign policy session at Camp David. She spoke enthusiastically about her lengthy discussion in Britain with Gorbachev just a week earlier.[98] Thatcher's contributions aligned her with Shultz rather than Weinberger (who had not been invited to the meeting), as when she stressed that 'it is correct to emphasize military balance, not superiority'.[99] In the last months before Chernenko's death in March 1985, the US–Soviet relationship had become less tense and confrontational than it was in 1983, though nothing of substance had changed. Notwithstanding opposition to engagement from within their own American administration, Reagan and Shultz, in company with Western European governments, hoped that some progress in US–Soviet relations would be made once a successor had been appointed to the evidently ailing Chernenko. No-one, however, predicted the scale of the transformation that was to occur.

Figure 3 Mikhail Gorbachev's first meeting with Margaret Thatcher, Chequers, December 1984. Front row: Denis Thatcher, Raisa Gorbachev, Mikhail Gorbachev, Margaret Thatcher. Second row (L to R): Aleksandr Yakovlev (face partly obscured), Geoffrey Howe, and Soviet ambassador to UK Viktor Popov (between Gorbachev and Thatcher). Back row (L. to R.): Soviet interpreter Nikolay Uspensky, Trade and Industry Secretary Paul Channon, Defence Secretary Michael Heseltine, UK ambassador to Moscow Sir Iain Sutherland, Minister of State at FCO Malcolm Rifkind, Minister of Agriculture Michael Jopling.

6

MARGARET THATCHER

The Moulding of the 'Iron Lady'

Margaret Roberts, as she was before her marriage to Denis Thatcher, came from a more modest background than have most politicians who went on to lead Britain's Conservative Party. Her early life was, though, more privileged than Reagan's, not to speak of Gorbachev's. She had a state grammar school education, supplemented by private tuition, and became an undergraduate at Oxford during the Second World War. Wartime rations made that experience more frugal than inter-war life in Oxford colleges had been, but incomparably less fraught than Gorbachev's daily struggle for survival during the war. It was, therefore, odd that Thatcher retained from the war years a residual anti-Germanism, whereas Gorbachev, when in power, appeared to be free of such animus. Her father, like Reagan's, worked in a shop, with the big difference that Alfred Roberts owned the grocery business and the apartment above it which served as the family's home in the Lincolnshire town of Grantham. Whereas both Gorbachev and Reagan were the first members of their families to have a higher education, this was not the case with Thatcher, for a Roberts cousin had gone to university. The future prime minister was at pains to point out, however, that she was the first member of the family to go to Oxford or Cambridge. For her part, she regarded Oxford 'as quite simply the best, and if I was serious about getting on in life that is what I should always strive for'.[1]

Born on 13 October 1925, Margaret Thatcher was much younger than Reagan and older than Gorbachev. Like Gorbachev, and quite unlike Reagan, she felt distinctly closer (in her case, *far* closer) to her father than to her mother. Alfred Roberts, a self-made small businessman who left school aged 13, read widely, became a local preacher in the Methodist Church, and was active in municipal politics, being first elected to the town council in 1927 as an 'Independent Ratepayer' (which usually meant Conservative, thinly disguised).[2] For more than twenty years he chaired the Grantham council's finance and rating committee, an impressively long stint which led the local newspaper to call him 'Grantham's Chancellor of the Exchequer'. He became an Alderman and Mayor of Grantham and over many years was a pillar of the local Rotary Club.[3] Alfred and Beatrice Roberts had two children, with Margaret four years younger than Muriel, who went on to marry a Scottish farmer whose attentions were first focused on the younger sister. She, however, passed him on to the elder sibling—'gently dumped by Margaret and pushed towards Muriel', in the words of Thatcher's major biographer, Charles Moore.[4] Many who have written about Thatcher have noted that in her *Who's Who* entry (based on information supplied by the reference book's subjects), she appeared as 'd. of late Alfred Roberts', but with no indication that she ever had a mother.[5] Although Beatrice Roberts was a meticulous homemaker, the narrowness of her interests and the absence of wider ambitions appeared to rile both daughters, especially the younger of the two. In later years, Muriel said that 'Margaret and I weren't close to her' and that 'Mother didn't exist in Margaret's mind'. Moore adds: 'Margaret always expressed herself more charitably and tactfully on the subject, but without much enthusiasm.'[6]

The family were staunch Methodists, and on Sundays the young Margaret not only attended the regular 11 a.m. service but also Sunday School beforehand and Sunday School again in the afternoon when 'from about the age of twelve, I played the piano for the smaller children to sing the hymns'.[7] At times she tried to get out of going to Sunday School, pointing out to her father that her friends went for walks and she would like to join them, to which Alfred Roberts, who was himself a frequent preacher, replied: 'Never do things just because other people do them.'[8] After attending her local primary school, Margaret won a scholarship to Grantham Girls' School, the best in the area. She was remembered by her contemporaries as a serious pupil, yet sporty enough to play for the school hockey team. Reagan's earlier career, and not only his political views, may have had a romantic appeal for her, for as a schoolgirl, she had a strong interest in films, writing enthusiastically about the latest 'picture' to reach Grantham. Although she was fond of poetry, at school she specialized in sciences rather than the arts, and chemistry became the subject of her application to the University of Oxford. At that time (and for many years to come), a qualification in Latin was one of the requirements for Oxford entry, and Margaret was annoyed that her headmistress did not allow her to take the Latin class at school. Her father, in contrast, fully backed her ambition to go to Oxford and paid for her to receive private tuition in Latin and for Oxford's general paper (as well as, earlier, for elocution lessons). Accepted by Somerville College, she embarked on study for an Oxford degree in 1943, and was fortunate that the tutor in her subject at Somerville was Dorothy Hodgkin, a brilliant scientist who went on to win the Nobel Prize for Chemistry in 1964.[9] The undergraduate Margaret Roberts spent most of each day in the laboratory and was a conscientious and good, rather than outstanding student. Still a Methodist (later she became an Anglican), she attended Oxford's Wesleyan Memorial Church, but her interest in politics, imbibed from her father, led her to join the Oxford University Conservative Association (OUCA) 'almost as soon as I came up to Oxford'.[10]

Margaret Thatcher was often in her later life described as a 'conviction politician', and many of those convictions had their roots in her youth. The certainty with which she held her beliefs surely owed something to her religious upbringing. The firmness of her attachment to a market economy, hard work, and self-reliance owed a great deal to the influence of her father, to life above the shop, and to seeing first-hand what it meant to run a small business. Nevertheless, during the war and immediately after, she shared the view of most Conservatives at the time that the state had an important role to play in ensuring fairness and she was some way off turning into the ideological free marketeer she later became under the influence, particularly, of Sir Keith Joseph.[11] In the late 1940s, she could still write to her sister, complaining about the accusation that 'if the Tories get back they will take off all the controls', for this, she wrote, was 'untrue'.[12] Her Oxford experience and active role in the university's Conservative Association (she became its president in 1946) brought her into contact with other future Tory politicians. This helped to give her a greater social assurance, although her letters to her sister revealed insecurities along the way.

The way she was remembered by some of her contemporaries in the association could hardly have been more different from the memories of those who served in the cabinets over which she much later presided. She was recalled by OUCA members during her Oxford years as a person 'who could be relied upon to do the donkey work', 'quiet', 'rather mousey', and devoid of 'star quality'.[13] The assertive personality she subsequently developed was partly in response to the difficulties of making a political career in the man's world of mid-twentieth-century British politics, especially in the Conservative Party in which it was an uphill task for a woman to become the adopted candidate in a winnable parliamentary seat.* Her closest friend in OUCA was Edward Boyle, an Etonian and hereditary baronet, later Education Minister in the government headed by Harold Macmillan, who moved to the centre of the British political spectrum, thereby putting himself on the left wing of the Conservative Party. But notwithstanding the wide gulf between their eventual political views, Thatcher and Boyle maintained their friendship right up to the end of Boyle's life in 1981. As an undergraduate, the future prime minister was impressed by Boyle's 'intellectual refinement and gentle good manners', by the opulence of his mother's London flat, and by 'his lack of snobbery towards her'.[14]

Thatcher's sense of the importance of the role that Britain could play in the world owed a lot to her reaching maturity during the Second World War and to her unbounded admiration for Winston Churchill. In a speech during the general election campaign of 1945, when she was aged just 19, she made clear her belief that Britain was a great power that should be considered an equal of the United States and

---

* Nevertheless, the Conservative Party, as of 2019, has produced two women prime ministers and is thus far the only UK-wide political party to have done so. At the time of writing, the first ministers of Scotland (from the Scottish National Party) and Northern Ireland (from the Democratic Unionist Party) are women. Yet the UK lags behind much of Europe (especially the Nordic countries) in terms of women's participation in the highest governmental posts and in legislative representation, although not so far behind in both these respects as do the United States and Russia.

the Soviet Union, and her devotion to the British Empire. It was, she said, 'the most important community of peoples the world has ever known' and it 'must never be liquidated'.[15] While still an undergraduate at Oxford, she had decided she wished to become a Member of Parliament, this at a time when women MPs were extremely thin on the ground of the British Parliament, especially in the ranks of the Conservative Party. Thatcher was also unusual for a British politician in her education in the natural sciences and in acquiring some practical experience of scientific work. Armed with her Oxford degree, she started work in 1947 as a research chemist in an Essex plastics factory. Unquestionably, however, she found politics much more fulfilling than her day job. Having become active in her local Conservative association, she succeeded in getting herself selected in 1948 as the prospective parliamentary candidate for Dartford for the election that was to take place in 1950. It was not a seat that the Conservatives were expected to win, and they did not. The 24-year-old Margaret Roberts came a respectable second to the Labour candidate, Norman Dodds, with the Liberal a distant third.

Dissatisfied with her humdrum job in industry, she had for some time thought about becoming a barrister, and in 1950 she began part-time study for the Bar exams and was admitted to Lincoln's Inn. Embarking on these legal studies was made easier by moving to a different job, though still as a research chemist, in West London, with Lyons, the food company. After a long search for a flat she could afford in an area she was content to live in, she eventually found one in Pimlico which at that time was viewed as a rather dowdy area. Her financial position was vastly improved after she agreed in 1951 to marry Denis Thatcher, a businessman whose previous marriage had been a short-lived wartime one. It was far from love at first sight. She had earlier told her sister, 'I can't say I really ever enjoy going out for the evening with him. He has not got a very prepossessing personality.'[16] But the marriage became mutually supportive, and politically they were at approximately the same end of the political spectrum, though Denis's private views could make those of his wife appear almost liberal.[17]

Her marriage, and the financial security it provided, made it easier for the new Mrs Thatcher to mix in wealthy Conservative social circles. In the 1951 general election (which took place before her marriage), she contested the Dartford seat once more and predictably lost again to Labour MP Dodds. Having served her political apprenticeship, she was determined that next time she would be the Conservative candidate in a seat that her party was expected to win. Having passed her final Bar examinations in late 1953, she was a practising barrister by the time she sought adoption in a suitable constituency. A combination of Conservative constituency associations' traditional reluctance to countenance a woman MP and the fact that by this time she had become the mother of twins meant that she did not succeed in contesting the 1955 election, at which a Conservative government was re-elected. By 1959, however, she was the candidate in the eminently winnable North London seat of Finchley, whose MP she remained until, having been removed from the premiership in 1990, she left the House of Commons at the time of the 1992 general election and became a peer.

Foreign Policy Influences

The development of Margaret Thatcher's views on foreign policy, and the influences on them, both before and especially after she became leader of the Conservative Party in 1975 and prime minister in 1979 are the most pertinent issues for this book. None of the front-bench positions Thatcher occupied before becoming party leader was concerned with foreign policy, but it is notable that she supported the choice of Sir Alec Douglas-Home* as Conservative leader and prime minister in succession to Harold Macmillan in 1963 and was sympathetic to the relatively hard line he had taken on the Soviet Union as Foreign Secretary.[18] Her relations with Edward Heath, Conservative prime minister from 1970 to 1974, were never warm, and after she successfully stood against him for the party leadership in 1975, they became distinctly hostile, particularly on Heath's part. Nevertheless, Thatcher strongly supported Britain's entry into the European Economic Community, still popularly known as the Common Market—later to become the European Union—though even in the early 1970s she was much less of a Europhile than was Heath.

Thatcher took a critical interest in Communism and the Soviet Union. Even before she entered Parliament, she had read the books that were influential with social democratic opponents of Communism, not only with conservatives, such as Douglas Hyde's *I Believed*, Arthur Koestler's *Darkness at Noon*, Karl Popper's *The Open Society and its Enemies* and *The Poverty of Historicism*, and George Orwell's *Nineteen Eighty-Four*.[19] Like Ronald Reagan, she also, however, read and was influenced by Hayek's *The Road to Serfdom* which viewed socialists of a social democratic type as wanting to take their societies on the road to serfdom, albeit more slowly than Communists.** Thatcher's fellow Conservative politician Keith Joseph, whose views she shared but who was temperamentally unsuited to be leader of a party, was the main influence on strengthening still further her commitment to freer markets and a bonfire of

---

* The fourteenth Earl of Home had given up his hereditary earldom in order to be a candidate for the prime ministership, since it had long been a firm convention that the premier must be in the House of Commons, not the Lords. Having been Foreign Secretary, 1960–3, he held that office again, as Sir Alec Douglas-Home, in the Heath government (1970–4). He then returned to the Upper House in 1974 as a life peer, becoming Lord Home, the last in a series of titles (before the Second World War he had been Lord Dunglass) long enough to mystify the outside world and, for that matter, most Britons.

** Orwell, in sharp contrast with Hayek, never ceased to regard himself as a 'democratic Socialist', even to the extent of consistently using the capital letter. Shortly before his death in early 1950, and referring to *Nineteen Eighty-Four*, he wrote: 'My recent novel is NOT intended as an attack on Socialism or on the British Labour Party (of which I am a supporter) but as a show-up of the perversions to which a centralized economy is liable and which have already been partly realized in Communism and Fascism' (quoted by Bernard Crick in *George Orwell: A Life* (Penguin, Harmondsworth, 1982), p. 569).

controls. To proselytize free market views, Joseph set up a Centre for Policy Studies (CPS), of which Thatcher became vice-chairman in 1974. A former Communist turned marketizing zealot, Alfred Sherman was the Centre's first director. Robin Harris, a major speech-writer for Thatcher and the drafter of her memoirs, has asserted that 'this highly intelligent woman only began to think once she joined her fate to Keith Joseph's at the CPS', although Thatcher herself observed that all her ideas about her own country were formed 'before I was seventeen or eighteen'.[20]

On foreign policy, Thatcher's thinking was guided by a very different personality from the highly strung Keith Joseph and the dogmatic Sherman. This was the urbane Hugh Thomas, who resigned as a Foreign Office official in 1956 in protest at the Anglo-French invasion of Egypt. Thomas was a member of the Labour Party until 1974, but he gravitated to the Conservatives and chaired the CPS from 1979 until 1991. (Disenchanted by growing Conservative Euroscepticism, he changed his party allegiance again in the 1990s, and sat on the Liberal Democrat benches of the House of Lords.) As Chairman of the CPS, he dismissed Sherman, who was notoriously difficult to work with, from its directorship in 1983. Thomas himself was a distinguished specialist on the Hispanic world and wrote an influential book on the Spanish Civil War. He had no particular expertise on the Soviet Union or Eastern Europe, but that did not prevent him from holding strong views. He exerted significant influence on Mrs Thatcher in the 1970s and 1980s by helping to introduce her to those leading specialists who advocated a harder line toward the Communist world. Their impact was the greater in the years before Thatcher became prime minister than once she occupied 10 Downing Street. In opposition, the advice she received came from people chosen because of their political stance, whereas in government she benefited (more than she appreciated) from Foreign Office expertise. Some of those who advised Thatcher when the Conservatives were still in opposition were, nevertheless, eminent scholars in Russian history and politics—London professors Leonard Schapiro and Hugh Seton-Watson (both of whom died before Gorbachev became Soviet General Secretary) and Robert Conquest (author of The Great Terror, on Stalin's purges), who moved in 1981 to the Hoover Institution in California, among them.

Another frequent participant in these meetings with Thatcher was George Urban who worked for Radio Free Europe for many years and became its director in 1983. He wrote a book on the group who advised her on the Soviet Union and Eastern Europe, in which he makes clear how his early enthusiasm for her abrasive attitude to Communism gave way to concern when she later became, in his view, excessively sympathetic to Gorbachev and to his attempt radically to reform the Soviet system.[21] A more extreme occasional contributor to the group meetings was Brian Crozier who, unlike Thatcher, failed to recognize the reality of change in the Soviet Union even after it had become obvious to all but the chronically blinkered. Crozier later claimed, however, to have had numerous individual meetings with Thatcher and to have told her in the mid-1970s things nobody else had 'about Soviet subversion in the United Kingdom and worldwide'.[22]

The loss of the 1974 general election after the Conservatives had been back in office for only four years made Edward Heath, their leader, vulnerable. Nevertheless, so long as he was determined to remain Leader of the Opposition, none of his most senior colleagues was willing to challenge him. There was, however, a strong movement among Tory backbenchers to get rid of Heath, and this required a plausible alternative leader. When Thatcher boldly decided to stand in the leadership election in February 1975, it was widely assumed that after she had lost the first round of this contest—but had done enough to demonstrate the decline in Heath's authority—more senior figures would enter the fray in the second round and one of them would be the victor. It did not work out like that. Thatcher's campaign among Conservative MPs—who comprised the selectorate—was well organized by Airey Neave, a former army and intelligence officer who was later assassinated by Irish terrorists in a car-bomb explosion at the Houses of Parliament.

To almost everyone's surprise, even on the first round of voting, Thatcher came top, with eleven more votes than Heath received. Since she did not yet have an overall majority among Conservative MPs, there had to be a second round. For Heath the game was up, though he never reconciled himself to being ousted by his own party (any more than Thatcher herself did when she was deposed more than fifteen years later). Heath's resignation, following his first-round humiliation, freed senior colleagues who had remained loyal to him, such as William Whitelaw and Geoffrey Howe, to enter the fray. The momentum, though, was with Thatcher. In the second round she got more votes than her five rival candidates put together.[23] The Conservative Party had, for the first time in its history, elected a woman leader and had paved the way for Britain's first female prime minister, which she became when the Conservatives defeated the Labour government, led by James Callaghan, in the 1979 election. Whitelaw, who had come second in the leadership stakes with 79 votes as against Thatcher's 146, was appointed deputy leader. After the election victory, he was appointed deputy prime minister as well as Home Secretary.

In a sign of things to come, the first major speech Thatcher made as Conservative Party leader was on policy towards the Communist world. She took a harder line than that of the Labour government and, indeed, that of the person she had appointed as Shadow Foreign Secretary, Reginald Maudling. Robert Conquest was called in to advise her and to draft the speech, on which she received complimentary comments from Lord Home, to whom she had shown the text. (When Foreign Secretary, Sir Alec Douglas Home, as he was known then, had presided over the expulsion in one fell swoop of more than a hundred Soviet diplomats and journalists in the UK who were engaged in various forms of espionage.) In contrast, Thatcher had deliberately not shared the speech in advance with Maudling. She was implicitly critical of the process whereby lengthy negotiation with the Soviet Union had led to an agreement known as the Helsinki Final Act, which was signed later in 1975. That document formalized recognition of the existing political borders of European countries and agreed that they could not be changed without the consent of their citizens. It also included a commitment to uphold a variety of human rights and freedoms. Needless to say, these were not observed by the pre-perestroika Soviet leadership and their Communist allies. The Helsinki Agreement became, nonetheless, a valuable tool in the hands of dissidents in the Soviet Union and Eastern Europe and, ultimately, played a modest role in the liberalization of the regimes.[24] In her speech Thatcher went on the ideological offensive against the Soviet regime in a manner that presaged some of Reagan's oratory in the early years of his presidency. She said that 'when Soviet leaders jail a writer, or a priest, or a doctor or a worker, for the crime of speaking freely', such acts showed that they did not dare to let people 'enjoy the freedoms we take for granted'. Furthermore, 'a nation that denies those freedoms to its own people will have few scruples in denying them to others'.[25]

In April 1975 Thatcher had her very successful and amicable meeting with Reagan, then governor of California, discussed in the previous chapter. Reagan had invited her to visit him in California when she came to the United States in September that year, but her schedule did not take her beyond the East Coast. She was primarily concerned to make contact with the key Washington politicians, including President Gerald Ford, a meeting which passed off pleasantly enough but with neither of them making much of an impression on the other. She also met Secretary of State Henry Kissinger, whom she had already encountered in London, Defense Secretary James Schlesinger, and Treasury Secretary Bill Simon, as well as members of the Senate and House of Representatives. She had begun the process of enhancing her international standing, and the success of the American visit helped to consolidate her authority within her own party.[26]

Thatcher embellished still further her anti-Soviet credentials with a speech written for her by the journalist, Robert Moss, a man Brian Crozier described as his 'disciple'.[27] Moss was recruited for the task by Thatcher's political secretary, Richard Ryder, and was aware that she wanted an emphasis (which fitted well with his own beliefs) on the great dangers the Soviet Union was posing. She gave the speech in Kensington Town Hall on 19 January 1976, just after returning from a visit to British troops in West Germany. Having noted that Warsaw Pact forces greatly outnumbered those of NATO in personnel, tanks, and aircraft in central Europe, Thatcher claimed that the Labour government was 'dismantling our defences at a moment when the strategic threat to Britain and her allies from an expansionist power is graver than at any moment since the end of the last war'. The only success 'the Russians' could boast of was their military power and they were 'bent on world dominance'.[28] This was the point at which the Soviet army newspaper, *Krasnaya zvezda* (Red Star), gave its unwitting impetus to Mrs Thatcher's reputation by publishing an article, highly critical of her 'threatening' speech, in which the author referred to her as the *zheleznaya dama*—the Iron Lady.[29] A few days later, and with a passing reference to the Duke of Wellington, who triumphed over Napoleon at Waterloo, Thatcher, addressing her Finchley Conservative Association, was happy to announce: 'Yes, I *am* an iron lady, after all it wasn't a bad thing to be an iron duke; yes, if that's how they wish to interpret my defence of values and freedoms fundamental to our way of life.'[30] The term stuck and did Margaret Thatcher much more good than harm. Even Nelson Mandela, who could not shift her opposition to sanctions against apartheid South Africa, came away from a meeting with her in July 1990 pleasantly surprised. In a recorded interview, he said, 'I was tremendously impressed by her…I was impressed by her *strength* of character—really an iron lady.'[31] (Mrs Thatcher's daughter, Carol, commenting on her mother's severity when her children got bad reports from school, said 'I'd twigged before the Russians that she was the Iron Lady.'[32])

Early Years of the Thatcher Premiership

The Conservatives winning the 1979 general election had much more to do with the unpopularity at that time of the Labour government than with public support for Margaret Thatcher personally. Of the two main party leaders, James Callaghan was far more popular with the British electorate than was Thatcher.[33] The workaholic new prime minister, however, lost no time in getting down to business, with the firm intention of prioritizing domestic over foreign policy. She told the Cabinet Secretary, John Hunt, that 'I'm going to have a very good Foreign Secretary [she was referring to Lord Carrington, who was Foreign Secretary from 1979 until 1982 and Secretary-General of NATO from 1984 to 1988] and I shan't go on any foreign trips at all. My job is to turn the economy round.'[34] While all prime ministers since the Second World War have had to involve themselves in foreign policy, even if their main interests lay elsewhere, Thatcher was, indeed, not as active in international affairs during her first term (1979–1983) as she subsequently became, with the very big exception of the Falklands War in 1982, an unforeseen conflict that arose from an Argentinian invasion of the islands that lay so much closer to their shores than to those of Britain.

In the month in which Ronald Reagan took office as president, Margaret Thatcher addressed the annual dinner of the Pilgrims' Society, an organization that celebrates ties of cooperation and friendship between the United States and Great Britain. She began by making much of the fact that she would be 'the first European Head of Government' to visit the new president, saying that it would 'mark the opening of a period of particularly close understanding between the two Governments and a particularly close understanding between the two Heads of Government'. After emphasizing how the government she led and the Reagan administration were united in their economic outlook and desire to reduce state regulation, she turned to foreign policy and warned of the dangers from the Communist world. The conventional forces of the Warsaw Pact were, she said, much larger than those of NATO and their

Figure 4 Aircraft meeting: (L to R) Geoffrey Howe, Margaret Thatcher, Michael Heseltine, and Robin Butler (private secretary to the prime minister).

nuclear armoury at least its equal. While the West should be ready to respond to evidence of real Soviet interest in détente, she could at present see no sign of it.[35] The speech went down well in Washington, and Reagan cabled the prime minister to thank her.[36] His response in private was to say that Margaret Thatcher is 'the only European leader I know with balls'.[37]

Thatcher's visit to the United States in February 1981 cemented the good relations she had already established with Reagan. In their briefings for the president, the National Security Council and the State Department told him that the Conservative government was at the time very unpopular and that their economic policies were not producing the expected results. The president himself, however, set aside these reservations, stressing his happiness with the coincidence of his and Thatcher's overall economic philosophies and view of international affairs, including an emphasis on military strength. Although Thatcher welcomed Reagan's 'zero option', whereby American intermediate-range nuclear missiles would not be installed in Europe if the Soviet SS-20s were removed, she did so on the same grounds as did Caspar Weinberger and Richard Perle in the Pentagon—on the assumption that the Soviet side would never agree to withdraw the missiles that were already in place. She wanted the American nuclear weapons to be in Europe to deter a Soviet attack by conventional forces.[38]

Although the president and prime minister greatly liked each other, Thatcher was not oblivious to Reagan's intellectual limitations. Lord Carrington accompanied the prime minister to a meeting in the Oval Office on her first day in Washington. When the conversation turned to South Africa, Reagan said, 'Well, of course, the South Africans are whites and they fought for us during the war. The blacks are black and are Communists.' Carrington noted that 'even Margaret thought this was rather a simplification'. When they left the White House, she pointed to her head, and said of the president, 'Peter, there's nothing there.'[39] She remained conscious that she was sharper than Reagan, but she shared his political instincts and was not immune to his charm. Her dismissive comment was far from being Thatcher's last word on Reagan or her abiding impression of him. From the second half of 1981 onwards they addressed each other as 'Margaret' and 'Ron', and in a lengthy 1990 interview (most of which was not published at the time), Thatcher said: 'I was prepared to use such talents and abilities I possess to do the utmost that I could to further what I believed in and one of the great coincidences of history...was that Ron Reagan and I were in power at the same time, believing the same things, having to some extent the same political, tactical approach as well as the same beliefs.'[40] Robin Harris has noted another aspect of her admiration for Reagan: 'She was particularly struck by the way in which he could articulate severe truths in a gentle manner—she knew that her own tendency was to do the opposite, and she fought against it, though with limited success.'[41]

Thatcher's style of leadership, concentrating as much power as possible in her hands and hectoring and intimidating ministers (while being considerate to her personal staff), in the end contributed greatly to her removal from office. Even some of her ideological allies were from quite early on concerned about the way in which she led the government. Sir John Hoskyns was Head of the Policy Unit at 10 Downing Street from the time of the Conservative election victory in 1979 until the spring of 1982 and regarded himself as a 'candid friend' of the prime minister.[42] He drafted what he called a 'blockbuster note' entitled 'Your Political Survival' in August 1981. It was co-signed by a colleague in the Policy Unit, David Wolfson, as well as by one of Thatcher's favourite speech-writers, Ronald Miller. The document said that because the Labour Party was in disarray, the Conservatives might win the next election, but that 'the Cabinet was divided and half-hearted', the prime minister was unpopular, and that she 'broke every rule of good leadership: bullying the weaker colleagues, criticising them in front of each other and in front of their officials', and that she was too ready to blame others when things went wrong. These things would not be forgiven once her position became weaker. It was time, when speaking of what the government had done to say 'We', not 'I'.[43] Hoskyns notes that 'the letter did not have the desired effect'.[44] A few weeks later she 'hissed' at him that 'No one has ever written a letter like that to a prime minister before', to which Hoskyns replied, 'Margaret, we're trying to help you.'[45]

Thatcher had a deep distrust of the British Foreign and Commonwealth Office (FCO) who saw managing the relationship with the Soviet Union as an important part of their responsibilities. Within the Foreign Office itself, there were different strands of opinion. A widespread notion was that the Soviet Union was largely immune from change, especially of a democratizing kind. (At a conference of officials, politicians, and academic specialists I attended in February 1985—just one month before Gorbachev became Soviet General Secretary—a British ambassador summed up the proceedings to general, but not unanimous, approval by saying, 'There's one thing we all know, the Soviet Union isn't going to change!') Some FCO officials concluded that, since attempts at radical change in Communist countries were doomed to failure, it was foolish even to try.* Diplomats often felt an affinity with those in Communist countries they regarded as 'technocrats' and believed that if change was to come, it would be through them. Sir Duncan Wilson, a British ambassador to Moscow at the end of the 1960s and beginning of the 1970s, time and again in his dispatches places his hopes in the 'technocrats' whom he contrasts with the 'ideologists'.[46]

In reality, when radical change came from within ruling Communist parties, whether in Czechoslovakia in 1968 or in the Soviet Union during perestroika, it was instigated by people who were interested in ideas and who were very much politicians, not technocrats. Wilson represented also, however, another strand of official thinking that was much more to the point, namely a policy of seeking more East–West contact in the belief that this would contribute over the longer term to a liberalization of the countries under Communist rule. That approach had quite broad support within the FCO, a striking manifestation of it being the seriousness with which FCO officials took the Helsinki process. Earlier, Wilson, in his valedictory dispatch from Moscow, indicated his strong approval for West German Chancellor Willy Brandt's *Ostpolitik*, noting that Brandt's 'own powerfully stated justification of this policy is essentially that, in the long term, it will assist peaceful evolution in Eastern Europe (including the Soviet Union)'.[47] Another, and minority, view within the Foreign Office—not usually to be found in its very highest echelons, but similar to that of some of Thatcher's informal advisers—was that Western countries should be much more aggressive in waging the Cold War against an unreformable Soviet Union, both through increased military and intelligence expenditure and by going on the ideological offensive.

---

* I had a very vigorous argument with two FCO exponents of such 'realism' in the early 1970s. One was a leading Foreign Office specialist on Czechoslovakia and the other, who also had a primary specialization on East-Central Europe, went on to become ambassador to one of the post-Soviet states. They both argued that Gustáv Husák was much to be preferred to Alexander Dubček as leader of Czechoslovakia and that the prevailing regime in that country was a great improvement on the 'Prague Spring' which they dismissed as a foolish endeavour that had done more harm than good. The chaos of 1968 had now been replaced by a commendable stability and improved living standards.

One element in the more mainstream FCO policy of tension-reduction and keeping lines of communication open was support for exchange visits of students and of more senior scholars as well as of theatrical groups and other representatives of the arts. Under the influence of such outside advisers as Robert Conquest, Thatcher was suspicious of that kind of exchange. She made known her displeasure in 1981 when the Foreign Secretary, Lord Carrington, gave the go-ahead to negotiations on a new Great Britain–USSR Cultural Agreement.[48] Carrington's political standing was, however, sufficiently high that the negotiations proceeded, and the subsequent Agreement was signed, regardless of Thatcher's misgivings. In this instance, the Foreign Office was right and the prime minister wrong. A highly authoritarian and ideocratic regime, such as that of the Soviet Union, had more to lose from the exchange of people and ideas—even to the limited extent facilitated by a Cultural Agreement—than had democracies. The more citizens, including Communist Party members, from the Soviet Union and Eastern Europe saw Western countries for themselves, the less satisfied they tended to become with their own political and economic systems. In contrast, Westerners who, under the terms of the Cultural Agreement, lived for extended periods in the Soviet Union and thus acquired first-hand experience of the censorship, the lack of political freedoms, and the paucity of goods and foodstuffs in the shops had their critical views of the Soviet political and economic system reinforced. At the same time, they usually returned with an appreciation of how great was the gulf between the stereotypes of official doctrine and the wide variety of opinion to be found in Soviet society.*

Some of those who advised Thatcher informally on what they perceived as an acute threat of Soviet subversion strengthened her tendency to regard the Foreign Office as a nest of 'defeatists, even collaborators'.[49] Rodric Braithwaite has recalled Thatcher's reaction when it was suggested in 1980 that she might usefully acquaint herself with the knowledge of the Soviet Union of a group of FCO specialists. 'Foreign Office? Foreign Office? What do they know about Russia?' was her response. But when she took part in the discussion and learned more about the serious problems the Soviet Union was facing, she remarked that if it was 'in such a parlous state, the system was bound to collapse before long'.[50] Thatcher distinguished the Foreign

---

* I speak from personal experience, having made from the 1960s to the 1980s quite a number of visits (the longest of which were three months in 1966, the entire academic year 1967–8, and two months in 1976) to the Soviet Union under the terms of various Great Britain–USSR Cultural Agreements, and having known many scholars both from the USA and from the UK who had similar extensive exposure to Soviet society. While first-hand knowledge of the system did not, so far as I could see, make anyone more admiring of it, it did facilitate a more nuanced understanding of how it worked, including insight into the roles and stratagems of those who worked for change from within the system. Ruling Communist parties, which generally embraced around 10 per cent of the adult population (and a far greater proportion of those with higher education), included people of different mindsets, values, and aspirations. Failure to understand this was a major reason why Western governments were so taken by surprise both by the 'Prague Spring' of 1968 and by the Soviet perestroika.

Office as an institution, which she continued to dislike and distrust, from some of its individual members who had served her well, not least those seconded to 10 Downing Street to work with her.

With Reagan in the White House, the American administration was especially sympathetic to Britain's request to buy the latest version of Trident nuclear missiles (although, as Charles Moore observed, it was ironical that the US 'could bestow or withhold what was supposed to be Britain's independent nuclear deterrent').[51] Defence Secretary John Nott warned Thatcher that two-thirds of Conservative MPs and two-thirds of the Cabinet were opposed to the renewal of the nuclear deterrent both on cost grounds and concern about a possible escalation of the arms race. The clinching argument had more to do with international status than with defensive capability. Carrington noted that failure to acquire Trident 'would have left the French as the only nuclear power in Europe' and that would have been 'intolerable'.[52] With Reagan's encouragement, the US Defense Department, for its part, struck a deal whereby the UK was exempted from paying for Trident research and development costs in return for retaining a stronger naval force than had been envisaged in Nott's forthcoming review of defence expenditure, leading Richard Perle to observe that 'we ended up subsidizing the Royal Navy'.[53]

Falklands War and Relations with Reagan

The Argentinian invasion and occupation of the Falkland Islands in early April 1982 became a defining episode of Thatcher's first term as prime minister. A setback that could have proved terminal for her premiership became a triumph which consolidated her position within her own party and the country. The Falklands were 8,000 miles from Britain, 300 miles from Argentina at the nearest point, and had a population of under 2,000 people, almost all of British descent and firmly committed to the idea that the territory they occupied was British, as it had been for some 150 years when the British reoccupied the islands in 1833 that had at various times come under Spanish, British, and French jurisdiction. The Argentinian military junta saw an opportunity to win popularity across the domestic political spectrum by seizing the islands which, known as *Las Malvinas*, were seen as rightfully belonging to Argentina.

The islands had not hitherto figured especially prominently in British consciousness or in that of the prime minister.* One politician who had taken the Falklands seriously as a potential source of conflict was Jim Callaghan, both as Foreign

---

* When Hugh Thomas told Margaret Thatcher that there was a scholar in Oxford, Malcolm Deas, who understands the history of the Falklands dispute, she replied, 'How nice to be Mr Deas and have the time for that sort of thing.' (My source is Malcolm Deas, quoting the late Lord Thomas.) Deas was subsequently introduced by Hugh Thomas to the prime minister who told him that he could communicate ideas to her via Thomas.

Secretary in the government led by Harold Wilson and, subsequently, as prime minister. He had insisted that HMS *Endurance* remain in the Falklands waters as a sign of the UK's readiness to resist any potential Argentinian occupation of the islands, and he protested when the Thatcher government withdrew it from the South Atlantic in early 1982.[54] The ship's presence was largely symbolic, but its departure was read by the Argentinian military junta as symbolizing Britain's unwillingness to defend the islands.

After the Argentinian invasion took place on 2 April 1982, pictures of the small British force on the islands surrendering (as they had been told to do by the Governor of the Falkland Islands in the face of the overwhelming numerical superiority of the occupiers) and being forced to lie on the ground were greeted with outrage in the House of Commons, especially from the right wing of the Conservative Party but also by Michael Foot who had succeeded Callaghan as leader of the Labour Party. The fact that it was a right-wing military junta in Argentina that had instigated the Falklands invasion helped to solidify cross-party support in Westminster for using all available political resources, and military means if necessary, to reverse this attempted take-over of the islands. Although the removal of HMS *Endurance* had been a decision of the Ministry of Defence opposed by the Foreign Office, Lord Carrington honourably accepted ministerial responsibility for the failure to foresee and avert the invasion and resigned as Foreign Secretary. It was indicative of Mrs Thatcher's weakened position at the time that she replaced Carrington by the colleague she 'least respected and least liked', Francis Pym.[55] As a former Defence Secretary, he had relevant experience as well as the requisite seniority.

The Foreign Office initially wished to pursue a diplomatic solution to the Falklands crisis, while the Ministry of Defence, following cuts to the navy, had serious doubts about the practicality of regaining control of the Falkland Islands by force, given that it would take three weeks to assemble a task force and get the British ships there. When the First Sea Lord, Admiral Henry Leach, informed Mrs Thatcher of the timescale, she said, 'Surely you mean three days' and was told that, on the contrary, he meant what he had said. It was Leach, however, who said that retaking the islands not only could be done but also 'must' be done. This was music to the ears of Thatcher who had earlier clashed with Defence Secretary Nott on the feasibility of the enterprise. When she told him, 'You'll have to take them back', he replied, 'We can't', and got the response, 'You'll have to.' If all the expert advice had been that this was mission impossible, Thatcher would have had to accommodate herself to it, and the Falklands episode would then have contributed to her downfall, whereas it proved her salvation.[56] It was Leach's insistence that the military option was both feasible and desirable that facilitated what became a resounding military success, in spite of serious British casualties which were described, oddly possessively, by Thatcher as 'some of my finest ships and some of my finest lives'.[57] Nevertheless, as Moore observed, she approached the operation 'modestly' and without the tendency to lecture which she commonly displayed. She had 'great respect for the armed forces' and 'had the good sense to trust them to do their job'.[58]

The reference to 'my ships' and 'my lives' was in a telephone conversation of 31 May 1982 between Thatcher and Reagan, in which the prime minister resisted American efforts to broker a ceasefire while hostilities were underway. Reagan received the kind of treatment Thatcher more commonly meted out to Cabinet colleagues, especially Geoffrey Howe. The president could hardly complete a placatory sentence before he was interrupted by the prime minister. A member of the NSC staff, Jim Rentschler, having listened in to the call, unkindly noted in his diary that Reagan 'came off sounding like even more of wimp than Jimmy Carter'.[59] While Reagan was personally sympathetic to the British effort and to Thatcher's determination to resist aggression, he was under pressure from within his own administration to secure a face-saving resolution that would preserve the US's good relations with Argentina and win support in Latin America, more broadly.

UN Ambassador Jeane Kirkpatrick, with her emphasis on the desirability of working with right-wing authoritarian regimes, seeing them as allies in the struggle with Communism, was an especially vigorous opponent of the British military operation. At a higher level, Secretary of State Haig and National Security Adviser Clark sought a compromise solution and urged Reagan to try to persuade Thatcher and the British government to accept a ceasefire rather than have the British forces continue the fight until they achieved the complete surrender of the Argentinian troops. In this respect, the US administration was in step with majority opinion in the United Nations. For many countries, the British action looked like old-fashioned colonialism.

A G7 economic summit in Versailles was scheduled to take place at the same time as a UN Security Council debate on a resolution in favour of a Falklands ceasefire. Reagan was briefed with points to put to Thatcher in favour of accepting such a compromise short of complete military victory in the Falklands. Against the advice of Haig and also that of the NSC, he decided he would meet Thatcher alone, unaccompanied by officials. He 'wanted to avoid the sharp edge of her tongue' and, still more perhaps, to avoid receiving sharp counter-arguments and rebukes in the presence of witnesses.[60] Reagan's own position on the Falklands dispute was somewhat closer to that of Weinberger, a firm supporter of Thatcher and the British military operation, than to the views of Kirkpatrick or even Haig. As usual on foreign policy, the Reagan administration spoke with a variety of discordant voices. Haig complained that 'my efforts in the Falklands ultimately cost me my job as Secretary of State', his shuttle diplomacy having been deemed to be a failure.[61] As the strongest supporter of the UK military response to the Argentinian junta's ill-advised adventure, Weinberger took personal responsibility for ensuring that all British requests for equipment and supplies were met affirmatively and promptly.[62]

What ultimately gave the British task force's victory its legitimacy in anti-imperial quarters was, first, that the occupation of the islands had been carried out by a military junta headed by General Leopoldo Galtieri and, second, that its reversal (at the cost of 255 lives of British servicemen and more than twice as many losses among Argentinian troops) hastened the overthrow of that authoritarian regime and of Argentina's return to civilian and democratic rule. Even critics of the British operation in many countries, including the Soviet Union, often admitted in private that they had been impressed by the skill with which a logistically demanding military enterprise had been organized at short notice as well as by the resolve which underlay the UK's response. At the very moment that the UN Security Council passed a resolution calling for a ceasefire—vetoed by the UK and, for the US, by a hesitant and embarrassed Jeane Kirkpatrick*—the G7 meeting in Versailles was being quite supportive of the British actions. As host of the leaders from the seven countries, French President François Mitterrand, affirmed his 'full solidarity with Great Britain' and earned the gratitude of Thatcher who said he had been 'most understanding and splendid throughout'.[63] The Argentinians had been using French-manufactured Exocet missiles, but when they sought replacements, Mitterrand made sure that they did not receive them in time, making up a story about 'technical problems'.[64]

After the British forces had prevailed in retaking the islands, differences between the UK government and the Reagan administration became more marked. Clark, in a memorandum for the president of 22 June 1982, emphasized that the president's 'main objective with Mrs Thatcher should be to reiterate our view that "a just war requires a just peace", one which both sides can accept'.[65] Having largely favoured their British ally, and having been perceived internationally (Kirkpatrick notwithstanding) to have been supportive of the UK position, the State Department in particular as well as the NSC were sensitive to the damage this was doing to the American reputation in much of Latin America. Following Haig's not-entirely-voluntary resignation, his successor George Shultz, much though he had admired the UK's willingness 'to fight for a principle' and stand up to aggression, persuaded Reagan to support 'a balanced' UN resolution on the Falklands and a search for a compromise solution. The British prime minister did nothing to disguise the fact that she was furious. Shultz felt that Thatcher was 'wrong to oppose us for taking a reasonable position on a critical issue in our neighbourhood'. He noted that Reagan and Thatcher 'were soul mates', and their personal relationship was 'as close as any imaginable between two major leaders'. On the issue of the Falklands settlement, however, Shultz observed that even the president 'was getting a little fed up with her imperious manner'.[66]

---

* Kirkpatrick, having been much more concerned about loss of American influence in Latin America than with Britain's loss of the Falkland Islands, had pressed for the US to abstain on the vote, rather than join the UK in vetoing the resolution. Haig, however, as Secretary of State took the decision that it should be a veto. He subsequently changed his mind, but too late for Kirkpatrick who had already cast her reluctant veto. She then asked if the veto could be changed to an abstention. The mix-up became the main story and reduced the level of criticism that the UK might otherwise have received for being the one country to veto a ceasefire resolution.

As such differences of opinion illustrated, Margaret Thatcher was fully prepared to stand up to the US administration, the president included, whenever she thought their arguments or policies were not in accord with British interests. Notwithstanding the ideological affinity of Reagan and Thatcher, the prime minister at times took issue with the president even when it came to dealing with the Soviet Union.[67] It was in the same year as their differences over the Falklands—1982—that they sharply disagreed on Western responses to Soviet actions. Sanctions had been applied to the USSR following the invasion of Afghanistan in December 1979, and Western countries watched the rise of Solidarity, the unofficial trade union which turned into a mass movement in Poland in 1980–1, with a mixture of excitement and trepidation.

When the Polish Communist authorities introduced martial law in December 1981 to crush Solidarity, there was pressure from Washington on its European allies for retaliation against Moscow. As noted earlier, the Soviet leadership had, over many months, pressed their Polish counterparts to institute a crackdown, but—in contrast with the Soviet invasion of Hungary in 1956 and of Czechoslovakia in 1968—they had this time not sent in their own army to suppress the people of a 'fraternal' Warsaw Pact country. Direct military intervention in Poland had been seriously considered by the Soviet leadership in August 1980, but quite quickly they decided against it.[68] The fact that the Polish regime, led by General Wojciech Jaruzelski, themselves eventually restored the *status quo ante* in their own country meant that European governments were less outraged by the crackdown than they would have been by a Soviet invasion. (The limited nature of the resistance within Poland to martial law owed much to Poles' perceptions that this internal repression was a 'lesser evil' than Soviet tanks on their streets. Not being privy to Kremlin discussions, they assumed such a foreign invasion to have been an all too likely alternative outcome.)

The Reagan administration favoured a strong response, especially in the form of economic sanctions, to the introduction of martial law in Poland. They saw this as an opportunity to put a stop to the planned construction of a pipeline which would supply natural gas from the Soviet Union to West European countries. While such economic interdependence could be viewed in Europe as promoting peaceful relations across the East–West divide, it was seen in Washington as both helping the Soviet Union increase its hard currency earnings and creating a dependence of Western Europe on Moscow. Such outcomes the Reagan administration viewed as detrimental to the United States. Britain, unlike West Germany, France, Italy, and other European countries, was not purchasing Soviet gas, but it had an economic interest in the pipeline project. John Brown, the Glasgow-based engineering company, had contracted to supply turbines for the enterprise, and a lot of jobs were at stake at a time when the British economy was in the doldrums. In a 30 July telegram to Reagan, Thatcher wrote: 'I can only reiterate my very serious concern about the outlook for this British company if it is prevented from exporting the equipment which it is under contract to supply.' She said that the UK would continue to support that company in fulfilling the contracts it had undertaken.[69] Reagan's reply was emollient. He said that he much appreciated 'the constructive framework in which you have placed our differences concerning the sanctions issue' and noted that 'on the broader security concerns posed by Soviet behavior and the crisis in Poland we think alike'.[70]

In general, Thatcher was more sympathetic to Reagan's desire to take a harder line against the Soviet Union than were other West European leaders. In 1980 Hugh Thomas and Leonard Schapiro had presented her with a paper in which they advocated 'economic warfare' to exploit Soviet weakness. The prime minister told them 'she was attracted to the idea but did not feel in a position to accept it'.[71] She was conscious of the risk of erosion of support at home if a tougher response came at the expense of Britain's economic interests and concerned also about the dangers of a rift between Britain and its NATO partners at a time when she was keen to maintain support for the deployment of American intermediate-range nuclear weapons in Europe. The hard line demanded by the Reagan administration in the early 1980s, whereby the West Europeans were to suffer economic damage in order to punish the Soviet Union, was compromised, moreover, by Reagan's simultaneous lifting of the grain embargo on the Soviet Union. It had been imposed by the Carter administration, but was anathema to Midwestern farmers, whom Reagan chose to appease. To win support in the Midwest, Reagan had promised to allow a resumption of US wheat sales to the Soviet Union, for the ban had damaged American farmers more than it had harmed Soviet consumers. He fulfilled that commitment and in 1983, with another presidential election looming the following year, he signed a new agreement with the Soviet Union that 'included a pledge never to repeat the grain embargo'.[72]

During his first term, when Reagan was sending out ambiguous messages on relations with the Soviet Union, he indicated at various times that he wished to meet with Soviet leaders and reach agreements with them, based on principles of mutual security. Yet within the National Security Council, he spoke about waging economic war on them—'just lean on the Soviets until they go broke' was the way he put it at the NSC in March 1982.[73] Such a policy was never, however, consistently pursued, and if it had been, it is highly unlikely that the Cold War would have ended when or as it did. It was when Reagan chose constructive engagement with the Soviet leadership during his second term, once Gorbachev was installed in the Kremlin, that the Cold War was wound down. Not only Midwestern farmers but also French and German leaders and even Margaret Thatcher, who enjoyed the closest relations with Reagan of any foreign head of government, were not prepared to damage what they perceived to be their own economic (and, in the case of the leaders, political) interests for the sake of making the Soviet Union weaker.

In November 1982 a compromise was reached on the pipeline issue, but one which seemed to involve greater concessions from the American than the European side. The United States accepted that one pipeline would go ahead, but a second strand of the pipeline that had been proposed would not. The UK view was that this had been a defeat for the Reagan administration, although British officials were instructed not to say so.[74] (US covert operatives had, however, inserted a bug in the software the Soviet Union had purchased for operating the pipeline which at a later date caused a massive explosion inside the Soviet Union.[75] Mrs Thatcher, and other European leaders, were unaware of this and would surely have disapproved.) John Brown Engineering was among the companies able to go ahead with its contribution to the pipeline, although there were to be some further restrictions both on high-technology exports and on low-interest loans to the Soviet Union.[76] Earlier, Reagan had been disappointed that the June 1982 G7 meeting at Versailles failed to back his attempt to secure tougher restrictions on granting credit to Soviet and East European states.[77]

While fighting was still continuing in the Falkland Islands, Reagan paid an official visit to the UK in June 1982, immediately after the Versailles G7 meeting. His British hosts had taken pains to ensure it would be a success, and in his diary Reagan described the visit as 'a fairy tale experience'.[78] He and Nancy spent the night at Windsor Castle, where Queen Elizabeth hosted a dinner, and the next day he was photographed horse-riding alongside the Queen in Windsor Great Park. The president delivered a major speech to a joint session of the two Houses of Parliament in the Royal Gallery of the Palace of Westminster that had conscious echoes of Winston Churchill's 1946 'Iron Curtain' speech. Reagan, too, focused on a divided Europe and a Soviet threat and spoke of consigning Marxism-Leninism to the 'ash-heap of history'.[79] In her memoirs, Thatcher attaches great significance to Reagan's Westminster speech, calling it 'the manifesto of the Reagan doctrine', meaning that 'the West would not abandon those countries which had had communism forced upon them'.[80] Like others in Reagan's audience, she was impressed that the president had apparently delivered the whole speech without a single note. Reagan told her he had read every word from the two perspex screens which she had assumed were some kind of security device. It was the prime minister's first acquaintance, and that of other British politicians, with a speech autocue (although Reagan told the prime minister it was a British invention).[81]

A sensitive issue in UK–US relations arose in early 1983. This was the question of whether US nuclear weapons based in Britain could be fired without the consent of the British government. The Reagan administration had a real dilemma, for the issue surfaced in the run-up to the June 1983 general election in Britain which the president was desperately keen for the Conservatives, under Margaret Thatcher's leadership, to win. The Labour Party, led at the time by Michael Foot, was highly critical of Reagan's foreign policy, and Reagan himself had no wish to exchange his ideological ally Thatcher for the unashamedly socialist Foot. A generation earlier an understanding had been reached between Prime Minister Winston Churchill and President Harry Truman that a decision to use nuclear weapons would be a joint one, but the American administration had a strong preference for avoiding public reference to the conditions under which nuclear weapons might be used. They preferred not to speak of the 'dual key', believing that this undermined the policy of nuclear deterrence, the more especially since every other country hosting American nuclear weapons would want a veto on their use if it were publicly known that the UK possessed it.

In a State Department internal memorandum to Under Secretary for Political Affairs Lawrence Eagleburger, Robert Blackwill wrote that Thatcher would be seeking the minimum necessary to manage her political problems in the UK and that she might settle for a reaffirmation of the 1952 Truman–Churchill communiqué which said that firing nuclear weapons based in the UK would be a joint decision. If, though, Thatcher wanted a UK presence at American bases in Britain, that 'could be highly troublesome'.[82] In the letter which followed on from this to UK Cabinet Secretary Sir Robert Armstrong, Eagleburger wrote that the US was 'aware of the difficulties your government has faced on this issue, and appreciate the firm public line which the Prime Minister, and Defence Secretary Heseltine have taken'. But it was important to avoid suggesting that the existing arrangements were unsatisfactory. Any replacement for them could not apply only to one ally or 'indeed to any one class of nuclear weapons systems'. The agreement they reached must avoid undermining deterrence and striking 'a major blow at Alliance cohesion'.[83] Yet Reagan was so anxious to give maximum help to Thatcher in her election campaign that he went much further than his officials wished and authorized her to tell Parliament that 'no nuclear weapons would be fired or launched from British territory without the agreement of the British Prime Minister'. And in public he admitted on 26 May that this constituted 'a sort of veto power'.[84]

The Falklands crisis had taken Thatcher by surprise, but the outcome of the conflict strengthened her political standing both at home and abroad. It led her to decide that she should have a foreign affairs and security unit in 10 Downing Street that would be the equivalent of the Policy Unit that had been headed by Hoskyns (succeeded by Ferdinand Mount in 1982) and which dealt only with domestic policy. The FCO as a whole and the Foreign Secretary, Francis Pym, in particular were vehemently opposed to this on the grounds that the UK did not have a presidential system and that, in the United States, which did, mixed messages from and conflict between the National Security Adviser and the Secretary of State were far from uncommon.

A compromise solution was reached. An entire new unit was not set up, but two senior posts were created in Number 10—that of foreign policy adviser and adviser on defence and intelligence. Thatcher was especially keen to enlist the services of Sir Anthony Parsons who, by general agreement, had performed brilliantly as the UK's ambassador to the United Nations (especially during the Falklands conflict) in the foreign policy post. He had just retired from the Foreign Office, but she succeeded in persuading him to take up the office. Roger Jackling, a less senior official from the Ministry of Defence, became the defence and intelligence adviser, but Defence Secretary Michael Heseltine simply forbade Ministry staff to take his telephone calls.

Jackling found himself frozen out. He was soon withdrawn, and advice on defence issues at No. 10 was subsumed in the Foreign Policy Adviser's portfolio.[85]

Parsons, an accomplished diplomat at home as well as abroad, successfully retained the trust both of the prime minister (with whom he was not afraid to disagree) and of the FCO. His successor, Sir Percy Cradock, defined the responsibilities of this office-holder as being to brief the prime minister when quick decisions had to be taken on Foreign Office recommendation and, in turn, to keep the FCO informed on the PM's thinking on international matters. This involved regular liaison with the Foreign Office.[86] Parsons was an especially important link between 10 Downing Street and the Foreign Office when Francis Pym was Foreign Secretary, given the strained relationship between Thatcher and Pym, who was to be peremptorily sacked by the prime minister in mid-1983. (As Pym observed: 'Whatever else may be said of it, my meeting with the Prime Minister on the evening of Friday, 10 June 1983 was brief and to the point. "Francis", she said, "I want a new Foreign Secretary".')[87] Pym's successor was Sir Geoffrey Howe who had hitherto been Chancellor of the Exchequer and who was to become a successful Foreign Secretary.

Following Reagan's 'evil empire' speech and launch of the SDI project in March of the same year, relations between the NATO countries and the Soviet Union and its East European allies had deteriorated further. The Foreign Office were concerned about this and so were two of its people who now held the most senior positions on the 10 Downing Street staff—Parsons and the private secretary to the prime minister, John Coles. They played an important part in persuading Thatcher that the time was ripe for a new analysis of Britain's relations with the Soviet Union and Eastern Europe. In the June 1983 election the Conservative Party had a convincing victory. Thatcher's political leadership during the Falklands conflict had been widely admired. Fighting a war was not an area in which she could claim any expertise, and so she interfered in policy detail much less than usual, leaving decisions to the military leadership and deferring also at times to Cabinet colleagues with military experience, several of whom had served in the Second World War. Her determination and resolve had, however, underpinned the operation.

Not coincidentally, in the 1983 general election campaign, opinion polls showed her to be substantially more popular than her party, the reverse of the situation in the run-up to the 1979 election. Increased unemployment during the first three years of the Parliament had made the government unpopular, but in the fourth year the economy picked up. The June 1983 general election saw the Conservative overall majority in Parliament rise from 43 to 144 seats. That was in spite of the fact that there was a swing of 1.5 per cent against the Conservatives and that well over half a million fewer voters supported them than in 1979. Although viewed as a triumph for Thatcher, a decisive contribution was made by the split in the anti-Conservative vote. A new Social Democratic Party (SDP) had been formed, led by formerly senior figures in the Labour Party—the 'Gang of Four': Roy Jenkins, Shirley Williams, David

Owen, and Bill Rodgers, all of whom had held Cabinet ministerial posts in Labour governments—who had become disillusioned by the party's leftward trajectory. Although the dramatic rise of the SDP was to be followed by almost as rapid a fall, it secured nearly as many votes (although far fewer seats) as did Labour in 1983— greater inroads into Labour support than the Liberal Party could muster over the previous half-century.

7

THATCHER AND THE TURN
TO ENGAGEMENT WITH
COMMUNIST EUROPE

A s she began the second term of her premiership in 1983, Margaret Thatcher
could count herself a lucky leader, greatly helped by a divided opposition, for
the scale of the Conservative victory strengthened her hand within the government.
Having emerged victorious, she decided that the time was right to take a strategic
look at different areas of policy. One of her strengths was always to do her home-
work. Although she had strong views on many subjects, she took pains to be well-
informed. Hitherto officials and politicians in the Foreign Office, including Foreign
Secretary Francis Pym before he was replaced by Geoffrey Howe, had been more
concerned than was the prime minister about the Cold War having got colder during
the Reagan presidency.[1] Her 10 Downing Street advisers Sir Anthony Parsons and
John Coles (both themselves career diplomats) helped her to reach the conclusion
that it was time to have a fresh look at current developments and future prospects in
the Soviet Union and Eastern Europe and at the policy implications for the UK. It was
agreed that a seminar would be held at Chequers,* the prime minister's weekend residence, on 8–9 September 1983.[2]

The overall scope of the seminar was strikingly broad—nothing less than 'to consider the Government's strategy in international affairs with a view to establishing
clear aims for the next few years and considering practical action in furtherance
of those aims'.[3] However, as Coles informed the Foreign Office: 'By far the most
important session in the Prime Minister's eyes will be that on East/West relations to
which we are now devoting virtually the whole of 8 September. Mrs Thatcher will
expect the discussion paper or papers to address *fundamental* questions' (emphasis in

---

* In a conversation I had with Sir Anthony Parsons at St Antony's College in the early 1990s, I asked him
if he thought that the September 1983 Chequers seminar had been important. He replied: 'It changed
British foreign policy.' Answering my question about who had initiated the seminar, he said that he and
John Coles had been the prime movers, and that 'it took a lot of preparation to reach that point'.
Of Thatcher, he said: 'She was a formidable guided missile, but she had to be pointed in the right direction.'
(I made a note at the time of these words of Parsons, but not of the date of that unplanned encounter
with him.)

the original).[4] Just how far-reaching her objectives were is indicated by Coles in the same memorandum when he notes that the prime minister 'would be inclined to see our objective in the long term as the replacement of Communist by democratic regimes'. And if the analysis indicated that fulfilling that aim lay a long way ahead, then she wanted to know 'how we can work towards it and what, meanwhile, our subsidiary aims should be'.[5]

The Foreign Office supported the idea of a fresh look at East–West relations, but their assumption was that the specialists who would advise the prime minister and other senior ministers present would be from the FCO itself. Thatcher's distrust of the Foreign Office came out strongly in her response.[6] Referring to 'my decision to arrange a seminar at Chequers on Thursday 8 September 1983 to pick the brains of experts on the Soviet Union', she had found herself instead 'presented with a list of the best minds in the Foreign Office' as proposed participants. Continuing her unambiguous riposte, she wrote, 'This is NOT the way I want it. I am not interested in gathering every junior minister, or everyone who has ever dealt with the subject at the FO. The FO must do their preparation before. I want also some people who have really studied Russia—the Russian mind—and who have some experience of living there. More than half the people on the list know less than I do.'[7]

Invitations were therefore issued to eight outside specialists (all but one of them a university teacher) who had expertise on different aspects of the Soviet system and society or on Eastern Europe.* In addition to their papers, sent to 10 Downing Street in advance of the seminar, much longer documents were sent from the Foreign Office and the Ministry of Defence. The substantial FCO paper on 'East–West Relations', unsurprisingly, said nothing to suggest that major change in the Soviet

---

* As one of those invited, I draw in this chapter not only on the archival documents but on my own conversations and contemporary notes. All the academics wrote papers of between six and eight pages that were read in advance by the prime minister (and by the other government participants) with close attention, as was clear from her annotations on the papers and her questions arising from them. At the seminar itself the eight outside specialists spoke for ten minutes each on the theme of their papers, elaborating them and making additional points. The seminar was divided into four sessions of an hour each: *System*: Archie Brown on the Soviet political system, Alec Nove on the economic system; *Society*: Alex Pravda on social problems, Michael Bourdeaux on religion; *Economy*: Michael Kaser on economic constraints, Ronald Amann on technological inertia; and *Power*: Christopher Donnelly on the military, George Schöpflin on the Soviet Union and Eastern Europe. On the other side of the table, Mrs Thatcher had the Foreign Secretary Sir Geoffrey Howe on her right and Defence Secretary Michael Heseltine on her left. Also present on the government side were Minister of State at the Foreign Office, Malcolm Rifkind (later to become Foreign Secretary in the government led by John Major); Sir Antony Acland, head of the diplomatic service; Sir Anthony Parsons, foreign policy adviser to the prime minister; both of the private secretaries to the prime minister, John Coles and Robin Butler (Coles later became head of the diplomatic service and Butler became head of the home civil service); Malcolm Mackintosh, the Soviet specialist within the Cabinet Office; Bryan Cartledge (at the time a Downing Street adviser to the prime minister, earlier British ambassador to Hungary, 1980–3, later, 1985–8, ambassador to the Soviet Union); and (in his capacity as an unofficial foreign policy adviser to the prime minister) Hugh Thomas.

Union and Eastern Europe was likely to occur any time soon. Summarizing its conclusions, the document declared that 'The time is ripe for a more active policy aimed at "the gradual evolution of the Soviet system towards a more pluralistic political and economic system".' Mrs Thatcher double-underlined 'more active policy' on her copy of the document, but inserted a question, 'by whom?'. The quotation about evolution toward a more pluralistic system was from US Secretary of State George Shultz. The FCO paper qualified the previous point by adding: 'Western leverage on the Soviet Union *is not great. Eastern Europe may provide greater opportunities for influence.* But in both cases the process of change will be long term' (words underlined by Thatcher in italics).[8] The Foreign Office submission for the seminar ran to eighty-four pages, fifty of them devoted to East–West relations. Yet, in her memoirs, the prime minister makes no explicit reference either to that paper or to the Ministry of Defence submission. She had greater respect for the Ministry of Defence than for the Foreign Office, but her relations with its political head, Michael Heseltine, were distinctly cool.* In her memoirs, she refers only to day one of the two-day seminar when the academics were present and says that 'by the time the seminar went ahead I felt that we did have the right people and some first-class papers'.[9]

In the run-up to the seminar, both Howe and Heseltine made clear that they were in favour of greater engagement with the Soviet Union and the countries of Eastern Europe. That was in spite of the fact that the international atmosphere had become more fraught, for it was on the night of 31 August/1 September, just over a week before the seminar took place, that Soviet air defence forces shot down Korean passenger aircraft KAL 007 which had flown off course and well into Soviet airspace. As noted earlier, the Kremlin leadership made a tragic error politically worse for themselves by initially refusing to confirm that the plane had been deliberately downed and then issuing a series of misleading statements about it.[10] President

---

* I noted Heseltine's willingness to disagree with the prime minister and to side with one or other of the academics in the note I made shortly after the 8 September meeting: 'The Prime Minister asked almost all the questions and expressed almost all the opinions from the Government side. Howe spoke the second most, but rarely and more than once tried and failed to get a word in. Heseltine was very much to the point when he spoke and on one occasion (referring to Donnelly's remark that he believed that almost the last thing the Soviet Union wanted was nuclear war, to which the Prime Minister had responded that it was one thing for him to believe that and another for her, with her responsibilities to assume that) said that the Soviet leaders, equally, could not simply assume that all the weaponry they were confronted with would never be used to attack them. In the light of their historical experience, especially of two world wars this century, their political and military leaders had to prepare for all eventualities. This was in reply to the Prime Minister's rhetorical question: how could the Soviet leaders seriously believe for a moment that the United States or other Western countries might attack them? When Alec Nove at one point said that in any arms control agreements the Soviet Union's security had to be taken into account as well as that of our side, Mrs Thatcher questioned why it should, but Heseltine intervened to agree with Alec Nove. He was the only person on the government side of the table who ventured to contradict her throughout the entire meeting.'

Reagan was also mistaken, however, in not only assuming but also publicly stating that the Soviet military had known all along that it was a passenger airliner they were destroying. Foreign Secretary Geoffrey Howe, who had the benefit, as had the prime minister, of intelligence supplied by the number two KGB officer in the Soviet Union's London Embassy, Oleg Gordievsky (who was working for MI6), later wrote: 'It took the Soviets several days to be sure that their blundering was the cause of this tragedy...Yet within hours the American authorities, at almost every level, were proclaiming it a piece of deliberately calculated, cold-blooded Soviet wickedness.' The main effect of this 'simplistic overreaction', observed Howe, was to come 'near to convincing Moscow, Andropov included, that the whole incident had somehow been contrived, as a cunning trap, by the CIA'.[11] At no point in the decision-making process about shooting down the aircraft was any Soviet politician involved, and the official policy was that if a passenger aircraft flew unauthorized over Soviet territory, it should be forced to land, not destroyed.[12]

When the prime minister opened the Chequers seminar on 8 September, she said that the shooting-down of the Korean airliner would be a preoccupation over the next few weeks, but that this meeting was concerned with the longer term. In a six-page memorandum to Thatcher dated three days earlier, Howe had written that if anyone wished to argue that the downing of the KAL flight proved that dialogue with the Russians was impossible, he would 'want to maintain the precise opposite'. It made it more imperative. The Soviet Union evidently felt threatened and this incident proved how dangerous it was when 'the two superpowers talk to each other more across the floor of the United Nations than they do on the Hot Line'.[13] On 1 September Defence Secretary Heseltine wrote to the prime minister that 'we have to ask ourselves' whether British involvement in arms control was merely 'cosmetic'—done 'not out of conviction but because it is expected of us' or was it a genuine attempt 'to make the future safer than it will be if the present arms build-up continues in both East and West'. Heseltine for one was convinced that 'the latter must be our objective'.[14] If 'a more broadly based dialogue with the Soviet Union were to begin', he would be very much in favour of it. He was worried by 'the absence of such dialogue for which I think there can be no substitute if we are truly to get the measure of the Russians and be able to derive the right policies for dealing with them'.[15]

The outside specialists at the seminar had no knowledge at the time of these views of the most senior ministers, but their analyses of the situation in the Soviet Union and Eastern Europe were essentially congruent with them, and when they were asked—as they were by Thatcher, in a more informal, after-lunch session, for their policy recommendations—so were the points they made. These included an emphasis on the importance and value of the BBC broadcasts to the Soviet Union and Eastern Europe.[16] More generally, they argued that the more East–West contacts the better and that these should be at all levels—from dissidents to general secretaries. Even where the specialists agreed with the Foreign Office view which, at best, they knew only partially from conversations with FCO officials, and not at all from contemporary classified documents, this was of some consequence. Thatcher was more open to influence by specialists whom she felt she had chosen—in preference to those whom the Foreign Office had wished upon her—and who, unlike her senior ministerial colleagues, could not be the remotest threat to her. Howe noted that in interaction with them the prime minister 'was unusually restrained and the experts were allowed to speak pretty fully to their briefs'.[17] The permanent head of the Foreign Office, Sir Antony Acland, reported to senior FCO colleagues that while 'the opening session with the outside experts' was 'fascinating, well structured and thoughtful', the 'level and tone' of discussion had 'deteriorated after lunch when the academics had departed'. The prime minister became reluctant to accept that dialogue with Soviet leaders could be useful. Nevertheless, 'she showed signs of interest in meeting Andropov, but not in Moscow'.[18]

When examining the potential for significant change within the Soviet Union, the outside specialists went beyond the more cautious judgements of the Foreign Office. The FCO paper prepared for the seminar made no mention of any possible future Soviet leader, whereas the academic paper on the Soviet political system (of which I was the author) referred to Gorbachev as a likely future general secretary who was not only the youngest but also 'the best-educated member of the Politburo and probably the most open-minded' and the person who 'might well be the most hopeful choice from the point of view both of Soviet citizens and the outside world'.[19] I made the more general point that 'a movement for democratising change can come from within a ruling Communist Party as well as through societal pressure'. The party intelligentsia had played a decisive part between 1963 and 1968 in bringing about the Prague Spring of '68, and while it would be rash to predict an 'early "Moscow Spring"', it would be 'carrying an historical and cultural determinism too far' to say that this could never happen in the Soviet Union.[20] It appeared that Thatcher had not heard of Gorbachev prior to the September 1983 seminar, and in her preparatory reading of the papers, as distinct from the seminar discussion, she did not pick up on his being 'the most hopeful choice'. During the seminar itself, at one point the prime minister turned to Howe and said, 'Should we not invite Mr Gorbachev to Britain?' No reference to this fleeting remark was made in the official report of the meeting, and it would, in fact, have been premature to invite Gorbachev at that stage. Konstantin Chernenko was number two to Andropov in the Communist Party hierarchy and Gromyko and Ustinov still dominated foreign and defence policy.

The seriousness of the problems facing the Soviet Union was emphasized in the paper on 'Technology' by Ronald Amann when he noted 'creeping stagnation' in the Soviet Union and Eastern Europe and added: 'It is appropriate to refer to this complex process as a "crisis" not because any East European society, least of all that of the

USSR, is on the point of immediate collapse but because it is a systemic disorder which shows no signs of substantial reversal either in principle or in practice.'[21]

The paper which raised most explicitly the possibility of 'the collapse of the Soviet system from within' was by a specialist on religion in Communist countries, Michael Bourdeaux, who linked this with signs of a religious revival in the Soviet Union. He highlighted the importance of the Polish pope and its significance for Lithuania particularly, but extended his generalization about the salience of religion to Russia.[22]

A 'New Policy'

Both the contemporary documents and the memoir literature make clear that the September 1983 seminar produced a shift of policy. The prime minister overcame some of her doubts and misgivings and was persuaded to embrace a policy of high-level dialogue with the Soviet Union and the countries of Eastern Europe. In advance of the seminar, Thatcher had been highly sceptical of the Foreign Office view that more active engagement with the Soviet Union was desirable. She took particular issue with the FCO statement that 'the West is faced by the task of managing a powerful military Empire in decline'. That phrase was double-underlined in her copy of the document and attracted double question-marks.[23] She evidently liked neither the notion of 'managing' (her instinctive preference was for confronting) nor the assumption that the Soviet adversary was in 'decline'. Yet, from September 1983 she accepted, and fully participated in, the move to closer engagement with both the Soviet Union and Eastern Europe.

Reporting to the Foreign Office on 13 September about the findings of the seminar as viewed from 10 Downing Street, the prime minister's private secretary, John Coles, wrote that, after lengthy discussion, it was now agreed that the 'aim should be to build up contacts slowly over the next few years'. Coles added that there 'would be *no public announcement of this change of policy*' (italics added).[24] He said that it was 'possible that the new policy of increased contacts' would lead within the next two to three years to a meeting between the prime minister and Andropov, but that Thatcher would not go to the Soviet Union for that purpose. The aim, rather, would be to persuade Andropov to visit the West, something that he had never done.[25] Furthermore, 'It might also be useful to arrange at the appropriate time for other senior members of the Politbureau, particularly potential successors to Andropov, to visit London.' The prime minister would, in principle, be prepared to meet with one or more such visitors, but that question needed further examination and recommendations to be made 'in due course'.[26] It was also agreed, as a result of the seminar, that ways of 'increasing the flow of information to the Soviet Union should be actively pursued' and that the FCO would focus on the role of the BBC External Services and the reach of their broadcasts to the Soviet Union and Eastern Europe.[27]

A day later, in a letter to the office of the Foreign Secretary, Coles re-emphasized the change of policy that had taken place. He noted that the discussions on arms control and disarmament at Chequers had not resulted in new decisions. However, 'The conclusions of the meeting on East/West relations are in a different category in that they relate to the formulation of *a new policy*' (italics added).[28] The more active diplomacy began right away. Hungary was at that time still highly authoritarian but, nevertheless, the least politically repressive of the European Communist states. It had also gone the furthest with economic reform, introducing some market elements. The Foreign Secretary was already due to visit Budapest within a week of the Chequers seminar, and Thatcher followed Howe to Hungary in February 1984.[29] 'The idea of the Iron Lady on the other side of the Iron Curtain', wrote Howe, 'made a great impression within Hungary, and also on Margaret herself. It was a media success, and whetted her appetite for more.'[30] In the course of the next twelve months Howe himself went on to visit all of the Warsaw Pact countries.[31]

Reflecting on the September 1983 seminar, Howe laid great stress on its significance. In his memoirs, he writes that while 'we failed to foresee the pace of change that was to follow in the Soviet Union and Eastern Europe...we concluded that we should treat each country individually, encourage greater diversity, recognizing that the possibilities were severely limited', while taking care not to induce repressive counter-action by the Soviet Union. Noting that it had been possible to convince the prime minister that a policy of deliberately destabilizing the Soviet Union or Eastern Europe would be counterproductive, Howe added:

> This important advance in understanding was probably to prove crucial to the successful outcome of Margaret's first encounter, still more than twelve months ahead, with Mikhail Gorbachev. The force with which Margaret later expounded this and argued the case for dialogue with Moscow was no less crucial in turning President Reagan away from the 'evil empire' rhetoric and encouraging him towards a similar relationship with Gorbachev. I sometimes think this may be seen by historians as her greatest achievement in foreign affairs. Our September seminar at Chequers was, therefore, more important than we knew.[32]

Sir Percy Cradock, whose lengthy period as the prime minister's foreign policy adviser lasted from 1984 until 1992 (the last two years spent counselling John Major) later noted that the September 1983 meeting, though 'just before my time, inaugurated a more open approach to Eastern Europe and led eventually to the first meeting with Gorbachev'.[33] Making a more general point, Cradock observed, 'It was very much to the Prime Minister's credit that she found time for these gatherings and deliberately raised her sights from the day-to-day action.' While Thatcher, in Cradock's assessment, was 'not perhaps a thinker herself, she had a respect for ideas and for those who purveyed them', and she 'also found the academics a useful foil to the Foreign Office and took pleasure in praising the first to the detriment of the second'.[34]

It is evident that a combination of the advice of the FCO, the Ministry of Defence, the outside specialists, and the officials with great foreign policy experience on the 10 Downing Street staff (especially Parsons and Coles) led to a change of policy. The prime minister herself in her memoirs focuses on the contribution of the academics rather than of the FCO, in keeping with her wariness of the Foreign Office as an institution. Of Gorbachev, she wrote, that 'what little we knew seemed modestly encouraging', that he was 'clearly the best educated member of the Politburo', and 'had acquired a reputation for being open-minded; but of course this might be just a matter of style'.[35] Later in September 1983 she visited Canada where she heard further favourable reports of Gorbachev from Canadian Prime Minister Pierre Trudeau, who had met the future Soviet leader earlier that year.[36]

Ups and Downs of the Relationship with Reagan

Travelling on to the United States after Canada, Thatcher met with President Reagan in the Oval Office on 29 September and told him that, while it was necessary to deal with the Soviet Union from a position of strength, she felt that it was time to engage. The official American report of the meeting records her telling Reagan that she believed it was important to 'strive to establish normal relations' with the Soviet Union, and the president replying that he 'shared her views'. The speech she made later that day was, in some respects, in contrast with those views. Typically hard-hitting, it included the remark that the Communist creed was 'immune to the promptings of good and evil'. She added, however, that 'We have to deal with the Soviet Union. But we must deal with it not as we would like it to be, but as it is. We live on the same planet and we have to go on sharing it.' Therefore, 'We stand ready', in the right circumstances, 'to talk to the Soviet leadership'.[37] In an interview in November of the same year, she complained that no-one had taken any notice of the conciliatory element in her speech.[38] Soviet concerns that the NATO exercise, code-named Able Archer, scheduled to take place in November, might be a cover for a real attack on the Soviet Union (as noted in Chapter 5) strengthened the British view that confrontation and high tension made for a dangerous state of affairs. Thatcher's conversion to the need for dialogue with the Communist world was underlined at a meeting of Commonwealth heads of government in New Delhi in late November 1983. 'It is only through contact', she told her colleagues, 'that we can hope to be able to influence others.'[39]

This was a view that President Reagan increasingly came to share in the course of 1983, but in October of that year the general warmth of the Reagan–Thatcher relationship was severely tested. The two leaders clashed when the president took the decision to send American troops into the Caribbean island of Grenada to crush a left-wing coup which had toppled the government and had, Reagan claimed, endangered American students who were present on the island. In the UK the coup was not seen as particularly threatening. A Marxist leader, Maurice Bishop, had been overthrown and killed by hardliners within his own government, but in a tiny island with a population less than that of the city of Oxford, it hardly merited an invasion. Grenada was a former British colony and a member of the Commonwealth, the Queen was Grenada's head of state, and the UK was represented on the island by a governor-general. The British government took the view that, at the very least, there should have been serious discussions with the UK before any military action was taken by the United States. In fact, Reagan—who admired Thatcher and hated to be in conflict with her—decided on action and deliberately left it too late for her to register her objections. The Washington view was that they were not going to tolerate a 'second Cuba' (although the idea that Grenada might pose a future threat seemed far-fetched)[40] and that Thatcher had greatly overreacted, the more especially since the United States had been helpful to Britain during the Falklands conflict the previous year.[41]

In a BBC World Service phone-in with the prime minister on 30 October 1983, Thatcher was provoked by a questioner from New York who suggested Britain had gone soft on international terrorism and who also brought up US cooperation over the Falklands. She sharply rejected the Falklands parallel, saying that Britain had gone in to get its own territory back and that she was 'totally and utterly against Communism and terrorism'. However, she went on, 'If you are pronouncing a new law that wherever Communism reigns against the will of the people…there the United States shall enter, then we are going to have really terrible wars in the world. I have always said…that the West has defensive forces in order to defend our own way of life and when things happen in other countries which we don't like, we don't just march in.'[42]

If Thatcher was exceedingly irked by being bypassed on Granada, leading figures in the Reagan administration were no less put out by her private and public anger over the invasion. National Security Adviser McFarlane wrote to the UK Cabinet Secretary, Sir Robert Armstrong, that the prime minister's comments in her BBC interview had been 'unusually harsh' and that, as they had been inflicted by 'one of our closest allies during a national anguish over the tragedy in Beirut' (the US Marine base in Lebanon had just been blown up with the loss of 242 American and 38 French lives), it 'was doubly wounding'. McFarlane highlighted American support for the UK during the Falklands War, even though the American government understood this 'would make relationships with our hemispheric neighbors far more difficult', adding pointedly, 'We make a critical distinction between strong private differences and public recrimination.'[43]

Thatcher found herself in the unfortunate position of being accused of harshness and ingratitude by her American allies at the same time as she was being portrayed as their poodle by her domestic opponents. Both the new Labour leader, Neil Kinnock, and the vastly experienced Shadow Foreign Secretary, Denis Healey, were able to mock Thatcher's pride in the 'special relationship' with the United States and with Reagan personally, given that the president had paid no attention to British views and that the Foreign Secretary had indicated, when speaking to the House of Commons, that the US would be unlikely to take military action. 'The truth is', said Howe, 'that the government had been humiliated by having its views so plainly disregarded in Washington.' The occasion had provided a field-day for the Opposition in which, wrote Howe, Healey had been 'at his destructive best'.[44] Kinnock, for his part, addressing the prime minister in the House of Commons, said that the relationship which had been said to exist between her and the president had 'turned out to be not so special', and asked whether, following 'the chaos and humiliation of the Grenada affair', she would now 'demonstrate a greater independence in furthering British interests and working for peace throughout the world?'[45]

In fact, Thatcher was already playing an active part in the new policy of enhanced engagement with Communist Europe. As already noted, she had paid a successful visit to Hungary at the beginning of February 1984, and just one week after she was in Budapest, Soviet leader Yury Andropov died. As Thatcher had chosen not to attend Brezhnev's funeral in 1982, she had never had the opportunity to meet Andropov. On the occasion of his death, however, she did not hesitate to fly to Moscow. She stayed in the British Embassy, a handsome building in a prime position opposite the Kremlin (now the British ambassador's residence, a new embassy building having been constructed). Thatcher observed that 'One of the few points on which the Foreign Office and I agreed was the need for British embassies to be architecturally imposing and provided with fine pictures and furniture.'[46]

Reagan had rejected State Department advice to attend, and the United States was represented by Vice-President George Bush who had a twenty-five minute encounter with the new Soviet leader, Konstantin Chernenko, compared with the more persistent Thatcher's forty minutes.[47] Leonid Zamyatin, a senior official in the Central Committee, two decades later produced a wholly fanciful story about Gorbachev noticing that Mrs Thatcher was feeling the cold during this 'working funeral' in the Russian winter and so escorted her to a warm room.[48] In fact, they did not meet until Gorbachev's visit to Britain in December 1984, three months before he became Soviet leader. Gorbachev would not have dreamt of indulging in such a breach of Soviet norms as to approach the British prime minister at Andropov's funeral. Chernenko was already in poor health when he was chosen by the Soviet Politburo to be general secretary and, since Gorbachev had his eye on succeeding him, he had every incentive to continue to abide by the rules of the Soviet game.

Early in Chernenko's leadership, which lasted only thirteen months, there was a behind-the-scenes struggle in which members of the old guard tried, unsuccessfully, to slow down the rise of Gorbachev who, nevertheless, became number two to Chernenko within the Communist Party hierarchy. The largely ceremonial post of Chairman of the Foreign Affairs Commission of the Soviet of the Union (one of the two houses of the Supreme Soviet, a legislature which met rarely, had no independent power, and rubber-stamped decisions taken elsewhere) went with the job of party second secretary. This gave the British government a way of inviting Gorbachev to the UK as leader of an 'inter-parliamentary' delegation. (It would have been inappropriate, and completely at odds with Soviet protocol, to have invited him as party second secretary and a likely successor to Chernenko.) While Andropov was still alive, the British government, in keeping with the new policy of engagement, had already drawn upon the services of the British branch of the Inter-Parliamentary Union and the presiding officers of both Houses of Parliament—the Speaker of the House of Commons and the Lord Chancellor in the House of Lords—to invite the Supreme Soviet to send a delegation to the UK from 3 to 7 December, 1984. That letter, sent in early February, expressed no preference regarding its composition or its leadership.[49] With Andropov on his deathbed at the time, the invitation got nowhere.

In contrast, when a new letter of invitation was sent, it was addressed specifically to Gorbachev—who, in his Supreme Soviet capacity, was invited to lead a delegation to Britain—and signed by Sir Anthony Kershaw, the Chair of the House of Commons Foreign Affairs Committee. Various names of possible future Soviet leaders, who might be invited as alternatives to or in addition to Gorbachev, had been bandied about in the Foreign Office and 10 Downing Street. Among them were two people who harboured aspirations to become party leader but who would have changed nothing for the better had they succeeded. One was an overbearing secretary of the Central Committee, Grigory Romanov, whom Gorbachev ousted from the top leadership team soon after he became general secretary. Another was the 70-year-old first secretary of the Moscow party organization, Viktor Grishin. Like Romanov, he did not last long once Gorbachev was leader. In early June 1984, however, the prime minister agreed to a Foreign Office proposal that Gorbachev, First Deputy Chairman of the Council of Ministers Heydar Aliev, and Foreign Minister Gromyko be invited. But priority was still given to Gorbachev, who should come in 1984, with Aliev and Gromyko to be invited for 1985. Although the FCO reported that Gromyko would come the following May, the decision by that time was no longer in his hands.[50] The letter of invitation to Gorbachev was drafted in June by FCO officials under the supervision of Minister of State Malcolm Rifkind.[51]

How eager the British side was to receive Gorbachev was evident in a series of messages sent by the Foreign Secretary to the British ambassador in Moscow, Sir Iain Sutherland. Thus, in a telegram of 14 June, Howe told the ambassador to make clear to his Soviet interlocutors that he would be received by Thatcher herself and have meetings with senior members of the government 'at which a wide range of questions could be discussed'.[52] In pursuing this policy of greater contacts with the Soviet Union and attempting to reduce East–West tensions, Thatcher was very much in tune with parliamentary and broader public opinion. The Opposition in the House of Commons had been critical of Reagan's hard-line policy and strongly favoured greater effort to improve relations with the Soviet Union. There was support also on the Conservative benches—as well as from the Foreign Office ministers—for a policy of engagement.[53]

Gorbachev's 1984 visit to the UK, dwelt on at greater length in Chapter 3, merits another look, this time more for its importance for Thatcher and the British side. Since Gorbachev headed what was officially a parliamentary delegation, one of his hosts at the airport to meet him was the Speaker of the House of Commons, Bernard ('Jack') Weatherill. Gorbachev lost no time in telling him, 'We accept Britain as it is, and hope that you will accept us similarly', adding that he had come 'to clear away the obstacles' in the way of better UK–Soviet relations.[54] When she met Gorbachev two days later, Thatcher told him about her Chequers seminar fifteen months earlier, and said she had 'decided "that she must try to do something" to engage with the Soviet Union'.[55] While there was no use, she added, in either of them trying to convert the other (a sentiment with which Gorbachev heartily agreed), it was important 'to diminish hostility and the level of armaments'. The prime minister added that the people who most realized the importance of avoiding conflict were those who had 'actually experienced the privations of the last war'. They were, she observed, coming to the end of the generations which remembered it: 'And I said to him, "I am a little bit older than you and you probably will not [remember the war]", and he said "Oh I do".'[56] As Gorbachev was aged ten when the Soviet Union was invaded and fourteen when the war ended, and since the privations he endured in those years were on a different scale from those experienced by the Grantham schoolgirl and Oxford undergraduate Margaret Roberts, there was little chance of him ever forgetting. He could, though, identify with the sentiments underlying her remarks. Thatcher made a point of emphasizing that 'Britain had a bigger influence with the United States than any other NATO member'.[57] Both the prime minister and Gorbachev were conscious that Thatcher's genuinely 'special relationship' with Reagan conferred an extra significance to this first meeting of the British prime minister with the man who was likely to be the next leader of the Soviet Union.

Gorbachev was impressed by the amount of time the British prime minister devoted to him. As usual, Thatcher had prepared herself very thoroughly. Her extensive reading included the political intelligence provided by the top secret reports of Gordievsky.[58] In addition to her reading, on the evening before Gorbachev and the Soviet delegation arrived in the UK, she held an informal seminar with a group of specialists at 10 Downing Street which was attended also by Howe.* It became clear during the meeting that the British government hoped that the visit would set in motion an improvement in UK–Soviet relations and, indeed, that it would do Gorbachev some good.[59] That hope would have been dashed if Gorbachev had turned out to be an assembly-line Soviet politician. But since all his interlocutors, and most importantly the prime minister, agreed that this was far from having been the case, the visit was viewed by the British side as a great success. By the end of his stay, Thatcher was able to say, in all sincerity, as well as with an element of political calculation, 'I like Mr Gorbachev. We can do business together.'[60]

For Anatoly Adamishin, the Head of the First European Department of the Soviet Foreign Ministry at that time (and in the 1990s Russia's First Deputy Foreign Minister and subsequently Russian ambassador to London), this was 'the memorable meeting' at which Thatcher 'especially singled out Mikhail Gorbachev' and, he added, 'was on his side to the end'.[61] The prime minister's reaction to the Gorbachev visit was every bit as positive in private as it was for public consumption. 'At the end, she felt very elated', her private secretary Charles Powell noted, and her British interpreter into and from Russian, Tony Bishop, went still further. Being, as he put it, not only an observer but 'one who had to be her voice and reflect her tone', he had felt that at times he 'was witnessing something akin to a flirtation between two people with much to gain from and offer to each other'.[62]

Having met Gorbachev at Chequers on Sunday 16 December, Thatcher flew the next day to Beijing to sign the agreement on Hong Kong that the UK government had reached with China. From there she went on to Hong Kong (still at that time a British colony). This was followed by a twenty-four-hour flight from Hong Kong to Washington for a Camp David meeting with Reagan on Saturday 22 December. While her private secretaries, Robin Butler and Charles Powell, tried to get some sleep, she announced that she was going to stay awake and 'study the ABM Treaty

---

* They were four academics and a businessman as well as the Cabinet Office Sovietologist Malcolm Mackintosh. As one of the academic specialists, I was invited to speak specifically about Gorbachev. Alec Nove was there to speak on the Soviet economy, Michael Kaser on economic relations within the Soviet bloc, and Lawrence Freedman on international relations and arms control. The businessman was Norman Wooding who had long been involved in East–West trade and commercial relations, especially with the Soviet chemical industry. To my saying that I thought Gorbachev wanted to go as far as the Hungarians with reform, but that he could not openly say so yet—he had to be careful—Mrs Thatcher responded, 'My goodness, he *will* have to be careful.' Earlier that year the prime minister had seen Hungary for herself, and her reaction reflected her pragmatic side. She was aware that a Soviet politician who aspired to the top job had to exercise restraint and self-censorship if he wished to get there. By implication, she accepted also that it would be a significant step forward if the Soviet Union were to move to even the degree of economic reform and relative political relaxation that had already by 1984 occurred in Hungary. In subsequent reality, while one might compare the liberalization in the Soviet Union of 1986 (perhaps even its further development by 1987) with that of Budapest in the mid-1980s, by 1988 Soviet change far exceeded anything seen in János Kádár's Hungary, and by 1989 Gorbachev's perestroika had gone well beyond even the reforms of the Prague Spring.

and Cap Weinberger's statements on SDI'.[63] She duly did so and was still alert enough to do more than her share of talking at the Camp David meeting. Weinberger had been deliberately excluded from the short list of those invited, but Secretary of State Shultz, National Security Adviser McFarlane, and Vice-President George Bush were there. Those invitees were somewhat more receptive than Weinberger would have been to Thatcher's upbeat assessment of Gorbachev and to the reservations she expressed about SDI.

As we know from the official American record of the Camp David meeting, Thatcher gave a detailed account of her conversation with Gorbachev, making clear that she had been no soft touch but not revealing the extent to which she had allowed Gorbachev to see how little she shared Reagan's faith in SDI. She mentioned some of the criticisms of Soviet practice she had made over the Chequers lunch, including the policy of refusing people the right to leave, whereas in the West many countries had 'to stop people from coming in'.[64] Thatcher reported that she had told Gorbachev that no great power in history had used 'its military strength so sparingly to advance political goals' as had the United States. She 'had also emphasized to Gorbachev that the President is an honorable man who sincerely wants to improve relations with the Soviet Union'. When she mentioned the 'personal handwritten letter to Brezhnev' which Reagan had written shortly after taking office, she found that 'Gorbachev did not appear familiar with it.'[65] She made clear that Gorbachev had impressed her, and she believed he was an advocate of economic reform and was willing to 'slacken government control over the Soviet economy'.[66] Furthermore, 'he was an unusual Russian in that he was much less constrained, more charming, open to discussion and debate, and did not stick to prepared notes'. (She had found his wife to be equally charming.) Perhaps to make sure that her hosts did not suspect her of going soft, Thatcher added that 'she often says to herself the more charming the adversary, the more dangerous'.[67]

On SDI, Thatcher trod a delicate path. She remained highly sceptical of its efficacy, but she was well aware how attached to it was Reagan. She observed that Gorbachev 'had spent an inordinate amount of time on SDI' and she had told him that Britain supports the US in its research effort in this field. She made a distinction between research and a possible future 'stage where production looked possible' when some 'serious and difficult decisions' would have to be taken.[68] Thatcher said she had some 'real worries' about 'SDI's impact on deterrence'. The official American report of the meeting noted that the prime minister had 'some doubts'. She observed that even 'if an SDI system proved 95 percent successful—a significant success rate—over 60 million people would still die from those weapons that got through'. In her view the West should emphasize that this was a 'research program' and that its point was to strengthen not weaken deterrence.[69]

Reflecting on this meeting at a later date, McFarlane said that Reagan was taken aback by what Thatcher said. Even though similar points had been made from within the administration, hearing it from her made a bigger impact. This, said McFarlane, was the first time Reagan 'had grasped that the person he respected above all others was making a very compelling case. It was passionate. He was very sobered by it.'[70] British officials attempted to insert in the meeting's conclusions (a document that became known informally as 'the Treaty of Camp David') a declaration that 'SDI-related testing and deployment would, in view of treaty obligations, have to be a matter for negotiation'. McFarlane, for the American side, removed 'testing' from that sentence, but the agreement that the US could not move to deployment without negotiating with the Soviet Union 'upset the Pentagon and pleased the State Department'. From that time on, the insistence of Weinberger and others that the US should please itself over SDI could be countered by referring to the statement that had been endorsed by the president along with the British prime minister.[71]

The year 1984 ended on a high note for Margaret Thatcher, with the successful visit of Gorbachev swiftly followed by her meeting with President Reagan and the top US foreign policy team at Camp David in which she not only impressed her hosts but won that significant concession in the debate over SDI. Just two months earlier, the prime minister had narrowly escaped being killed in a terrorist act perpetrated by the Irish Republican Army (IRA) at the Conservative Party conference in Brighton. She was still working on her speech to be delivered the next day when the bomb went off at about 2.50 in the morning of 12 October. The bathroom of her suite was badly damaged, but she and her husband were uninjured. Five people were killed in the explosion and thirty-one injured. The IRA issued a statement which made clear that their intention had been to kill the prime minister. It read, 'Today we were unlucky, but remember, we have only to be lucky once. You will have to be lucky always.'[72] To lose friends and colleagues in a terrorist act which was aimed primarily at her hardly amounted to luck. She went ahead with her speech although she had not slept, and her coolness under fire (she seemed calmer in fact than she usually was before a major speech) won her the respect even of political opponents and a thunderous standing ovation from her party members. She had told the assembled delegates that 'the fact that we are gathered here now—shocked but composed and determined—is a sign not only that this attack has failed, but that all attempts to destroy democracy by terrorism will fail'.[73]

PART II

8

BREAKING THE ICE (1985)

Early in 1985, while Konstantin Chernenko was still alive, there was a sign of modest improvement in American–Soviet relations when Foreign Minister Andrei Gromyko agreed to restart Geneva arms control discussions which had been suspended. Negotiations proceeded at snail's pace, however, not least because there were those on both sides who had no interest in acquiescing with any reduction in their country's military arsenal, whether or not it was matched by the other side. The head of the large American delegation, Max Kampelman, and Warren Zimmermann, a career diplomat who joined him as his deputy in 1985, were tough negotiators, but they did wish to reach agreements. Zimmerman later explained why so little progress was made. Hitherto, those who wished to block progress on arms control had relatively little difficulty in doing so. On the American side, said Zimmermann, there were people who had been sent from the Pentagon to ensure that no progress was made: 'This is of course not what they would admit except after a few drinks, but that was indeed what they were sent to do. They would report back to their de facto leader Richard Perle in the Pentagon every night or every two nights about the progress of the negotiations or in their eyes the lack of progress in the negotiation.'[1]

For their part, the Soviet delegation were not ready to reach an agreement unless it included a curb on SDI, since some of them, at least, feared it might actually work and they had been misled by misinformation about successful American tests which, said Zimmermann, had been faked.[2] 'The Russians', he added, 'had their own restraints on doing very much', since, if SDI were to be built and if it worked, it 'would give the United States and their allies a first strike capability' and this they were determined to prevent 'at all costs'.[3] The Soviet Union, Zimmermann noted, also considered that SDI would be a violation of the 1972 ABM Treaty and 'most objective American observers agreed with them on that'.[4] It was precisely for its capacity to undermine arms control agreements that some hard-liners within the Reagan administration welcomed the president's commitment to SDI, even though hitherto they had no faith in its technical viability. Richard Perle was a case in point. In the words of Frances Fitzgerald, 'it occurred to Perle that it might have its uses—not as a bargaining chip or, certainly, as a Star Wars defense, but, rather, as the ultimate weapon against arms control'. It could be used to block Shultz's plans and 'to wreck the ABM Treaty as well'. Perle thus became 'a vigorous advocate of the SDI program and took to delivering reports on great progress and the promise of technical marvels to come'.[5]

In both the United States and the Soviet Union there were powerful interests supportive of defence-related industry and the jobs that depended on them. It was an American president with a distinguished career as a soldier, Dwight D. Eisenhower, who made the notion of a 'military-industrial complex' part of the vocabulary of politics. One of Eisenhower's speech-writers, Malcolm Moos, had thought of putting into the president's last State of the Union Address the 'military-industrial-congressional complex', but the term that got into the drafts of the speech and stayed there (although Eisenhower always did a lot of rewriting) left out the complicity of the legislature.[6] Thus, in his 1960 State of the Union address, Eisenhower said they must 'guard against the acquisition of unwarranted influence, whether sought or unsought, by the military-industrial complex' and the danger of a 'disastrous rise of misplaced power'. This combination must never be allowed to 'endanger our liberties or democratic processes'. Taking nothing for granted, they had to recognize that only 'an alert and knowledgeable citizenry can compel the proper meshing of the huge industrial and military machinery of defense with our peaceful methods and goals, so that security and liberty may prosper together'.[7]

The military and their allies in military industry were a powerful lobbying group within the Soviet Union as well, the vast differences between the political systems of the USA and the USSR notwithstanding. The Soviet military-industrial complex was at least as influential a claimant on state financial and political backing as was its American counterpart. The absence of any choice of political party, or of political pluralism more generally, in the Soviet Union did not prevent institutional interests within the system competing with each other for a greater share of scarce resources. Defence Minister Dmitry Ustinov, who had spent years managing military industry, set up a body within the Council of Ministers called the Commission on Military-Industrial Issues. The former head of Soviet space research, Roald Sagdeev, later wrote, 'With a name like that, I was never able to understand how our propagandists could ever have denied the existence of our own military-industrial complex.'[8]

Progress on armament reductions needed political will at a higher level than that of the arms control negotiators. The context began to change when Chernenko died on 10 March 1985. In the speediest leadership transition in Soviet history, Mikhail Gorbachev was installed as new Soviet leader within twenty-four hours of his predecessor's death—chosen, first, by the Politburo and, subsequently, by the Central Committee, unanimously in both cases.[9] Gorbachev gave his Politburo colleagues no hint of the extent to which he would favour a change of course. His language could not have been more platitudinously reassuring. 'We do not need to change our policy', he assured them. 'It is a faithful, correct, fully Leninist policy. We need to speed up the tempo, move forward, expose shortcomings and overcome them, and clearly see our radiant future.'[10] Gorbachev believed that his priority at this moment was to appear unthreatening to the aged oligarchy responsible for selecting a new leader. And even those on the Politburo who were worried that the youngest man in the top leadership team would wield a new broom that would sweep them away, accepted it was too late to stop his further rise. The best chance opponents and doubters, such as Viktor Grishin, Grigory Romanov, and Nikolay Tikhonov, had of keeping their positions was to back the winning side, although their hopes were soon dashed. All three were ousted by Gorbachev before the end of 1985.

In the selection of the new general secretary, the Central Committee had followed the Politburo's lead, as was its habit. This time, though, they did so enthusiastically, for after three elderly leaders in a row who had been wilting before their eyes, they warmly welcomed the energetic younger man who stood before them. They had no idea what was in store. Gorbachev himself did not yet know how far he would eventually go in domestic and foreign policy; still less could he foresee some of the unintended consequences. From the outset, however, he was more of a reformer than anyone else in that 1985 Politburo and the most determined to seek qualitative change in East–West relations. It would have been political suicide before he became party leader for Gorbachev to criticize the conduct or direction of Soviet foreign policy, and he had not done so. Thus, his colleagues in the Soviet leadership had very little notion of the policies he would pursue, and in foreign policy least of all. The idea, sometimes mooted, that the Politburo consciously picked a 'soft-liner' because they were so worried by Reagan's hard-line policy is devoid of substance.[11]

Chernenko's funeral gave American leaders their first opportunity to meet with Gorbachev. Reagan, according to George Shultz, did not have 'a thought in his mind' about going to Moscow himself, but he accepted Shultz's suggestion that he invite Gorbachev to visit the United States in a letter that Vice-President Bush would hand-deliver. The way Reagan put it in his diary on 11 March was rather different from Shultz's later recollection. He wrote that he had been awoken at 4 a.m. to be told that Chernenko was dead, so 'My mind turned to whether I should attend the funeral. My gut instinct said no. Got to the office at 9. George S. had some arguments that I should—he lost.'[12] The American representation at the funeral was, accordingly, led by Bush and Shultz.

In contrast with Reagan's reluctance to go to Russia, no-one could have stopped the head of the British government from travelling to Moscow. It was a chance for Margaret Thatcher to meet again with Gorbachev and build on the head-start she had over other leaders (Pierre Trudeau excepted) in getting to know him.[13] Geoffrey Howe, who accompanied her, noted that the scheduled meeting of fifteen minutes with Gorbachev lasted for almost an hour, and that 'Margaret enthused over Gorbachev's recent London visit' which, she told the new Soviet leader, had been 'one of the most successful ever'. Howe remarked that not everyone in the FCO approved of the bonhomie: 'One hard-boiled Foreign Office official who read the note of the meeting expressed himself "bothered" that "the PM seems to go uncharacteristically weak at the knees when she talks to the personable Mr Gorbachev".' Howe thought their worries were needless. 'Certainly', he wrote, 'the two leaders were attracted to each other', and 'relished each other's company', but 'neither Margaret nor Mikhail ever completely lowered their guard'.[14]

Gorbachev's meeting with Bush and Shultz was potentially more significant for East–West relations, but that encounter lasted just half an hour. (The queue of leaders seeking time with the new man in the Kremlin was very long.) Bush did the talking from the American side, although Gorbachev spoke still more. Shultz watched and listened intently. He concluded that Gorbachev's 'free-flowing monologue showed a mind working at high intensity, even at the end of a long, hard day' and that 'In Gorbachev we have an entirely different kind of leader in the Soviet Union than we have experienced before.' Speaking to the press, Shultz added a cautionary note. He told them that 'Gorbachev is totally different from any Soviet leader I've met', but that 'the U.S.–Soviet relationship is not just about personalities'.[15]

Shultz was nonetheless well aware that 'personalities'—the character and outlook of particular leaders—were far from inconsequential. Reagan, Thatcher, and Gorbachev were individuals who mattered a lot, albeit in varying degrees. After Gorbachev was installed in the Kremlin, all three shared some modest optimism about the prospect of extricating East–West relations from the deep freeze in which they had been locked since the late 1970s. And they viewed the relationship with each other as crucial for any such improvement. Now that she had met Gorbachev both in Britain and in Russia, Thatcher was more optimistic than in the past about the possibilities of 'doing business' with the Soviet leadership. She had already played a significant part in helping to persuade Reagan that, in the person of Gorbachev, this could be a realistic prospect. None of the three, of course—or, for that matter, any-one else in 1985—envisaged the scale and speed of what lay in store. The transforma-tion of the Soviet political system by the end of the decade, the peaceful transition to non-Communist rule in Eastern Europe, and the replacement of confrontation between two armed camps by a new level of East–West trust and cooperation con-stituted change of a different order from what was imagined when this triangular relationship got underway.

Stereotypes and Realities

Moreover, all three leaders in 1985, and for some time thereafter, retained stereotypes about the other side. In Gorbachev's case this concerned Reagan specifically, and the United States more than Western Europe, for he had seen half a dozen West European countries, most recently the UK, for himself. The predominant view in Moscow was that Reagan was incorrigibly hostile to the Soviet Union and such a dyed-in-the-wool anti-Communist that there was little or no chance of having useful discussion with him. The American president sent out mixed signals and the parts of his speeches and his letters to Soviet leaders which stressed the need for dialogue and for peaceful relations were taken less seriously than the rhetoric about the Soviet threat and the importance of American military build-up. While Gorbachev remained sceptical of Reagan, he was unwilling to accept that nothing could be done to improve Soviet–US relations. An optimist by nature, he was at the same time more acutely sensitive to the dangers inherent in the continuing East–West impasse than were most Soviet or, for that matter, American politicians.

Reagan and Thatcher, for their parts (and especially Reagan), had long assumed that the Soviet Union was bent on world domination—with the goal of establishing Communist systems everywhere—and that the Communist Party of the Soviet Union (CPSU) itself was every bit as monolithically united as its own propaganda claimed it to be. This represented a failure to understand two developments that had taken place gradually within the CPSU over the post-Stalin period. The first was that, in spite of lip-service to the idea that Marxism-Leninism and 'socialism' (as defined in Moscow) would be the future of mankind, no Soviet leader after Khrushchev had seriously thought of the creation of Communist systems in the Western world as a policy goal. Second, behind the monolithic façade the CPSU tried to present to the outside world, and to the 90 per cent of the Soviet adult population who were not party members, there were fundamental differences of opinion within the mass membership. (There were more than 18.5 million members, out of a total population of 273 million, at the beginning of 1985.)[16]

Reagan's and Thatcher's image of the Communist Party was of a body composed of either zealots or conformists. They had long believed that different and critical ways of thinking were confined to small bands of dissidents and religious believers who had distanced themselves from the party, but were persecuted by it and its punitive agency, the KGB. In reality, the heterodox opinion which ultimately made the greatest difference emanated from within the ruling party itself. Although the overt dissidents were a significant moral force, their political influence was negligible— until the liberalizing reforms introduced by Gorbachev had made the Soviet Union safe for dissent. Then a dissident of the stature of Andrei Sakharov could in 1989 become a member of the new Soviet legislature and, more remarkably, the long-banned works of Aleksandr Solzhenitsyn, including *The Gulag Archipelago*, were published in large editions. That, however, was a phenomenon of the late 1980s. As of 1985, KGB pressure had reduced dissident numbers and effectiveness to lower levels than they reached in the 1960s and 1970s, and even in those years their impact was limited. The Soviet Union was a very different country from Poland, where the impetus to change did, indeed, come from outside the ranks of the ruling party, with Solidarity becoming a mass movement and in 1980–1 forcing major concessions from the party-state—before, under immense pressure from Moscow, the Polish party leadership cracked down on the opposition and imposed martial law in December 1981. Opposition to the ruling party in the Soviet Union turned into a mass movement only at the very end of the 1980s, following Gorbachev's liberalizing and democratizing reforms from above that reflected his growing commitment to social democratic change.[17]

Ideas mattered in a highly ideological system and the writings of the most notable dissidents were surreptitiously read by some party intellectuals. There was, however, no shortage among the latter of people fully capable of developing a critical analysis of Soviet domestic and foreign policy themselves. Those who worked in the international institutes, such as the Institute of the United States and Canada, the Institute of World Economy and International Relations (IMEMO) and the Institute of Economics of the World Socialist System (better known as the 'Bogomolov institute', after its long-serving director, Oleg Bogomolov), had the advantage of knowing one or more foreign languages and of access to Western specialist literature. These institutions contained educated specialists who were relatively well-informed about both domestic and international developments. The same was true of quite a number of the social science institutes, among them the Institute of Economics and Organization of Industrial Production of the Siberian Academy of Sciences in Novosibirsk and the Central Economic-Mathematical Institute (TsEMI) in Moscow, two institutions from which Gorbachev drew at different times his principal economic advisers.[18]

Important though ideas were, if they were to be effective in a Communist system they needed power-holders who would implement them. Even before perestroika, some officials in the Communist Party apparatus played that role within the strict limits imposed by the institutions and norms of an unreformed Soviet Union. So hierarchical was the system that much depended on the positions adopted by the general secretary who could embolden and empower some groupings and institutional interests within the party and weaken others. Under Brezhnev the military-industrial complex prospered, and Russian nationalists were accorded a greater tolerance than was extended to other deviants from Communist orthodoxy. Under Gorbachev, it was not long before a wide array of different tendencies became readily discernible as a result of the new tolerance and glasnost that developed by the late 1980s into freedom of speech. The main beneficiaries of encouragement from above were Westernizers, political and economic reformers, and social scientists who wished to be free of ideological shackles. Emboldened by this support, tacit at first but before long explicit, their analyses and proposals became more radical. In contrast, Russian nationalists, inflexible hard-liners, and conservative Communists found themselves being increasingly sidelined.

Unaware of such conflicting tendencies within the CPSU, Reagan was, nevertheless, ready in principle to engage with his Soviet counterpart. His letter to Gorbachev of 11 March 1985 expressed the 'hope that we can in the months and years ahead develop a more stable and constructive relationship between our two countries'. They would need 'to proceed in a way that takes both differences and common interests into account in seeking to resolve problems and build a new measure of trust and confidence'. Reagan added, 'history places on us a very heavy responsibility for maintaining and strengthening peace' and that he believed 'our differences can and must be resolved through discussion and negotiation'. Assuring Gorbachev of 'my personal commitment to work with you and the rest of the Soviet leadership in serious negotiations', he invited him to Washington at his 'earliest convenient opportunity'.[19]

Gorbachev replied on 24 March, thanking Reagan for the invitation to Washington, but requesting that they 'return to the question of timing and venue for a summit' at a later date. Shultz made the point to Reagan that Gorbachev's letter was 'notable for its non-polemical tone'.[20] Gorbachev had been positive about the president's proposal, and accepted that such a meeting should take place even if it was not going to end with their 'signing some major documents'.[21] The last summit between the leaders of the United States and of the Soviet Union had been as long ago as 1979, when President Carter met Leonid Brezhnev, so the agreement, in principle, that Reagan and Gorbachev should get together, even without necessarily having any dramatic breakthrough to announce, was a significant step forward.

Gorbachev's response was influenced by Aleksandr Yakovlev who, following his decade of diplomatic experience in Canada, had headed the major international relations institute, IMEMO, for the past two years. When he became party leader, Gorbachev had lost no time in bringing Yakovlev back into the party Central Committee building, appointing him head of the Department of Propaganda in July 1985. As early as 12 March that year, the day after Gorbachev became Soviet leader, Yakovlev wrote a memorandum to the new general secretary in which he noted that Reagan wanted to be regarded as a peacemaker and that Gorbachev should be ready to meet him, but without haste, and the venue should be somewhere in Europe, not in the United States. Moreover, while the US would remain the most powerful country over the next quarter of a century, and therefore required their close attention, there should be a simultaneous reorientation of Soviet foreign policy towards development of relations with Western Europe, Japan, and China.[22] Yakovlev was primarily concerned with domestic rather than international policy during the first three years of Gorbachev's leadership—until in 1988 he became the senior secretary overseeing international relations within the Central Committee—but in both policy areas his views carried a lot of weight with Gorbachev in the middle and late 1980s.

Tensions *within* the Three Governments

Within his own administration, Reagan was still being pulled in different directions. Shultz, in particular, believed that it was both desirable and necessary to improve the US relationship with the Soviet Union, whereas Caspar Weinberger, running the Defense Department, was profoundly suspicious of any such move, deeming it a threat to the further enhancement of American military might. Bud McFarlane occupied a position in between that of State and Defense, but he was somewhat closer to Shultz's view than to Weinberger's. Within the NSC, the person who knew by far the most about the Soviet Union, Jack Matlock, was firmly in favour of dialogue. He was also insistent (both at the time and subsequently) that it was no part of Reagan's policy to bring down the Soviet Union, but, rather, to alter Soviet behaviour. In contrast, Richard Perle complained that Thatcher's 'do business' statement was being used by people who wanted, as he later put it, 'to change US policy fundamentally from the President's policy—of bringing the Soviet Union down—to more of a détente'.[23] Even within the Defense Department, there were, nevertheless, minds more open to the idea that something might be changing in Moscow. One of them belonged to Weinberger's military assistant, General Colin Powell. His attitude to the British prime minister's positive assessment of Gorbachev was, as he remarked years later, 'Jesus, if dear old Margaret thinks there's something here we'd better take a look.'[24] Thatcher's credentials as a Cold Warrior made her support for engagement with the Soviet Union and her relative optimism about Gorbachev all the more useful for those in the State Department, including Shultz himself, whom hard-liners in the Reagan administration regarded with suspicion. The position she took became a significant element in intra-administration debates, for her opinions, noted Shultz, 'had weight even with those who were dubious about the merits of dialogue'.[25]

Whereas Shultz was to remain Secretary of State for the remainder of Reagan's presidency and Howe kept his post as Foreign Secretary until July 1989, there was no comparable continuity in the Soviet Union. In a characteristically bold move, Gorbachev replaced Andrei Gromyko in June 1985 with a novice in the conduct of international relations—Eduard Shevardnadze, the first secretary of the Georgian Communist Party organization. Gromyko had not only occupied the post of Foreign Minister continuously since 1957, but his vast knowledge and personal experience of East–West relations stretched back to the Second World War. He was Soviet ambassador to the United States from 1943 until 1946 and he took part in the 1944 Dumbarton Oaks conference on the founding of the United Nations. He was a member also of the Soviet delegation at the Yalta and Potsdam conferences in 1945. Over the years, he had become an increasingly important political player, especially since his promotion to membership of the Politburo in 1973. For that very reason, his continued presence in the Foreign Ministry would have made it difficult for Gorbachev to pursue an innovative international policy.[26]

Gromyko had been content to move from the Foreign Ministry to what was in principle a higher office when Gorbachev offered him the chairmanship of the Presidium of the Supreme Soviet. This meant that from 1985 he was the titular head of the Soviet state. (Gromyko kept that position until he relinquished it to Gorbachev in 1988. His Politburo membership came to an end in the same year.) Notwithstanding the formal authority of the Presidium of the Supreme Soviet chairmanship, far greater political power accrued to Gorbachev's office of General Secretary of the

Central Committee of the Communist Party. Gromyko's readiness to move from the Ministry of Foreign Affairs had been the greater because of his assumption that he would be succeeded by one of his own protégés in that ministry. When Gorbachev mentioned whom he had in mind for the post, Gromyko's reaction was 'close to shock'.[27] In proposing Shevardnadze as Foreign Minister to the Politburo in late June 1985, Gorbachev was aware that his choice was liable to be controversial, not only because of Shevardnadze's lack of foreign policy experience but also on account of his nationality. He was a Georgian, not a Russian, and a party official who had never hitherto worked in Moscow or outside his native Georgia. Picking his words carefully in the Politburo, Gorbachev astutely linked Gromyko with the nomination. They had, he informed his colleagues, discussed together various names, but 'In the end we settled on Eduard Amvrosievich Shevardnadze.'[28]

That the new minister should *not* be a Gromyko protégé, and thereby beholden to him, was one reason for Gorbachev's choice. Shevardnadze's lack of foreign policy experience was an advantage in Gorbachev's eyes. The new general secretary had every intention of being the principal foreign policy-maker and he wanted someone with whom he saw eye to eye and who would willingly go along with his initiatives. International affairs specialist Andrei Grachev, who became Gorbachev's presidential press spokesman during the final phase of his leadership, later wrote that Gorbachev's choice of Shevardnadze was 'proof of his determination to recruit a

Figure 5 An early meeting between Eduard Shevardnadze and George Shultz, with Pavel Palazchenko interpreting and Ronald Reagan observing.

Foreign Minister who would conduct no policy other than that of the General Secretary'.[29]

For his part, Shevardnadze was taken aback by Gorbachev's desire to make him Foreign Minister, pointing to his lack of experience. Gorbachev responded that this was 'a good thing'. Soviet foreign policy needed a 'fresh eye, courage, dynamism, innovative approaches'.[30] A second reason for Gorbachev's choice was that the two men, party bosses of neighbouring territories in the Soviet Union, had known each other for many years and had good personal relations. These had become sufficiently frank that they had shared with each other their opinion that the Soviet invasion of Afghanistan was a tragic error. Later, and still more tellingly, they agreed privately that things had gone 'rotten' in the Soviet state.[31] A third factor (although linked to the first) was that Gorbachev was 'categorically opposed to the appointment of a diplomat—he wanted a politician'.[32] In that he was successful. Geoffrey Howe, speaking informally while he was still Foreign Secretary, said that when he was talking with Shevardnadze, he felt he was speaking to a fellow politician, not a bureaucrat.[33] George Shultz felt the same way.[34]

Shultz's view mattered significantly more than that of his British counterpart. In the first place, East–West relations at the highest level were conducted between the United States and the Soviet Union. Second, Thatcher was much more of a hands-on foreign policy-maker, interested in every detail, than was Reagan. Thus, Shultz had a much larger impact on American policy and on Reagan's thinking than Howe had on Thatcher's. For Shultz, it was 'always a puzzle' why Thatcher 'seemed to pay little attention' to Howe. The American Secretary of State thought that his British opposite number was 'a wonderful Foreign Secretary', someone whom he saw 'a great deal of and came to admire'.[35] Thatcher's attitude to Howe had several components. It was coloured by her hostility to the Foreign Office as an institution. She also, however, had a prejudice against Howe's diffident manner, even though it only partly masked considerable toughness and a formidable intellect. Somewhat paradoxically, Thatcher thought him timid and yet also a potential political rival. Since he long put up with her abrasiveness towards him, and yet in 1990, with a devastating resignation speech to the House of Commons, set in motion the process that led to her ousting as prime minister, that judgement (as distinct from the way she treated him) may not have been entirely wrong.[36]

Howe incurred the wrath of the prime minister when he made a speech on 15 March 1985 at the Royal United Services Institute (RUSI) in London, in which he laid out a number of objections, widely shared by British and other European politicians, to Reagan's SDI. He had sent a copy for approval to 10 Downing Street just before leaving with Thatcher for Chernenko's funeral. Private secretary Charles Powell, having taken only a cursory look at the text, told the Foreign Office that the prime minister had 'seen and approved the speech'. The only problem was that she hadn't.[37] Howe's RUSI speech was well-argued and entirely reasonable. However, it greatly irritated Richard Perle, who happened to be in London at the time. In a public put-down, Perle said that the speech proved that 'length is no substitute for depth'. The London *Times*, which was going through an intransigent phase which put it at odds with most European opinion and allied it with the most obtuse hard-liners within the Reagan administration, absurdly pronounced that the speech 'may have done untold damage' and that it was 'mealy-mouthed, muddled, negative, Luddite, ill-informed'.[38]

The phrase in Howe's speech which was most quoted was that 'there would be no advantage in creating a new Maginot Line of the 21st century' in space (referring to France's line of defence against Germany in the 1930s which the Nazis simply bypassed by entering France in 1940 through Belgium), for it to be 'outflanked by relatively simpler and demonstrably cheaper countermeasures'.[39] Years later it became even clearer than it was at the time that SDI was an expensive pipe-dream. Indeed, there was not much in the substance of Howe's critique which Thatcher herself privately disagreed with. She saw it, however, as undercutting her policy of supporting President Reagan to the hilt in public, even finding some positive things to say about SDI, while attempting to modify his attachment to it in private. This was, though, a two-way process. Reagan—who, as Bud McFarlane emphasized, admired Thatcher and felt at one with her ideologically—was miffed by her opposition to SDI. In response to her arguments, McFarlane and Charles Powell had put together the compromise statement at Camp David in December 1984, at which Thatcher had tried to rein in SDI, and which was accepted as a joint policy position of the American and British governments. In particular, it stipulated that any move from research on SDI to deployment 'would be negotiated and terms agreed upon among the allies'.[40] Reagan, however, shared some of the misgivings of the Defense Department about this and told McFarlane that Thatcher 'was missing the point on SDI' and 'doing us a lot of damage with all this sniping about it'. He asked his National Security Adviser if he could 'find a way to get her to come off this position, or at least modify it a little bit'.[41]

McFarlane believed that he found a way. When he called on the prime minister in 10 Downing Street in January 1985, she reiterated her worry that SDI would be seen as 'seeking a first-strike capability', that there was no guarantee that the system would work, and that it would cost too much.[42] When, wrote McFarlane, she 'came up for air', he seized the opportunity he had been waiting for, to say that Reagan believed that $300 million a year in SDI research and development 'ought to be subcontracted to British firms'. This, he maintained, led the prime minister to change her tune and to her speaking in support of SDI when she addressed the US Congress a month later.[43] For the government, and for Britain's 'military-industrial complex'— small in comparison with those of the United States or the Soviet Union, but large by West European standards—a promise of a big injection of additional investment in the defence sector was a strong inducement to second thoughts. Not only did it modify Thatcher's opposition to SDI, but opinion in the Ministry of Defence became notably, and unsurprisingly, more sympathetic. The UK Defence establishment had been almost wholly sceptical about SDI until the United States came up with the offer of a share in its research and development. They then seized the opportunity to obtain additional funding.[44]

Although the British prime minister somewhat softened her line on SDI, being especially careful to do so when speaking in public, she did not, in fact, retreat from the substance of what had been agreed at Camp David. McFarlane, pleased though he was with what he took to be a modification of Thatcher's position in response to his offer of a role in the investment spoils, noted the limits to the policy change. When Mrs Thatcher spotted him entering a room at the G7 economic summit in Bonn five months later, she immediately detached herself from the group she was with and marched up to him. McFarlane recounts: '"Now, Bud", she began from several feet away, without even saying hello, "are you keeping SDI under appropriate restraint, adhering to the ABM treaty and so forth?"' She nodded with satisfaction when he replied 'Yes, Prime Minister.'[45] For his part, in spite of their differences, he regarded her as 'a formidable—and brilliant—political leader'.[46]

Though she took pride in being seen as a 'conviction politician', in her role as a 'persuader' in Washington, Thatcher modulated her tone and came uncharacteristically close to displaying diplomatic skills.[47] In a letter to Reagan, following Geoffrey Howe's RUSI speech, she assured him of Britain's continuing support. 'Our position has *not* changed, *whatever* you may have heard or read' (her emphasis).[48] Within Parliament, the great majority of MPs backed a policy of engagement with the Soviet Union and remained sceptical, to say the least, about SDI. Thus, Howe's publicly expressed position had broad support and, to the extent that Thatcher was pursuing a new policy of dialogue with the Soviet Union and attempting at times to mediate between Moscow and Washington, she, too, was in line with a broad swath of parliamentary and public opinion.

Approaches to the Summit

Much of the East–West diplomacy of 1985 was concerned with the lead-up to the first summit meeting between Reagan and Gorbachev which took place in Geneva in November of that year. Gorbachev had lost little time in taking foreign policy initiatives, although domestic policy occupied still more of his attention. In April he announced a halt to the further deployment of Soviet intermediate-range SS-20 missiles in Europe, but the Reagan administration was unimpressed, seeing this as no more than a repackaging of earlier offers of a moratorium by Brezhnev and Andropov. In his first few months as Soviet leader, Gorbachev had meetings in the Kremlin with Fidel Castro; an American Congressional delegation led by Speaker 'Tip' O'Neill; former German Chancellor Willy Brandt; the Italian Prime Minister Bettino Craxi; and several of the East European Communist leaders. O'Neill helped to persuade Gorbachev that Reagan was serious about wishing to engage with him, and returned to Washington with a positive verdict on the new Soviet leader. He described him as 'a master of words and a master of the arts of politics and diplomacy' and said he had flair, charisma, and 'a Western style'.[49]

Reagan and Shultz obtained a stronger sense that things might be changing in Moscow after Shevardnadze replaced Gromyko in late June. The new Foreign Minister conveyed an immediate impression of greater open-mindedness, even admitting that he still had much to learn about international affairs.[50] It was quite a contrast with the world-weary caution of his predecessor. The change of tone and style in Soviet foreign policy strengthened the qualified optimism in the State Department about the prospects for fruitful dialogue. Reagan, however, was still getting plenty of advice to be wary of the Soviet leadership, and not only from the Defense Department and from the CIA. One acquaintance informed him that the Russian word, *mir* (pronounced meer), meant both 'peace' and 'the world'. That was perfectly true, but the gloss which the acquaintance put on the linguistic point was an extrapolation too far. What this meant, he said, was that 'when the Soviets use the word MEER they mean that they want the WORLD and not Peace…The Soviets always dominated and oppressed their people and continue trying to take over the world.'[51]

In a letter to Reagan of 10 June 1985, Gorbachev had made it clear that he was seeking qualitative change in US–Soviet relations, for to aim simply at 'containing tensions within certain bounds and trying to make it somehow from one crisis to another' was not 'a prospect worthy of our two powers'. He wrote that it is 'the Soviet Union that is surrounded by American military bases stuffed also by nuclear weapons', not the US by Soviet bases. He urged Reagan to 'try to look at the situation through our eyes', so that Soviet concerns would become clearer to him.[52] One of the issues which Reagan had raised in correspondence with Gorbachev was the Soviet invasion of Afghanistan in 1979 and its continuation of the war in support of the pro-Moscow regime. 'Isn't it long overdue', he wrote to Gorbachev, 'to reach a political resolution of this tragic affair?'[53] The president was unaware of the extent to which Gorbachev agreed with those sentiments. As we have already seen, Gorbachev and Shevardnadze had shared their private thoughts at the time of the Soviet intervention in Afghanistan that this was a huge mistake.

From the outset of his general secretaryship Gorbachev wanted to get the Soviet troops out of that neighbouring country, but not in such a precipitate way as to give the appearance of a Soviet defeat. That would have raised the politically unsettling question of why so many young soldiers' lives had been lost in vain.* His first

---

* It was a dilemma that at various times faced American presidents—from the Vietnam War to the invasion of Iraq and its aftermath. Indeed, for the United States, it applied also in Afghanistan where, in the twenty-first century, it was Western, rather than Russian, troops who were attempting, with very limited success, to support an Afghan government lacking authority in large parts of the country.

Figure 6 Reagan with National Security Adviser Robert (Bud) McFarlane and White House Chief of Staff Donald Regan (centre), aboard Air Force One, July 1985.

public hint that he was determined to bring an end to Soviet military operations in Afghanistan came later when, in his major speech to the Twenty-Seventh Congress of the Communist Party of the Soviet Union in February 1986, he referred to that war as a 'bleeding wound'.[54] Their Afghan allies had, however, been warned several months earlier that they would soon have to get used to doing without Soviet military assistance. Gorbachev told the Afghan leader Babrak Karmal in October 1985 that his government would have to learn by the following summer how to defend their revolution themselves and that they needed to 'lean on the traditional authorities' and broaden the base of their regime. This had 'dumbfounded' Karmal. However, Gorbachev insisted, 'With or without Karmal we will follow this line firmly, which must in a minimally short time lead to our withdrawal from Afghanistan.'[55]

Reagan and Gorbachev's agreement in principle that they should meet, already established in March, became concrete at the beginning of July. It was decided that the summit talks would take place in November in Geneva. Gorbachev's first journey to a Western country after he became Soviet leader was, however, to France which he visited the month before the Geneva summit—in early October 1985. For Gorbachev a keen interest in Western Europe was not new, but officials in the International Department of the Central Committee interpreted the Paris visit as the beginning of a fresh focus on Europe and a break with Gromyko's overwhelming concentration on the United States.[56] To the extent that Gorbachev wished to demonstrate to the Americans that he had other sympathetic interlocutors, should the US prove obstructive in Geneva, he had, however, little to show for his talks in France. In contrast with his visit to Britain the previous year, before he became the Soviet leader, he was not given the opportunity to address members of the French parliament.[57] While President François Mitterrand was impressed by the Soviet leader's abilities, the French government responded only lukewarmly to Gorbachev's talk of their sharing a 'common European home' (with its echoes of former President Charles de Gaulle's invocation of 'Europe from the Atlantic to the Urals').

Over time Mitterrand became more receptive to this concept, accepting that for Gorbachev it was more than propagandistic, that it had an idealistic component, and reflected the views of those who wished to see Russia restoring its European identity.[58] France was jealously protective of its status as a nuclear military power and, accordingly, wary of Soviet pressure for nuclear disarmament in Europe. Notwithstanding Moscow's willingness to exclude the French and British nuclear arsenals 'for the time being' from disarmament talks, and Gorbachev's offer to have a separate negotiation with France from that with the United States on nuclear weapons, the French government wished to avoid getting swept up in a process that would end with them losing their nuclear deterrent which they saw as a major pillar of their political autonomy.[59] In Britain opinion was more divided on the utility and morality of spending large sums of money on nuclear weapons, although the Conservative government was firmly committed to them, no-one more zealously than Margaret Thatcher.

The British prime minister was regularly consulted by Reagan and lobbied by Gorbachev, and she corresponded frequently with both of them. Thus, Gorbachev wrote to Thatcher in August 1985, seeking her support for the Soviet decision announced earlier that month to impose 'a unilateral moratorium on all nuclear explosions' and getting the US to do the same. Gorbachev's argument that without tests, existing nuclear arsenals would 'be doomed to gradual obsolescence' had limited appeal for Thatcher who set great store on Britain's nuclear capability.[60] She was, however, seriously engaged in East–West diplomacy. In a long letter of 12 September 1985 to Reagan, she expressed concern that Gorbachev was making 'all the running' in East–West relations and that it was important that the forthcoming Geneva summit must be more than a 'getting to know you' session.[61] If the meeting were to be successful, it must get into the substance of issues and give an impetus to arms control.[62] She was also attempting to break the deadlock on SDI, saying that the 'key element' would be 'deep cuts in offensive weapons' and a 'clarification of activities which are permitted and prohibited under the ABM Treaty'. She believed that further progress on arms control would be maintained 'only if there is direction from the top by you and Gorbachev' and that 'you should be thinking in terms of a further meeting at your level within a reasonable time'.[63]

Thatcher wrote that she was sure that Reagan would wish to raise human rights and, although she supported this, it could 'too easily lead to an argument about the fundamentals of our two systems, or the trading of particular accusations, neither of which in my own experience is likely to get us anywhere in terms of better Soviet behaviour'. Thus, she thought that the best approach was to get across to Gorbachev 'two parallel convictions'. The first was that 'we in the West are *not* in the business of undermining the Soviet state'.[64] The other point Reagan should convey was that 'human rights in the Soviet Union *are* our business', and 'not just because both East and West have committed themselves to them at Helsinki' but 'because justice at home is more likely to produce stability and responsible behaviour abroad'.[65] On her fifth and final page, Thatcher said that the letter had become longer than she had intended and 'I certainly don't want you to feel that I am lecturing (perish the thought)', but—continuing to lecture—she stressed the importance of the US showing serious intent to make maximum progress at Geneva. Conscious that Reagan's National Security Adviser, rather than Reagan himself, would be the person concerned with the detail, she added that 'I should be very ready to discuss these points more fully with Bud McFarlane if you were able to spare him for a day or so to come over as my guest.'[66] McFarlane was duly spared. The first item on the prime minister's briefing cards for a 23 October meeting with Reagan was 'Thanks for sending McFarlane'.[67]

Thatcher's letter to Reagan was sent on the day that the defection of Oleg Gordievsky from the Soviet Union was made public. His extraction from Moscow, when he was already under suspicion and surveillance, was a blow for the KGB and a coup for Britain's MI6. The British government chose that moment to expel from the UK twenty-five Soviet officials whom they knew to be spies. The Soviet Union promptly reciprocated by expelling twenty-five British nationals, including some who were not connected with the intelligence services.[68] The British ambassador to Moscow, Sir Bryan Cartledge, feared that the exchange of expulsions would scupper the possibilities for serious diplomacy. They did, indeed, put a temporary dampener on the Thatcher–Gorbachev relationship, but neither leader allowed spies to get in the way of their broader objectives. Reagan, too, kept in mind the bigger picture. In his reply to Thatcher's letter, the president accepted most of what she had argued and told her he admired the way she had handled the Gordievsky case. He made clear that he shared her desire to balance 'intolerance of Soviet hostile international activities' with 'our desire to build a constructive relationship with the Soviet Union'.[69]

On the same day, 12 September, as Mrs Thatcher wrote to Reagan about his forthcoming summit with Gorbachev, the Soviet leader sent the president an even longer dispatch about their forthcoming Geneva meeting. Military confrontation, he said, 'would be catastrophic for our countries, and for the world as a whole'. Preventing it was their 'mutual and, for that matter, primary interest'.[70] Gorbachev proposed, among other things, an end to the testing of nuclear weapons, a ban on space weapons (meaning SDI), and a 50 per cent reduction of nuclear arms.[71] In a letter to Thatcher on 12 October, which made no mention of the unpleasantness over spies but focused entirely on limiting nuclear arms and easing tensions, Gorbachev made three specific proposals (the first of which related to SDI): (1) 'to ban the development, testing and deployment of strike space weapons'; (2) 'to cut in this case by 50 per cent nuclear armaments of the USSR and the USA which are capable of reaching the territories of each other'; and (3) to establish 'equal total levels of nuclear charges—6000 units each'.[72] Gorbachev noted that these points had been 'the subject of serious conversation' in their previous contacts, that he had raised them with President Mitterrand on his recent visit to France, and that they would figure in the forthcoming Soviet–American summit.[73]

It took Reagan until the end of October 1985 to reply to Gorbachev's letter of 12 September. That was mainly because argument had been raging throughout that time within the administration about the positions the president should take in Geneva and on whether and how the United States should abide by the ABM Treaty. George Shultz observed that 'Cap Weinberger, Richard Perle, and others at the Pentagon...wanted to press forward with SDI at full speed no matter what' and saw 'the ABM Treaty as an obstacle to be sidestepped'. He was firmly opposed to that view.[74] In his letter of 31 October to Gorbachev, Reagan mentioned 'specific language for our consideration' that Shevardnadze had proposed on his recent visit to the United States for talks with Shultz, during which he had also met with the President. 'I have repeatedly made clear', wrote Reagan to Gorbachev that 'it is indeed my view that a nuclear war cannot be won and must never be fought'. He continued to believe in eliminating all intermediate-range nuclear missiles (which the Soviet side was not yet ready to accept) and, indicating his firm attachment to SDI, Reagan said that he envisioned 'a cooperative transition to more reliance on defenses' and he 'would like to see a more developed dialogue on how such a transition could be jointly undertaken'.[75]

Reagan prepared unusually thoroughly for his first summit meeting with Gorbachev, reading papers from the various government agencies which were filtered by NSC Soviet specialist Jack Matlock. The preparation included a rehearsal the day before Reagan's first meeting with Gorbachev, with Matlock playing the part of Gorbachev and presenting the arguments he expected the Soviet leader to make.[76] Reagan was at his most attentive when the discussion was about people rather than more abstract data. He wanted to know more about Gorbachev as a person and about Russians as individuals. It was because Suzanne Massie, although uninformed about high politics, could evoke ordinary Russians that Reagan found her an engaging interlocutor. She was invited to the White House for a third time in early September as part of Reagan's preparation for the Geneva summit.[77] More important for Reagan, even before he met Gorbachev, were his own first-hand impressions of the Soviet officials he encountered. He found Soviet ambassador Dobrynin quite agreeable, but his optimism about the prospects for improved US–Soviet relations became greater after he met Shevardnadze.[78]

Reagan had also sought further advice from Thatcher. When they met with other allied leaders on 24 October, he asked her to put in writing points she had made orally about the line to take with Gorbachev. She handed a letter to the president that same evening, giving a copy also to McFarlane. The first of Thatcher's points was one which Reagan was to make on other occasions to Gorbachev (it does not appear in the record of the Geneva discussions, but did at the 1986 Reykjavik summit)—that there was a time when the United States had nuclear weapons and the Soviet Union did not, but they never 'made use of that superiority to attack the Soviet Union or to threaten it'. On the contrary, 'We want to live in peace with you.'[79]

Most of the Thatcher recommendations concerned the presentation of the American position on SDI. They reflected her own reservations about the project, not only because she still saw SDI as a potential threat to nuclear deterrence but also as an obstacle to progress on reducing tensions in the East–West relationship. She advocated a view of SDI which was very much in line with that of Shultz and the State Department—and, unsurprisingly, far too restrictive to find favour with Weinberger and the Department of Defense. Thatcher suggested that Reagan give Gorbachev 'an absolute assurance on four points', these being first, that the goal is balance not superiority; second, 'the U.S. will not do anything in its research and testing which contravenes the ABM Treaty'; third, if the work moved into new areas, the Soviet Union would be consulted as called for by the Treaty; and, fourth, 'we shall not deploy strategic defence weapons without prior negotiation with you in accordance with the ABM Treaty'.

The manner in which Thatcher thought Reagan should sum up his position to Gorbachev was diplomatic and conciliatory. Her conclusion (as aspiring Reagan speech-writer) was in words she would hardly have used prior to the coming to power of Gorbachev: 'I hope you will find what I have said reassuring. We have no designs on you. We recognise you as equals. We know that you are entitled as we are to feel secure. Let's find that security for both of us by spelling out our intentions with clarity, explaining our motives with frankness and accepting that the world cannot be safe for one of us unless it is safe for both of us.'[80]

A few days later Reagan wrote to Thatcher, seeking her public backing for the American view that the Soviet Union had been in breach of its obligations on a number of existing agreements, including the ABM Treaty, the Limited Test Ban Treaty, the Geneva Protocol on Chemical Weapons, and (most obviously) the Helsinki Final Act. At Geneva Reagan intended to make clear to Gorbachev that such violations were unacceptable and he hoped the British government would support the US position.[81] The prime minister gave Reagan the assurances he had asked for, and a week later McFarlane wrote to Cabinet Secretary Sir Robert Armstrong to say he was 'extremely heartened' by Thatcher's response. He told Armstrong, as one of the prime minister's close advisers, more about the American negotiating position than he was prepared to share with the UK Foreign Office and Ministry of Defence.[82] McFarlane was very concerned about how the summit would be perceived by American and European public opinion. He noted that 'we sincerely want to engage the Russians on the issue of the relationship between offensive and defensive forces—not that we will ever convince them but we may be able to diminish the credibility with our publics of their scare tactics'.[83]

Thatcher's contacts with Gorbachev were less frequent than with Reagan, but on 7 November, the anniversary of the Bolshevik revolution, she responded to the Soviet leader's letter of 12 October, having in the meantime acquired a detailed knowledge of the American negotiating stance. Concerned, as ever, to maintain British nuclear weapons, she welcomed Gorbachev's readiness to continue exchanges of view on arms control. The British nuclear missile force, which was 'strategic in character', was 'the minimum size consistent with its requirements as a deterrent force'. However, 'if Soviet and US strategic arsenals were to be very substantially reduced and if no significant changes had occurred in Soviet defensive capability, we would want to review our position in the light of the reduced threat'. She noted 'with satisfaction' that until such time Gorbachev accepted that negotiation would not involve the British forces. She added that she wanted to keep in touch with him and that 'you and President Reagan carry all our hopes and good wishes for the success of your meeting'.[84]

Geneva, November 1985

Since no great breakthroughs were expected from the Geneva summit, each side paid particular attention to winning the support of public opinion. The Soviet Union sent a large contingent of sophisticated commentators, many of whom spoke good English, and their PR was on a qualitatively different level from the crude propaganda of pre-Gorbachev years. Nevertheless, the American media counted it as a coup for their man when, on a cold Geneva day, Reagan stood in the open air, hatless and coatless, awaiting a Gorbachev who was dressed in hat and overcoat.

When the talks got going, Reagan emphasized the long-standing absence of trust between the US and USSR. Incorrectly, however, he said that in the Second World War American planes had been denied permission to refuel at Soviet bases after they had bombed targets in Nazi Germany. The Soviet deputy foreign minister, Georgy Kornienko, told Shultz that he had been stationed at a Soviet base during those years and American bombers had been allowed in to refuel. On checking the story, Shultz found that Kornienko was right, although negotiating permission had been arduous. It was, said Shultz, very difficult to correct one of Reagan's inaccurate stories once he had got the narrative into his head, and it usually contained 'an underlying kernel of truth'.[85]

Reagan referred to Soviet 'intervention and troublemaking' in Afghanistan, Cambodia, and Nicaragua, but did not pick up on Gorbachev's broad hint that they wished to put an end to their Afghan venture. The Soviet leader said that they would like to see a settlement in Afghanistan under United Nations auspices and that the US could help, but that it did not want to. 'You say', he countered, 'the USSR should withdraw its troops, but actually you want them there, and the longer the better.'[86] A large amount of time on the first day was spent in argument about SDI, in which Reagan and Gorbachev did not come close to a meeting of minds. Gorbachev observed that there were a lot of people in both the United States and the Soviet Union who had a material interest in the military sector, but that this was not the most efficient method of economic advance. Japan and West Germany had 'experienced an economic upsurge' while spending little on the military.[87] Reagan's response was that 'if the two sides are to get down to reducing the mountains of weapons, then both must get at the cause of the distrust which has led to them'.[88]

There was much sparring on human rights, with Reagan emphasizing the Soviet Union's lack of observance of the Helsinki agreement it had signed in 1975. Reagan told Gorbachev that he was under a lot of pressure on these issues by people in the United States with connections to Soviet citizens who had been discriminated against. The president said that it would be easier for him to reach and fulfil agreements with the Soviet Union 'if he were not beset by people in the U.S. Congress and by organizations that hear of their relatives and friends and complain about the restraints which they consider should not be imposed upon them', such as 'the right to live in other places or the right to emigrate'.[89]

Throughout the two days of talks, SDI kept cropping up in the conversation, more often than not on Reagan's initiative. His belief in it was becoming an article of faith. He insisted that what he had in mind was a defensive shield, not first-strike capacity with offensive weapons, and that, once it had been established that the system would work, he was prepared to share the technology with the Soviet Union. At that point they could sit down together 'and decide if deployment was desirable'.[90] Reagan's promise to share SDI with the Soviet Union was never taken seriously by Gorbachev, who pointed out that the United States did not share its most advanced technology even with its allies and that a great many less sensitive things than SDI were on the list of items that it was prohibited to export to the USSR. Within the Reagan administration there were in fact many, not least in the Defense Department, who had come to believe in 'space dominance' as well as those in the State Department and the NSC, notably their chiefs, Shultz and McFarlane, who regarded SDI primarily as a negotiating chip that could be bargained away.

In spite of the total lack of agreement on SDI, which was the main obstacle to Gorbachev and his team supporting a 50 per cent cut in each side's stock of strategic offensive nuclear arms, there had been a melting of the ice in the American–Soviet relationship. At the dinners, the two leaders, accompanied by their wives, spoke informally and at times amusingly. Reagan mentioned receiving a letter from a little girl who told him exactly what she wanted him to do and ended, 'Now go into the Oval Office and get to work.' Raisa Gorbachev told of her husband getting a letter from an 83-year-old woman in a provincial Russian city, expressing approval of the anti-alcohol measures the Soviet Union had adopted in 1985 (far from popular with a majority of Soviet men), who had written that she kept Gorbachev's picture next to an icon. She also gave her telephone number, but said he should only call early in the morning, for she was 'busy at all other times'.[91] For Secretary of State Shultz, the big story was that Reagan and Gorbachev 'had hit it off as human beings'.[92] The two leaders agreed that they would meet again, in Washington in 1986 and Moscow in 1987. In fact, each of those meetings took place a year later than planned, but before then, having broken the ice, they were to meet in Iceland!

The joint Soviet–US statement at the end of the summit meeting managed to identify a number of shared positions and common aims, even though no fundamental breakthrough occurred. It included the declaration that 'a nuclear war cannot be won and must never be fought' and that neither the Soviet Union nor the United States will 'seek to achieve military superiority'.[93] They agreed to accelerate work on arms control and called for early progress on 50 per cent reductions in the nuclear arms of the US and the USSR and on an interim INF agreement. Effective measures for verification would be agreed upon. The leaders reaffirmed their commitment to the Treaty on the Non-Proliferation of Nuclear Weapons and to the complete prohibition of chemical weapons and the destruction of existing stockpiles. There would be meetings of experts to work out the means of verification. There was also agreement on broadening cultural, educational, and scientific interaction.[94]

An exchange of letters between Reagan and Gorbachev before the end of the year underlined the improvement of the atmosphere between the two military superpowers, while illustrating how far apart they still remained on key issues. Reagan wrote, 'We genuinely enjoyed meeting you in Geneva and are already looking forward to showing you something of our country next year.' He returned, however, to some of his favourite themes. He called again for Soviet forces to leave Afghanistan and defended at length his SDI project, saying that its goal was 'to eliminate any possibility of a first strike from either side'. The Soviet Union, he wrote, currently had 'a three to one advantage in warheads that can destroy hardened targets with little warning' and that, he said, was what lay behind the programme. Reagan observed that, in Geneva, 'I found our private sessions particularly useful' and 'in the final analysis, the responsibility to preserve peace and increase cooperation is ours. Our people look to us for leadership, and nobody can provide it if we don't.'[95]

In his reply, Gorbachev said that only a country that was preparing for a first strike capability needed a 'space shield' and that if the US proceeded with the implementation of their SDI programme, the Soviet Union would be forced to develop further their nuclear forces and increase their capability of neutralizing the threat. It would, as a result, keep both countries in a 'whirlpool of an ever-increasing arms race'.[96] Near the end of his letter, Gorbachev wrote that with regard to Afghanistan, the US seemed to be ignoring the 'open door' that could lead to a political settlement.[97] He finished, however, on a positive note, saying that he would 'truly like to preserve not only the spirit of Geneva, but also to go further in developing our dialogue'.[98] In a letter to Gorbachev of 26 December, Reagan returned to the subject of Afghanistan, confirming American 'readiness to reach a political settlement'.* He continued: 'Three elements could form the basis for a lasting solution: A process of negotiations among the warring parties including the Soviet Union; verified elimination of the foreign military presence and restraint on the flow of outside arms; and movement toward political self-determination and economic reconstruction.'[99]

Reagan himself was encouraged by his Geneva encounters with Gorbachev. He began a post-summit meeting at the White House by saying, 'Maggie was right, we can do business with this man.'[100] His administration took pains to keep the British prime minister and Foreign Secretary informed about Geneva and what they hoped would be the next steps. George Shultz came to 10 Downing Street in December, accompanied by Assistant Secretary of State for Europe Rozanne Ridgway and the US ambassador to the UK, Charlie Price, to report to Margaret Thatcher and Geoffrey Howe. Shultz told his British colleagues that the next summit would provide a useful deadline for making progress both on arms control and on human rights. The recent resignation of Bud McFarlane, which was regretted by Thatcher, was, Shultz acknowledged, a 'major loss', for while his successor, Admiral John Poindexter, was 'capable' he did not have McFarlane's expertise on arms control issues.[101] (McFarlane was, in effect, an early scapegoat for what became known as the Iran–Contra Affair, an ill-thought out plan to provide arms to supposed opponents of hard-liners in Iran in return for the release of American hostages. McFarlane had been deeply sceptical about important aspects of the venture. His abrasive relationship with Reagan's Chief of Staff, Donald Regan, was also 'undeniably part of the reason' he left the White House.[102])

---

* Jack Matlock, who was the main drafter of Reagan's letters to Gorbachev during his years at the NSC (in April 1987, he became US ambassador to the Soviet Union), gave a press conference, along with Robert Gates of the CIA, following the Geneva summit, at which Gates said that the US government believed that the Soviet Union would never leave Afghanistan. Matlock pointed out to Gates afterwards that this made nonsense of American policy which was to urge the Soviet Union to leave Afghanistan, saying that America would not exploit that to its advantage. Matlock, like Shultz, thought that the CIA's political analysis was very poor, but his personal relations with Gates were good. 'Gates is a decent person', said Matlock, 'who did not do things behind your back—so, in that respect, was quite unlike Weinberger—but as late as 1990 Gates did not realize that anything fundamental had changed in the Soviet Union'. (I am quoting from one of the conversations I had with Ambassador Matlock each day between 15 and 18 March 2016 when we were both working in the archives of the Reagan Presidential Library at Simi Valley, California.)

The American administration, Shultz told Thatcher, had noted that Gorbachev thought of SDI as a programme to put weapons in space to strike targets on earth. To respond to this, the president had instructed that an attempt be made 'to design a Treaty which would prohibit offensive weapons in space while permitting defensive weapons', although it 'remained to be seen whether it was possible to draw a firm line between the two sorts of weapons'.[103] Shultz and Thatcher were on the same wavelength in supporting research on SDI (with the prime minister more firmly on board now it was clear that British companies could benefit from some of the bounty) and in their concern not to breach existing treaties by going further than that. Shultz told the prime minister that he had found her contributions, particularly the points she had made at the Camp David meeting in December 1984 which had become agreed policy, 'invaluable'.[104] Thatcher implied she did not think much had been achieved at Geneva, for she told Shultz that 'substantial progress' needed to be made in the arms control negotiations and on other issues' before the next summit meeting. It would 'not be manageable to have a second getting-to-know-you session'.[105] The prime minister could not foretell that, far from having the inconsequential exchange she feared when Reagan and Gorbachev next met, they were to come close to agreeing to get rid of their and other states' nuclear arsenals altogether, an objective she abhorred, regarding it as both impractical and dangerous.

9

NUCLEAR FALLOUT

Chernobyl and Reykjavik (1986)

The year 1986 was one of 'nuclear fallout' in more senses than one. First, and most literally, there was massive radioactive fallout in April when a nuclear reactor at the Chernobyl atomic power station in Ukraine exploded. The eruption, and the fire which followed, produced contamination that was especially severe in Ukraine and Belarus but spread far beyond Soviet borders. It was an event that underlined for the world—and for no-one more than Mikhail Gorbachev—how utterly catastrophic nuclear war would be. The second was a summit meeting in October which took place not in Washington or Moscow but in Reykjavik, Iceland, at which Reagan and Gorbachev came close to agreeing to banish offensive nuclear missiles entirely, but then fell out over Reagan's insistence on pressing ahead with SDI.

Many of the initiatives aimed at a breakthrough in East–West relations came from Gorbachev. While the Soviet leader had one eye on international opinion and the propaganda effect, he was seeking a genuinely new relationship and joint efforts to eliminate the danger of nuclear war. In a letter to Reagan of 14 January 1986, he proposed that there should be no more nuclear weapons on earth by the end of 1999. What was new about this particular proposal was that it went beyond previous generalities and outlined a timescale that would proceed in three stages.[1] In the first phase, which would last between five and eight years, the Soviet Union and the United States would reduce by half their long-range nuclear weapons, those capable of reaching each other's territories. They would also agree not to conduct any nuclear tests. The reductions in the number of nuclear warheads would be 'on the basis of the mutual renunciation of the development, testing and deployment of attack space weapons'. That part of the proposal was aimed at SDI, and it was predictable that Reagan would resist both the substance and the terminology in which it was couched, since he always insisted that the envisaged missiles were not 'attack' weapons but 'defensive'. The second stage which, in Gorbachev's proposal, should start 'no later than 1990 and last 5–7 years' would bring Britain, France, and China into the nuclear disarmament process and produce agreement on the elimination of their medium-range and tactical nuclear weapons. A final stage, to start not later than 1995, would be devoted to reaching agreement on eliminating all remaining nuclear weapons and an understanding also that 'these weapons shall never be resurrected again'.[2]

Just one day after writing to Reagan, Gorbachev, in a lengthy public statement, set out his proposal for the elimination of all nuclear weapons by the year 2000.[3] For Jack Matlock, as the Soviet specialist on Reagan's National Security Council, the speed with which the Soviet proposal was made public suggested that Gorbachev 'had nothing more than propaganda in mind'. However, John Poindexter, the recently appointed National Security Adviser, told Matlock on 15 January that 'the president has already looked at it and likes the part about getting rid of nuclear weapons. He believes it's the first time a Soviet leader has suggested a certain date.'[4] Reagan rejected the bit of the proposal designed to stop SDI, but insisted that the tone of the US response should be reasonably positive. In his diary entry for 3 February 1986, Reagan referred to discussions within the administration about 'Gorbachev's proposal to eliminate nuclear arms': 'Some wanted to tag it a publicity stunt. I said no. Lets [sic] say we share their overall goals & now want to work out the details.' The US should proceed with SDI, though 'if research reveals a defense against missiles is possible we'll work out how it can be used to protect the whole world not just us'.[5]

More than a fortnight earlier Secretary of State Shultz had, in fact, told Reagan that they should not simply reject the Soviet proposal, for it was 'our first indication that the Soviets are interested in a staged program toward zero'. Reagan's response was, 'Why wait until the end of the century for a world without nuclear weapons?'[6] Reagan had set out his 'zero option' of nuclear missiles in Europe as long ago as November 1981, a far-reaching proposal, although less grandiose than Gorbachev's. Even within his own administration, Reagan's zero option was seen as more propagandistic than serious, for it meant exchanging the removal of Soviet missiles already in place for American missiles which had still to be developed for future deployment. Moreover, the US was already facing opposition to them from within West European countries which could conceivably become strong enough to stop their placement.

Shultz shared Margaret Thatcher's view that 'we could not "uninvent" nuclear weapons and that nuclear deterrence had kept the peace'.[7] However, he respected Reagan's and Gorbachev's desire to eliminate these weapons, believing that, though complete abolition was probably unachievable, a serious attempt to reach that goal could lead to massive reductions in their numbers.[8] That was a minority view within the administration and it had its opponents even within the State Department. For the Defense Department, it was especially unwelcome. Richard Perle, Shultz recorded, thought the whole notion of a world without nuclear weapons 'a total delusion'.[9] One reason why many Western politicians as well as arms control professionals were wary of Gorbachev's proposal was that the Soviet side had a numerical advantage over the West in conventional forces. That was why none other than the Chief of the Soviet General Staff Marshal Sergey Akhromeyev was a prime mover in this big initiative. Whereas Reagan's 'zero option' meant no intermediate-range nuclear missiles in Europe, this was a 'bigger zero'—no nuclear weapons at all. General Viktor Starodubov, one of the Soviet negotiators in SALT talks, said that in the higher echelons of the Soviet Ministry of Defence, they were sure that the Americans would reject the proposal, thus giving it propaganda value; but in the unlikely event that they accepted, the Soviet side would be content with its advantage over the West in conventional forces.[10] Even though Akhromeyev was far more sceptical than was Gorbachev of the chances of the proposal ever becoming a reality, he was sensitive to the dangers of complacency over the existence of 'thousands of strategic missiles with tens of thousands of warheads' that were standing 'on trigger alert' and of their capacity to 'incinerate all life on Earth within ten minutes'.[11]

Margaret Thatcher, in common with François Mitterrand, was scarcely less dismissive of the Gorbachev proposals than was Perle. She called them 'pie in the sky'.[12] Perle reported Thatcher saying to him, 'It is inconceivable that the Soviets would turn over their last nuclear weapon. They would cheat. I would cheat.'[13] Shultz, who had told Reagan that the arms control community 'disagrees with your desire to get rid of nuclear weapons', was soon made aware that anyone trying to talk the president out of this goal was 'wasting his breath'.[14] Reagan was ready, in principle, to embrace not only the European zero but a worldwide zero of nuclear arms. In public, Reagan's initial response to the Soviet proposal was cautious, not least because of its implications for SDI. Gorbachev's plan was, he said, 'at first glance constructive', although it contained parts that caused the US 'serious concern'. The American side would give the proposal 'careful study'.[15]

Limited deals were even at this stage being done between the United States and the Soviet Union. On 11 February there was an exchange of spies from each side which the US agreed to only on the condition that it was accompanied by the arrival in West Berlin of Anatoly Scharansky (Natan Sharansky from 1986 onwards), a Soviet Jewish dissident who had been in prison since 1977, accused of treason and espionage. There had been a vociferous campaign for his release in America and Western Europe as well as in Israel, and his case had been raised frequently with the Soviet authorities by the Reagan administration.[16] Although exchanges of prisoners had taken place in the past, the Soviet Union had long taken an intransigent line over Scharansky. The agreement to allow him to emigrate from the Soviet Union was interpreted by Shultz as part of a trend whereby 'the Soviets were moving in our direction'.[17] Among the senior figures in the administration, Shultz felt, however, that he was in a beleaguered minority. To his relatively upbeat assessments, 'Cap Weinberger would then say that we were falling for Soviet propaganda. CIA director Bill Casey or his deputy, Bob Gates, would say that CIA intelligence analysis revealed that Gorbachev had done nothing new, only talked a different line. And most of those present would try to stimulate the president's fear that any U.S. diplomatic engagement with Moscow would jeopardize the future of SDI.'[18]

Thatcher's earlier enthusiasm for Gorbachev was temporarily dampened when he appeared to be working towards the removal of Britain's nuclear weapons, although the prime minister and the Soviet leader continued to correspond with each other respectfully. She received a long letter from Gorbachev at the same time as he wrote to Reagan (14 January) in support of the new Soviet proposals in which he paid attention to a particular concern of the British—achieving progress in the chemical weapons talks taking place in Geneva. Gorbachev wrote that the Soviet Union would 'actively work towards finding a solution to the problem of complete liquidation of chemical weapons and of the industrial base for its production'.[19]

In a letter to Reagan of 11 February 1986, Thatcher was very far from encouraging Reagan to 'do business' with the Soviet leader. She said that Gorbachev was 'clearly a more astute operator' than his predecessors, but beneath the 'veneer' he was the same kind of 'dedicated Soviet Communist that we have known in the past, relentless in pursuing Soviet interests'.[20] At this point her tone was closer to that of Weinberger than of Shultz. She played on the president's commitment to SDI, saying that Gorbachev would 'rely on a steadily mounting volume of pressure from Western public opinion' to get rid of SDI. She did, nevertheless, remind Reagan of the 'Camp David Four Points' which would 'meet some genuine Soviet anxieties as well as Soviet propaganda' and show that 'we continue to seek a stable international environment' and adherence to the ABM Treaty.[21] Within the British government, Foreign Secretary Geoffrey Howe and the FCO showed a greater responsiveness to the Soviet overtures than did Thatcher and her closest 10 Downing Street advisers. Percy Cradock, in a memorandum to his colleague Charles Powell, observed of a Foreign Office paper, that it identified so many 'legitimate Soviet concerns' that 'we appear on more than one occasion to be acting as Soviet apologists'. That was incorporated by Powell in a note the following day to Thatcher.[22]

When Reagan wrote to Gorbachev on 12 February, he addressed himself more to a handwritten letter Gorbachev had sent him on 24 December 1985 (in response to a letter in Reagan's hand) than to the 14 January communication, since the substance of the latter was already in the public domain and advised the Soviet leader 'to keep our private communications separate'. Striving to find grounds for optimism, Reagan suggested that 'some of the obstacles to an agreement on intermediate-range missiles seem to be falling away' and he hoped that by 'concentrating on practical solutions, we can give greater momentum to this process'.[23]

The president continued to defend the SDI programme and returned to the attack on the Soviet military involvement in Afghanistan, adding that if the Soviet troops were removed from that country, the United States would have 'no desire or intent to exploit a Soviet military withdrawal from Afghanistan to the detriment of Soviet interests'.[24] It would be difficult to argue convincingly that the US stuck to that intention. The United States continued to back Islamist fighters in Afghanistan, supplying them with advanced weaponry. The use of militant Islam as a weapon to be used against the Soviet Union went back to the Carter administration, in which Zbigniew Brzezinski was a vigorous proponent of that policy. The Cold War mindset, as the Spanish historian Gil Guerrero has observed, was ill-suited 'for understanding the forces behind radical Islam'. If the Carter administration was trapped in a 'Soviet-centric worldview',[25] this remained at least as true of the Reagan administration and, indeed, that of President George H. W. Bush. The American policy of providing financial and military support for political Islam undoubtedly complicated (but did not ultimately frustrate) Gorbachev's policy of extracting the Soviet Union from its Afghan quagmire. For the United States, however, it had many unintended consequences. Militant Islamists, radicalized in the fight against the Soviet Union in Afghanistan, were ready to take on the US once the Soviet Union no longer existed. Thus, American support for the mujahidin who morphed into the Taliban was a short-sighted policy that came back to haunt the United States.[26]

New People and New Thinking in Moscow

Shultz and Assistant Secretary of State Rozanne Ridgway were impressed not only by Gorbachev but by his new foreign policy team. Ridgway remarked to Shultz, 'We used to be able to count on their stodgy bureaucracy; now I think we have the stodgy bureaucracy.'[27] Although there was, in fact, no shortage of bureaucratic resistance to Gorbachev's domestic reforms and to elements of his foreign policy, in each year in which he held the highest political office, both the theory and practice of Soviet policy changed more dramatically than it had done in the year before. Modest though the changes in 1986 were, compared with what lay in store, that year saw Soviet policy move beyond the boundaries of the first nine months of Gorbachev's leadership. Party congresses, which were held every five years, were always big events in the Soviet calendar, not because they were forums for great debate (that had ceased after the 1920s), but because they were expected to produce major statements of policy. This imposed a deadline by which positions had to be worked out in advance by teams of officials and specialists over the several months immediately preceding the grand gathering in Moscow. The Twenty-Seventh Congress of the Communist Party of the Soviet Union (CPSU), held in late February and early March 1986, came too soon in Gorbachev's leadership for it to be as radically innovative as he would have wished, but it did provide an important opportunity for promotion of different people to high positions within the leadership.

The Communist system was such that party general secretaries increased their power over time as they gradually replaced the team they had inherited with people who were loyal to them or closer to their outlook.* Gorbachev's personnel changes came significantly quicker than those, for example, of Leonid Brezhnev who was the longest-serving of his predecessors apart from Stalin. But unlike Brezhnev (who promoted acolytes with whom he had formed good relations when he was their party boss in Ukraine, Kazakhstan, and Moldova), Gorbachev did not advance to the Politburo or Secretariat of the Central Committee (CC) any of his subordinates in Stavropol. He avoided nepotism and cliques, yet his appointments were far from wholly successful. Some of those he promoted were not subsequently distinguished either by their commitment to far-reaching reform or by their personal loyalty. In the area of foreign policy, however, he succeeded in identifying and advancing talented like-minded people to positions of major influence. Gorbachev noted in his memoirs that the general secretary could not single-handedly change Soviet foreign policy, and that when he assumed that office, the International Department of the CC, the Ministry of Foreign Affairs and the KGB were no less conservative and ideologically 'drilled' than were the bureaucrats dealing with domestic policy. But there were, he added, analysts and specialists on international affairs who were open to the idea of change in Soviet foreign policy, so one of his first tasks was to promote such people to leadership positions in this area.[28] At the Twenty-Seventh Party Congress he completed the change of the top foreign policy-making team. Moreover, the international policy section of Gorbachev's lengthy report to that Congress was among the document's more innovative components. It aired publicly, for the first time, doubts about the wisdom of the Soviet military presence in Afghanistan not only by the reference to the conflict as a 'bleeding wound' but also by expressing the hope that Soviet troops would be able to return to their homeland in 'the very near future'.[29]

On the eve of the Congress, Aleksandr Yakovlev, the main author of that part of Gorbachev's report to the assembled delegates and the outside world, was not in formal terms even one of the top 470 members of the CPSU. Having been appointed a head of department in the Central Committee, and in view of Gorbachev's respect for his knowledge and judgement, Yakovlev was very influential, but at the beginning of 1986 he was neither one of the 319 full members of the CC nor one of the 151 candidate members. By the end of the Congress, thanks to Gorbachev's backing, he had received extraordinarily fast promotion. He had become not merely a CC member but also a

---

* The fact that Gorbachev was fast losing power in 1990–1 in no way contradicts that generalization. In each year from 1985 until 1989, the Soviet leader was able to introduce ever more fundamental change in the USSR, change that made the system different in kind. By promoting competitive elections for a legislature with real authority in 1989, Gorbachev himself reduced the unique power that accrued to the office he held of party general secretary. By the end of 1989 it was no longer meaningful to call the Soviet system Communist, since 'democratic centralism' within the party had given way to heated intra-party debate, while the 'leading role of the party' (a euphemism for its monopoly of power) had been vitiated by contested elections; by the development of civil society; freedom of speech and, increasingly, of publication; and by the rise of pressure groups, new political movements, and embryonic parties.

secretary of that body, a position of real power which was to lead to his jointly over-seeing ideology along with a much more conservative colleague, Yegor Ligachev. Another Gorbachev ally, Vadim Medvedev, less radically reformist than Yakovlev but closer to his position than to Ligachev's, likewise became a secretary of the CC and was put in charge of its 'Socialist Countries' department which supervised relations with the rest of the Communist world. Medvedev replaced an older and more hide-bound party official, Konstantin Rusakov who, already in failing health, died later that year.

The long-serving head of the still more important International Department (ID) of the Central Committee, Boris Ponomarev, an impeccably orthodox Communist, was sent into overdue retirement and succeeded by Anatoly Dobrynin, another new CC secretary, whose long service as Soviet ambassador in the United States had made him more familiar with the corridors of power in Washington than those of Moscow. He was, first and foremost, a pragmatist, much more interested in keeping relations with other states, the United States above all, on an even keel, than with the spread of Communist ideas in the capitalist and developing world, which had been part of the remit of the ID. In addition, Lev Zaykov (a Leningrad party official with a background in military industry), who had been promoted to a secretaryship of the CC already in 1985, became a full and significant member of the Politburo as the overseer of the military-industrial complex. He chaired meetings of the 'Big Five' (bol'shaya pyaterka), whose other members were the Minister of Foreign Affairs, the Minister of Defence, the Chairman of the KGB, and the head of the International Department of the CC. They worked out compromise positions on arms control and draft positions on defence-related foreign policy. Zaykov was skilful at building consensus, and his role within the 'Big Five' kept Gorbachev, especially in this early period of his leadership, at arm's length from wrangles with the military.[30] A lot of the policy detail was thrashed out in another group known as the 'Little Five' (malaya pyaterka), consisting of the deputies of those ministers and departmental heads who were joined, in prac-tice, by other experts and officials (so that sometimes as many as forty attended the meetings). The pyaterka system for consensus-seeking in defence policy was not new. It had been established during the years in which Gromyko was in charge of foreign policy and Ustinov of defence.[31] What made the biggest difference to the outcomes of their deliberations in the perestroika era was the change of personnel at the top, especially Shevardnadze's presence and the proximity of his views to Gorbachev's.

At the beginning of February 1986, Gorbachev made a less high-profile appoint-ment than that of Shevardnadze, but one of no less significance when Anatoly Chernyaev began to work for him as his principal adviser on foreign policy. He replaced Andrey Aleksandrov-Agentov who had occupied that position since Brezhnev's time. Chernyaev became exceptionally close to Gorbachev and went on to play a greater part than anyone else in the drafting of his foreign policy pronounce-ments and letters to foreign leaders. Born into a cultured intelligentsia family, with some aristocratic antecedents (including a General Chernyaev who served in Tsar Alexander II's army),[32] Chernyaev not only survived in the Communist period, but became a party official. He fought in the Red Army throughout the Second World War and joined the Communist Party in 1942. After the war he graduated in history from Moscow University and taught there before entering the apparatus of the party Central Committee. He spent 1958 to 1961 in Prague on the staff of the *World Marxist Review*, a journal aimed at promoting Soviet orthodoxy within the international Communist movement and which, paradoxically, incubated the reformism of some of the leading proponents of perestroika. Most of the Soviet representatives returned to Moscow with their intellectual and political horizons broadened.[33]

Chernyaev later wrote that he did not know any member of the Soviet 'Prague group' who supported the invasion of Czechoslovakia in August 1968 (to put an end to the 'Prague Spring'), although only a few of them criticized it openly. A majority, including Chernyaev, vented their feelings just among friends and trusted colleagues, thus (wrote Chernyaev) branding themselves as 'unwilling accomplices in this historic crime'.[34] Only in that less-than-heroic way were people of heterodox views, like Chernyaev, able to continue to work within the system. From 1970 until early 1986, when he answered the call from Gorbachev, Chernyaev was a deputy head of the ID. If people such as Chernyaev, or Georgy Shakhnazarov (another Prague alumnus who went on to become a deputy head of the Socialist Countries department and later an important aide to Gorbachev whose influence was second only to Chernyaev's) or Yakovlev had not in the pre-perestroika years continued, for the most part, to observe the rules of the game in Soviet politics, the 'revolution from above' of the second half of the 1980s would scarcely have been possible. Since there was no way in the mid-1980s that Gorbachev could have brought overt dissidents into his team, even had he so wished, it was those 'within-system reformers' (known also as 'intrastructural dissenters' or 'intrasystemic dissidents'[35]) who made it possible for the new general secretary to change Soviet foreign and domestic policy fundamentally in the second half of that decade. And during this period, the views of these critical insiders continued, like Gorbachev's, to evolve far beyond their previous limits.

The International Department was generally considered by Western Sovietologists to be a bastion of ideological conformism and the same scholars tended also to exaggerate its dominance over Soviet foreign policy.[36] In reality, the ID was less influential than the Ministry of Foreign Affairs in state-to-state relations. This was partly because of the weight carried by Communist Party rank. Foreign Minister Gromyko had been a full member of the Politburo since 1973, whereas the ID head Ponomarev remained a candidate (non-voting) member of that highest collective policy-making body within the CPSU. In the perestroika period, differentiation of status and authority continued. Shevardnadze had become a full member of the Politburo in 1985 when he was appointed Foreign Minister, thus outranking Dobrynin, now a secretary of the Central Committee but not a member of the Politburo. Of the two men,

Shevardnadze was also far closer to Gorbachev, and that was of critical significance. Sergey Tarasenko, who was Shevardnadze's principal adviser within the Foreign Ministry, has noted that Dobrynin would have liked to dominate foreign policy from the ID, but the endeavour was doomed to failure for yet another reason: the Ministry of Foreign Affairs had better access to information from all over the world and this 'gave it substantial superiority over other internal agencies', for 'we could decide whether to disseminate that information or not'.[37] Over the course of the post-Stalin period, the Ministry had come to include many highly capable and well-educated people with an excellent knowledge of foreign languages. Those who had served in Western countries could hardly fail to be conscious of the higher living standards there and be no less aware of the freedoms Westerners enjoyed.

The International Department was also not all it seemed on the surface. Far from being a citadel of orthodoxy, even in the 1970s and first half of the 1980s, it contained people of widely differing views—from orthodox Leninists and dreary conformists to a significant number of officials who were privately critical of the party leadership and of the conservatism of Soviet foreign and domestic policy. In the second half of the 1980s no institution provided more recruits for Gorbachev's team of advisers than did the ID.* Compared with most departments of the Central Committee, ID officials were better educated, in many cases knew one or more foreign languages, and were comparatively well-informed about the outside world. After the Soviet Union had ceased to exist, Chernyaev (by some distance Gorbachev's most import-ant recruit from the ID) allowed his hitherto secret diary entries from the 1970s and the 1980s to be published,[38] and it became abundantly clear that he had long held iconoclastic views. In the volume of his memoirs devoted to his pre-perestroika life, Chernyaev entitled one chapter 'In the regime of Doublethink (the International Department of the Central Committee)'.[39]

By the time of the first anniversary of his elevation to the party leadership in March 1986, Gorbachev had a new foreign policy team in place. He was able to take control of Soviet foreign policy in a way in which he could *not* determine the country's eco-nomic policy.[40] Half a dozen different people in key positions facilitated radical change of foreign policy. In contrast, there were far more politically influential actors with an institutional and personal stake in the existing economic system, ranging from Gosplan (the State Planning Committee) and the Ministry of Finance to the ministers responsible for every branch of industry and to the economic departments of the Central Committee which oversaw them. Moreover, an important part in the implementation of economic policy was played by regional party secretaries and

---

* There was also some blurring of the lines between the party and ministerial *apparatchiki*. A few senior officials, most notably Dobrynin and Georgy Kornienko (who had been First Deputy Foreign Minister to Gromyko and had hoped to be his successor), moved from the Foreign Ministry to the International Department. Kornienko was First Deputy Head of the ID during the two years, 1986–8, when Dobrynin was in charge of the department.

managers of large industrial enterprises, and the latter were overseen by their branch ministers in Moscow. Above them stood the Chairman of the Council of Ministers who, for the greater part of the perestroika era, was the technocratic Nikolay Ryzhkov. Gorbachev was only intermittently engaged with economic policy and, though the backwardness in many respects of the Soviet economy (with the defence sector and space programme important exceptions) had been one of the stimuli to perestroika, the transformation of the economic system was a lower priority for Gorbachev than were foreign policy, political reform, and, at a later stage of perestroika, the need to convert a pseudo-federal Soviet Union into a genuine federation (or even loose confederation). That last objective was pursued in what turned out, ultimately, to be a vain attempt to hold the state together in the face of rising ethnic nationalism that had been enabled and emboldened by the new tolerance and burgeoning political pluralism.

Although Chernyaev became Gorbachev's principal foreign policy aide at the beginning of February 1986, the Twenty-Seventh Congress, which opened later that month, arrived too soon for him to be as influential on Gorbachev's thinking as he became before long. It was Yakovlev to whom Gorbachev entrusted preparation of the international section of his report to the Congress, and it was the only part of the draft report the general secretary accepted without major changes.[41] Yakovlev, in turn, relied on just two people to help him with the production of the text—Valentin Falin, an intelligent Central Committee official who had been a successful Soviet ambassador to West Germany, and Nikolay Kosolapov, an innovative thinker at the Institute of World Economy and International Relations (IMEMO) who had worked closely with Yakovlev (as well as with his predecessor as IMEMO director, Nikolay Inozemtsev) when Yakovlev led that institute.

Perestroika turned out to be the golden age of the *institutchiki*.[42] Academics, especially those who worked in the policy-oriented research institutes, had never in Russian history been as politically influential as they became in the second half of the 1980s.

Some of these thinkers and researchers were the Soviet equivalent of American in-and-outers, who would serve in a particular administration and then return to academia, legal practice or business, with Henry Kissinger, Zbigniew Brzezinski, and George Shultz especially notable examples. Within the Soviet Union, a number of the full-time consultants working in the International Department of the Central Committee in the 1980s came there from academic institutes and sometimes returned to academia. Most notably, Yakovlev and Evgeny Primakov, both of whom held high party and state positions under Gorbachev, had been directors of IMEMO (with Primakov succeeding Yakovlev in that role in 1985), while Vadim Medvedev, who had earlier worked in the Department of Propaganda of the CC as a subordinate of Yakovlev, served as Rector of the Academy of Social Sciences of the CC from 1978 to 1983 when he re-entered the party headquarters as Chief of the Department of

Science and Education. These people, in turn, drew on the expertise of their former academic colleagues. Under Gorbachev's leadership, the *institutchiki* were encouraged to abandon self-censorship and to say what they really thought should be done. Thus, the ideational change, which had gradually been taking place in think-tanks for some years before Gorbachev became general secretary, was empowered and embodied in what became known as the New Political Thinking (*Novoe politicheskoe myshlenie*) or, simply, New Thinking.[43]

Although a good deal of the rhetoric in Gorbachev's Twenty-Seventh Congress speech on international issues was along familiar lines, there were new emphases which few in the West picked up. These included the argument that the only security worthy of the name was mutual security[44] and that the Soviet goal should be to keep down the military potential of states to a 'reasonable sufficiency'.[45] Subsequently, Gorbachev was to make still clearer that a 'reasonable sufficiency' need not involve matching the other side weapon for weapon in order to deter any possible aggression. (One of Gorbachev's fiercest opponents, General Albert Makashov, later wrote that the most serious blow against the armed services of the Soviet Union came from their commander-in-chief, Gorbachev, as 'the initiator of the doctrine of "reasonable sufficiency"' which set in motion 'the planned reduction of the military potential of the country, and later even its destruction'.[46]) In a striking reference to one of Reagan's favourite hypothetical examples, Gorbachev noted the American president's contention that if 'our planet was threatened by another planet, the USSR and the USA would quickly find a common language'. But, the Soviet leader asked rhetorically, did not 'nuclear catastrophe' and 'the great ecological threat' constitute more real and present dangers than the arrival of mysterious extraterrestrials?[47]

Even before he became Soviet leader, Gorbachev had been well aware that nuclear war posed a catastrophic threat to the very existence of human life on the planet. His perception of the peril was, however, greatly reinforced by the accident at the Chernobyl nuclear power station in April 1986 which caused radioactive contamination of wide swaths of Ukraine and Belarus and raised radioactivity levels in a variety of European countries, even (on account of the prevailing winds) as far away from the Soviet Union as parts of Britain. The accident strengthened his conviction of the need to banish nuclear weapons completely. Later in 1986 he told the Politburo that 'it is now necessary to expand further the battle for the liquidation and complete prohibition of nuclear weapons and to actively conduct our peace offensive'.[48] The term, 'peace offensive', had in the past signified Soviet campaigns that had more to do with propaganda than with serious policy, but Gorbachev was in earnest. After Ronald Reagan and George Shultz, accompanied by their wives, spent an evening at the home of Mikhail and Raisa Gorbachev in 1988, during Reagan's visit to Moscow, Shultz sent the president a memorandum which Reagan reproduced in his memoirs. It was obvious, wrote Shultz, that Gorbachev had been 'deeply affected' by Chernobyl and that it had left 'a strong anti-nuclear streak' in his thinking.[49] Aleksandr

Bessmertnykh, an influential participant in arms reduction talks and later, in the first eight months of 1991, Soviet Foreign Minister, has spoken of Gorbachev's 'discovery' in 1985–6 that 'many leaders in both camps' had dangerously 'pre-nuclear notions of the world' at a time when 'thirty thousand nuclear warheads were sitting in storages on both sides'.[50] Gorbachev frequently referred to Chernobyl in the context of the need to recognize the interdependence of the countries of the world and the necessity of arms reduction. In one of his interviews, he noted that in just one rocket there 'lurked a hundred Chernobyls'.[51]

As for SDI, Gorbachev was made aware that it would not work as an effective means of defence, not only by physicists of the calibre of Roald Sagdeev, the head of Soviet space research, but by Marshal Akhromeyev. There was, therefore, no need to waste money trying to replicate it, for it could be frustrated at a fraction of what the Americans were spending. Yet, that advice notwithstanding, SDI occupied more of Gorbachev's attention and of internal Soviet debates than it merited.[52] As Sagdeev put it, 'if Americans oversold SDI, we Russians overbought it'.[53] Sagdeev observed that he and his colleagues felt the need to expend a lot of energy fighting against those who wanted a Soviet equivalent.[54] This was because large sections of the Soviet military-industrial complex, including Oleg Baklanov, the minister responsible for the nuclear weapons programme, played up the threat of SDI. Doing so was for them a device for getting increased military investment at a time when Gorbachev was intent on curtailing the bloated Soviet defence budget. When a space industry official, Aleksandr Dunaev (an ally of Baklanov), told Gorbachev that 'We are losing time while doing nothing to build our own counterpart to the American SDI program', Sagdeev, who was in the small group of experts being consulted by Gorbachev in his Kremlin office, said that he 'almost died from suppressing my laughter'.[55] Rather than being persuaded by such self-interested lobbying, Gorbachev accepted the informed judgement of those who assured him that SDI could not succeed even remotely in the way Reagan imagined. Yet, he and others in the Soviet leadership remained concerned about SDI breaching the existing ABM Treaty, about possible technological spin-offs from the American research, about what looked like the United States seeking a first-strike capability, and because of the serious doubts it raised on whether the Reagan administration shared his belief on the necessity of reversing rather than accelerating the arms race.

In discussion with a small group of those with major responsibility for foreign policy, consisting of Shevardnadze, Dobrynin, Yakovlev, KGB Chairman Chebrikov, Vadim Medvedev, and Chernyaev on 24 March 1986, Gorbachev noted that the means of countering the American space weapons programme would involve as little as 10 per cent of the cost of the American programme. While, therefore, the Soviet Union must continue to oppose such an acceleration of military competition, they should stop being afraid of SDI.[56] It was the following year, however, before Soviet public diplomacy became less obsessive about SDI. Gorbachev and the Soviet leadership by then understood that by overreacting to it, they had inadvertently provided encouragement for its sponsors in the United States and led even sceptics within the Reagan administration to see SDI as a useful bargaining counter in future negotiations. American and British specialists, especially those who did not have a material interest in the research and development funding that SDI's sponsors offered, had, however, come to exactly the same conclusions as Soviet experts—that SDI could be countered by the Soviet Union and at a fraction of the cost being incurred by the United States. Thus, military technology expert Bill Perry, who had first been called from California to Washington to assess the threat from Soviet missiles in Cuba in 1962 and was appointed US Defense Secretary a generation later, noted that SDI could be overwhelmed by sheer numbers. He wrote: 'The Soviets could deploy thousands of decoys with their warheads, thereby multiplying the number of targets the SDI must deal with, a huge problem of target-discrimination. And the Soviets could build more missiles and warheads, at a much lower cost than SDI. So even if we never deployed the SDI system, simply starting it could precipitate a new and more dangerous phase of the nuclear arms race.'[57] That last point was what most agitated Gorbachev.

The Soviet leader delivered a particularly significant speech to diplomats in the Ministry of Foreign Affairs (MFA) in late May 1986 that remained unpublished until after the Soviet Union ceased to exist.[58] Those who heard it were impressed not only by the freshness of its content but also by its underlining that Gorbachev was in charge of foreign policy and intent on taking it in a different direction. Addressing the Soviet officials responsible for foreign policy implementation, he insisted that peace was the 'highest of all values' and that, in the nuclear age, world war had become an 'absolute evil'. The nuclear arms race must be halted, even though the United States, which was the 'locomotive of militarism', wished to keep it going to prevent the Soviet Union from switching expenditure to civilian needs.[59] By arguing, as he had in the Politburo on other occasions, that it was US policy to make the Soviet Union spend more on armaments, he was able to make the patriotic case for reducing military expenditure. In his MFA speech, Gorbachev suggested that there was a strong element of deception in the way in which the United States boasted about the progress and successes of SDI. If they were doing as well as they claimed, there would be more secrecy about it. So it was necessary to study what was a real programme and real danger and what was bluff.[60]

Gorbachev added that the Ministry had become excessively fixated with the United States. They needed to pay attention to other parts of the world—in particular, Europe and the Asia-Pacific.[61] On Afghanistan, he said that while they could not permit the Americans to establish themselves on the USSR's southern border, it was also clear that 'our forces cannot remain there for long'.[62] Gorbachev called for a qualitative change in the Soviet relationship with other Communist states (the 'countries of the socialist commonwealth', in Soviet discourse). They had become 'full-blooded states' with their own way of life and their own achievements—'in many ways superior to ours'.[63] As the most powerful state in the 'socialist commonwealth', the Soviet Union needed to display modesty and respect for others' attempts to resolve their problems independently.[64] It was also time to stop putting 'human rights' in quotation marks, as if they weren't real. Soviet policy should treat them seriously and not place itself on the defensive.[65] Distancing himself from post-war Soviet diplomacy, and from Andrei Gromyko's long tenure as Foreign Minister, Gorbachev said they had to get away from the 'senseless obstinacy' that led to 'our being called "Mister NYET" [Mr No]'.[66]

Chernobyl and its Impact

In the immediate aftermath of the explosion and fire at the Chernobyl nuclear power station in Soviet Ukraine on the night of 25/26 April, the response of the central authorities to the disaster was tardy and glasnost was conspicuous by its absence. Gorbachev and the Soviet Politburo were themselves ill-informed initially about the scale of the disaster. They held an emergency session on 28 April when Vladimir Dolgikh, the Central Committee secretary who oversaw heavy industry and the energy sector, reported on what he knew of the catastrophe, noting that 'at this point, we only have hypotheses' about the causes of the accident and the most appropriate measures to 'eliminate the consequences'. Chairman of the Council of Ministers Nikolay Ryzhkov said that a radioactive cloud had reached the Lithuanian capital Vilnius the previous day. Gorbachev and Yakovlev were the first to stress the need for an early public statement about the accident, with Gromyko warning that it 'should be written in such a way that it does not cause excessive anxiety or panic'.[67] Later that day a minimally informative announcement came from the Soviet official news agency, TASS, and was read out on the evening television news. But the outside world had already been alerted to greatly increased radioactivity levels by reports from Sweden, for a northwesterly wind had carried the contamination from Ukraine to Belarus and on to Lithuania, Sweden, Finland, and Denmark.[68] Already it was clear that this was a major disaster, but it was several days later before Gorbachev and the Moscow leadership were made aware of just *how* bad it was.

Quite soon, however, the general secretary came to see the accident—and obfuscation of its gravity—as a reflection of much that was wrong with the Soviet system. In a Politburo meeting of 3 July, Gorbachev criticized the lack of responsibility that had led to the accident and the slow response in the immediate aftermath. Neither the civil defence nor the medical services had been prepared, he said, and people simply did not know what to do. Weddings in nearby towns went ahead the following day and children were playing on the streets, oblivious to the hidden menace of the high levels of radiation. The ministry with responsibility for the atomic power industry had been a law unto itself. They kept information away from the Central

Committee and covered things up. As a result, 'we have suffered huge losses, not only economic but also human', and what happened at Chernobyl had discredited the USSR, Soviet science and technology, and the atomic energy industry. Berating the first deputy minister responsible for that sector, Aleksandr Meshkov (who was dismissed from his post), Gorbachev said that the accident could have been prevented, but 'we were faced by extreme irresponsibility'.[69] Meshkov's wasn't the only head to roll. Later the Minister of Medium Machine Building (as the Soviet nuclear power ministry was euphemistically named), the 88-year-old Efim Slavsky, was belatedly eased into retirement.

In spite of the initial mishandling of the tragedy, the Soviet leadership soon focused on the task of addressing the accident's consequences. Marshal Sergey Akhromeyev observed a few years later (at a time when he had already become critical of Gorbachev's handling of foreign and defence policy) that both Gorbachev and Ryzhkov worked tirelessly to deal with the aftermath of the disaster, and the civil and military personnel, politicians, economic planners, and scientists operated together with a cohesion he had not seen since the Second World War.[70] As the overlord of the Ministry of Medium Machine Building, Ryzhkov, along with Yegor Ligachev, flew to Kiev on 2 May and then by helicopter to the most affected area. They met with officials and the workers who were courageously, and with considerable success, doing their best to mitigate the worst effects of the disaster (for many of them, at the cost of their lives). Local Ukrainian officials were less impressed than was Akhromeyev by Moscow's response to the disaster. Ligachev's 'Well, it's certainly a great misfortune, but we'll learn from your experience' went down badly, leading even to wild speculation that there had been a delay in evacuating people from the acute danger area because 'the Moscow bosses wanted to see how radiation would affect the health of Ukrainians'.[71] Some learning of a different kind, nevertheless, took place. Both in the Politburo and outside it, Gorbachev went on to use the Chernobyl tragedy as an argument against cosy personal relationships, narrow departmentalism, the persecution of critics and whistle-blowers, and excessive secrecy. Chernobyl became for him a further argument for change that involved moving beyond glasnost as an attractive concept to promoting glasnost in action.

The Reagan administration was not united in its response to the Chernobyl disaster in Soviet Ukraine and, even in retrospect, those closely involved in the American reaction have given conflicting accounts of it. When news of the accident reached the outside world—from Scandinavian, not Soviet, reports—Reagan was in Japan, accompanied by National Security Adviser John Poindexter, McFarlane's successor. Jack Matlock notes that, from the NSC in Washington, he sent an urgent message to Poindexter asking if the US should offer assistance, and within minutes got a reply that the president wanted that to be done 'without delay'.[72] Messages with this offer were sent both to the Soviet Embassy in Washington and via the American Embassy in Moscow, but were not taken up by the Soviet authorities. Shultz recalled the US response differently. In his memoirs, he says that he drafted a message for Reagan to send to Gorbachev, offering expert help with the clean-up, but that Poindexter wished to delay its sending until a study had been conducted by the NSC. In the Secretary of State's version, it was Shultz himself who argued the need to show a sense of urgency and carried the day. A message was sent in Reagan's name on 29 April, the day after the brief announcement of the accident on Soviet television.[73]

Chernobyl was such a dominating concern for the Soviet leadership that it was followed by a brief pause in Gorbachev's activist diplomacy. Shultz wrote to Reagan on 19 May that 'as a result of Chernobyl and other events since last year's summit, the Soviets are becoming increasingly defensive and withdrawn'. He was concerned that a 'prolonged deadlock' in US–Soviet relations might 'increase the electoral difficulties' of such 'strong supporters' of the president as Thatcher and Helmut Kohl. The Secretary of State urged Reagan to send a 'forward-looking personal letter to Gorbachev'.[74] A letter was duly sent four days later in which Reagan referred to the work of the American physician Dr Robert Gale in treating victims of Chernobyl and praised 'the sacrifices and skill with which your experts are dealing with the human and physical consequences of the disaster'. Reagan hoped that dealing with the disaster wouldn't slow progress to 'resolve our differences', for they were living 'in a time of historic and possibly unique potential' and, at his next meeting with Gorbachev, the president was 'eager to achieve tangible practical results'.[75]

Reagan Administration Wrangles over Soviet Policy

The extent to which Soviet foreign policy was changing was, nevertheless, unclear to Western governments, and the very idea that significant movement might be underway was dismissed by large sections of the Reagan administration. Notwithstanding a few exceptions within their ranks, the Defense Department and the CIA remained especially set in their ways and narrowly protective of their institutional interests. Shultz complained that every White House meeting on foreign policy when Reagan was not present turned into a battle with those who were arguing for a harder American line, prominent among them Defense Secretary Weinberger, director of Central Intelligence Bill Casey, and (at a lower level) the president's director of communications Pat Buchanan.[76] Casey, Shultz observed, had views that were 'so strong and so ideological that they inevitably colored his selection and assessment of materials', to the point that he doubted the objectivity of the intelligence.[77] Scepticism that anything could be changing for the better in Soviet policy was, Shultz noted, a constant refrain of the CIA. This reflected the view of deputy director of Central Intelligence and the CIA's top Soviet expert, Robert Gates, who viewed the Soviet Union as 'a despotism that works' and saw Gorbachev 'as just another in the succession of hidebound Soviet leaders'.[78] Shultz noted that some of the younger CIA analysts who had been invited in late May 1986 to a Saturday seminar, took a different view, so 'I saw that there was at least healthy ferment in the agency.'[79]

For his part, Gorbachev was being pulled in many different directions at once, and increasingly so as time went on. Yet, by mid-1986, he was devoting an increasing amount of time to foreign policy. That summer he had visits in quick succession from French President François Mitterrand and Richard Nixon. According to Chernyaev, Mitterrand helped to persuade Gorbachev that he should not equate Reagan's intentions 'with the goals of the U.S. military-industrial complex' and that the American president was 'intuitively striving' to find a way out of the stand-off. Gorbachev took Mitterrand's assessment of Reagan the more seriously because it was accompanied by a Gallic disdain for the American political class. (Mitterrand had added that, 'Unlike many other American politicians, Reagan is not an automaton.'[80]) In Chernyaev's view, the French president helped to erode the remaining stereotypes that had coexisted in Gorbachev's mind alongside his 'new thinking'.[81] Nixon, for his part, emphasized Reagan's seriousness about improving relations with the Soviet Union, noting that the president's popularity at home made it easier for him to succeed in this endeavour. He told Gorbachev that Reagan felt that he had established a personal connection with him at Geneva. It would, therefore, be unwise to wait three or four years in order to deal with his successor. This advice had an impact on Gorbachev, reinforcing his own preferences.[82]

Reagan, however, continued to put greater faith in the Strategic Defense Initiative than in arms control agreements. He held a meeting in July with private sector supporters of SDI aimed at consolidating that support and mobilizing them to do more. Reagan said that for three decades American strategy had been based on mutually assured destruction (MAD), but mankind still lived under the 'awesome threat' of nuclear war. It was time 'to do something about nuclear weapons, rather than simply live with them in fear'.[83] He was dismissive of those who thought that what was required was not SDI but reaching arms control agreements: 'Trust and understanding, it is said, will lead to arms control. Hearing people say that is like meeting grown-ups who still believe in the tooth fairy.'[84]

While sceptical of *arms control* agreements, Reagan made clear that he was very much open to *arms reductions* which he regarded as a more ambitious and more worthwhile project, to which he believed that SDI was complementary. 'Let's not kid ourselves', Reagan said, 'it's realism, not trust, that is going to make it possible for adversaries, like the Soviet Union and the United States, to reach arms control agreements'. SDI, he held, could become a catalyst for a major reduction in the number of nuclear weapons.[85] As he had done before, and would do again, Reagan insisted that he would be willing to share the defensive technology with the Soviet Union.[86] To many, this was far removed from the 'realism' of which he spoke in the same address. Understandably, Gorbachev regarded it as inconceivable that the American administration would permit the sharing of the latest military technology, even if (as appeared to be the case) Reagan was sincere in his intention.

The relationship with Moscow continued to be a central preoccupation for the president. In spite of his aloofness from policy detail, Reagan was a willing pupil when it came to acquiring a somewhat better understanding of Soviet politics. 'More than other U.S. presidents', Matlock has observed, Reagan 'was aware of the many things he didn't know, and welcomed education', but he was also selective and relied on people he trusted, such as Shultz, to handle 'the details that bored him'.[87] Matlock provided the president with spoof memoranda from Chernyaev to Gorbachev. Although at that time he had no idea what Chernyaev was advising Gorbachev—in the post-Soviet era all was revealed—Matlock believed that this device helped Reagan 'to understand that Gorbachev was a fellow politician forced to deal with a lot of domestic pressures, even though his political system was quite different from Reagan's'.[88] The memos included jokes and anecdotes and Reagan liked them so much he asked for extra copies to share with friends. The president was still hoping to have another summit meeting with Gorbachev in 1986, but two episodes put this in jeopardy. The first involved America's allies as well as the Soviet Union. The United States had not ratified a Treaty imposing limits on strategic nuclear arms known as SALT II, but had, nevertheless, up to this point stayed within its limits. The predominant view within the Reagan administration was that the Soviet Union had, in minor ways, breached that agreement and that, more seriously, it was infringing the ABM Treaty by the construction underway of a radar facility at Krasnoyarsk.[89] It was argued also that SALT II was flawed because its basic unit of account was launchers rather than the number of warheads. Shultz argued against abandoning the Treaty's limits, but on this occasion Weinberger carried the day, to the dismay of most of America's foreign friends.

Nevertheless, in June Weinberger surprised Shultz and pleased Reagan by coming up with a proposal to eliminate all ballistic missiles.[90] This was highly unlikely to be acceptable to the Soviet Union, for Weinberger was proposing elimination of those weapons which posed the gravest danger to the United States, namely intercontinental ballistic missiles (ICBMs) and submarine-launched ballistic missiles (SLBMs), while retaining strategic bombers where the Americans had an advantage. The US and its allies would also retain its medium-range cruise missiles that gave them the means of attacking the Soviet Union.[91] Although the proposal seemed certain to be rejected by the Soviet side, it had fierce opponents even among hawks in the United States. Paul Nitze, was one. Throughout Reagan's second term, Nitze had the title of Special Adviser on Arms Control to the President and Secretary of State, and his opinion carried weight. He was firmly in favour of the programme of modernization of the US nuclear arsenal and feared that Congress would be unlikely to fund a new generation of ballistic missiles if they appeared to be at risk of being banned. Nitze was also concerned that the proposal seemed to embrace British, French, and

Chinese missiles. The Chinese were not his problem, but the state of the Atlantic alliance concerned him. He was acutely sensitive to the likely reaction in London and Paris, and when he went there to have his views confirmed, he was able to report to Shultz that the British and French governments wanted no part in the plan.[92]

When the US proposal went to the Soviet Union on 25 July, it mentioned only American and Soviet missiles. Weinberger, meantime, remained as committed as was Reagan to SDI and 'worked ceaselessly to convince the president that any negotiation that even mentioned SDI would kill the program'.[93] Shultz, wearying of the constant internal opposition to his diplomacy, gave Reagan a letter of resignation on 5 August which the president refused to accept and the Secretary of State allowed himself to be talked into staying on. It was the third time he had offered to resign, and though he was ready to follow through on the proposal, his preference was to remain, but without being undermined (as he saw it) by the Defense Department, the CIA, and the White House and NSC staffs.[94]

The American decision no longer to abide by the SALT limits, a change of policy Shultz opposed, had further strained US–Soviet relations, and a 'spy scandal' later in August greatly added to the discord. A number of Americans had been convicted in US courts for selling secrets to the Soviet Union and when a Soviet employee in the United Nations Secretariat, Gennady Zakharov, recruited an American defence contractor to supply information, he was unaware that person was cooperating with the FBI. Zakharov did not have diplomatic immunity for actions that went beyond his UN brief, and the FBI proposal that he should be arrested was approved both by the CIA and the State Department. The Soviet Union retaliated by arresting Nicholas Daniloff, an American journalist working in Moscow. Reagan asked CIA director Casey whether Daniloff had ever been employed by American intelligence and was told that he had not been. He had once, completely unknowingly, assisted them by delivering an envelope addressed to the American Embassy that had appeared in his Moscow mailbox, but was unaware that inside it was another envelope for the CIA.[95] A CIA agent in Moscow had also muddied the waters by purporting to be a friend of Daniloff, whom he had never met, in a telephone conversation with a Soviet informer which was listened to by the KGB. So, though Daniloff was no spy, bad luck and what Shultz called 'CIA incompetence' had made him vulnerable.[96]

The stand-off was eventually resolved when a Soviet dissident physicist, Yury Orlov, was released from custody by the Soviet authorities and officially became the exchange for Zakharov. Daniloff was also freed and allowed to return to the United States, in what Matlock described as a 'thinly disguised trade' of Zakharov for Daniloff. The deal was negotiated by Shultz and Shevardnadze. In the NSC Matlock disapproved of the State Department's handling of the episode which, once Daniloff had returned to the US, was followed by American expulsions of Soviet officials that, in turn, led to Soviet retaliation with a round of expulsions of Americans from the USSR.[97] Reagan had been angered by the treatment of Daniloff, and the prospects for a summit meeting between him and Gorbachev in 1986 (a year in which he had earlier hoped that Gorbachev would visit the United States for the first time) seemed bleak. Yet Gorbachev was anxious to re-engage with the United States, provided decisions of substance could be taken, and not allow a whole year to pass without another top-level meeting. Thus, part of the deal between Shultz and Shevardnadze involved haggling over the summit, with the Secretary of State insisting that any such meeting could only take place after Daniloff was safely back in the United States. 'In our private talks', said Shultz, 'I stressed Daniloff; Shevardnadze stressed a summit.'[98]

Reykjavik

Normally, a summit involved many months of preparation. The meeting of Reagan and Gorbachev at Reykjavik was very different. It was not even intended to be a summit in the full sense, but a brief get-together to prepare the way for a more substantive meeting in Washington. When he left for a vacation in Crimea in late August, Gorbachev took Chernyaev with him, as was to become his custom from then until 1991. His vacations always included time set aside for political reflection and policy-related discussion. Exchanging ideas with his main foreign policy adviser became as important to him as the change of air. Early on in this stay on the Crimean coast, he told Chernyaev to prepare a draft letter to Reagan proposing that they meet in late September or early October either in London or Reykjavik. 'Why Reykjavik?', Chernyaev asked, to which Gorbachev replied that it would be a good location, 'Halfway between us and them, and none of the big powers will be offended!'[99] The subsequent letter from Gorbachev to Reagan, dated 15 September 1986, said that 'the entire world' was expecting them to have a 'really productive and fruitful' second meeting, and he concluded: 'That is why an idea has come to my mind to suggest to you...that in the very near future and setting aside all other matters, we have a quick one-on-one meeting, let us say in Iceland or in London, may be just for one day, to engage in a strictly confidential, private and frank discussion (possibly with only our foreign ministers present).' The aim would be to demonstrate political will and to prepare the ground for a Washington summit.[100]

Shultz as well as the NSC (where Matlock was an especially influential voice) advised Reagan to accept the invitation, provided Daniloff was speedily allowed to return to the United States. The invitation was hand-delivered by Shevardnadze in Washington on 19 September and the first session in Reykjavik opened on 11 October, an exceptionally short preparatory period. By the point at which the American condition for the summit had been met, time was still shorter—little more than a week between the announcement and the arrival of the two delegations in Reykjavik. It was meant to be merely a 'meeting', Shultz noted, though 'in the eyes of the world, Reykjavik would become the epitome of the very word "summit"'.[101]

Figure 7 Reagan makes clear to Gorbachev his disappointment at the end of the October 1986 Reykjavik summit. Veteran Soviet diplomat (by this time a Secretary of the Central Committee) Anatoly Dobrynin is in the background between them.

On the Soviet side, the impetus to make a breakthrough, by bringing far-reaching proposals to Reykjavik, came from Gorbachev, *not* from the Ministry of Foreign Affairs, even under its new leadership. When the MFA were asked to prepare a paper for the meeting, Shevardnadze was on holiday and the task fell to First Deputy Foreign Minister, Anatoly Kovalev. Gorbachev read it and asked Chernyaev what he thought of it. 'It's no good, Mikhail Sergeyevich', replied Chernyaev, to which Gorbachev added, 'Simply crap!' He complained that the Ministry had 'still not learned to think big', for they were 'afraid of being accused of softness, of losing face'.[102] Chernyaev passed on to Kovalev Gorbachev's dissatisfaction with the paper and asked for another document of proposals for the meeting with Reagan that would have a particular focus on disarmament. The trust Gorbachev already reposed in Chernyaev meant that his aide could adopt quite a sharply critical tone in the letter he sent to Kovalev. As an aside, he said that 'by mistake some ideas intended for Reykjavik almost showed up in the letter which Comrade Shevardnadze was supposed to deliver to Reagan', but Gorbachev had caught that error in time. Chernyaev mentioned this 'only because it shows that the people who are preparing materials for Reykjavik already have Gorbachev's ideas on paper', yet the document the MFA had produced for him 'is not what the general secretary had in mind for the summit'.[103]

A senior official in the MFA who supported Gorbachev's intention to tackle the bloated size of the Soviet military budget, Anatoly Adamishin, noted that, even after the new general secretary had come to power, the military-industrial complex had powerful advocates within the Ministry.[104] Very conscious of this, Chernyaev, in his letter to Kovalev, said that the military had their own logic and interests but 'this doesn't mean that the military should define our general policies'.[105] The MFA seemed to have completely forgotten Gorbachev's goal of 'a nuclear-free world by the end of the century'. Consistent with that memory lapse, 'the issue of strategic arms limitation has been pushed into the background', although it constituted the primary danger to humanity, as Gorbachev had observed on many occasions.[106] In Chernyaev's view, Reagan would not make concessions at Reykjavik. Getting him to change his stance meant the Soviet Union had to exert influence via Western Europe and 'turn public opinion against him'. However, 'by keeping our SS-20s in Europe', wrote Chernyaev, 'we'll certainly never get the West Europeans on our side'. He also expressed incredulity at the assumption in the MFA that there were circumstances in which Thatcher or Mitterrand 'or whoever follows them' would 'press the button to launch their missiles against us'.[107] Chernyaev emphasized that 'the summit in Reykjavik would be aimed not at experts who know all the fine points of modern weapons', but at 'the world community', so 'big politics should be in its forefront, not negotiating minutiae'.[108]

Gorbachev and Chernyaev were no more satisfied with a subsequent draft, jointly produced by the Ministry of Foreign Affairs, the International Department of the Central Committee and the Ministry of Defence. It had been prepared by Yuly Vorontsov who (along with Kovalev) had the rank of First Deputy Minister of Foreign Affairs, his counterpart in the International Department of the CC Georgy Kornienko, and the Chief of the General Staff (and First Deputy Head of the Ministry of Defence) Akhromeyev. In a long memo to Gorbachev, Chernyaev said the foreign and defence establishment draft seemed to be based on the principle that 'If there is a war, both sides should have equal means', whereas what was needed was a completely different approach (one, he said, that had been set out at the Party Congress earlier that year), namely that 'War is madness, therefore it should not and will not happen.'[109] The draft from the three senior officials contained nothing that had not already been said at Geneva by the Soviet chief negotiator, Viktor Karpov. It referred, yet again, to 'the danger that the French and English arms present to us', but it was 'completely impossible to imagine the circumstances' in which those governments, 'no matter how close their relations with the United States', would 'launch a nuclear attack against us'.[110] Reducing and then liquidating strategic arms, with a 50 per cent cut in the first instance, should be the main goal, and reductions should not be made conditional on an agreement on space weapons. Banishing nuclear tests should also, however, be an objective at the summit, and 'if there is no testing, there will be no SDI'.[111] Whereas Chernyaev had assumed that Reagan would not accept proposals as bold as those

Gorbachev wished to put to him, the general secretary himself had an open mind regarding Reagan's response. What was impermissible, he told the Politburo on 22 September, was that they should make proposals knowing that they would be rejected by the other side.[112]

For the Soviet Union to exclude British and French nuclear weapons from the INF negotiations was a major concession. As we have seen, it had been a prime aim of the British government to make sure that they could not be negotiated away. But the Soviet position hitherto, and under successive leaders, had been that balance meant an approximate equivalence between the two military blocs, not just between the USA and the USSR. From a NATO standpoint, it was the Soviet deployment of SS-20 missiles that had upset that balance, whereas the Soviet military took the view that this was simply restoring parity between the blocs. They did not see how British and French nuclear forces could fail to be considered alongside US forward-based systems in Europe and American Poseidon submarines. Akhromeyev's predecessor as Chief of Staff and First Deputy Minister of Defence (from 1977 until 1984), Marshal Nikolai Ogarkov, had firmly held that 'with the deployment of SS-20s in the latter part of the 1970s and early 1980s an approximate balance existed in Europe at the nuclear level'.[113] Thus, when Gorbachev changed the Soviet position on British and French nuclear weapons, he was doing something that was almost certainly necessary to obtain an INF agreement, but he was putting at risk his standing with the Soviet military.

Akhromeyev complained that Gorbachev had acted unilaterally, while on vacation in August, when he decided to exempt British and French nuclear weapons from negotiations on arms reductions. (If, of course, the Soviet leader's more far-reaching proposals for nuclear disarmament had made progress, this would have been merely a change in the timetable for their removal.[114]) In contrast, once Gorbachev got down to preparing very thoroughly for the Reykjavik summit, he had, said Akhromeyev, acted collegially. The general secretary had convened a series of meetings at which important decisions had been taken and, 'as distinct from the decisions concerning England and France', these had been agreed in a spirit of unity.[115] The meetings Akhromeyev had in mind were of an ad hoc committee which, in addition to Gorbachev, consisted of Politburo members Lev Zaikov and KGB Chairman Viktor Chebrikov, First Deputy Foreign Minister Kovalev, Akhromeyev, and Chernyaev. Emphasizing the importance of getting rid of all intermediate-range nuclear weapons in Europe, Gorbachev said everyone understood that a hundred missiles were enough to destroy 'all of Europe and a large part of the Soviet Union'.[116] Chebrikov, however, was reluctant to remove all of the Soviet Union's intermediate-range nuclear weapons because unlike their ICBMs, whose locations the Americans knew, they were mobile. He also cautioned Gorbachev against using the term 'concessions' when negotiating with the Americans.[117] But, responded Gorbachev, 'by solving these problems, we will not weaken our security, but rather strengthen it'. At the same time all of them, as well as the Politburo and the Ministry of Foreign Affairs, must understand that 'nothing will come of it if our proposals lead us to a weakening of U.S. security', for the 'Americans will never agree to it'.[118]

In striving to persuade his colleagues of the need for a far-reaching agreement, Gorbachev pointed to the threat to the Soviet economy. In the absence of compromise on some points, 'we will be pulled into an arms race beyond our power, and we will lose this race, for we are presently at the limit of our capabilities'—a line of argument he was to deploy at a Politburo meeting four days later (on 8 October).[119] The general secretary was much more conscious than were most other members of the top leadership team of the damage the size of the Soviet military-industrial complex budget inflicted on the Soviet economy. The military competition was a greater strain on the Soviet economy than on the much larger American economy, although it was one which hitherto the Soviet leadership had always been prepared to bear. While stressing the importance of avoiding a new round of the arms race, even the most pacific Soviet leader in the history of the USSR was not prepared to allow 'US superiority' through their development of SDI. If a new round of military competition did begin, said Gorbachev, 'We should concentrate all our resources on our own anti-SDI system.'[120]

Among the positions eventually agreed by the Soviet side was a readiness to cut by 50 per cent their heavy ICBMs, the SS-18s, although there had been heated discussions about this in the Ministry of Defence. The Americans could not match those weapons and this was a major concession by the Soviet side.[121] Less than a week before the Reykjavik conference was due to begin on 11 October, Gorbachev phoned Akhromeyev and told him that he intended to include him in the Soviet negotiating team at the summit, for there would be a lot of discussion of military matters. It was not only the Americans who were to be surprised to find Akhromeyev at Reykjavik and playing a very active part in the proceedings. The Soviet marshal himself had not expected to be there. In the event, the main officials in Gorbachev's team at the summit were, as Akhromeyev noted, Shevardnadze, Yakovlev, Dobrynin, Chernyaev, and himself.[122]

The American delegation therefore arrived in Iceland with little notion of what was in store. Reagan, said Matlock, came to Reykjavik intending to propose essentially incremental steps, although he was ready to agree a reduction in the arsenal of all strategic nuclear weapons provided Gorbachev was both willing to abandon linkage of this with SDI and prepared to include a 50 per cent reduction in the Soviet land-based ICBMs.[123] Shultz later complained that Reykjavik had exposed 'how poor the quality of our intelligence was about the Soviet Union'. The CIA message 'about what to expect in Reykjavik was exactly contrary to what transpired'. On this occasion Shultz was expecting too much of the intelligence agency. While the CIA did, indeed, greatly underestimate the increasingly fundamental change that took place in both Soviet foreign and domestic policy in the second half of the 1980s, it was hardly fair to blame them for failing to know what had been decided within the small preparatory group for Reykjavik which Gorbachev had assembled or for not anticipating his late decision to accord a prominent role to Akhromeyev, for it was the marshal who led for the Soviet side when the expert groups got to grips with the arms control part of the summit negotiations.

Akhromeyev's real opposite number, Admiral Bill Crowe, the Chairman of the Joint Chiefs of Staff, had been left in the United States. The American military experts on the opposite side of the table to Akhromeyev were, accordingly, led by the veteran American arms specialist Paul Nitze. Not only Shultz but harder-liners also within the American delegation were pleasantly surprised by Akhromeyev's reasonableness.[124] One of them was the director of the US Arms Control and Disarmament Agency, Ken Adelman, whose views were close to those of Jeane Kirkpatrick and Richard Perle. Adelman believed that by agreeing to '50 percent strategic cuts down to equal levels' in each side's nuclear weapons, Akhromeyev was responsible for an arms control breakthrough that 'could not have happened with any other Soviet official in that center seat'.[125] In reality, not only had that position been worked out in advance of the meeting by the Soviet side, but Akhromeyev had been influential in toughening up the Soviet response to American proposals by insisting that the strategic arm in which the Americans had an advantage would be cut by the same percentage as that where the USSR had superiority.

During a break in the Reagan–Gorbachev discussions on 12 October, the final day of the summit, Gorbachev told Akhromeyev that Reagan had proposed a 'double zero' in strategic nuclear weapons, removing all land-based intercontinental ballistic missiles and the submarine-based missiles within ten years and asked the Soviet marshal if he thought that was acceptable. It was unacceptable, Akhromeyev responded, unless it became a 'triple zero' and included the US strategic bombers in which the Americans had an advantage several times over. Gorbachev's priority was achieving a political breakthrough in Soviet–US relations and he did not instantly accept this important addendum to Reagan's proposal. Akhromeyev pointed out that it was wholly consistent with the Soviet proposition of 15 January that year that *all* the nuclear weapons on the planet should be liquidated by the end of the century, whereupon Gorbachev instructed Akhromeyev, Shevardnadze, Yakovlev, Dobrynin, and Chernyaev to turn the 'triple zero' into a concrete proposal. They produced a written text that did just that.[126]

Aside from the fact that everything that had been provisionally agreed on 11–12 October at Reykjavik foundered in the final session, mainly on the rock of SDI, Akhromeyev had been fully involved in the preparations of the Soviet side leading up to Reykjavik and was operating within the agreed parameters of Gorbachev's policy initiatives, including the fall-back positions. He also played a key role in adapting Soviet military doctrine to the change in the country's foreign policy. When Akhromeyev outlined the new defence doctrine in a major post-Reykjavik speech at the Academy of the General Staff, it was greeted with incomprehension, disbelief, and alarm.[127] Although he was able to allay some of the concerns in the question-period, there is no doubt that his flexibility was greater than many in the military were ready to countenance. 'Stormy discussions', Akhromeyev observed a few years later, 'continued in the Academy for more than a month.'[128] The marshal's close involvement in elaborating the new Soviet military doctrine meant that at Reykjavik itself he could argue his case flexibly, demonstrating a complete command of the complex issues. His prominent role in the summit appeared to indicate that, thus far, Gorbachev had kept the Soviet military on side. At that time, the authority of the general secretary remained very great, and the armed forces, although a powerful institutional interest, accepted their subordination to the top party leadership. Moreover, as noted earlier in the chapter, Akhromeyev did not jib even at complete nuclear disarmament, if that could be achieved, since the Soviet Union possessed superiority in conventional forces.

The Reykjavik summit became a much bigger affair than Gorbachev's mid-September letter to Reagan proposing it had initially suggested. The Soviet group was larger than the American, but even the US team was jocularly referred to as the 'core thirty-four', although 'the key working members of the delegation', in Shultz's view, numbered 'about twelve'.[129] No-one for Gorbachev had a higher priority to accompany him to Reykjavik than his wife Raisa, who was given her own separate programme in Iceland, but with whom Gorbachev could, as was their custom, discuss the day's events. One thing Gorbachev and Reagan had in common was a close relationship, by any standard, with their spouses and both were averse to being separated from them. Matlock had advised Reagan against bringing Nancy to Reykjavik since there were to be only working meetings, with no joint dinners or other social occasions, and it was advice he came to regret. Neither the president nor Mrs Reagan were happy when it appeared that the Soviet side had secured a public relations advantage, with Raisa charming both the Icelanders and the international media.

Nancy's contribution on this occasion extended no further than consultation with her astrologer friend in California on what would be the most auspicious day for the president to depart for Reykjavik and was told that this would be 9 October, two days before the meeting was due to begin. At 9.45 a.m. that day Air Force One, carrying Reagan, duly took off.[130] For Matlock it was not the PR aspect that bothered him, but the strong feeling that if Nancy had been there, Reagan might have been more willing to stay in Reykjavik for another day. Gorbachev, having made significant concessions, was prepared to stay longer in order to clinch an agreement, provided the Americans made the required compromise on SDI, and it was Reagan who called a halt to the meeting. Matlock believed that another day would have made possible a major agreement to which the parties had come close.[131] That conjecture is disputed by others in the American delegation, such as Adelman (although he was a far less central figure), who maintained that it was not a question of time but of substance— the inviolability of SDI—that separated the leaders.[132]

Matlock does not dispute the strength of Reagan's commitment to the idea of SDI. His point is that in consideration of implementation of policy, Reagan always relied on others. Thus, he could have been persuaded that by agreeing to Gorbachev's insistence that there be no testing in space of SDI over the next ten years, during which time there would be a drastic reduction in the number of nuclear weapons on both sides, he would not be giving up on the project. Since SDI had made little headway a generation later (never mind a decade after Reykjavik), the concession would have been of less practical import than Reagan imagined. 'Ten years in laboratories', wrote Matlock, 'would not have killed SDI; it could have preserved the concept since there was at least that much research needed to determine what technologies were the most promising.'[133] He also believed that Shultz could have persuaded Reagan to sign up to the far-reaching arms reductions Gorbachev was proposing by making this theoretical concession, but the Secretary of State did not attempt to do so. Shultz respected Reagan's SDI obsession, even though he did not share it. Matlock further believed that if McFarlane, rather than Poindexter, had still been National Security Adviser, he would have persuaded Reagan that signing up to deep cuts in offensive weaponry, which Reagan wished to see, made a modest compromise on the hypothetical SDI timetable a small price to pay.[134] And finally, had Nancy Reagan been present, her counsel would have been on the side of those who favoured making such a small concession for the prize of a far-reaching agreement on arms reductions. She was determined that her husband should be remembered as a peacemaker, not a warmonger, and such influence as she exerted on appointments to and departures from the Reagan administration was never to the advantage of its hardest-liners. Her credulity on astrology notwithstanding, she was generally sensible enough on matters of peace and war.

Of the various discussions that took place at Reykjavik the most dramatic were, naturally, between Reagan and Gorbachev, sometimes accompanied only by their translators and a notetaker, at other times reinforced by Shultz and Shevardnadze. The leaders had five meetings in two days in the mornings and afternoons, with a final evening session on the 12th in a last desperate attempt to secure an agreement. The military experts—the groups headed by Akhromeyev and Nitze—held their negotiations all through the night in the middle of the summit. Arms were not the only issue discussed by Reagan and Gorbachev. Human rights issues and cultural relations also came up and on these there was a good deal of give and take, as there was, indeed, on arms reductions until each of the leaders made SDI a deal-breaker. But arms issues and Gorbachev's insistence on a strict interpretation of the ABM Treaty, preventing the development of SDI, which the Soviet side interpreted as being aimed at securing a first-strike capability, were at the heart of the discussions. Reagan repeated his willingness to share SDI technology with the Soviet Union, to which Gorbachev gave the same answer that this was something he could not take seriously (nor, for that matter, could members of Reagan's entourage). 'You don't', Gorbachev told Reagan, 'want to share even petroleum equipment, automatic machine tools or equipment for dairies.' Sharing SDI would be a 'second American revolution', he told Reagan, and 'revolutions do not occur all that often'. To this Reagan responded, 'If I thought that SDI could not be shared, I would have rejected it myself.'[135]

Gorbachev had come to Reykjavik ready to make substantial concessions for the sake of a far-reaching agreement that would dramatically diminish the danger of war, whether by design or by accident, and enable the Soviet Union to reduce the size of its excessive defence budget. Thus, the concessions that Akhromeyev was authorized to unveil at the meeting of military experts were highly attractive to the American side. In the triad of strategic weapons, the Soviet Union had an advantage in ICBMs but less in SLBMs and especially not in heavy bombers. Equal percentage cuts would have left the Soviet side with continuing superiority in ICBMs because of their numerical advantage in the first place. The interim agreement reached was, there-fore, for equal ceilings, with a limit of 1,600 launchers and 6,000 warheads.[136] That was more than enough to make life uninhabitable in either 'superpower'. This Soviet concession was, however, predicated on American acceptance of a ten-year period of non-withdrawal from the ABM Treaty during which work on SDI would be con-fined to the laboratory.[137]

The issue of anti-ballistic missile defence was a constant throughout the two days of intensive discussions. On the morning of the second day, Reagan told Gorbachev that he did 'not understand the charm of the ABM Treaty', since all it did was to guar-antee mutual destruction, whereas they were now talking about elimination of mis-siles. 'The genie is already out of the bottle', he said. 'Offensive weapons can be built again. Therefore I propose creating protection for the world for future generations, when you and I will no longer be here.'[138] To this Gorbachev responded, that the issue of anti-missile defence had a long history and the 1972 ABM Treaty was the product of many years of debate among leaders and experts in the United States, the Soviet Union, and other countries. They recognized that large-scale anti-missile defence would simply 'spur on the arms race in offensive weapons'. Thus, if it were to be built, they could forget any talk of trying to reduce nuclear weapons. Gorbachev added that, 'as the American saying goes, "It takes two to tango". And it takes two to control arms, to reduce and eliminate nuclear weapons. Our national interests will not be preserved if we retreat from consideration of the interests of the other side.'[139]

In the final session of the second day, SDI was again a dominant feature, with Reagan returning to his favourite analogies. 'Our aim', he told Gorbachev, 'is to safe-guard ourselves from a revival of missiles after they have been destroyed, in order to make a kind of gas mask against nuclear missiles and deploy a defense system' and 'I have also spoken of the danger of nuclear maniacs.' To this Gorbachev responded, 'Yes, I've heard all about gas masks and maniacs, probably ten times already. But it still does not convince me.'[140] A little earlier the two leaders, managing to set SDI temporarily aside, had agreed not only to deep cuts in offensive nuclear weapons over the next decade, but also to the complete banishing of nuclear weapons.[141] As a State Department summary of the proceedings, written immediately after the summit had ended, laconically put it: 'Reykjavik came unexpectedly close to an unexpectedly ambitious agreement.'[142] Gorbachev was the first of the participants off the mark with a post-summit press conference, while he was still in Reykjavik. Overcoming his disappointment and initial inclination to attack Reagan, he chose to emphasize the positive and portrayed the summit as the beginning of a breakthrough.[143]

Reaction to Reykjavik in Moscow, Washington, and London

Reporting back to the Politburo two days after the summit ended, Gorbachev emphasized how close he and Reagan had come to 'the liquidation of nuclear weapons' which would have had been of huge significance 'both for us and for the whole world'.[144] He was also, however, much more scathing about Reagan than he had been in public. He was not only a 'class opponent' (as distinct, however, from 'class enemy')[145] but he had displayed 'extreme primitivism, a caveman cast of mind and intellectual feebleness'.[146] As this suggests, the rapport between Gorbachev and Reagan, especially before 1987–8, is often overstated. From the time of the Washington summit a year after their Reykjavik encounter, Gorbachev developed a liking for his American counterpart (while still finding him at times exasperating) and he appreciated the sincerity of Reagan's anti-nuclear sentiments. As of 1986, though, he regarded the president as remarkably obtuse.

Several members of the Politburo showed a readiness to revert to hard-line Soviet positions. For Politburo member (and future President of Azerbaijan) Heidar Aliev, the summit had 'unmasked the United States'.[147] Gromyko said that they needed to write more about SDI, exposing the idea that it was a shield, when it was nothing of the kind.[148] KGB Chairman Viktor Chebrikov declared: 'The Americans understand only strength. We need to set against them the unity of our people with the party and to strengthen the patriotic education of the workers.'[149] Nevertheless, the Politburo members gave their strong approval to Gorbachev's conduct of the negotiations and, with his authority in its wake high, he retained sufficient leeway to move in a different direction from that in which Chebrikov was pointing.

In most of the Western world, the reaction to Reykjavik among a broad public was one of disappointment that a far-reaching agreement between the Cold War's two leading antagonists had been within their grasp and yet they had failed to seize the opportunity. In Western Europe public opinion placed most of the responsibility on Reagan for the failure, whereas in the United States he emerged with his standing enhanced for refusing to give way on Star Wars, for which he had been a persuasive domestic salesman. Initially hugely disappointed by the failure to clinch the far-reaching agreement with Gorbachev, Reagan took to the campaign trail and portrayed

Reykjavik as a turning-point in disarmament negotiations, which, to a significant degree, it had been.[150] The percentage of Americans who thought that the summit had been a success increased daily during the first post-summit week. By 17 October 70 per cent of the American public believed that the US and the Soviet Union had made 'major progress towards arms reductions'.[151] And in mid-October, US public approval of SDI reached 73 per cent.[152] Leading Democrats in Washington—among them, Senators Gary Hart, Sam Nunn, and Claiborne Pell—were critical of Reagan for refusing to limit SDI in return for deep cuts in offensive nuclear weapons.[153] But within large sections of the political and defence establishments of Washington and London, there was much more concern that the leaders had actually come close to agreement on the elimination of nuclear weapons than about the ultimate break-down of the talks.[154]

National Security Adviser Poindexter led the charge against what Reagan had agreed at Reykjavik, handing a memorandum to the president just four days after the summit ended in which he pulled few punches. 'Mr President,' it began, 'my purpose in this note is to strongly recommend that you step back from any discussion of elim-inating *all nuclear weapons* in 10 years, and focus attention on the proposals that you handed over to General Secretary Gorbachev in writing in Iceland which were focused on the elimination of all *offensive ballistic missiles* in 10 years.'[155] Arguing at length against leaving the US dependent on conventional forces, Poindexter recog-nized that the president might feel that he had committed himself to this idea, but, he concluded, 'I strongly feel that you should step back—and do so now.'[156]

When the American Joint Chiefs of Staff met in the immediate aftermath of Reykjavik, they were firmly against the elimination of all ballistic missiles and it fell to their head, Admiral Crowe, to explain to Reagan their objections. He confessed to being 'quite nervous telling the President that his proposal was a terrible idea', but at an NSC meeting on 27 October he read out a statement that had been agreed upon with his colleagues. It included contentions that the elimination of ballistic missiles would endanger the security of the nation and that compensating for their removal would involve substantially *increasing* the military budget. Crowe expected the presi-dent to address the issues he had raised, but Reagan went off at a tangent, saying how much he loved the American military. They were, he said, 'not adequately appreci-ated' and he was constantly trying to get the country to recognize their true value. Whether Reagan had failed to grasp the arguments Crowe was making or whether, having done so, he was deliberately changing the subject to avoid conflict remained unclear.[157]

There were many in the Reagan administration eager to retract much that the president had agreed to in Reykjavik. The major exception was Shultz who was still willing to let Reagan (as peacemonger) be Reagan and who largely shared the presi-dent's instincts on nuclear weapons. Taking a minority position within the adminis-tration, he argued against those who were enamoured of the status quo, saying that he did not see what was 'so good about a world where you can be wiped out in thirty minutes', adding: 'I had never learned to love the bomb—or the ballistic missile that carried it.'[158] The majority in the administration who were alarmed by the sweeping nature of the cuts Reagan had countenanced were forcefully augmented by Margaret Thatcher. In advance of the summit, Shultz had informed Foreign Secretary Geoffrey Howe that given that Reykjavik was a 'preparatory meeting', no agreements were expected.[159]

In fact, what came so close to being agreed at Reykjavik filled Thatcher with horror. For her, 'its failure was the only good thing about it'.[160] She put things more tactfully to Reagan by making points he and Gorbachev had agreed to as if they had entirely emanated from the latter. In a telephone conversation with Reagan just after the summit, she said that 'the Soviet idea to eliminate all nuclear missiles in return for a 10-year agreement to restrict SDI research to the laboratory is extremely dangerous'.[161] For her, it was not the restriction on SDI that was the problem, but the elimination of the missiles. Thatcher's view of the matter was expressed candidly in her memoirs: 'My own reaction when I heard how far the Americans had been prepared to go was as if there had been an earthquake beneath my feet.' She was shocked that 'the whole system of nuclear deterrence which had kept the peace for forty years was close to being abandoned'. Thatcher hated the idea of Britain losing its nuclear weapons and, in her memoirs, she declared that she had always disliked the INF 'zero option'. She believed it left Western Europe vulnerable to massive attack by Warsaw Pact forces, and she had only 'gone along with it in the hope that the Soviets would never accept'.[162]

On this issue Howe and the British Foreign Office were in step with the prime minister. In his memoirs Howe notes that Shultz portrayed Reykjavik as a 'near triumph'. The Foreign Secretary took the contrary view, shared (as he noted) by Thatcher and French President Mitterrand and some other European leaders, that Reagan had 'narrowly avoided falling into a Russian trap, which would have led to American abandonment, within ten years, of their entire strategic deterrent'. The 'supreme irony' about it all, as he noted, was that 'the only reason why Reagan had hung on to his own strategic deterrent (which the alliance cherished) was his deep attachment to the SDI programme (which many in the alliance deeply mistrusted)'.[163]

Even before the Reykjavik summit, it had been agreed that Thatcher would have further discussions with Reagan in 1986 and a meeting at Camp David was arranged for 15 November. In a lengthy note to the president, Poindexter reminded him that 'While she remains one of your most ardent supporters, Mrs. Thatcher is concerned about the strategic implications of your Reykjavik proposals.' She was worried about the UK Trident programme being called into question and, moreover, about this undermining her electoral chances. Since Thatcher's views tallied with Poindexter's, the National Security Adviser was happy to remind the president that the prime minister had called him the day after Reykjavik to express her concerns. Thatcher did not wish to separate the issue of nuclear weapons from that of 'redressing conventional and chemical weapons imbalances'. She also feared that elimination of ballistic missiles would 'undercut her domestic political position', since the British Labour Party at that time was in favour of the UK giving up its nuclear weapons and removing all US nuclear missiles from British soil.[164] Poindexter noted that on other arms control matters, Thatcher remained critical of the 'so-called broad interpretation of the ABM Treaty' and of the United States ceasing to observe the SALT II limits on weaponry.[165]

The British prime minister liked to bypass both the Foreign Office and the State Department bureaucracies in her relationship with Reagan. The NSC normally safeguarded the president's weekends and Reagan was exceedingly sparing about inviting visitors to Camp David, but he sent a handwritten note to his aides agreeing, in Thatcher's case, to her wish for a Saturday meeting at her preferred location. She said she would be accompanied only by the UK ambassador to Washington, Sir Antony Acland, and her private secretary, Charles Powell. A notable absentee was her Foreign Policy Adviser, Sir Percy Cradock, whom she respected but who was a less close confidant than was Powell. A still more prominent absentee was Geoffrey Howe. It was Powell on whom she relied to craft the arguments she would use with Reagan, with the Foreign Secretary playing no part in that process. Howe was kept informed but not invited to contribute arguments to be deployed, even though on Reykjavik he saw eye to eye with the prime minister. Reminding Thatcher that she had 'a bilateral with the Foreign Secretary' coming up, Powell referred to Howe as 'the plump chap with glasses…whom we haven't seen for a long while!'[166]

Thatcher was very demanding. Even after the Americans had arranged separate meetings for her on the Friday with Shultz and Weinberger and a Camp David meeting and working lunch with Reagan on the Saturday, a memo from two NSC officials to Poindexter noted that the British 'would like to start earlier', although no other European head of government could have expected as much top-level time. 'There is also a basic principle', the officials added, for 'the President is, after all, the host'.[167] A briefing memorandum from a senior State Department official for Shultz ahead of his meeting with Thatcher noted that 'her strongly held views point up the challenge which we will face in reconciling the President's proposals with the Prime Minister's positions and her political and financial commitment to Trident and to a nuclear deterrent'.[168] In a note Shultz made on 14 November after 'My meeting with Prime Minister Thatcher' (deposited in the State Department archives), he records her dismay at the absence of advance consultation on the proposal to get rid of ballistic missiles, a policy that would 'undermine the security of Western Europe' and, if pursued, would 'cause you to lose me and the British nation'.[169]

That was strong stuff. With Reagan himself, Thatcher was more measured. Iran–Contra was turning into a major crisis undermining confidence in the president just at the time of her visit. The prime minister flew into Washington the day after Reagan, under pressure, had given his first major speech on this affair. Reagan's expressed intention was to tell the truth, but a detailed specialist study of Iran–Contra described the resulting text as 'an amalgam of misleading and untruthful statements'.[170] Although aware (through GCHQ cooperation with the American NSA) of the president's own role in the affair, Thatcher made clear her personal support for him. She emerged from Camp David well satisfied that she had got what she came for. It included a statement that the United States would continue with its strategic nuclear modernization programme which would embrace Trident.[171] Reagan lost Poindexter over Iran–Contra in that same month and he was replaced as National Security Adviser by Frank Carlucci. Much though he admired and liked Thatcher, Reagan was wary of being at the receiving end of her admonitions. Carlucci, in line with the majority of senior officials in the Reagan administration, tried to ease the president away from his nuclear disarmament proclivities. 'I finally said', Carlucci recalled, 'if you move to get rid of nuclear weapons, Margaret will be on the phone in five minutes.' 'Oh, I don't want that', Reagan replied.[172]

10

BUILDING TRUST (1987)

Nineteen eighty-seven was the year in which it became clearer that Mikhail Gorbachev was committed to reform of the Soviet system. Yet, there was no shortage of influential voices in Washington, not least within the Defense Department and the CIA, as well as politicians in Europe (including German Chancellor Helmut Kohl), still maintaining that no more than stylistic or cosmetic change in Soviet foreign and domestic policy was involved. How far reform might go remained a matter of more serious debate. Among those who saw Gorbachev as a reformer, most assumed that economic reform was his top priority. What became evident in the course of 1987 (and clearer still the following year), however, was that Gorbachev's higher priority was political reform.

Emblematic of the change was the return to Moscow on 23 December 1986 of Andrei Sakharov, the renowned physicist and human rights campaigner, who had been exiled to the city of Gorky (later restored to its old name of Nizhny Novgorod) in 1980. He and his wife, Elena Bonner, an equally active dissident, had been deprived of a telephone in their Gorky apartment throughout their compulsory exile. It became clear that something was up when a phone was installed out of the blue on the evening of 15 December. Sakharov was told to expect a call the following day. When the telephone rang on the 16th, Gorbachev was at the other end of the line to tell the exiled scientist that he and his wife were free to return to their apartment in Moscow and that he should resume his 'patriotic work'.[1] Sakharov made it clear that, for him, any definition of devotion to his country would include continuing to speak his mind about the rights of citizens. Even in the course of this surprise call from Gorbachev, he appealed for an end to the imprisonment of prisoners of conscience. The general secretary's response was that many had already been released and the situation of others had improved.[2]

A sizeable segment of the Soviet intelligentsia held Sakharov in high esteem, both as a scientist and as a man of courage and integrity. Thanks to publicity in the Western mass media and to the attention paid Sakharov by Western politicians—Reagan and Thatcher among them—he had still more fame and support in Europe and North America than in his homeland. The ending of his administrative exile was thus a matter of both domestic and international political significance. In the remaining years of his life, Sakharov, who died suddenly in December 1989, never became an unconditional supporter of Gorbachev—at times he was a sharp critic—but he was a valuable and particularly well-informed ally of the general secretary in his opposition to ballistic missile defence. During his very first trip abroad in 1988, Sakharov told an American audience that 'SDI fosters escalation from conventional to nuclear warfare…encourages dangerous and desperate adventures, and complicates disarmament negotiations.'[3]

Putting Political Reform on the Soviet Agenda

In his major speech to the January plenum of the party's Central Committee, Gorbachev frequently used the word, 'democratization'. It remained unclear how far he would be prepared to take this process, and his own understanding of what was needed became more expansive over time. To invoke the concept of 'democratization' was in itself significant, for it tacitly acknowledged the inadequacy of the 'socialist democracy' that had supposedly already been created in the Soviet Union. Describing 'the democratization of Soviet society' as the 'party's urgent task', Gorbachev also insisted on the need for *glasnost* (transparency) and *otkrytost* (openness). He emphasized the need for a rule of law and the independence of judges and called for reform of the electoral system. Although these aspirations were set out in general rather than specific terms, he concluded his address by calling for a special party conference to be held the following year, whose task would be 'to consider questions of the further democratization of the life of the party and of society as a whole'. The very act of holding such a conference, said Gorbachev, would constitute a serious step in the path of democratization.[4] This was a valid contention, for convening such a major event would impose a deadline by which new positions had to be reached.

Gorbachev's speech to the January plenum focused on domestic rather than foreign policy, but he made up for that with a major speech on 16 February at an international forum in Moscow called 'For a nuclear-free world and for humanism in international relations'.[5] Incongruously, it was being held on the same day as the Soviet Union, in a concession to the Soviet military and in the absence of American agreement to end its testing of nuclear weapons, was resuming its own testing.[6] Gorbachev's speech to the forum pointed in a different direction. In place of the familiar Soviet language of class struggle, irreconcilable ideological differences, and the correlation of forces between 'capitalist and socialist countries', he posited a new age, one in which those who operated in different political and social systems would find ways of working together in an interdependent world. The competition in nuclear arms was, he said, a threat to the continued existence of humanity. Soviet foreign policy would henceforth be determined more than ever by the priority of 'improving our country', and that was linked to a constructive approach to international relations.[7]

Among those invited to participate in the forum was Sakharov who, in a posthumously published volume of memoirs, described it as 'a well-organized undertaking, staged primarily for propaganda purposes'.[8] It was certainly intended to influence international opinion. Nonetheless it represented a further advance by Gorbachev and those who were not in thrall to the Soviet military-industrial complex, but who believed, rather, in the possibility of deep armament reductions and a qualitative improvement in East–West relations. Sakharov himself ensured that not all of the Russian contributors to the forum said the same thing. In one of his speeches, in flat contradiction of the Soviet foreign policy line hitherto (and the position Gorbachev had taken at Reykjavik), Sakharov came out against making deep cuts in intercontinental, medium-range, and battlefield nuclear weapons dependent on reaching an agreement on the imposition of limitations on SDI. He argued that a compromise on SDI could be reached later and, in that way, 'the dangerous deadlock in the negotiations could be overcome'.[9] Sakharov told the forum that any ABM system, including SDI, was of little use against cruise missiles and missiles launched from close range. It could be overcome by increasing the number of operational warheads and of decoys and amounted only to a 'Maginot line in space'. It was both expensive and ineffective.[10]

With his reference to the Maginot line, which Hitler's army had easily circumvented, Sakharov echoed the comparison Geoffrey Howe had made in his March 1985 speech that had incurred the wrath of the more excitable among Britain's cold warriors and had greatly irritated Margaret Thatcher. The prime minister's awareness of the depth of Reagan's attachment to SDI had made her uncharacteristically restrained and subtle when discussing that particular topic with the president.

Sakharov noted in his memoirs, without claiming cause and effect, that two weeks after he had spoken at the forum in favour of decoupling agreement on SDI from the issue of deep cuts in the number of missiles on each side, 'the USSR renounced the package principle for intermediate range missiles', and soon after that 'proposed the elimination of shorter-range missiles'.[11] Gorbachev did, indeed, issue a public statement at the beginning of March in which he said that eliminating medium-range nuclear weapons in Europe would no longer be linked to agreement on SDI.[12] He was coming closer to acceptance of Reagan's zero option, which had been supported by many members of the Washington administration and, reluctantly, by Margaret Thatcher in the UK only because they felt confident that the Soviet Union would never agree to removal of both sides' missiles from the European continent.

The argument for a change of approach that carried most weight with Gorbachev was made by Aleksandr Yakovlev in a lengthy memorandum of 25 February.[13] Yakovlev stressed the importance of doing a deal with Reagan in 1987, while the president still had the requisite political authority. Moreover, he argued, it was always valuable to have 'the maximum freedom of manoeuvre', and the 'package' (the firm linkage of deep cuts in missile numbers to American acceptance of restrictions on the testing and development of SDI) was tying the Soviet side's hands.[14] A public announcement of the untying of the package, if it was made soon, might compensate in the eyes of world opinion for the resumption of Soviet nuclear tests. Gorbachev needed no further convincing. Since this would be both a unilateral concession by the Soviet side and a departure from their previous policy, discussion preceded the Politburo meeting at which the change was approved. Once Gorbachev was persuaded, thanks primarily to Yakovlev, of the need for this concession, others fell into line.

The day after Yakovlev's memo, Gorbachev invited Politburo members to offer their thoughts, but only after telling them that a new level of discussion with Western countries was needed. Getting Politburo members to identify themselves with the policies he espoused (which sometimes led the Soviet leader to make temporary retreats and to return to the proposal at a later date) was one of Gorbachev's political arts. Once the Politburo as a whole had accepted collective responsibility for a policy, they were in a weak position to object to its implementation. The Politburo members were aware that Gorbachev no longer wished his hands to be tied by insistence on a package deal, and in 1987–8 the general secretary's personal as well as institutional authority within the top Soviet leadership team was still very high. Consequently, every Politburo member who spoke, including Yegor Ligachev and Marshal Sergey Sokolov (both later critical of the agreement Gorbachev signed with Reagan in Washington that incorporated this decision of 26 February), supported the separation of an agreement on missile cuts from a compromise on SDI. Andrei Gromyko was among those who spoke up for the change of line as, less surprisingly, did Eduard Shevardnadze and Anatoly Dobrynin.[15] This enabled Gorbachev to sum up: 'So let's untie the package.'[16]

Thatcher and the Puzzle of Perestroika

No Western head of government took greater pains to follow Soviet developments than did Margaret Thatcher. She had no access to Politburo discussions, but she followed Soviet public pronouncements closely. Alarmed by how near Reagan and Gorbachev had been to outlawing nuclear weapons at their Reykjavik summit, but eager to know more about the extent of change that might be underway in Moscow, she prepared assiduously for a visit she made to the Soviet Union in late March 1987. Did perestroika mean that they had embarked in Moscow on really substantive or essentially cosmetic change? The prime minister studied Gorbachev's major speeches, including his lengthy report to the January plenum of the Central Committee which Charles Powell, who had already marked what he took to be the key passages, passed on to her. She also read articles by academics and was briefed by Oleg Gordievsky, the former Soviet KGB agent now in protected exile in the UK. From Gordievsky she learned what would make an impact on the Soviet public if she were given the opportunity to get the facts across to them.[17]

The prime minister noted in her memoirs that 'I was able to have some influence on President Reagan on fundamental issues of alliance policy' and that Gorbachev, therefore, had 'as much reason to do business with me as I with him'. Moreover, she had struck up 'such a good personal relationship with Mr Gorbachev at Chequers before he became leader', it was no surprise that she was 'soon invited to Moscow'.[18] As she noted, 'I prepared myself very thoroughly.' In late February she held an all-day seminar on the Soviet Union at Chequers.[19] This meeting brought together a small group of officials and academics.[20] The only politician present, apart from the prime minister herself, was Foreign Secretary Geoffrey Howe. Sharper differences of opinion and of interpretation were aired at this meeting than at the September 1983 Chequers seminar that had been the starting-point of the attempt by the UK government to step up their engagement with the Soviet Union and Eastern Europe.* The discussion was summarized by Powell early on in his report of the event as reflecting 'a difference between those, principally the experts on the Soviet Union, who were impressed by the scope and energy of Gorbachev's reforms; and those, principally non-specialists, who were not convinced that real change would be either possible or allowed and were sceptical of Gorbachev's motives. To simplify: between enthusiasts and sceptics.' The prime minister's annotations of the report began with her underlining of 'enthusiasts' and 'sceptics'.[21]

Powell's report was more sympathetic to the 'sceptics' than to the 'enthusiasts' and, thus, in line with the views of the prime minister at the time. In February 1987, notwithstanding her liking for Gorbachev personally, Thatcher's sympathies were primarily with those who were wary of the idea that anything substantive could be changing in the world's most powerful Communist state.[22] She was to return, however, from her exhilarating March visit to the Soviet Union closer in her thinking to the 'enthusiasts'. That applied, in particular, to her positive assessment of the extent to which change was already underway in the USSR and to her recognition that Gorbachev was serious about domestic reform. She had yet to be similarly convinced that there was going to be qualitative change in Soviet foreign policy.

Sir Percy Cradock, although he was the prime minister's official foreign policy adviser and though he had good relations both with Thatcher and with his colleague Charles Powell, accepted that it was Powell, her private secretary, who had become her closest adviser. Indeed, he observed, it was sometimes 'difficult to establish where Mrs Thatcher ended and Charles Powell began'.[23] In an apt summing-up of Powell's

---

* As a participant in both of these Chequers seminars, I can attest that the 1987 participants (a minority of whom had also been part of the 1983 group) disagreed among themselves much more radically than did those invited to the meeting held in Andropov's time. Given that there was more secrecy in the Soviet Union of 1983 than of 1987, and that analysis of opaque political developments was correspondingly more difficult then, it would be fair to say that the earlier seminar was the more perspicacious of the two. The very range of opinion expressed in February 1987 was, nevertheless, of value for the prime minister. It avoided the dangers of groupthink.

attributes and significance, Cradock wrote that he was highly efficient at transacting business and displayed intense industry. He would be 'at his desk from six in the morning until late at night'. But he was also a courtier, with 'an easy, engaging manner' and 'a well-developed sense of humour'. One of his assets was the ability to 'sense the wishes of the Prime Minister and to convey her views. His own and hers were often indistinguishable.'[24]

Powell's division of the participants in this Chequers seminar into 'enthusiasts' and 'sceptics' was fair. But when he drew 'conclusions' that 'seemed to command broad assent', he tilted the balance of the argument very firmly in the direction of the 'sceptics'. Indeed, in a covering note to his report, Powell acknowledged that he might have erred 'slightly on the side of conveying too negative a view of what is happening in the Soviet Union'.[25] Among the supposedly broadly accepted conclusions were the view that there was no prospect of 'a pluralist society' being 'just round the corner', 'no sign of adoption of market principles in the Soviet economy', and 'no likelihood that Soviet ideology would change fundamentally'. There would be 'only limited change which fully preserved the powers and guiding role of the Party' and in twenty years or so 'the Soviet system might at best evolve' into 'something resembling Yugoslavia today'.[26] Every political projection in those 'conclusions', several of which were far from commanding the 'broad assent' of the academics present, was spectacularly wrong. The only one which turned out to be even partly true was the point about transition to the market. Even in that instance, market criteria were accepted *in principle* by Gorbachev and his allies in the Soviet leadership by 1990, but they were only to a very limited extent implemented. Political reform throughout the perestroika era outpaced economic reform.

A handwritten note on Charles Powell's report of the Chequers seminar by Michael Lewellyn Smith, the head of the FCO Soviet Department, drew on the classification of the two groups of people made by Cabinet Office Sovietologist Martin Nicholson who attended the seminar.[27] In contrast to the 'enthusiasts' and the 'sceptics', Columbia University specialist on Soviet politics Seweryn Bialer (who had arrived hotfoot from Moscow where he had met senior people in Gorbachev's team) occupied what Nicholson called 'the judicious centre ground'.* It was especially significant that the British ambassador to Moscow, Sir Bryan Cartledge, was, as a result of his day-to-day contacts and observation in Russia, the one government official to

---

* The people Nicholson identified as falling into Powell's category of 'enthusiasts' were, in addition to the author of this book, Ronald Amann of Birmingham University, Peter Frank of Essex University, and Sir Bryan Cartledge, UK ambassador to the Soviet Union. The 'sceptics' were Hugh (later Lord) Thomas, Robert Conquest, who had flown in from the Hoover Institution at Stanford, and the Oxford historian, Sir Michael Howard. The seminar was restricted to fifteen people. The only participants not already mentioned were, on the academic side, Christopher Donnelly, director of the Soviet Studies Research Centre at Sandhurst, and from the officials, Sir Percy Cradock and David Ratford who was Assistant Under-Secretary of State (Europe) in the FCO.

identify with those who were most convinced that significant change was underway. All the more so because Cartledge had throughout his career been regarded as a hard-liner vis-à-vis the Soviet Union and a pessimist about the prospects for positive change. At the Chequers seminar he said, 'Gorbachev is trying to create a moral and psychological revolution. The changes he is seeking are not simply cosmetic but radical.'[28]

If one compares the arguments and projections of the optimists ('enthusiasts') and the pessimists ('sceptics') with what was to occur over the following three years (not to speak of twenty, and the wildly inappropriate Yugoslav comparison), it is clear that everyone present underestimated the subsequent speed and scope of change. Yet, it is no less evident, in the light of imminent developments, that it was the optimists who had come closest to getting things right, that the pessimists were wrong, and that the occupier of the 'judicious centre ground' was, at least, not as far off the mark as were the sceptics. The Polish-American scholar Bialer's views were, in fact, much closer to those of the optimists than to the pessimists. At the seminar he said that, speaking with pro-reform officials in Moscow, he had put all the arguments against the likelihood of democracy to them—the weight of Russian history (no experience of democracy), the legacy of Lenin, and so on—and got the reply that democracy has to start somewhere, 'even if in England it was with Magna Carta and in Russia only now!'[29] Bialer's relative optimism had emerged still more clearly in his private briefing of the prime minister on his Moscow conversations two days ahead of the Chequers seminar. In that conversation, Bialer said that until his most recent visit to the Soviet Union he had been 'deeply sceptical about the prospects of significant change and reform', but now 'he had radically revised his opinion'.[30]

The prime minister took these views on board but was also much influenced by Robert Conquest, a seminar participant whom she had known for years, and who was, by some distance, the most sceptical of the Soviet specialists about the possibility of serious reform in the Soviet Union, although the non-expert Hugh Thomas was still more dismissive of the idea that substantial change could be underway. Conquest's position was more nuanced than Thomas's, and succinctly expressed in an article written shortly after the Chequers seminar, published in a symposium in the American journal, *The National Interest*, in which 'eight leading authorities on Soviet affairs from both sides of the Atlantic' were asked 'What's Happening in Moscow?' Conquest wrote that 'Gorbachev stands for radical reforms *within* the system—that is reforms which are not really radical' and opined that '"democratization" will be largely cosmetic'.[31] Writing in the same symposium, Alec Nove* wryly observed that

---

* Nove, a notable contributor to the September 1983 Chequers seminar, was invited by the prime minister to participate in the February 1987 meeting. He would have been an important addition to the ranks of those who detected serious change underway in the Soviet Union, but, based as he was in California during that semester, he felt obliged to decline the invitation.

the same people who believed that 'the Soviet Union is an expansionist monster in its very essence unless and until there is a fundamental change in the system' simultaneously insisted that fundamental change in such a system was impossible. Therefore, 'any change that has actually occurred cannot be fundamental because it has occurred'.[32]

Thatcher heard a wide variety of views on the scope and potential of Soviet change and consulted widely before her visit to the USSR, including with other Western leaders, although less so on this occasion with Reagan than with others. 'I knew President Reagan's mind', she said, 'and had, I knew, his confidence. I therefore limited myself to sending him a lengthy message.'[33] And it was only a very few months since she had given Reagan the benefit of her post-Reykjavik thoughts at Camp David. She made a point, however, of meeting separately with François Mitterrand and Helmut Kohl just five days before setting off for Moscow on 28 March. The prime minister and the French president saw eye to eye on nuclear weapons. Mitterrand, Charles Powell informed the FCO, had said that 'the point to get across to Mr Gorbachev was that in practice all Soviet strategic weapons were capable of striking Western Europe; and that if Europe were asked to give up its nuclear weapons, then the Soviet Union must logically give up all of theirs too. Since this was obviously not feasible, we should make clear from the outset that the de-nuclearisation of Europe was simply not on the agenda.'[34] On the prospects for change in the Soviet Union, Mitterrand told Thatcher that Gorbachev was trying to have it both ways—searching for reforms which would make the Soviet economy more efficient while preserving 'the Leninist system' and he doubted that was tenable. But he believed that Gorbachev was prepared to take risks to achieve results and that internal change would be accompanied by changes in Soviet foreign policy, notably in Afghanistan and in the Middle East.[35]

Thatcher later remarked that one of Mitterrand's 'shrewdest and most perceptive observations was that the Soviet leader would find that "when you change the form, you are on the way to changing the substance"'.[36] The German Chancellor, in contrast, found no such grounds for optimism. Kohl had not yet met Gorbachev and was to be kept waiting until October 1988 for an invitation to Moscow on account of an ill-advised interview he had given in the autumn of 1986 in which he described Gorbachev as a propagandist of the 'Goebbels type'.[37] The prime minister's own notes from her conversation with Kohl make clear that the German Chancellor remained much more negative about Soviet developments than was Mitterrand. Gorbachev was running high risks, Kohl said (and in that he was right), but he wanted a 'modern Communist system, not a democratic system', and the Soviet Union had become 'more anti-religious than ever before'.[38] This last point was particularly ill-informed.

The prime minister was determined to be the supreme foreign policy-maker in British government. She even attempted to prevent Howe from accompanying her to

Moscow, but had to give way on this in the face of strong protests from the Foreign Office.[39] Nevertheless, for her main meetings with Gorbachev, she made sure that Howe would be meeting Shevardnadze at the same time in another building.[40] Prior to the Soviet visit, she ignored the suggestion of the Foreign Secretary that she should focus on getting 'the Russians and Americans to sink their differences over SDI', and the draft of a Howe article, written in the Foreign Office for publication in the Soviet magazine, New Times, was much too conciliatory for her taste. She was offended also by Howe giving himself equal billing with her by writing of their impending Soviet trip that 'Mrs Thatcher and I see this visit as an important opportunity.' She circled 'Mrs Thatcher and I' and wrote 'No no no'.[41] Her disdain for the FCO was not diminished when she discovered that they had chosen as her official gift for Gorbachev two silver-handled hairbrushes. 'But', she objected, 'he's completely bald.'[42]

Thatcher's 'Most Fascinating and Most Important Foreign Visit'

Margaret Thatcher spent five days in the USSR, arriving on Saturday 28 March to a welcoming ceremony in the Kremlin and ending on 1 April when she flew to Tbilisi in the morning, spent the day in Soviet Georgia, and left on a direct flight to London late that night. The prime minister's visit was extensively covered by state television. Her biggest impact on Soviet citizens was in a lengthy and uncensored TV interview in which, it was generally agreed, she got much the better of her three Soviet interviewers. While she and Gorbachev argued fiercely at times, each came away with enhanced respect for the other. Thatcher's arguments made Gorbachev better aware than he already was of how the Soviet Union was perceived in Britain and in Western Europe. He appreciated the extent to which the prime minister had so comprehensively informed herself about recent Soviet developments and policy pronouncements. Although ideologically Thatcher was close to Reagan and very different in her outlook from Gorbachev, they had some attributes in common. Each liked to talk at length (while being capable also of listening attentively and absorbing information). They combined an attachment to a number of firmly held principles with mastery of detail, and took pleasure from vigorous debate. In those various respects, Thatcher and Gorbachev were more akin to each other than either of them was to Reagan.*

The prime minister's speech at a Kremlin banquet on 30 March was a mixture of the conciliatory and the outspoken. Arms control agreements, she said, depended less on the skill of negotiators than on how governments and peoples in East and West viewed each other, what they believed about the other's intentions and their readiness to honour commitments, and on 'how they judge each other's long-term

---

* Over lunch, during the break in the Chequers seminar of 27 February 1987, Mrs Thatcher said that Gorbachev was 'the only Soviet politician I can have a good argument with'.

Figure 8 Margaret Thatcher, who made a big impression during her 1987 visit to the Soviet Union, being greeted warmly in Soviet Georgia. Behind her and a Georgian official are (L to R) Charles Powell (private secretary to the prime minister), Anatoly Kovalev (Soviet First Deputy Foreign Minister), British Ambassador to the USSR Sir Bryan Cartledge, and interpreter Richard Pollock (behind Thatcher, face partly obscured).

objectives in the wider world'. She said that the extent to which the Soviet government met the commitments it had 'freely undertaken in the Helsinki Final Act' would determine the confidence placed in them by other countries, as would their readiness to withdraw their armies from Afghanistan. She attempted to portray SDI in a less threatening light by emphasizing the commitment (made at Camp David) that 'any deployment would be a matter for genuine negotiation'.[43] In her Kremlin speech, Thatcher made her usual defence of nuclear weapons, saying that the knowledge of how to make them could not be erased and that conventional weapons 'have never been enough to deter war'. She concluded with a flourish: 'There is a famous passage in Shakespeare which speaks of a tide in the affairs of men which when taken at the flood leads on to fortune; perhaps Mr General Secretary, you have already caught that tide, you have certainly embarked upon a great endeavour and we most earnestly wish you and your people well. Your success would bring in other tides on other shores far beyond your own.'[44]

Earlier that day Thatcher and Gorbachev had met for discussion which overran because each got so involved in the arguments, and the prime minister returned somewhat late to the British Embassy for a lunch at which she hosted Andrei Sakharov and Elena Bonner and other former dissidents whose rights to criticize were on the verge of being accorded official Soviet recognition. Thatcher urged them to continue to support Gorbachev when the going got tough, saying that 'the costs of reforms would be apparent long before the benefits'.[45] While still suspicious of Soviet foreign policy, she identified with Gorbachev as a 'fellow reformer'. In the view of her foreign policy adviser Cradock, from the time of this Moscow visit onwards, Thatcher became 'dangerously attached to Gorbachev in his domestic role', so much so that 'the Soviet leader, at least in his internal capacity, was becoming something of an icon'.[46]

This would not have been immediately obvious to Gorbachev when Thatcher engaged him in hammer-and-tongs argument during their morning meeting. They swapped horror stories of the crimes of the other side and argued about the dangers posed by their opponents' weaponry. When Thatcher said that Western Europe was not a very large territory and that the Soviet intermediate and medium-range missiles posed a huge danger to it, Gorbachev responded that NATO had 1,100 planes and 300 rockets, to which Thatcher said that missiles and planes should not be compared, and that for Europe the issue of shorter-range battlefield missiles was also of great importance. Gorbachev replied: 'But we are ready to resolve that question', at which point Thatcher switched to the attack on chemical weapons before moving on to make a qualified defence of SDI. She emphasized the vulnerability of Europe in comparison with the United States which was an ocean away, bringing up the Soviet invasions of Hungary in 1956 and Czechoslovakia in 1968. Gorbachev, in retaliation, mentioned the Falkland Islands, Chad, and Nicaragua, and got a predictably dusty response on the Falklands. They were, said Thatcher, British lands with a British population. 'They were occupied, and we threw out the occupiers.'[47]

For Anatoly Chernyaev, Gorbachev's close adviser and his notetaker, this was the 'most interesting' of all the many meetings Gorbachev held with foreign politicians and public figures in the course of 1987.[48] The two leaders argued about capitalism, socialism, Communism, and colonialism and at one point, said Chernyaev, 'began going around in circles'. When Gorbachev accused the prime minister of being such an ardent supporter of nuclear weapons that she was prepared to accept the risk of war, she 'became so excited', said Chernyaev, 'that the conversation got completely out of hand. They started to interrupt each other, repeat themselves, assure each other of their best intentions.' Although their arguments were 'particularly heated', this 'strangely enough', added Chernyaev, 'only strengthened their mutual sympathy'.[49]

The meeting between the two leaders, with only notetakers and interpreters present, continued after lunch, with Gorbachev now doing most of the talking.[50] Later in the afternoon, they were joined in a plenary session by their foreign ministers and a larger group. There were further meetings between Gorbachev and Thatcher over dinners, and their parting at the end of the Russian stage of the prime minister's Soviet visit was a cordial one. Gorbachev was accompanied only by his wife. Thatcher's interpreter Richard Pollock saw this as connoting the Gorbachevs' 'sincere personal commitment to the relationship' and possibly also 'Gorbachev's increasing confidence in his own position'.[51] On arms control, observed Pollock, Gorbachev 'seems to devise what he believes are "fair" proposals, try them out (on his interlocutor), but—if rebuffed—not to sulk, but to be willing to think again and possibly modify the proposal'.[52] In his telegram to the FCO, reporting on the visit, British Ambassador Cartledge noted that seven hours of official talks between Thatcher and Gorbachev plus a further four hours over two dinners was an investment of time by the general secretary in a visiting head of government that was 'without precedent'.[53] 'The outstanding characteristic of all the discussions', Cartledge added, 'was the degree of frankness in which both the Prime Minister and Gorbachev felt able to indulge without throwing them off the rails or impairing a personal relationship which, in fact, improved steadily throughout the visit'.[54]

The warmth of the farewells suggested that Gorbachev had been not in the least put out by the prime minister's performance in her television interview which had attracted a huge audience. Many Soviet viewers were delighted by this latest manifestation of glasnost and Thatcher's vigorous rebuttal of Soviet propaganda, while many others were annoyed, not so much with Thatcher as with the home team who had been so thoroughly routed. Cartledge, in his report to the Foreign Office on the prime minister's visit, noted that this 'prime media event' was probably seen 'by a Soviet audience of at least 120 million people'. Although it had been recorded in the late afternoon, it was broadcast uncut at 11 o'clock on the evening of 31 March and 'trailed in advance on the evening news programme'. Among the things that the great majority of Soviet viewers learned for the first time from the interview were that it was their government's deployment of SS-20s which had provoked the stationing of Cruise and Pershing 2 missiles in Western Europe and that the Soviet Union had the only operational anti-ballistic missile system in the world, deployed around Moscow.

The ambassador quoted a senior Soviet Ministry of Foreign Affairs official who told one of his colleagues, 'She walked all over them.' One of Thatcher's interviewers told a Soviet TV chat show that he and his colleagues had received complaints from the public not only that they had been too feeble in rebutting the prime minister's arguments but also, on the contrary, that they had been rude to her by interrupting. Could they not agree, he pleaded, that what had occurred was 'in essence an unprecedented experiment in glasnost by Soviet television'. 'Indeed it was', Cartledge concurred.[55] He had 'no hesitation in describing the visit as historic'. It had 'established a new bench-mark for the quality of East–West dialogue' and would 'remain a reference point of East–West relations'.[56]

Thatcher's own summing-up in her memoirs was that it had been 'quite simply, the most fascinating and most important foreign visit I made'.[57] The British Embassy in Washington reported on the extensive publicity given to the visit by the mass media in the United States. The Moscow correspondents of several American

Figure 9 Gorbachev with his two most influential aides, Anatoly Chernyaev (on right) and Georgy Shakhnazarov (centre).

newspapers were joined in Russia by their London correspondents. The *New York Times* comment, as summarized by the British Embassy, was that Thatcher 'returned home with three messages: first, that there was hope for a meeting between Reagan and Gorbachev and an agreement on medium-range missiles by the end of this year; second, that Gorbachev was serious about internal change; and third, that Gorbachev could be trusted'. They also noted the prime minister's 'bravura 50 minute performance' on Soviet TV. The same newspaper observed that the visit had stretched the boundaries of glasnost and raised 'the possibility that Mr Gorbachev may have planned all along to use his outspoken visitor to help him define the ground rules for a new kind of public discourse'.[58]

In a letter of 2 April to Gorbachev, thanking him for the welcome she received and for his 'great kindness in devoting so much time to it', the prime minister returned to the theme of trust. After saying that she wished Gorbachev well with his policies of openness, restructuring, and democratization, she added that they 'point the way to the greater trust and confidence which we both want to see'. She told him that her visit had been 'an exhilarating experience' and that she hoped they could 'continue to communicate directly with each other on matters of concern to us both'.[59]

Gorbachev, in turn, was very satisfied with Thatcher's visit. In a conversation with senior colleagues and advisers—Yakovlev, Shevardnadze, Dobrynin, Chernyaev, and Vadim Medvedev—on her last day, by which time she had departed for Georgia, he recounted the sharpness of their exchanges on nuclear weapons. He had told her that the logic of her position that they guaranteed a country's peace and security was that every country should be free to have them and that they should, accordingly, spread throughout the world which would create a 'terrible situation'.[60] But, in spite of the differences in their views, Gorbachev added, Thatcher had been pleasantly surprised by the reception she got from the Soviet public whose sympathy for her had grown still more after her TV appearance, for 'she won the battle of the screen'. For his part, Gorbachev said that he very much valued the directness of their conversation and he was left feeling respect and even goodwill towards her.[61]

Gorbachev spoke at length also in the Politburo about Thatcher's visit. He told the members what the prime minister had said about the Soviet Union undermining trust, citing the invasions of Hungary, Czechoslovakia, and Afghanistan. She was, moreover, 'sure we have not given up the Brezhnev doctrine'.* Rather than simply dismiss out of hand Thatcher's concerns, as his predecessors would have done, Gorbachev said, 'This is really something to ponder, comrades. We can't just brush it aside.'[62] In Chernyaev's view, Thatcher's visit had another significant consequence— Gorbachev's 'sharp turn toward Western Europe'.[63] The general secretary told the Politburo that nothing could be decided without Europe, and that 'we haven't studied Europe enough and don't know it very well'. The Soviet leadership needed to see Europe in all its diversity, and to realize that 'Western Europe is our basic partner.' He mooted the idea of setting up a European Research Centre.[64] Shortly afterwards, an Institute of Europe was duly set up under the auspices of the Soviet Academy of Sciences.

Shultz's Battles in Washington and Progress in Moscow

While Gorbachev and Thatcher were further strengthening their good relations, the Reagan administration in the early months of 1987 was in some disarray. Frank Carlucci had succeeded John Poindexter as National Security Advisor in December and there was a tussle between him and the Secretary of State. Shultz was wary of Carlucci's desire to be the principal foreign policy coordinator and of the NSC penchant for back-channel communications of their own with Moscow. The two men got off to a bad start in early January. Shultz told Carlucci that when Gorbachev became Soviet leader, the CIA had 'said he was "just talk", just another Soviet attempt to deceive us'. They had insisted that the Soviet system was incapable of being

---

* The 'Brezhnev doctrine' gained its name from the justification that the Soviet leadership produced for their armed intervention in Czechoslovakia in August 1968 to halt and reverse the radical political reforms being pursued by the leadership of the Czechoslovak Communist Party, urged on by a revitalized society. The 'doctrine' stated that the Soviet Union had a right and duty to intervene 'to defend socialism' wherever 'socialism' (as defined in Moscow) was under threat.

changed, although it soon became evident that it was, in fact, changing.[65] Shultz detected that, with his 'attack on the agency', he had offended Carlucci who was a former deputy director of the CIA. For his own part, Shultz was unhappy about what he took to be Carlucci's desire 'to rebuild the NSC staff into analysts, policymakers, arbiters, and operators all rolled into one'.[66] A more sympathetic account of Carlucci's activities viewed them as a necessary reorganization of 'the battered NSC staff' and an attempt 'to find a way to cope with the rival baronies at Defense and State'.[67] There was, however, little sign of a slackening of the tension between the State Department, on the one hand, and Defense and the CIA, on the other. The only good news for Shultz in Washington was the replacement in February 1987 of Donald Regan by Howard Baker as White House Chief of Staff. Baker was the recently retired Senate majority leader and he and Shultz had enjoyed friendly relations ever since the days of the Nixon administration.[68]

Even within the American military establishment, there were some sharp disagreements, especially over SDI. General James Abrahamson, who was in charge of the programme invariably exuded optimism about it, and Caspar Weinberger talked up the progress that was being made, especially when he was briefing Reagan. At one point, after announcing the results of some tests, he said, 'Mr President, your dream is here.' When he heard this, the Chairman of the Joint Chiefs of Staff, Admiral Bill Crowe, who was sceptical both about SDI and the credibility of the tests, wrote that he thought he was 'going to choke'. After Weinberger started calling for early deployment, Crowe 'flatly contradicted him in public, telling the Congress in so many words that there was nothing to deploy'.[69]

Crowe was also firmly opposed to the broad interpretation of the ABM Treaty which would allow greater freedom to develop anti-ballistic missile defences. There was support for his position in Congress where Senator Sam Nunn, who became Chairman of the Armed Services Committee of the Senate in 1987 (and retained that post until 1995), was an influential opponent of the broad interpretation, and his stance mattered, since Congress held the purse-strings. The Joint Chiefs of Staff, who had earlier been frustrated by their lack of control over the SDI project, succeeded in 1987 in bringing it within the purview of the Defense Acquisitions Board, which was able to scrutinize progress. They found that there was little prospect of it moving beyond a research programme and that, on 'optimistic' assumptions, it would 'cost billions upon billions of dollars and still let 70 percent of Soviet missiles through'.[70]

Shultz was an especially important SDI sceptic, though as noted earlier, prepared to use it as a bargaining chip. He wanted to build on what had almost been achieved at Reykjavik, although the domestic political climate in early 1987 was not propitious. Whereas Thatcher could rely on strong support in Britain for the improvement in UK–Soviet relations her visit to Moscow had appeared to presage—with the main criticism in Parliament from the Opposition benches being that she had been excessively intransigent, rather than too accommodating*—US–Soviet relations had been soured by another spy scandal. There was concern also that the Reagan administration had been so weakened by the Iran–Contra affair—which had dragged on for months—that it would be in a poor bargaining position if it re-engaged with the Soviet Union. Iran–Contra had cast a long shadow. 'A big problem', noted Shultz in his memoirs, 'was that President Reagan kept saying—and he truly believed it—that we had not traded arms for hostages. I had to keep trying to make him realize that indeed we had.'[71] Shultz said he 'knew that a wounded president would have a big impact on my own effectiveness'.[72]

Shultz was unhappy with the NSC's use of Senator Ted Kennedy and especially his aide Larry Horowitz for 'back channel communications' with Moscow. With Reagan's approval, the Secretary of State appointed Max Kampelman, the coordinator of US–Soviet arms control negotiations at Geneva, to be the person who would perform that informal role, and he would be reporting to Shultz. It was 'idiotic', Shultz believed, that Carlucci 'wanted to work with former Ambassador Dobrynin in a separate U.S.–Soviet channel and wanted to travel to Moscow to conduct negotiations'. He told Mike Armacost, the Undersecretary of State for Political Affairs, that the White House was 'going to screw everything up again!'[73] Reagan's agreement that Kampelman and his Soviet counterpart Yuli Vorontsov would form the only private channel did not resolve the problem of massive disagreements among key players in the administration. When Weinberger opened a discussion among them by 'saying, "Max [Kampelman] and the Communists want to…" I hit the roof', wrote Shultz, 'and so did Max'.[74]

Like others, Carlucci had his reservations about Suzanne Massie's rapport with Reagan and foresaw risks if she were to be used as an informal channel between Reagan and Soviet officials. Whereas Massie's influence on Reagan usefully reinforced the president's own inclination to engage with the Soviet Union, she had overstepped the mark by proposing that she become US ambassador to the Soviet Union. This was never on the cards and when the pre-eminently qualified Matlock was appointed to the post, Massie's fallback request was for Reagan to meet with her 'a little more regularly than every six months or so' and to give her 'a specific task to accomplish', since, as she put it in a letter to the president, 'I believe that Russians trust me and I could make a contribution.'[75] Carlucci reminded Reagan about Massie's ambassadorial ambitions and said that while it was fine for the president to be talking with her, giving her 'specific tasks' was another matter. Carlucci was sure the Soviets would use her and that this was potentially dangerous.[76]

---

* In particular, Thatcher was criticized by the Leader of the Opposition, Neil Kinnock, for her attempts to thwart both Reagan's and Gorbachev's desire to get rid of nuclear weapons. Kinnock asked in the House of Commons whether the prime minister still maintained 'her belief that a world without nuclear weapons would be less stable and more dangerous than one with them, despite the clearly different convictions of both our ally and her new friend' ('Soviet Union, Prime Minister's Visit', https://www.margaretthatcher.org/document/106787, pp. 1–19, at p. 5).

In the face of opposition from both within and outside the administration, but with the crucial support of the president, Shultz went to Moscow for talks with Gorbachev and Shevardnadze in mid-April. After an American marine sergeant, who had formed an unwise relationship with a Soviet young woman working for the KGB, compromised some of the security of the US Embassy, the United States prohibited Soviet citizens from working in that building (even though they were excluded from the more sensitive parts). The American staff were left with all the routine tasks that had been performed by 260 Soviet employees. The US ambassador to Moscow, Arthur Hartman, was sharply criticized by George Bush, among others, for the security breaches, with the vice-president recalling a cable Hartman 'had sent some months earlier disparaging the criticism of embassy management'.[77] All this caused a furore in American political circles but, as Matlock, who succeeded Hartman as American ambassador in Moscow in the spring of 1987, later pointed out, any information Soviet agents got via the marine sergeant was trivial in comparison with what they were receiving directly from their American moles in Washington, particularly Aldridge Ames in the CIA and Robert Hanssen in the FBI, as well as from a CIA defector to Moscow, Edward Lee Howard.[78]

In fact, between 1985 and 1986 the United States lost every covert intelligence source it had in the Soviet Union.[79] Attempting to explain this devastating loss for American intelligence, and more drastic consequences for those arrested, American security agencies focused on the marines who had been guarding the embassy. There were stories about them having given the KGB access to the embassy at night which turned out to be untrue. A confession of collaboration with the KGB had been extracted from a second marine by the Naval Investigative Service by methods, said Matlock, 'just short of torture'. He had written his 'confession' under duress and retracted it immediately.[80] It was not until years later that Americans learned that it was the Washington moles, Ames and Hanssen, who had betrayed the US's Soviet agents and sources.[81] The scandal of the supposed infiltration of the embassy became, however, the main story at the time, and Congress supplied 'unlimited funds' for shipping back home under close guard every sensitive piece of equipment in the embassy for detailed examination.[82] Washington was 'boiling mad', according to Shultz, and the head of the National Security Agency, General William Odom, said there was no way the US could provide secure communication facilities for Shultz in time for his Soviet visit.[83] In this atmosphere the Senate passed a resolution by an overwhelming majority advising the Secretary of State not to go to Moscow. Reagan, however, supported Shultz's desire to resume discussions with Gorbachev and Shevardnadze. In doing so, he was at odds with his party. Only ten Republican Senators opposed the resolution calling on Shultz to stay at home.[84]

Shultz flew first to Helsinki where he always stopped on his way to Moscow. Ambassador Matlock joined him there, and they discussed the forthcoming Moscow meetings without having to worry about being bugged. The Secretary of State arrived in Moscow on 13 April and had a meeting the same day with Shevardnadze. Conscious that his Soviet counterpart was a proud Georgian, Shultz got a translation made of 'Georgia on My Mind' (Georgia, for this purpose, moving from the American south to the Caucasus) and persuaded Matlock and other Russian speakers from the American Embassy to sing it at the lunch Shevardnadze hosted. The Soviet Foreign Minister professed to be delighted. Although both Shultz and Shevardnadze knew that sociability alone would not resolve the problems that divided their countries, they developed a mutually respectful and increasingly warm relationship which, said Matlock, 'helped them weather potential crises'. This had a knock-on effect lower down the diplomatic hierarchy, so that by 1989, according to Matlock, American and Soviet diplomats were working in many areas 'virtually as colleagues'. Matlock added that this 'could never have occurred unless Gorbachev had decided to open Soviet society and to begin respecting what he called "the human factor" in political relations'.[85]

Shultz met with Gorbachev on 14 April and began by handing over a letter to him from Reagan. It referred only obliquely to the spy furore as 'a recent incident that has caused problems between our two countries'. Reagan welcomed 'the improved dialogue on arms reductions' and 'some progress on human rights', while expressing concern about lack of progress on regional issues, especially Afghanistan. He wrote that military competition stemmed from 'fundamental mistrust between our governments' and said that if 'we are able to eliminate that distrust, arms reductions negotiations will be much easier'.[86] This was almost the exact opposite of the message he delivered to American private sector supporters of SDI the previous year when, as noted in the previous chapter, he compared the suggestion that 'trust and understanding' would lead to arms agreements to belief 'in the tooth fairy'.[87]

The emphasis on trust was, however, in line with the view of Shultz, who was accompanied at this Kremlin meeting by Assistant Secretary for European Affairs Rozanne Ridgeway and by Paul Nitze and Matlock. Sitting alongside Gorbachev were Shevardnadze, Dobrynin, and the latter's successor as Soviet ambassador to the United States, Yury Dubinin. When the conversation turned to detailed argument on arms reductions, they were joined by Marshal Akhromeyev. The meeting got off to an argumentative start. Gorbachev echoed Reagan by observing that there was a 'shortage of trust' and Shultz brought up the spying scandals. Gorbachev saw this as an artificial issue because both sides were doing it.[88] Shultz retorted that when seventy Senators had voted against him coming to Moscow, there was nothing minor about the problem. The account in Shultz's memoirs suffers, according to Matlock, from imprecision. When the Secretary of State asked Gorbachev if he could tell the president that 'it is against your policy and rules to allow your intelligence agencies to physically penetrate our embassy building', Gorbachev (in Shultz's version) said 'Yes, that is precisely so.' Matlock, who was at the meeting, recorded in his notes Gorbachev's reply as 'Ya dumayu, chto eto tak', a somewhat less categorical 'I think that is so.'[89] In reality the KGB had not physically penetrated the sensitive parts of the existing American Embassy in Moscow for several years. They had started installing a sophisticated listening system in the new embassy building that was being constructed, but that work remained incomplete. Matlock later wrote that Gorbachev's best response would have been to say, 'Yes, we tried to bug the new embassy, but you caught us before we finished the job. You tried to bug ours, but we fixed it. So what else is new, and what's the big deal?'[90]

When they got on to armaments, Gorbachev tried to get Shultz to agree with him that the two sides already had a rough military parity, but Shultz stressed areas where the Soviet Union had an advantage and had modernized their forces, thus justifying Reagan's 'stepping up of U.S. efforts in this sphere'.[91] The Soviet transcript quotes Gorbachev responding: 'You are saying that you feel especially threatened by our ICBMs. We feel even more threatened by your side's SLBMs because they are less vulnerable, equipped with MIRVs [multiple independently targetable re-entry vehicles], and very accurate. And even though you have undermined the last mechanism limiting the strategic arms race—the SALT II Treaty—we abide by its limits.'[92] Strategic parity could be maintained, Gorbachev went on to insist, by reducing the number of all offensive strategic weapons by 50 per cent.[93]

On intermediate and shorter-range missiles with nuclear warheads, Shultz and Gorbachev made more progress. Referring to INF, Gorbachev reminded Shultz that at Reykjavik the US had agreed to limits of 100 on each side globally and none in Europe, and was that still the case? Shultz confirmed that the US did and would agree to that, although they would prefer 'zero globally', for 'verification of zero was easier and more certain than of any finite number'.[94] He pointed out that he was speaking only for the United States, being aware that not all of America's European allies would enthusiastically agree with the elimination of all intermediate-range nuclear weapons. Shultz reported the results of his meeting to Reagan by saying that he had 'consolidated all of the concessions we had achieved at Reykjavik on INF and START and had made great progress on short-range INF missiles'. When the president asked about the likely reaction of European allies, Shultz said some of them wanted to keep a certain number of the American missiles that had been installed (and though he did not mention her name, Thatcher was among those he had in mind, as was the German government which had survived a domestic political battle to have these missiles on its territory), but, he added, they 'would have a hard time arguing for something other than zero'.[95] More questionable was Shultz's assumption that Gorbachev (as distinct from many in the Soviet military-industrial complex) was less keen on these arms reductions than was the American side.

Shultz had prepared a useful digression in his talks with Gorbachev. In an interlude from the argumentative discussions, he unrolled charts on the predicted growth of different countries up to the year 2000 and conducted an informal seminar on the impact of scientific and technological developments—more specifically, on the 'information revolution'. The key was going to be knowledge-based productivity, even in defence, and, Shultz suggested, the Marxist dichotomy between capital and labour was becoming obsolete, for the most important capital had increasingly become human capital. Gorbachev, being interested in ideas, 'interjected occasionally' but 'listened carefully' and was fully 'engaged and interested'. He told the Secretary of State: 'We should have more of this kind of talk.'[96]

A highlight of Shultz's visit was an uncensored interview on Soviet TV. According such an opportunity to Margaret Thatcher had set a precedent and it would have been a real setback for US–Soviet relations had Shultz's interview been cut when hers was not. Like Thatcher's, the Secretary of State's recorded interview was broadcast in full. Shultz's translated remarks included, 'The Afghan people want you to leave their country; they do not want your armed forces to be in their country. How many soldiers do you keep there, 120,000?'[97]

Later in 1987 Shultz discovered that what he called 'the great marine scandal' had been overblown. 'Seven months after my extraordinary April visit to Moscow', he noted, it turned out that 'the KGB had *not* penetrated our embassy, after all'. What must Gorbachev and Shevardnadze have thought was going on in Washington? 'The marine spy scandal', wrote Shultz, had 'been whipped up and fueled by investigative zealots interacting with a media and Congress all too ready to believe, even relish, wrongdoing.'[98] It was another illustration of the opposition to engaging with Gorbachev's Soviet Union which lasted throughout the Reagan administration. The policy Shultz pursued, with Reagan's support, was far from being a unified position within the administration and Reagan did not exert the type of control over it that Thatcher maintained within her government. Hard-liners within the administration had their allies among conservative commentators in the mass media who were adept at finding reasons for remaining intransigent.

Shoring up the Domestic Base—Gorbachev and Reagan

Gorbachev had domestic hard-line opposition of his own, although it was far less outwardly visible in 1987 than it became later in his leadership. He was prepared to make deeper cuts in the Soviet military arsenal for the sake of removing American nuclear missiles from Europe, and for the larger aim of producing a qualitative change in the East–West relationship, than the defence sector found acceptable, but an unpredictable event in May offered him the opportunity to strengthen his political supremacy over the military. The chance occurrence was the arrival of a foreign single-engine plane in the heart of Moscow. The young West German pilot Matthias Rust (who was still a few weeks short of his nineteenth birthday) had refuelled in Helsinki and then cut off communication with air traffic controllers. His flight was uninterrupted by Soviet air defences and he landed the light aircraft on the edge of Red Square. Rust declared that he was on a bridge-building peace mission, and he certainly posed no threat to the Soviet Union (other than the risk of unintentionally crashing his plane in the Soviet capital). Many Russians were amused by his distinctly unusual method of travelling to within a stone's throw from the Kremlin, but neither the Soviet political nor the military leadership found it funny. Rust was arrested and imprisoned, although pardoned and released after fourteen months.

His unscheduled flight acutely discomfited the Soviet Ministry of Defence in particular, and Gorbachev made the most of their embarrassment. Summoned to the Politburo, the Chief of the Air Defences, Aleksandr Koldunov, admitted that he learned about the aircraft only after its arrival, which led Gorbachev to ask him if it was the Moscow traffic police who informed him.[99] Koldunov was removed from his post and, more importantly, so was the Minister of Defence (and candidate member of the Politburo), Marshal Sergey Sokolov, who had been resistant to what he viewed as the excessive flexibility of Gorbachev's foreign and defence policy. Sokolov was replaced by General Dmitry Yazov who was much more reluctant to challenge Gorbachev—until, very late in the day, when he was recruited by those attempting to overthrow the Soviet leader in August 1991 (and who succeeded merely in hastening the end of the Soviet state).[100]

The head of the International Department of the Central Committee, Anatoly Dobrynin, who himself grew increasingly critical of the radicalism of Gorbachev's domestic political reforms and of his foreign policy, noted that Gorbachev had initially been very wary of the military and careful to avoid a direct clash with them, but Rust's unheralded arrival in central Moscow played into his hands. Gorbachev, in Dobrynin's words, 'made perfect use of the military's state of confusion and its badly damaged prestige'. Yazov 'knew little about disarmament talks, and had nothing to do with them', so Gorbachev accomplished 'a quiet coup'.[101] Dobrynin added that an additional hundred or so conservative military leaders 'who also opposed Gorbachev's reforms and his concessions to the Americans' were pushed into retirement, but 'the military establishment by and large remained discontented with Gorbachev, and this would show time and again'.[102]

As Andrei Grachev, a foreign policy adviser to the general secretary, observed, Gorbachev's reaction to the startling incursion into Soviet airspace, while untypically harsh, was 'a calculated political move intended to curtail the excessive political role that the military had acquired'.[103] Yazov, Grachev noted, showed little ambition 'to interfere in the political debate, even over aspects of foreign policy that directly affected the strategic situation of the USSR'. The Chief of Staff Marshal Akhromeyev, however, continued to do so and Yazov largely ceded the responsibility of voicing the military view of the disarmament process to him.[104]

In the United States there were many more overt critics of improving relations with the rival superpower.* Conservative Republicans were worried by what they saw as

---

* The USSR was still perceived as a superpower at that time and in the military sphere it was, being the only country capable of utterly destroying the United States within a few hours. Economically, it was far from a superpower, as its civilian economy was backward and the country relied excessively on its rich natural resources, making its exports susceptible to the fluctuating world price of oil and gas (which was declin-

George Shultz's willingness to do a deal with the Soviet leadership and they believed that he was wielding an excessive influence over Reagan. Columnists William Buckley and William Safire and actor Charlton Heston were among those worried that the president might be going 'soft on Communism' in order to secure an arms deal.[105] Even Richard Nixon and Henry Kissinger, more conservative 'realists' than ideologues, opposed Reagan's desire for an INF Treaty and were concerned that he would be outwitted by Gorbachev. Reagan agreed to Nixon's request for a meeting with him, at which the former president did his best to undermine Reagan's faith in Shultz. Nixon proposed that Reagan strengthen his standing with his own 'Hawks', and at the same time win concessions, by telling Gorbachev that he had to pursue a 'real conventional balance' because of them. Nixon told Reagan that he did not have a high regard for Shultz as Secretary of State. He was a 'great Secretary of Treasury', but whoever became head of the State Department was 'brown nosed by FSO's [Foreign Service Officers]'. Moreover, said Nixon, Shultz had 'never negotiated' with 'commies'.[106]

Given that this Reagan–Nixon meeting took place in late April 1987, by which time Shultz had been Secretary of State for almost five years (during the first three of which Gromyko was Soviet Foreign Minister), what Nixon said about Shultz's lack of negotiating experience with Communists made little sense. Nixon, according to Carlucci's notes of the meeting, told Reagan that 'I don't buy nonsense that you will make bad treaty', but that he needed to 'make a strong stand' and not facilitate 'opposition to the right' of him in the United States.[107] Later, in his own private reflections on his conversation with the president, Nixon struck an entirely different note on Reagan's capacity. He wrote, 'There is no way he [Reagan] can ever be allowed to participate in a private meeting with Gorbachev.'[108]

In the early part of 1987, support for the view that Reagan and Shultz were too keen on nuclear disarmament was reinforced when Fritz Ermath of the CIA succeeded Jack Matlock as the Soviet specialist within the NSC. Much later Ermath was to admit to being wrong in thinking that 'this kindly old gentleman', as he described Reagan, was going to be 'suckered' by Gorbachev.[109] As the year went on, the balance of influence within the administration switched again. CIA director Bill Casey had been ill since December 1986 and died in May. He was succeeded by William Webster, who was moved from heading the FBI. Initially a Carter appointee, Webster had less influence with Reagan than had Casey and his appointment meant that Robert Gates, the deputy director of the CIA and a Soviet specialist deeply sceptical of the extent of change in the Soviet Union, had been passed over for the top post. When Weinberger resigned as Defense Secretary in November and was succeeded by Carlucci, with General Colin Powell taking over from Carlucci as National Security Advisor, the

ing during the second half of the 1980s). Politically, however, the early years of perestroika saw the Soviet Union winning new friends abroad, with a shift in public opinion in a number of democracies towards viewing the Reagan administration as more of a threat to world peace than was Gorbachev's Soviet Union.

shift towards those ready and willing to engage with the Soviet Union became more marked. The president had, of course, even more critics from the ranks of liberal opinion in the US than from conservatives. Powell, who was sympathetic both to Reagan's military build-up and to his peacemaking proclivities, later observed: 'The mistake Ronald Reagan's liberal critics made was to assume that because he was a conservative and because he supported a huge defense buildup, he was some sort of dude-ranch warmonger.'[110]

In any case Reagan paid heed to Nixon's suggestion that he should re-establish his good standing with the American 'right' and took a familiar route to strengthening his authority. Like other political leaders under attack at home (for the Iran–Contra affair as well as from Cold War hard-liners), he sought solace by addressing foreign audiences. (A generation earlier, British Prime Minister Harold Macmillan observed that he was a 'politician' at home but was seen as a 'statesman' as soon as he went abroad.) The part of Reagan's European travel which made the greatest media impact was a speech of 12 June, close to the Berlin Wall and the Brandenburg Gate, when he famously declared, 'Mr Gorbachev, open this gate! Mr Gorbachev, tear down this wall!' Those words had been put into Reagan's mouth by a speech-writer, Peter Robinson, and there was pressure both from the State Department and from within the NSC to have them removed on the grounds that they were not in keeping with the new spirit of dialogue with the Soviet Union. But Reagan liked them and insisted on keeping that clarion call in his text.[111] It went down well with many Germans and badly in Moscow, but the most important audience Reagan had in mind was his Republican base back home.

As it happens, Gorbachev and Shevardnadze had suggested to the East German leadership a fortnight *before* Reagan's speech that they dismantle the wall. In late May 1987 the Soviet leaders were in Berlin for a meeting of the Warsaw Pact organization and they broached the subject when speaking with their German Democratic Republic (GDR) hosts just after it. Gorbachev and Shevardnadze, as the Foreign Minister's aide, Teimuraz Stepanov-Mamaladze, noted at the time, had 'proposed to remove the Wall'. They even mentioned the possibility that Reagan would make an issue of this in his forthcoming visit. 'Our friends' (meaning GDR leader Erich Honecker, in particular), Shevardnadze told his assistants, 'reacted very negatively.'[112] Gorbachev and Shevardnadze evidently did not press the matter further. It was an important component of the 'new thinking' that, while the Soviet leadership tried to exert influence, it no longer gave orders to the leaders of other Warsaw Pact countries. Even had the Soviet leader wished to make an exception of that self-denying ordinance with respect to the wall, Reagan's speech was shortly to make it harder, rather than easier, for him to do so. Gorbachev's own preference was for evolutionary rather than revolutionary change inside 'the Soviet bloc', since upheaval in Eastern or Central Europe had the potential to derail Soviet reforms and his own leadership. When the wall was, in fact, comprehensively breached in 1989, this came about through a mix-up within the East German administration rather than by deliberate action in Moscow, Washington, or even Berlin. What mattered then was that Gorbachev accepted the new reality.

The Washington Summit

Nineteen eighty-seven was a year of improvement in East–West relations, notwithstanding ups and downs. It culminated with the Reagan–Gorbachev Washington summit at the end of it. Gorbachev and Reagan both wanted a summit meeting at which the signing of the INF Treaty would take place. Reagan was extremely keen 'to get Gorbachev over to the land of the free', as Carlucci put it in an internal NSC note of 5 May, but anxious not to give Gorbachev 'leverage by seeming too eager'. Shultz was to repeat the basic line that the 'welcome mat is out, no conditions, we can talk about dates anytime the Soviets want to'.[113]

In the months immediately preceding the summit, which took place in December, Gorbachev encountered an internal problem that ultimately was to damage him far more than any domestic difficulty did Reagan. This was Boris Yeltsin's clash with the Soviet leadership. Yeltsin had been promoted to be first secretary of the Communist Party organization in Moscow with the acquiescence of Gorbachev, but on the recommendation of the conservative Central Committee secretary who supervised the party organization, Yegor Ligachev. The relations between Ligachev and Yeltsin, both forceful characters who liked to get their own way, soon soured, and Yeltsin used a CC meeting of 21 October to make an unscheduled and critical speech in which he said that the people had gained nothing during the first two years of perestroika. This went down particularly badly because the main purpose of that plenum had been to approve the text of a major address Gorbachev was to deliver on the seventieth anniversary of the Bolshevik Revolution the following month. Yeltsin's political outlook at the time was a mixture of relative conservatism and developing populism.

At a Politburo meeting less than a week earlier, at which defenders of the old order criticized as alien to Soviet ideology the phrase, 'socialist pluralism', in the draft of Gorbachev's seventieth anniversary speech, Yeltsin likewise appeared to be more conservative than reformist. He complained that the draft paid too much attention to the 'bourgeois-democratic' February revolution at the expense of the October (Bolshevik) revolution.[114] Whatever the motivation for Yeltsin's intervention at the Central Committee session six days later—and a big part of it was his dissatisfaction at still being a candidate rather than full member of the Politburo, along with his unwillingness to accept subordination to Ligachev—his break with the party hierarchy was to grow in significance over the next few years. It ultimately played a large part not only in ending Gorbachev's leadership of his country but also in the disintegration of the Soviet Union.

Although now facing criticism from more than one direction at home, Gorbachev continued to win friends abroad. His book on perestroika and the 'new thinking', published at the beginning of November, became a best-seller worldwide.[115] Of the several party reformers who worked on the manuscript, Chernyaev was the most closely involved, but Gorbachev himself was thoroughly immersed in the project. The general secretary, noted Chernyaev in his diary, worked on the text 'with passion' and 'dictated it two or three times over'. He foresaw that the book would create a new image for him and for the Soviet Union and it 'would help to win the West's trust', which, Gorbachev believed, would 'become the new and most important factor in transforming international relations'.[116]

Gorbachev had told Shultz in April that, in order to get rid of nuclear missiles in Europe, the Soviet Union was willing to destroy not only its Europe-based intermediate-range missiles but also those in Asia (for the Americans and Europeans had pointed out that these could potentially be moved to Europe) and that he was prepared to include tactical missiles—notably the SS-23 (known as 'Oka' in Russia)— as part of the INF Treaty deal. Shultz could not fully respond to the offer without consulting America's allies, but NATO formally adopted this 'double zero' aspiration at a meeting on 12 June. Only after that—on 9 July—did Gorbachev seek and get Politburo approval for this shift in the Soviet position. As part of the argument for his Politburo colleagues, he said that getting rid of the missiles in Asia would make a good impression on China and Japan and Asia as a whole.[117]

Gorbachev's top priority was to make progress with START, for he and Reagan had agreed at Reykjavik on the need for deep cuts in the strategic arsenals of both sides. Shultz, however, was relatively unresponsive on the START issue when, accompanied by Carlucci, Nitze, Roz Ridgway, and Matlock, he met with Gorbachev on 23 October, six weeks before the Washington summit.[118] Weinberger had already given notice that he would be resigning as Defense Secretary. When Carlucci sought Shultz's support for the idea that he become Weinberger's successor, Shultz agreed. Relations between them had improved and it was with Carlucci's prospective new post in mind that Shultz invited the National Security Advisor to accompany him to Moscow. Carlucci accepted enthusiastically, for he had never been to the Soviet Union.[119] Gorbachev was in an edgy mood because the row over Yeltsin at the Central Committee had occurred just two days earlier and he was troubled by its possible consequences. The American side had expected to fix a date for the forthcoming summit at Shultz's Kremlin meeting, but Gorbachev indicated that for him to come to Washington just to sign the INF Treaty was not enough.[120] Gorbachev's English-language interpreter Pavel Palazchenko was convinced that the Yeltsin affair had affected Gorbachev's state of mind and that, feeling the main danger to him was going to come from Soviet conservatives, he had to make an effort to prevent his foreign policy being attacked as 'too soft'.[121]

The meeting did not end in total failure. Gorbachev said he would write Reagan a letter, and both sides hoped that this would result in a date for a Washington summit being agreed. A week later Shevardnadze arrived in Washington and hand-delivered a letter from Gorbachev to the president, giving an advance copy on his arrival to Shultz. The Secretary of State was, therefore, able to give Reagan his gloss on the letter before the president had seen it. Shultz described it as 'fairly positive' and told Reagan that Gorbachev had proposed a summit in the first ten days of December.[122] In the letter itself, Gorbachev wrote, 'Our position is clear and honest: we call for the total elimination of the entire class of missiles with ranges between 500 and 5,500 kilometers and of all warheads for those missiles.'[123] Gorbachev also called for progress towards a treaty on strategic offensive weapons and for taking advantage of the opportunities for 'solving at last the problem of the complete elimination of chemical weapons globally'. There was scope also, he wrote, for retaining stability at lower levels of conventional forces which could be achieved 'through substantial reductions in armed forces and armaments, through removing the existing asymmetries and imbalances'. Time, he wrote, was precious and he hoped that Shevardnadze's visit to Washington would facilitate practical solutions to key problems.[124]

The Reagan–Gorbachev summit meeting might even have been aborted had a draft joint ministerial communiqué, handed to Shevardnadze on the plane by Deputy Foreign Minister Aleksandr Bessmertnykh and arms control specialist Viktor Karpov, been delivered unamended to Shultz. It contained demands on ABM that were liable to be sufficiently ill received in Washington that they could have put the summit in jeopardy again. With Shevardnadze's approval, the draft was rewritten by his aide Sergey Tarasenko and quickly translated by Palazchenko, and preparation for the summit went ahead. Shevardnadze's major difficulty on this American visit was with the constant questions he faced from the American mass media about Yeltsin.[125]

The Washington summit between Reagan and Gorbachev—their third such meeting in as many years—took place in December, and the Soviet leader accepted an invitation from Margaret Thatcher to break his journey for a brief meeting with her at the Brize Norton military base in Oxfordshire. In spite of her liking for Gorbachev personally, and her acceptance that he was a serious reformer, the prime minister fluctuated between optimism and scepticism in her attitude to change in the Soviet Union. A meeting with Gorbachev usually left her feeling more optimistic. On this occasion, Gorbachev was strikingly frank, given that he was speaking to someone who had earned the title of the 'Iron Lady' for her anti-Sovietism. His openness on domestic policy was greater with Thatcher than with most foreign leaders because he respected the effort she made to inform herself so thoroughly on Soviet developments. Indeed, Gorbachev spoke more critically of the Soviet system with Thatcher than he ever did with Reagan or even with Shultz.

At the Brize Norton meeting the British prime minister congratulated Gorbachev on his recently published 'bestseller' which she had already read, and Gorbachev apologized for not having a copy with him to sign for her.[126] Gorbachev told her that up to the present 'we have not been able to cross the threshold beyond the Stalinist system of administrative government'.[127] The boldest attempt thus far to change things had been made by Nikita Khrushchev and there had been some half-measures taken in Leonid Brezhnev's time. Now something completely different was being undertaken. It was a policy of 'democratization, glasnost and economic transformation, including the decentralization of the economy',* but every step had to be calculated carefully.[128] Thatcher was by now identifying with Gorbachev as a reformer and comparing her own reforms with Gorbachev's. When the Soviet leader said that his most difficult opposition was 'the old psychology', the prime minister said she understood him completely.[129] Gorbachev volunteered that there was no unity of views on all questions 'even in our Politburo', to which Thatcher responded that the same was true of the British Cabinet.[130]

The leaders were two-thirds of the way through their conversation before the first note of discord was struck. Predictably, this was when the discussion turned to nuclear weapons. Thatcher stuck to her oft-repeated view that they had 'already kept the peace in Europe for more than forty years', whereas Gorbachev expressed his concern about their proliferation and wanted to know when Britain would be ready to take part in the process of nuclear disarmament.[131] The prime minister also raised the issue of Afghanistan, to which Gorbachev responded that the political decision about ending the Soviet military presence there had already been taken and that the sooner 'your American allies' end their interference there, 'the sooner that problem will be resolved'.[132]

The Brize Norton meeting ended on an amicable note, with Thatcher expressing her regret that the time had been so short and asking Gorbachev to let her know the results of his meeting with Reagan. Gorbachev replied that he would certainly pass on that information and added: 'Then you may compare it with what your American friends say.' He thanked her for 'the reminder about my visit to England', an invitation which he would certainly take up.[133]

Then came Washington. Gorbachev's meeting with Reagan took place on 8–9 December, and on the 10th he had a conversation with Vice-President George Bush, who accompanied him to the airport. Although there were arguments at the summit on human rights and on Afghanistan as well as on armaments, it was the most harmonious meeting thus far between Reagan and Gorbachev. From the outset, they

---

* The June 1987 plenum of the Central Committee had inaugurated an economic reform that devolved significant power from the industrial ministries in Moscow to large industrial enterprises throughout the country and a 1987 Law on the State Enterprise codified the change. The shift in policy, however, had unintended consequences in the absence of a move to market prices. The reform, heavily influenced by Chairman of the Council of Ministers Nikolay Ryzhkov, remained essentially technocratic and ineffective. Powerful interests within the Soviet system blocked more radical economic reform and Gorbachev had far more success in introducing far-reaching political reform and in transforming Soviet foreign policy than he had with regenerating the economy, over which he had less control.

agreed (for the first time) to call each other 'Mikhail' and 'Ron'. Both leaders faced domestic criticism for coming to an agreement on banning intermediate-range nuclear missiles. The critics were less publicly vocal in the Soviet Union than in the United States, for the Soviet system had not yet evolved in 1987 as far as it had two years later, when vigorous political debate was out in the open. Domestic dissatisfaction at high levels was, nevertheless, potentially more serious for the general secretary than for the American president. Gorbachev could have been replaced as Soviet leader by the simple device of a vote in the Politburo, followed by a confirmatory vote by the Central Committee. He had, therefore, to tread carefully and build alliances at home as well as abroad. Reagan, in contrast, knew he was secure in the White House until his second term came to an end in January 1989.

Although Gorbachev's aspiration was to use the Washington summit to make progress on START, drastically reducing (with a view ultimately to eliminating) strategic nuclear weapons on both sides, he was wholly persuaded of the desirability of the INF Treaty. In his memoirs, he blamed former Defence Minister Dmitry Ustinov for persuading Leonid Brezhnev to agree to the installation of SS-20 missiles. They had not given serious consideration to the likely American response, and, to the limited extent they had thought about it, they had relied too much on the possibility of mobilizing West European opinion to reject equivalent American weapons on their soil. Marshal Akhromeyev, he noted, was aware from the outset that this deployment was a mistake, for the Soviet Union would have no defence against American Pershing-2 missiles, and the Chief of Staff played an important part in negotiating the INF Treaty which removed that category of weapons on both sides.[134]

Like the rest of the Soviet military, however, Akhromeyev had been deeply unhappy about one important concession Gorbachev and Shevardnadze had already made to American demands in order to secure the INF Treaty. They had agreed to include SS-23 ('Oka') missiles in the list of those to be destroyed, even though it had a maximum range, in the view of the Soviet military, of 400 kilometres, whereas the Treaty covered missiles with a range between 500 and 2,000 kilometres.[135] The Americans argued that its range could be at least 500 kilometres, and Vitaly Kataev, a former designer in military industry who was deputy head of the Defence Department of the Central Committee in Moscow, shared that view. He believed that the Oka range could be extended to 600 kilometres.[136] Gorbachev wished to discourage the Americans from deploying their Lance II missiles which had a 400-kilometre range, and, in the end, the United States did not.[137] The SS-23 concession had been made earlier in the year, first by Shevardnadze in discussion with Shultz, and later confirmed by Gorbachev at a meeting which Akhromeyev attended only after this item had been discussed. The Soviet military were dismayed about having to destroy all 239 of these shorter-range missiles. Defence Minister Sokolov had been vehemently opposed to the destruction even of the SS-20s, never mind the SS-23s, before

Figure 10 Gorbachev and Reagan, each holding copies of the INF Treaty, at the December 1987 Washington summit

the arrival of Rust's light aircraft in Moscow provided Gorbachev with the opportunity to replace him by a more malleable minister.[138]

The SS-23 apart, Akhromeyev welcomed the signing of the INF Treaty and rejected the notion that this was a capitulation by the Soviet Union to a policy that Reagan had enunciated as long ago as 1981—his 'zero option'. That, after all, had neither been taken seriously nor had it been desired by most leading members of Reagan's own administration or by major West European leaders. In Akhromeyev's widely shared view, Reagan's 1981 proposal was made on the assumption that the Soviet Union would reject it.[139] The extent of the opposition in the United States to the signing of the INF Treaty underlined that point. Critics of Reagan's willingness to sign it included former Secretaries of State Henry Kissinger and Alexander Haig, and a significant number of Republican Senators, among them the Republican leader in the

Senate, Bob Dole, who was quoted as saying on the very day the Soviet leader arrived in Washington that he did not trust Gorbachev.[140] Matlock noted that the Treaty's opponents argued that the missiles covered by it were needed in Europe to provide a 'ladder of deterrence' in keeping with NATO's 'flexible response' strategy. Yet they ignored the fact that the Soviet Union was eliminating many more missiles than the United States and thus reducing the threat to the US more than proportionately. Ironically, Matlock added, many of the people opposing the INF Treaty had been original supporters of the zero option, but this merely underlined the fact that the zero option was acceptable to them 'only as long as the Soviet Union rejected it'.[141]

No real progress on strategic arms was made at the Washington summit, with the two sides' different interpretations of the ABM Treaty again a sticking point, and the usual SDI arguments on both sides aired once again. Yet, the signing of the INF Treaty did take place, and it was not the only positive result of Gorbachev's visit. The good impression that the Gorbachevs, husband and wife, made on most Americans and the impact on the couple of the warmth of their reception on this, their first-ever, visit to the US further eased Cold War tensions. On the way to the White House, Gorbachev stopped his motorcade, got out and mingled with the crowd, shaking hands. 'Gorbachev', said Shultz, 'with his open manner, easy repartee, and spontaneity, proved to be a captivating figure in the United States and around the world.'[142] The jovial encounters played well both on Soviet and American television.

Reagan was less attuned than Thatcher had become to reformist trends in the Soviet Union that were likely to develop much further. The one time Gorbachev did embark on a discussion of Soviet problems and began to speak about reforms, Reagan interrupted him with a joke about a Russian-speaking young American in discussion with a student in Moscow. Asked by the Russian what he was going to do, the American replied 'I haven't decided yet.' He put the same question to the Russian and got the answer, 'They haven't told me yet.' Reagan said, 'That's the difference between our systems.'[143] In addition to being diplomatically tactless, this was factually inaccurate, for Russians did have a substantial choice of profession. Gorbachev simply changed the subject from internal Soviet developments to arms control. Shultz was 'disturbed and disappointed' by Reagan's insensitivity and later told him so. 'Discussion', he noted, 'of Soviet internal problems and Gorbachev's ideas for dealing with them would have been revealing to us and possibly helpful to him.'[144] Colin Powell, who was present at the meeting, remembered the context differently. He wrote that Gorbachev was talking about weapons systems when Reagan interrupted him with his joke. He, too, however, was embarrassed. As Reagan finished his story, 'the Americans', said Powell, 'wanted to disappear under the table, while Gorbachev stared ahead, expressionless'.

After the meeting ended, Powell reported, 'George Shultz courageously said what had to be said: "Mr President, that was a disaster. That man is tough. He's prepared. And you can't just sit there telling jokes."'[145] Shultz could be equally frank with

Reagan's opposite number. Gorbachev knew that Shultz had watched on TV his press conference at the end of the summit and he asked him what he thought of it. 'You went on much too long', Shultz replied. Gorbachev laughed, clapped him on the back and said he was glad that there was someone 'who tells you what he thinks'.[146] Part of the problem in Reagan's formal meetings with Gorbachev was not only the president telling rather feeble jokes about the Soviet system but also his excessive reliance on other members of his entourage to answer concrete questions from the Soviet side.[147] Shultz told Reagan that he did much better in small groups than in large formal discussions. He was also in his element hosting a White House dinner for Gorbachev and the visiting Soviet delegation, an event described by Shultz as 'marvelous in every way'.[148]

Although little specific progress was made in the discussions of the ABM Treaty, START, or on regional issues during the summit, the INF Treaty was itself a notable achievement. Moreover, taken as a whole, the summit had produced a closer rapport between the world's two most militarily powerful states. Reagan called it 'a clear success' and, before he left the US, Gorbachev said he detected 'a growing desire in American society for improved Soviet–American relations'.[149]

Back in Moscow, Gorbachev's report to the Politburo was very different in tone from that which he made following the Reykjavik summit when he had spoken of Reagan's 'caveman' mentality. His changing attitude to Reagan was evident when he spoke, as he was to continue to do, of the importance of 'the human factor' in world politics. Earlier the Soviet leadership had seen Reagan 'only as the embodiment of the most conservative part of American capitalism and the masters of the military-industrial complex'. But it turned out that 'the politicians, including the leading heads of state, if they are truly responsible people, also represent the purely human qualities, interests, and the hopes of the common people' and that they 'can be guided by the most normal human motives and feelings'.[150] The INF Treaty was, he said, the central achievement of the summit, and he praised Akhromeyev and Deputy Foreign Minister Bessmertnykh for their role in 'untying the truly difficult military-technical knots'.[151] What was also important was the goodwill they encountered in Washington. The enemy image was beginning to crumble and the 'Soviet military threat' being seen to be mythical.[152] The logic of disarmament would dispel fears and suspicions, and this would be 'especially relevant for Europe, since we were primarily dealing with European nuclear weapons'.[153]

Anatoly Chernyaev, who had accompanied Gorbachev to all his important meetings with foreign politicians in 1987 and had been present throughout the Washington summit, reviewed the year in his diary. He concluded that it had seen a breakthrough in the Soviet Union's relations with the outside world. 'A new and powerful factor', he wrote, 'arises in foreign policy—*trust*. This factor will later make possible the end of the Cold War.'[154]

11

THE END OF THE IDEOLOGICAL DIVIDE (1988)

The end of the Cold War owed more to change in the Soviet Union than to developments in America. That should not be a cause for surprise, as the Soviet Union *needed* to change more than did the United States if this goal was to be achieved. That is not to say that the United States had been particularly restrained in using the resources at its disposal to influence political outcomes in other countries. Successive administrations had moved to undermine governments they thought were acting contrary to American interests (instances included the overthrow of the Iranian government of Mohammad Mossadeq in 1953, several attempts to remove Fidel Castro in Cuba, and support for the military coup which overthrew the government of Salvador Allende in Chile in 1973). The United States did not, however, impose identical political and economic systems on countries within its sphere of interest in the way in which the Soviet Union exercised its control over Eastern Europe. Among the NATO countries, there were governments of different political complexions. The US was more open to a charge of hypocrisy than of imposition of uniformity, since the 'Free World', whose defence successive American governments saw themselves as leading, embraced at various times highly authoritarian regimes in Latin America, the Middle East, and Asia. The governments of the countries concerned had, however, the overriding merits in Washington eyes that they sided with the United States in the Cold War and presided over essentially capitalist economies.

In contrast, Moscow demanded that countries within its military alliance, the Warsaw Pact, maintain Communist political and economic systems of the Soviet type. The official ideology up to the time Gorbachev entered the Kremlin highlighted irreconcilable class conflict and ideological struggle between the 'socialist' and 'capitalist' worlds. In the Soviet lexicon, 'peaceful coexistence' did not connote cooperative interaction. Rather, it combined a realistic need to avoid the calamity of nuclear war with the aim of advancing Communist influence by other means. Peaceful coexistence with the West, far from meaning ideological coexistence, involved intensification of the battle of ideas. Only during the perestroika period of Soviet history did the obsession with permanent ideological struggle cease, as the break with past thinking became more striking in each successive year. Gorbachev's choice of a new top foreign policy-making team and innovation in Soviet international and defence policy were hugely important, but they constituted only part of the decisive change. No less crucial for the Cold War's ending were the liberalization and partial democratization of the Soviet political system and cardinal change in the content of Soviet ideology.

Intra-Elite Differences in Moscow

Although the Moscow summit between Gorbachev and Reagan at the end of May and beginning of June 1988 was of symbolic consequence, it was a much less momentous political event than the Nineteenth Conference of the Communist Party of the Soviet Union held a few weeks later which put the pluralization of the political system firmly on the agenda. (Even though he was Gorbachev's main adviser on foreign policy, Chernyaev devoted only a single paragraph in his voluminous diary to the Reagan–Gorbachev Moscow summit, but had far more to say about the Party Conference.[1]) The conference made plain to attentive observers that Soviet ideology was undergoing far-reaching change. This became even clearer in a speech Gorbachev delivered at the United Nations in December. In essence, that UN speech marked the end of the Cold War in its ideological dimension. Before this point was reached, however, the Soviet leader faced a serious domestic backlash against the change of both domestic and foreign policy he had initiated. Rather than make a tactical retreat, as he felt obliged to do on some other occasions, Gorbachev chose in the first half of 1988 to take on those who wished to turn the clock back and who were ready to revert to the familiar armoury of repressive powers to uphold strict party dictatorship.

The resistance to Gorbachev's perestroika* was signalled by an article in the newspaper, *Sovetskaya Rossiya*, on 13 March 1988. Its nominal author was a hitherto unknown Leningrad chemistry lecturer called Nina Andreyeva.[2] Her commentary on perestroika, which included praise of Stalin (and had an anti-Semitic undertone), attacked the elements of pluralism that had been developing and which were undermining 'the leading role of the party'. What mattered most was that the article had been edited and approved by officials within the Central Committee (CC), with the blessing of one of the Politburo's most powerful members, Yegor Ligachev. Shortly after the article's appearance, Ligachev, who was the party's overseer of ideology, called the heads of television and radio and the editors of the major newspapers to a conference in the CC building, said he hoped they had all read this 'wonderful

---

* Perestroika, while the accepted shorthand way of referring to the entire Gorbachev era, was an elastic term which initially was a euphemism for reform at a time when there was still a taboo on the use of the very word 'reform' in relation to the Soviet Union. Over time the meaning of perestroika evolved alongside changing practice. In the last two years of the Soviet Union's existence, the concept had largely outlived its usefulness, but it had come by then to stand for a root-and-branch transformation of the Communist system.

article', and told them that they should be guided by its ideas in their work.[3] The publication was timed to appear just when Gorbachev was leaving for Yugoslavia and when his most radically reformist ally within the top leadership team, Aleksandr Yakovlev, was in Mongolia. On the flight to Yugoslavia, Gorbachev's aide Georgy Shakhnazarov drew his attention to the newspaper article. For Gorbachev, Yakovlev, and Shakhnazarov it was abundantly evident that these were not just the views of Andreyeva. Had they been no more than that, the article would not have become a major political issue. But, as Gorbachev was quickly able to establish on his return to Moscow, CC officials had orchestrated this attack, telling regional party secretaries to republish the article and make it widely known.[4]

Interviewed in 1991, Shakhnazarov noted that the article had brought into the open the extent of 'opposition to Gorbachev's line' within the party and 'this prompted him to be more resolute and firm' in defending the path taken.[5] Significantly, in the three weeks that elapsed between publication of the Andreyeva article and its authoritative rebuttal, glasnost came to an abrupt halt. Old habits of self-censorship reasserted themselves, and the few writers who tried to publish counterblasts to the *Sovetskaya Rossiya* publication found their access to the media barred. On his return from Yugoslavia, Gorbachev convened a meeting of his closest associates and concluded that the episode called for a showdown at a meeting of the Politburo. That became all the clearer in the course of an informal discussion with Politburo members during a break at a conference ten days after the Andreyeva publication. Gorbachev let others speak about the Andreyeva article before he indicated where he stood. It soon became obvious that at least half the Politburo members approved of the publication. Ligachev pronounced it to be a 'very good article' and 'our party line'.* Gromyko, who at the time was the formal head of state as Chairman of the Presidium of the Supreme Soviet, said it was 'a good article' that 'put everything in its place'.[6] The institutional power and authority of Gorbachev's office remained such, however, that once the general secretary had intervened to say 'And I have a different opinion', the tenor of the discussions changed.[7]

The Politburo devoted two whole days to the Andreyeva affair. At one level, this was a discussion about a newspaper article but, in reality, it was about a far more

---

* At the formal meeting of the Politburo later that week, Ryzhkov proposed that Ligachev be removed from his duties as 'curator' of Soviet ideology. In a carefully calculated compromise, designed to keep everyone on board, Gorbachev took away some of Ligachev's responsibilities in this sphere and handed them to Yakovlev. As the joint curators of ideology, they made an odd couple and took such different positions in public as well as private that it became far from clear what the 'party line' was. In the course of a major reorganization and contraction of the Central Committee apparatus in the autumn of 1988, Gorbachev removed them both from ideology, put Vadim Medvedev in charge of it, made Yakovlev the secretary responsible for international affairs within the CC, and, in what amounted to a demotion, placed Ligachev in charge of agriculture.

fundamental issue—the direction in which the Soviet Union should move. During the meeting, held on 24–5 March, the Andreyeva article was strongly attacked not only by Gorbachev but also by Shevardnadze, Ryzhkov, Medvedev, and especially cogently by Yakovlev, who was allocated the task of drafting the official party response to what was effectively an attempt at counter-reformation. Yakovlev had come to the Politburo meeting armed with a written text, his own lengthy analysis of the dangers posed by the Andreyeva article which he characterized as the 'anti-perestroika manifesto' of the 'most conservative forces' in Soviet society.[8] On this occasion, and for some time thereafter, the hierarchical and disciplined nature of the Soviet Communist Party, which Gorbachev's own reforms were in the process of undermining, still worked to the party leader's advantage, buttressing the authority of the general secretary's pronouncements. In time-honoured manner, even those who a mere two days earlier had been full of praise for the article agreed unanimously to condemn it and assented to its rebuttal in *Pravda*. The article was published anonymously in that newspaper (the most authoritative organ of the Communist Party) to indicate that this was not simply the opinion of a particular writer, but the settled position of the party.[9] Fully reflecting Gorbachev's view, its precise formulation owed much to Yakovlev who regarded the preceding discussion and its outcome as 'a turning-point in the history of perestroika'.[10]

Deep divisions remained within the highest echelons of the Soviet system, but in the first half of 1988 those supportive of far-reaching change gained ground. Gorbachev had already got the agreement in principle of the Politburo for the Soviet Union to withdraw from the war in Afghanistan, though there was still a difference of view between those who wished to keep a small force in that country to support the current government led by Mohammad Najibullah and those who held that nothing short of a complete withdrawal would suffice. At a Politburo meeting on 18 April 1988, Shevardnadze and KGB Deputy Chairman Vladimir Kryuchkov (who became head of the KGB in October of the same year) were somewhat unlikely allies on this question. Both favoured the retention of a smaller Soviet force. Shevardnadze generally saw eye-to-eye with Gorbachev, but he was less prepared for a clean break from the Afghan quagmire from a sense of obligation to Najibullah, appearing to believe that to keep between 10,000 to 15,000 Soviet troops in Afghanistan was consistent with his support for withdrawal. Gorbachev observed that even with the vast number of troops they had kept in Afghanistan up to that point, they were not succeeding in saving the regime. For both domestic and international political reasons, there should be no ambiguity about their departure. He was especially strongly supported by Yakovlev, who said they had promised their own people they were getting out and should leave completely. He wanted 'no more funerals' (of young Soviet servicemen).[11] The decision to move towards complete withdrawal was upheld and the last Soviet soldier left Afghanistan in February 1989.

Harmonizing Western Approaches

In the United States meanwhile, relations at the top of Reagan's foreign policy-making team had become notably more harmonious. With Frank Carlucci as Defense Secretary, Colin Powell as National Security Adviser, Howard Baker as White House Chief of Staff, and George Shultz continuing as Secretary of State, the country now had a team capable of working together. They had 'confidence and trust in each other', recalled Shultz, and Reagan could see and appreciate the improvement over what had gone before.[12] Furthermore, as Shultz noted, he, Powell, and Carlucci met early every morning they were all in town—in Powell's White House office at 7 a.m.— and developed an understanding of their respective problems and were able to agree on 'who would handle what and how'.[13] At a dinner in Shultz's honour in January 1989, during the final days of the Reagan administration, Colin Powell said that 'the NSC adviser and the secretary of state had not gotten on so well since the days when Henry Kissinger held both jobs simultaneously'.[14]

In foreign policy, the focus of Reagan, Gorbachev, and Thatcher in the first part of 1988 was on the Moscow summit due to be held in late May. Thatcher would not, of course, be there, but during the months of preparation for that event, she was determined to use to the full the influence she could exercise over Reagan. Gorbachev and Shevardnadze had hoped that a START agreement might finally be signed and that this would be the summit's high point. There was much more hesitation on the American side, with the main exception of Shultz, who was keen to reach an agreement on drastically cutting the numbers of strategic nuclear weapons. In the meantime, however, Shultz had to work quite hard to get the INF Treaty ratified by the Senate. Given the political experience and standing of some of its American opponents, this was no straightforward task. Many of these objectors, who included Richard Nixon, Henry Kissinger, and Brent Scowcroft (who the following year became National Security Adviser to President George H. W. Bush), argued that the Treaty would 'lead to a denuclearized Europe, leaving the West vulnerable to superior Soviet conventional forces'.[15] In fact, the INF Treaty left Europe very far from denuclearized. As Shultz had pointed out the previous year, when he was responding to the arguments of Nixon and Kissinger against the Treaty, there were still going to be more than 4,000 US nuclear weapons in Europe 'on aircraft that could retaliate deep into the Soviet Union and on remaining missiles and nuclear artillery'. Several of these systems were undergoing modernization. There were also 'several hundred submarine-launched ballistic-missile warheads' that would remain available to the Supreme NATO Commander. Thus, even after eliminating intermediate-range nuclear weapons, there was more than sufficient 'flexible response' deterrent capacity that didn't involve 'relying exclusively on strategic systems' (meaning ICBMs).[16]

Denuclearization had also been Margaret Thatcher's fear, but she had accepted the INF agreement, while remaining worried about possible further developments that would call into question the UK's nuclear weapons. Concerned, as she had been, ever since the Reykjavik summit, about Reagan's desire, shared by Gorbachev, to get rid of nuclear weapons entirely, she worried that the president might concede too much on his first-ever visit to Moscow. The French government had been even more reluctant than was the British prime minister to accept the removal of both NATO and Soviet intermediate-range nuclear weapons from Europe, stipulated by the INF Treaty. Defence Minister André Giraud went so far as to describe the INF negotiations as a 'nuclear Munich'.[17] Ironically, it was SDI, of which Thatcher had been sceptical from the outset and to which President Mitterrand of France was even more opposed,[18] that limited the process of denuclearization and helped both countries to retain their own nuclear forces. The United States refused to go along with Moscow's demands for a ban on all nuclear tests and, as Gorbachev's interpreter at the summit talks Pavel Palazhenko observed, it appeared to the Soviet side that 'the administration's goal was to have a free hand to continue testing for creating a new generation of nuclear weapons and for SDI experiments'.[19]

A summit meeting of NATO leaders in Brussels, the first such in six years, took place in early March. It was held mainly at Thatcher's instigation. She was concerned to avoid a 'third zero' on shorter-range nuclear weapons unless and until 'parity on conventional weapons and a ban on chemical weapons had been achieved'.[20] The Federal German government, especially Foreign Minister Hans-Dietrich Genscher, had a more flexible position on this issue than she cared for, but she was satisfied with the final communiqué in which the heads of government agreed on 'a strategy of deterrence based on an appropriate mix of adequate and effective nuclear and conventional forces which will continue to be kept up to date where necessary'.[21] After this meeting broke up, Thatcher met with Reagan, eager to press on him her views on what the summit had achieved. Citing the wording of the communiqué, she said that 'these were the only circumstances in which NATO should negotiate on short-range systems', and she reported Reagan as agreeing with her.[22] She also urged caution on a START agreement, saying that while she accepted it as a goal, 'it was more important to get the right agreement than to have it quickly'.[23]

Reading between the lines of an interview Thatcher gave to CBS News just before the summit, it is not difficult to see that while her primary concern was that Europe should not be weakened militarily vis-à-vis the Soviet Union, her related aim was to limit Reagan's options in Moscow. The prime minister said that the NATO summit would make clear to the Soviet Union 'that the President of the United States always consults his NATO allies and that he even comes to Europe to do so…It is to show that we are absolutely behind the President in the Intermediate Nuclear Weapons treaty and to show that we believe that what is now vital, after the 50 per cent reductions that are being negotiated, is the next stage and we want to give him our views about that.'[24] As was not unusual, Thatcher talked more than anyone else at the summit. Reagan was reported to have looked on 'with visible admiration and affection', although at other times he seemed to fall asleep.[25] At a press conference after the NATO meeting ended, he admitted he did not recall whether or not he had seen the final text of the draft communiqué. This led to a hasty intervention by his Chief of Staff Howard Baker to confirm that the president had, indeed, signed off on the final wording.[26]

The growth of trust between the two superpowers which had occurred in 1987, notwithstanding ups and downs, developed further in 1988. Caspar Weinberger's departure from the Reagan administration helped that process along. Weinberger himself remained a sceptic. In his memoirs, first published in 1990, he expressed shock at a 'recent, rather startling poll' which 'indicated that 71 per cent of Republicans and 74 per cent of Democrats believe that the United States can trust the General Secretary of the Soviet Union, Mikhail Gorbachev'.[27] 'Trust', he rhetorically inquired, 'that Mr Gorbachev will turn his back on the goals of the Soviet state?' And 'Trust that Mr Gorbachev is diametrically opposed to the precepts of the Communist Party that he leads (precepts that are of course diametrically opposed to Western values and principles)?'[28] The idea that a Soviet politician could evolve from being a reformist Communist to a socialist of a social democratic type—in other words, to embracing the kind of socialism of leaders who had formed democratic governments in alliance with the United States (from Clement Attlee in early post-war Britain to contemporary France under President Mitterrand or Spain with its socialist Prime Minister Felipe González)—was something a number of people in the State Department understood but was evidently beyond the comprehension of Weinberger. In a 1998 interview for an oral history of the Cold War, years after the Soviet Union had ceased to exist, the former Defense Secretary said that Gorbachev's 'only real contribution' was making the Soviet Union recognize 'that they couldn't win a war' which led him to change his rhetoric. But, Weinberger went on, 'I don't think he ever changed his philosophy. He was, and I think to this day still is, a firm believer in communism. He talked a lot about perestroika, glasnost, all of those things, but he never really changed.'[29]

Compared with obtuseness on that scale, Reagan was flexibility personified. One of Europe's leading social democrats, Denis Healey, an innovative and formidable UK Secretary of State for Defence in the 1960s and Labour Shadow Foreign Secretary in the 1980s, described Reagan's and Thatcher's change, in response to Gorbachev's initiatives, with a pinch of hyperbole and partisan panache in his own memoirs published in 1989, in which he argued that Gorbachev had 'transformed President Reagan and Prime Minister Thatcher from fanatical anti-Soviet crusaders into champions of détente and disarmament'. 'God moves in mysterious ways His wonders to perform', continued Healey, 'and sometimes chooses unexpected vessels for His grace. The alchemy of history can change the basest metals into gold.'[30]

Senate ratification of the INF Treaty came just in time for Reagan and Gorbachev to exchange the formal documents when they met in Moscow at the end of May. The worry had been not that the Senate would reject the agreement outright, for almost all Democrats and a good number of Republican Senators were in favour, but that they would attach crippling amendments which would require further negotiation with Gorbachev, and undermine Reagan's credibility with the Soviet side.[31] The new unity in Reagan's foreign policy-making team helped to avert this danger, and both Shultz and Powell played significant parts in the eventual securing of an overwhelming Senate vote in favour of ratification, and without the insertion of any damaging reservations.

In the last year of his presidency, Reagan was able to ride out the criticism that had come his way from former allies and admirers who believed he was compromising too much with the Soviet adversary. For Gorbachev, the growing dissatisfaction of Soviet critics, concerned that he was on a path which would undermine the Communist system, was more seriously threatening. After all, a vote in the Politburo, backed by the Central Committee, was in 1988 still sufficient to remove him from office. This meant that the Soviet leader had to tread carefully, taking pains to carry the top leadership team with him. He went beyond the ranks of the Politburo and held meetings with the provincial party bosses who formed the largest component of the CC. He divided them into three separate groups and tried to persuade members of each group (people who in their own region were, in effect, provincial governors) of the need for far-reaching change. The transcripts of the meetings indicate deep misgivings among these party officials about the way things were going. There was more sympathy with Andreyeva's conservative, even neo-Stalinist, gloss on current developments than with the official *Pravda* rejoinder. Gorbachev did not hold back on the need for further reform, making clear his own dissatisfaction with what had passed for 'socialist democracy' in the Soviet Union hitherto. In an oblique reference to the need for contested elections, he said (in an April meeting with one of the groups of regional officials) that it was not only in the West that the question was posed, 'on what basis do 20 million [members of the CPSU] rule 200 million?' and gave his answer, 'We conferred on ourselves the right to rule the people!'[32]

Notwithstanding the wariness of party officials, for whom talk of democratization raised concerns about their own future security of tenure, Gorbachev succeeded in advancing the agenda for change following the Andreyeva episode, as preparations went ahead for Reagan's visit and, more significantly, the Nineteenth Party Conference due to take place a month later. The radicalization of the reform agenda was worked out in a series of meetings Gorbachev held with his aides Georgy Shakhnazarov, Ivan Frolov, and Anatoly Chernyaev, together with the most enlightened Secretaries of the Central Committee Yakovlev and Medvedev, who were joined by various specialists. The results of their deliberations were published as 'theses' for the party conference almost on the eve of Reagan's arrival in Moscow. The first draft of the document was prepared by Shakhnazarov and Frolov.*

Reagan in Moscow

When the Russian text was published, the US Embassy faxed it to Ambassador Matlock who was already in Helsinki, where he had gone to brief the president who, along with Nancy Reagan and a large entourage, had arrived on 25 May. Reagan was not due to travel on to Moscow until the 29th. As Matlock read the Soviet 'theses', discovering 'one new element after another', his excitement grew. 'Never before', as he wrote in his 1995 memoir, 'had I seen in an official Communist Party document such an extensive section on protecting the rights of citizens or such principles as the separation of powers, judicial independence, and presumption of a defendant's innocence until proven guilty.' It all sounded like 'something closer to European social democracy'.[33] The next morning Matlock met with Reagan, at a meeting attended also by George Shultz, Colin Powell, and Roz Ridgeway, in a hotel room with an acoustic seal that had been assembled by American security specialists to ensure that their deliberations remained confidential. Matlock began his briefing on the current political scene in the Soviet Union with the proposals for the party conference. He summarized them and then 'told the president that if they turned out to be real, the Soviet Union could never again be what it was in the past'. Although the 'theses stopped short of democracy as we would define it', said Matlock, 'they contained the seeds of the liberation of the country'.[34] How much of an impact this made on Reagan is unclear. In his diary entry on that Helsinki discussion, the only substantive comment Reagan makes is that he is going to tackle Gorbachev 'on religious freedom—not as a deal with us but as a suggestion to him as an answer to some of his problems'.[35]

The Moscow summit did not register any substantial achievements, other than helping to erode in the minds both of Russians and Americans their stereotypes of each other. Russians saw on their TV screens a genial Reagan who seemed far removed from the ogre of Soviet propaganda (especially that disseminated during the president's first term which was before Gorbachev became party general secre-

---

* Shakhnazarov, who had been a deputy head of the Socialist Countries department of the Central Committee since 1972 (First Deputy Head from 1986) and president of the Soviet Association of Political Sciences since 1974, became a full-time aide to Gorbachev early in 1988, but before that he was already an influential ad hoc adviser. Frolov was a former editor of the main Soviet philosophy journal, *Voprosy filosofii*, and in 1986 he was appointed chief editor of the theoretical journal, *Kommunist*, which he turned into a readable publication containing diverse viewpoints. In 1987 he became an aide to Gorbachev with special responsibility for ideological questions. Both Shakhnazarov and Frolov had in the past spent time in Prague, working on the *World Marxist Review*, whose alumni constituted a group of influential and seriously reformist party intellectuals.

Figure 11 In Moscow's Red Square during the American president's 1988 visit, Gorbachev lifts a small child from his mother's arms and asks him to 'shake hands with Grandpa (*dedushka*) Reagan'.

tary). Americans, for their part, saw not only a friendly Soviet leader who exuded charm (they had already witnessed that during the Washington summit) but also lots of Russians who did not look so different from themselves and who clearly welcomed the great improvement in US–Soviet relations.

The working sessions of the summit were a disappointment, especially for the Soviet side. Reagan duly brought up the issue of religious freedom which, said Gorbachev, in spite of past 'excesses', now existed in the USSR.[36] There was a good deal of sparring on human rights, with Reagan raising both general and particular humanitarian issues in the Soviet Union, and Gorbachev referring to the unemployment statistics of America Blacks and Hispanics and the per capita income difference between Whites and Blacks in the US. In the Soviet Union, he said, they had recently 'become much more self-critical', but it appeared that 'the U.S. had not'.[37]

On arms control it was no longer the Soviet Union but the United States that was hesitating over verification, with the administration buckling under pressure from the US military, and the navy in particular who, Shultz said, 'found the idea of people tramping around inside [their] nuclear submarines' to be 'not attractive'.[38] As Svetlana Savranskaya and Thomas Blanton have written, the 'U.S. military's recalcitrance on the very issue that previously had been an American strong suit ("trust, but verify", Reagan kept repeating) held up the arms cuts that Moscow—more so than Washington—was ready to make'.[39] Gorbachev made the most of the change of tack. The president, he said, had 'earlier been a strong advocate of verification', but now 'the Soviet side had to talk the U.S. into it', raising the question of whether the earlier position was a bluff. The Americans were now reluctant to have inspections for chemical weapons as well as on-site inspection of missiles on their ships. 'What', Gorbachev asked, 'was to be inspected? The White House and Kremlin? The two leaders had now visited both sites themselves.'[40] He also proposed large cuts in conventional forces—500,000 on each side—but Shultz said that this was something on which the US would have to consult their allies.[41]

The American side were on stronger ground when they complained that the Soviet radar installation at Krasnoyarsk was a violation of the ABM Treaty. The United States accepted that the limited anti-missile defence installed around Moscow was compatible with the Treaty but, as Shultz insisted at the summit, they had long held this did not apply to Krasnoyarsk. Gorbachev said part of the problem was their failure to agree on the scope and limits of the ABM Treaty. He was conciliatory over Krasnoyarsk, saying that it could be totally dismantled if they reached a broader agreement. He related the issue to SDI. Speaking 'amiably' (according to the official American transcript), Gorbachev said that he could give the president free advice, 'even though Henry Kissinger would have charged him millions' for it, which was that he had been deceived by former Defense Secretary Weinberger and, now possibly, by Carlucci (who was present at the discussion) into thinking that 'it was possible to put something in space that would give the U.S. an advantage'. It was 'one thing', said Gorbachev, 'for SDI to defend against a certain number of missiles; it was another for it to stop that number times X. But if both sides devoted all their national wealth to such a competition, the discussions the two sides were having were meaningless.'[42] What remained unspoken was that the military burden was already much greater on the smaller Soviet economy than on that of the United States, although it was also true that countering American ballistic missile defence with a Soviet proliferation of multiple-warhead missiles (MIRVs), some with nuclear warheads and some without, was a far less costly project than SDI.

When the discussion turned to Afghanistan, Reagan complimented Gorbachev on the decision to withdraw Soviet forces. He said that the United States favoured 'a stable, neutral, and non-aligned Afghanistan' and that 'we are prepared to work with you to ensure it'.[43] This was an intention that remained unfulfilled—at great subsequent cost to the US and to its closest allies. Gorbachev said that he was not against a new coalition government in Afghanistan, but that the Soviet possibilities of influencing its composition were limited. His fear was 'the creation of a fundamentalist, Moslem government'. That was why 'we need to cooperate', he said, for 'if we don't', acting instead only in what each side took to be its own specific interests, 'we won't be able to achieve anything—anywhere'.[44]

Reagan had been prepared to accept a formulation for the communiqué on the summit proposed to him by Gorbachev, but during a break in the proceedings,

Shultz, Ridgway, and others in the American team voiced strong objections. There was an understandable unwillingness to accept the inclusion of 'peaceful coexistence', given its past connotations. Apart from its subtext of ideological, as distinct from military, struggle, the term had explicitly applied to states with different 'social systems'. Quirkily, it did not, therefore, rule out military action against a fellow 'socialist' state, such as had happened with the Soviet invasions of Hungary in 1956 and Czechoslovakia in 1968. Such adventures were far removed from Gorbachev's intentions, but those in the American delegation who were better versed in the history of the concept than was Reagan were right to object to those words. Gorbachev quite readily agreed to remove 'peaceful coexistence', but he found the American objections to 'freedom of choice' for all peoples harder to understand.

For Pavel Palazchenko, the likely reason was that the US side 'did not believe Gorbachev meant it', for 'they thought in the usual geopolitical terms and could not imagine we would ever abandon Stalin's "conquests" in Europe'. He added that the Americans 'were not alone in having these doubts'.[45] In the end, as the official US transcript of the summit talks makes clear, Gorbachev gave further ground on the terminology and accepted wording that had been agreed between Soviet deputy foreign minister Aleksandr Bessmertynykh and his American counterpart, Ridgway.[46] 'All that we are asking for', said Gorbachev, 'is a statement that confirms there are to be political solutions, not military solutions, to international problems.'[47] The Soviet leader was disappointed by the American reaction, one which Matlock also believed had been excessively negative, for he took the view that Gorbachev was simply 'using some old bottles for his new wine'.[48] This was something Chernyaev had noted even before he was working full-time as Gorbachev's closest aide. 'Peaceful coexistence Gorbachev-style', Chernyaev wrote in his diary on 16 November 1985, is 'in contrast to what we had before (regardless of whatever we said and wrote, and however we swore that we are against war and strong-arm tactics)'. It now meant taking seriously the maxim, 'to live and let live' and 'without attempts to cheat' or to pursue superiority.[49] True though that was of Gorbachev's understanding of 'peaceful coexistence', he was also using distinctly new formulations whose significance was insufficiently grasped by the American side.

The most striking events during Reagan's Moscow visit were not in the formal discussion sessions of the summit. The president hosted a lunch, to which prominent Soviet dissidents were invited, at the American ambassador's residence, Spaso House. The distinction between 'dissidents' and those who worked for change from within the system was on the verge of breaking down, especially as the pluralization of the system itself gathered pace in the following year. The NSC, understandably enough, continued to call them 'dissidents', and Shultz described them as 'refuseniks and human rights activists'. Matlock suggested that, given that Gorbachev was talking about democratization, it would be better to rename them 'democratic activists'. He noted that it 'took a while for this idea to catch on'.[50] Reagan addressed a meeting of writers, artists, and musicians at the Writers' Club, praising the advent of glasnost, but calling for the publication of banned works that had still not appeared, such as Aleksandr Solzhenitsyn's The Gulag Archipelago. Sergey Zalygin, the editor of the leading Soviet literary monthly journal, Novy mir, told Matlock to tell the president that they agreed with him and that this Solzhenitsyn book would soon be published in the Soviet Union.[51] (It was serialized in Novy mir in 1989.)

Reagan had hoped to meet the Patriarch of the Orthodox Church, but the church bureaucracy, which had over the years actively collaborated with the KGB, was more conservative than the reformist wing of the Communist Party leadership, and the Patriarch was only prepared to greet the president if he avoided contact with priests who were out of favour with the hierarchy. For Reagan that was an unacceptable condition, and he chose to meet with Father Gleb Yakunin, who had long been a brave critic of the compromised church leadership, in preference to the Patriarch.[52]

As a symbolic break with the past, no event was more striking than Reagan's speech to students and faculty at Moscow State University. The sight of the arch-enemy of Communism speaking in front of a huge bust of Lenin, and being warmly received by a packed and attentive gathering of Soviet young people, was one which few of his supporters back home, and probably even fewer of his liberal critics, had ever expected to behold. Reagan's speech had been skilfully crafted and went down well. It was in sharp contrast with a speech he delivered at Springfield, Massachusetts earlier in the year, on the very day in April when George Shultz, accompanied by Colin Powell, arrived in Moscow for a meeting with Gorbachev, and which had got the meeting off to a bad start. On that occasion, Reagan had repeated many stereotypes about the Soviet Union and seemed to pay little heed to how much the country was changing. The 21 April speech, in which Reagan, among other things, cast doubt on whether the Soviet Union was serious about getting out of Afghanistan, had received cursory attention from National Security Adviser Colin Powell, but the NSC staff had regarded it as 'a perfectly normal effort by White House speechwriters to anchor the Republican right wing before the summit'.[53] Gorbachev had the advantage over Shultz of having read the Springfield speech (the Secretary of State knew nothing about it), for it had been speedily translated for his benefit.

The Moscow State University speech was very different. This time both the Secretary of State and the National Security Adviser had been involved and wholeheartedly approved of the text, on which, of course, Reagan had the last word. For Shultz, it 'was precisely the message to deliver' and 'Ronald Reagan delivered it magnificently.'[54] The president told his Russian audience that the key to progress is 'freedom—freedom of thought, freedom of information, freedom of communication' and observed that 'no single person, no single authority or government has a monopoly of truth'. He alluded also to economic freedom and cited the technological progress that had been made in the Republic of Korea, Singapore, and Taiwan, noting also a growth of economic freedom in Communist China.[55] He drew the

Soviet students' attention to the range of local television and radio stations and newspapers in the United States, 'each one an independent, private enterprise, fiercely independent of the Government'.[56] He did not confine himself to presenting the United States in the best possible light, but cited many of the great figures of Russian culture, among them Lomonosov, Gogol, Dostoevsky, Kandinsky, Scriabin, and Pasternak. He had begun by saying that he was in Moscow 'to meet with one of your most distinguished graduates'. Gorbachev would be satisfied also to hear him tell his mainly young audience: 'Your generation is living in one of the most exciting, hopeful times in Soviet history. It is a time when the first breath of freedom stirs the air and the heart beats to the accelerated rhythm of hope, when the accumulated spiritual energies of a long silence yearn to break free.'[57] The president emphasized how important it was 'to institutionalize change—to put guarantees on reform'.[58]

His speech over, Reagan answered questions from the students with an adept and light touch. When asked what he would be doing when he ceased to be president, he replied that when he was in Hollywood it was said that 'if you didn't sing or dance, you wound up as an after-dinner speaker. And I didn't sing or dance.' That got the laughter he hoped for, and Reagan continued, 'So I have a hunch that I will be out on the speaking circuit, telling them about a few things that I didn't get done in government, but urging the people to tell the Congress they wanted them done.'[59] The students saw also an idealistic side of Reagan that was very different from Soviet stereotypes and, indeed, from the Reagan perceived by many liberal Americans. The president told his Moscow State University audience that he had been speaking recently to seventy-six students, half of whom were American and half Russian. 'They had held a conference here and in Finland and then in the United States', he said, and 'I couldn't tell the difference looking at them, which were which, but I said one line to them. I said I believe that if all the young people of the world today could get to know each other, there would never be another war.'[60]

The only somewhat hostile question Reagan got was from a student who wanted to know why he had received 'refuseniks or dissidents', one of whom, the questioner claimed, was a Fascist collaborator. Reagan said he knew nothing about that last point, but explained the American interest on the grounds that the US was a country made up of people from every nation of the world and that 'Americans all feel a kind of kinship to that country that their parents or their grandparents or even some great-grandparents came from.' That was why he had come with a list of names given to him by relatives or friends of people they believed had been mistreated in the Soviet Union and who should be allowed to emigrate. He tactfully added that this was the kind of case that was 'brought to me personally so I bring it to the General Secretary' who 'has been most helpful and most agreeable about correcting these things'. Still in diplomatic vein, Reagan added, 'Now, I'm not blaming you; I'm blaming bureaucracy', adding that problems arose also with the American bureaucracy.

So, 'every once in a while, somebody has to get the bureaucracy by the neck and shake it loose and say, Stop doing what you're doing!'[61]

The Moscow State University occasion was, as Jack Matlock saw it, 'the centre-piece' of Reagan's visit to the Soviet Union. The ambassador said that the speech 'rang out as a paean to Gorbachev's perestroika' and the response to the president—a standing ovation—was 'probably the most enthusiastic he had witnessed since the demonstration that followed his nomination at the Republican convention'.[62] In his memoirs, Reagan devoted as much space to his Moscow University speech as to the rest of his Soviet visit put together. It had been, he recorded, 'an extraordin-ary day I never thought possible'.[63] For television viewers in the Soviet Union, in the United States and throughout the world, the only event at the Moscow summit that made a bigger impression was when Gorbachev and Reagan strolled amicably together in a sun-drenched Red Square, and spoke with bystanders. Gorbachev took a small child from his mother's arms and invited him to 'Shake hands with *dedushka* [grandpa] Reagan'.[64] Back in the grounds of the Kremlin, a reporter asked Reagan if he still believed the Soviet Union was an 'evil empire'. In an answer which reverberated around the world, he replied, 'No, I was talking about another time, another era.'[65]

Reagan left Moscow on 2 June and, accompanied by the principal members of his entourage, flew to London. After lunch with Ambassador Charlie Price, who was a friend, and four hours of rest, he and Nancy Reagan had tea with the Queen at Buckingham Palace. 'From there', Reagan wrote in his diary, 'it was over to 10 Downing St for a tête-à-tête with Margaret Thatcher—I gave her a report on our summit in Moscow aided by Colin, George S. etc.'[66] The following day Reagan delivered a speech at a ceremonial occasion in London's Guildhall, with the prime minister and numerous dignitaries in attendance.

Back in Washington, Reagan wrote a 'Dear Mikhail' thank-you letter which con-cluded by sending Gorbachev 'warmest regards' and was signed 'Ron'. In the letter itself, he said that not only he and Nancy but everyone was still talking about 'the warmth of our greeting and the hospitality' they had received. In the most interest-ing paragraph of the short but very friendly letter, Reagan wrote, 'You would have been surprised at the responses I received during my meeting with "dissidents and refuseniks". I'm speaking now of what I was told by a number of those individuals who favored your proposals for glasnost and perestroika. They were outspoken also in their approval of you and their support for what you are doing as the leader of your country.'[67] Reagan added that none of those mentioned had 'made any suggestion that I pass on their words but I felt you'd appreciate knowing of their attitude'.[68]

Gorbachev made the same point with a different slant when on 6 June he reported to the Politburo on the Reagan visit (probably before he received Reagan's letter). He said that bringing the president together 'with our dissidents' had backfired on those who devised the idea of that meeting.[69] In general, he took a positive view of Reagan's first visit to the Soviet Union. Its extensive coverage on American TV had, said Gorbachev, given ordinary Americans the chance to see normal Russians. Americans had been impressed by 'the friendliness of our people on the streets of Moscow towards the president', adding that the tone of Western propaganda had changed.[70] The visit marked, he said, a turn for the better in Soviet–American relations. Reagan had assessed what he saw realistically, had spoken honestly about his impressions, and had not hesitated 'to correct his previous offensive evaluations' (with Reagan's consignment of the 'evil empire' to an earlier time no doubt foremost in Gorbachev's mind).[71] In a post-summit memorandum to Gorbachev, the director of the Institute of the USA and Canada, Georgy Arbatov, said that the summit's most obvious, and perhaps main, result, was that it had helped the United States and the West in general to discover, as no other event before it had, 'the character, scale, and meaning of the changes taking place in the Soviet Union'.[72]

When the Politburo met on 24 June to consider the draft report which the general secretary was to present to the Nineteenth Conference of the CPSU at the end of the month, Gorbachev pointed out that in the first draft of the passage on the reduction of the threat of nuclear war, this was attributed 'to our military strength'. But that, he insisted, was incorrect. It was 'thanks to the new thinking'.[73] Gorbachev described the change of emphasis as constituting 'realism',[74] although the switch of emphasis from military power to ideational change, and an embrace of the notion that there were both universal interests and 'all-human values', was not how the concept was understood by most of those (on both sides of the Cold War divide) who described themselves as 'realists'. In a later summing-up of what the new thinking, both on foreign policy and on domestic politics, amounted to, Gorbachev described it as 'an attempt to think and act in accordance with normal human *common sense*' (italics in the original),[75] phraseology that would have had Marx turning in his grave and Lenin, too—but for the fact that he had not been given a burial, but was still available for public inspection in the mausoleum on Red Square.

While the Moscow summit—and the improvement in US–Soviet relations it consolidated—was popular back in America, among those who were far from euphoric was Vice-President George Bush. He told a reporter soon after Reagan's Russian visit that 'The Cold War isn't over', a view strongly shared by Brent Scowcroft.[76] The future National Security Adviser was especially sceptical. Scowcroft thought that Gorbachev 'was trying to kill us with kindness', saying 'things we wanted to hear' and making 'numerous seductive proposals to seize and maintain the propaganda high ground in the battle for international public opinion'. What Gorbachev wanted, as Scowcroft saw it, was 'to restore dynamism to a socialist political and economic system and revitalize the Soviet Union domestically and internationally to compete with the West'. And this made him 'potentially more dangerous than his predecessors' who had been 'periodically hitting us between the eyes to remind us of their aggressive ambitions'.[77]

Gorbachev and Radicalization of the Programme for Change

What Scowcroft, Bush and a great many foreign observers failed to appreciate was the fundamental difference between the kind of 'socialism' that was more accurately described in the West as 'Communism' and the socialism of a social democratic type espoused by many political parties in Western Europe, several of whom had at various times formed governments that were no less, and arguably more, democratic than those of the United States. To the extent that Gorbachev's 'socialism' was in transition from that of reformist Communism to a social democratic variant of socialism, and in the light of his foreign policy emphasis on political solutions and eschewal of military entanglement, it made Gorbachev not a 'potentially more dangerous' adversary, as Scowcroft had put it, but an already more constructive partner. In the second half of 1988 the direction of Gorbachev's travel became clearer, first in his major report to the Nineteenth Party Conference and then, in December, in his speech at the United Nations. The focus of the first was primarily on domestic change and, in the latter, on international policy.

The theses prepared for the Nineteenth Party Conference which, as Matlock had informed Reagan, broke important new ground in the development of Soviet reform, were surpassed by the decisions Gorbachev persuaded the conference to adopt. As Ivan Laptev, the chief editor of *Izvestiya* at that time, observed, there was a tactical reason for this: if you mention in advance everything you want to do, the enemies of such radical change can prepare their defences.[78] The most important reform, the move to contested elections for a legislature with real power, had been only obliquely hinted at prior to the conference and the decision to break with the Soviet tradition of non-competitive pseudo-elections was momentous. It had unintended as well as intended consequences. It was, as Gorbachev and his closest advisers on political reform wanted it to be, a substantial step forward in the democratization of the Soviet Union. It also meant, however, that in parts of the Soviet Union—and most notably the Baltic republics of Estonia, Lithuania, and Latvia—competitive elections gave voters the opportunity to support the candidates most disposed to demand greater sovereignty (if, not yet, full independent statehood) for their republic.

The conference, held from 28 June to 1 July, witnessed, for the first time since the 1920s, radically different views not only being expressed in a major party forum but also being reported in the Soviet mass media. In another break with tradition, much of the discussion was televised. That included criticism from the floor of current members of the Politburo. A majority of the delegates, many of them party officials at the regional and local level, were less keen on radical change than was the reformist wing of the party leadership which was in the driving seat of the conference. Speakers who criticized recent developments from a conservative Communist or Russian nationalist standpoint, such as the writer Yury Bondarev, who compared the launch of perestroika to a plane taking off without any idea where it was going to land, received louder applause than those who stressed the need for radical reform. If the foot-dragging and covert opposition to transformative change from those with a vested interest in the status quo were to be overcome, bold and skilful leadership was required. Gorbachev made full use of the authority conferred by his office, allied to his natural ability, powers of persuasion, and political skills in manoeuvring.

Boris Yeltsin seized the opportunity to address the conference and made a plea for 'party rehabilitation'. Although he had been marginalized and took no part in any of the decisions made during 1988 which paved the way for the pluralization of Soviet politics, Yeltsin had never been expelled from the Communist Party or even from the Central Committee. Essentially, therefore, he was pleading to be restored to a position within the top party leadership. This being denied him, he resigned two years later from the CPSU on his own initiative and added to his popularity by doing so, since by 1990 the party had become increasingly unpopular. In 1988 it was still, realistically, seen as the only instrument for effecting political change. Yeltsin's conference speech brought him into direct conflict once again with Ligachev who began his response by noting that it was he who had recommended that Yeltsin become a secretary of the CC and subsequently a candidate member of the Politburo.[79] He made it clear that it was a decision he had come to regret, but refrained from alluding to his misplaced assumption that Yeltsin would become his loyal follower within the top leadership team. Gorbachev unwisely allowed himself to join in the criticism of Yeltsin, partly in response to promptings from his wife.[80] This was counterproductive, for the more Yeltsin was attacked by the party hierarchy, the more popular acclaim he increasingly garnered for standing up to officialdom.

Four days after the conference ended, the lengthy and detailed resolutions it approved were published in the Soviet Union. The resolution on 'democratization of Soviet society and reform of the political system' spoke of the need radically to 'strengthen socialist legality' in order to 'preclude the possibility of usurpation of power and abuses'. In elections to soviets, the resolution said there must be no control over the nomination of candidates and encouraged the inclusion of more candidates than seats on the ballot paper. Intra-party democratization was also on the agenda, including the abandonment of the nomenklatura system of party appointments, whereby those who occupied 'elected' posts at all levels had in fact been appointed by higher party organs. In future, party secretaries—including, importantly, the General Secretary of the Central Committee—could be elected to the same post for no more than two successive terms. The resolution on relations between the nationalities promised a democratization of the Soviet federation whereby greater independence would be granted to the republics and regions (although the precise centre-periphery institutional arrangements were not specified). The conference resolution on glasnost was among the most important, for it emphasized that this was a developing process and that its 'consistent expansion' was a necessary part of democratization. Glasnost was portrayed as a necessary condition for, inter alia, 'encapsulating all the diversity of interests existing in Soviet society and the socialist pluralism of opinions'.[81]

Decisions to cut the size of the party bureaucracy and to take serious steps toward the democratization of the political system had been outlined in Gorbachev's major speech to the party conference and accepted in principle by the delegates, in many cases on the happy assumption that these measures would take years to come to fruition, if they ever did. Gorbachev, however, sprung a surprise on them just when everyone thought the conference had completed its deliberations and the delegates were getting ready to leave their seats. He produced a piece of paper from his pocket with the text of a resolution which called for a reform of the structure of the party apparatus to be carried out before the end of the current year, and for the next session of the Supreme Soviet to formulate an electoral law that would enable the competitive election of deputies to a new legislature, the Congress of People's Deputies, to take place in April 1989. Ligachev, who was chairing the session and was also taken somewhat by surprise, asked if anyone was against. No-one was. The resolution was passed unanimously. Yet, as *Izvestiya* editor Ivan Laptev observed, delegates who had thought that any changes would come slowly, and that they would be comfortable enough for another decade, were shocked when they realized what they had been bounced into accepting. He heard a number of senior provincial officials saying, as they left the conference, 'what have we done?' For Laptev, this was 'the most dramatic moment' of Gorbachev's first five years as Soviet leader.[82]

Although the main focus of the Nineteenth Party Conference was on internal Soviet developments, the report Gorbachev presented included a section on international policy which foreshadowed his UN speech later in the year. Gorbachev noted the progress that had been made in the preceding three years in reducing the threat of war, mentioning also the decision taken to withdraw Soviet forces from Afghanistan. He spoke optimistically of a 'gradual demilitarization and humanization of international relations' and said that 'Soviet foreign policy, notwithstanding some blunders and errors in the past, had on the whole rendered great service for the country, for socialism and for all humanity.'[83] He stressed the importance and value of the increased contact with other countries—not only between heads of government but between ordinary citizens, scientists, cultural figures, political party leaders, parliamentarians, social organizations, and movements (mentioning specifically 'social-democratic leaders')—and in that way opening the Soviet Union to the outside world.[84] He reiterated the aim of removing all nuclear weapons, by stages, by the year 2000, and said that the Soviet Union was ready for disarmament to proceed under conditions of thoroughgoing mutual supervision.[85] In a passage which was largely overlooked in the West, and certainly not given the attention it deserved by Western politicians at the time, Gorbachev said that 'the concept of freedom of choice occupies a key place in the new thinking' and 'we are convinced of the universal applicability of this principle for international relations'.[86] He added that any intrusion from without, by whatever means—never mind military intervention—belonged to the armoury of former years. Sovereignty and independence, equal rights, and non-interference were becoming, said Gorbachev, the generally accepted norms of international relations. 'That is why', he declared, 'the use of force in all its forms and manifestations has become historically obsolete.'[87]

No Soviet leader had ever spoken in such overwhelmingly pacific terms at a major party forum. The ideas and sentiments Gorbachev expressed could be regarded as excessively idealistic or even naively unrealistic in the light of subsequent developments. Nevertheless, if Western politicians had displayed a greater awareness of the qualitative change in Soviet thinking (and the Bush administration was slow to acquire even the level of understanding on this that the Reagan administration had reached), more progress in deep and verified arms reductions on both sides could have been achieved sooner. At a minimum, had Western leaders realized that Gorbachev meant what he said about freedom of choice, they would not have been taken so much by surprise when the peoples of Eastern Europe took him at his word the following year and their countries became independent and non-Communist, while Soviet troops remained in their barracks.

Margaret Thatcher's Diplomacy

The changes in Moscow were beginning to have an effect in Eastern Europe, where both governments and peoples had become accustomed to the Soviet Union establishing the limits within which they could manoeuvre. The exceptions were Yugoslavia and Albania, which were not members of the Warsaw Pact and where the Yugoslav system had hitherto been more liberal and the Albanian harder line than the Soviet, and Romania, which did belong to the military alliance but pursued a somewhat independent foreign policy combined with harsh domestic dictatorship. Romania's puffed-up autocrat, Nicolae Ceaușescu, was the Communist leader Gorbachev found the most arrogant and insufferable.[88] Even in those societies, news of what was happening in Moscow filtered through and offered glimmers of hope for citizens who dreamt of reformist change. In the other Central and East European Communist states, the impact of the Soviet perestroika and of improved East–West relations was significantly greater. That applied, in the first place, to Poland and Hungary but also to Czechoslovakia, East Germany, and Bulgaria. In Poland and Hungary leaders as well as citizens reacted positively to the atmosphere of greater tolerance, whereas the Czech, East German, and Bulgarian party leaderships, in contradistinction to many of their citizens, viewed the new tolerance and liberalization in Moscow as a threat to their stability and security of tenure.

Margaret Thatcher combined her personal esteem for Gorbachev, and her belief that he was serious about introducing significant change in the Soviet Union, with encouragement of economic reform and greater political freedom in Eastern Europe. In November 1988 she visited Poland on the invitation of the country's leader, General Wojciech Jaruzelski, who had imposed martial law in Poland in December 1981, when under intense pressure from Brezhnev's Soviet Politburo to crush Solidarity, but had subsequently been presiding over a gradual relaxation of the hard-line regime reimposed then. Of the Warsaw Pact leaders, he was the one with whom Gorbachev had the warmest relations. The goal of Thatcher's visit was, as she put it, to continue with the strategy of engaging with Eastern Europe that had begun with her visit to Hungary in 1984. She wanted 'to open up these countries—their governments and peoples—to western influences and to exert pressure for respect for human rights and for political and economic reform'.[89] In pursuit of those aims, she had lengthy meetings with Jaruzelski and, separately, with Prime Minister Mieczyslaw Rakowski. Jaruzelski, who was both president of the country and party leader, told Thatcher that the government was ready to talk with Solidarity and she said she hoped they would take up that invitation.[90] She flew to Gdansk with Jaruzelski to lay a wreath at the Westerplatte, where the first fighting between the Poles and the Nazi invaders took place in 1939.

Thatcher then went to Gdansk shipyard, where she was met by cheering workers (not the sort of greeting that would have awaited her in a shipyard or factory back home). That was followed by a meeting with Lech Wałęsa and other Solidarity leaders, where Thatcher's long-standing anti-Communism was tempered by her sense that political progress would be furthered by Solidarity's constructive engagement with the party-state authorities. She was struck, as she later told Jaruzelski, by the moderation of Solidarity's position, with their goal being described by Wałęsa as 'pluralism'—a state and society 'in which the Communist Party was not the sole legitimate authority'. Thatcher felt, however, that the Solidarity leadership were lacking in 'immediate practical objectives' and when she told them she thought they should attend the talks proposed by Jaruzelski and that Solidarity should submit its own proposals and produce a detailed agenda with supporting papers, 'my hosts looked quite astonished'.[91] They discussed Solidarity's negotiating stance and agreed that 'the most important point I could make to General Jaruzelski was that Solidarity must be legalized'. At one point, after listening to the Solidarity leaders, Thatcher said, 'you really must see that the Government hears all this'. 'No problem,' Wałęsa replied, pointing to the ceiling, 'our meetings are bugged anyway.'[92]

The British prime minister duly put the points that arose from her Gdansk meeting with Solidarity's leaders to Jaruzelski in a subsequent meeting with him and thanked him for not putting obstacles in the way of her meeting Wałęsa. Although she found Jaruzelski a 'slightly awkward interlocutor until you got to know him' (with his dark glasses necessitated by an eye problem and rigid stature imposed by a back support), she was confirmed in her view that he 'was a Pole and not just a communist' when he made a completely unscheduled reappearance. Just before her plane to London took off, Jaruzelski's car screeched to a halt next to the plane and he leapt out carrying a huge bouquet of flowers.[93]

Two weeks later, Thatcher was in Washington for her last meeting as official guest of Ronald Reagan. By this time, Reagan was in the final stage of his lame duck period, for it was just a fortnight after George H. W. Bush's presidential election victory. Nevertheless, Reagan was determined to mark his special relationship with Thatcher and he authorized a particularly elaborate state dinner in her honour. Thatcher had been his first foreign guest at the White House, and it seemed to Reagan only right that she should be accorded the privilege of being the last.[94] The British prime minister had enjoyed Reagan's unstinted admiration and the two leaders felt a great affinity. On this final visit to Washington during the Reagan presidency, Thatcher was greeted with a nineteen-gun salute. The prime minister believed that she and Reagan had both taken a hard anti-Communist line at a time when others had been too conciliatory in their dealings with the Communist world, yet they had both come to believe that significant change was now underway in those countries partly as a result of their own efforts.

During her Washington visit Thatcher said, 'We are not in a Cold War now', for East and West were enjoying 'a new relationship much wider than the Cold War ever was'.[95] Whereas George Bush had said in one of the presidential debates that the jury was still out on Soviet reforms, Thatcher announced that she expected Gorbachev to push for further reform. What was more, London and Washington should be ready to help him 'both verbally and in practice'.[96] The warmth with which she was received by Reagan notwithstanding, Thatcher was well aware that her meetings with Bush and with other senior members of the incoming administration, now being put together, had become much more politically important.

She soon discovered that, though the British government remained a very significant ally of the United States, her personal influence in Washington would never again be what it was during the Reagan administration. She did not enjoy as congenial a relationship with Bush as she did with Reagan, and though the incoming Secretary of State James Baker was 'always very courteous' to her, relations with him were not as close as they had been with 'the admirable George Shultz'.[97] As Thatcher noted in her memoirs, 'I later learned that President Bush was sometimes exasperated by my habit of talking nonstop about issues which fascinate me and felt that he ought to have been leading the discussion.'[98] After observing Reagan listen contentedly as she expounded her views, this obviously came as a surprise to her. In her own account, her relationship with Bush had become better by 1990, for by then 'I had learned that I had to defer to him in conversation and not to stint the praise' which she was prepared to do if it served 'Britain's influence and interests'.[99]

Well into 1989, Bush's National Security Adviser Brent Scowcroft, who was close to the incoming president both personally and in outlook, was suspicious of Gorbachev, concerned that the Soviet leader might talk the US into disarming without also fundamentally changing military policy in the Soviet Union. So far as Scowcroft was concerned, Gorbachev 'remained a communist', for whom the political changes were no more than a device for circumventing those in the party who were blocking economic reform.[100] It worried Scowcroft that 'Everyone was tired of the Cold War, and even leaders such as British prime minister Margaret Thatcher were now declaring it over.'[101]

It was not only Thatcher's more positive attitude to the changes that had taken place in the Soviet Union that dampened the incoming administration's enthusiasm for her. It was also her increasingly acerbic relationship with Britain's West European allies. By the time she left office, she was more admired in Prague, Warsaw, and even Moscow than she was in Paris, Brussels, and Berlin, and that process was well underway by late 1988. One of her close associates and speech-writers, Robin Harris, said that those who viewed the speech Thatcher delivered in Bruges on 20 September 1988 to 'an unappreciative Europhile audience' as 'marking the beginning of a new policy' were correct, for it did. The Bruges speech (to whose composition Harris contributed but whose main writer was Thatcher's private secretary Charles Powell) reflected Thatcher's fears that the European Economic Community (EEC), as the European Union was then called, was becoming a 'Euro-federalist project'.[102] The speech was also in part a reaction to one delivered earlier in September by the President of the European Commission Jacques Delors which appeared to presage a 'new wave of interventionism'. Thatcher's speech further soured her relations with Geoffrey Howe, for he was among those who had persuaded her to embrace the single market within the EEC, and Howe, for his part, greatly disliked her growing Euroscepticism. Even when he was still Chancellor of the Exchequer, before becoming Foreign Secretary, Howe regarded support for Europe as 'a mark of "decency" within the Conservative Party'.[103]

It was not only the leadership of the British Foreign Office who were disturbed by Thatcher's increasingly difficult relationship with the EEC but also their Washington counterpart. The State Department and their incoming political head James Baker were supportive of greater European integration, as was Bush. This was not a matter on which Reagan had strong views but one, rather, where he was inclined to go along with Thatcher's judgement. The incoming US administration lost little time in ending that cosy accord. Thatcher complained of the State Department under Baker 'briefing against me and my policies—particularly on Europe' and of a shift towards putting the US relationship with Germany, rather than that with Britain, as the main focus of their concerns.[104] Given the centrality of 'the German question', as it was to develop in 1989–90, this was hardly surprising, but Thatcher's ill-disguised hostility to German unification, a unity that was sought and eagerly endorsed by Washington, became another reason for the Bush administration to accord her judgement substantially less respect than it received from Ronald Reagan.

The New Thinking Comes to New York

In the second half of 1988, following Reagan's visit to Moscow and the Nineteenth Party Conference in the Soviet capital, relations between Washington and Moscow were warmer than ever before. There was a rapid expansion of contacts between senior American and Soviet officials. They included Secretary of Defense Frank Carlucci and the Soviet Minister of Defence Dmitry Yazov.[105] Even more remarkably, between 1988 and 1990 Marshal Akhromeyev met his American counterpart, Admiral William Crowe, on no fewer than six occasions.[106] According to Akhromeyev, they had constructive, detailed, and open discussions and acquired a better understanding of each other's view of the world and of the international situation.[107] Yet, notwithstanding the extension of diplomatic activity, the efforts of Shultz and Shevardnadze to achieve an agreement to reduce strategic offensive nuclear weapons (START) while Reagan was still in the White House ended in failure. Although both the Secretary of State and the Soviet Foreign Minister wanted the agreement, the kind of strategic defence Reagan had in view was still an issue for the Soviet side and the Reagan administration were, moreover, 'unwilling to accept the sort of limitations on cruise missiles that Soviet negotiators demanded'.[108]

For many within the American establishment, and for European leaders, a big issue remained Warsaw Pact superiority in conventional forces. A majority of Reagan administration officials, as well as key senators, were opposed to a START agreement before an accord had been reached on a reduction of conventional weaponry in Europe to equivalent levels on both sides. Moreover, Bush did not want any agreement to be made at the tail-end of his predecessor's administration, thus tying him into a policy towards the Soviet Union that would look like a continuation of Reagan's. He and his closest advisers wished to take time to reassess the relationship.[109] Given that Bush had been Vice-President for eight years and had been kept in the loop on US foreign policy, including all the key discussions with the Soviet leadership, he could have been expected to know his own mind by this time. Whereas, however, Reagan's conservative credentials were long established, Bush felt vulnerable vis-à-vis the right wing of the Republican Party.[110]

The issue of the imbalance in conventional forces was about to be addressed in spectacular fashion by Gorbachev in his speech of 7 December at the United Nations. He had come to understand the centrality of this issue for Western leaders, as part of a learning process in which Margaret Thatcher had been an especially insistent and influential teacher.[111] The unilateral cuts in Soviet conventional forces which Gorbachev announced were dramatic and they were what grabbed the headlines. Over the next two years the Soviet armed forces would be reduced by 500,000 personnel. Six tank divisions would be withdrawn from the German Democratic Republic (East Germany), Czechoslovakia, and Hungary and disbanded. There would be 50,000 fewer Soviet troops left in those countries and 5,000 fewer tanks. On the

Figure 12 Gorbachev making his ground-breaking speech to the United Nations in New York, 7 December 1988.

European part of Soviet territory and on the territory of their European allies, the cuts over the following two years would amount to 10,000 tanks, 8,500 artillery systems, and 800 combat aircraft. There would also be substantial cuts in the size of the armed forces on the Asian part of Soviet territory and many of the troops stationed in neighbouring Mongolia would return home. In making this move, Gorbachev was essentially meeting Western concerns about Soviet superiority in conventional force numbers.

What made still more of an impression on defence officials in Western Europe than the scale of the cuts was their composition. They particularly applied to forces that would be deployed in rapid offensive operations deep into West European territory. This initiative was a concrete manifestation of the new Soviet security doctrine of 'non-offensive defence'. Overall, Gorbachev framed the large-scale reductions of conventional Soviet forces in terms of 'demilitarization of international relations' and, still more ambitiously, of 'transition from an economy based on armaments to an economy [resting on] disarmament'.[112]

Even more important than the unilateral arms reduction initiatives was, however, what George Shultz called the 'philosophical' part of Gorbachev's UN speech. In Shultz's view, 'if anybody declared the end of the Cold War, he did in that speech. It was over.' And yet, as Shultz put it, 'the press walked by that'. Gorbachev's interpreter Pavel Palazchenko, citing these remarks made by Shultz at a conference held at

Princeton in 1993, observed that, though Shultz was criticizing the media, he could just as well have been referring to 'almost the entire U.S. foreign policy establishment'.[113] In the first half of his UN speech, Gorbachev abandoned central tenets of Marxism-Leninism and virtually all of the dogma of Soviet foreign policy that had prevailed prior to the second half of the 1980s. For Palazchenko, it was the speech of a man who 'was thinking in terms of a single global civilization, of one world whose problems could not be solved on the basis of our outdated "theology"'.[114]

Gorbachev declared that it was time to give priority to those values that united all of humanity (as distinct from those of any one class, nation or group). With an idealism verging on the utopian, he said they had to seek an 'all-human consensus on movement towards a new world order', but progress must not be at 'the expense of the rights and freedoms of the individual or of nations or at the expense of the natural world'.[115] Earlier than most politicians (not only Soviet politicians), Gorbachev was a leader who took ecological issues seriously. Later in the same speech, Gorbachev spoke about the need to overcome 'the worldwide ecological threats', saying that in this respect the situation in many regions had become 'simply frightening'.[116] Among his suggestions for doing something about it was the setting-up of a centre for ecological assistance under the auspices of the United Nations.[117]

A 'one-sided emphasis on military strength', observed Gorbachev, 'in the final analysis weakens other components of national security'. He went on to stress the cardinal importance of 'freedom of choice' as 'a universal principle' from which there must be no exceptions.[118] Gorbachev made clear that the emphasis on 'all-human' values and interests was not to deny the variety and legitimacy of different socio-political systems. It was, though, better to recognize and tolerate diversity than to try to teach others one's own brand of democracy, the more especially since, when democratic values took the form of an 'export order', they frequently and quickly became degraded.[119] The times, he said, demanded a 'deideologization of interstate relationships'. This did not mean giving up one's convictions, philosophy, or traditions but it meant not shutting oneself off from the experience of others. 'It goes without saying', said Gorbachev (although what followed was something no previous Soviet leader would have said), that 'we are far from laying claim to indisputable truth'. They needed their common humanity to prevail over the multiplicity of centrifugal forces in order to preserve 'the viability of a civilization that is possibly the only one in the universe'.[120]

On a less lofty plane, Gorbachev noted the need for more intensive and open political dialogue and said, little by little, a mutual understanding had started to develop in US–Soviet relations, along with elements of trust, without which it was very difficult to make progress. These features were still more apparent in the Soviet Union's relations with Europe. 'The Helsinki process', he said, 'is a great process.' It needed to be strengthened and deepened and to take account of new circumstances.[121] For the Brezhnev leadership, the main point of the Helsinki Final Act of 1975 had been recog-

Figure 13 Vladimir Kryuchkov (left) in conversation with Aleksandr Yakovlev. Kryuchkov cultivated Yakovlev to win his support for making him KGB Chairman. The radical differences in their outlooks before long made them political enemies.

nition of the existing borders of the countries of Europe and they had downplayed or ignored the stipulation that these could be altered with the consent—and only with the consent—of the populations. They had also disregarded the articles which insisted on respect for human rights and freedoms. Gorbachev took the view that the Soviet perestroika was leading to a new respect for rights and liberties within his own country. It was high time, therefore, to stop being defensive in the face of Western attempts to remind the Soviet leadership of what they had signed up to in Helsinki and, on the contrary, to embrace that agreement in its totality.

A huge amount of effort went into the preparation of Gorbachev's December 1988 UN speech. The first draft was written by Chernyaev, who sought contributions from Yakovlev, Shevardnadze, Dobrynin, Valentin Falin (who, two months earlier, had succeeded Dobrynin as head of the International Department of the Central Committee of the CPSU), and Akhromeyev.[122] Gorbachev himself reworked the whole text which he consciously set out to be an 'anti-Fulton'.[123] By this he meant that, whereas Churchill's famous speech in Fulton, Missouri, with its stress on the 'iron curtain' which had descended across Europe, had signalled that the world had entered a period of Cold War, he would be pointing the way to a reunited world and, in effect, announcing the end of the Cold War, especially in its ideological capacity. Within less than four years of becoming the leader of his country, Gorbachev had introduced a dramatically different political discourse that broke with all previous Soviet ideology. In its ambition and idealism, his new thinking raised the question whether Western leaders would be capable of responding to such fundamental challenges to their conventional wisdom.

In its practical implications, the new doctrine raised questions at home as well. For the Soviet military the huge troop reductions proposed by Gorbachev were a bitter pill to swallow. Akhromeyev had the difficult task of acting as a go-between with the Soviet High Command and of seeking to persuade them to accept the movement from Soviet superiority to an approximate parity with the West in conventional forces in Europe. The leadership of the general staff believed that such huge defence cuts as the political leadership proposed would have a seriously adverse effect on their military strength. 'For us, in the military leadership to accept the decision about the reduction was', said Akhromeyev, 'very difficult.'[124] Moreover, for many officers and their families it was a painful experience and for some even a tragedy.[125] The discussion of the proposed cuts continued in the Ministry of Defence over two weeks in the first half of November but, in the end, Gorbachev got his way, and on 24 November the broad lines of his UN speech were approved also by the Politburo.[126]

The extent of the argument behind the scenes in the lead-up to Gorbachev's speech was proof enough of the seriousness of the proposed military cutbacks. The conceptual change the speech encapsulated made a big impact on Gorbachev's United Nations audience, who gave it a rapturous reception. In Moscow the word British Ambassador Rodric Braithwaite used in his diary to describe Gorbachev's New York speech was 'stunning'.[127] It was variously received, however, by those who mattered most in American politics. For Shultz, it was a clear declaration that the Cold War had ended. He appreciated also the sentence in Gorbachev's speech in which he said, 'We acknowledge and value the contribution of President Ronald Reagan and the members of his administration, above all Mr George Shultz.'[128] As Shultz was about to demit office, he was, however, concerned that the incoming administration (albeit of the same party) 'did not understand or accept that the cold war was over'. He feared also that their planned 'top-to-bottom policy review' would put at risk the 'real momentum' that by this time characterized US–Soviet relations.[129]

Shultz's fears were well-founded. Although there were career analysts of the Soviet Union within the CIA who understood the magnitude of the change represented by Gorbachev's UN speech, higher up, in the person of Robert Gates, there remained profound scepticism. Still more importantly, Scowcroft dismissed the speech as 'a largely rhetorical flourish' that had created 'a heady atmosphere of optimism'. This made an early summit meeting between the incoming president and Gorbachev undesirable because it would 'only abet the current Soviet propaganda campaign'.[130] In a television interview the following month, Scowcroft suggested that Gorbachev's foreign policy 'might be secretly intended to throw the West off its guard' and that until the United States had better evidence to the contrary, that was what their assumption should be. 'I think', he added, 'the Cold War is not over.'[131]

Gorbachev had meetings both with Reagan and with Bush while he was in New York, but nothing of substance could be agreed with the outgoing president at this stage and his successor was non-committal. Reporting to the Politburo, Gorbachev said that when 'I managed to tear myself away from Reagan, I spoke to Bush about this indecisiveness.' Bush retorted that he could not say anything until the formal transfer of power had taken place. Gorbachev told the Politburo that he understood that convention, but that they would, nevertheless, need to 'take into account that Bush is a very cautious politician'.[132]

The euphoria engendered by the UN speech did not last long. Apart from concern over whether the Bush administration would be ready to engage, Gorbachev had to end his foreign travel abruptly when news came through of a major earthquake in Soviet Armenia with massive loss of life and destruction. He decided to postpone the planned visits to Cuba and then to Britain which had been due to follow immediately after New York. Reporting to Margaret Thatcher would have to wait, although she was the first foreign leader to express her sympathy to him, and British aid for the victims of the earthquake promptly followed. Even if the incoming US administration was not ready to take up relations with the Soviet leadership where Reagan had left off, there was no diminution of Thatcher's esteem for Gorbachev. Shortly before taking up his ambassadorial post in September, Braithwaite had tea with the prime minister. Thatcher stressed the closeness of her relationship with Gorbachev and saw a parallel between his political role and her own. In language about a Soviet leader which was a far cry from the rhetoric which earned her the sobriquet of the 'Iron Lady', she said that if Dukakis won the forthcoming American presidential election, 'Gorbachev will be my only friend left.'[133]

12

THE END OF THE COLD WAR (1989)

Mikhail Gorbachev's peaceful demolition, in his United Nations speech, of what was left of the ideological wall between Communist Europe and the West was to be followed in 1989 by the demolition of real walls. Yet, at the beginning of 1989 Europe was still politically and physically divided between Communist and non-Communist states which meant that one of the Cold War's principal features remained in place. The incoming American administration also *believed* they were still engaged in a Cold War. There was a strong feeling within the Bush administration that Ronald Reagan and George Shultz had put too much faith in personalities—in Gorbachev in the first instance but also (in Shultz's case) in Eduard Shevardnadze.

Yet Gorbachev had removed the rationale for ideological struggle with fresh thinking backed up by such real and substantial changes as growing freedom of speech within the USSR, the withdrawal of Soviet troops from Afghanistan, and his announced large-scale reduction in the size of the armed forces. The Soviet leader had made it more difficult to portray his country as the enemy. Following Gorbachev's speech at the UN, 54 per cent of Americans believed that the Soviet Union was either 'no threat' or 'only a minor threat', and two thirds thought that the Soviet concern was primarily with their own national security, as against 28 per cent who believed the USSR was 'bent on world domination'. In Britain, West Germany, and Italy those perceiving the Soviet Union to be a threat were still fewer.[1]

It was, however, one thing to renounce long-standing Communist dogma, as Gorbachev had effectively done the previous year, and even to embrace 'freedom to choose' as a concept, and another to tolerate an actual end to Communist rule in the eastern half of the European continent. The East–West divide in Europe was the Cold War's most visible manifestation, and Soviet control over a buffer zone between the USSR and the West had long been regarded in Moscow as a legitimate geopolitical reward for the decisive role their country played in defeating Nazi Germany. Even those in the West who thought Gorbachev was sincere about radically reforming his own country and about pursuing peaceful and constructive relations with the non-Communist world could not be sure what would happen in the event of a threat to the hegemony of a ruling Communist party in a Warsaw Pact country or in the Soviet

Union itself. It was widely assumed that any serious challenge to Soviet-style Communist rule would be met with force. Indeed, it had long been taken for granted in Washington, London, and other Western capitals that maintenance of 'the leading role of the party' (and of East European leaders' loyalty to the Kremlin) was for the Soviet leadership in Moscow non-negotiable.

If that was the assumption not only of Soviet and East European leaders but also of their Western adversaries, the peoples of Central and Eastern Europe had every reason to share it. Yet, during 1989 those same peoples, in one country after another, tested the hypothesis that Gorbachev had meant what he said when he spoke of the citizens of every country having the right to choose the kind of system they wished to live in. The East–West stand-off had begun with the Sovietization of eastern and central Europe. And since a majority of the people who lived there regarded Communist rule with varying degrees of disillusion, distaste, or disgust, the Cold War could only truly be said to have ended when they were able to remove their Communist governments and establish, or re-establish, independent statehood. Whether Gorbachev would be true to his 'freedom to choose' words of the previous year was one question. Another was: supposing Gorbachev did allow any attempt at regime change in an East European country to take its course, could he survive politically? Was there not every likelihood that he would be overthrown by hard-liners in Moscow who would then lose no time in restoring Soviet hegemony over the recalcitrant client state?

The Bush Administration's Soviet Policy: A Sluggish and Uncertain Start

The Bush administration provided neither early recognition of, nor encouragement for, Soviet change. Both Secretary of State James Baker, an old and close friend of the president, and National Security Adviser Brent Scowcroft, who had also become a trusted friend and adviser of Bush, urged caution on dealing with Gorbachev. Scowcroft was profoundly sceptical of Reagan's embrace of Gorbachev and his favourable assessment of his intentions and sincerity.[2] Gorbachev's peace initiatives, in Scowcroft's view, amounted to no more than trouble-making for the Western alliance.[3] Since Bush was, as Gorbachev had correctly informed the Soviet Politburo, cautious by nature, this merely reinforced the American president's own inclinations and led to a prolonged period of non-engagement with the Soviet Union.

By the time the Bush administration decided on more active diplomacy, which was not until May 1989, further profound change had taken place in the USSR which made a big impact in Europe, both East and West. Those close to Bush were concerned that Gorbachev had become the most highly esteemed world statesman, eclipsing Bush.[4] American re-engagement was aimed more at impressing domestic and international audiences than with improving East–West relations. Even Baker, who was sympathetic to the Soviet perestroika, as it was explained to him first by Shevardnadze in March and subsequently by Gorbachev when he had his first Moscow meeting with him in May, saw the relationship at this point as adversarial. 'Gorbachev's strategy', Baker later wrote, 'was to weaken Western cohesion through high-profile, publicly attractive proposals and thus to gain economic benefits from the West.'[5]

The deputy national security adviser to Scowcroft was Robert Gates, previously deputy director of the CIA and a long-time Soviet specialist, a man deeply distrustful of the idea that Gorbachev's reforms would change anything basic in the Soviet Union. In a November 1987 memorandum, during the Reagan administration, he had written that it was hard to detect any fundamental change either taking place in the Soviet Union or in prospect, and that the Communist Party 'certainly will retain its monopoly of power and the basic structures of the Stalinist economy will remain'.[6] When he took up his new post, his scepticism about Gorbachev's intentions persisted, and he saw Soviet force reductions as 'a threat to "Alliance cohesion" rather than a gain for security in Europe'.[7] Within the CIA, there were senior analysts such as Fritz Ermath (who spent the last two years of the Reagan presidency as the top Soviet specialist on the NSC) whose preconceptions similarly dulled their capacity to recognize basic change, even when the evidence was unfolding before their eyes. At a less elevated rung of the hierarchy, there were, however, others with a more open mind who could recognize that what was happening in Moscow was a dramatic break with the past.

A National Intelligence Estimate (NIE) produced in April 1989 admitted the depth of the disagreement in 'the Intelligence Community'. There was a substantial group who 'see current policy changes as largely tactical', driven by the need for a breathing space from competition. They placed great weight on the continuing relevance of Marxism-Leninism for their Soviet adversary and held that this ideology guaranteed continuing hostility towards capitalist countries. On the other side were those intelligence analysts who viewed Gorbachev's policies as reflecting 'a fundamental rethinking of national interests' and who argued that ideological tenets hitherto regarded as fundamental in the Soviet Union were already being revised.[8] Douglas MacEachin, a senior CIA analyst of the Soviet Union who maintained that Gorbachev was serious both about reform and about wanting to wind down the arms race, ran into bitter opposition to his views.[9] Ultimately, however, the disputes within the CIA did not matter unduly. In the first place, not much of their arguments got through to successive presidents by the time they had been filtered in the NSC. Second, and more important, the judgements Reagan and Shultz and, subsequently, Bush and Baker made of the character and aims of their Soviet counterparts counted for far more than all the NIEs put together.[10]

Secretary Baker and Condoleezza Rice, who became the Soviet and East European specialist in Scowcroft's NSC, give strikingly divergent accounts of the much-heralded reassessment of policy towards the Soviet Union which Bush authorized. But one thing they do agree on was its uselessness. For Baker, the 'so-called strategic review was neither strategic nor a proper review'. Launched in mid-February, it was meant to produce a reassessment of US foreign policy from top to bottom. The appraisal was, he said, largely carried out by Reagan administration holdovers who by seeking 'bureaucratic consensus' produced a 'mush'.[11] Rice, who was intimately involved in the series of policy reviews, had a quite different perspective on them. Their purpose, she observed, was 'to give time to get new people into place and, in the case of European and Soviet policy, to slow down what was widely seen as Ronald Reagan's too-close embrace of Mikhail Gorbachev in 1988'.[12]

Baker's assessment that the reviews were insufficiently critical of the Reagan administration's priorities is hard to reconcile with Rice's account. The series of reviews, two of which 'I personally managed', recalled Rice, 'seethed with distrust of the changes taking place in Eastern Europe and the Soviet Union'.[13] To her credit, she admits the lack of insight and of prescience in their findings. The reviews were over-taken by events that took the Bush administration completely by surprise. The real changes in the Communist world were soon on a scale, observes Rice, that 'got our attention in time to overcome our inherent caution'. Self-deprecatingly, she added that 'no one remembers that we wrote policy guidance questioning Gorbachev's motives and setting up careful "tests" of Moscow's intentions months before the collapse of Soviet power in Eastern Europe and the unification of Germany'.[14]

Bush and Baker, being none the wiser after the official policy reviews, held three meetings in the NSC at the end of March and beginning of April 1989 specifically devoted to the Soviet Union and Eastern Europe. Bush also met with Sovietologists from outside the administration in February, with no discernible effect, and Baker held a seminar in the State Department in April, to which three academic specialists (George Breslauer, Stephen Meyer, and Stephen Sestanovich) were invited to contribute. The Secretary of State noted that the basic disagreement among the experts, mirrored in the administration, was between those of hawkish disposition, who thought that Gorbachev's perestroika was merely the seeking of a breathing-space before the Soviet Union would re-emerge, strengthened, and thus a still greater threat in the years to come, and the 'more dovish analysts', for whom 'perestroika was a fundamental shift in Soviet policy'.[15] Baker remained unimpressed, dismissing the contrasting viewpoints as 'mainly academic theology' and believing that, as of the spring of 1989, 'both views had analytical strengths and weaknesses'.[16] The Secretary of State observed that he and his senior advisers, to a much greater extent than the Department of Defense or the NSC, favoured an 'activist' view, as he put it, seeking to find out how far Gorbachev would be willing to go 'by moving forward ourselves'.[17] To the extent that he pursued that policy, Baker was following in the footsteps of

Shultz, but much more tardily. And Baker viewed the relationship with the Soviet Union as a battle for international influence to a greater extent than Shultz had done. 'Gorbachev's strategy', the new Secretary believed, 'was premised on splitting the alliance and undercutting us in Western Europe', by courting popularity with their peoples.[18] While it was true that Gorbachev was interested in appealing to European public opinion, he was much more concerned with obviating the need for a military alliance hostile to the Soviet Union than with splitting it.

Aside from a more pessimistic assessment of Soviet intentions, Baker broke with the policy of Reagan and Shultz with his desire, strongly shared by Defense Secretary Dick Cheney and National Security Adviser Scowcroft, to de-emphasize arms negotiations. Baker's account of Soviet military might is at odds with the narrative which sees Reagan's arms build-up as having forced a Soviet Union which could not compete into pursuing a concessionary foreign policy. In Baker's words: 'Given Soviet massive advantages in almost every type of weapons system, we felt the numbers game was a losing game; we preferred the concept of arms "control" to arms "reduction".'[19] Baker told Shevardnadze, when they met in Moscow in May, that while the Americans did not wish 'to sidetrack arms control', they had no desire to get bogged down in technicalities or to focus simply on numbers. They preferred a broader political approach to the problem of attaining strategic stability.[20] Since that was in accord with Gorbachev's and Shevardnadze's own outlook, it was a path forward which could have been taken earlier. Gorbachev's unilateral arms reduction initiatives had been influenced, as we have seen, by his desire to reduce the size of the Soviet military budget but also by his having come to appreciate the significance of Western concerns about the Soviet advantage in conventional forces, not least as a result of the forceful advocacy of Margaret Thatcher. The Soviet leader's own preoccupation was, nevertheless, far more with the big political picture than with the technical minutiae of arms negotiations (capable, though he was, as General Colin Powell in particular noted, of mastering them).[21]

Virtually the only key member of Reagan's team with a significant role in the making of America's policy toward the Soviet Union to keep his job was Jack Matlock. Having been the NSC specialist on Russia and Eastern Europe and subsequently, from 1987, US ambassador to Moscow, Matlock remained in the latter post until the summer of 1991. In the early months of 1989 he was greatly frustrated by the unwillingness of the Bush administration to carry on where Reagan had left off and engage in constructive dialogue with the Soviet leadership. In the ambassador's interpretation, Bush's 'weakness with the right' tempted him 'to play the tough guy to please his potential critics'.[22] Having worked in the White House for three years, Matlock was also well aware of the tensions between the 'Reagan people' and the 'Bush people', though he tried to stay on good terms with both.[23] Yet it took a lot of lobbying before the ambassador succeeded in having a meeting with Bush in March 1989 and the president remained unresponsive to Matlock's urging upon him the merits of holding an early superpower summit.[24]

Gorbachev and the Pluralization of the Soviet Political System

While the Bush administration was still dithering over foreign policy, Gorbachev pressed ahead with radical political reform in the Soviet Union. It had already been foreshadowed at the Nineteenth Party Conference in mid-1988, but the breakthrough to real political debate and contested elections for a new legislature in the Soviet Union made less of an impression in Washington than it did in European capitals. At this stage of the Soviet perestroika, Gorbachev was still very much in the driving seat, and he sanctioned a momentous change in Soviet politics by tacitly accepting the abandonment of the doctrine of democratic centralism which had mandated strict party discipline and the subordination of every CPSU member to higher party organs. In the elections, held in March 1989, for a new legislature called the Congress of People's Deputies (which was, in turn, to elect indirectly a smaller body, the Supreme Soviet, that would meet for longer periods each year than the larger Congress), an overwhelming majority of the candidates were Communist Party members. Meeting as the party group, they decided that decisions of the highest party organs would not be binding on them.[25]

Two new features made these elections utterly unlike the pseudo-elections that had existed in the Soviet Union hitherto when there was one candidate, and one alone, for each seat in the legislature. In the great majority of constituencies in 1989, there were more candidates than there were deputies' positions to be filled. Seats were also set aside to be chosen not by the electorate as a whole but by such social organizations as the Academy of Sciences, but the deputies chosen from those bodies included some of the most talented and independent-minded of the new legislators—among them Andrei Sakharov. (The bureaucratic leadership of the Academy had tried to prevent Sakharov from being one of their representatives, but the will of rank-and-file academicians prevailed.) The second fundamentally new feature was that those candidates who (unlike Sakharov) were Communist Party members, far from observing a party line laid down centrally, opposed one another while espousing sharply divergent policies. They did so in the election campaign and continued to do so when the legislature was in session. The CPSU had long contained people of very different views, but hitherto that diversity of political opinion emerged only between the lines of official publications and, much more freely, in conversation between trusted friends. Now the differences were out in the open and could be seen and heard on TV in broadcasts of debates in the legislature.

The new political environment made life more difficult for the KGB. In the report (delivered to Gorbachev in February 1989) on their activities in 1988, Vladimir Kryuchkov, who succeeded Viktor Chebrikov as the KGB chief in that year, walked a fine line between paying lip service to the political change already effected and the organization's traditional distrust of nonconformist activity. On the one hand, the report spoke of the KGB's 'devotion to steadfast maintenance of socialist legality and guaranteeing the real rights of the individual', of implementing legal reforms, and the rehabilitation of the victims of 'groundless repression' in the 1930s, 1940s, and the early 1950s.[26] On the other hand, in addition to giving numbers on the arrests of terrorists, spies, their collaborators, and a variety of politically hostile elements, the report stressed the threat posed by American and other intelligence agencies as well as 'foreign anti-Soviet centres, and antisocialist, nationalist, extremist and other elements' within the USSR. They were, Kryuchkov reported, 'taking advantage of the democratic transformation' to destabilize the country.[27] In order to move from Deputy Chairman to Chairman of the KGB, Kryuchkov had lobbied hard, and successfully, to get the support of Aleksandr Yakovlev, presenting himself as a reformer, in contrast with Chebrikov. His real views were very different, although he adapted them for different interlocutors.*

Almost on the eve of the elections to the Congress of People's Deputies, Gorbachev put the finishing touches to a new book manuscript written in 1988 and early 1989. A team assembled by Chernyaev had been working intensively on it, but it was a project on which Gorbachev expended a lot of effort, writing and amending in spare moments. Chernyaev, at one point, believed its impact might be still greater than that of Gorbachev's 1987 book, *Perestroika: New Thinking for Our Country and the World*, which became a worldwide bestseller.[28] Yet, in the end, Gorbachev decided not to publish the manuscript. Events were moving so fast that it was becoming out of date, and Gorbachev's own views were evolving, too. The manuscript was very different from what any previous Soviet General Secretary would or could have written. It displayed commitment to democratization and reform, and attacked Stalin and Stalinism. Yet it was a mixture of the new and the old inasmuch as it linked perestroika to the ideas that Lenin was formulating in the last few years of his life. The manuscript both idealized the 'late Lenin' (whose last works, wrote Gorbachev, 'were permeated by anxiety') and made conscious use of him to legitimate perestroika.[29] While no reform of the Soviet system could have got off the ground with a frontal attack on Lenin, 1989 was the year in which political debate was leaving Lenin behind. It was the start of a

---

* Immediately after the failed coup against Gorbachev in August 1991, in the organization of which the KGB Chairman was heavily involved, Kryuchkov wrote Gorbachev a grovelling letter of apology in which he said he was 'very ashamed' and concluded by offering Gorbachev, 'as in the past', his 'deep respect'. (The original of the letter was for a time kept on public display at the Gorbachev Foundation in Moscow.) What Kryuchkov had been saying to his co-conspirators was very different and in post-Soviet Russia he virulently attacked Gorbachev (and Yakovlev also) as a traitor. He did so in his memoirs and at a round-table conference in Moscow in June 1999, jointly organized by the Mershon Institute of Ohio State University and the Institute of General History of the Russian Academy of Sciences. At that conference, Kryuchkov said that 'Gorbachev struck one blow after another at the Military Industrial Complex, making it out to be a monster that we needed to settle accounts with at all costs.' The former KGB chief went so far as to assert: 'It seems to me that if we were to dig into human history, then we would probably not find a single example of a powerful government official who, while in power, essentially carried out the sort of treasonous policy we see with Gorbachev' (Transcript of Moscow Cold War Conference, Tape 3, pp. 26 and 33).

Figure 14 Eduard Shevardnadze with new US Secretary of State James Baker, 10 May 1989 (Baker's first visit to Russia). Also in the picture US ambassador to Moscow Jack Matlock (behind Baker) and US government Russian interpreter Dimitry Zarechnak (on right).

period in which Gorbachev was beginning to see that his growing attraction to the democratic socialism of social democratic parties was incompatible with a belief in Leninism, however refined or redefined. While the pluralization of Soviet politics owed more to Gorbachev than to anyone else, the new pluralism, and the intellectual and political debate it generated, influenced also its progenitor—one of whose most important characteristics was the possession of an open mind.

Echoing the language of Lenin, Gorbachev had referred, in the unpublished manuscript, to Boris Yeltsin's '"infantile" disease of ambition'.[30] However, the March 1989 election gave Yeltsin the opportunity to launch a political comeback, one which he seized with both hands. Still a member of the Communist Party, he overwhelmingly defeated the favoured candidate of the party hierarchy in a Moscow-wide constituency. Jack Matlock later wrote that he had found Yeltsin's victory 'less astonishing than the fact that *the votes had been counted fairly*' (italics Matlock's).[31] Some of the most anti-establishment votes were recorded in Moscow and Leningrad. In an outcome that would have been unthinkable even a year or two earlier, Russia's second city saw the defeat of the first secretary of the Leningrad regional party organization and candidate member of the Politburo, Yury Solovev. An anti-apparatchik vote was also discernible in the Ukrainian capital, Kiev, while the people of the Baltic republics took the opportunity to make known what they thought of their current republican bosses. The chairmen of the Council of Ministers of Latvia and Lithuania were among the candidates who failed to be elected.[32]

The elections fell well short of being fully democratic. For example, 100 seats out of the 2,500 in the Congress of People's Deputies (of whom a third were chosen by social organizations) were reserved for a list of party figures whose approval was required only by the Central Committee of the party. Gorbachev himself was on that list, though at this point he was still by far the most popular politician in the country and could easily have won in an openly contested seat. (Even at the end of 1989, Yeltsin was a distant second to Gorbachev when people were asked to name the most outstanding political figure in the Soviet Union.[33] It was during 1990—most specifically, in May–June of that year—that Yeltsin overtook him as the country's most popular politician.[34]) Nevertheless, the contestation in the majority of seats made these elections qualitatively different from anything that had gone before in Soviet politics.

Addressing the Politburo on 28 March, after the elections were over, Gorbachev characterized them as 'the most outstanding step' thus far 'in the implementation of political reform and the further democratization of society'.[35] In the discussion which followed, however, sharp differences emerged within this highest party body about their recent electoral experience. There was more criticism than praise for the process, with those who agreed with Gorbachev on seeing the elections as a positive step forward—most notably, Yakovlev and Shevardnadze—less numerous than the Politburo members who expressed concern about the number of party secretaries who failed to get elected and who voiced their discontent with the mass media whom they accused of whipping up negative sentiments about party officialdom. Ligachev described the situation as 'very dangerous', saying that they should remember that in Hungary and Czechoslovakia (in 1956 and 1968) 'everything began with the mass media'. He said that 'repression' was not necessary, but they 'must retain order' and be ready to use the instruments of power, especially against some publications.[36] Given that expectations had been aroused in Soviet society, restoration of traditional Soviet-style order would, in fact, have meant repression. It was of decisive importance that the minority within the Politburo who resisted that course of action included the most powerful person in their midst, General Secretary Gorbachev.

For Yakovlev, those Politburo members who blamed the mass media for the defeat of many party officials were getting 'too emotional' about the press. He saw the elections as a vote in favour of perestroika and against stagnation, against the command-administrative system and against bad management.[37] Gorbachev, always conscious of the fate of Nikita Khrushchev who was overthrown by his Politburo colleagues, had to keep on board the majority who feared that radical reform was threatening to destroy pillars of the system. Indeed, it was, but the difference between them and Gorbachev was that the general secretary had come to believe that the Soviet political system needed to be dismantled and rebuilt on new foundations. He later wrote: 'The presence of a strong conservative tendency in the

Politburo, and in general in the higher echelons of the party, led to our not infre-quently being late in taking urgent decisions.'[38] Writing more than twenty years after he became general secretary, he reflected that he should have been ready earlier to take the risk of splitting the Communist Party and also, in defiance of the wishes of the party hierarchy, to have stood for direct election as president by the people as a whole, rather than being indirectly elected president by the Congress of People's Deputies, as he was in March 1990.[39]

If the 1989 election itself was a major step in the pluralization of Soviet politics, so were the public arguments which followed on the floor of the Congress of People's Deputies. As Gorbachev's aide and adviser on political reform Georgy Shakhnazarov noted, the deputies immediately divided into several groups, thus demonstrating how illusory was the idea that the party consisted of like-minded people.[40] Gorbachev was elected chairman of the new legislature, although a Leningrad deputy, Aleksandr Obolensky, stood against him, thus forcing a vote. In the earliest weeks of the fledg-ling parliament's existence, Gorbachev chaired its proceedings. He did so, according to Shakhnazarov, because he wanted to foster a culture of parliamentarism. Deputies of critical views, including Sakharov, were given more speaking opportunities than were proportionate to their representation within the legislature. By taking on what was in effect the role of speaker in the new assembly, Gorbachev not only added a huge burden to the almost intolerably heavy load of responsibilities he already car-ried, he also, in the view of one of the shrewdest members of his circle, 'inflicted damage on his personal authority'.[41] When, observed Shakhnazarov, millions of people, sitting in front of their television sets, could see some unknown young dep-uty contradicting and even openly insulting the head of state, they concluded that this boded ill for the country and for that leader.[42]

What was taken for granted in parliamentary democracies was an unfamiliar experience in the Soviet Union and Russia. For a prime minister to be scathingly criticized in, for example, the British Parliament has long been par for the course—Margaret Thatcher for one was well accustomed to it—but Russian political expect-ations and norms were very different. Shakhnazarov viewed Gorbachev's tolerance of deputies publicly contradicting him as being, at one and the same time, a plus in terms of the democratizing process and a minus in that it began a process of under-mining the authority of the person who had launched the reforms and who still had a decisive role to play. Gorbachev was both party leader and head of state, having succeeded Gromyko in the latter role (as Chairman of the Presidium of the Supreme Soviet) in October 1988. But public criticism of him in 1989 made clear to the popula-tion that the top leader's authority was no longer unquestioned and unquestionable. And that turn of events was at odds with a deeply embedded assumption in Russian political culture (which Shakhnazarov had in mind) that the country's interests were best served by having an overwhelmingly strong leader at the helm. Whether Russia, or any other country, is well served by such a widespread belief is quite another matter.[43]

Gorbachev's priority was domestic change, though he continued to seek a qualitative improvement in Soviet relations with Western countries—and, indeed, worldwide, including China and Japan. The last Soviet soldier duly left Afghanistan in February 1989. The pro-Soviet leadership in Kabul nonetheless continued to look to Moscow for support. Gorbachev did not wish to see the collapse of a friendly government in Afghanistan though, in contrast with Shevardnadze, he was resistant to pleas from the Afghan leader Mohammed Najibullah to send further Soviet military assistance. As early as March, Najibullah requested Soviet air support for the Afghan government forces during critical battles, and both Foreign Minister Shevardnadze and KGB Chairman Vladimir Kryuchkov were strongly in favour of acceding to this request. Gorbachev convened an informal meeting of Politburo members and Secretaries of the Central Committee at the Novo Ogarevo dacha on the evening of 10 March to discuss the fragility of the military situation in Afghanistan and Najibullah's request. Minister of Defence Dmitry Yazov was more cautious than Shevardnadze, who spoke passionately in support of helping Najibullah, saying that to do anything else would be a betrayal and would lose the Soviet Union friends in the Third World.[44]

As on previous occasions when Afghanistan was discussed, the most vigorous proponent of putting an end to Soviet military involvement in that country was Yakovlev. When Shevardnadze said that Pakistan was contravening the Geneva agreement which had brought to an end the Soviet military intervention in Afghanistan, Yakovlev responded, 'But we are not Pakistan. With great difficulty we have won international trust, as a result of the new thinking.' Why throw it away, he asked, and for what?[45] More Politburo members supported Yakovlev than the position taken by Shevardnadze and Kryuchkov. Summing up, Gorbachev said he was 'categorically opposed' to providing the kind of air support requested by Najibullah. Furthermore, 'As long as I am general secretary, I'll not tolerate trampling on our word which we gave to the whole world.'[46]

Gorbachev's concern was not only to reduce the risk of war and the disproportionate share of Soviet resources taken by the military-industrial complex but also to secure a more benign international environment for radical domestic change. Closer connections with Western Europe, in particular, would be conducive to the success of Soviet reforms. As was clear from the alarm expressed by Politburo members at the defeat of numerous party officials in the recent elections, there was no shortage of people in positions of institutional power who believed that political change had already gone too far. For Gorbachev, as for his closest advisers on political reform— notably Yakovlev and Shakhnazarov—it still had a long way to go, although there was debate within the leader's inner circle about the precise institutional forms further democratization should take.

Gorbachev–Thatcher Diplomacy Deepened

For Gorbachev, Margaret Thatcher remained an exceptionally significant interlocutor. Not only was Britain one of Europe's most influential countries, it also prided itself on its 'special relationship' with the United States. More special at some times than others, the term was particularly applicable to the sharing of intelligence information. And it was true of the political and personal rapport of Margaret Thatcher and Ronald Reagan. On 19 January 1989, as Reagan demitted office, the two leaders exchanged letters. Thatcher told Reagan that he had been 'a great President, one of the greatest, because you stood for all that is best in America'. She praised his convictions and faith and added that his 'unassuming courtesy was the hallmark of the true and perfect gentleman'.[47]

Reagan's letter to Thatcher praised their partnership and how they had improved the world's 'prospects for peace and security', adding: 'You have been an invaluable ally, but more than that, you are a great friend. It has been an honor to work with you since 1981.'[48] Although she was of course still strongly opposed to the goal of complete nuclear disarmament which Reagan shared with Gorbachev, Thatcher was consistent in her pressure on her American counterparts to engage with the Soviet leader. She reinforced the pacific and diplomatic side of Reagan's 'peace through strength' policy and was a valuable ally of George Shultz in the arguments within the Reagan administration about the desirability of entering into negotiations with the Soviet Union. Even Reagan administration hard-liners could hardly dismiss Thatcher as a peacenik.

The British prime minister shared Gorbachev's concern that the Bush administration was not building on the achievement of more constructive East–West relations that had occurred during Reagan's second term. Still ready to play the role of go-between, she tried to assure Gorbachev of Bush's good intentions. Yet the American administration seemed more concerned about Bush's international standing than with issues of substance. Thatcher, while far from oblivious to her own standing, was much more actively following the progress of Soviet reform. In between the March election of the Congress of People's Deputies and the convening of its first session in May, Gorbachev made the visits to Cuba and to Britain he had to postpone in December of the previous year when the scale of the disastrous Armenian earthquake led him to cut short his foreign travel.

In the lead-up to Gorbachev's London visit, Thatcher gave an interview to the editor of *Izvestiya*. It was published a week ahead of Gorbachev's departure for Britain. When British Ambassador Braithwaite called on *Izvestiya* editor Ivan Laptev on 3 April, he found him 'still reeling from the effect of his meeting with the PM: she seems to charm all Russians into near-insensibility. He didn't change a word of the interview she gave him ten days ago, which was published on 29 March and was one of the best she's done.'[49] In what he described in his diary as his 'curtainraising telegram to London', Braithwaite noted that the UK visit really mattered for Gorbachev. 'The PM', he wrote, 'is perhaps the only foreign leader with whom he can discuss domestic and foreign policy on equal terms. She can help him understand what is going on in Atlantic and European affairs by virtue of her own special role there'. Gorbachev would be hoping that Thatcher could provide him with 'some clues in interpreting the continuing silence from Washington, about which the Russians are clearly nervous'. The prime minister, Braithwaite added, 'remains an object of intense fascination and admiration throughout the Soviet Union. Gorbachev gains by his association with her; especially when, and in her recent interviews with Izvestiya and Ogonek,* she is saying what he probably wants the Soviet people to hear.'[50]

Braithwaite made clear in his telegram to London that the Soviet economy was still languishing, with its reform lagging far behind that of the political system. Whereas Gorbachev's ending of the Soviet military intervention in Afghanistan, his constitutional change, and the big reduction in the size of the armed forces demonstrated his 'courage, strategic imagination, and tactical cunning', he had been indecisive, wrote Braithwaite, in his handling of economic matters. (Day-to-day supervision of the economy was the primary responsibility not of Gorbachev but of the Chairman of the Council of Ministers, Nikolay Ryzhkov). A few days earlier, the leading British specialist on the Soviet economy, Alec Nove, had called on Braithwaite after spending 'a fascinating time in Leningrad during the elections'. Excited by the political change and cultural renaissance that had occurred in Russia, Nove was 'very gloomy' about the economy. He told Braithwaite, 'Not only can't I see the light at the end of the tunnel. I can't even see the tunnel.'[51]

In his memoirs, Gorbachev refers to Britain's 'special relationship' with the United States and his hope, which he believed was fulfilled, that the British prime minister would use that relationship to persuade the Bush administration to re-engage with the Soviet Union.[52] Gorbachev arrived at London's Heathrow airport at 11 o'clock at night on the fifth of April, accompanied as always by Raisa, and with a large group in tow which included his aides Chernyaev, Shakhnazarov, and Frolov; Politburo members Shevardnadze and Yakovlev; IMEMO director Evgeny Primakov; Marshal Akhromeyev; the head of the CPSU International Department, Valentin Falin; the cosmonaut, Valentina Tereshkova; and writer Mikhail Shatrov. Notwithstanding the lateness of the hour, Thatcher (and her husband Denis) was at the airport to greet the Gorbachevs, and discussions between the prime minister and general secretary began at once. Their main meeting took place at 10 Downing Street the next morning (with only notetakers Anatoly Chernyaev and Charles Powell and interpreters present), followed by a working lunch for almost as small a group. The only additions were

---

* *Ogonek* was a weekly Soviet magazine. In the perestroika era—in common with another weekly, *Moscow News*—it was in the vanguard of glasnost, regularly disregarding hitherto sacred taboos.

Soviet ambassador to the UK, Leonid Zamyatin, and his British counterpart, Rodric Braithwaite, plus Raisa Gorbachev and Denis Thatcher. The foreign ministers Howe and Shevardnadze were not present.[53]

At the morning meeting Gorbachev complained to Thatcher about the increasingly negative reaction of Washington, in the persons of Bush and Baker, to the change in the Soviet Union and said he detected a greater reservation also on the prime minister's part.[54] This Thatcher vigorously denied, saying how much Western countries welcomed the widening of the rights of the individual in the Soviet Union and the growing freedoms of speech, assembly, and movement, saying that the West strongly supported the transformation the Soviet Union was undergoing. Gorbachev later wrote that 'Thatcher spoke sincerely' and, while he did not accept that the Western position was as united as she suggested, he believed the line she took continued to have influence in Washington. He saw a link between the successful London discussions and the visit of US Secretary of State Baker to Moscow a month and a half later which took place in 'a constructive spirit'.[55] Gorbachev and Thatcher disagreed, as usual, on nuclear weapons, with Gorbachev arguing for movement towards their complete elimination and stressing the danger to peace of their retention and modernization. If the existing nuclear powers were intent on keeping these weapons for ever, what would prevent 'some dictator or other' getting his hands on a nuclear weapon?[56]

Both sides were satisfied with the way the meeting went, with Chernyaev especially smitten by the prime minister. He wrote that 'Margaret Thatcher was marvellous, as always. I sat across from them for three hours in her office in 10 Downing Street, admiring her again.' He observed that 'In public she was lavish in her praise' for Gorbachev and that she 'did it bravely, sometimes even in defiance of her own establishment and other Western leaders'.[57] At one time the prime minister lagged behind the Foreign Office in any desire for engagement with the Soviet leadership. Now, as Chernyaev correctly surmised, the boot was on the other foot. Braithwaite noted that British officials were 'not very happy' about Gorbachev making what was already his third visit to Britain and were 'worried that European public opinion was being carried away by Gorbymania'.[58] For Thatcher, in Chernyaev's view, it was partly a matter of principle and recognition of the historic significance of the change underway in the Soviet Union, but in part also the response of a 'politician who, having placed her bet on Gorbachev, had a personal interest in his success'.[59] What was especially important, he wrote, was that 'Thatcher, and later [Helmut] Kohl, did much to ease Gorbachev's suspicions that Bush would veer off the course that he and Reagan had established.'[60]

While the Thatcher–Gorbachev discussions were taking place in Downing Street, Geoffrey Howe was having official talks with Eduard Shevardnadze in the Foreign Office. The five hours they spent together was the Foreign Secretary's fifteenth meeting with Shevardnadze, testimony to the intensity of UK–Soviet engagement during the perestroika period. Howe noted that their dialogue was 'by now very informal but very direct'. In retrospect, he also observed that at the time of this April 1989 visit 'Mikhail Gorbachev was probably nearing the high point of his undeservedly short but remarkable reign.'[61] (In that month, Howe's own period of office as Foreign Secretary was closer to ending than he had any reason to expect. He was demoted to the post of Leader of the House of Commons just three months later. He came close to resigning from the government then, but was persuaded to remain a member.[62] His resignation was delayed until November of the following year when it triggered Margaret Thatcher's own political demise.[63]) Braithwaite, who was present at the meeting between the two foreign ministers, recorded in his diary how the British Foreign Secretary 'attacked Shevardnadze politely' over chemical weapons (for the British believed the Soviet stocks were higher than they admitted) and for supplying 'medium range Fencer bombers to Libya'. Shevardnadze's response was to 'congratulate' Howe on Britain's '£14 billion air defence deal with the Saudis'—a riposte Braithwaite summed up as 'A neat and urbane performance.'[64]

In a speech at the dinner hosted by the prime minister on the evening of 6 April, Gorbachev spoke again of his aim of moving towards the complete liquidation of nuclear weapons and noted that 'Mrs Thatcher considers this to be a lot of romanticism', whereas he, on the contrary, believed his position was strictly in accord with realities of the times in which they were living. There would be many difficulties on the way to a nuclear-free world, but that was the goal towards which they should be moving.[65] He thanked the prime minister and her colleagues for their attention, goodwill, and hospitality, and recalled that 'the British leadership was one of the first in the West to detect the drawing near of major change in the Soviet Union', adding that the Soviet side valued the interest the British government was continuing to show in Soviet developments which were leading to a transformation and enrichment of UK–Soviet relations.[66]

Addressing an invited audience at London's Guildhall the following morning, Gorbachev reminded them that it was now four years since the Soviet leadership had launched their change of course, and he emphasized that perestroika and new thinking applied both to domestic and foreign policy. They were now experiencing 'the contradictions of the transition period', but were undertaking 'a profound transformation of everything—the way of life, the relationship to work, and to civic duty'.[67] The most powerful lever for resolving their problems was reform of the political system, and they were in the process of creating 'an open, democratic and free society'.[68] The recent elections, he said, had been held in a democratic atmosphere without precedent in the whole of Soviet history.[69]

On foreign policy, Gorbachev emphasized the interconnectedness of the world's problems. Embarking on disarmament would release resources for tackling the world's environmental problems.[70] He referred to his UN speech and said that as he had already announced, 'our armed forces will be reduced by 500,000'. The military budget was being cut by 14 per cent and 'I take this opportunity to tell you that we have recently decided to cease this year the production of enriched weapon-grade uranium.'[71] Stressing the importance of eliminating chemical weapons, he said, 'We appreciate the position of Great Britain which has eliminated its chemical weapons unilaterally and was the first to raise this issue at an international conference.' He noted that Soviet experts had already visited the British scientific research centre at Porton Down and that their British counterparts had been 'to our centre'.* They needed to work for 'the complete prohibition and elimination of chemical weapons'.[72] He compared the main components of NATO and Warsaw Pact personnel and armaments and concluded that there was an 'approximate parity' between them which meant that the Western perception of a 'Soviet military threat' was without foundation.[73]

Following the Guildhall speech, Gorbachev and his wife had lunch with Queen Elizabeth at Windsor Castle. He invited the Queen to pay a visit to the Soviet Union, something no British monarch had done in the years since the Bolsheviks killed the last tsar (a cousin of the Queen's grandfather) and his family. Somewhat incongruously, Gorbachev's next engagement after meeting the Queen and Prince Philip was with the General Secretary of the Communist Party of Great Britain, Gordon McLennan, who doubtless had mixed feelings about the relative warmth, in particular, of the Gorbachev–Thatcher relationship. Varying his themes for different interlocutors, Gorbachev told McLennan about his recent meeting with Fidel Castro. Referring to his current UK visit, Gorbachev said that in the past Britain had often complicated international relations, but now there was a new realism that had been embraced by the British prime minister. He stressed, nevertheless, his differences with Thatcher over nuclear arms.[74] The meeting with McLennan was Gorbachev's last before he and his wife departed for Moscow. The previous day the Soviet leader had met representatives of the British business community. He also had an amicable meeting in the Soviet Embassy with Labour Party leader Neil Kinnock to whom he emphasized his readiness for a new level of cooperation between (reformed) Communists and social democratic parties.[75]

Reporting on the Gorbachev visit to the British Cabinet, Howe summarized the Soviet leader's objectives as seeking support for his radical internal reforms, trying to establish whether the Bush administration was going to engage with the Soviet

---

* A group of twelve Soviet specialists visited the British chemical research centre, Porton Down, in late May 1988, and there was a return visit by British scientists and technologists to the Soviet Shikhany facility in June of the same year. The investigative journalist David Hoffman, in his study of Soviet weaponry, notes that 'the Soviets had amassed at least forty thousand tons of chemical agents, and the United States thirty-one thousand tons'. Hoffman accepts that Gorbachev was sincere in wanting to stop the Soviet production of chemical weapons and to rid the world completely of them. He notes also, however, that the generals in charge of chemical weaponry continued their manufacture without the knowledge of Gorbachev or, in the 1990s, that of Yeltsin (Hoffman, *The Dead Hand: The Untold Story of the Cold War Arms Race and its Dangerous Legacy* (Doubleday, New York, 2009), esp. pp. 309 and 420).

Union in the way in which Reagan had, and presenting 'a positive picture of new thinking in Soviet foreign policy'. The visit had been 'extremely useful for the Anglo-Soviet relationship, marking the critically important role played by the United Kingdom and the Prime Minister personally in the Soviet perspective on East/West relations'.[76] Nevertheless, said Howe, the 'Soviet strategic aim remained to detach the United States from Europe by means of the slogan of denuclearisation'. He warned that Gorbachev, 'in his programme of political reform, was riding a tiger' and that events 'might well outstrip his own expectations'. Thus, 'Western policy' should remain one of 'support for the internal Soviet reform programme coupled with resolute determination to maintain Western defence'.[77]

On the return flight to Moscow, Chernyaev expressed surprise that Gorbachev had not responded more enthusiastically than he did during his meeting with Thatcher, adding that perhaps he was 'thinking of those back in Moscow who won't understand' his good relations with her. Gorbachev, wrote Chernyaev, 'glared at me for that' and said, 'See, Anatoly disagrees.' Chernyaev responded, 'Of course I disagree. First of all, it's wrong not to respond appropriately to her good intentions. She's doing us a favour. She raised the prestige of perestroika, and of you personally, so much that Kohl, Mitterrand, and even Bush will have to try and keep pace.'[78] In fact, Gorbachev both in London and when reporting to the Politburo, was very positive about the relationship he had established with Thatcher. He was less carried away in his admiration for the British prime minister than was Chernyaev, but he undoubtedly respected her. He was conscious also that, as Chernyaev later put it, 'for decades our relations with Britain had not only been cold to the point of hostility, they were also usually on Moscow's back burner'. So, in Chernyaev's words, it was 'even more amazing that, "by the will of fate", they became Gorbachev's door into European politics. Thatcher's position on perestroika set the pace for our recognition by the West.'[79]

As if to prove to Chernyaev that he was not going to worry about 'those back in Moscow' who would disapprove of his good relations with a Conservative premier, Gorbachev told the Politburo on 13 April: 'I like Thatcher's independence. You can talk to her about anything. And she understands everything. She's a trustworthy person.' He naturally added that, as usual, they argued 'very sharply' about nuclear weapons. Gorbachev maintained that Thatcher was seen in Europe and in America as aspiring to be the leader of the West which did not please Bush and Kohl. But to talk with her was, he said, 'always interesting' because she favoured 'direct and lively conversation'. Gorbachev reported positively also on his meeting with the Queen whom he described as 'a placid and good person' who did not exclude visiting the Soviet Union. 'Leningrad', he informed the Politburo, 'she continues to call Petersburg'.[80] In that respect the Queen was a bit ahead of Gorbachev, enjoying, perhaps, what Trotsky called 'the privilege of historic backwardness'. In September 1991 Leningrad returned to its pre-First World War name of St Petersburg.

Gorbachev's Activism at Home and Abroad

Gorbachev's December 1988 New York visit had ended, as we saw, with the tragedy of the Armenian earthquake. A tragedy of a different sort occurred just after the Soviet group returned to Moscow from London in April 1989. There had been demonstrations in the Georgian capital, Tbilisi, over several days while Gorbachev was away. The protesters were overwhelmingly young people and fired by nationalist sentiments. They were opposing Abkhazia's separation from Georgia, which many Abkhaz were seeking. The Georgian demonstrators were demanding also greater autonomy for their republic within the Soviet Union or even outright Georgian independence. When Gorbachev was briefed on the developments after his plane had landed in Moscow, he said (as Eduard Shevardnadze confirmed) that the stand-off must be resolved by political means, not by the use of force.[81]

Gorbachev proposed that Shevardnadze (as the former first secretary of the Georgian party organization and a man whose role on the international stage as Soviet Foreign Minister was a source of pride for Georgians) fly to Tbilisi, along with Georgy Razumovsky (a younger member of the top leadership team whom Gorbachev had put in charge of the country-wide Communist Party organization the previous autumn), to secure a peaceful resolution to the crisis. Shevardnadze, having just returned from the long journeys to Cuba and Britain, and being due to fly to Berlin for a meeting of Warsaw Pact foreign ministers on 10 April, was relieved to be told by the Georgian party first secretary, Dzhumber Piatashvili, when he called him, that there was no need to hurry to Tbilisi, for everything was under control. But on the night of 8/9 April the peaceful demonstration was ended viciously. Nineteen of the young demonstrators were killed and several hundred were injured. The Leningrad law professor, Anatoly Sobchak (a politician who belonged to the group of deputies closer to Yeltsin than to Gorbachev) was chosen by the new legislature to chair a committee of inquiry into the Tbilisi tragedy. He noted later that Shevardnadze was deeply shaken by what had happened, not only as a Georgian sensitive to national feelings, but also because of his awareness that if he had flown to Georgia on 8 April, as Gorbachev had suggested, the slaughter in Tbilisi could have been avoided.[82]

The brutal treatment of the young protesters was a huge stimulus to nationalist and separatist tendencies in Georgia. The pluralization of Soviet politics and the new tolerance had, on the one hand, enabled significant progress to be made in democratization but, on the other, it brought to the surface of political life all the suppressed aspirations and resentments that could not be articulated prior to the advent of glasnost and perestroika. Throughout 1989 Gorbachev was able, albeit with difficulty, to retain his authority and he wielded more power than any other individual within the Soviet Union both in foreign and domestic policy. Nevertheless, as a result of reforms he himself had sponsored, he could now be challenged politically with impunity by those who (unlike many of Gorbachev's Politburo and Central Committee col-leagues) had no power to lose, and the fault-lines within the Soviet multinational state were becoming increasingly evident. It was easier for Gorbachev to manipulate and control the ruling party than to secure anything like consensus within the broader society on the speed and direction of change. Little more than a fortnight after the Tbilisi killings, Gorbachev showed that he was still pulling the strings within the CPSU by securing the retirement of seventy-four full members and twenty-four candidate members of the Central Committee. Among those to be, in effect, compul-sorily 'retired' were such senior conservative Communists as Andrei Gromyko, Nikolay Tikhonov, Vladimir Dolgikh, and Boris Ponomarev.[83]

Gorbachev had also embarked on the hugely significant task of transferring power from the Communist Party to the Soviet state, and especially to the new legislature. In official Soviet doctrine the party congress had always been the highest political authority in the land even though, in day-to-day practice, power had been wielded by the Politburo and Secretariat of the Central Committee and, at times, by the general secretary alone.[84] Speaking to a group of Politburo members and Secretaries of the Central Committee on 29 April, Gorbachev said that the legislature 'must rank higher' than the party congress to show that we have 'really arrived at a new stage of social development'.[85] They needed to look at the 'Leviathan' they had created over seventy years and see 'democracy as both a goal and a means', for only through democracy would it be possible for the country to 'develop normally'.[86] The norms which constituted 'normal' had, increasingly, become for Gorbachev and for a good many like-minded Russian reformers those of the democracies they had seen else-where on the European continent. The transformation of the political system was, more than ever, at the top of Gorbachev's domestic agenda, even though he had to cajole exceedingly doubtful colleagues and circumvent suspicious officials at lower levels of the hierarchy anxious about the consequences for them.

Gorbachev's dominance was, if anything, still greater in foreign policy than in the transformation of the political system. It was certainly much easier for the general secretary to determine foreign than economic policy. There were fewer major players within the former sphere and the most important of them—Shevardnadze, Yakovlev (now the overlord of international policy within the CPSU Central Committee), and Chernyaev—had been hand-picked by Gorbachev. In contrast, most heads of eco-nomic ministries owed their position to Chairman of the Council of Ministers Ryzhkov rather than to the general secretary and there were countless regional party officials and factory managers who could drag their feet or even sabotage economic reform. To make matters worse, the political leadership had failed to reach an agreed position on how far or how fast they should move in the direction of a market econ-omy. Although by 1990 and especially 1991, when Gorbachev himself and the state he led were engaged in a struggle for political survival, he sought direct Western eco-nomic assistance, this was not the case in 1989. In the early months of that year he had told both the first secretary of the Italian Communist Party and the Foreign Minister of Spain (in separate private meetings) that, in spite of shortages in the Soviet Union, Western credits were not the answer and he did not seek them.[87]

With the United States still apparently unwilling to return to the intensity of US–Soviet relations of the later Reagan years, Gorbachev combined his supervision of domestic political change with intense diplomatic activity of his own in the first half of 1989. He reported to the Politburo on 13 April not only about his Cuban and British visits, but also about a 'very interesting meeting' he had held in Moscow on 11 April with Hans-Jochen Fogel, the leader of the German Social Democratic Party. In an observation that would have been regarded as heresy a few years earlier, Gorbachev told this ruling group within the CPSU that even more interesting than his own conversation was what Fogel had said to Yakovlev, namely that 'the international Communist movement in fact no longer exists' but 'socialist thought continues to live on within social democracy'.[88] Rather than distance himself from that view, Gorbachev saw this as meaning that a democratizing CPSU and social democrats must go forward together.[89]

Gorbachev became the first Soviet leader since Nikita Khrushchev to visit China, doing so in May 1989, the same month in which he met James Baker in Moscow. Since mid-April young people, mainly students, had been demonstrating in Beijing's Tiananmen Square in support of democratization. Gorbachev's impending visit heightened an already keen interest among Chinese intellectuals in the reform process in the Soviet Union.* While in Beijing, Gorbachev was kept well away from the protesters, and he did not attempt to avoid the restrictions imposed on him, for the purpose of his visit was to end the tense relationship between the Soviet and Chinese parties and governments which had existed ever since Khrushchev's time. Gorbachev met the 82-year-old Deng Xiaoping who was no longer officially the leader of the country but, from his semi-retirement, still the person who had the last word on the biggest issues. He met also the General Secretary of the Chinese Communist Party, Zhao Ziyang, who impressed him with his relative openness. That included the Chinese party leader revealing to Gorbachev that major decisions were still referred to Deng and Zhao's raising what was an extremely important question for both general secretaries, 'Can a one-party system ensure the development of democracy, and will it be possible in this system to have effective control over negative phenomena and to fight the corruption which is to be found in party and government institutions?'[90]

The immediate aim of Gorbachev's China visit was realized, for Deng told him that the very fact he was meeting with Zhao indicated that Sino-Soviet relations could now be regarded as normalized.[91] Deng had also not wanted to spoil the rapprochement

---

* In China in September 1988, when I was part of a small group of Oxford scholars who were guests of the Chinese Academy of Social Sciences, I was asked to speak about the Soviet perestroika in every research institute we visited in Beijing and Shanghai.

by using armed force against the demonstrators prior to or during Gorbachev's visit. But shortly after Gorbachev returned to Moscow, tanks and armoured personnel carriers moved into Tiananmen Square and the surrounding area. Estimates of the numbers killed in the crackdown vary between several hundred and several thousand. A temporary statue, known as the Goddess of Democracy, which the students had erected, was flattened on 4 June. This was the same day in which Communism essentially ended, entirely peacefully, in Poland as a result of contested elections sanctioned by Jaruzelski. There is no doubt about which of the responses to political opposition Gorbachev preferred, although many of his post-Soviet Russian critics hold that against him and believe that a Tiananmen Square-type crackdown would have nipped separatist movements in the Soviet Union in the bud. Zhao, for his part, paid a price for his attachment to political reform, reluctance to use violence against the demonstrators, and his frankness with Gorbachev. Not only was he replaced as leader of the Chinese Communist Party, he also spent the rest of his life under what was, in effect, house arrest (although, like Khrushchev—in similar circumstances after being ousted as Soviet leader in 1964—Zhao taped memoirs which were subsequently smuggled out of the country and published abroad).[92]

Baker's First Visit to Moscow

Henry Kissinger, always eager to play a role in international politics, came to Moscow in January 1989 as a member of a Trilateral Commission delegation, whose other leading members were former French President Valery Giscard d'Estaing and former Japanese Prime Minister Yasuhiro Nakasone. Kissinger made proposals that were later interpreted in the mass media as suggestive of 'a second Yalta—some kind of grand bargain on Eastern Europe'.[93] Pavel Palazchenko, Gorbachev's interpreter at the meeting, did not find the visit or Kissinger's remarks 'particularly helpful to Gorbachev'. Doubts on both sides lay not far below the superficial cordiality of the meeting.[94] Gorbachev, in his meeting with the visiting delegation, spoke of Eastern Europe's 'freedom of choice', and he repeated those words in a post-mortem on the Trilateral Commission discussion with his advisers. Vadim Medvedev, although he was a close ally of the general secretary, warned that there would be 'a crisis in Eastern Europe', to which Gorbachev responded, 'Whatever it is, they will have to decide themselves how they will live.' Palazchenko was confident 'he meant it', but, he added, 'I don't know whether everyone on Gorbachev's side of the table, in the Central Committee and elsewhere, thought so.'[95]

If that was the case within the Soviet elite, it is not surprising that Gorbachev's rhetorical commitment to 'freedom of choice' was not yet taken at face value by the Americans. Nevertheless, it would have made sense for the US to treat Gorbachev's expressed commitment to 'democratization' and 'freedom of choice' *as if* he meant what he said unless and until his actions proved otherwise. Scowcroft and Baker, not

Figure 15 (L to R) Soviet Defence Minister Marshal Dmitry Yazov, US Secretary of Defense Frank Carlucci, and Soviet Chief of the General Staff Marshal Sergey Akhromeyev in Moscow, May 1988.

to speak of Gates and Cheney, too readily assumed that when Gorbachev spoke of 'democratization' or 'freedom of choice', he could hardly be serious.

Baker, who had his first meeting as Secretary of State with Shevardnadze in Vienna at the opening of talks on Conventional Forces in Europe (CFE) in March, noted that the CFE's predecessor, the Mutual Balanced Force Reduction talks (MBFR) had 'languished for fourteen years, and produced very little movement'.[96] Unless political momentum was provided by heads of government or foreign ministers, the meetings of experts from countries of different ideological orientations could drag on endlessly. Shevardnadze was glad to hear from Baker that because of the good relations the principals within the Bush administration had established, 'there would be no repeat of the internecine warfare that had made the conduct of foreign policy so difficult in many previous administrations'.[97] The Secretary of State did not need to spell out that this had been true throughout much of the Reagan administration—although not, as we've seen, of its final phase. The Vienna meeting was the beginning of a good relationship between Baker and Shevardnadze and also of their assistants, Dennis Ross on the American side and Sergey Tarasenko, Shevardnadze's right-hand man, who acted as notetakers on this occasion and went on to develop a friendship.[98] Palazchenko, Shevardnadze's interpreter, thought Baker's speech in Vienna, advocating an end to the division of Europe, was consistent with what Gorbachev had said in his UN speech, but that the tone of 'imperious demand' made what he said 'more difficult to accept'.[99]

In the run-up to Baker's May visit to Moscow—the first time he had ever set foot in Russia—Defense Secretary Dick Cheney made things more difficult for him by saying in a CNN interview on 29 April that he thought that Gorbachev would 'ultimately fail'. Baker did not necessarily disagree with that speculation, but he objected to Cheney publicly intruding on his foreign policy bailiwick. He discussed the problem with Bush who agreed that Scowcroft should distance the White House from Cheney's remarks.[100] When the Secretary of State met Shevardnadze in Moscow on 10 May—it was the following day before Baker saw Gorbachev—the Soviet Foreign Minister took issue with Cheney's assessment. Baker responded that the Defense Secretary was just giving his own 'prognosis for success' and that 'the President made clear he did not share this view'.[101] Shevardnadze went on to make light of the issue, saying that he was not surprised by what Cheney had said, for the Secretary of Defense had his budget to think of. 'How would he finance his defense programs if there were no Soviet threat?'[102] Shevardnadze was well aware, from Soviet experience as well as from what he had learned about American politics, that the military and military industry would always see dangers ahead and pressing reasons for being allocated more resources.

Baker had been 'perfunctorily introduced' to Gorbachev in Washington on earlier occasions, but when he met him in the Kremlin on the morning of 11 May, it was their first real discussion. 'Gorbachev bounded into the room', Baker recalled, 'beaming as always with energy and confidence.' His 'upbeat attitude' seemed to fill the room and it reminded the Secretary of State of Reagan. The optimism they shared was, he reflected, perhaps 'one reason Gorbachev and Reagan were able to work together so successfully'.[103] Gorbachev himself referred to his optimism during the conversation with Baker. He was convinced that real cooperation between the United States and the Soviet Union could continue on every question. 'In that relationship', he added, 'I am an incorrigible optimist, and that optimism is based not only on philosophical considerations, but on the experience we have already had.'[104] Shevardnadze had more of an air of foreboding. His shoulders, observed Baker, seemed to carry 'the burdens of the world'. Baker came to believe that 'Shevardnadze was the more realistic' of these two Soviet political allies of broadly similar views but of different temperament.[105] While many subsequent events might appear to bear out that assessment, it is likely that only an optimist by nature would have taken the risk of introducing fundamental change in Soviet foreign and domestic policy, undermining the authoritarian pillars that supported the multinational Soviet state.

When the discussion turned to economic issues, Baker couched his advice tactfully. His years as Secretary of the Treasury had taught him that a country's leadership was the best judge of what was politically viable, but his own experience suggested that on such a matter as price reform, it would be better 'to move sooner rather than later'.[106] State-determined rather than market prices were, indeed, at the heart of Soviet economic problems, leading to shortages and lengthening queues which, in the last few years of the Soviet Union's existence, became worse rather than better. The planned economy, which had worked after a fashion, was breaking down but a market economy (whether regulated in the manner favoured by social democrats or as capricious as the 'Wild East' capitalism of 1990s Russia under Yeltsin) had not yet been created. Gorbachev's reply to Baker indicated awareness of the problem but also the higher priority he accorded political over economic reform. 'We were', he said, 'twenty years late on price reform, so two or three more years won't hurt.'[107] In fact, its absence did matter, although marketizing reform, entailing higher prices for currently subsidized basic foodstuffs, would have been at least as unpopular as the shortages characteristic of the basically unreformed Soviet economic system.

On armaments there were sharper disagreements. Gorbachev, Shevardnadze, and Akhromeyev (who participated in part of the discussion) objected to American plans to modernize short-range missiles to be deployed in Europe. Although they were a little below the 500-kilometre range that would have made them illegal under the INF Treaty, to the Soviet side they seemed remarkably similar to the SS-23 (or 'Oka') missile which Gorbachev had agreed to scrap to secure that agreement. As first Shevardnadze and then Gorbachev admitted, that had led to a strongly critical reaction from the Soviet military.[108] This was an awkward issue for both general secretary and foreign minister, and it was not until a year later, by which time the political map of Europe had changed utterly, that the American modernization plan was abandoned. In his account of the meeting, Baker focuses especially on a Gorbachev proposal to withdraw 500 tactical nuclear weapons from Eastern Europe that year and, if the United States were to reciprocate, to remove all of them by 1991. Since the US was engaged in sensitive discussions with its European partners on short-range nuclear weapons, this proposal irritated Baker, especially when it became a major story in the American media. He was concerned that 'George Bush risked being upstaged diplomatically by Gorbachev.'[109]

Head of Government Diplomacy in Europe

Slow though he was to engage with Moscow, Bush was far from idle in European diplomacy. A NATO summit at the end of May provided him with a good opportunity for visits to West Germany, Italy, and Britain. His boldest and most important speech was in the German city of Mainz where he introduced the notion of a 'Europe whole and free' which, he said, had been 'a distant dream' at the time of the founding of NATO but was now its mission. He also defined the end of the Cold War in terms of a reunited Europe, saying 'The Cold War began with the division of Europe. It can only end when Europe is whole.' Alluding to Gorbachev's concept, he added that 'there cannot be a common European home until all within it are free to move from room to room'.[110]

By mid-July Bush was in France, meeting in the Elysée Palace with President Mitterrand, just nine days after Gorbachev had sat in the same room. Mitterrand urged Bush to meet with the Soviet leader, offering his view that Gorbachev was 'more imperilled than ever before' and that he not only 'detested the Chinese course'—referring to the crushing of the Tiananmen protest—but 'feels threatened by it'. He reminded Bush that 'Gorbachev established a personal relationship with Ronald Reagan and desired one with President Bush.' Mitterrand also urged caution, given the risks Gorbachev was running, and said it was 'too soon to talk about dissolving the Warsaw Pact'.[111] Mitterrand had his reservations about the American president. Earlier that month, he told Gorbachev that 'Bush, as a president, has a very big drawback—he lacks original thinking altogether.'[112]

Bush had been urged by Thatcher as well as by Mitterrand to meet with Gorbachev, but it was during a visit to Poland and Hungary in July that he was finally persuaded that this was essential. He thought of it as a preliminary get-together for a proper summit that would take place in 1990, but the political map of Europe changed so rapidly in 1989 that the meeting between the American and Soviet leaders, which eventually took place in Malta in December that year, certainly counted as a summit. It was, above all, reforming Communist leaders in central Europe, notably Jaruzelski in Poland and Miklós Németh in Hungary, who succeeded in persuading Bush that if he wished the process of peaceful change in Europe to continue, it was high time he engaged with Gorbachev. Bush wrote to his Soviet counterpart on 21 July on his way back from Europe and said that until then he had felt that they should not have a meeting, for if it did not include a major agreement, it would 'disappoint the watching world'. Now his thinking was changing: 'Perhaps it was my visit to Poland and Hungary or perhaps it is what I heard about your recent visits to France and Germany—whatever the cause—I just want to reduce the chances there could be misunderstandings between us. I want to get our relationship on a more personal basis.'[113] Bush suggested an informal, 'no agenda' summit, preferably somewhere 'secluded', such as at Camp David or at the Bushes' seaside home in Maine. Eventually the 'secluded place' Bush was keen on became Malta, and the plan was that alternate sessions would take place on two warships (one American, one Soviet).

Gorbachev was at least as active as Bush in his European travel prior to the summit. He spent time both in West Germany and East Germany as well as France and Italy, the last of those visits in November 1989 involving also Vatican City and a friendly conversation with Pope John Paul II. Gorbachev established a good rapport with Helmut Kohl during his visit to West Germany from 12 to 15 June and his reception from the population was close to rapturous.[114] The two sides produced an agreed declaration which included condemnation of 'any hankering after military superiority', commitment to seek a 'stable balance' of armaments at 'a lower level which suffices for defence but not for attack', and affirmation that they were both 'striving for the elimination of existing asymmetries through binding agreements subject to effective international control'.[115] Not everyone saw it as accomplishing much. On the copy of the document he passed on to Margaret Thatcher, Charles Powell wrote that 'It strikes me as rather flatulent, & worth a good deal less than is claimed for it.'[116] Nevertheless, given the twentieth-century history of German–Russian relations, the levels of agreement and amount of goodwill the declaration embodied were far from inconsequential.

Kohl phoned President Bush on the day of Gorbachev's departure to report positively on the visit. He had found 'Gorbachev in very good shape' and 'much more optimistic' than when he had met him in Moscow in October 1988. Kohl noted Gorbachev's closeness to Jaruzelski in Poland and 'the enormous distance' between him and the leaderships in East Berlin and Bucharest. He also told Bush that 'Gorbachev was dismayed about developments in China.' As a flattering way of encouraging Bush to engage with the Soviet leadership, Kohl said that Gorbachev had 'greater hope for establishing good contact with the President than he had with President Reagan' and that he wanted to 'deepen contacts with the U.S. and the President personally'.[117]

In his assessment of the Gorbachev visit for the UK Foreign Office, the British ambassador to West Germany, Sir Christopher Mallaby, described it as a 'Gorbachev tour de force of confidence, skill and charm'. His 'characteristic verve' had been in striking contrast with Bush's recent visit. Even in advance of Gorbachev's arrival, Mallaby reported, West German opinion polls showed him to be more popular than Bush or any German politician save Richard von Weizsäcker, the president (titular head of state) of the Federal German Republic (FRG) from 1984 to 1994. The popular welcome for Gorbachev had been so ecstatic, reported Mallaby, that it was 'seen by many as the most enthusiastic for any foreign political leader since the visits of de Gaulle in 1962 and Kennedy in 1963'.[118] The overwhelming emotion driving this support for Gorbachev was the 'intense relief' of the German people at 'the reduction in the threat' for which Gorbachev 'is widely felt here to be personally responsible'.[119]

More significant than the generalities of the joint declaration, Mallaby suggested, was Gorbachev's 'pledge to Kohl' that 'the Soviet Union will not interfere in the reform process in Eastern Europe.' Moreover, even on the issue of the Berlin Wall and the broader German question, Gorbachev had left the impression that there was hope of progress in the future. Apart from a couple of observations by the Soviet leader on short-range nuclear weapons, there had been 'a marked absence' of 'wedge-driving tactics'.[120] The visit had resulted in 'a great leap forward' of Gorbachev's popularity in West Germany and it had raised expectations of East–West progress.[121] Whether it was because the German government were claiming that the Gorbachev visit had increased their influence and that the FRG was 'accepted now by both superpowers as a partner in leadership' or because Gorbachev's popularity in West Germany outstripped that of any other European or American politician (Weizsäcker being above the fray), Powell, rather oddly, wrote on the copy of Mallaby's report he passed to Thatcher, 'A profoundly depressing account'.[122]

In early July Gorbachev spent three days on a visit to France in which 'the Mitterrand–Gorbachev chemistry was good' but, in the view of the British ambassador to Paris, Sir Ewen Fergusson, it had never been on the cards that the visit would match the importance of Gorbachev's visit to Bonn. Although French relations with the Soviet leader were generally good, said Fergusson, 'Gorbophoria does not rule here.'[123] In his talks with Mitterrand, Gorbachev showed 'no concern about developments in Poland and Hungary' but, in contrast, in private he made clear his disapproval of the Tiananmen crackdown. He could not say much about this in public, lest he 'undo any of the difficult work achieved in restoring and improving Soviet–Chinese relations'.[124] The French noted Gorbachev's repeated warnings about the dangers of the United States 'exploiting developments in Eastern Europe' which they interpreted as betraying his concern that opponents at home would then use this against him. Fergusson added that Gorbachev's Strasbourg speech would repay careful study, for it was revealing of changing Soviet attitudes to Eastern Europe and the 'Brezhnev doctrine'.[125]

In that significant speech to the Council of Europe in Strasbourg, Gorbachev set out his aspiration for a 'European common home'. Referring to noble dreams of a voluntary and democratic community of European nations, Gorbachev quoted Victor Hugo as saying the day would come when all the nations of Europe—France, Germany, Italy, England, and Russia—would 'merge indissolubly into a higher form of society and form a European brotherhood' and when 'the only fields of battle will be markets open for trade and minds open to ideas'.[126] (As it happens, all of the countries mentioned by Hugo, with the exception of Russia, had already, by the time Gorbachev spoke, come together in the European Economic Community, known from 1993 as the European Union.)

Gorbachev said he did not have a blueprint for what he called the 'common European home' but in his recent discussions with the continent's leaders, they had begun to address the architecture of that home, the methods of its construction, and even its 'furniture', though he provided little in the way of specifics.[127] In the process, common European values should, he said, occupy the first place and the traditional balance of power should be replaced by a balance of interests. The last few years had seen intensive dialogue among European states, and it was time leaders started discussing progress towards a European community of the twenty-first century, in which—although this was not an immediate prospect—there would be a high level of integration within the vast economic space stretching from the Atlantic to the Urals.[128] Gorbachev noted the 'huge, revolutionary significance' of the changes taking place in the Soviet Union, as a result of which governments, parliaments, and peoples would soon be dealing with a 'completely different socialist state from what it has been up to now'.[129]

When addressing primarily Western audiences Gorbachev stressed that what was occurring in the Soviet Union was *systemic change*. He was more cautious when speaking with East European Communist leaders. Conscious of growing unhappiness within the Soviet power elite and of the danger of their mounting a successful counter-reformation, he hoped for evolutionary rather than revolutionary change in Eastern Europe. Gorbachev's concern was that the rapid ending of Communist rule in Eastern Europe would undermine him and his project. For that reason, he did not go out of his way to undercut the existing leaderships or to offer support to democratic oppositional forces in central and eastern Europe. Gorbachev's old friend Zdeněk Mlynář chastised him for this. Accepting that Gorbachev had indeed renounced the 'Brezhnev doctrine', Mlynář told him, in a conversation they recorded in the early 1990s, that he had, nevertheless, disillusioned those seeking change in Czechoslovakia when in his visit in spring 1987 he had failed to condemn the Soviet invasion of 1968. In essence, Gorbachev's response was that (a) he did not wish to tell a fraternal party what to do and destabilize the existing leadership under Gustáv Husák; and (b), the Soviet Politburo had an agreed position on Czechoslovakia that he could not single-handedly change, especially at such an early stage of perestroika.[130] Crucially, however, Gorbachev stayed true to his 'freedom to choose' mantra, and did not countenance the use of force to prevent the rapid dismantling of Communist systems in what had until recently been called 'the Soviet bloc'.

Figure 16 Mikhail Gorbachev with his favourite foreign leader, Spanish Prime Minister Felipe González, Madrid, October 1990.

Gorbachev's preference was for like-minded leaders who would move towards a social democratic variant of socialism. His problem was that they were more readily identifiable in Western than in Eastern Europe—in the persons, most notably, of former German Chancellor Willy Brandt and Spanish Socialist Prime Minister Felipe González, with both of whom Gorbachev had struck up a real friendship. Speaking with Brandt in Moscow in October 1989, Gorbachev suggested that perhaps the time had arrived to end 'the schism' within 'socialism'—between Communist and (democratic) socialist parties.[131] In conversation with González in Madrid in October 1990, Gorbachev said that when they first met in 1986, the Spanish prime minister had been virtually the only Western leader with whom he could have a confidential exchange of views. At their 1990 meeting, Gorbachev said that if by socialism what was meant was a totalitarian regime in which people were no more than cogs in machines, then they were unquestionably getting rid of it. 'For me', said Gorbachev, 'socialism is movement towards freedom, the development of democracy, the creation of conditions for a better life for the people' and 'raising the humane individual'. Defined in those terms, Gorbachev said, 'I was and remain a socialist.' González told Gorbachev that he agreed with him, adding that this necessary conversation was one he would not be able to have with Thatcher.[132]

Gorbachev's remarks to González illustrate how right was Jacques Lévesque, the author of one of the best books on 1989, when he noted that 'for Gorbachev and his circle, the socialist idea became constantly more open, elastic and eclectic'.[133] In Eastern Europe, however, where Communist rule had been imposed by force, with the Soviet military machine as the ultimate guarantor of its continuing existence, the very term, 'socialism', had been tarnished by Communists' use of it to describe their party dictatorships.

Although the meaning of socialism was not a subject for Thatcher–Gorbachev conversations, they had plenty of other topics to discuss, and the British prime minister could not resist the opportunity of another get-together with Gorbachev when she was returning to London from a visit to Japan. Their meeting on 23 September lasted for two and a half hours, followed by further discussion over a lengthy lunch. Later she held a press conference in the Soviet Ministry of Foreign Affairs press centre in which she spoke enthusiastically about Gorbachev and about the changes in the Soviet Union and Eastern Europe. She noted that she had been in touch with President Bush beforehand, given that meetings were currently taking place between James Baker and Shevardnadze. Thatcher spoke of her 'very strong support for the historic changes which are taking place in the Soviet Union' under Gorbachev's leadership. Glasnost and political reform had gone 'far further, far faster than any of us could ever have thought' and they had 'transformed the whole atmosphere'. Political reform was perhaps easier than economic reform, for a government could bring it about by 'taking the requisite action', although it needed 'a great deal of boldness and courage and vision, all of which were forthcoming from Mr Gorbachev'. In contrast, economic reform required a great many people to show initiative and take responsibility, but she believed that the prospects of 'prosperity for the people of the Soviet Union are greater than they have been at any time during the last 70 years'.[134]

Even the expulsion of eight Soviet officials and three Soviet journalists from Britain only a few weeks after Gorbachev's London visit earlier in the year had done little damage to the Thatcher–Gorbachev relationship, though it led to expulsions of British diplomats and journalists in retaliation. On that occasion, British Ambassador Braithwaite had broken the news, first, to Chernyaev who 'did not bother with recriminations', but asked if the British were sure they really had the evidence of illegitimate intelligence activities and that they had picked the right people. He also wondered why Thatcher hadn't warned Gorbachev during his visit to London.[135] Braithwaite (and, at a higher level, Geoffrey Howe) believed that warning should have been given then, but the prime minister was reluctant to risk spoiling the atmosphere of a meeting with Gorbachev.[136] As he wrote in his diary, Braithwaite suspected that 'our action did indeed embarrass Gorbachev and make him look a fool in front of hardliners who think that Mrs T has taken him for a ride'.[137] If that were so, the prime minister came close to overcompensating in her September press conference in Moscow. Even her closest confidant, Charles Powell, remarked afterwards to Braithwaite that 'she perhaps went a bit overboard, and risks being made fun of by the British press, who will draw a contrast with the tough words on defence she has only just uttered in Tokyo'.[138]

The Transformation of Central and Eastern Europe

In every one of the Warsaw Pact countries, with the probable exception of the Soviet Union itself, a majority of the population would have discarded their Communist rulers years earlier, had they believed this was possible. But as Alexis de Tocqueville observed, 'The evil that one endures patiently because it seems inevitable becomes unbearable the moment its elimination becomes conceivable.'[139] There had, though, been occasions when hopes and expectations had been raised, only to be brutally dashed. The Hungarian Revolution was crushed by Soviet tanks in 1956, the Prague Spring suppressed by half a million Soviet-led Warsaw Pact troops in 1968, and the Solidarity mass movement, which threatened to end Communist rule in Poland in 1980–1, halted by the Polish regime's own imposition of a martial law insistently pressed upon them by the Soviet leadership.

Democratizing change in the Soviet Union and the new tolerance in Moscow provided the decisive stimulus to change in Eastern Europe, but once it began it was contagious. The people in other central and east European states could see what the Poles and Hungarians were getting away with. For countries which, in principle, already enjoyed national independence but, in reality, had been subject to Soviet overlordship and constraints imposed by Moscow, the risks of demanding an end to Communist rule now appeared significantly lower than at any time in the previous forty years. Western influence had long been substantial within these societies, in spite of regime efforts to control the flow of information, with widespread awareness of both the higher standards of living in the West and of political freedoms denied in Communist states. There was nothing new about that factor in 1989. Nor was there anything new about Western proselytizing for economic and political freedoms, although Margaret Thatcher and Ronald Reagan engaged in this more actively than did many of their predecessors. What *was* radically new was far-reaching political reform in the Soviet Union and the fact that the Soviet Union by 1989 had a qualitatively better relationship with the countries of Western Europe and with the United States than ever before. East Europeans could be tempted to assume that Gorbachev (although not his conservative Communist opponents) would be reluctant to undermine the emergent East–West accord through aggressive action, even in a region that had long been regarded as the Soviet political backyard.

The first contested national elections of 1989 in any of the Communist states were those in the Soviet Union in March, as we have seen. The spectacle of public political argument and of senior members of the Communist Party being defeated in the ballot constituted a remarkable break with the Soviet past. An even more dramatic

Figure 17 (L to R) Raisa Gorbachev, Polish President Wojciech Jaruzelski, Mikhail Gorbachev, and Barbara Jaruzelski in the Kremlin, April 1990.

election was held in Poland in early June. Solidarity, having spent most of the 1980s in the shadows, surviving only as a much-weakened underground organization, began to reassert itself from early 1988. General Jaruzelski, with Gorbachev's blessing, agreed to the holding of round-table talks between the Polish opposition and the government. These led in April 1989 to the legalization of Solidarity, full legal status for the Catholic Church, and an interim agreement on constitutional change. As a compromise, it was accepted that approximately half of the seats in the forthcoming parliamentary election would be contested. The scale of Solidarity's success surprised even themselves. In the less powerful upper house of the parliament, they won 99 out of 100 seats, and elected 161 out of 460 members of the lower house. By the end of 1989 the Communist party's 'leading role' had been removed from the Constitution. With the agreement of Solidarity, Jaruzelski continued in the presidency even while power was moving into the hands of the opposition. This helped to reassure the Soviet leadership, the more especially since Jaruzelski was the only leader of a Warsaw Pact country for whom Gorbachev had a warm regard. It was yet another sign of the changing times that the Soviet leader's rapport with several West European heads of government (his favourite being Felipe González)[140] was based on more genuine goodwill and mutual esteem than were his relations with East European counterparts (Jaruzelski excepted.) In 1991 Solidarity leader Lech Wałęsa replaced Jaruzelski in the Polish presidency, and in the same year Solidarity won a majority in both chambers of the legislature in free elections.[141]

In Hungary, reformers within the ruling party as well as the burgeoning opposition outside the party were encouraged by the change of Soviet foreign policy and by far-reaching political reform in Moscow. Hungary had been well ahead of the Soviet Union with economic reform, but by the end of 1988 change in the political system lagged behind that initiated in Moscow. Once, however, radical change got seriously underway in Hungary, as it did in 1989, there were fewer deeply entrenched interests to be overcome, and weaker resistance, than that faced by Gorbachev and his reformist allies. In February the legislature in Budapest passed laws permitting a multiparty system. In the same month the Central Committee voted to give up the party's 'leading role'. Three months later the party leadership agreed to begin round-table talks with the democratic opposition. These led to acceptance of free elections for a new and powerful parliament and direct election of a president. By October Hungary was no longer a Communist state and its name was changed from Hungarian People's Republic to the Hungarian Republic.

The toughest test of Soviet tolerance was the GDR (East Germany), given that the division of Europe was a consequence of the war with Nazi Germany in which many more Soviet citizens than Germans lost their lives. For Erich Honecker and the hardline leadership of the GDR, their domestic crisis began in May when the Hungarians enabled thousands of East Germans to travel to the FRG via Hungary and Austria.

The tight controls on travel that the GDR imposed were further undermined as East Germans, who could visit other East European Communist states but not Western countries, inundated the West German embassies in Prague and Warsaw with requests to travel to the FRG. The celebration of the fortieth anniversary of the founding of the GDR on 7 October did Honecker more harm than good. Gorbachev accepted his invitation to attend, and in a coded warning to Honecker told the East German Politburo, with a resentful Honecker beside him, that 'Life itself will punish us if we are late' in responding to demands within the society.[142] The East German crowd chanted 'Gorbi! Gorbi!' and gave him a demonstrative welcome, while offering no similar support to Honecker. Less than a fortnight later the Politburo replaced Honecker as party leader by Egon Krenz, though nothing could stem the erosion of authority of the regime.

The beginning of the end for the GDR came with the opening of the Berlin Wall. The East German leadership, under the pressure of public opinion, agreed to relax the regulations on travel abroad but they had no intention of opening their borders completely. On the evening of 9 November, the party press spokesman inadvertently left the wrong impression that citizens were now being offered freedom of travel and this interpretation was picked up and promptly broadcast by West German television which was widely watched in the GDR. One broadcaster went so far as to say that

Figure 18 Young people from East and West Berlin taking over the Berlin Wall after it was breached with impunity in November 1989.

'the gates of the Berlin Wall stand wide open'.[143] It was an example of how a statement that was wrong in fact can change perceptions and if people act on those perceptions, they, in turn, can change the reality. Thousands of Germans, believing that it was now possible to travel from East to West Berlin arrived at the wall. Faced by overwhelming numbers, and with no clear instructions on what they should do, the senior Stasi officer in charge of the border guards at each crossing had to decide for himself. One by one, they concluded that it was preferable to open the gates than to use force against large numbers of peaceful but emboldened citizens.[144] It was late at night in Germany (and already the small hours of the morning in Moscow) when the trickle of people allowed out became a flood. In most cases, the East German citizens returned home again, but with their appetite for further change—of the system as well as of their freedom of movement—whetted.

The Soviet leadership quite literally slept through the dramatic events in Berlin. When Gorbachev was informed on the morning of 10 November by a nervous East German ambassador that, faced by thousands of Berliners expecting to be allowed through, they had opened all the border crossings along the wall, the Soviet leader responded that they had 'taken the proper action' and said he should pass on his approval to the GDR leadership.[145] That the large-scale breaching of the wall resulted from accident rather than design was not conveyed to Gorbachev, although once Gorbachev's approval of the decision to open the crossings became known, Krenz mendaciously claimed to have given the order for it.[146] The fall of the wall came as a surprise not only to Gorbachev but to the leaders of East Germany, West Germany, and the United States. German Chancellor Helmut Kohl was at the time on a visit to Poland which, in the light of German–Polish history, had great significance. Nevertheless, he abandoned his Polish programme and returned home with undiplomatic if understandable haste.

George Bush and James Baker were equally unprepared for the event which set in motion another fundamental change in German history. The president's initial reaction was characteristically cautious and restrained. Bush welcomed what he (inaccurately) termed 'the decision by the East German leadership to open its borders', but told journalists that 'there will be no gloating from the White House'.[147] On this occasion Bush's caution served him well. On the day the opening of the wall became known, Gorbachev cabled the American president urging him 'not to overreact' (and sent a message also to Kohl warning him to stop talking about reunification).[148] Gorbachev was worried about 'unforeseen consequences' of the events in Berlin and conscious that, without American restraint, it would be much harder for him to control his own hard-liners. Bush was therefore right to be critical of American senators who had urged him 'to go to Berlin to "dance" on the Wall'. This, Kohl told him later, would have been 'outrageously foolish'. It would, wrote Bush, 'have poured gasoline on the embers' and have been 'an open provocation to the Soviet military to act'.[149] Gorbachev, said Bush, had been remarkably relaxed up to this point about what was happening in Eastern Europe, but he clearly felt that the German question had the capacity to derail the entire process of change in the Soviet Union.*

The demonstration effect of Soviet troops staying in their barracks, while Poland and Hungary became non-Communist and the Berlin Wall was breached, emboldened citizens in the remaining Warsaw Pact states. In Bulgaria the long-serving party leader Todor Zhivkov was deposed one day after the fall of the Berlin Wall, and in early 1990 the Communist Party's leading role was removed from the constitution. In Czechoslovakia, the fundamental change began later but was completed at remarkable speed. A student demonstration in Prague on 17 November was suppressed, but the opposition to Communist rule came together under a new grouping called the Civic Forum, in which Václav Havel was quickly recognized as its informal leader. Havel had earned widespread respect in Czech society—as well as several terms of imprisonment—for standing up to the state authorities and providing eloquent defences of democracy and freedom over a period of more than twenty years. Massive demonstrations in Prague in December, in which Havel was joined by Alexander Dubček, the leader of the Communist Party during the Prague Spring, put intense pressure on the existing party leadership. With Gorbachev and his allies in Moscow firmly opposed to the use of force, resignations from the Czech government came thick and fast during December. A predominantly non-Communist government was formed, and on 28 December Dubček was co-opted to the parliament and chosen to be its Speaker. The following day that Federal Assembly elected Havel as President of Czechoslovakia. Within the space of six weeks, in what Havel famously termed the 'velvet revolution', the country had made a transition from orthodox Communism (lagging far behind the Soviet perestroika) to democracy.[150]

Only in Romania did the state authorities use extreme force in order to preserve the status quo, albeit in vain, and only there did the outgoing dictator face execution. This, however, was the Warsaw Pact country over which the Soviet Union had least influence, for Nicolae Ceauşescu had long governed the country as a family fiefdom. He and his wife were shot by firing squad on Christmas Day 1989. Half a year earlier, in discussion with French President François Mitterrand, Gorbachev had remarked that 'Ceauşescu is scared of democracy' after Mitterrand said that 'we all understand that Romania is a real dictatorship', adding that the 'only unclear point is whose dictatorship it is—Ceauşescu's or his wife's'.[151]

---

* In a memorandum to Gorbachev, written in October 1988, Shakhnazarov said that the problems in East Europe were rooted in the imposition on them of the 'same economic and political model of socialism' as that of the Soviet Union and in any future crisis in the region the Soviet leadership must exclude the use of force. He even raised the question (well in advance of the upheavals of 1989) whether it served Soviet interests still to have troops on the territories of those countries, except in the case of East Germany (*krome GDR*). The memories and legacy of the war meant that Germany remained a special concern (Shakhnazarov, *Tsena svobody* (Rossika Zevs, Moscow), 1993, pp. 367–8).

The Malta Summit

Shevardnadze was kept waiting for his first meeting with Bush as president until the second half of September, just weeks before the Berlin Wall fell. The Foreign Minister spoke reasonably frankly to the president about the 'painful' nationalities problem in the Soviet Union which they sought to resolve through moving towards self-government in each of the country's fifteen republics. Referring also to economic difficulties, he said that the Soviet leadership was trying 'to reduce the incompatibility of our economy with those of the West' and had established 1,500 joint ventures, including 80 with the United States. They were working on legislation that would promote more economic interaction, adding that they were not looking for 'aid' but 'equal cooperation'.[152] Bush and Baker pressed Shevardnadze on Soviet arms in Nicaragua which Baker thought had come via Cuba, to which Shevardnadze responded, 'I have no reason to suspect the Cubans but, in any event, the Soviet Union cannot be held responsible for all countries with whom we have good relations.'[153]

Some two weeks after the fall of the Berlin Wall Bush wrote to Gorbachev setting out an informal agenda for their supposedly 'no agenda' meeting in Malta scheduled for early December. It had six main points: Eastern Europe; regional issues (including Central America, Afghanistan, and the Middle East); the defence spending of both countries; 'your vision and mine of the world 10 years from now' and what the differences might be between Gorbachev's 'Common European Home' and Bush's 'Europe Whole & Free'; human rights; and arms control, in a broad sense. (The president had been warned by the relatively hard-line General Ed Rowny, long an important American participant in Strategic Arms Limitation Talks, against engaging in discussions of substance on armaments. In a memorandum, Rowny asserted that 'there are potential risks and few gains in discussing START'.[154]) Bush wrote to Gorbachev that he wanted also to hear about his expectations from perestroika and where it would lead. Writing on the eve of Thanksgiving, he concluded, 'I will give thanks that you are pressing forward with glasnost and perestroika; for, you see, the fate of my own family and yours is dependent on perestroika's success.'[155]

Scowcroft, in his joint memoir with Bush, pointed to the differences within the US administration in the run-up to the Malta summit. Baker was the most optimistic among the leading figures 'concerning Gorbachev's sincerity about reform', supported by Deputy Secretary of State Lawrence Eagleburger who said that Gorbachev deserved credit for his courage in pursuing far-reaching change and, in any case, since he was the leader of the Soviet Union, there was no alternative to working with him. Robert Gates was much more pessimistic, and Defense Secretary Dick Cheney 'was negative', arguing that 'it was premature to relax Cold War-style pressure'. He believed that it was 'hard-line policies that had brought us to this point'. Colin Powell, now Chairman of the Joint Chiefs of Staff, was 'on the moderate side of Cheney', while Vice-President Dan Quayle 'was the most conservative of all', coming close to saying that was happening in the USSR was little more than a 'ploy to lull us into thinking the danger was over and we could dismantle our security structure'.[156]

Bush, for his part, was impressed by a CIA analysis arguing that reforms in the USSR had been 'strong enough to disrupt the Soviet system, but yet not strong enough to give the Soviet people the benefits of a market economy'.[157] The president was, however, more optimistic than were Scowcroft or Gates about Gorbachev's reformist intent and about his prospects for political survival.[158] Margaret Thatcher came to Camp David for a discussion with Bush, Scowcroft, and Eagleburger on 24 November. Alongside her high regard for Gorbachev, she remained extremely hard-line on defence. Bush had inherited a large budget deficit from Reagan and wanted to cut American military expenditure. Ironically, since it was mainly dollars she was talking about, Thatcher took a harder line on avoiding defence cuts than did Cheney and Powell and was, in Bush's words, as 'rigid as she can be on this'.[159] In her press conference afterwards, she combined praise for NATO with support for Gorbachev. She thought he was 'very firmly in the saddle' and that the achievements of greater freedom and change of atmosphere in the Soviet Union had already been enormous.[160]

The Americans were coming around to this view. Just before the Malta summit, Baker wrote to Bush that the general secretary's 'political position within the Soviet leadership appears stronger than ever'.[161] Gorbachev was, indeed, in the process of moving power from the party to the state and in that sense was becoming less dependent on the Politburo. But there was growing domestic opposition to him from within the CPSU apparatus and their allies in the military-industrial complex as well as from forces outside the Communist Party. The latter were more visible to the watching world. Baker correctly noted that 'While democratization is moving forward in the USSR, it has unleashed some dynamic forces that are beyond Gorbachev's ability to control.'[162]

Baker implicitly recognized that Gorbachev, rather than Bush, had set the pace for Soviet–American relations and was seen internationally as the more significant leader. In his memorandum to the president, he wrote that 'Malta could promote a public sense, here and abroad, of a *new* pace and purpose to the U.S.–Soviet dialogue with you leading *as much as* Gorbachev' (italics added).[163] Although Gorbachev had already demonstrated his aversion to the use of military force, Baker told Bush he should 'stress our interest in reform through a peaceful, democratic process' and 'remind Gorbachev that a violent crackdown (in Eastern Europe as well as in the USSR) would inevitably harm our relations'.[164] He reiterated the US's non-recognition of the Baltic states as part of the Soviet Union, but said that the president 'should emphasize that we are not out to destabilize the USSR' and that the US did not have any preconceived ideas about what kind of agreements the Soviet leadership might reach with the Baltic states in facilitating their progress toward self-determination.[165] Finally, arms control agreements should be left for a summit meeting planned for 1990, by which time Baker hoped that all the major issues dividing the two sides on strategic arms would have been resolved and a START treaty could be signed.[166]

There was a last-minute readjustment of the venue of the leaders' talks at the Malta summit. The idea of the meetings taking place, in turn, in the American and Soviet battleships off the Malta coast had to be abandoned. Stormy weather made the journeys to those ships so potentially dangerous that the meetings were held instead on the Soviet cruise ship, the *Maxim Gorky*, which was moored in the harbour. Gorbachev began by noting that the summit was being held on Bush's initiative which was true, in a formal sense, although Gorbachev had been anxious for direct talks at the highest level to resume long before Bush had come round to the idea of reviving them. Bush acknowledged that 'this particular meeting was my idea' and that his 'change of heart has been well received in my country, for the most part'.[167]

Both the Soviet and the American official reports of the Malta summit talks are available, the Soviet version emanating from the Gorbachev Foundation well over a decade before a Freedom of Information request led to the declassification of the American document. The editors who oversaw the publication of both sets note that the accounts are not contradictory, but that the Soviet document, produced by Chernyaev, 'is significantly more detailed' than Scowcroft's American variant.[168] No great breakthroughs occurred at the summit and Gorbachev and Bush were true to form inasmuch as Gorbachev wanted to look at the big picture, whereas Bush focused on particular issues. Some of these were music to the ears of Gorbachev. The president said he would move to ease trade restraints, to end the link between Soviet emigration policy (which had become much freer) and bestowal of 'most favored nation' status, expand American technical cooperation with the Soviet Union (which Bush and Baker had agreed in advance they must not call technical 'assistance'), and support Soviet participation with observer status in the General Agreement on Tariffs and Trade (GATT) talks.[169] Taken together, these shifts in the American position assuaged Gorbachev's doubts about whether Bush really wanted perestroika to succeed.

Bush also brought up his concerns about Nicaragua and especially Cuba, to which Gorbachev responded that no-one could give orders to Fidel Castro, 'absolutely no one'.[170] He passed on, however, a remark by Castro which Scowcroft duly reproduced—'Find a way to make the President aware of my interest in normalization' of relations with the United States. Bush admitted that America's allies could not see why the administration was so bothered by Cuba and Nicaragua, but 'for the fledgling democracies in Latin America and the U.S. right it is a gut issue' and the Cuban émigrés in Florida had 'strong emotions' about Castro. Gorbachev, in response, urged Bush to give some thought to changing the American policy towards Cuba. The Soviet Union's long relationship with the island was in response to the economic blockade and they would like 'to put it on a more normal basis, especially economic'. But 'the most important thing', said Gorbachev, 'is that we have no plan for Latin America—no bridges, no bridgeheads. That is not our policy—you have it from me.'[171]

On Eastern Europe there was a fair measure of mutual understanding. Bush said that he had tried not to complicate Gorbachev's life by jumping up and down on the Berlin Wall, and the Soviet leader responded that he had noted this and appreciated it.[172] Gorbachev proposed a 'Helsinki II Summit', attended by leaders of all the countries who signed the Helsinki Final Act. He objected, however, to a concept of American origin, that the 'division of Europe should be overcome on the basis of Western values'.[173] Baker replied that what was meant was 'openness and pluralism', and Gorbachev maintained that those were values they shared. He noted that the Soviet Union was becoming more open and they were abandoning the things that divided them. 'Let us not', he said, 'make it a theological debate. That led to religious wars and we should have learned from that.' Baker resolved the disagreement by suggesting 'democratic values', to which Gorbachev immediately assented.[174]

The German question was brought up by Gorbachev. It had also been raised with Bush by Margaret Thatcher shortly before the summit. There was too much talk of German unification, she told him. Gorbachev, she said, should be their main concern, for this wouldn't have happened without him. Destabilize Gorbachev and the possibility of democracy in the Soviet Union would be lost.[175] In his memoir, Bush said he did not share Thatcher's distrust of a united Germany, but he, too, had worries about 'the adverse political effect reunification could have on Gorbachev'. Scowcroft had still more 'lingering sympathy for Thatcher's position' and for her priorities, seeing German unification as 'potentially the most destabilizing issue of all'.[176]

What made the German question especially salient at the Malta summit was that just a few days before the Soviet and American leaders met, Chancellor Kohl had raised the stakes with a speech in the Bundestag in which he set out ten points on inter-German relations which suggested movement toward a confederation in the first instance. Kohl had been prodded into urgent action by a private initiative of Valentin Falin, the head of the International Department of the Central Committee of the CPSU, using a fellow Germanist and long-standing friend from their student days, Nikolay Portugalov, to raise with Kohl's right-hand man, Horst Teltschik, the possibility of movement towards a German confederation. Portugalov was both conveying official Soviet policy to Kohl, as agreed with Chernyaev, and pursuing a more surreptitious approach designed by Falin. Before becoming an official in the party's International Department, Portugalov had been a KGB officer, so the dual role came easily to him. Since, however, it led to Kohl stepping up the tempo of the drive towards German unity, taking Gorbachev by surprise, Falin's initiative had unintended consequences.[177]

Kohl took the unofficial kite-flying to mean that it was possible to move faster than he had hitherto realized on unification and he wanted to be in the driving seat. His sudden initiative had been a bolt from the blue not only for Gorbachev but also for Bush. To avoid leaks, Kohl had told none of his NATO allies, not even the most important of them, the United States, of his impending speech. He did not even tell the German Foreign Minister, Hans-Dietrich Genscher. Bush, who knew nothing of Falin's initiative, believed that the timing of Kohl's intervention was dictated by his wanting to be sure that the president and the Soviet leader did not come to an agreement of their own on Germany. That was probably an additional factor. Bush called Kohl the day after his Bundestag speech and the chancellor pledged his solidarity with Germany's allies and indicated that he still saw the process he envisaged as one that would take a number of years.[178]

In the course of 1989 Gorbachev had established what he believed to be good relations with Kohl and had been impressed by what he thought was his prudence. He was, therefore, taken aback by Kohl's sudden raising of the stakes. Bush had, of course, a still closer relationship with the chancellor. Partly because of the sheer importance of the German question, Kohl was in the process of taking over as the American president's most favoured West European interlocutor, a role which Margaret Thatcher had enjoyed during the Reagan presidency.* Talking regularly both with Bush and with Gorbachev, Kohl performed also some of the same functions of go-between, but (from the time of the fall of the Berlin Wall) with his eye very firmly on movement toward German unification. Gorbachev understood that this was now on the political agenda, but he told Bush that Kohl was not acting 'seriously and responsibly'. Surprisingly, nonetheless, at the Malta summit he posed the question, 'Would a unified Germany be neutral, not a member of any military-political alliances, or would it be a member of NATO?' He hoped that everyone would 'understand that it is still too early to discuss either of these options'.[179] Bush said that Kohl had responded emotionally to the events in East Germany and that he was influenced also by electoral considerations, but the chancellor was aware that 'some Western allies who paid lip-service to reunification' were in reality 'quite upset by the prospect'. Gorbachev said he, too, knew that.[180] (Margaret Thatcher had made clear to him in private, what she could not say anything like as plainly in public, that she was opposed to a united Germany.)

Though it didn't result in major breakthroughs, the Malta summit was, for the US ambassador to Moscow, Jack Matlock, the point at which Bush at last 'resumed the active policy Reagan had followed during his final years in office'. Throughout the year it had been obvious that Gorbachev was acting on the principles he had set out in 1988.[181] Up until the last minute before the Malta summit, Gorbachev was uncertain, as Chernyaev noted, whether 'Bush and Baker would be prepared to establish a relationship of trust with him of at least the sort he had with Thatcher, Mitterrand, Kohl, or [Italian Prime Minister] Andreotti'.[182] In the course of the summit talks, Gorbachev and Bush agreed to give a joint press conference on the results of their

---

* In his unpublished diary, Bush wrote on 21 November 1990 (when Margaret Thatcher was about to be ousted from the premiership) that he had a 'good relationship with Thatcher', 'great respect for her, and I like her', but 'I don't feel the warmth for her as I do to say Helmut [Kohl], or even Mitterrand' (Charles Moore, *Margaret Thatcher: The Authorized Biography, Volume Three: Herself Alone*, Allen Lane, London, 2019, p. 690).

discussions—the first time this had ever been done by an American president and Soviet leader side by side. In the context of the time, observed Chernyaev, it was 'something extraordinary'. It reflected a 'deep change' in their personal relations. For Chernyaev, who was present throughout as notetaker on the Soviet side, what was striking at the summit was 'the complete and well-meaning frankness' that marked the exchanges. The level of trust that had been achieved at the highest levels of the US and Soviet administrations during Reagan's last two years in the White House was revived and even enhanced at Malta.

What was most consequential of all, however, was the dismantling of Communist regimes in Eastern Europe and the acceptance of that process by the Soviet leadership. The Cold War had begun with the Soviet take-over of Eastern Europe. It ended ideologically with Gorbachev's embrace of the principle of 'freedom to choose' in 1988. It ended on the ground with the political transformation of Eastern Europe in 1989. In that year East Europeans, West Europeans, and Americans all learned that Gorbachev was true to his non-interventionist word.

13

WHY THE COLD WAR ENDED
WHEN IT DID

I f I was right in concluding the previous chapter by asserting that the Cold War
essentially ended in 1989, now is the point to interrupt the chronological narrative
in the second part of this book with a more systematic explanation of the reasons for,
and the timing of, such a political transformation. This chapter both adds to and
sums up salient points on the Cold War's ending that have emerged in the book thus
far. It also briefly addresses alternative explanations that have been offered for the
most remarkable international phenomenon of the second half of the twentieth
century.

The political transformation of the Soviet Union, of Eastern Europe, and of
East–West relations in the space of five years occurred on a scale, and in a manner,
widely assumed to be impossible until it happened. Prior to the perestroika era, most
Western conservatives, many liberals, and the majority of Russian dissidents scorned
the idea that a serious reformer—and one intent on ending the Cold War—could rise
to become General Secretary of the Communist Party of the Soviet Union or that far-
reaching change could be initiated from within that ruling party. In the West, however, a 'retrospective determinism' had got to work by the early 1990s.[1] Such a Soviet
leader and such a change had ceased to be surprising. Politicians and analysts were
finding a variety of reasons why the previously impossible—the negotiated ending
of the forty-five-year stand-off, on terms congenial to the West which, they believed,
the Soviet leadership had no option but to accept—had either been inevitable all
along or had needed only additional American military and economic pressure on
Moscow to make it happen.

Explanations for the end of the Cold War which emphasize that American military
strength left the Soviet Union no realistic option but, in effect, to concede defeat are
among the least convincing. That has not prevented them occupying a significant
place in the thinking (especially the post-hoc rationalizations) of many members of
the Reagan administration and of some academic specialists on international relations.[2] Yet, such 'realism' betrays little understanding of the substance of political
struggle and political change in the Soviet Union during the perestroika period and
of the mindset of members of the Politburo Gorbachev inherited from Brezhnev,
Andropov, and Chernenko. The increased military spending, including that on SDI,

of the Reagan administration was, indeed, for Gorbachev an additional incentive to take steps to end the Cold War, but for every other member of Chernenko's Politburo it was a reason why the Soviet Union should not lower its guard for a moment and why it must build yet more ballistic missiles.

Reagan has even been credited with stimulating 'the emergence of New Political Thinking in Moscow after the death of Brezhnev in November 1982'.[3] Yet new thinking was well underway in Soviet research institutes in the 1970s, before Reagan came to power.[4] It had to be expressed cautiously, however, and it had very limited influence on actual Soviet policy prior to Gorbachev becoming general secretary. As leader, he positively encouraged a greater intellectual boldness, and the scope of critiques of the status quo became far more radical. Another misconception of those who see the hard-line component of the Reagan administration as instrumental in producing far-reaching change in the USSR is the erroneous assumption that the 1985 Politburo chose Gorbachev as leader 'precisely because they recognized a need for some reform'.[5]

If it were superior military strength that forced the Soviet Union to come to the negotiating table and meet the United States more than half-way, this 'realist' interpretation of the end of the Cold War fails to explain why the stand-off did not end much earlier. At a time when the USSR had been economically devastated by the quite disproportionate toll taken on that country by the Second World War, and when it was militarily incomparably weaker than the United States, the Soviet leadership expanded the frontiers of Communism to embrace almost the whole of eastern Europe and a sizeable part of central Europe. This was quite notably the case during the period when the United States had nuclear weapons and the Soviet Union had not yet developed them.* During the 1950s and 1960s, when the US military strength still clearly exceeded that of the USSR, Communist expansion continued. Even when, as in the case of the Cuban revolution, it was not initiated from Moscow, it was supported by the Soviet side. From the early 1970s until the 1980s, there was an approximate military parity between the Warsaw Pact forces, headed by the Soviet Union, and those of NATO, led by the US. If the Soviet leadership was not compelled to make concessions for the sake of achieving a constructive relationship with the West at a time when it was far weaker than America in military terms, it is an odd claim that they were obliged to do so in the mid-1980s when each side was aware that the rival superpower had enough missiles with nuclear warheads to devastate the other in a single day.

---

* When the war ended, Soviet armed forces, who had driven the Germans out, were present in large numbers in most of the countries that shortly thereafter became Communist—and that was of decisive importance for those states' incorporation in the Soviet bloc. However, at home the USSR was faced by a monumental task of economic and physical rebuilding at a time when the USA had emerged from the war with the strongest and largest economy in the world and with its infrastructure undamaged.

The major concern of this chapter is with the *how* and *why* of the Cold War's ending and, accordingly, why it happened *when* it did. Some of those who argue that economic pressures and constraints on the Soviet Union made it likely that the Cold War would end on Western terms emphasize that they do not claim any insight on the timing of this happening. In due course, it is suggested, the differential growth rates, technological lag, and other material incentives would force the Soviet Union to accept that their system had failed.[6] Few would deny that the problems identified were real or that command economies were less efficient, and did less to raise the standard of living of their people, than market economies, the problems and inequities of the latter notwithstanding. However, in a highly authoritarian regime, the populace, by definition, had very little say in the matter. In the higher echelons of the CPSU—party apparatus, ministries, and military-industrial complex—Stalinists and authoritarian nationalists had a larger presence than would-be free marketeers or social democrats. In the longer term, the number of unknowns increases, making greater confidence about long-term than short-term outcomes somewhat curious. It is very rash to assume that a real crisis in the Soviet Union years later than the 1980s, with no Gorbachev in power, would have yielded a result congenial to the West, rather than support for an order-restoring 'strongman' who would see harmonious relations and extensive interchange with Western countries as a threat to authoritarian rule.

Although Ronald Reagan and, more surprisingly (given the vast discrepancy between American and British global power), Margaret Thatcher made significant contributions to ending the Cold War, it was transformative change in the Soviet Union that was by far the most crucial development, though a degree of Western reciprocity to that change was a necessary condition for its peaceful conclusion. This response came more quickly from Western Europe (where Gorbachev was more popular than Reagan) than from the United States. Besides Britain—and the formidable part played by Thatcher—France[7], Italy, and Spain were among the earliest European countries to engage with the new Soviet leadership. And in West Germany, Gorbachev's popularity grew rapidly, although Chancellor Kohl for several years lagged behind German public opinion. After his first meeting with Gorbachev in October 1988, Kohl made up for lost time.

The liberalization and evolving democratization of the Soviet political system, accompanied by the new freedom of speech, contributed greatly to the growth of international trust. The later 1980s witnessed a remarkable degree of ideational convergence, with both sides expressing commitment to 'democratic values' and (what was most extraordinary in the light of Soviet history) understanding approximately the same things by that terminology. This did not mean that Gorbachev and his closest collaborators favoured adopting the precise institutional structures of the United States or the United Kingdom (whose institutions, after all, differed radically from one another) or of any other country.[8] More importantly, however, there was now an appreciation by the Soviet leader and his key domestic allies that political democracy meant, among other things, contested elections, a rule of law, and the political accountability of governments to legislatures and to the people. Insofar as this meant an East–West convergence of views, it was clear that the Soviet Union had done most of the 'converging'.

This was partly a consequence of the engagement of West European and American leaders (especially Reagan and Shultz in the US case) with their Soviet counterparts. It was related also to a longer-term interaction of an influential minority within the Soviet foreign policy establishment with Western officials and researchers, a process that intensified during the perestroika years. Specialists in Soviet research institutes concerned with international affairs had been developing elements of what became known as the 'new thinking' well before perestroika, but their ideas were empowered only after Gorbachev became party leader.[9] For the 'new thinkers' now given a voice in the decision-making process, a major goal was to wind down the competition in armaments and reach further agreements on the limitation and reduction of weapons of mass destruction. There was a new emphasis on 'reasonable sufficiency' in defence, as distinct from parity at the existing costly level. Mooted in research institutes before being embraced by Gorbachev, these notions caused alarm in military circles.[10]

Both in principle—with Gorbachev's insistence, especially from 1988, that all countries must have the freedom to make their own choice of political and economic system—and, in practice, as was seen equally clearly in 1989, the Soviet Union was no longer imposing Communist systems on the countries of Eastern Europe. Those states regained their independence and most of them began rapidly democratizing. What is more, the radically reformist wing of the Soviet leadership, which had the incomparable advantage of having the party leader on its side, were dismantling, pillar by pillar, the Communist political structures in their own country.

Leadership, Power, and Ideas

While there are many contributory causes of the end of the Cold War, it occurred when and how it did due to a combination of leadership, power, and ideas—most specifically, in the Soviet Union. The coming to power of Gorbachev in March 1985 provided innovative and adroit political leadership. In the strictly hierarchical Communist system, the power and authority of the general secretary was very great. And what made this particular leader's authority so decisively important was that he had a different mindset from that of any of his predecessors in the Kremlin and was remarkably open to new ideas.[11]

While no Soviet party leader had a completely free hand within the ruling oligarchy, the general secretary's authority was such that he could change the balance of influence among the various opinion groupings that existed within the CPSU. He had a larger say than anyone else on appointments, but only a leader as bold and ambitious as Gorbachev could effect a complete change in the top foreign policy-making team within a year of taking office. Typically, Soviet leaders used their patronage to gradually bring into the ruling circles people who had been their trusted subordinates at earlier stages of their careers. Gorbachev did not fill any of the major political posts in this way. What made his appointments so important was that he very deliberately brought into the international policy-making team people who were eager to do things differently from in the past. That was especially true of Chernyaev, Yakovlev, and Shevardnadze.

Throughout the post-war period the Soviet leadership was prepared to spend a disproportionately large share of national income (precisely how much, members of the Politburo themselves did not know) on defence, and the military-industrial complex was a hugely influential institutional interest within the system. The response of the Soviet Politburo to the American military build-up during Reagan's first term was to carry on as before. There was no dissent from Defence Minister Ustinov's insistence at a Politburo meeting less than two months after Reagan had announced his Strategic Defense Initiative that 'Everything we are doing in relation to defence we should continue doing', that all planned missiles must be delivered, and that they must actively oppose 'the imperialist intrigues of our enemies'.[12] This was the firm stance of the Soviet leadership prior to Gorbachev's becoming general secretary (as was noted in Chapter 5). Anatoly Dobrynin, the long-serving Soviet ambassador to Washington (and subsequent head of the International Department of the Central Committee), was in no doubt that Reagan's policy produced the opposite effect from that intended. His stepping-up of military spending and waging an ideological offensive merely consolidated a hard line within the Soviet leadership.[13]

For those who had neither an ideological commitment to, nor a material stake in, SDI, its limitations were obvious. Even Robert Gates joked that 'there appeared to be only two people on the planet who actually thought SDI would work—Reagan and Gorbachev'.[14] Gorbachev's concern about SDI was very real, but it was not based on the supposition that it would work in anything like the manner Reagan imagined. It was clear that the Soviet Union could combat any SDI deployment more cheaply but effectively (if one can use the word, 'effectively', about a conflict in which countless millions on both sides would be killed) by overwhelming any missile defence system through sheer numbers. As former Defense Secretary Bill Perry observed (and as was discussed more fully in Chapter 9), the Soviet Union could, much more cheaply than the cost of SDI, deploy thousands of decoys with their nuclear warheads, greatly multiplying the number of targets SDI would have to cope with.[15] Andrei Sakharov made the same point as Perry in his 'Maginot line in space' speech at a Moscow forum in February 1987, mentioned in Chapter 10.[16] Sakharov, who (like Perry) knew what he was talking about on nuclear weapons and their delivery systems, was fully convinced of the feasibility of an asymmetric response to SDI, but, nevertheless, viewed the American attempt at comprehensive missile defence as an extremely dangerous error. It was a stimulus to the development of offensive systems, and 'attacks on space-based elements of hostile ABM systems during a nonnuclear stage of a major war could provoke escalation to a global thermonuclear war, in other words, to the destruction of the human race'.[17]

Moreover, said Sakharov, addressing the 1987 Moscow Forum, 'The claim that the existence of the SDI program has spurred the USSR to disarmament negotiations is also wrong. On the contrary, the SDI program is impeding those negotiations.'[18] On this particular point the dissident and nuclear scientist Sakharov, the shrewd but traditional Soviet diplomat Dobrynin, and a leading 'new thinker' Anatoly Adamishin, who became a Soviet deputy foreign minister under Shevardnadze, are at one. Adamishin observed that Reagan's policies gave 'unnecessary arguments to our "hawks" and created difficulties for Gorbachev', making it harder for him 'to over-come the great internal resistance to his steps towards the lessening of tension'.[19] Former Thatcher speech-writer John O'Sullivan's claim, cited in the Introduction to this book, 'without Reagan, no *perestroika* or *glasnost* either', was specious. Indeed, noted Adamishin, the idea that Reagan's hard line led to the new thinking and to perestroika was the precise opposite of the truth. It was grist for the mill of the con-servative majority of officials within the departments of the Central Committee and the ministries. Their view was expressed by KGB Chairman Viktor Chebrikov at a Politburo meeting in 1986: 'The Americans understand only strength.'[20] Even in the Ministry of Foreign Affairs in the mid-1980s, advocates for the Soviet military-industrial complex retained a strong voice.[21]

That SDI did not lead to disaster owed much to Gorbachev. The Politburo col-leagues who chose him, and the Central Committee members who were happy to endorse him, as general secretary in March 1985 were completely unaware that they were electing the most pacific leader in Soviet history (a 'pacifist', Anatoly Gromyko, the son of the Foreign Minister, called him,[22] though that was an exaggeration). Since the logic of SDI development was to lead an adversary to increase its production of offensive weapons, and then use a mixture of nuclear warheads and decoys, Bill Perry was right to say that 'even if we never deployed the SDI system, simply starting it could precipitate a new and more dangerous phase of the nuclear arms race'.[23] Although Gorbachev was persuaded by Soviet experts that SDI could be readily combated, it was clear that this meant ratcheting up rather than winding down the arms race and that it carried with it a heightened risk of nuclear war by accident or misadventure.

Thus, for Gorbachev and for the like-minded people he appointed to key foreign policy posts, the folly of SDI called for diplomatic efforts to prevent its deployment and render unnecessary the inevitable countermeasures the Soviet Union would take if it went ahead. Having tried to persuade Reagan of the serious arguments that had convinced both sides in earlier years to abandon the idea of large-scale missile defence—and had led to the Antiballistic Missile (ABM) Treaty signed in

1972—Gorbachev initially made the withdrawal of Soviet intermediate-range weapons from Europe conditional on concessions from Reagan on SDI. Faced with Reagan's obduracy at Reykjavik, however, he embraced the zero option and signed the INF Treaty in 1987. That agreement could have been reached sooner in the absence of the SDI threat to the ABM Treaty. But the fact that SDI was never likely to work in the manner Reagan envisaged was a good reason for decoupling the arms reduction agreement from Reagan's Strategic Defense Initiative. It was also reasonable for Gorbachev to suppose that the more the US and the USSR cooperated both in arms reductions and in other areas, the less incentive either side had to embark on vastly expensive military projects. Well over a generation after Reagan gave SDI the green light, such a comprehensive missile defence system still does not exist.

There is no adequate reason to imagine that either Soviet foreign or domestic policy would have changed fundamentally if a leader other than Gorbachev had become general secretary. We must bear in mind that only a full member of the Politburo at the time of Chernenko's death could be a candidate for the party leadership. That was a small and conservative group. Georgy Shakhnazarov, a long-serving senior official in the Central Committee apparatus (and president of the Soviet Association of Political Sciences) who later became a key Gorbachev adviser both on domestic political reform and on Eastern Europe, observed that 'everything would have remained the same as before if Viktor Vasilevich Grishin [a senior member of the Politburo who aspired to the top job] had been elected general secretary in March 1985'.[24] There was, Shakhnazarov notes, a large element of pure chance in someone as different from his Politburo colleagues as Gorbachev being in the prime position at the right time to seize the most powerful post in the country.

The most any of the others would have aspired to achieve internationally was the kind of détente that existed for a time in the 1970s, but with Reagan in the White House, that would have been far from easy to attain. Both sides would still have had an existential interest in avoiding nuclear catastrophe, but neither would have been prepared to make the compromises that would have ended the Cold War. In particular, no other plausible contender to be leader of the USSR in 1985 would have permitted, still less espoused, the development of political pluralism or, in 1988, have declared that the people of every country without exception had the right to decide for themselves what kind of political and economic system they wished to live in. Without the ideational change that occurred with Gorbachev as general secretary, and a new Soviet practice that accorded with it, both rulers and ruled in Eastern Europe would have assumed, with good reason, that they still lived under limited sovereignty. They would have continued to be aware that to go beyond those limits was too dangerous a path to take, and that the limits included respecting the monopoly of power of the Communist Party and their country's alignment with, and loyalty to, the leadership of the Soviet Union.

Even within the party intelligentsia of the Soviet Union, not to speak of the Communist Party as a whole, Westernizers—whether as social democrats (like Shakhnazarov) or would-be free marketeers (such as Yegor Gaidar)—and supporters of political pluralism were in a minority. And reform-minded *mezhdunarodniki* (Soviet specialists on international affairs) were far from advocating or even envisaging in 1985 a USSR which would calmly accept the demise of Communism in Eastern Europe and the dissolution of the Warsaw Pact. A significant minority among party intellectuals favoured a cultural liberalization and some measures of economic reform, but transformation of the political system, including contested elections for a legislature with real powers, seemed too remote from reality to contemplate. Visiting scholars to the Soviet Union in the mid-1980s were told by those serious reformers prepared to speak frankly to them in private that pluralism was not on the political agenda. Gorbachev's openness to political change substantially exceeded the expectations in the mid-1980s even of those intellectuals who a few years later were to berate the Soviet leader for not going fast enough with his reforms. In the later years of perestroika, this segment of the intelligentsia was frequently more radical than the general secretary. But Gorbachev had to consider how far he could go at a given time while avoiding overthrow by a coalition of conservative bureaucrats, the KGB, and the military-industrial complex, an outcome he staved off until August 1991.

Arguments about the relative importance of interests or ideas in politics, and most specifically in the Soviet Union during the period which led to the ending of the Cold War, often oversimplify interests and present a false dichotomy. We need to ask: in whose interests specifically would particular major changes be, whether we are talking about movement from authoritarian one-party rule to political pluralism, transition from a command economy to a market economy, the accountability of the military-industrial complex and the security forces to a freely elected legislature, or the end of the Cold War for the party-state and military hierarchy. Western politicians and journalists tended to assume that all these things were self-evidently in the interests of the Soviet people.

Yet only with radical reform of the political system were the people given a voice, and when they used it, nationalist grievances and discontent about material shortages in the last years of the Soviet Union bulked larger than complaints about the pace of democratic institution-building. For the party apparatus and the ministerial bureaucracy who administered the country—without the inconvenience of checks by an independent judiciary, an autonomous legislature, or a free and critical press—it is far from clear why political liberalization, not to speak of democratization, should be in their interests. Officials in Gosplan (the State Planning Committee), the economic ministries, and the economic departments of the Central Committee, together with regional party secretaries at lower levels of the hierarchy, who all had important roles in making the command economy work, believed that they had much to lose from marketizing reform, and they resisted it. (A significant number of party and state officials later converted their administrative control over property into ownership, but that was something they could scarcely imagine, still less count on, in advance.)

For the military, the KGB, and the Ministry of Interior—the *siloviki*, as they came to be known, from the Russian word, *sila* (meaning 'force' or 'power')—both pluralization of the political system and a dramatic improvement in East–West relations promised nothing but trouble. And that promise was fulfilled in the perestroika years. The people who led these organizations were not averse to a modus vivendi with other countries. They would have had to be mad consciously to pursue policies leading to nuclear war but, unsurprisingly, they believed that the vast resources devoted to military expenditure and the security forces constituted money well spent. The prominent Western specialist on the Soviet economy, Alec Nove, was far from alone in observing that 'the arms race doubtless contributed to economic overstrain' in the Soviet Union, but he perceptively added, 'paradoxically the Cold War may have helped the system to survive, by providing a *raison d'être* for its continuance', along with 'the dominant role of the military-industrial complex'.[25] The latter had to be persuaded, cajoled, browbeaten, and sometimes bypassed by Gorbachev in order to get them to acquiesce, very reluctantly, with policies—including the loss of closely aligned governments in Eastern Europe—which, among themselves at the time, and publicly later, they frequently denounced as treachery.*

There was huge discontent on the part of military leaders with Gorbachev's and Shevardnadze's willingness to give up the SS-23 ('Oka') missiles as part of the concessions from the Soviet side in the INF negotiations, a concession to US Secretary of State Shultz in discussion with Gorbachev that the Chief of the Soviet General Staff,

---

* Oleg Shenin, a Politburo member and secretary of the Central Committee with responsibility for the party organization who participated in the attempted coup against Gorbachev in August 1991, said that 'Multifaceted and large-scale state treason was committed in Malta at the meeting between Gorbachev and Bush in December 1989.' Oleg Baklanov, the Central Committee secretary overseeing the military-industrial complex, asked, 'How is one to evaluate the work of Gorbachev as General Secretary and that of the Politburo members who continued to support him and carried out his policy?' and answered, 'I think that it can be seen as the highest form of betrayal of the interests of the state and its leaders.' I have already, in Chapter 12, cited KGB Chairman Vladimir Kryuchkov describing Gorbachev's behaviour as the most 'treasonous policy' in 'human history'. According to the transcript of this 1999 Moscow conference (at which these remarks were made and in which I participated at the invitation of its co-sponsor, the Mershon Center of Ohio State University), I posed the following question: 'A number of participants, both here and in statements and writings elsewhere, have said that Gorbachev was a traitor. If in fact a traitor held the office of general secretary for almost seven years and was not arrested—if we exclude Foros in 1991—was this not the biggest failure in the history of the KGB?' Kryuchkov was slow to respond, but eventually said he did not think 'appropriate action' would be taken 'if there were a leader of this sort in England or the United States', but added that 'our system, at that time and now, is seriously flawed in that it prevents the timely punishment of those who have acted to the detriment of our state'.

Marshal Akhromeyev, learned about only the next day when it was too late to retract it.[26] The military were angry also about the exclusion of British and French nuclear weapons from the INF negotiations. Overlord of military industry Oleg Baklanov objected strenuously and recalled that he made 'categorical objections and wouldn't sign the proper documents or would sign them with reservations' which 'caused a great hullabaloo', but he was overruled.[27]

It is sometimes asserted that Gorbachev's role was not decisive because there was little open advocacy in the Soviet Union in 1989 of force to be used to prevent the East European countries abandoning Communist rule, or demands for military intervention in East Germany in 1989 or 1990 to prevent unification. That misses the most important points. Gorbachev's hard-line opponents had already been outmanoeuvred. To explain the relative absence of pressure to crush anti-Communist movements in Eastern Europe, including the GDR, in 1989, we need to understand, first, the fundamental significance of the power and authority which accrued to the general secretary, and, second, that democratic and nationalist hopes would not have been instilled in the first place in the allied Warsaw Pact countries if any member of the Politburo other than Gorbachev had been chosen as party leader in 1985. Communist regimes in Eastern Europe would have continued for the same reason that they had persisted for four decades—because the people who lived in those countries had every reason to believe that there was no viable alternative. In the absence of the new thinking empowered by Gorbachev and the radically new policies he had already pursued by the end of 1988, expectations would not have been aroused, and it would have been a very different 1989.

It is worth considering briefly one quite popular alternative view—that it was a Polish pope who made the momentous changes at the end of the 1980s possible. This became a widespread view in Poland, but it has more to do with national pride there and faith elsewhere than with political reality. What is true, and significant, is that the elevation of the Polish Cardinal Karol Wotyła to the papacy in 1978 as Pope John Paul II was a source of inspiration in the rise of Solidarity, culminating in something close to dual power in Poland in 1980–1. Yet, even in a country where over the years, Marxist-Leninist rulers had less authority than in most other Communist states, and where there was a much more vibrant civil society, the Polish government was strong enough to impose martial law in December 1981. This was partly because Poles assumed that the might of the Soviet army stood behind their own unpopular rulers and that further resistance could lead to intervention and make a bad situation worse. That is why their changing perceptions in the late 1980s of where the Soviet leadership stood, and what Moscow would be liable to do, were so important. There was strong Western support for Solidarity in 1980–1 (not least from Reagan and Thatcher), but this was no more effective than the support of the Pope had been in preventing the crackdown on the movement and the imprisonment of its leaders. It was the Soviet liberalization and new political tolerance in the second half of the

1980s, and Gorbachev's willingness to let central and east European governments and peoples sort out their political differences themselves, that facilitated the dramatic break with the past. It smoothed the way for the re-emergence of Solidarity and its rise to power at the end of the 1980s.

Victor Hugo famously wrote, 'Greater than the tread of mighty armies is an idea whose time has come.'[28] But that bold statement raises big questions. How do we know an idea's time has come? Who provides the idea? And who can implement it? In authoritarian regimes, even more than in democracies, ideas need institutional bearers if they are to acquire political substance. In a Communist system they had to be espoused by the top leader, and for ideational innovation to result in far-reaching political change required leadership renewal. The death of Mao and the emergence of Deng Xiaoping as his de facto successor led to profound change in China— marketizing reform of the economy and an opening of China to the world, although no concessions to political pluralism. Change on the Chinese scale has been historically rare.

Yet, even more profound change occurred in the Soviet Union and Eastern Europe in the second half of the 1980s. It was inextricably connected with the opportunity which befell the youngest member of the Politburo when he became general secretary in 1985 to decide that the time for ideas (in the plural) had come. Indeed, Vladislav Zubok, a leading Russian historian of the Cold War (now a professor at the London School of Economics, after teaching for some years in the United States), argues that Gorbachev 'took ideas *too seriously*' (italics in the original).[29] The various components of the 'new thinking', to which Gorbachev became deeply attached, took precedence, Zubok argues, over state interests. Unlike his predecessors, for whom 'a "realism" based on strength, coercion and balance of power was even more important than communist ideology', Gorbachev was prepared 'to give up diplomatic and military positions the USSR had retained and expanded' through his commitment to ideas and ideals such as the demilitarization of international relations, all-human values, universal interests, a common European home, a new global order, and his growing attachment to a social democratic variant of socialism.[30]

It was Gorbachev's openness to ideas hitherto deemed heretical in the Soviet Union that enabled him to initiate change that went against the personal inclinations and judgements, and even the interests, of other members of the party-state hierarchy. Gorbachev did not change policy instantly and unilaterally but gradually and by persuasion. If there was a clear majority of the Politburo in the early years of perestroika sceptical about, or opposed to, a change he favoured, he would at times make a tactical retreat, saying that they needed to think further about it. He would then exercise persuasion behind the scenes, bring the matter back to the Politburo at a somewhat later date, and secure agreement for it. With Yakovlev as an overseer of the media in the early years of perestroika, editors supportive of far-reaching reform, and ready to question past domestic and foreign policy, were backed, encouraged and given some protection from the frequent attacks coming their way from more conservative Communists. The circulation of the journals and newspapers in the vanguard of glasnost rose dramatically and helped to create a newly vitalized political society.

The Military and the Economy

Gorbachev's ability to win the intra-party arguments owed much to his exceptional persuasive skill, but it was decisively bolstered by his political power and authority. It was not only that he had the privilege of chairing meetings he attended, whether the Politburo or Central Committee—and even, initially, the new parliament—but that, especially up to the end of 1989, the conditioned reflex of officials was, ultimately, to comply with his wishes. This was in keeping not only with seven decades of experience of Communist rule but also with a still longer tradition in Russia of submission to the country's leader. Central Committee secretary Baklanov and Minister of Defence Dmitry Yazov were frequently opposed to what Gorbachev and his foreign policy appointees were doing, and sometimes took their objections to the general secretary. According to Yazov, Gorbachev would say, 'Why are you opposed? What do you want, nose to nose, bayonet to bayonet?' He told Yazov, 'You have to look ahead!' Some years later, the (by then) former Defence Minister was asked by an interviewer whether he had inquired in which direction that was? Yazov responded, as if this were answer enough: 'At that time Gorbachev was general secretary.'[31] Referring to the period up to the end of the Cold War in 1989, Anatoly Gromyko remarked that foreigners seemed to have a hard time realizing just how influential was the office of general secretary 'in the Soviet mentality', adding that 'to object to the general secretary, or even worse, to debate his opinions in public—at that time I don't think anyone dared to do that.'[32]

To believe that the Soviet Union had no option but to pursue the kind of foreign and defence policy that Gorbachev sought to implement is either to underplay or to overlook the misgivings and behind-the-scenes resistance to his policies which he overcame, with a mixture of guile and use of the authority derived from his office.[33] Oleg Grinevsky, a senior Soviet diplomat who led the Soviet delegation at the Conference on Security and Co-operation in Europe (CSCE) talks in the 1980s, observed that 'Gorbachev seriously coerced the military.' There was 'a big struggle', he said, over the 500,000 cut in the armed forces that Gorbachev announced at the UN in December 1988.[34] An especially important example, observes Grinevsky, of Gorbachev 'coercing' the defence establishment (one I noted in Chapter 10, citing Dobrynin's stress on its significance) was his use of the young German Matthias Rust's 1987 arrival in Red Square in a light aircraft as 'a pretext for settling scores with the military'. Gorbachev seized the opportunity to remove Marshal Sokolov, the Minister of Defence who had been resistant to his foreign and defence policy, as well as '150 other military personnel'.[35] Gorbachev took this chance, observed Vladimir Kryuchkov, who succeeded

Chebrikov as Chairman of the KGB in 1988, 'to strike a blow' at the Ministry of Defence, which, the general secretary believed, had been insufficiently subordinate to him and didn't 'follow his train of thought'.[36]

Complementary to the argument that the Soviet Union had no alternative but to pursue a constructive, and often concessionary, foreign policy in the second half of the 1980s as a result of Reagan's military build-up is the view that this was necessitated by the dismal state of the Soviet economy. The context of a long-term decline in the rate of Soviet economic growth and of the country's technological lag (except in military production and space research and development) is, indeed, important. For Gorbachev and a number of his allies, it was one of the stimuli to embark on perestroika. However, economic slowdown which might lead to a change of government in a democracy (although not always even there), can be explained away, as a necessary belt-tightening response to external threat, by an authoritarian regime. Gorbachev spoke in the mid-1980s about the existence of 'pre-crisis phenomena' in the Soviet Union. In response to events moving out of control during 1990–1, he sometimes understandably, but inaccurately, suggested that the country was already in crisis in 1985.[37] This was, however, a retrospective judgement. In the last two years of its existence the USSR *was* in crisis—at imminent risk of disintegration—as an unintended consequence of reforms that the general secretary had introduced. Gorbachev has, on a number of occasions, noted (perfectly correctly) that if his only concern had been to remain in power, he could have done so without embarking on radical reforms. Economic sluggishness notwithstanding, all had, in fact, been remarkably calm in 1984–5. Even under the lacklustre Konstantin Chernenko, people had simply put up with shortages, grumbling in private rather than engaging in public protests.

Western economists who studied the Soviet Union were well aware of the declining rate of Soviet economic growth and of the country's technological backwardness in many areas, and some of them used the term 'crisis' to describe it. Even the latter who did so were not assuming there was anything inevitable about a turn to radical reform. As the American specialist Marshall Goldman, who called his 1983 book *U.S.S.R. in Crisis*, observed, 'The present situation is bad, but the consequences of reform may be even worse.'[38] What makes the argument that dire economic necessity, reinforced by the policies of the Reagan administration, *compelled* the Soviet Union to embark on reform especially unpersuasive is that, after becoming Soviet leader, Gorbachev was before long according a far higher priority to political reform (which did nothing to enhance economic performance) than to economic reform. It was as late as 1990 before he clearly accepted the principle that the Soviet Union should become an essentially market economy, though even then he baulked at putting it into practice. It was also evident that he was much more impressed by European social democracy and by the German social market economy than by the anti-statist model favoured by Reagan and Thatcher.[39] And the problem of *how* to make the transition from command economy to market economy remained acute. A move to market prices would raise the cost of essentials and was liable to increase, rather than reduce, popular discontent which was growing fast in 1990–1.

Because of the institutional obstacles in the way of radical economic reform, it was reasonable for Gorbachev to believe, as he told Thatcher, that economic reform was dependent on political reform.[40] Yet it is quite wrong to interpret political change as no more than preparation of the ground for economic reform. Gorbachev himself wrote years later that 'In the heat of political battles we lost sight of the economy, and people never forgave us for the shortages of everyday items and the lines for essential goods.'[41] From as early as 1986 he came to value political liberalization and, subsequently, democratization for their own sakes. At a time when his agenda was grossly overloaded, reform of the economy fell below transformative change of the political system and of Soviet foreign policy in Gorbachev's order of priorities. Latterly the growing nationalities problem and his successive attempts to reconstruct the Soviet pseudo-federation as a loose and voluntary federation, underpinned by a new Union Treaty, also occupied more of his time than did the economy. Political reform could be radicalized from month to month in a remarkably speedy evolution. But only a sharper break would work for transformation of the economic system. There was a basic contradiction, which remained unresolved, between improving the existing economic system and moving to one based on different principles.

Some commentators maintain that the Reagan administration successfully went out of its way to exacerbate Soviet difficulties by collaborating with Saudi Arabia to reduce the international oil price.[42] The USSR was heavily dependent on the revenue it received from the export of oil and gas, but as the author of a well-informed study of the Soviet economy during the perestroika years has pointed out, 'the oil-price fall, though important, explains little by itself' and was just one of several contributors to a growing budgetary crisis.[43] Much of the problem was a direct result of policies pursued by the Soviet leadership. Thus, the state monopoly on the manufacture and sale of alcoholic drinks (with vodka the main component) was a huge contributor to the budget. The anti-alcohol campaign launched in 1985 meant that by 1987 the budgetary losses resulting from restrictions on the sale of liquor were approximately the same as those resulting from the decline in the world market price of oil.[44]

Moreover, Soviet state subsidies on the price of food cost the exchequer several times more than either the drop in the oil price or the loss of tax revenue from alcohol sales.[45] The scale of those subsidies was one reason why the Soviet leadership hesitated to move to market prices, since they would lead to a sharp rise in the price of basic foodstuffs. Non-market prices meant shortages of products, but market prices would mean people paying very much more. There was no easy way out, especially since, as Gorbachev recognized, perestroika had not brought the population benefits in their material lives, as distinct from conferring a vast increase in freedom (including a new tolerance of their right to express outrage).[46]

The share of the budget taken by the military-industrial complex was, of course, greater still (although somewhat offset by foreign earnings from Soviet arms sales) and this was an area where Gorbachev wished to make savings. Yet, by the end of the 1980s there had been no reduction in the cost to the country of the defence sector. Savings from arms and troop reductions had transitional costs, with benefits slower to accrue.

Western Power and Western Influence

I have argued that neither the American military build-up nor economic pressure forced the Soviet Union to embark on systemic change and to call a halt to the Cold War. That is not, however, to deny that for Gorbachev specifically, and for the like-minded people he appointed as key players in the foreign policy-making team, the cost of maintaining military parity with the United States and other economic pressures were reasons—in addition to their desire to eliminate the danger of the two sides sleepwalking into a war which neither side could win—for seeking qualitatively better relations with NATO countries. Gorbachev was at least as interested in improving relations with the major countries of Western Europe as he was with the United States. Indeed, he found more that attracted him in the politics, economies, and societies of the former than of the latter. He also found Western Europe, and his relations with its leaders, more interesting than his dealings with the Soviet Union's Communist allies in Eastern Europe.

Within the top foreign-policy-making group, Gorbachev's willingness to change Soviet positions in pursuit of these new priorities was shared especially by Shevardnadze, Yakovlev (who was influential on both foreign and domestic policy), and Chernyaev, with the successive heads of the International Department of the Central Committee, Anatoly Dobrynin and Valentin Falin both more cautious. And there were many far harder-liners than Dobrynin and Falin in the ruling circles of the Soviet party-state. That was particularly true of its major institutional interest, the military-industrial complex. Their view of the appropriate response to military and economic pressures was to maintain high defence spending, tighten discipline at home, and intensify anti-Western propaganda. Since the policies Gorbachev pursued had, along with their many positive achievements, the unintended consequence of the disintegration of the Soviet state and a Russia in the post-Soviet era (especially its first decade) which was weaker both militarily and economically vis-à-vis the United States than it was in the 1980s, the hard-liners could argue, and have subsequently done so, that their policy of 'no change' to the fundamentals of Soviet foreign policy was in the country's interest.

In his 'Long Telegram' of 22 February 1946 from the American Embassy in Moscow to Washington, George Kennan wrote of 'a type of insecurity' which afflicted Russian rulers who 'have invariably sensed that their rule was relatively archaic in form, fragile and artificial in its psychological foundation', and unable to stand comparison with the political systems of Western countries. Thus, they were afraid of direct contact between the Western world and their own, fearing what would happen if Russians learned the truth about the 'world without' or if foreigners discovered the truth about the 'world within'.[47] On the eve of the Soviet perestroika some forty years later, that view of the world still had a lot of purchase within the Soviet leadership. Admiration of Western technological achievements was nothing new, but Gorbachev's growing esteem for the freedoms, tolerance, and political accountability that existed in Western countries was a clear break with the Soviet past. Having come to share an appreciation of those political values, Gorbachev did not of course wish to announce this as an acceptance of 'Western values', but he was ready to embrace them as 'democratic values' or as 'universal values'. Westernizers had, ever since the nineteenth century, been a significant strand or grouping within the Russian intelligentsia, but never before had the mainstream beliefs of Western democracy been embraced and promulgated by the holder of the highest post within the Russian or Soviet political system.

Over the long run, from the time of the Soviet takeover of Eastern Europe in the 1940s, to the 1980s, Western military power and the NATO alliance had provided a necessary discouragement to Soviet political and military leaders who might be tempted to expand their hegemony to include one or more existing Western democracies. However, it was Western democratic example, far more than the threat of military power, that had the greater influence on Gorbachev and his radically reformist supporters.[48] The same George Kennan who, in Stalin's time, urged the American government to be militarily strong enough to pursue a policy of 'containment' of the Soviet Union, noted also in his 'Long Telegram' that a lot depended on the 'health and vigor of our own society', that 'we must have courage and self-confidence to cling to our own methods and conceptions of human society', and that 'the greatest danger' in dealing with Soviet Communism would be to 'allow ourselves to become like those with whom we are coping'.[49]

Policy choices are linked to perceptions and there can be different perceptions of what is in the national interest of any country that depend on the values of political actors as well as on identifications, beliefs, and habits of mind to which they have long adhered. Politicians in any country are more likely to use their reason to defend their existing beliefs and prejudices than to make a careful calculation of the costs and benefits of engineering a major policy shift.[50] New experiences, especially those with a positive emotional component, can, however, promote belief change in people with the self-confidence and self-esteem to value evidence they see with their own eyes and to reassess what they had hitherto been taught to believe. This was conspicuously true of Gorbachev.[51]

His visits to half a dozen different European countries in the 1970s, adding Canada in 1983 as well as a return visit to Italy and his first visit to Britain in 1984, made a big and favourable impression on him. At the time of his election as general secretary,

Gorbachev had seen more of the West than had any other member of the 1985 Politburo apart from Andrei Gromyko. Once he became party leader, Gorbachev lost no time (as has already been noted) in bringing Aleksandr Yakovlev into the Secretariat of the Central Committee and before long into the party's highest policy-making body, the Politburo. Yakovlev had spent a year in New York in 1959 and, more significantly for the development of his heterodox ideas, an entire decade in Canada. As an ambassador, he could have continued to live in a Soviet bubble, but he took the opportunity to fully engage with the host country and also to find time for reflection. In the relatively relaxed atmosphere (even during the Cold War) of Ottawa, he came to admire Canadian pragmatism and 'common sense' and, speaking frankly to Gorbachev on an Ontario farm in 1983, told him 'how primitive and shameful Soviet policy looked from here'.[52] First-hand experience of the Western world was significant not only in these two outstanding cases, but also for a segment of the party intelligentsia, including some party officials (particularly from the International Department of the Central Committee), who spent time in non-Communist Europe or in North America. These researchers and officials could not fail to notice the strikingly higher standard of living in Western countries and, in a good many cases, they came to appreciate the advantages of permitted dissent, political competition, and a rule of law. They were a minority within the party, but a minority which became more influential than ever before as a result of Gorbachev's accession to the general secretaryship.

During the perestroika period interaction between the Soviet Union and the West greatly increased. There was far more interchange at elite level in both directions and it became easier for ordinary Soviet citizens to visit the West. There had long been more English-language books, novels included, translated into Russian than of Russian into English, but with no pre-perestroika possibility of translating books critical of the Soviet system or its ideology. During perestroika, a withering-away of the censorship allowed hitherto banned works by Soviet writers (among them, Varlam Shalamov and Aleksandr Solzhenitsyn who had portrayed the horrific conditions of political prisoners in the USSR) to be published officially. Even such a long-anathematized Western writer as George Orwell was translated into Russian in large print-runs. Western politicians, diplomats, and scholars were questioned on Soviet radio and television with increasing frequency from 1987 onwards. Margaret Thatcher's visit in March of that year and her forthright TV interview marked the breakthrough. By 1990–1, US Ambassador Jack Matlock and his UK counterpart Rodric Braithwaite, both fluent Russian speakers, were being interviewed by Soviet media and treated as respected experts on international developments.

Since Gorbachev's elevation to the party leadership was unconnected with the policies of the Reagan administration, and as his open mind and reformist disposition were both a natural endowment and a product of his Soviet experience and of his encounters with different political cultures on foreign visits, it is hard to sustain the argument that the Cold War would not have ended when it did had the assassination attempt on Ronald Reagan in March 1981 achieved its aim. A prominent historian of the Cold War, John Lewis Gaddis, argues, however, that had Reagan died, and his 'vice president, George H. W. Bush, succeeded him at that point, the Reagan presidency would have been a historical footnote and there probably would not have been an American challenge to the Cold War status quo', since 'Bush, like most foreign policy experts of his generation, saw that conflict as a permanent feature of the international landscape.'[53] Gaddis puts Reagan in the company of other leaders who did not accept the Cold War's permanence and were prepared to do something about it. It is a list in which he includes Margaret Thatcher and Pope John Paul II but, remarkably, does not mention Gorbachev.[54]

Gaddis is, nevertheless, far from dismissive of Gorbachev's human qualities. Observing that 'he gave up an ideology, an empire, and his own country, in preference to using force', he continues: 'He chose love over fear, violating Machiavelli's advice for princes and thereby ensuring that he ceased to be one. It made little sense in traditional geopolitical terms. But it did make him the most deserving recipient ever of the Nobel Peace Prize.' But for Gaddis, 'Gorbachev was never a leader in the manner of Václav Havel, John Paul II, Deng Xiaoping, Margaret Thatcher, Ronald Reagan, Lech Wałęsa—even Boris Yeltsin', for they, he suggests, 'all had *destinations* in mind and maps for reaching them' (italics in the original).[55]

At best, that is a highly dubious generalization and it misunderstands the nature of Gorbachev's development and achievements. He could not have changed the Soviet system, and its relations with the outside world, as much as he did but for the fact that his own views evolved greatly during his less than seven years in the Kremlin. An open mind and ability to improvise were among his most valuable assets. In contrast, any route-map that could be devised in 1985 would either have taken him no further than the destination of a mildly reformed, economically less sclerotic Communist system or, if bolder from the outset, to prison or worse. No-one could become General Secretary of the CPSU with a destination in mind of pluralist democracy, a market economy, independence for the East European states, and the transformation of a purely formal federation into a genuine and voluntary federal state. Gorbachev's original aims were much more modest than that, as they had to be. If he had stuck with the more limited reformist aims he espoused in 1985, it is hard to see how the Cold War would have ended, for the Soviet Union would still have been a Communist state, albeit with a degree of cultural liberalization, a widening of the limits of the possible for political discussion, and some economic revitalization, while the countries of Eastern Europe would have remained within the Soviet orbit.

Firm views about destinations and maps for getting there were part of the Leninist tradition, from which Gorbachev was gradually liberating himself and his country. It was precisely his capacity for learning and an ability to adjust not only his tactics but also his goals which sustained the political transformation of the Soviet Union and the dialogue on ending the Cold War. A less flexible and adaptable leader, if determined from the outset to question the fundamentals of the system, would have been rapidly ousted by his Politburo colleagues. The leader of the CPSU had great power so long as he did not undermine the pillars of the Communist system or threaten the most entrenched institutional interests. Gorbachev did not begin, and could not have begun, by doing so. It was the gradual nature of his realization that those pillars needed to be dismantled and the major interests tamed (and made accountable to a parliament and people) that enabled him to last as long as he did.

Adam Smith, in the middle of the eighteenth century, warned against 'the man of system' too enamoured with an 'ideal plan of government', and he wrote critically of the kind of leader who 'seems to imagine that he can arrange the different members of a great society with as much ease as the hand arranges the different pieces upon a chess-board', without appreciating that 'in the great "chess-board" of human society, every single piece has a motion of its own'.[56] Firm views about political destinations and a map for reaching them are liable to be a chimera in any political system. In the largest country by far in the world, in which there were more than a hundred different nationalities, grievances which had been suppressed for seventy years were all liable to come to the surface of political life with a liberalization of the society or pluralization of the political system.[57] The idea that any leader could set out with a map for navigating the rough and dangerous terrain ahead is wholly fanciful.

Reagan helped to make the end of the Cold War possible, but not primarily through military build-up, still less through waging economic warfare, but especially through his willingness to engage with a new Soviet leadership. It was his good fortune that early in his second term (and unconnected with the policies pursued in his first term), a Soviet leader unlike any of his predecessors took charge in the Kremlin. Gorbachev was the first head of the CPSU to regard the accelerated American military build-up not as impetus to the manufacture of still more Soviet missiles but, rather, as yet another reason for ending a Cold War which was becoming ever more senseless since the new thinking he espoused, and which itself evolved, was narrowing the ideological divide. And this ideational change was accompanied by concrete and far-reaching reform of the Soviet political system. From Gorbachev's standpoint—and, over time, that of his Western interlocutors—the Cold War was becoming anachronistic, given the scale of the transformation underway in the Soviet Union.

But, as I have argued, some of the policies that emanated from Washington during those years slowed, rather than hastened, the ending of the Cold War. The Reagan administration spoke with a variety of discordant voices, and on many issues the president stayed above the battle. Relations with the Soviet Union were, however, one subject on which he remained focused. It mattered enormously that, in the debates within the administration, he usually came down on the side of those who wished for dialogue and engagement with their Soviet counterparts. He heard arguments both for and against this within the NSC as well as from the CIA and the Defense Department, on the one hand, and Shultz's State Department, on the other. In the final analysis, he usually sided with the position espoused by Shultz. On occasion, indeed, he was readier to accede to a Soviet formulation than were the State Department. That was the case with his willingness to accept the terminology of 'peaceful coexistence' in a proposed Soviet text at the Moscow summit in 1988. On this issue Shultz and Assistant Secretary of State Rozanne Ridgway were the 'hawks' who (understandably, given the concept's history) refused to agree. The previous year it had been the other way round when Reagan made no concession to the State Department's unhappiness with his call in Berlin to Gorbachev to 'tear down this wall'.[58]

For a time the improvement in East–West relations, which made people in the Soviet Union feel safer, worked to Gorbachev's advantage. That was very much the case in 1988, the last year of the Reagan presidency, when Gorbachev was still highly popular in his own country as well as abroad. War had impinged on every Soviet family in the 1940s in a way in which it had not done for every American household. The dread of war in subsequent years was a more tangible reality in the USSR and a more distant and abstract worry for the average American. Improved East–West relations played well for politicians in all countries, including Reagan himself and also Margaret Thatcher in Britain, but it was especially advantageous for Gorbachev and helped him to gain ascendancy over Soviet hard-liners, since public opinion was on his side. This was changing fast by 1990–1, but that was after the end of the Cold War when Gorbachev was struggling with the unintended consequences of democratization, including national independence movements at home which were related also to the end of the Cold War—in particular, its most important manifestation: the transition to fully independent statehood of the countries of Eastern Europe. Thus, Reagan's engagement with the Soviet Union, the agreements he and Gorbachev co-signed, and the president's explicit refusal to apply the 'evil empire' epithet to a changed Soviet Union bolstered Gorbachev on his risky journey that took him from reformer of the existing system to systemic transformer within the space of four years.

It was useful in the American context that Reagan's conservative and anti-Communist credentials were so well established that when he was attacked for having 'gone soft' on Communism, he could shrug off such criticism, although at times he was accused of naivety not only by ultra-conservatives but by such mainstream foreign policy 'centrists' as Richard Nixon and Henry Kissinger. George Bush felt more vulnerable than Reagan did to any suggestion that he was insufficiently hard-line, which at least partly explained the loss of momentum in improved US–Soviet relations during the first year of his presidency. Baker, who initially shared Bush's caution but who eventually carried on from where Shultz had left off, had a meeting shortly after becoming Secretary of State with Rozanne Ridgway who had been in charge of European policy under Shultz. 'Tell me, Roz,' said Baker, 'don't you think that you all went too fast?'. 'No, sir,' she replied, and she was right.[59]

If we return to the counter-factual history in which the assassin's bullet killed Reagan in March 1981, Bush—and, in all probability, Baker—would have had some experience of dealing with the Soviet old guard, Brezhnev, Andropov, and Chernenko in quick succession, as well as with Soviet Foreign Minister Gromyko. Far from feeling that Reagan had become too close to his Soviet counterpart, they would have come to office at a time when he had never met a Soviet top leader, a time of high tension between the United States and the Soviet Union. March 1981 was, however, two years before Reagan's embrace of SDI, and that would have been one complication fewer. Contrary to the view that Reagan was uniquely necessary for the Cold War's ending, I find it hard to believe that Bush and Baker would have been incapable of recognizing the difference embodied by Gorbachev and Shevardnadze in 1985 and that they would have been so intimidated by conservative American critics that they would have failed to respond to the evident change of style, and subsequently of substance, represented by incoming General Secretary Gorbachev and by his new foreign policy-making team. For in reality, by the later months of 1989 they had begun to engage with the Soviet Union in a manner reminiscent of Reagan and Shultz, notwithstanding their desire to distinguish the Bush administration from Reagan's.

Margaret Thatcher's role in international affairs peaked during the years in which Reagan, Gorbachev, and she were all at the helm in their respective countries. She was not one of nature's diplomats, but she was able, nevertheless, to be an effective advocate of Reagan to Gorbachev and of Gorbachev to Reagan. Never hesitating to disagree with either of those leaders on matters on which she felt strongly, she still succeeded in establishing excellent relations with both. She played a significant part in getting serious East–West dialogue going from the mid-1980s and her role as intermediary was particularly important during the year in which she had already met with Gorbachev, but Reagan had not yet had his first encounter with the new Soviet leader (his first, indeed, with *any* Soviet general secretary) in Geneva in November 1985. From 1987 onwards, Thatcher was sufficiently clear-sighted to recognize that serious reform was underway in the Soviet Union and, among conservative leaders worldwide, there was none more supportive of Gorbachev.*

Notwithstanding the constructive contribution to ending the Cold War made by these and other Western leaders, the crucial changes which made this outcome possible took place in the Soviet Union, and as a result of an interdependent mixture of

---

* Reagan's speech-writer Peter Robinson was among those who noted that Margaret Thatcher gave Reagan 'cover', especially at a time when American conservatives 'were afraid that Reagan was going soft' on the Soviet Union. Since Thatcher continued to be the foreign leader most highly regarded by the Republican right, her positive approach to dealing with Gorbachev offered them reassurance on Reagan's changing stance (Charles Moore, *Margaret Thatcher*, Vol. III, p. 175).

bold leadership, political power, and new ideas (new, at any rate, in the Soviet context). Harry Truman's frustration at times with the limitations on the power of the American president was famously rephrased by Richard Neustadt as 'Presidential *power* is the power to persuade.'[60] Mikhail Gorbachev had formidable powers of persuasion, but to a still greater extent than any American president, operating within a separation-of-powers system, these were bolstered by the vast authority and power of his office. Gorbachev made use of those political resources to steer Soviet foreign and domestic policy in a radically different direction from hitherto. The constructive engagement of Reagan and Shultz—and, after a lengthy pause, of Bush and Baker—played an important part in ending the East–West stand-off. But much more decisive was the coming to power of Gorbachev, his selection of a new foreign policy team who shared his values, his willingness to liberalize the Soviet system, and his subsequent embrace of democratization. Gorbachev's rejection of the ideological underpinnings of the East–West conflict led to a new emphasis on freedom of choice, accompanied by his firm rejection of the use of force to uphold Communist regimes loyal to Moscow. The end of the division of Europe, which followed from this, marked the end of the Cold War.

PART III

14

UNINTENDED CONSEQUENCES
(1990)

The events of 1990 and 1991 were scarcely less momentous than those of the second half of the 1980s, but, as I will argue, they were consequences of the Cold War's ending rather than an intrinsic part of it.* Among them were the further democratization and the interrelated disintegration of the Soviet Union and more active US–Soviet diplomacy than had characterized the first year of the Bush presidency. The enormous geopolitical change represented by the reunification of Germany in September 1990 was followed by an even more momentous geopolitical event—the break-up of the Soviet Union into fifteen separate states in December 1991. Although Mikhail Gorbachev's power was ebbing away during his last two years in the Kremlin, his foreign policy decisions still mattered. How the Soviet Union reacted in 1990 to the growing demand for unity within the two German states was crucial. With some 380,000 Soviet troops stationed in the GDR,[1] the USSR had the power to prevent it, but at the cost of losing most of the international goodwill that had been generated since Gorbachev became Soviet leader.

When Gorbachev complained to Bush that Helmut Kohl was stirring up dangerous emotions in Germany, the president defended the chancellor, saying that Kohl accepted a 'step-by-step approach to change in the GDR and the need to avoid destabilizing the situation in Europe'. Bush also appositely observed that 'Gorbachev's own commitment to reform in the USSR had played a decisive role in encouraging Soviet allies to embark on a similar path.'[2] In American filmed images of the fall of the Berlin wall, Ronald Reagan's June 1987 Berlin speech in which he said,

---

* Ultimately, there cannot be a definitive end-date of the Cold War, since choosing one involves a judgement about what constitutes the core of the conflict. During a period of fairly stable détente between the United States and the Soviet Union in the 1970s, when there was a modus vivendi between the Nixon and Ford administrations, on the one hand, and the Brezhnev leadership, on the other, there were those in the West who deemed the Cold War to be already over even then. In my understanding, as noted earlier in the book, the Cold War began with the forcible Soviet takeover of eastern Europe. The corollary is recognition that it was over when (and only when) the perestroika-era Soviet leadership eschewed the use of force to prevent the rapid de-Communization of the region during 1989, in line with the ongoing change in Soviet theory and practice. Different criteria will produce a different end-point. Thus, for example, if the division of Germany is judged to be the principal defining feature of the Cold War, its ending will be placed in the autumn of 1990.

'Mr Gorbachev, tear down this wall!', is frequently juxtaposed with scenes of jubilant young Germans crossing through or climbing on the wall in November 1989, as if this were cause and effect. Brent Scowcroft, who was critical of that Reagan speech, correctly noted that when an American president issued a peremptory public instruction to Gorbachev, far from facilitating the desired outcome, that made it more difficult, politically and psychologically, for Gorbachev to press the East German leadership to dismantle the wall.[3]

When the wall was comprehensively breached with impunity, this was, as we have seen, a response neither to American nor Soviet pressure but, at its most immediate and prosaic level, a result of a bureaucratic communication failure in East Berlin. More fundamentally, it was a consequence of East Germans' raised expectations, their knowledge of the extent of political change in Moscow (in sharp contrast with the rigidity of the GDR), the example set by Hungary and Poland, and their awareness that the Soviet leadership had accepted the transformations which had already occurred in those two countries. And, as was noted in Chapter 10, Gorbachev and Shevardnadze had actually broached the subject of removing the wall with the East German leadership prior to Reagan making his 1987 Berlin speech, but Honecker was recalcitrant on the issue, and concerned about the size of the prospective emigration. (Ten years after the fall of the wall, George Shultz recalled a German joke about Honecker. The story was that the Communist leader of the GDR had 'a new girlfriend who was very vivacious and pretty' and 'he was crazy about her'. He said: 'I love you so much I'd just do anything for you.' She said, 'How about knocking down the Berlin Wall?' Honecker thought about it for a minute and said, 'Ah ha! I see you want to be alone with me.'[4]) For its part, the Soviet Union stuck to the new policy of leaving it to the leaderships and peoples of Eastern Europe to sort things out for themselves.

The German question was just one of a range of hugely important issues Gorbachev had to wrestle with throughout 1990. On that subject, his discussions with Helmut Kohl and with George Bush mattered very much more than his conversations with Margaret Thatcher.[5] Although the British prime minister made clear to Gorbachev that she was opposed to German unity, she could not prevent it. Her importance in East–West dialogue was already on the wane compared with the Reagan years, although far from negligible, as can be discerned from the number of times communication with her crops up in the documents and reflections on 1990 of both Bush and Gorbachev. Unbeknown to her, however, she was at the start of that new decade entering her last year in 10 Downing Street. As Bush went on to lose the presidential election of 1992, the British prime minister, Soviet leader, and American president were to be deprived of government office in three successive years, and in a manner none of them would have considered likely just a year or two earlier. Of the three, only Bush was defeated in a general election, but after the euphoria of the negotiated end of the Cold War, as well as the speedy victory over Saddam Hussein's army—following the Iraqi incursion into Kuwait—in the Gulf War of 1991, it was an election an incumbent US president would have expected to win.

In normal times the person at the top of the governmental hierarchy—president, prime minister, general secretary, chancellor (in the German case) or hereditary ruler—will have greater opportunities to set the political agenda than any other political actor. In a democracy, it should, nevertheless, go without saying that this depends on the leader retaining the confidence of those whom he or she aspires to lead. Loss of the support of the electorate curtailed Bush's presidency to one term. Losing the backing of a substantial number of her cabinet and parliamentary colleagues led to Thatcher's removal from office by her own party rather than by the people as a whole, although her ousting was connected not only with her leadership style but also with the fact that she had become increasingly unpopular with the electorate.

Gorbachev's support at home was also on the wane. Soviet domestic and foreign policy mutually reinforced one another in a positive way up until 1989, but that ceased to be so in 1990 (and was even less so in 1991) in the immediate aftermath of the Cold War's ending. Although still the key foreign policy-maker, most crucially in negotiation with the United States and with the Federal Republic of Germany, Gorbachev found his bargaining position weakened by the growth of separatist tendencies within the USSR and by the deteriorating economy. It was a period of conflicting tendencies. On the one hand, there were genuine advances in democracy and in the freedom and vigour of political discussion. The ordinary person in the USSR was no longer a powerless subject, but a citizen with rights, including meaningful votes. That transition was already well underway in 1989 but was consolidated over the following two years. On the other hand, freedom and developing democracy exposed injustices and long-suppressed grievances. With the economy in limbo—neither a fully functioning command economy nor yet a market economy—and shortages getting worse, people were no longer inhibited from giving angry voice to their discontent.

Similarly, contested elections allowed voters, if they so desired, to opt for the most nationalist or anti-establishment candidate on the ballot paper. The development of an autonomous civil and political society meant that mass movements within Soviet republics of peoples seeking national autonomy grew in influence and numbers. Those most obviously bent on independent statehood were the citizens of the Baltic states, but developments in the Russian republic, and the role of Yeltsin, were ultimately the most dangerous for Gorbachev. Since Russia occupied three-quarters of the territory, and contained half of the population, of the USSR, Yeltsin's assertion in May 1990 that Russian law had supremacy over Soviet law was a hugely significant step towards what became his professed goal of outright Russian independence from the union.[6] His prime aim, however, was to remove Gorbachev from power and to take his place in the Kremlin. If that could have been done while preserving Soviet statehood, Yeltsin would have been more than happy to preside over the larger state. If his surest path to power involved the break-up of the union, it was one he was ready to follow.[7] After accompanying British Foreign Secretary Douglas Hurd to a meeting with Yeltsin during Hurd's September 1990 visit to the Soviet Union, UK Ambassador Rodric Braithwaite noted in his diary that Yeltsin had 'very little interest in policy matters'. He continued: 'He is interested in power, and his current tactic is to destroy Ryzhkov, emasculate and discredit the Union government, and so isolate Gorbachev—as a step towards eliminating Gorbachev as well', adding that 'he evidently believes in the Triumph of the Will'.[8]

The Soviet Domestic Context

One of the defining characteristics of the Soviet system was of course the domination of the Communist Party over all state as well as societal institutions. The introduction of contested elections in 1989 began to alter that fundamentally, not yet through competition from other parties but by exposing the vast differences of political position within the CPSU itself and allowing voters to choose among them. The change in the party's status was only formalized, however, when its guaranteed 'leading role' was cut out of the Soviet Constitution in March 1990—a large step towards replacing party by state power. Gorbachev had, with difficulty, persuaded the CPSU leadership to agree to this and the change was formally made at a meeting of the Congress of People's Deputies of the USSR, the legislature created the previous year.

At that same March session of the new parliament, Gorbachev was elected President of the USSR, while retaining his position as party leader. His indirect election by the legislature, rather than by the people as whole, was criticized by a minority of radical deputies, but got majority support on the grounds that the problems facing the country were so great that the need to establish strong central state authority was urgent. Future presidential elections every five years were to be by universal suffrage, but this policy remained a dead letter, for less than two years later, there was neither a Soviet president to be elected nor a USSR. The creation of the presidency did little to resolve the growing conflicts within the Soviet state, but it was of more than symbolic significance. That is because, as has been noted in earlier chapters, Gorbachev could have been suddenly replaced by a majority in the Politburo who would then hastily convene a meeting of the Central Committee to endorse their decision (as happened when Nikita Khrushchev was deposed in October 1964). Now the Politburo did not have that degree of power. They could initiate the removal of the party general secretary, but only the state legislature could take away his presidential power.[9]

Along with the new presidency, two novel collective bodies were created—a Presidential Council and the Federation Council. The first of these contained the senior state office-holders, such as Ryzhkov, Shevardnadze, and Kryuchkov, as well as Aleksandr Yakovlev (a senior secretary of the CPSU who did not, however, hold a state office) and several outsiders. The most surprising choices were of two writers of different political orientation, the Russian nationalist and religious believer, Valentin Rasputin, and the highly regarded Kyrgyz novelist, Chingiz Aitmatov, who, in a notable speech to the First Congress of People's Deputies in 1989, had (with some poetic licence) named Norway, Spain, Canada, and even Switzerland as fine examples of socialism.[10] The Presidential Council did not, as its supporters hoped at the time, turn out to be the successor to and functional equivalent of the Politburo, for it became no more than an advisory body to Gorbachev, having neither power of its own nor supporting structures capable of carrying policy into effect.

The Federation Council lasted somewhat longer. The heads of the Supreme Soviets of the union republics were, ex officio, members of that body and so it, at least, had some representative status. While the Politburo was a loser in the creation of these two new organs, Gorbachev personally was only very partially the winner. With state institutions such as ministries now more independent of party control, it would have served him better to have had more committed supporters of democratization and several knowledgeable advocates of a 'social market economy' in key ministerial posts.[11] That would, however, have involved first removing Ryzhkov as prime minister. (When Gorbachev did finally part company with Ryzhkov at the end of 1990, he replaced him by Valentin Pavlov who, far from being an improvement, joined the conservative camp and participated in the attempted coup against Gorbachev in August 1991.)

Gorbachev was irked by ill-informed criticism from some radicals suggesting that he had created the presidency in order to exercise dictatorial power, for as he remarked to his aides, he had undermined the truly dictatorial powers he inherited when he became General Secretary of the Communist Party, as he proceeded to make both the party and its leader accountable to an elected parliament.[12] Some foreign observers, including participants in a seminar on Germany which Margaret Thatcher held at Chequers in March 1990, also expressed their concern that Gorbachev was accumulating excessive power—in the hyperbole of one of them, George Urban, 'powers far in excess of those Stalin himself had possessed'—but Thatcher would have none of it. 'As long as Gorbachev is president', she responded, 'I have no fear at all that he would abuse his powers. He's not that sort of a man.' Pertinently, she added: 'If dictatorial power had been Gorbachev's ambition, he would have been content with his position as party general secretary. That is all Stalin had, and look at the use *he* made of it.'[13]

In Russia, Anatoly Sobchak, a law professor who became a prominent member of a group of radically reformist deputies in the legislature and later the mayor of St Petersburg, took a similar view, observing that 'Dictators, arriving in power, do not begin with democratic reforms and with attempts to place legal limits on their own absolute authority.'[14] Sobchak differed from some of his radical colleagues—as did a distinguished authority on Russian culture, Academician Dmitry Likhachev—in arguing for Gorbachev's speedy election by the Congress of People's Deputies, rather than by universal franchise, to overcome what the future St Petersburg mayor called the 'undoubted paralysis of state executive power'.[15]

Gorbachev himself, however, later concluded that he had probably been mistaken in not pushing for the choice to be made by the electorate as a whole.[16] A majority in the higher party echelons could see that legitimacy conferred by the people would make him, or any other president, more independent of them, and so they were opposed to it. Another factor in the delay in moving to presidential election by universal suffrage was concern about the popularity of Boris Yeltsin who had adopted a populist, egalitarian, and anti-establishment line which had growing appeal. He was now on an upward trajectory, and Gorbachev on a downward slide, in public opinion. But in March 1990, Yeltsin had not yet overtaken the general secretary as the most popular politician in the USSR. That occurred some two to three months later.[17] The likelihood is that Gorbachev would have won a popular presidential election in March 1990. He could have made much of the fact that he would have been the first leader in the whole of Russian history who, after inheriting great power, had placed his political future in the hands of the people. In many respects, through an accumulation of reforms, he had been doing just that, but not so directly or overtly. Even if he had lost a presidential election, he would have gained prestige by accepting defeat and would have been in a stronger position to make a comeback than he was, after being in office but not wholly in power, over the next year and a half.

Elections for new legislatures in all fifteen union republics of the USSR were held in 1990, and they gave those who demanded far greater independence for their republic, or even separate statehood, the chance to win support. Pro-independence candidates were highly successful in the Baltic republics, especially in Lithuania where the nationalist movement Sajudis won 90 out of 114 seats. A dedicated advocate of Lithuanian independence, Vytautas Landsbergis, was then elected as chair of the legislature. Nationalists also enjoyed success in Georgia, Armenia, and Western Ukraine. They had least success in the Soviet Central Asian republics, where there was far less competition among candidates than in the European parts of the USSR.[18] In the Russian election, Yeltsin's popular appeal was again evident. Still a member of the Communist Party, and even of its Central Committee (although a lonely and uninfluential figure within it), he had an anti-establishment appeal in the wider society which won him 80 per cent of the votes cast in his native Sverdlovsk.[19]

There is no getting away from the fact that the most profound unintended consequence of the transformation of Soviet foreign policy and of the political system was the disintegration of the Soviet state. The calm acceptance by Gorbachev of the countries of Eastern Europe acquiring independence from the Soviet Union raised the expectations of the most disaffected nations within the USSR. And the novel freedom to speak out, combined with competitive elections for new and meaningful legislatures, provided the domestic facilitating conditions. That is not to say that democratization made the creation of fifteen separate states in place of the USSR inevitable. Whereas Gorbachev was the principal author of political freedom and a burgeoning democracy in the Soviet Union, Yeltsin was the prime mover in the state's comprehensive dissolution. The old USSR, which had been federal in form but unitary in substance, could have been replaced by a genuine federation (or by a looser confederation), embracing more than half of the existing republics, including, crucially, Russia and, probably, Ukraine. It would certainly have been a smaller state, for the three Baltic republics, in particular, would not have consented to belong to it. Nothing was more important in preventing the creation of a smaller, looser but genuine federation than Yeltsin's putting the pursuit of personal power ahead of negotiating in good faith with Gorbachev and the federal authorities—ahead also of longer-term Russian interests.

There was a temporary détente between Gorbachev and Yeltsin in the late summer and early autumn of 1990 when a team of economists, half of them nominated by Yeltsin and half by Gorbachev, worked intensely throughout August at a dacha outside Moscow and reached agreement on a radical programme for transition to a market economy. The 38-year-old economist Grigory Yavlinsky (later to be leader of the liberal party, Yabloko, in early post-Soviet Russia) headed the Yeltsin group, which included also the still younger Yegor Gaidar, 34 at the time, who subsequently became acting prime minister in the first post-Soviet Russian government. The older economists nominated by Gorbachev were, like their younger colleagues, convinced of the need to move to a market. They were led by Stanislav Shatalin, a member of the Presidential Council (the final report of the team was often called 'the Shatalin plan'), and a prominent member of the team was Gorbachev's economic aide, Nikolay Petrakov. The group united behind a programme which aimed to speedily move the USSR from a command economy to a market economy.

They came up with proposals for a staged transition, including a timetable for what should be achieved in each phase. The word 'socialism' did not appear even once in the 238-page report, 'Transition to the Market: Conception and Programme'.[20] Neither, for that matter, did 'capitalism'. The declared aim of achieving a market economy within 500 days was certainly over-optimistic. One of the economists in the team, Yevgeniy Yasin, noted that it was essentially 'a daring polemical slogan' and 'Yeltsin seized upon it instantly', although he did not read even a single page of the report.[21] Leonid Abalkin, the director of the Institute of Economics in Moscow who became a Deputy Chairman of the Council of Ministers, advising Ryzhkov on economic reform, said that if the 'Transition to the Market' team really could bring the country out of economic crisis in 500 days, he would raise a monument to them and regularly lay flowers at it.[22]

Thoroughly convinced by now of the need to move to a market economy, Gorbachev was initially enthusiastic about the economists' plan. Faced, however, by concerted resistance both from the government under Ryzhkov's chairmanship and from the USSR Supreme Soviet, and concerned also about the economic pain that would be inflicted at least in the short run, he retreated from that position and asked another of his economic advisers, Abel Aganbegyan, to devise a compromise between the '500 days programme' and that of Ryzhkov and Abalkin. Thereby, he forfeited the support not only of the most radical economic reformers but also of some of his erstwhile democratic supporters who linked movement to the market with democracy. Gorbachev's retreat from the '500 days programme' put an end to his uneasy cooperation with Yeltsin, driving a wedge yet more firmly between them. Yasin noted that 'Yeltsin did not seem to be very upset by the end of his alliance with Gorbachev', for he 'clearly saw new political opportunities in Gorbachev's being guilty for the failure of their joint program'.[23]

Gorbachev was simultaneously coming under increasing criticism from within the higher echelons of the Communist Party, the economic ministries and the security organs. After March 1990—with the creation of the presidency, Presidential Council and Federation Council—the Politburo remained the principal policy-making body in the party, but it had ceased to be the highest policy-making institution in the country. That was especially true after the Twenty-Eighth Party Congress (the CPSU's last-ever) was held in July. It approved a big reduction in the staff of the Central Committee, and led to a radical overhaul of the Politburo, with most of the members who held high state positions, such as Ryzhkov, Shevardnadze, and Kryuchkov no longer members. Neither was Yakovlev. This underlined that the most important decisions on state policy were going to be taken elsewhere. Gorbachev was strongly attacked at the congress (as were Yakovlev and Shevardnadze), with almost a quarter of the delegates refusing to vote for his re-election as general secretary.

Gorbachev's aide, and adviser on political reform, Georgy Shakhnazarov, proposed in the run-up to the congress that he should change the Communist Party's name to Social Democratic Party of the USSR and then tell those CPSU members who disagreed with that decision to 'stay away' from the forthcoming gathering. By 1994 Shakhnazarov had come to believe that Gorbachev was right in not following that high-risk strategy, for it would have resulted in 'dual power'* and left the CPSU in the hands of those intent on turning the clock back.[24] It is, indeed, highly likely that the office of general secretary of the rump CPSU would, along with all the old levers of power, have been used to stifle the liberalization and democratization already achieved and have led to a harder-line foreign policy. Gorbachev's dilemma was that

---

* In fact, what developed in the Soviet Union over its last two years was not only the 'dual power' (*dvoevlastie*) of the all-union administration headed by Gorbachev and the Russian legislature and embryonic government led by Yeltsin, but a multiplicity of powers (*mnogovlastie*). Even at the federal level, the prime minister and ministers who composed the Soviet government were often pursuing very different aims from those embraced by Gorbachev and his most enlightened advisers, and almost half of the Soviet republics were, like Yeltsin's Russia, increasingly going their own way and disregarding the federal centre.

conservative Communists were in a large majority within the apparatus of the CPSU, while within the population as a whole there was now a majority who had become increasingly disillusioned with the party, even though it had enjoyed a notable revival of support with the enthusiasm and optimism engendered in the earlier years of perestroika. Yeltsin benefited more from the congress than Gorbachev did by publicly renouncing his party membership and demonstratively walking out of the hall.[25] Gorbachev's policy was one of 'revolutionary change by evolutionary means', but although this did succeed in producing massive changes, both intended and unintended, it did not prevent his support within the population at large from declining rapidly during the last eighteen months of the Soviet Union's existence. And it could not bring about the social democratization of the country which had become Gorbachev's ideal domestic goal.[26]

The Soviet leader had to make some tactical concessions to the conservative majority within the Soviet government and take account of their organizational support throughout the country as well as responding to the radical forces within the society. One of the most formidably knowledgeable of Soviet traditionalists was Marshal Sergey Akhromeyev. Contacts between senior officials in the United States and the USSR had expanded to such a degree that Admiral Bill Crowe (Chairman of the Joint Chiefs of Staff until 1989 when he was succeeded by General Colin Powell) had come to think of Akhromeyev as a friend. This was reciprocated to the extent that Akhromeyev spoke relatively frankly with Crowe and did not hide the fact that he was depressed by what was happening within the Soviet Union. He told Crowe in March 1990 that 'the population would not tolerate Gorbachev giving in to Lithuania's demands for sovereignty, and that if pushed to the limit, Moscow would crush Lithuania'. Crowe's impression was that Akhromeyev was fed up with being 'continually overruled on decisions and had become tired and disillusioned'.[27]

Akhromeyev told his former American counterpart that he had believed in what Gorbachev was doing, but the country was not ready for so many changes. He was distressed by the decline in the prestige and unity of the Communist Party and said that 'we wrecked it ourselves', adding that this had 'shattered his heart hundreds of times'.[28] Akhromeyev was a vastly experienced and intelligent soldier, a Soviet patriot, and a conservative Communist, but far from an extreme reactionary. One of his allies among highly placed party officials, Valentin Falin, described Akhromeyev as a person of 'exceptional personal integrity' who had been against the Soviet military intervention in Afghanistan and who was an important new thinker on military doctrine.[29] He had been regarded by the Americans as a creative partner in arms-control negotiations. But while radicals who attacked Gorbachev for not moving faster with reform gained far more publicity in the West, Akhromeyev was representative of a powerful body of opinion within the Soviet establishment that was becoming increasingly agitated by the course of events. Gorbachev was better aware than his critics from the ranks of the radical democrats or of the separatists of the dangers to his position from the other side. What is remarkable is that he made only temporary and tactical retreats from the process of democratization, even though the zig-zags meant that, increasingly, he was satisfying neither side.

Anger with the general secretary, expressed in a manner unthinkable in earlier years, was uninhibited at a Politburo meeting on 16 November 1990. When Gorbachev spoke of wanting to form 'a democratic coalition',[30] the first secretary of the CPSU for Ukraine Stanislav Gurenko retorted that they were still a ruling party and coalitions were formed when a party did not have a majority. Therefore, they should be making no concessions 'to the pretensions of some extremists'.[31] Oleg Shenin, the secretary of the Central Committee in charge of the party organization, spoke in favour of 'presidential rule', meaning a crackdown on all separatist forces, and said, 'I support Comrade Gurenko: are we a ruling party or are we not?'[32] Ivan Polozkov, who had been elected to the newly created post of first secretary of the Communist Party of the Russian Federation (the CPRF having been formed as a result of pressure from conservative Communists seeking a counterweight both to Gorbachev and to Yeltsin's influence over the Russian Supreme Soviet) attacked Gorbachev still more bluntly, telling him, 'Your guilt lies in the fact that now you do not operate through the party.' Gorbachev readily agreed that he no longer did so, adding that his problem was that he did not have the presidential structures that would take the party's place.[33] Even moderate members of the Politburo, such as the first secretary for Kazakhstan, Nursultan Nazarbayev, argued that it was time to scrap the Presidential Council, and Gorbachev himself had come to the conclusion that it served little useful purpose.

Having sat up until 4 o'clock in the morning preparing a speech and a package of institutional changes, Gorbachev addressed the Supreme Soviet of the USSR the day after the acrimonious Politburo meeting.[34] He called for the abolition of the Presidential Council; the replacement of the Council of Ministers by a Cabinet of Ministers to be headed by a prime minister subordinate to the president; the strengthening of the Federation Council; and the creation of a Security Council. The last of these institutional innovations was a concession to the *siloviki*. It did not, however, square the circle of keeping both hard-liners and radical democrats happy. Neither side was satisfied. During the winter of 1990–1, Gorbachev's domestic popularity was in fast decline, not least by now in the eyes of radical democrats who had been the main beneficiaries of his policies. For their part, the hard-liners were only temporarily appeased. Of the nine members appointed to the new Security Council in November 1990, six were active participants in the attempted coup which placed Gorbachev under house arrest just nine months later.[35]

The German Question

For the leaders of the United States, the Soviet Union, and Great Britain, there was no more important international issue in 1990 than the German question. For Chancellor

Helmut Kohl, that was, of course, still more true, and Kohl seized every opportunity to move as quickly as possible towards his goal of German unification. Margaret Thatcher argued against haste, making clear, especially in private discussions, her more general opposition to a united Germany. She feared that such a state would be too dominant both economically and politically in Europe and she nurtured a deep-seated distrust of Germans. One of her more respectable arguments, employed when she was speaking with Presidents Bush and Mitterrand, was that German unification would undermine Gorbachev. For Kohl, however, it was precisely the fact that Gorbachev was vulnerable to potential overthrow which created the urgency. There was a window of opportunity for the peaceful unification of the two Germanies with Gorbachev in the Kremlin which might vanish if he fell victim to Soviet hard-liners.

The triangular relationship of Margaret Thatcher with Ronald Reagan and Mikhail Gorbachev has been a central theme of this book. During Reagan's second term, the British prime minister had been the most important interlocutor of the leaders of both 'superpowers' (apart from their direct relationship with each other). By 1990 there was a new triangular relationship, one in which Kohl, Gorbachev, and Bush, in that order, were the key policy-makers where the future of Germany was concerned. From early in 1990 Gorbachev was increasingly involved with the German question.

Figure 19 Gorbachev with French President François Mitterrand during Gorbachev's visit to Paris, October 1985.

To deliberate on it, in the context of a broader discussion of what was happening in Europe, he brought together on 26 January a group of people who came from different parts of the CPSU spectrum of opinion. Those present were senior members of the Soviet government Ryzhkov, Shevardnadze, and Kryuchkov; party officials Yakovlev, Valentin Falin (head of the Central Committee's International Department), and Rafael Fedorov (first deputy head of that department); as well as Akhromeyev and Gorbachev's aides Chernyaev and Shakhnazarov. Gorbachev mentioned in passing each of the Warsaw Pact countries, and what was happening there, until he came to Poland which was, he said, a 'special case' (but, he added, they had nothing to fear from the new Polish Prime Minister Tadeusz Mazowiecki), before coming finally to the 'completely special case—the GDR'.[36] Gorbachev rehearsed what he would say to Kohl—that they would need to bring him together with the four victorious powers from the Second World War, even though he (Kohl) and Willy Brandt regarded France as only an 'honorary victor'. It was Chernyaev who reminded Gorbachev that they needed to bring together 'not 5 but 6'—the four victorious powers (USSR, US, the UK, and France) and *both* of the German states. Gorbachev immediately agreed to that formulation.[37]

The Soviet formula of 4 + 2 was, then, born shortly before an almost identical American version of 2 + 4 was brought to the attention of Secretary of State Baker on 30 January. It had been devised by State Department officials Dennis Ross and Robert Zoellick, and while many in the American administration, including both Bush and Baker, regarded 'the Four Powers as largely an anachronism from World War II', they recognized its appeal in Moscow, London and Paris.[38] Putting 'the two' first meant that the German states themselves (especially, of course, the FRG, for the GDR was in an advanced stage of dissolution) would determine internal developments, but the other four powers would play a role in external aspects of unification. Baker believed that the advantage of this for the US was that it made it difficult for the Soviet Union and the Germans to cut a deal 'disadvantageous to Western interests' and that it would create 'a diplomatic process for unification that could keep pace with events'.[39]

Bush had by now established a good relationship with Gorbachev and had no wish to undermine him, but both the president and Baker were determined to do what they could to facilitate the absorption of East Germany in a united and democratic German state. Yet, highly important as US–Soviet and US–FRG talks on the future of the two German states undoubtedly were, the most crucial decisions were made in Germany itself, in the Soviet Union, and in direct negotiation between Gorbachev and Kohl.[40] Once it became clear that there was overwhelming support both in East and West Germany for unification, Gorbachev's publicly declared position that the people of every country had the right to determine their own future made it highly likely that he would acquiesce with German unity. The questions that remained were whether he would survive politically if the most politically sensitive of all the Soviet

Union's East European allies was given leave to depart from the Soviet camp, whether a united Germany would be a member of NATO, and what price in economic help to the Soviet Union (which was by now badly needed) would be paid by the West, and West Germany in the first instance, for Moscow's concessions.

A substantial literature has accumulated over the question of whether the Soviet Union was or was not promised by the United States that if a united Germany joined NATO, there would be no further expansion of the organization eastwards. In reality, that latter aspect was not seen as a big issue by either side at the time, for there was little or no expectation among the principal political actors that this would happen. Nevertheless, some assurances were given by the Americans and Germans that helped persuade Gorbachev eventually to go along with a united Germany in NATO. Of post-Soviet NATO enlargement (which will be touched on in the final chapter), the least that can be said is that Western countries breached the spirit of those assurances and, in some cases, the letter.[41] In a speech in Bavaria at the end of January 1990 the West German Foreign Minister Hans-Dietrich Genscher said that the German unification process should not impair 'Soviet security interests'. NATO, accordingly, should rule out 'an expansion of its territory towards the east, i.e. moving it closer to the Soviet borders'.[42] When Gorbachev said to Secretary of State Baker when they met in Moscow on 9 February, 'Of course, it is clear that an expansion of the NATO zone is unacceptable', Baker replied, 'We agree with that.'[43] Even the declassified, and substantially redacted, American transcript of that same discussion, records Baker saying, 'If we maintain a presence in Germany that is a part of NATO, there would be no extension of NATO's jurisdiction for forces of NATO one inch to the east.'[44] Earlier on the same day, in a meeting with Shevardnadze, Baker said that 'a Germany that is firmly anchored in a changed NATO', by which he meant 'a NATO that is far less of military organization, much more of a political one', would have no need for an 'independent nuclear capability'. And he added: 'There would, of course, have to be iron-clad guarantees that NATO's jurisdiction or forces would not move eastward.'[45] The following day Chancellor Kohl told Gorbachev that, while NATO membership for Germany was essential, he understood the security interests of the Soviet Union and 'We consider that NATO must not expand the sphere of its activity.'[46]

The argument that the Americans put to Gorbachev on the German question was that it was in the Soviet interest that there should be continuing influence over a united Germany from the American and European members of the North Atlantic Treaty Organization, and that this could best be achieved by German membership of NATO. At a meeting with Baker in Moscow on 18 May 1990, Gorbachev was still resistant to the idea. He suggested that there was a contradiction between Baker's saying that the Germans had proved themselves trustworthy and his insisting that they needed the constraints of NATO. 'You respond', said Gorbachev, 'that if Germany does not become a part of NATO, it could create a problem in Europe. So it turns out you do not trust Germany.'[47] Gorbachev said they should continue their discussion in Washington, but 'if none of my arguments convince you, then I'll suggest to the President and announce publicly that we want to join NATO too', since, after all, 'you say that NATO is not directed against us, that it is just a security structure that is adapting to the new reality'.[48] Baker did not respond to the suggestion of Soviet admission to NATO, but on German membership said that there would be 'resentment in Germany' if it was put into 'some kind of special category, if it is forced to do something against its will'.[49]

Acceptance of the principle of NATO membership for a united Germany came a step closer when Gorbachev arrived in the United States for a summit meeting with Bush at the end of May and beginning of June 1990. Among Gorbachev's advisers, Chernyaev had been especially relaxed about the prospect of Germany joining NATO, for he did not see Western countries constituting a danger to the Soviet Union. In a memo to Gorbachev of 4 May, he reminded him of his desire for good relations with Germany and said there was no need to think in Cold War terms about security. He went so far as to add that even if Poland joined NATO, that would not be a threat.[50]

Gorbachev's position at the summit was not clear-cut. He still objected to the principle of this extension of NATO's role, saying that 'if NATO does not plan to fight with us, then with whom?' Bush replied, 'with instability', to which Gorbachev responded, 'Do you really think that the more weapons [you have] the more robust stability would be?'[51] Yet, to the visible consternation of some of his accompanying delegation, especially Falin, who was not only the head of the CC's International Department but a German specialist, and Marshal Akhromeyev, Gorbachev twice agreed with Bush that the Helsinki Final Act gave countries the right to choose their own alliances. Bush noted that Akhromeyev looked angry and Falin was at least as agitated. He joined the discussion and, in Bush's words, 'launched into a lengthy filibuster on why Germany in NATO was unacceptable to the Soviet people' in a 'virtually open rebellion against a Soviet leader'.[52]

In mid-April Falin had sent Gorbachev a strongly argued memorandum against German membership of NATO, although he noted the influence that West Germany had already exerted over the GDR, so that even their East German ally was 'trying to convince the Soviet Union that a united Germany must join NATO'.[53] In the post-Soviet era, Falin complained that almost the entire Politburo, government, and chairmen of the parliamentary committees were bypassed on the issue of German unification and that the role of Minister of Defence and the general staff had been strictly circumscribed.[54] It was true that this policy was made within a very narrow circle. Significantly, the two aides on whom Gorbachev most relied, Chernyaev and Shakhnazarov, had both come to accept the principle of the whole of Germany being 'under the wing of NATO', but the final decision was very much his own.[55] Writing a decade after Germany was reunited, Falin claimed to have warned Gorbachev that including the territory of the GDR in NATO would lead to an expansion of that organization to the east which, he added, 'soon occurred'.[56]

Falin knew more about Germany than did either Chernyaev or even Shakhnazarov (whose earlier responsibilities in the 'Socialist Countries' department of the Central Committee had included oversight of the GDR) and he resented both Shevardnadze's lack of interest in his views and Gorbachev's failure to act upon them.[57] Earlier than most members of the Soviet elite, Falin had seen the disintegration of the GDR coming. Over a lengthy period he had discussed with such prominent West German Social Democrats as Willy Brandt and Egon Bahr the idea of a very gradual coming together of the GDR and the FRG.* After the fall of the wall, as noted in Chapter 12, he engaged in some freelance diplomacy of his own, bypassing Shevardnadze and hoping to impress Gorbachev, using back-channels to propose to the Germans a confederation of the two German states. This had the entirely unintended consequence of galvanizing Kohl in late November 1989 into seizing the initiative and pushing for speedy reunification.[58]

Pavel Palazchenko, Gorbachev's and Shevardnadze's top English-language interpreter, has suggested that, in the new atmosphere whereby old Cold War tensions had disappeared, even in the Soviet army there was a majority who did not object to a united Germany or to its membership of NATO. In the absence of survey data of army opinion, that assessment remains open to doubt. But Palazchenko goes on to make clear that, even if his supposition was correct, it was politically irrelevant. Gorbachev's problem was that 'among the high-ranking members of the still powerful Soviet institutions—the army, the KGB, the party apparat—the prevailing opinion was quite different'. They were vehemently opposed to unification of Germany and its membership of NATO. This meant that Gorbachev had to proceed with caution on the issue, even though he himself 'accepted the idea of unification'.[59] Viewing German unification and its inclusion in NATO as the 'great prize' for the West, Rodric Braithwaite later wrote that it was 'not at all clear that Gorbachev would or could agree to either'. Conscious that domestic Soviet opposition to such developments might overwhelm Gorbachev, Western negotiators 'were anxious to nail the deal down before things fell apart in Moscow'.[60]

Kohl was especially determined that a unified Germany would be in NATO, and the United States, Britain, and France strongly supported that position. On 30 May, the day before Bush was due to begin discussion with Gorbachev at the Washington summit, the German chancellor called the president and asked him to tell Gorbachev that Germany and the US 'will stand side by side' and that a sign of this cooperation

---

* What Falin would have discovered was that it is one thing to plan evolutionary rapprochement and another to keep it gradual once expectations, especially nationalist expectations, have been aroused. Gorbachev also favoured more gradual change in Germany, and, for that matter, in the Soviet Union, but the freer the country, the less scope the leader has to regulate the pace of change—unless he backtracks on those freedoms and reaches for the old instruments of oppression and control.

must be 'the future membership of a united Germany in NATO without any limitations'. The president should, said Kohl, 'make this clear to him, but in a friendly way'. He went on to say that Gorbachev needed economic help 'very much', that it should be provided, and that it was of 'immense importance that we make further progress in disarmament'.[61]

In fact, little progress was made on arms control at the Washington summit, but Gorbachev got the US–Soviet trade treaty and most-favoured-nation trade regime which he keenly desired for symbolic reasons, though a large upsurge in trade between the two countries seemed unlikely.[62] Symbolic also of new relations of trust between Bush and Gorbachev was the invitation to the Soviet leader and his immediate entourage to spend a day of informal talks in the more relaxed atmosphere of Camp David. Gorbachev asked Akhromeyev to take notes of a conversation he and Shevardnadze held with Bush and Baker. But, as Palazchenko, who was interpreting the conversation, rightly surmised, it was not for his skill as a notetaker that Gorbachev wanted the marshal there (his notes turned out to be incomplete and difficult to decipher) but 'as someone who was trusted by the military and the conservatives and could confirm that nothing "improper" happened during those private discussions—no capitulation, no sellout'.[63]

Bush had embarked on the summit meeting well informed on the pressures Gorbachev faced at home, not least by a long cable from Ambassador Matlock of 11 May. It began by saying that the Soviet Union was 'in a crisis of political power and facing fundamental choices—of Gorbachev's making if not of his design'. Matlock noted that party factions 'now exist in all but name' and that a bitter struggle was underway within the CPSU 'not so much for its soul as for its property and resources'.[64] The US ambassador made clear that Gorbachev was under intense domestic pressure, but noted that for five years he had 'confounded the doomsayers'. He had 'moved boldly and outmaneuvered his opponents while radicalizing and accelerating reform across the board'.[65] That was still his probable inclination but, the ambassador added, 'there are limits to the bold departures Soviet society will tolerate, especially if they do not produce the promised economic well-being'. Moreover, wrote Matlock, Gorbachev's continuing with the reform process would ultimately mean accepting 'a truncated Union'.

Chancellor Kohl was aware that, in spite of the principle of choice of alliance being extended to Germany, which Gorbachev had appeared to concede during his talks with Bush, unification was not yet a done deal. Now vulnerable at home, Gorbachev would expect the Germans to provide substantial financial compensation to the Soviet Union as a quid pro quo. The crucial meeting between Gorbachev and Kohl took place on 15–16 July, in a relatively informal atmosphere for momentous discussions, in the village of Arkhyz in Gorbachev's home region of Stavropol in southern Russia. The day before, Falin managed to attract the Soviet leader's attention for a moment and asked if he could have a word with him. Gorbachev

Figure 20 A break in the Gorbachev–Kohl discussions on German unification in the southern Russian village, Arkhyz, July 1990. Seated (L to R): West German Foreign Minister Hans-Dietrich Genscher, Mikhail Gorbachev, and German Chancellor Helmut Kohl.

said he had no time right then, but he would call Falin that evening, which he did. Falin had a number of demands for Gorbachev to put to the German side, including no nuclear weapons on German soil (and he cited a survey suggesting that 80 per cent of Germans were in favour of a denuclearized Germany). He reiterated the case against a united Germany's membership of NATO or, as a fallback, not being part of its military structure, as had been the case with France on de Gaulle's initiative. 'I'll do what I can,' Gorbachev replied. 'I'm only afraid that train has already left the station.'[66]

In fact, it was at Arkhyz that both the principle and some of the key details of a unified Germany in NATO were established. The German side agreed that they would finalize the status of their current borders (an important issue for the Poles, in particular, given the extent of former German territory that was now part of Poland), that they would reduce the size of the German army to 370,000 military personnel, pay between 11 and 12 billion deutschmarks to cover the withdrawal of Soviet troops from the GDR, and sign a treaty on good neighbourly relations with the USSR. Bargaining continued up to the signing of the 2 + 4 agreement on 12 September. Gorbachev decided that he had not asked for enough financial compensation and demanded 15–16 billion deutschmarks. Kohl agreed on a further three billion as an interest-free loan, and the deal was sealed.[67]

Margaret Thatcher and German Unification

Since communication between Chancellor Kohl and the prime minister was 'virtually non-existent', wrote British Foreign Secretary Douglas Hurd,* 'each was willing to compensate by extending courtesies to the other's Foreign Minister'.[68] In Hurd's several meetings in 1990 with Kohl, the chancellor 'emphasised again and again his admiration for Churchill' and 'quoted and requoted Thomas Mann's phrase about aiming for a European Germany not a German Europe'.[69] Hurd liked Kohl, even though the chancellor was not really a man 'for graceful courtesies', and he did not blame him for 'driving ahead with unification as fast as he could'. This was a legitimate exercise of leadership and Kohl knew that the opportunity 'might be fleeting'.[70] Just two days after Hurd had an amicable meeting with Kohl in Bonn, Thatcher delivered what the Foreign Secretary described as a 'tirade against German unification' during a cabinet meeting on 8 February. In conversation with her that evening, Hurd recalled, 'she brushed aside my arguments and continued to talk about the need to work with the Russians against Kohl'.[71]

Baker's 2 + 4 proposal was presented by the Americans at a meeting of foreign ministers in Ottawa a week after Margaret Thatcher had delivered her tirade, and though smaller European countries who were left out of the 2 + 4 process were critical of it, for Hurd it was 'a godsend'. Britain's seat at the table as of right, being one of 'the four', helped to assuage at least some of Thatcher's concerns. The process involved a series of well-prepared meetings over a period of seven months in different European cities with each country represented by its foreign minister. For Hurd—and the British more generally—it meant that there was 'no longer a danger of deals, particularly any affecting NATO or the rights of the Poles, being done behind our back'.[72]

Characteristically, the workaholic Thatcher, with her interest in expert opinion outside government, held an all-day Chequers seminar on Germany on Sunday 25 March 1990, to which she invited specialists on German history and politics.** The Foreign Secretary was present, as was the prime minister's private secretary, Charles Powell, as notetaker. Unlike the seminars on policy toward the Soviet Union, the existence of this one was leaked, with detailed quotation from the internal government account of it written by Powell. A majority of the outside experts subsequently went on record complaining that the minutes of the meeting reflected the anti-German bias in the

---

* Hurd was not Geoffrey Howe's direct successor. Following Thatcher's demotion of Howe in July 1989, John Major held the post of Foreign Secretary for three months, but when Nigel Lawson resigned as Chancellor of the Exchequer in October of that year, Thatcher moved Major to the Treasury and appointed Hurd to the FCO. He continued to hold that office during the greater part of Major's premiership (for almost six years in total).

** Two US-based scholars were invited—Fritz Stern and Gordon Craig. The British participants were historians Hugh Trevor-Roper (Lord Dacre), Timothy Garton Ash, and Norman Stone plus the writer and broadcaster, George Urban, a former director of Radio Free Europe.

questions that were posed to the contributors in advance of the seminar rather than the answers they gave. They maintained that Powell's account more faithfully recorded Thatcher's (and perhaps Powell's) views than the arguments of those whose advice she sought.[73] The minutes included some extraordinarily patronizing generalizations on 'the Germans themselves and their characteristics'.[74] Along with the publication of an anti-German article by a British government minister, Nicholas Ridley (which led to his resignation),* Powell's minutes of the seminar (when they became public) received widespread and aggrieved attention in Germany. *Der Spiegel* reproduced about 90 per cent of the text, and *Die Welt* saw the article and seminar report as evidence of 'the UK's difficulty in adjusting to its current position in the world'.[75]

By this stage of her premiership, Thatcher's belief that she knew better than her interlocutors had become increasingly evident. (The president of the Hungarian Academy of Sciences Ivan Berend unfavourably contrasted Thatcher's explaining to him 'what was really happening in Hungary', when they met in August 1990, with the 'brilliant questions' he was asked a few months earlier by the Spanish Prime Minister Felipe González.)[76] George Urban, a prominent East Europeanist who admired Thatcher and had taken part in numerous briefing meetings with her from the very early 1980s onwards, bemoaned what he now called her 'overweening self-confidence and self-importance'.[77] He dictated his account of the March 1990 Chequers meeting for his personal archive the day after it occurred and devotes more than forty pages to it in a book about his various encounters with Thatcher.[78] The arguments for a united Germany were put clearly. All the outside experts, according to Urban, were in accord with Hugh Trevor-Roper, one of the specialists, when he reminded the prime minister that after the Second World War, both the British and the Americans wanted a united and free Germany. The country had been split into two states because of 'the unyielding nature of Stalinism'.[79] Why, then, was there any need to be horrified now that this part of the original post-war Allied aims was being achieved without war, bloodshed, or crisis? There were, apparently, 'muttered voices of approval around the table' and Thatcher was 'a little taken aback'. Trevor-Roper, responding to a friend's inquiry in August about the March seminar, said it had been 'noted that the PM, in her public utterances, was much less anti-German' and that this 'was commonly seen as a result of our meeting'.[80] The fact that the outside experts' views reinforced those of the Foreign Office may, indeed, have had an influence. More importantly, with each passing month, it became ever more evident that German unification was going to happen, and the prime minister had little option but to accommodate herself to that reality.

The Foreign Secretary, wrote Urban, had been 'subdued and mostly silent', and appeared 'visibly unhappy about the prime minister's emotional tone and her

---

* Ridley resigned as Secretary of State for Trade and Industry on 14 July 1990 in the wake of the uproar caused by an article he published in *The Spectator* in which, among other things, he described European monetary union as 'a German racket designed to take over the whole of Europe'.

reluctance to go along with some of our reasoning'.[81] Hurd's memoirs (published six years after Urban's death) made clear that he was, indeed, unhappy with Thatcher's views on Germany. He described the Chequers seminar as 'the one more shot in her locker'. She had hoped that her 'own instinctive opinions' would be 'buttressed with outside expert support', but the prime minister's 'robust statement of her anxieties' had found scant support from the academics. The seminar had 'passed into popular history for the wrong reasons', wrote Hurd, for it was Powell's vivid account 'of the Prime Minister's views which caught the imagination', whereas little attention was paid to his conclusion that 'the weight of evidence and the argument at the seminar favoured those who were optimistic about life with a united Germany'.[82]

Wit was not one of Thatcher's strong points. Otherwise, she might have echoed the remark attributed to the French writer François Mauriac, 'I love Germany so much that I'm glad there are two of them.'[83] As it was, her extreme reluctance to accept a united Germany puzzled the Americans, as well as angering Kohl. But the 2 + 4 process meant that Bush kept in close touch with her. Although their relationship lacked the warmth of that between Thatcher and Reagan, both Bush and Scowcroft acquired a respect for her grasp of detail which emerges clearly in their co-authored volume of memoirs. The closeness of the contacts between the UK and the US in those years was indicated when Lawrence Eagleburger and Robert Gates came to 10 Downing Street to brief her on the latest American thinking on European security and the German question and she invited them to 'take their accustomed chairs' after which, as they informed Scowcroft, 'a long and searching conversation' ensued in which Thatcher 'manifested a daunting familiarity with U.S. deployments in Europe'.[84] Bush, understandably, had much greater respect for the knowledge she had acquired and the position she took on the Soviet Union than for her views on Germany. He quoted an April 1990 conversation with her in Bermuda in which she said that the Soviet military had been treated badly, they had been obliged 'to destroy decent weapons', and the army was 'fragmenting along ethnic lines'. Significantly, she observed that the Soviet military was 'no longer on Gorbachev's side'. As a result, though Gorbachev was 'a sensible politician', he had been hardening his position in recent weeks.[85]

When Thatcher visited the Soviet Union in June, she added her support for a united Germany being a member of NATO, having by then fully accepted that unification was going to happen. She did not hide her apprehensions about it, which were, she said, shared by President Mitterrand, although he had not gone public with them.[86] Reporting to the Foreign Office on this visit, Charles Powell wrote that Gorbachev's views on Germany and NATO were still evolving. Rather than say at any stage that a united Germany in NATO was unacceptable, he seemed to be searching for ways to make such an outcome 'more palatable and explicable to his own people'.[87] Thatcher was by this time far more popular in the Soviet Union than she was in Germany. Reporting to the Foreign Office in October 1990, after German unification had been achieved, the British ambassador to Bonn, Sir Christopher Mallaby, noted that while

Hurd was well regarded in the Federal Republic, Thatcher was resented by leading German politicians on account of her attitude to unification. This, together with her hostility to further European integration, had reduced British influence in Germany.[88]

Diplomacy or War in the Middle East?

From early August, with the German issue virtually resolved, the United States had another major international preoccupation—the invasion of Kuwait by Iraq. The Bush administration was determined not to allow Saddam Hussein to take over this Middle Eastern ally and control its oil resources. Whereas in the past, the US would have wished to isolate the USSR from the process, Bush made strenuous—and ultimately successful—efforts to gain Gorbachev's reluctant support for American military intervention. On Bush's initiative another summit meeting with Gorbachev was convened at short notice, this time in Helsinki on 9 September. He was accompanied not only by Shevardnadze but also by Akhromeyev and by Evgeny Primakov, an adviser with formidable knowledge of the Arab world who was becoming a prominent politician in his own right.

Bush assured Gorbachev that if military action was needed to dislodge the Iraqi troops from Kuwait, American troops would not remain in the Gulf region on a long-term basis. There was agreement on the aim of ending the Iraqi occupation of Kuwait but marked disagreement on whether this could be achieved by diplomacy. The differences notwithstanding, relations between Bush and Gorbachev were friendly, and the Helsinki summit marked the point at which the two leaders began to address each other by their first names.[89] Bush, moreover, told Gorbachev that he saw this as the beginning of a new era of Soviet–American cooperation in the Middle East, in which they would make 'more positive collaborative efforts to regulate not only this problem, but the rest of the issues in the Middle East'.[90] Later in the conversation Bush conceded that Soviet experts on the region might know more than their American counterparts, but on one point he would disagree with them. While Saddam wanted the West to believe that he spoke on behalf of the entire Muslim world, he had not succeeded in 'becoming a symbol of the Arab struggle with the infidel'.[91]

True to his values, Gorbachev tried hard to avert the need for a war, and Soviet specialists on the Arab world were firmly opposed to Moscow siding with Washington against Iraq, a long-standing Soviet ally. Shevardnadze took somewhat less persuasion than Gorbachev to agree that US military force to remove the Iraqi troops from Kuwait was both necessary and justifiable. Baker had a long meeting with the two of them in Moscow on 8 November, in which Shevardnadze 'came close' to the American position that a UN Security Council resolution authorizing force should be passed before the end of that month. In a cable to Bush, Baker wrote, 'While I think Shevardnadze is not enthusiastic about using force, he is more inclined to think it will have to be used eventually.' Gorbachev remained sceptical.[92] He wished

Figure 21 Margaret Thatcher and President George H. W. Bush at 10 Downing Street, July 1990. Private secretary Charles Powell is seated to Thatcher's left and US National Security Advisor Brent Scowcroft on Bush's right.

to persuade Saddam Hussein to see sense and avoid a war by ordering the withdrawal from Kuwait. Much to the annoyance of Shevardnadze, Gorbachev involved Primakov, with his Middle Eastern expertise and long acquaintanceship with Saddam (he had first met him as long ago as 1969 and many times since), to act as an intermediary with the aim of averting an American attack.[93]

The mission with which Gorbachev entrusted Primakov was to secure Iraq's withdrawal without a war, and that was also the declared preference of the Bush administration. Nevertheless, Primakov's diplomacy, which took him repeatedly to the Middle East and also to the United States, was regarded with disfavour in Washington. For his part, Shevardnadze saw it as trespass on his territory and it led to a cooling of his hitherto close relationship with Gorbachev and to acrimonious argument with Primakov, one of whose ideas was to link Iraqi withdrawal from Kuwait with a new initiative to resolve the Palestinian question, partly as a face-saving cover for Saddam's retreat. Shevardnadze told Primakov that his mission was a recipe for disaster in the Middle East and endangered the whole of Soviet foreign policy. This enraged Primakov who said, 'How dare you, a graduate of a correspondence course from a teachers' college' [in Georgia] 'lecture me on the Middle East, the region I've studied since my student days!' Gorbachev, who was present, raised his voice, saying 'Yevgeny, stop right now!'[94]

The Soviet Union, against the advice of their Arabist specialists, did support a UN resolution demanding that Iraqi forces withdraw from Kuwait and empowering states to use 'all necessary means' if they failed to do so by a deadline of 15 January 1991. (China abstained from the vote—but did not veto the resolution—notwithstanding Bush's efforts to achieve unanimity among the permanent members of the Security Council.)[95] Up to the moment at which the American attack on the Iraqi forces began in January 1991, Gorbachev continued to try to broker a resolution of the conflict by diplomatic means, ultimately irritating the Bush administration in the process. Primakov had encountered a mildly sceptical response from the president when he met with Bush in the White House in mid-October, but in a separate Washington meeting, Dennis Ross of the State Department told him that the Israelis would not accept his proposed linkage of an Iraqi withdrawal from Kuwait with a new initiative on the Palestinian question. On the way back to Moscow, Primakov stopped off in Britain on Gorbachev's instructions and at the request of Margaret Thatcher. She saw him at Chequers on a Saturday and listened carefully to what he said before speaking for almost an hour herself. She was in full 'Iron Lady' mode and told him it was not enough to get Saddam's forces out of Kuwait; they needed to destroy Iraq's military in a crushing blow. There was no alternative to military action. 'The conversation with Thatcher', Primakov concluded, 'had been designed to be a cold shower for us.'[96]

In the same month Gorbachev was awarded the 1990 Nobel Peace Prize, not for his efforts to prevent the Gulf War—although, having been unwilling to resort to force to defend what many in the Soviet military-industrial complex regarded as vital Soviet concerns, it would have been strange had he viewed with equanimity what they saw as the US defending *its* economic and geopolitical interests—but for 'his leading role in the peace process', in which 'confrontation has been replaced by negotiations' in the ending of the Cold War. The Nobel citation added, 'The greater openness he has brought about in Soviet society has helped promote international trust.'[97] All too conscious of the problems facing him at home, and aware that being feted abroad while domestic economic difficulties and inter-ethnic tensions continued unabated in the Soviet Union, would do him more harm than good, Gorbachev, though appreciative of the award, chose not to pick it up in person.[98] Chernyaev noted that Gorbachev had a disdain for awards to politicians because they had been 'cheapened and discredited under Brezhnev'.[99] There was, however, a big difference between the prizes awarded Brezhnev by Soviet toadies—for everything from his hitherto overlooked outstanding military valour during the Second World War to the major Soviet literature prize for his slim volumes of ghosted memoirs—and recognition by a highly prestigious and independent international body. Gorbachev postponed his Nobel lecture until 11 June 1991, which was just before the ultimate deadline for its delivery. Chernyaev contrasted the warm approval in 'the international media' for what Gorbachev said then with the relative silence on it of the Soviet press.[100]

Departure of Thatcher and Shevardnadze

The departure of two major figures in the Cold War's ending before the year 1990 was out came as a surprise to most of the other protagonists. The first to go, in November, was Margaret Thatcher when she was ousted from office by her Conservative colleagues. The second exit came with the resignation of Eduard Shevardnadze in December. He had been under increasing attack from Soviet hard-liners but the decision, when it came, was his own. His resignation surprised his colleagues at home and abroad—and no-one more than Gorbachev who, some five years earlier, had astonished the Soviet political elite by choosing Shevardnadze to be Minister of Foreign Affairs.

Thatcher's political demise was triggered by Geoffrey Howe's resignation from his Cabinet post as Leader of the House of Commons and, more particularly, by his 13 November speech to the House, explaining his decision. There was no criticism in that speech of Thatcher's Soviet policy, for Howe had embraced engagement with Communist countries somewhat earlier than Thatcher did, and he shared her admiration for the role Gorbachev had played in their political transformation. He was, however, highly critical of her attitudes to Britain's partners in the European Economic Community (as the EU was still known), contrasting her scepticism about European organizational cooperation with Harold Macmillan's realization in the early 1960s that it was essential for the UK 'not to cut ourselves off from the realities of power; not to retreat into a ghetto of sentimentality about our past and so diminish our own control over our own destiny in the future'.

The prime minister's attitude towards Europe was, said Howe, 'minimizing our influence and maximizing our chances of being once again shut out'. If the Conservatives as a party or Britain as a country were to become detached from 'the middle ground of Europe' the consequences would be 'incalculable and very hard ever to correct'. Howe made clear that, unlike the prime minister, he was open to the idea of a common European currency. More generally, he was critical of her hectoring style of government which he contrasted with his 'commitment to government by persuasion'. Howe concluded by saying that, in resigning, 'I have done what I believe to be right for my party and my country. The time has come for others to consider their own response to the tragic conflict of loyalties with which I have myself wrestled for perhaps too long.'[101] The quietly devastating last sentence appeared to be a call to Conservative Cabinet members and the parliamentary party to put the good of their political party and the UK ahead of loyalty to the person who had led the party for fifteen years and the country for more than eleven. Enraged by the speech, Thatcher later asserted that Howe's 'long suppressed rancour' gave his words 'more force than he had ever managed before'.[102]

The very next day former Secretary of State for Defence Michael Heseltine, who had resigned from the Cabinet in 1986, launched a leadership challenge. At that time the choice was in the hands of the parliamentary party, and in the first ballot Heseltine secured 152 votes against Thatcher's 204. As she did not have an overall majority, there had to be a second round. Thatcher was taking part in a CSCE conference in Paris in the run-up to the ballot, thereby missing the chance to win over the four more MPs she needed to win outright.* Her first inclination was to fight on into the second round, but when she took soundings with each member of the Cabinet in turn, she was shocked to discover that the tide had so turned against her that almost all of them told her she would lose. Accordingly, she resigned her party leadership and premiership on 22 November and departed, tearfully, from 10 Downing Street.

Among the messages Thatcher received was a letter from Gorbachev, sent on the very day of her resignation to the Soviet Embassy in London. He wrote that 'with a feeling of great warmth and deep satisfaction I recall our working meetings which played such a great role in the development of the relations between the Soviet Union and Great Britain'. He highly valued the way they had developed a mutual understanding on many issues and wrote that it was symbolic for him that his 'international activities' in practice 'started with our conversations as far back as 1984'. Every political figure, he continued, is assessed both by contemporaries and by future generations. He was in no doubt that her 'enormous contribution as a politician' would be recognized in British and world history.[103]

Following Thatcher's resignation, the candidates for the party leadership in the second round were Michael Heseltine, Douglas Hurd, and John Major. Thatcher, who was determined to stop Heseltine, used what influence she had left—and it included a considerable body of support on the Conservative backbenches, far less in the Cabinet—in Major's favour. He won fifty-four more votes than Heseltine, who was runner-up, just two short of an overall majority. Heseltine, however, immediately conceded defeat, and Major became prime minister, an office he held until 1997, leading the Conservatives to victory in the 1992 election and to heavy defeat by the Labour Party five years later.

One consequence of the shock removal of a UK prime minister who had been in office so long and who, for better or worse, had made a bigger impression on the outside world than any of her predecessors since Churchill, was its overshadowing of an agreement at the CSCE Paris conference she had been attending which could be regarded as a codification of the end of the Cold War.** Known as the Charter of Paris for a New Europe, it was a document signed by the heads of government—in some

---

* The conference provided the opportunity also for bilateral meetings, and Thatcher met with Gorbachev. Anatoly Chernyaev, who was present, compared the occasion to Churchill at Potsdam (when he left for London, expecting to return, only to discover that the electorate had brought his premiership to a close). Chernyaev was, as ever, fulsome in his appreciation of the British prime minister, as a politician and as a woman. 'I sat opposite her and feasted my eyes on her', he wrote in his diary. 'Beautiful! She likes the fact that I admire her', Chernyaev diary entry (in Russian) of 24 November 1990, https://nsarchive2.gwu.edu/rus/text_files/Chernyaev/1990.pdf.

** The CSCE (Conference on Security and Co-Operation in Europe) grew out of the Helsinki Conference and its Final Act of 1975. In 1995 it changed its name to OSCE (Organization for Security and Co-Operation in Europe).

cases heads of state—of the countries of Europe, including the USSR and, from outside Europe, by the US and Canada.[104] Gorbachev and Bush, as well as Thatcher, were, naturally, there, although at one point Gorbachev, believing that things were becoming so fraught at home that he had better cancel all his foreign trips, had told his entourage he wouldn't attend, but was persuaded by Chernyaev that this would be a big mistake. Gorbachev had been especially disconcerted by an aggressive speech by Yeltsin in which he said that Russia would no longer be subordinate to 'the centre' and by warnings that Ukraine was also showing signs of greater restiveness.[105] Gorbachev and Bush were among the twenty-two representatives of their countries who, during the Paris visit, signed the Treaty on Conventional Armed Forces in Europe (CFE), another step along the path of arms reductions. It imposed ceilings both on troop numbers and on different categories of military hardware.

All the signatories to the Charter of Paris agreed to adhere to 'democratic government' expressed through regular free and fair elections and to the 'pluralist character' of that democracy which 'entails accountability to the electorate' and the understanding that 'no one will be above the law'.[106] The signatories reaffirmed their 'commitment to settle disputes by peaceful means' and to 'develop mechanisms for the prevention and resolution of conflicts among the participating States'.[107] One may detect, however, a potential contradiction between the declaration that 'Security is indivisible and the security of every participating State is inseparably linked to that of all the others' and the statement that 'we fully recognize the freedom of States to choose their own security arrangements'.[108] The post-Communist enlargement of NATO was justified on the latter principle, for it was something that many of the states in east and central Europe wanted, but it was viewed in Russia as being far from 'inseparably linked' to *their* security but, rather, antithetical to it.

The signatories expressed their determination 'to co-operate in defending democratic institutions against activities which violate the independence, sovereign equality or territorial integrity of the participating States', adding that these included defence against 'illegal activities involving outside pressure, coercion and subversion'.[109] Another section emphasized a commitment to cooperate to tackle environmental threats and welcomed the creation of the European Environment Agency (EEA).[110] The document concluded with a section on the new structures and processes to be developed to further the process of European cooperation across the old dividing lines. The 'Heads of State or Government' would meet to review CSCE progress every two years (next time in Helsinki in 1992) and the Ministers for Foreign Affairs would meet, as a Council, at least once a year. A 'Committee of Senior Officials' would be set up and a Conflict Prevention Centre in Vienna established 'to assist the Council in reducing the risk of conflict'.[111] These could have constituted the first building blocks of new security arrangements to be developed within the CSCE process and which, crucially, would have embraced Russia, but (and it is a point to which I return in Chapter 16) the opportunity was missed.

Turmoil within, and the eventual break-up of, the Soviet Union played a part in that. Following Thatcher's abrupt removal from office which unsettled her White House and Kremlin interlocutors came the greater shock for Gorbachev and, arguably, for Washington, of Shevardnadze's resignation. The British premier and the Soviet Foreign Minister had in common the fact that they were becoming the target of ever stronger criticism within their own parties and countries. And just as Thatcher felt that her immediate colleagues had lamentably failed to rally in her support, so Shevardnadze felt that Gorbachev had not defended him from the attacks of hard-liners anything like as boldly as he should have done.* Yakovlev felt similarly let down, but much of the criticism of Shevardnadze and Yakovlev from conservative and reactionary Communists was also an indirect way of attacking Gorbachev at a time when some of his opponents still hesitated to make a frontal public attack on the top leader.

At the 7 November parade celebrating the Bolshevik Revolution, an attempt was made to assassinate Gorbachev. Security guards wrestled a man to the ground just as he was aiming for him and two shots went harmlessly into the air. Several days later, and more alarming politically for Gorbachev, he had a meeting with more than a thousand military officers who were members of legislatures or other Soviet public bodies. He got a very hostile reception and the officers were so openly critical of his leadership as to give grounds for believing that the army would be willing partners of those conservatives within the CPSU who were pressing for a 'strong hand' against separatists and demonstrators.[112] A few days later came the Politburo meeting of 16 November, discussed earlier in the chapter, at which Gorbachev came under sustained attack and, following which (as a result not only of that but of an accumulation of problems and pressures), he wound up the ineffective Presidential Council and created the Security Council as well as making the prime minister more explicitly responsible to him as president. The institutional changes were not necessarily bad in themselves. The real retreat came in the more conservative language Gorbachev used during this period and, still more, in his personnel changes.

He succumbed to pressure to remove from his post as Minister of Internal Affairs Vadim Bakatin, the one head of a power ministry of liberal disposition and a man who preferred a genuine rule of law to the iron fist, and replaced him by the hard-line former first secretary of the Latvian Communist Party, Boris Pugo. When Kryuchkov and others were pressing for emergency rule to be introduced throughout the USSR, Bakatin said he was 'categorically against' this. This, as Bakatin acknowledged in his

---

* Shevardnadze recognized that Gorbachev was far from free of constraints, but he needed to recognize that his reactionary opponents were burying his life's main work, 'saying his ideas were worthless, and it was necessary to go back to the old but still fearsome artillery'. Shevardnadze said he could imagine why Gorbachev did not speak up, for 'a politician has to size up the actual situation and the balance of forces'. However, 'in the early days of perestroika, while acknowledging the existence of an opposition, he wasn't afraid to go against the grain. He appealed to the people and won their support' (Shevardnadze, *The Future Belongs to Freedom*, Sinclair-Stevenson, London, 1991, p. xviii).

memoirs, was in accord with Gorbachev's own position.[113] It was a sign of the extent to which Gorbachev was worried by the hard-liners that he, nevertheless, replaced Bakatin by Pugo. Informed by Gorbachev that he was relieving him of his ministerial post, Bakatin responded that he had not sought to be the Minister of Internal Affairs; Gorbachev had put him there and so he was entitled to remove him, but he was making a mistake. Gorbachev said that matter had already been settled, but he wanted Bakatin to continue his membership of the recently created Security Council.[114]

Pugo's was just one of a number of bad appointments Gorbachev made in the last months of 1990 and in early 1991. Tactical retreat though this was, it understandably worried both his foreign partners and those at home most committed to democratic progress. Many of the latter did not regard Gorbachev's apparent backsliding as temporary and tactical, while the hard-liners, though they could be far from sure that Gorbachev had decisively moved in their direction, were sufficiently encouraged not to make a serious attempt to depose him in the winter of 1990–1 when their chances of success would have been greater than they were in the summer of 1991, by which time they had to reckon with the popularity and legitimacy Yeltsin had gained from his election to the Russian presidency. During this period of retreat, in addition to ill-advised appointments to high state offices, Gorbachev elevated to high party positions a number of conservative Communists, a step back which looked all the more mistaken in August 1991. Most of the people in that category—among them Oleg Shenin and Gennadiy Yanaev (who were fast-tracked to full Politburo membership and secretaryships of the Central Committee and, subsequently, in Yanaev's case to the office of vice-president)—were active participants in the attempt forcibly to seize the reins of power, as were Prime Minister Valentin Pavlov and Internal Affairs Minister Pugo.*

Two aggressively reactionary opponents of Gorbachev's policies among members of the Congress of People's Deputies of the USSR, Colonels Viktor Alksnis and Nikolay Petrushenko, boasted that they had succeeded in ousting Bakatin as Minister of Internal Affairs and that Shevardnadze was next in line for the chop. It was at a session of the Congress on 20 December (the day after he had been attacked by Alksnis and Petrushenko) that Shevardnadze made a dramatic intervention, announcing his resignation. He defended the Soviet Foreign Ministry's policy on Iraq's invasion of Kuwait. A number of speakers had severely attacked the attempt to thwart Saddam Hussein's land-grab, but Shevardnadze's response was that 'we have no moral right at all to reconcile ourselves to aggression and the annexation of a small, defenceless country'.[115]

Broadening the scope of his counterblast, Shevardnadze pointed to the forces of reaction that were developing strength within the party and accused democrats of

---

* Whereas Shenin and Yanaev were jailed after the putsch collapsed, Pugo, having been the minister who oversaw Soviet prisons, avoided acquiring first-hand knowledge of them by committing suicide.

'scattering'. 'Is it an accident', he asked, 'that two members of the legislature made a statement saying the minister of internal affairs was removed successfully and the time has come to settle accounts with the foreign minister?' How could young colonels get away with saying this? 'Who stands behind these comrades...?', he demanded to know. The part of his speech which attracted the most attention was the warning of a coming dictatorship. 'No one knows', he said, 'what kind of dictatorship this will be and who will come—what kind of dictator—and what the regime will be like.' He made it clear that he was not thinking that Gorbachev would perform that role, saying: 'I express profound gratitude to Mikhail Sergeyevich Gorbachev. I am his friend. I am a fellow thinker of his. I have always supported, and will support to the end of my days, the ideas of perestroika, the ideas of renewal, the ideas of democracy, of democratization.' He added, 'I cannot reconcile myself to the events taking place in our country and to the trials awaiting our people', but dictatorship would not succeed, for 'the future belongs to democracy and freedom'.[116]

Shevardnadze did not have any specific information about an impending coup, but he was concerned about the concessions Gorbachev had made to the conservative forces. The Soviet leader believed that his zig-zags were part of the price to be paid for evolutionary transformation of the system. Shevardnadze's view, as his adviser Sergey Tarasenko put it to Matlock (and it was an opinion shared by Yakovlev, Chernyaev, and Shakhnazarov), was that this was playing into the hands of groups determined to hold the Soviet Union together by force. Thus, 'Gorbachev might think he was buying time, but he would eventually be cast aside by those he depended on.' In those circumstances, Shevardnadze said he could not remain in the government.[117] The outgoing Foreign Minister told no-one, apart from his wife and children, other than his two closest aides, Tarasenko and Teymuraz Stepanov, of his intention to resign.[118]

Bush was surprised that he had not breathed a word about it to Baker, for he knew how close they were.[119] Baker himself told the press, 'I have known Eduard Shevardnadze to be a man of his word, a man of courage, conviction, and principle' and that they had done significant things together. 'I'm going to miss him,' he added.[120] Shevardnadze said that he would not have resigned had he not believed that 'the positive course in U.S.–Soviet relations was irreversible', although improvements might now come more slowly. He also wrote to Baker to apologize for not giving him any advance warning, to which the Secretary of State replied that he understood that this was not possible and praised him for being 'true to his values and convictions'.[121] Shevardnadze told Baker that Gorbachev had spent two hours trying to persuade him to remain as Foreign Minister, but Shevardnadze had insisted his decision was final. Gorbachev sent Aleksandr Bessmertnykh to Washington with a letter to Bush, telling him of his disappointment with Shevardnadze's resignation, but assuring the president that everything in their relationship was unchanged.[122]

It had been in Gorbachev's mind to offer the vice-presidency to a non-Russian in the interests of preserving the union and he had particularly in mind either the Kazakh leader Nursultan Nazarbayev or Shevardnadze. Nazarbayev turned the offer down and it is likely that Shevardnadze would have done the same. Either one of them would, though, have been an improvement on the colourless Russian apparatchik Yanaev. According to Shakhnazarov, 'Everybody in Gorbachev's circle was categorically against Yanaev. Everyone saw he was a grey person, although no-one thought he would be all that important.'[123] But Gorbachev described him as 'straightforward' and appointed him in the belief that he would at least be loyal—a serious misjudgement of the future putschist. The vice-presidency was not a particularly attractive post for an abler or more ambitious politician than Yanaev, especially at this stage of declining popular support for the Soviet federal authorities. The prime ministership (as distinct from the vice-presidency) might have been a more appropriate office for Shevardnadze, but Gorbachev would, at best, have faced insuperable opposition from the USSR Supreme Soviet to making such an appointment or, at worst, risked provoking a coup d'état there and then.

Shevardnadze did not leave Gorbachev entirely in the lurch. He agreed to postpone his departure from the Foreign Ministry until January to facilitate a smooth transition and continuity of Soviet foreign policy. It was mid-January before it was announced that his successor would be the experienced diplomat, Bessmertnykh, who had been First Deputy Foreign Minister from 1988 to 1990, when he became Soviet ambassador to Washington. Bessmertnykh was not only very knowledgeable about international policy but also a supporter of the direction in which Gorbachev was taking both political reform and foreign policy. Although he was more cautious than Shevardnadze, the choice came as a great relief to the Americans. In Matlock's words, 'We knew Bessmertnykh well and held him in the highest regard.'[124] Back in Brezhnev's time, Matlock recalled, a message had been sent to the United States from Gromyko, demanding that American cinemas not show a European film about Lenin which 'Moscow considered disrespectful'. Bessmertnykh was one of the most senior Soviet diplomats in the Washington Embassy and, at a reception there, Matlock took him aside and 'berated him for not explaining to Moscow how ridiculous this message made them all look'. Bessmertnykh didn't try to defend the message but said it was a 'very emotional' issue in the Kremlin. He added that 'it would probably be ten years or more before Lenin could be assessed dispassionately'. For Matlock this indicated that Bessmertnykh was 'a man who could think for himself' and, in the context of that time, 'was trying to be as honest as his job permitted'.[125]

From January 1991 Bessmertnykh was to have the task of representing Soviet interests abroad while they were being undermined by competing nationalisms, institutions, interests, and personalities at home.

15

FINAL YEAR—OF THE USSR AND OF GORBACHEV'S POWER (1991)

Relations between nationalities and between republics and the centre in the Soviet Union were not at the top of Gorbachev's list of pressing issues—until they forced their way there. It was the political reform he had sponsored and overseen, and the new thinking which underlay a new foreign policy, that turned the national question into the most serious of all. On the Soviet leader's grossly overloaded political agenda, it had become an even greater danger to the future of the state and to the process of political transformation than was the deterioration of the economy, grim enough though this was, with the economic system stuck in a no-man's land between plan and market.

By the beginning of 1991, Soviet citizens had for several years been able to air their national grievances without fear of arrest and imprisonment. Since 1989 they had even been free to elect to new legislatures deputies who were intent on seeking national sovereignty for their republics. Moreover, the Soviet leadership's tolerance in that same year of the East European states breaking free from Soviet hegemony raised expectations among the most disaffected nations within the USSR. Reacting to the nationalist upsurge, Gorbachev's starting-point was that it was in the interests of every Soviet republic to remain within (or, more aptly, join) a renewed union in which they would be powerful components of a genuine federation. It was one in which ever greater powers were being devolved to the republics in each successive draft of a proposed new Union Treaty.

Although Gorbachev continued to be active in foreign-policy-making—and relations with the Soviet Union remained a high priority for the Bush administration—the Soviet leader's room for manoeuvre internationally was by now severely constrained by the fissiparous tendencies at home, not only in the Baltic republics and Georgia but, more dangerously, in the Russian republic led by Yeltsin and by a growing national movement in Ukraine.

The National Question in the USSR

Nationalist demands for full sovereignty emanated from approximately half of the Soviet Union's republics. The main exceptions were in the Central Asian part of the

USSR (where the local party bosses, who remained in firm control, feared that independence would lead to an Islamic surge that would sweep them aside) and, until very late in the day, Belarus. But the pressures on Gorbachev came not only from separatists and radical democrats. They were at least as great from the opposing, and centralist, side which contained the big battalions in the most literal power-wielding sense. Within the party-state machine, and especially in the ranks of the *siloviki*—the army and the military-industrial complex, the KGB, and the Ministry of Internal Affairs—there was fierce opposition to losing any part of the Soviet Union, following the loss of Eastern Europe which had been a bitter enough pill for them to swallow. The fact that the vice-president, the prime minister, the Chairman of the KGB, the Minister of Defence, and the head of military industry were among the principal plotters who placed Gorbachev under house arrest in August 1991 was evidence enough of the impossible task the Soviet Union's last leader faced in trying to reconcile the aspirations for sovereignty of a number of nations within the multinational USSR with the opposition to this of the leading representatives of the most powerful institutional interests within the country, determined as they were to maintain the integrity of the USSR at all costs. Gorbachev also strove to hold together *a* union—as distinct from *the* Soviet Union in the form it had taken up until the mid-1980s—but *not* at *all* costs.

In the early months of 1991, the pressure on Gorbachev to institute a general crackdown on national separatism in the Baltic states was intense. KGB chief Vladimir Kryuchkov and other hard-liners had a more than useful ally in Gorbachev's Chief of Staff, Valeriy Boldin. He fed Gorbachev with one-sided and exaggerated information on the dangers to Russians in the non-Russian republics. The Soviet leader was presented with enormous piles of telegrams and letters from Russians living in Latvia, Lithuania, and Estonia, speaking of reprisals against them in the Baltic states and warning of a danger of civil war if order were not speedily restored.[1] Gorbachev made a speech on 10 January in which he used meaningless language of the past, warning of a danger of 'restoration of the bourgeois order' in Lithuania.

There were several instances where Soviet troops used violence in Lithuania and Latvia on the orders of some of those who later in the year were actively involved in the coup against Gorbachev.[2] In the worst incident, at least fourteen people were killed and many more wounded when Soviet troops took over the television station in the Lithuanian capital, Vilnius, on the night of 12/13 January. Among those involved in the repression in the Baltic states were Generals Valentin Varennikov and Viktor Achalov, both of whom were later to be active participants in the August putsch.[3] On the night of the Vilnius attack, the Lithuanian president, Vytautas Landsbergis, tried to telephone Gorbachev, but not only was he not put through to the Soviet president's dacha, Gorbachev was not even told about the call.[4] On the eve of the Vilnius attack, Kryuchkov, Pavlov, Baklanov, and Shenin met in Boldin's office. Their evident intention was to link Gorbachev with the violent suppression of the separatist movements in such a way that there could be no turning back. The Vilnius attack, Gorbachev observed later, was a political provocation aimed at destroying both perestroika and him 'in the eyes of the local population and abroad'.[5]

The killings by the security forces took place at night and, on learning about them the next day, Gorbachev made sure that the violence was halted. From the point of view of the hard-liners, he willed the ends of keeping the Soviet Union intact but would not allow them to deploy the means. His actions and inactions in the earliest months of 1991, during which he was playing for time, dissatisfied all but a minority who understood how vulnerable his position had become and the real danger of reversion to the old order if he were to be overthrown. They tolerated what they took to be one step back and trusted that it would be followed by two steps forward. But after Vilnius, Gorbachev lost his economic aide, Petrakov, and almost lost his closest adviser, Chernyaev, who wrote him a very long letter explaining why he would have to resign. The letter, however, was never delivered. Chernyaev's secretary, Tamara Alexandrova, told him that this was no time to 'desert Mikhail Sergeyevich' and demanded to know if he wanted 'to look good' at the leader's expense. She then locked the letter away and disappeared for a week, leaving Chernyaev with no access to his composition. By the time she returned to work, he had reached the conclusion that she was right. He reacted also against 'the public persecution of Gorbachev that instantly took place in the newspapers, on radio and TV, and at public rallies'. The liberal weekly *Moskovskie novosti* drew attention to the numerous people of intellectual distinction who had in recent days publicly denounced Gorbachev, while the Soviet leader was now preferring 'the company of mediocrities'. Chernyaev, with characteristic stubbornness, observed that 'to be promoted from mediocrity to great intellectual I only had to sign one of those manifestos. Now I was glad that Tamara hadn't let me send my letter of protest and resignation.'[6]

Nevertheless, Gorbachev was, indeed, abandoned by large numbers of his former supporters. He had given ammunition to his critics on all sides by trying to hold to a centrist position in a situation and at a time when there was little appetite for centrism. Yeltsin issued a strong statement condemning the use of force in Lithuania and told the American ambassador that he had done so because 'If they can use force against an elected assembly in Lithuania, they can do so against the Russian parliament.'[7] Yeltsin visited Estonia, Latvia, and Lithuania and signed a joint statement with the leaders of the three republics, announcing that they would develop relations 'on the basis of international law' (rather than of the Soviet Constitution). He also called on soldiers from Russia in the armed forces not to obey any orders to use force against civilians in the Baltic states.[8]

The broad umbrella organization of pro-democracy Russians called 'Democratic Russia' held a massive demonstration on 20 January protesting against the use of violence both in Lithuania and Latvia, and the placards and speeches were highly critical of Gorbachev. Western leaders added their voices to those who wished

Gorbachev to crack down not on those who peacefully sought national autonomy but on the agencies intent on using force to suppress them. Gorbachev's press secretary at that time, Vitaly Ignatenko, who later discovered that his telephone was being tapped by the KGB, wrote just after the collapse of the Soviet Union that Gorbachev was definitely not involved in the decision to use tanks and armed force in Vilnius but that he failed to act decisively enough in the immediate aftermath of the killings and should have dismissed those responsible.[9] Aleksandr Yakovlev, who was critical of Gorbachev's appointments and tactical retreat, nevertheless observed that, in spite of the *siloviki*'s desire to use force and to involve the Soviet leader in their 'many provocations', Gorbachev always insisted that national and other conflicts should be resolved without the use of violence and that he had gone into history 'without blood on his hands'.[10]

On 24 January Ambassador Matlock delivered a confidential letter from President Bush to Gorbachev, saying that he had accepted Gorbachev's earlier assurances that force would not be used in the Baltic states, but that he was coming under increasing pressure in the US over the latest violence. Cooperation with the Soviet Union on economic reform would not be possible unless the violence ceased. Bush said that if the use of force continued, the US would freeze its economic ties with the USSR and would not support Soviet associate membership of the International Monetary Fund and the World Bank.[11] When the ambassador had finished translating the letter line by line for the Soviet president, Gorbachev surprised him by saying, 'Tell me, Jack. How do you read the situation here?' Although it was an unusual question from a national leader to an ambassador, Matlock seized the opportunity offered and spoke for about fifteen minutes while Gorbachev listened without interrupting him. He told the Soviet president that he 'could not square his repeated verbal attacks on the democrats and on Yeltsin with the professed goal of perestroika' and observed that President Bush was under great domestic pressure to distance himself from the Soviet leadership. Matlock noted that the elected leaders in the Baltic states had been pursuing their goals by non-violent means and that the violence had been 'perpetrated by Soviet forces under Moscow's command'. He did not doubt Gorbachev's 'attachment to a peaceful, negotiated solution to these problems', but he was 'finding it impossible to explain to my government how his recent actions were consistent with his aims'. Gorbachev 'listened intently throughout my monologue', wrote Matlock, and 'he thanked me for my candor without a trace of irony'.[12]

Gorbachev then explained to Matlock how *he* saw things. He believed that the Soviet Union was 'on the brink of civil war' and his overriding task was to prevent this. There would, accordingly, be 'a period of "zigs" and "zags"'. The Soviet Union suffered from 'a low political culture' with no tradition of compromise, but he was intent on keeping the political process on a constitutional path and he was 'not a hostage to anyone'. He was ready for dialogue with all the Baltic leaders, and had made progress with the Latvians, but he doubted this would be possible with

Lithuania 'as long as Landsbergis was in charge'. As for Yeltsin, he was very difficult, for he would make agreements, then renege on them, but Gorbachev would keep trying. The Soviet president asked Matlock to tell 'my friend George' that he would stick with what he had promised with regard to the Gulf War, the German question, and the ratification of the conventional arms agreement, and that domestically his main desire was to ensure that change was not accompanied by violence. He had not abandoned the goals he had earlier set for himself.[13]

Although far from persuaded that Gorbachev's tactical retreats and zig-zags were what was needed, Matlock was impressed by that measured response. Many political leaders, he noted, who projected a calm public image were irascible in private. Gorbachev appeared to be the reverse. Lately, he had been irritable and less cogent in public than in the past (reflecting, no doubt, the intensity of the cross-pressures he felt), but he reacted equably and judiciously to Bush's letter. He had made two import-ant points—that he would keep his promises on the Gulf War, Germany, and the CFE agreement, thus subtly reminding the American president of the continuing importance of Soviet cooperation for US foreign policy goals but without any threat to withdraw cooperation should Bush change his policy towards Moscow. Second, he had empha-sized that his recent statements and apparent ambivalence over the crackdowns had been tactical, not a change of fundamental policy.

One consequence of the events in the Baltic states, nevertheless, was that a summit meeting that Bush was due to hold with Gorbachev was postponed from February until later in the year. Although the delay was, indeed, connected with Bush's con-cern about the criticism he would face if he went ahead so soon after the Baltic vio-lence with a visit to Moscow, the explanation given by the White House (in deference to Gorbachev) was that the president had to remain in Washington to give his full attention to the Gulf War.[14] Whereas previous Soviet leaders would have indignantly dismissed the American president's critical letter, still more the critique of an ambas-sador, as unwarranted interference in the internal affairs of the Soviet Union, Gorbachev kept the new and greatly improved relations on track by listening and then calmly explaining his actions and inactions in the knowledge of 'the full seri-ousness' of the situation he faced with its 'high tensions and high emotions' and forces that were very difficult to control.[15]

Gorbachev expended a great deal of time and energy trying to hold together by persuasion a reformed union which would be a genuine federation with many devolved powers. He held a referendum on the future of the union in March 1991. Such was the extent of the change which had already occurred in the USSR that six of the fifteen republics—Estonia, Latvia, Lithuania, Georgia, Armenia, and Moldova—refused to conduct it. Yet, more than 80 per cent of the total Soviet population did take part, and more than 76 per cent of them answered 'yes' to the question, 'Do you believe it essential to preserve the USSR as a renewed federation of equal sovereign republics in which the rights and freedoms of a person of any nationality will be fully guaranteed?' In the nine republics which held the referendum, support for this prop-osition was more than 70 per cent in every case, including Russia and Ukraine.[16] A momentous supplementary question attached to the ballot in the Russian republic asked voters whether they were in favour of having a directly elected president of their republic, and 70 per cent of them said 'yes'.

In order to get agreement on a new and voluntary Union Treaty, Gorbachev embarked on talks with the leaderships of the nine republics who had been prepared to cooperate in March to the extent of holding the referendum. The negotiations were held at the Novo-Ogarevo country house near Moscow and became known both as the 9 + 1 talks and as the Novo-Ogarevo process. Gorbachev was still General Secretary of the Communist Party, as well as President of the USSR, and to that limited extent the party was involved, but in essence the CPSU and its principal insti-tutions—the Politburo and the Secretariat of the Central Committee—were com-pletely bypassed. Gorbachev had succeeded in persuading Yeltsin and the Russian republic and Leonid Kravchuk representing Ukraine to take part in the talks, for the participation of the two gigantic Slavic territories (Russia, of course, in particular) was crucial for the viability of any treaty.

Four drafts were produced between November 1990 and August 1991, but only the versions agreed after the Novo-Ogarevo process was underway—specifically, those of June and August of 1991—were the product of negotiations fully involving the republics. Each draft devolved more power than did its predecessor, Yeltsin having been particularly difficult to satisfy at each stage. In the version that was published on 14 August and was due to be signed on 20 August 1991, the USSR no longer stood for the Union of Soviet Socialist Republics but for the Union of Soviet Sovereign Republics. It was the imminent signing of that document which determined the tim-ing of the attempted coup against Gorbachev.

International Politics before the Coup

The international organizational links between the Soviet Union and Eastern Europe ended in 1991. This was a logical consequence of the countries which composed East Europe acquiring their independence in 1989, followed by the disappearance of the GDR into the Federal Republic of Germany in 1990. There was no way that the cen-tral and east European former Communist states were going to coordinate their eco-nomic policies with their previous political overlord. Thus, to no-one's surprise, what Western observers called Comecon, and what was officially the Council for Mutual Economic Assistance (CMEA), was wound up on 28 June 1991 at a meeting in Budapest. The Warsaw Pact—Comecon's military-political equivalent, which had been the more formidable of the two institutions—was formally brought to an end by the member states, meeting in Prague on 1 July.

These decisions, which would have caused a sensation a few years earlier, produced hardly a ripple in international politics, although for the Soviet military and for Russian nationalists, they seemed like significant manifestations of their country's diminishing power. The big question—little raised at this point, still less answered—was: where does that leave NATO? And given that the countries which had in earlier years been Soviet satellites were now looking westwards, how and where would the Soviet Union, or Russia, fit into what Gorbachev called 'the common European home'?

Political turmoil in the Soviet Union—especially the tensions between a number of the republics and the centre, and the reciprocal antipathy between Yeltsin and Gorbachev—greatly weakened the Soviet negotiating position in 1991. When Gorbachev visited Japan in April, he hoped to improve Soviet–Japanese relations by persuading the Japanese to follow the path by which Willy Brandt and the Federal Republic of Germany improved relations with the Soviet Union (which ultimately led to a united Germany). In that way, he believed, a compromise agreement on the disputed Kurile islands (Japan's 'Northern territories' in the Tokyo version) could be reached. He was undermined by Yeltsin and those around him who insisted that the islands belonged to the Russian republic and so Gorbachev had no right to enter into negotiations affecting them.[17] Later that month Gorbachev wrote to Bush asking for a loan of $1.5 billion to the USSR for the purchase of American grain on the world market. Bush was dismissive of the request at a White House meeting with Baker, Scowcroft, and Treasury Secretary Nicholas Brady, saying, 'The guy doesn't seem to get it. He seems to think that we *owe* him economic help because we support him politically. We've got to give him a lesson in basic economics. Business is business.'[18] Speaking publicly, Bush said that 'regrettably' the Soviet Union had not begun the market reforms that 'I think Gorbachev aspires to' and that 'I know…Mr Yeltsin aspires to.'[19]

Gorbachev was bitterly disappointed, telling his aides that when they started the Gulf War, the US had 'no problem finding 100 billion', but 'when it's not a matter of going to war but assisting a new strategic partner it becomes problematic'.[20] The Soviet position was also being undermined by Yeltsin's team whose members had become more active internationally, as well as domestically, in opposition to Gorbachev. Andrey Kozyrev, who later in 1991 was to be appointed Russian (as distinct from Soviet) Minister of Foreign Affairs, travelled to Washington on Yeltsin's behalf in May and urged the US administration 'not to give any subsidies to the central government in Moscow, arguing that the credits would not be used efficiently'.[21] (Bush was pleasantly surprised when Yeltsin came to Washington and met him on 20 June, shortly after having been elected Russian president, and restrained his normal impulse to criticize Gorbachev, saying that he was ready to work with him, which was what the Bush administration wanted to hear.[22])

Margaret Thatcher, by now out of power and translated to the House of Lords as Lady Thatcher, tried to use what influence she had left. She came to Moscow in late May as a personal guest of the Gorbachevs, and gave a well-received speech to a thousand students at the elite international relations college, MGIMO, in the morning of 27 May. Ambassador Braithwaite was present and noted in his diary that Thatcher had been 'at her best'. She improvised on the theme of 'the importance to economic success of democracy and the rule of law' and said that if Russia could grow faster than America in the 1890s, there was no reason why it should not do so again.[23] That afternoon she had a two and a half hour meeting with Gorbachev—a lot of time for the Soviet leader, during a period of intense pressure, to spend with a *former* prime minister. This was followed by a meal in her honour with Mikhail and Raisa Gorbachev at their dacha on the same evening.

In the one-to-one afternoon meeting with Gorbachev, Thatcher was accompanied only by her favourite British interpreter, Richard Pollock, but a very full record of the meeting was kept by the Soviet side.[24] It was indicative of how good British–Soviet relations had become that when Braithwaite requested a copy of the Soviet transcript of the conversation, it was promptly delivered.[25] Gorbachev began the one-to-one with Thatcher by light-heartedly suggesting that it would be not a bad idea if she would 'agree to be prime minister here', for 'we could certainly work well together'.[26] (Since, both in the late Soviet and post-Soviet system, the prime minister ranked lower than the president, Gorbachev doubtless knew Margaret Thatcher well enough by this time to be aware how far-fetched was the idea of her happily adjusting to the role of number two. Somewhat more plausibly—*but* for the small matter of neither leader knowing the language of the other country—it was joked in the Soviet Union in 1990, with Thatcher still in power, that a straight swap between president and prime minister would be ideal, since Thatcher was now more popular in the Soviet Union than was Gorbachev and more popular there than in her own country, whereas Gorbachev was more popular in Britain than he was in the USSR and more popular in the UK than was Thatcher.)[27]

Gorbachev spoke frankly with Thatcher about the political problems he was encountering. He outlined what he was trying to do in getting an agreed division of powers between the federal centre and the republics. He told her also about how, when under fire at the Central Committee in April, he had threatened to resign, a majority of the members had drawn back from accepting his resignation through an 'instinct for self-preservation'. If the party had split then, he was sure that the larger and healthier part of it would have gone with him.[28] The two leaders discussed economic reform, and they moved on to the Soviet Union's relations with the United States. Gorbachev said that he had serious discussions with Bush, but that the complications of the current situation in the USSR were better understood in Europe than in America where Cold War stereotypes still persisted, including the view that the worse things were in the Soviet Union, the better for the United States.[29] Thatcher assured him that Bush, at any rate, was his 'strong supporter'.[30]

Jack Matlock, who had met Thatcher on several occasions when, as the Soviet specialist on the NSC, he had been the notetaker at some of her meetings with Ronald Reagan, did not expect her to remember him. It was, therefore, a surprise when Braithwaite called him to say she would like to discuss her meetings with Gorbachev with him. The British ambassador suggested that Matlock have dinner with them so that he would be on hand when Thatcher returned to the embassy after dining with the Gorbachevs at their dacha.[31] When the former prime minister arrived shortly before 10 in the evening, she lost no time in urging Matlock to 'get a message to my friend George'. 'We've got to help Mikhail', she said. 'Of course, you Americans can't and shouldn't have to do it all by yourselves, but George will have to lead the effort, just as he did with Kuwait.'[32]

She made a strong case, to which Matlock had some practical objections but with which he fundamentally agreed. 'Just a few years back', Thatcher said, 'Ron [Reagan] and I would have given the world to get what has already happened here.' Now that Gorbachev had played such a big part in ending the Cold War and changing so much in the Soviet Union, history would 'not forgive us' if other countries did not now come to his support. Her evening of conversation with Mikhail and Raisa Gorbachev had persuaded her that extensive private property rights would be forthcoming in the Soviet Union, though Gorbachev did not yet consider it timely to say so in public. Thatcher 'also had the impression', Matlock reported, that Gorbachev's political position had 'become desperate'. She was strongly in favour of his being invited to the G7 meeting of leaders of the major economic powers due to be held in London in July and that 'he not be sent home empty-handed'. Matlock argued that the Soviet Union still had 'no strategy for building the institutions necessary for a market system' and so to 'pour money into the country at this time would do no good and might do a lot of harm'. Thatcher glared at Matlock and told him he was talking like a diplomat, finding excuses for doing nothing. 'Why', she demanded, 'can't you think like a statesman? We need a political decision to support this process, which is so much in everyone's interest.'[33]

In spite of their apparent disagreement, both Thatcher's points and the American's response had substance. When Matlock returned to the ambassadorial residence, Spaso House, he drafted a telegram to the president conveying Thatcher's views and then wrote in his journal that he thought she had been right. Supporting openness and the movement toward democracy in the Soviet Union was in the West's 'vital interest', adding: 'Our leaders will simply be bereft of wisdom, or courage, or both, if they fail to respond to the challenge.'[34] Matlock noted that Bush wanted to support Gorbachev politically, but he lacked vision and was acting too cautiously.[35]

At the same time, there were genuine worries about the absence of a coherent economic policy in Moscow with Prime Minister Pavlov at odds with the market-oriented reformers. Moreover, there were many in the party and state bureaucracy who were now siphoning off national assets to enrich themselves or set up private ventures that would guarantee their future. Even a considerable portion of the large sums paid by the German government to cover the costs of finding accommodation for the several hundred thousand Soviet troops returning to the USSR did not reach those who needed it.

An internal Russian development with hugely consequential international implications was the direct election of Yeltsin as President of Russia on 12 June. On the same day two democratic reformers, Gavriil Popov and Anatoly Sobchak, were elected as mayors of Moscow and Leningrad, and in the latter city a majority voted also in favour of reverting to the old name of St Petersburg. Six candidates competed in the freely conducted presidential election, and there was no need for a second round, for Yeltsin won a clear majority on the first round with just over 57 per cent of the vote. Former prime minister of the Soviet Union Nikolay Ryzhkov came second and the clownish populist Vladimir Zhirinovsky (who continued to survive comfortably in the twenty-first century as a supporter of the presidential establishment) was third. The liberal former Minister of Internal Affairs Vadim Bakatin came bottom of the poll with 3.24 per cent. He suffered from still being a member of the Communist Party, albeit a very independent-minded one, at a time when the party had become discredited. In sharp contrast, Yeltsin's exit from the party the previous summer stood him in good stead.

The new Russian president lost no time in capitalizing on his enhanced authority. He wanted to be as much like an American president as possible (minus, as it later turned out, the checks and balances) and Gorbachev had to dissuade him from having a grand ceremony on Red Square at which he would take an oath of office with his hand on the bible. Gorbachev said they had millions of Islamic citizens, so why not the Koran—or the Torah in deference to citizens of Jewish religion?[36] Gorbachev did, however, grant Yeltsin's wish to occupy rooms in the Kremlin, that symbolic seat of Russian authority, albeit not—more precisely, not yet—its most prestigious part.

Just five days after Yeltsin was elected to the Russian presidency (and shortly after Thatcher's visit), Soviet Prime Minister Pavlov was a central figure in an attempt to curb Gorbachev's powers. Thus, Gorbachev had Yeltsin, on the one side, striving to weaken his powers and hand them to the republics, especially to the President of Russia with the enhanced legitimacy accorded him by popular election. On the other side were Pavlov, Chairman of the Supreme Soviet of the USSR Anatoly Lukyanov, KGB chief Kryuchkov, Minister of Internal Affairs Pugo, and Minister of Defence Yazov, all of them striving to strengthen the central government not only to put a stop to the growing assertiveness of the republics but also to weaken Gorbachev. On 17 June, in an open session of the Supreme Soviet of the USSR, Pavlov made a superficially plausible argument that because Gorbachev had too much to do, and was already working fourteen hours a day, the prime minister and the government should be given the right to initiate legislation, not least to deal with a deteriorating economic situation.[37]

The Supreme Soviet then went into closed session, but the speeches of Kryuchkov, Pugo, and Yazov were leaked by some members of the liberal minority within the legislature. The power ministers all spoke of the country being in crisis and Kryuchkov claimed that the CIA had over a lengthy period been recruiting Soviet citizens and seeing them move into leadership positions, so that the point had now been reached when Soviet policies had been 'devised across the ocean'. Yakovlev was already a bête noire of Soviet conservatives and they were aware that he had spent a year in New York and ten years in Canada. On this occasion, Kryuchkov did not mention him by name, but his audience knew which member of the top leadership team he had particularly in mind.[38] When he was seeking the chairmanship of the KGB, Kryuchkov had cultivated Yakovlev because of his closeness to Gorbachev, especially in the earlier years of perestroika, and Yakovlev, as he later rued, went on to recommend Gorbachev to appoint the future putschist to be head of the KGB.[39] Kryuchkov, needless to say, never acknowledged his debt to Yakovlev, thus not needing to explain why *he* should be the preferred choice as head of the Soviet intelligence agency of someone who was following the instructions of the CIA. Yakovlev, though, subsequently saw through Kryuchkov much earlier than Gorbachev did and, with good reason, he held that the general secretary had given the KGB chief more credence than he deserved.[40]

Pavlov and the government were granted the special powers the prime minister requested, with many of the Supreme Soviet deputies erroneously assuming that Gorbachev must have been aware of the move. But even as late as June 1991, Gorbachev could exercise his political authority. That became clear when he came to the Supreme Soviet on 21 June, said that Pavlov had overstepped the mark, and insisted on a reversal of the decision they had made four days earlier. The deputies duly complied. Gorbachev dealt gently with Pavlov in public, though was much more scathing in private.[41] He had already decided that Pavlov's appointment had been an error on his part and he had every intention of replacing him. He wished, however, to leave that until after the signing of the Union Treaty when, if the vice-president were a Russian, he believed the premiership should go to a prominent politician from a non-Russian republic to assist the task of holding the multinational Soviet state together by political means rather than coercion.

Embattled domestically, Gorbachev placed a lot of hope in the London G7 summit of mid-July, to which he had sought an invitation. Prime Minister John Major and most of the other leaders readily agreed to his request. Bush was hesitant, for he did not want to commit to economic help or to damage Gorbachev through a high-profile rejection of it.[42] It was agreed that the G7 leaders would have a special session with Gorbachev outside the main conference, though as Bush acknowledged, the lion's share of attention was on Gorbachev throughout the London event. The Soviet leader, noted Bush, made but one reference to financial assistance in his remarks. He referred to finding '$100 billion for a war', but was, Bush observed, evidently unaware 'that the Gulf countries, Japan, and others... had dug deeply to help defray the cost of the war'.[43] Oblivious to what lay in store for him just over a month later, Gorbachev told the G7 leaders in London on 17 July, 'We had a dramatic situation late last year and early this year. We had to maneuver between the ultra-radicals and those who would slow down or reverse reform.' Therefore, he had been, as he put it, 'playing for time' to preserve perestroika, with the intention not of suspending change but of radicalizing it.[44]

When Gorbachev and Bush met for a private discussion on 17 July in London, Matlock thought that, in spite of the good personal relationship they had already established, they were talking past each other.[45] Gorbachev spoke at excessive length—a persistent foible which many Russians by now held against him—and he did not fully appreciate how the lack of coherence of the economic policies emanating from Moscow was off-putting even for those in the West who believed that economic engagement might help keep the Soviet Union on the road to democracy.*

Hesitant though Bush was on economic support, he did take some risks with his domestic constituencies in order to assist Gorbachev politically when he visited the Soviet Union in late July and the beginning of August. Both Bush and Baker wanted Gorbachev to retain his presidential power and to succeed in creating and preserving a radically reformed and genuine federation. The only republics whose departure from the Soviet Union they desired were Estonia, Latvia, and Lithuania. Even in those cases, their preference was for this to happen as a result of dialogue between the Balts and Moscow. Before coming to the Soviet Union, Bush turned down an invitation from Landsbergis to include Lithuania in his itinerary, but he decided to make a brief visit to Kiev (Kyiv).** That was almost as sensitive a location, for in the months since March, when a majority of Ukrainians had expressed support in a referendum for their continuing membership of a reformed Soviet federation, nationalist sentiments had been fast developing.

Gorbachev told Bush that a Heritage Foundation report had recommended that the president visit Ukraine to encourage separatist sentiments there, to which Bush

---

* At a dinner with British politicians on the evening after the G-7 meeting, over which John Major had presided, Gorbachev, however, impressed his fellow professionals. He spoke about 'the sea change in international relationships' already achieved, about the need for transformation of the Soviet economy—but he could not go 'faster than the people will bear', and he was not prepared to use 'the forcible methods of the past'—and of his support for a market of a mixed economy type. The British, who listened with rapt attention, saw a man 'seriously devoted to overcoming the hideous difficulties that he and his country face', although Soviet ambassador to the UK Leonid Zamyatin and First Deputy Prime Minister Vladimir Shcherbakov whispered 'snide remarks to each other throughout' (Rodric Braithwaite, Diary 1988–1992 (manuscript), entry for 18 July 1991). According to Major, and again in contrast with the one-to-one with Bush, Gorbachev's dinner discussion with the G-7 leaders the previous evening 'was even more successful' than that of 18 July (ibid.).

** Kiev is a transliteration of the Russian spelling and Kyiv transliterates the Ukrainian name of the capital city. Throughout the Soviet period, in Kiev and many Ukrainian cities (as distinct from the countryside), Russian was spoken more than Ukrainian. Kiev became the standard spelling in the English language, and remained so during the entire Soviet period, including, therefore, the perestroika years.

Figure 22 Gorbachev in conversation with Bush at 1991 summit at Novo-Ogarevo (near Moscow), July 1991. On right is US National Security Adviser Scowcroft, on left US interpreter Zarechnak, and Soviet interpreter Palazchenko (speaking).

responded that he was unaware of that report, and 'in no way do I intend to support separatism'. Kiev was included in his itinerary only after Foreign Minister Aleksandr Bessmertnykh had said that the Soviet side was 'completely satisfied with this choice'.[46] The president assured Gorbachev that, when in Ukraine, he would do nothing to exacerbate his problems. The American media, Bush observed, had moved on from criticizing him for being excessively cautious about engaging with the Soviet Union to accusing him of being 'too fond of Gorbachev, almost like Thatcher'.[47] For his part, Gorbachev told the president that the new Union Treaty, agreed between the centre and the republics, would be incorporated in a rewritten Soviet Constitution.[48]

One reason, among many, the Bush administration wished to see the greater part of the Soviet Union hold together (though with an unprecedented devolution of power to the republics) was that the USSR, in the person of Gorbachev and his closest associates, had become constructive partners in arms control negotiations. A centrepiece of the 1991 Moscow summit meeting of Gorbachev and Bush was the signing of the Strategic Arms Reduction Treaty (START) by the two leaders on 31 July. This limited the number of nuclear warheads each side could deploy to a maximum of 6,000 (quite fearsome enough) and also restricted each country to a total of 1,600 intercontinental ballistic missiles and bombers. This agreement had been long in the making, and the Bush administration did not wish it to be endangered by disintegration and chaos on the territory of the Soviet Union and the dreadful possibility of 'loose nukes'.

At the first of their meetings on 30 July, Gorbachev brought up, as he frequently did, the COCOM* restrictions on sale of high-technology equipment to the Soviet Union. These were so extensive that, as Gorbachev had remarked to Bush's predecessor, he could hardly fail to be sceptical of Reagan's professed desire to share SDI with the Soviet Union, if and when it had been established that it would work. On this occasion Bush was non-committal, but said that it could be a legacy of the Cold War and that they would look into it.[49] The following day, Bush (accompanied by Baker and Scowcroft) continued a wide-ranging discussion with Gorbachev in the more relaxed surroundings of Novo-Ogarevo. Built in Khrushchev's time, it served the same purpose for Soviet leaders as Camp David does for American presidents and Chequers (the least informal of the three) for British prime ministers.

In the middle of Bush's 31 July conversation with Gorbachev at Novo-Ogarevo, the American delegation received word from the US Embassy, which Baker read out to the meeting, that 'unknown assailants had attacked a Lithuanian customs post during

---

* COCOM stands for the Co-ordinating Committee for Multilateral Export Controls. A group of seventeen Western countries headed by the United States not only imposed an arms embargo on Comecon countries, but also a ban on export of goods that might be of military use, as well as products deemed to be of an excessively high-tech nature to be appropriate for export to a country in the Communist bloc. Armaments apart, it was not unreasonable for Gorbachev to argue that many of those prohibitions were anachronistic at a time when there was already no Comecon or Warsaw Pact.

the night and brutally murdered all six customs officers'.[50] Gorbachev was outraged by the shooting and embarrassed that it had been brought to his attention by the Americans rather than by Soviet ministers or officials. Gorbachev immediately told Chernyaev to go and call Kryuchkov to find out what had happened. The KGB chief got the number of deaths wrong—he said four, whereas the Associated Press report, which had been Baker's source, correctly said six—and came up with three implausible versions of who might have been responsible, none of which involved the Soviet power ministries.[51] Palazchenko, who was interpreting the conversation, wrote: 'The sense all of us had then...was that it was a cruel provocation in order to, at the very least, mar the summit and make Gorbachev look bad—helpless and embarrassed—on what ought to have been his day of triumph.'[52]

The feeling of triumph should have been all the greater because the night before Bush arrived in Moscow, Gorbachev had met in Novo-Ogarevo with Yeltsin, as President of Russia, and with Nursultan Nazazarbayev, who was both first secretary of the Communist Party in Kazakhstan and president of the republic's Supreme Soviet. They hammered out an agreement on the main lines of the Union Treaty and they discussed also the need for changes in the federal government. The three leaders agreed that it would be necessary to remove from their posts various conservative members of the federal government after the ceremony of signing the Union Treaty which was due to take place on 20 August. They were at one in their view that Prime Minister Pavlov, KGB Chairman Kryuchkov, Minister of Internal affairs Pugo, Vice-President Yanaev, and Defence Minister Yazov would be among those to be removed. What Gorbachev did not know, but what Yeltsin correctly suspected, was that the KGB, on Kryuchkov's instructions, had bugged the room in which they met and recorded their entire conversation (which did not conclude until 3 o'clock in the morning).[53] Once Kryuchkov had shared with the others scheduled to lose their offices what was on the way, they had a strong personal as well as political incentive to prevent the Union Treaty from being signed.

In his conversation with Bush, Gorbachev noted the part played by transformative change of the Soviet political system and of foreign policy in stimulating democratic developments not only in the USSR but elsewhere, saying that 'totalitarian and authoritarian regimes are on their way out' and that this flowed from the changes in the Soviet Union which they wanted to continue. What remained necessary was keeping this process 'in a constitutional and legal framework' and not allowing it 'to spill over into turmoil and chaos', for that would have dangerous consequences.[54] When the discussion turned to South Africa, Bush tried to persuade Gorbachev to give up Soviet support for Nelson Mandela, whom he saw as 'out of touch'. The president complained about Mandela's respectful attitude to Gaddafi and Castro, which he found 'impossible to understand'.[55] It was, in fact, quite simple to understand. Those leaders had consistently supported the fight against apartheid of the African National Congress (ANC). While Mandela was, as he subsequently demonstrated, an

Figure 23 Margaret Thatcher and Mikhail Gorbachev in 1989. On left of the picture British ambassador to Moscow Sir Rodric Braithwaite; between Thatcher and Gorbachev is interpreter Richard Pollock.

exceptionally inclusive democratic leader, who chose to serve only one term as president (thus utterly different from Gaddafi and Castro), he remained grateful to the Cubans, in particular, for their staunch support for the ANC. Bush, however, wanted Gorbachev to do more to support South African State President F. W. de Klerk.[56]

When the discussion turned to the implementation of arms control agreements, Soviet Foreign Minister Bessmertnykh and Secretary of State Baker played prominent parts. Bessmertnykh brought up the practical problem of finding locations in which to destroy chemical weapons. Gorbachev added that one plant used for this purpose in Armenia had been shut down, one of well over a thousand factories closed through the pressure of the 'green bloc'. Gorbachev himself was extremely alert to ecological concerns. When Baker asked whether chemical weapons could not be disposed of 'somewhere in the Arctic', Gorbachev replied, 'That would be even worse.' Scientists had warned that it was 'a place where the ecological balance cannot be disturbed under any circumstances'.[57]

Gorbachev was rapidly approaching the end of his time in power (although he did not yet know it), but his intellectual and political horizons were much longer than those of most heads of government. Earlier in the discussion, he had raised 'the problem of resources, water, the environment, demographic processes that could lead to a doubling of the Earth's population in 30–50 years'. He posed the question of 'what role should our countries play' in dealing with these realities and tendencies.[58] It was not a question that Bush, who was scarcely thinking any further ahead than the US presidential election of 1992, chose to answer.

Bush was, however, as good as his word to Gorbachev when he spoke in Kiev the day after the Novo-Ogarevo meeting, though what he said brought him acerbic criticism at home which was carried into the presidential election campaign. The speech he made in the Ukrainian parliament on 1 August was poorly received by the nationalist deputies (who were still outnumbered by Communists) and by the leaders of the separatist movement, Rukh. Ukrainian public opinion had turned against Gorbachev, and the welcoming crowds for Bush were pro-American and hostile to Moscow. Some carried posters in English with wording such as 'Moscow has 15 colonies' and 'The empire of evil is living.'[59] In his speech, Bush said that there were those who 'have urged the United States to choose between supporting President Gorbachev and supporting independence-minded leaders throughout the U.S.S.R', and this he considered to be 'a false choice'. He went out of his way to praise Gorbachev who 'has achieved astonishing things' with glasnost, perestroika, and democratization and movement 'toward the goals of freedom, democracy and economic liberty'.[60] That was clearly not what Rukh wanted to hear, although it was Gorbachev who had opened the door for their political activity which had long been kept firmly shut by Ukrainian party officials such as the old Brezhnevite Volodymyr Shcherbytsky. As party first secretary in Ukraine, Shcherbytsky had maintained Leninist discipline, aided and abetted by such party officials as Leonid Kravchuk, who had risen through the ranks of the Ukrainian party bureaucracy to become propaganda chief.[61] As Speaker of the Parliament (and future Ukrainian president), Kravchuk in 1991 was in the process of reinventing himself as a champion of his nation's independence.

Bush's address became more notorious after New York Times columnist William Safire labelled it the 'Chicken Kiev' speech (which subsequently become the standard way of identifying it). Safire's statement that the president had been 'foolishly placing Washington on the side of Moscow centralism and against the tide of history' was a misrepresentation. Bush had made clear that what he wished to see was a negotiated agreement between the federal centre and the republics. Indeed, he had been told by Boris Yeltsin, whom he met separately from Gorbachev, that 'all the Union Treaty problems have been resolved' and that the Treaty would be 'open for signature' in August.[62] The president told his Kiev audience that the US would 'not try to pick winners and losers' between one Soviet republic and another or between republics and the centre, for that was 'not the business of the United States of America'.[63]

A passage in Bush's speech which went down particularly badly with nationalists was the observation that 'freedom is not the same as independence' and that 'Americans will not support those who seek independence in order to replace a far-off tyranny with a local despotism. They will not aid those who promote a suicidal nationalism based upon ethnic hatred.'[64] That separate statehood neither equates with nor guarantees freedom is no more than an elementary political truth. Bush's observation could be seen as a warning against nationalist extremism, but it was hardly a contemporary commentary either on Rukh, which was pursuing its political aims by peaceful means, or on the Gorbachev-led Soviet leadership (which Bush was far from viewing as a 'tyranny', even if some Ukrainians with short memories did so). Safire, whose columns displayed minimal understanding either of the way change had come about in the Soviet Union or of the intensity of the cross-pressures between which Gorbachev manoeuvred, benefited in his 'Chicken Kiev' article from hindsight. His column appeared on 29 August 1991, a week *after* the coup against Gorbachev had failed. The collapse of the coup gave a huge boost to national separatism and, for a time at least, put conservative supporters of authoritarianism on the defensive. Bush was speaking several weeks *before* the coup when it was not unreasonable to hope (although even then uncertain) that a voluntary agreement would be reached between a majority of republics (including Ukraine) and the centre and that Gorbachev, a man the president much preferred to Yeltsin, would still be the principal foreign-policy-maker.

Crisis of the Party and the State

Neither the Bush administration nor, more importantly, Gorbachev himself realized just how menacing was a document published on 23 July in the newspaper, *Sovetskaya Rossiya*. Called 'A Word to the People', it was essentially an advance justification for the overthrow of Gorbachev, as well as of his allies in the country's leadership, together with the abandonment of the policies they had espoused. What made the declaration so serious was that the signatories included senior members of the government and of the armed forces.

The 'Word' was drafted by a Russian nationalist writer with close ties to the military, Aleksandr Prokhanov, and signed by two other nationalist authors, Valentin Rasputin (who the previous year had been a member of Gorbachev's short-lived Presidential Council), and Yury Bondarev, who at the Nineteenth Party Conference in 1988 had compared 'our perestroika' to an aircraft which had taken to the air without any knowledge of where it would land.[65] Those who put their name to the declaration included General Boris Gromov, who had earlier commanded the Soviet army in Afghanistan and, at the time he signed this letter, was First Deputy Minister of Internal Affairs. He was an atypical signatory inasmuch as he was not a participant in the coup against Gorbachev the following month. A less surprising name was that of General Valentin Varennikov, a Deputy Minister of Defence and an admirer of Stalin. The statement attacked unnamed leaders of the Communist Party who were destroying their own party and handing power to 'frivolous and clumsy parliamentarians'. In a thinly disguised reference to Gorbachev, the document (published just a week after Gorbachev's meeting with the G7 leaders in London) asked rhetorically how the country had allowed into power those 'who seek advice and blessings across the seas'. The signatories expressed their conviction that the army would not allow the destruction of the fatherland and would act as 'a reliable guarantor of security and as the mainstay of all the healthy forces of society'.[66]

Whereas Gorbachev in 1987 had been able to dismiss scores of senior military officers, including the Minister of Defence and Politburo member Marshal Sergey Sokolov, for allowing a harmless light aircraft piloted by a young West German to fly unhindered to Moscow and land on the edge of Red Square, by late July 1991 his power and authority were incomparably diminished. He was thus inhibited from ordering the instant dismissal of Gromov and Varennikov from their ministerial offices, which their insubordination and thinly veiled threats merited. Gorbachev was biding his time until a different coalition could be constructed, following the signing of the Union Treaty. Then, he would be able to sweep aside all the hard-liners with whom he had taken a step back in the winter of 1990–1 before taking two steps forward with the 9 + 1 talks in April.

In the run-up to the August coup, Gorbachev had also been lulled into a false sense of security by the relative ease with which he persuaded the Central Committee of the CPSU to give its imprimatur to a social democratic draft party programme. That document was published on 23 July (the same day as 'A Word to the People') and approved as a basis for discussion at an extraordinary Party Congress meant to take place in November.[67] Although some amendments were accepted in response to con-servative Communist objections, the Central Committee approved the draft pro-gramme by 358 votes to 13. Almost certainly, a majority of those who voted for the programme had no intention of implementing it, since they subsequently either posi-tively welcomed the attempt to overthrow Gorbachev the following month or did nothing to interfere with it. If there had been no coup, the likelihood is that the party would have split irrevocably at that 'Twenty-Ninth Congress' (a congress that never took place, for the August coup, and its defeat, so transformed the political atmosphere in the country that the party itself had ceased to exist before the summer was over).

Some of Gorbachev's advisers (notably Shakhnazarov and also Yakovlev, who resigned as a senior adviser to the president on 28 July but rejoined him immediately after the failed coup) thought that the split was overdue. For his part, Gorbachev regarded the party programme as the optimal means for effecting a 'civilized divorce' between socialists of a social democratic type and unreconstructed Communists who (along with a variety of other tendencies) now constituted the main currents within the CPSU, an institution which still had approximately 15 million members in July 1991, although that meant the membership had dropped by more than 4 million over the previous eighteen months.[68]

The summer of 1991 saw Gorbachev engaged in an epic struggle to preserve the union by peaceful means. Yet, he devoted a lot of time to the content of the party programme, bypassing most of the official CPSU structures and relying especially on Shakhnazarov and Ivan Frolov (his former aide, now *Pravda* editor) for its composition.

The draft programme spoke of the 'conversion of the Soviet multinational state into a democratic federation of sovereign republics'. It embraced a multiparty political system, separation of powers, a mixed ownership economic system and 'regulated market economy', the rule of law, and working exclusively 'within the framework of parliamentary democracy'.[69]

In his speech to the Central Committee plenary session commending the draft programme, Gorbachev went further than the document. He said that the previous theoretical and practical model of socialism had proved to be bankrupt and, so far as the economy was concerned, socialism and the market were not only compatible but fundamentally indivisible. He accused those who expressed concern about the 'social-democratization of the CPSU' of 'communist fundamentalism', and he argued that the old criteria for confrontation with social democrats had lost their former meaning. He accepted that in future the Communist Party could lose office, in which case they must confine themselves to political methods and 'form a constructive opposition', supporting a government's 'sensible measures' and opposing when that was necessary for 'the defence of working people'.[70]

These aspirations were to be rendered void by the coup and its consequences. Even before then the deep divisions within the party mattered less to many Russians and non-Russians within the USSR than the struggle for national sovereignty and for a notion of 'democracy' which linked it with the rapid achievement of Western standards of material prosperity and a domestic change of ruling elite. The inverted commas are used because while the non-party opposition included genuine democrats who understood very well that meaningful democracy involved such principles as the rule of law, free and fair elections, an independent judiciary, party contestation, and protection of minorities, there were numerous self-proclaimed 'democrats' who had much less of a grasp of what democracy entailed than those counterparts in the broad democratic movement—much less also than had Gorbachev. A scholarly study of their documents and belief systems concluded that traditional Soviet ideology had exercised a more profound influence on the political outlook of 'democratic' activists than they themselves realized. Many of them, far from seeing democracy as involving compromise, accommodation of different groups and interests, and a separation of powers, viewed it 'as the unlimited power of the "democrats" replacing the unlimited power of the Communists'. They were also suspicious of state power as such and were ill-equipped to create the institutional structures of a democratic state or to appreciate that without state power—accountable state power—there can be no democracy.[71]

The August Coup

From Kryuchkov's recording of Gorbachev's meeting with Yeltsin and Nazarbayev, the hard-liners knew that their days were numbered, and that they had better strike before the signing of the Union Treaty if they wanted to save themselves and (so they believed) the Soviet Union. As it turned out, they became accomplices in the complete destruction of any kind of union among the fifteen republics which had composed the USSR. Before the attempted coup, there was still a distinct possibility that more than half of the republics, including the geographically and numerically most important ones, would join a voluntary federation with so much power devolved to them as to come close to a confederation. With, however, the conservative and reactionary opposition to Gorbachev by now placing far more emphasis on Soviet statehood than on ideology, there was plenty of support for their 'Word to the People' sentiments within the 'power ministries' and in the Central Committee of the CPSU. At the same Central Committee session which, to all appearances, condoned the draft party programme, two reformist members, Andrei Grachev and Otto Latsis, were shouted down when they explicitly attacked 'A Word to the People'.[72]

The fourth draft of the Union Treaty, published on 14 August, promised still greater devolution of power from the centre to the republics.[73] It was to be signed in Moscow on 20 August. Gorbachev had flown to the Crimea on 4 August for a much-needed holiday (which, as usual, he combined with work on speeches and other writing). He was accompanied by his family and close aides. He was due to return to Moscow on 19 August in time for the signing of the Treaty the following day. At the official holiday complex at Foros, on the Black Sea coast, Gorbachev swam every day, but also worked with his aides, especially Chernyaev, on a long article on the situation in the country (in which, ahead of the coup, he had explicitly rejected the idea of declaring a state of emergency) and on his speech to be delivered at the Union Treaty ceremony (of which Shakhnazarov wrote the first draft).[74]

On the afternoon of 18 August, Chernyaev handed Gorbachev the latest retyped version of the Treaty speech, with their final amendments incorporated, about one hour before a delegation of the coup plotters arrived to present Gorbachev with an ultimatum—either back their self-appointed State Committee for the State of Emergency or resign. Gorbachev flatly refused to do either. The next day the 'State Committee' announced to Soviet citizens and the outside world that the president was too incapacitated to carry out his duties.[75] In reality, aged 60, Gorbachev was remarkably fit, robust, and resilient.

Unquestionably, it was the imminence of the signing of the draft Union Treaty which determined the precise timing of the coup.[76] Gorbachev and his family (as well as Chernyaev) were not allowed to leave Foros or communicate with the outside world. Gorbachev kept his own bodyguards, who remained loyal to him, but a larger outer ring of guards brought in by the putschists surrounded the perimeter. Ships took up positions just off the coast to make sure there was no escape route by sea. On his arrival on 4 August, Chernyaev found that he had not been allocated his usual quarters in the 'Yuzhny' complex of superior Foros accommodation close to Gorbachev's dacha, but assigned less comfortable rooms some considerable distance away. KGB General Yury Plekhanov, the person responsible for the security of Soviet political leaders, had taken that decision and refused to budge when Chernyaev complained. He was, moreover, 'touchy and rude' in contrast with his former 'lackey-like' behaviour.[77] The Communist Party, however, still retained some residual authority over the security organs and Chernyaev went over Plekhanov's head to the latter's Central Committee overseer, Oleg Kruchina, whom he had known for years, and prevailed upon him to overrule Plekhanov.*

Chernyaev moved into his usual Foros accommodation, located just 50 metres away from Gorbachev's, which meant that a fortnight later—in contrast with, for example, Shakhnazarov and Primakov who, lodged somewhat further away, succeeded in returning to Moscow shortly after it became apparent that their communications with Gorbachev had been cut off—he was stuck within the cordoned-off area and unable to leave the complex once the putschists, and their contingent of armed guards, had arrived. One useful result was that Chernyaev was subsequently able to corroborate Gorbachev's account of his reaction to this sudden house arrest and of the way Anatoly Virgansky, the husband of the Gorbachevs' daughter Irina, managed to secretly film at night his father-in-law's statements condemning the coup. As a perceptive observer and indefatigable scribe, Chernyaev was also to add important details of his own on the nature of their captivity and on how different members of the Gorbachev family responded to the shock.[78]

The coup began for Gorbachev when he was told that a delegation to see him had arrived out of the blue. He picked up first one telephone and then another to find out more. All six, including the one for use in his capacity of commander-in-chief of the armed forces, were dead. The deputation made their way, uninvited, to Gorbachev's part of the residence, led by Plekhanov, whom Gorbachev immediately ordered out. Plekhanov obeyed. CPSU secretary Oleg Baklanov, the overseer of military industry, acted as if he were the senior figure in the group. He tried to persuade Gorbachev to let the 'State Committee' do the 'dirty work', after which the president would be free to return to Moscow. Gorbachev categorically rejected their blend of coercion and cajolery. As he wrote a few weeks later, 'I told them where to go in the language that Russian people use in such circumstances.'[79] That Gorbachev did not mince his words was confirmed by General Varennikov (earlier a leading figure in the violent overnight crackdowns in Soviet republics and a signatory to 'A Word to the People') who saw fit to complain to the legal investigator of his case that Gorbachev had used 'unparliamentary expressions' in addressing him and the other members of the delegation.[80]

The attempted overthrow of Gorbachev and reversal of the policies he had pursued, which had begun for him on 18 August, became known to the rest of the country

---

* Even though he was not part of the plot to topple Gorbachev, Kruchina committed suicide a few days after the coup failed by jumping from the window of his apartment. He was, however, the person in charge of the party finances and involved in siphoning funds in various directions which would not stand up to critical examination, now that it was clear that they would become the subject of hostile scrutiny. In a suicide note, Kruchina wrote that he was not a conspirator but that he was a coward.

only on the morning of 19 August. Soviet citizens woke up to an announcement that a state of emergency had been declared, accompanied by the lie that Gorbachev was too ill to be able to carry out his duties. One of the many accusations levelled against Gorbachev by his conservative opponents was that he was indecisive and irresolute (in later years some of them upgraded this to 'traitor'). But when they attempted to seize power, the putschists themselves were remarkably indecisive, irresolute, and disorganized. They allowed Yeltsin to make his way to the Russian White House which was at that time the home of the Russian parliament. Although they had cut off all Gorbachev's communications, they failed to prevent communication with the Russian parliamentary building, and Yeltsin was able to hold telephone conversations with foreign leaders. Tens of thousands of Muscovites, horrified by the attempted coup, surrounded the White House. Many of them stayed there all night during the three days the coup lasted. Their presence raised the political cost of storming the building and of arresting Yeltsin. With the legitimacy of his recent election fortifying him in the eyes of Russians and the outside world, Yeltsin became the visible face of resistance to the coup. Tanks were brought into the Moscow city centre, but their commanders had been affected by the changed atmosphere of recent years and they were reluctant to fire on their own people. Indeed, the order to do so never came from Minister of Defence Yazov. If Varennikov had been in charge, it might have been a different matter, but Yazov, who was berated by his wife for allowing himself to be drawn into this escapade, soon came to regret his involvement. Varennikov, in contrast, urged more decisive measures for 'the liquidation of the group of the adventurist Yeltsin'.[81]

When some of the self-styled Committee members held a press conference on 19 August, it did them more harm than good. Yanaev, as acting president, repeated the lie that Gorbachev was ill and so he, as vice-president, had assumed the presidential powers. But his shaky hands and trembling voice betrayed unease. Those around him made no more favourable an impression. One absentee was Prime Minister Pavlov, who had drunk himself into a stupor. Several of the commanders and tank crews in the centre of Moscow, including some at the Russian White House, switched sides and gave their support to those in the Russian parliament who were opposing the putsch. When Yeltsin emerged from the White House and denounced the coup from the top of a tank, this became a defining image of the resistance and of the putschists' impending defeat.

Chernyaev, however, was among those who thought that the coup failed on day one, when on 18 August Gorbachev refused to collaborate in any way with the plotters who had believed they could either persuade or intimidate him into acquiescence with their restoration of order. They had hopes also of using the distrust between Gorbachev and Yeltsin to enlist one against the other. Neither politician took the bait. For the few days the coup lasted, so did the solidarity between the Soviet and Russian presidents. Yet, the failure of the putschists was not preordained, even if in the longer run they would have encountered vast problems. Greater ruthlessness on their part—of the kind displayed by Deng Xiaoping when he ordered the clearing of demonstrators from Tiananmen Square in Beijing in 1989 with whatever level of force was required—would have been one way of turning the clock back. A more sophisticated approach might have been *not* to bring troops into the centre of Moscow at all. Both an active putschist, Pavlov, once he had sobered up, and an active opponent, Aleksandr Yakovlev, who had made his way to the Russian White House to join the resistance, believed that without the troops and armoured vehicles (which ran over and killed three young men, provoking outrage), 'the resistance would have been much less focused and the overall impression much more business as usual'.[82] If that had been combined with the arrest and isolation of Yeltsin as speedily as Gorbachev was isolated, this might have worked. Enthusiasm for Yeltsin was still high at the time, and it is an open question whether the desire for stability, order, and even the late Brezhnevite level of material provision would have prevailed over the belief that democracy plus economic reform presaged a better future. Unarmed protesters, or a weighing up of popular reactions, would hardly have been insuperable obstacles to a more efficiently conducted military-political coup.

The coup collapsed on 21 August. A combination of the resistance of Gorbachev and of Yeltsin and the irresolution and incoherence of the putschists led the plotters to conclude that the game was up. When it became known that a group of them were flying to Foros to speak with Gorbachev, Raisa Gorbachev feared that it was with the aim of making her husband's health as bad as they had told the world it was. She suffered a stroke (or mini-stroke) and lost the power in one arm for a time. Her health never totally recovered from the Foros ordeal and her fears during those days for the safety of her husband and family.[83] The putschists flew to Foros with the hope of mitigating the consequences of their actions. Gorbachev refused to see those who had incontrovertibly been part of the coup—most notably, Baklanov, Kryuchkov, and Yazov. They were put in different aircraft for their return to Moscow, and Kryuchkov and Yazov were immediately arrested on their arrival. Because Baklanov was a member of the USSR Supreme Soviet, his arrest had to await the removal of his parliamentary immunity which was duly rescinded.

Gorbachev did agree while still at Foros to see Chairman of the USSR Supreme Soviet Anatoly Lukyanov, whom he had known, although they were never close, since they were both students at Moscow University. Lukyanov's involvement in the coup was at the time less certain, but Gorbachev berated him for not standing up to the putschists, with whom, as it later transpired, he had been more than a passive collaborator. Another plane brought to Foros the far friendlier faces of those who had actively resisted the coup—Primakov, former Minister of Interior Vadim Bakatin, and two members of Yeltsin's team, Vice-President of Russia Aleksandr Rutskoy and Ivan Silayev. When those emissaries, along with Gorbachev and his family and immediate entourage, were on a flight back to Moscow during the night of 21/22

August, Kryuchkov was put at the back of the aircraft between armed guards as a discouragement to pro-putsch forces who might conceivably be tempted to shoot the plane down.

While the coup lasted, only two foreign heads of government wholeheartedly welcomed it—Saddam Hussein in Iraq and Muammar Gaddafi in Libya. Some Western leaders were more categorical in their condemnation from the moment they learned of the coup than others, none more vigorously so than Felipe González, although John Major also took a strong line from the outset.[84] González called Bush and said he should demand that the putschists 'allow telephone communication with Gorbachev', adding: 'Above all, don't refer to Gorbachev in the past tense!'[85] President Bush's initial response was characteristically cautious. Concerned though he was for Gorbachev's safety, both at a personal level and at the prospect of dealing with a very different Soviet Union, he and Baker still wanted to keep lines of communication open with the Soviet authorities, whoever they might be, in order to safeguard as much as possible of the agreements reached since Bush became president. Neither man dared assume that the putschists would be as incompetent, especially in failing to isolate Yeltsin, as they turned out to be.* Nevertheless, Bush's initial description of the coup as 'extra-constitutional' and 'a disturbing development' seemed unduly mild.[86] He was influenced by Scowcroft who urged caution. The National Security Adviser, noting that on 19 August they 'didn't know the current status of the coup', wrote, 'The President's inclination was to condemn it outright, but if it turned out to be successful, we would be forced to live with the new leaders, however repulsive their behavior.'[87] Of the Western leaders who had good relations with Gorbachev, the first to write him off and accept 'the new Soviet leaders' while the coup was underway was François Mitterrand. He was criticized within France for suggesting, during Gorbachev's Crimean isolation, that it would be possible to do business with those who had taken power if they continued to pursue economic and political change.[88]

Unsurprisingly, Margaret Thatcher, although no longer in office, rallied to the support of Gorbachev and of Yeltsin, since the latter, to her surprise during the days of the coup, turned out to be contactable. She was 'dismayed by the willingness of some Western leaders apparently to "wait and see" whether the coup leaders were successful'. She held a press conference and gave a series of interviews. She declared that what had happened in Russia was unconstitutional and they should not assume that it would succeed. The Russian people should 'now take their lead from Boris Yeltsin as the leading democratically elected politician'.[89] Thatcher wanted to speak by

---

* They did not manage to isolate even Gorbachev from independent sources of information. First of all, his bodyguards found some old radios in the service area of the building, fixed up aerials and began to pick up foreign broadcasts, especially the BBC and Radio Liberty. His son-in-law Anatoly Virgansky also succeeded in listening to Western stations on his pocket Sony radio. Thus, Gorbachev and those with him learned of the resistance to the coup in the Soviet Union and of its condemnation in other countries.

phone to Gorbachev but was told by the Soviet ambassador to London, Leonid Zamyatin (who supported the coup and was later recalled from his post) that this was impossible.

Informed by a Russian-speaking Conservative member of the European parliament, Nicholas Bethell, that Galina Staravoitova (an academic ethnographer who became active in the democratic movement, especially as a defender of minority national rights and who had recently become an adviser to Yeltsin) was in London, Thatcher immediately asked Staravoitova and Bethell to come and brief her. She told them that she had tried and failed to speak to Gorbachev, whereupon Staravoitova* asked her if she would like to speak to Yeltsin instead. When Thatcher accepted the suggestion with alacrity, Staravoitova searched through her handbag and produced the direct line to Yeltsin's office in the Russian White House. After several failed attempts, the former British prime minister was—'to my astonishment'—put through.[90] With Bethell interpreting, she had a lengthy conversation with Yeltsin in which the Russian president asked her to 'chair a commission of doctors to investigate the truth about Mr Gorbachev's allegedly poor health'. She promptly agreed to do so and spent the rest of the day liaising with the Foreign Office and the UK Department of Health 'to compile a suitable list of distinguished doctors'.[91] The question of their access was never put to the test, for the coup was soon crumbling.

From Coup to Collapse

Within the USSR itself, most of the leaders of the republics were shocked and alarmed, although some temporized during the coup. One who did so was Leonid Kravchuk in Ukraine who had received a visit from the formidable General Varennikov. In a television interview on 19 August Kravchuk indicated that he was ready to cooperate with the new 'central authorities', observing that 'What had to happen has now happened.'[92] When the coup collapsed, he promptly resumed his rapid transition from orthodox Communist to cheerleader for Ukrainian independence.[93]

Among highly placed officials in Ukraine, it was, in fact, an ethnic Russian from Kharkiv in eastern Ukraine, himself a supporter of preserving the union, deputy speaker Volodymyr Hryniov who took the firmest stand against the putschists, going on the radio on the morning of 19 August to condemn the coup 'in the strongest possible terms'.[94] The incentives to seek separate statehood had, however, become stronger for those in every republic who did not wish for a return to the pre-perestroika political order. Although the coup collapsed after a few days, the knowledge that the old strictly centralized, highly authoritarian system might well have been reintroduced,

---

* Staravoitova continued to be a courageous and independent-minded politician and campaigner in post-Soviet Russia. She was assassinated just outside her St Petersburg apartment in November 1998.

speeded up the dissolution of the USSR—ironically, since putting a stop to the separatist process had been at the very top of the putschists' agenda.

Most Soviet ambassadors either actively supported the coup or supinely acquiesced with it, in preference to speaking out against those who had forcibly seized power. A typical example was Nikolay Uspensky, the ambassador to Sweden who had been an interpreter for Gorbachev before the Soviet leader rightly (from every point of view) replaced him by Palazchenko. Uspensky announced that the removal of Gorbachev was understandable and that the 'new authorities' had acted properly.[95] His predecessor in Sweden, Boris Pankin, who by 1991 was the Soviet envoy to Czechoslovakia, acted differently. His reward for taking the risk of coming out against the coup while it was still in progress was a massive promotion to the post of Soviet Foreign Minister. The vacancy in that office occurred because Gorbachev dismissed Bessmertnykh once he discovered that he had not come out openly against those who were keeping him isolated in Foros. Although Bessmertnykh certainly did not support the putschists, he had declined to join his fellow-members of the Security Council Bakatin and Primakov in signing an open letter, which the latter two had composed, condemning the putsch while Gorbachev was still being held prisoner on the Crimean coast.[96] (In the post-Soviet period, Bessmertnykh re-established good relations with Gorbachev and took part in a number of conferences chaired by the former Soviet leader on perestroika and on the end of the Cold War.)

Among the fatal casualties of the coup was Marshal Akhromeyev. Some eight months earlier he had been one of twenty Soviet marshals and generals who had delivered a handwritten ultimatum to Gorbachev which reflected their concern about the growing assertiveness of oppositional and centrifugal forces and warned against the loss of any part of the Soviet Union.[97] Akhromeyev had struggled with a conflict of loyalties—to Gorbachev whom he had advised, to the Communist Party to which he had long belonged, to the Soviet army in which he had served from the Second World War onwards, and to the Soviet state in which he deeply believed. The last three loyalties overrode the first. Akhromeyev had not been involved in the organization of the coup, but when it occurred, he flew from Sochi to Moscow to lend his support. Following the failure to restore the old order, the 67-year-old marshal hanged himself on 24 August. In a suicide note, he wrote: 'I cannot live when my Fatherland is dying, and everything that has been the meaning of my life is crumbling.'[98] His death in this manner saddened not only his Russian admirers but his American interlocutors from the Reagan and Bush administrations, among them President Bush himself and the successive chairmen of the Joint Chiefs of Staff Admiral Bill Crowe and General Colin Powell, who respected and liked Akhromeyev, as well as the US arms-control specialist, Ken Adelman.[99] 'I felt a deep sense of sadness', Bush said later, 'over Marshal Sergei Akhromeyev's suicide', adding that he was 'an honorable and honest professional soldier, who had, as he once told Brent [Scowcroft], witnessed the destruction of everything he valued and worked for all his life'.[100]

After the failure of the coup, Gorbachev resumed his struggle to hold together some kind of union, but the momentum was now with Yeltsin and with the republics seeking independent statehood. The Soviet president would have benefited politically from going straight from the airport to the Moscow White House to express his solidarity with those who had occupied that focal point of resistance to the coup. None of the emissaries who had come from the Russian parliament building, however, suggested that he do so, and when the plane from Foros touched down in Moscow, bringing with them an exhausted Gorbachev family, his immediate concern was about his wife's health.[101]

When Gorbachev appeared before the Russian parliament the following day, Yeltsin went out of his way to humiliate him. He insisted that the Soviet president read in public the minutes of a government meeting held on 19 August which made clear that almost every minister had either supported or acquiesced with the coup. Yeltsin made much of the fact that these were Gorbachev's own appointees. In fact, most ministers, especially those who headed the numerous economic ministries, had been chosen by Ryzhkov, but the decisions on the most politically significant senior positions had, indeed, been Gorbachev's. That was true of Ryzhkov's successor, Pavlov, as well as of the Defence Minister, Interior Minister, KGB Chairman, and Foreign Minister, among whom only the last-named was not part of the coup plot.

Attempting to steer between utterly opposing currents in Soviet politics, Gorbachev had made compromises and, even allowing for the real constraints on his choice of personnel, he had made some very bad (as well as good) appointments. With the collapse of the coup, a spring in the steps of democrats, and the discrediting of conservatives and hard-liners (now weaker than they ever had been),* he had

---

* The last months of 1991 were the lowest point for ideological or conservative Communists in seventy years and the lowest point for the putschists. The leading figures—apart from Pugo who shot his wife and then himself—were arrested and imprisoned. Kryuchkov (who, as already noted, in later years denounced Gorbachev as a traitor) wrote a sycophantic letter to the Soviet president on 22 August in which he pleaded for the coup plotters not to be imprisoned in view of their age and health. Could they not have a lesser penalty, such as 'strict house arrest'? In the letter (which is preserved in the archives of the Gorbachev Foundation), he said he had heard Gorbachev's interview the previous day and asked rhetorically whether his condemnation of them had been deserved. Kryuchkov underlined his next short sentence which read: 'Unfortunately, deserved'. Later, the putschists (all of whom were released from prison quite early in post-Soviet Russia, serving not more than eighteen months or so of imprisonment) claimed that Gorbachev was complicit in the coup and could have left Foros at any time—as if Gorbachev could have turned up in Moscow, fit and well, thus demonstrating to the world that the self-appointed members of the 'State Committee' were fools as well as liars. None of them came up with their implausible story about Gorbachev's voluntary incarceration at the time of their arrest, or when under interrogation for their crime against the state, although to have said so then would have been an effective way of mitigating their offence and of ingratiating themselves with Yeltsin. The fact that they concocted this account only much later has not prevented a few conspiracy-fanciers in the West from choosing to believe it. The most detailed account of the reality of Foros and of the remoteness from truth of the putschists' revised version is in Anatoly Chernyaev, *My Six Years with Gorbachev* (Pennsylvania State University Press, University Park, PA, 2000), pp. 371–8 and 401–23; see also Archie Brown, *Seven Years that Changed the World: Perestroika in Perspective* (Oxford University Press, Oxford, 2007), pp. 319–24.

a freer hand in choosing his most senior colleagues, albeit in consultation with Yeltsin on some of the sensitive posts. One of the most important decisions was to invite Vadim Bakatin to become Chairman of the KGB. Despite, or thanks to, having no experience of that organization, Bakatin made an impact on it. One of his more controversial actions, for which he was to be blamed in post-Soviet Russia once the security services reasserted themselves, was to give the United States full information on where the listening devices had been placed in their new embassy building.[102] That was testimony to the qualitatively new level of trust between the Soviet and American leaderships, although the latter did not provide reciprocal information.

Accepting a suggestion from Aleksandr Yakovlev, Bakatin brought in former KGB General Oleg Kalugin to advise him, not least on whom he could trust and whom he should not trust in the KGB's Lubyanka headquarters. Kalugin had become a critic of his old organization and was under surveillance himself before and during the coup, having spoken out at democratic rallies.[103] He had been friendly with Yakovlev ever since they were fellow-students at Columbia University in 1959. Kalugin had been included in this Soviet–US academic exchange as a young KGB officer and Yakovlev as an ideologically reliable but genuine student. Already then in his mid-thirties, Yakovlev had served at the front in the Second World War before being invalided out, badly wounded. He walked with a limp for the rest of his life.

Among other major post-coup appointments, Ivan Silayev, who had been premier and in charge of the economy in the Russian republic, became Pavlov's successor as head of the USSR ministerial network, with particular responsibility for the Soviet economy, but at a time when the powers to do anything very much were fast slipping from the grasp of the federal government. The economist Grigory Yavlinsky, who had previously worked with Yeltsin, also joined the team as an adviser. The new Foreign Minister, Pankin, did not make much of an impression, and in November Gorbachev persuaded Shevardnadze to return to his old job. It was a short-lived stint since the post of Soviet Foreign Minister, along with the state Shevardnadze was once again representing, ceased to exist at the end of the following month.

Being a biological optimist, Gorbachev still believed that a union could be preserved or recreated, but so many members of the all-union government had participated in the coup that its failure worked much more to Yeltsin's advantage than to Gorbachev's. Moreover, Gorbachev's power during the first five years of his party general secretaryship had rested on the leverage and authority that office gave him. Even after he had established the executive presidency in March 1990, some of his residual power rested on his ability as Communist Party leader to control, albeit incompletely and with increasing difficulty, the party machine which had run the country for seven decades. Gorbachev had held on to the party leadership with a view to winning over a large segment of its membership as the nucleus of a new democratic socialist party and to prevent the organization's recapture by those who were eager to move in the opposite direction, restoring all too familiar highly authoritarian one-party rule.

The political clock moved fast in the immediate aftermath of the failed coup. Before August 1991 ended, the Communist Party of the Soviet Union had effectively ceased to exist. Gorbachev had, indeed, already removed the party's governmental powers, but it was Yeltsin who pronounced the party's death sentence, fortified by a shift in public opinion whereby Communists were becoming increasingly reviled. By the end of August, Yeltsin had suspended the activity of the Russian Communist Party on the territory of the Russian republic and nationalized party property; Gorbachev, accepting that the CPSU was no longer a body with the potential of being turned into a socialist party of a social democratic type, resigned as General Secretary of the CPSU and called on the Central Committee to dissolve itself; and the Central Committee building in Moscow was taken over at short notice by the Russian state authorities in such a way that even leading reformers like Chernyaev had to hurriedly gather together their belongings and abandon their offices.[104]

Once Gorbachev learned of the extent to which the higher party organs had colluded with the putschists (of which immediately after his return to Moscow from Foros he was still unaware), he was content to see those party structures dismantled. What remained of the party in the country was left leaderless and rudderless. Yeltsin administered the *coup de grâce* in early November when he banned both the CPSU and the Russian Communist Party on Russian territory in a decree of highly questionable legality, but which put paid both to the all-union and the harder-line Russian republican party (although a Communist Party of the Russian Federation re-emerged early in the post-Soviet era).[105]

The balance of power had irrevocably shifted from the federal centre to the republics. The independent statehood of Estonia, Latvia, and Lithuania was, in the new atmosphere, quickly accepted by Gorbachev as well as by Yeltsin. By mid-September, they had been joined by Armenia. Moldova and Georgia insisted they were independent already and nobody gainsaid them. But the most ominous development for the preservation of a union, which would, nonetheless, include most of the territory and the overwhelming majority of the population of the USSR, was the Ukrainian parliament's post-coup support for independence and their decision to hold a referendum on 1 December on the creation of an independent Ukrainian state. Both Gorbachev and Yeltsin agreed that a union without Ukraine was unthinkable. In Gorbachev's case, this was because he refused to believe that Ukrainians would vote for separate statehood, in view of their support for the union in the March 1991 Soviet referendum and in the light of the long ties of history and family between Russians and Ukrainians. Gorbachev's own mother was of mainly Ukrainian descent and his wife Raisa's father was Ukrainian. His belief that Russia and Ukraine were inextricably linked was not only an intellectual and political position but a deeply felt emotional one.

Yeltsin was also reluctant to see Ukraine in the same light as he viewed the Baltic republics. Just two days after he had recognized the latter as independent states, he authorized his press spokesman to say that the Russian republic reserved the right to discuss border revision with all republics contiguous to Russia except those of the Balts. Indeed, the Ukrainian-American historian Serhii Plokhy goes so far as to say that Yeltsin, who had prevented the coup plotters from preserving the USSR, 'now adopted that mission himself'.[106] A statement Yeltsin approved made a distinction between self-determination within a continuing union and separate statehood. Ukraine and Kazakhstan were singled out by Yeltsin's spokesman as republics where the borders were of particular concern. Yeltsin's allies, such as Gavriil Popov, who had been elected mayor of Moscow, referred to Crimea and Odessa as the parts of Ukraine which would come up for renegotiation.[107] Crimea had been transferred from the Russian republic to Ukraine in 1954 on the whim of Nikita Khrushchev at a time when a majority of its inhabitants were ethnic Russians. The latter were not consulted on the change, but at that time it did not make a vast difference which republic the peninsula belonged to, since all the big decisions in the pre-perestroika USSR were taken in Moscow.

Gorbachev succeeded in restarting the Novo-Ogarevo process, with the Kazakh leader Nazarbayev a strong supporter, and Yeltsin prepared, for a time, to go along with the idea of the Soviet state evolving into a confederation and common market (a kind of European Union of the East). In its last draft form, this was to become not a USSR—even in the August 1991 variant of Union of Soviet Sovereign (rather than Socialist) Republics—but a USS, the Union of Sovereign States. There was support for this from the Central Asian republics as well as from foreign leaders who hoped to continue to have Gorbachev at the helm as a reliable international partner and who feared the consequences of complete break-up of the Soviet Union. The more support Gorbachev won for a continuing union, the less, however, Yeltsin liked it.[108] The Soviet president was far readier than was the Russian president to share power. As Plokhy notes, Gorbachev was prepared to make far-reaching concessions to Ukrainians to keep them in a renewed union, whereas Yeltsin and his entourage offered only a 'Russia-dominated confederation'.[109]

Between the end of August and the end of December, Gorbachev was engaged not only with domestic politics, and above all the effort to preserve a union, but also with intensive international diplomacy. He met all the major Western leaders and took part in a conference on the Middle East in Madrid at which Israeli Prime Minister Itzhak Shamir thanked him for establishing the right to leave the Soviet Union. In response, Gorbachev said he had 'always emphasized that I am against anti-Semitism, as I am against all manifestations of nationalism and chauvinism'.[110] While Gorbachev was on his way to Madrid, Yeltsin sprung an unpleasant surprise by announcing dramatic cuts in Russian contributions to the Soviet budget, including a 90 per cent cut in the funding for the Soviet Foreign Ministry, as well as a programme for economic reform which he had coordinated neither with Gorbachev nor with the leaders of the Soviet republics. This undermined Gorbachev's position in Madrid. His meetings with Bush there constituted the last US–Soviet summit.[111]

In conversation outside the formal sessions of the conference, the fate of the Soviet Union and of Gorbachev occupied the other leaders at least as much as did the Middle East peace process. King Juan Carlos and Felipe González held a dinner to which they invited only Presidents Bush and Gorbachev. For Gorbachev this was a relaxed and friendly conversation in contrast with the tense discussions in which he was involved at home. The fact that González was the political host made Madrid all the more agreeable. When Andrei Grachev asked Gorbachev which foreign politician he felt closest to, 'he answered, without hesitation, González'. He 'immediately added that he had friendly as well as good professional relations with Bush, Kohl, Mitterrand, Thatcher, and more recently, Major, but 'especially with González'.[112] The Spanish prime minister said that his support for a continuing union was not just a matter of backing Gorbachev but for the continuation of a presidency of the union 'invested with full constitutional powers', to which Gorbachev responded, 'Felipe, I promise you that I will die with my boots on in the battle for the union.'[113]

With or without boots, it was a task beyond him. At one point in the Madrid dinner conversation, Gorbachev turned to Bush and said they had known each other for quite a long time, first of all during his vice-presidency and now they were in the third year of his presidency. He asked, 'Has there ever been a single occasion when I did not keep my word to you?' Without hesitation, Bush replied, 'No, never.' Shaking his head, Gorbachev said, 'I often find myself faced with the opposite phenomenon in my relationships with the leaders of the [Soviet] republics.'[114]

Yeltsin had been one of seven republican leaders who had, along with Gorbachev, signed an agreement on economic cooperation in the Kremlin on 18 October, and he was to be one of the seven who agreed at Novo-Ogarevo on 14 November to create a Union of Sovereign States with the Union Treaty to be signed before the end of the year. Ukraine held back, pending the result of their 1 December referendum. It was the result of their referendum which made it almost certain that such a union would not be created. Yeltsin and his advisers (most notably State Secretary Gennadiy Burbulis) were unwilling to proceed *without* Ukraine and *with* Gorbachev. The turn-around in Ukrainian opinion in the months since the March all-union referendum was such that, with over 84 per cent of the electorate participating, more than 90 per cent of voters opted for independence.[115]

The final blow for the union—and for Gorbachev—was administered by Yeltsin, Kravchuk (who, following the referendum, had become President of Ukraine), and Belorussian leader Stanislaŭ Shushkevich, meeting in Belevezha in Belarus on 8 December, at which they unilaterally announced the dissolution of the Soviet Union and its replacement by a Commonwealth of Independent States (CIS). The CIS, although its numbers were to expand to take in most of the former Soviet republics, never amounted to very much organizationally or as a collective body acting in unison. The more important decision was to abandon the union—thus no union treaty and (importantly for Yeltsin) no Gorbachev.

It was not only Gorbachev and his entourage who were shocked by the decision of the Slavic triumvirate. So were some of Yeltsin's supporters, including his vice-president, Aleksandr Rutskoy, who rushed to Gorbachev's Kremlin office when he heard the news from Belarus and 'demanded the arrest of the "drunken threesome" on charges of treason'.[116] Gorbachev shared his outrage—exacerbated by the fact that Yeltsin informed the American president of the trio's decision before Shushkevich (given the more thankless task) had called the Kremlin to tell him—but he did not adopt the policy Rutskoy advocated. Although in the post-Soviet era, a majority of Russians have consistently expressed regret about the break-up of the union (only in December 1991 was there a temporary majority in favour), there was by this stage little or nothing that Gorbachev could have done to prevent it. If the second last thing he wanted was the complete break-up of the union, the last thing was civil war. The end of the Soviet Union and the creation of the CIS were formalized at a 21 December meeting in Kazakhstan (held there in deference to Nazarbayev who had been upset by the decision sprung on him, without consultation, by the presidents of the three Slavic republics earlier in the month). Only the Baltic states and Georgia did not participate.*

In broader context, the dissolution of the USSR was an unintended consequence not only of the ending of the Cold War but also, and still more, of the liberalization and pluralization of the Soviet political system. Yet the most decisive blows against the attempts of Gorbachev and his allies to achieve agreement on a new and voluntary federation, or even, as a last resort, a confederation, were delivered by Boris Yeltsin. As Chairman of the Supreme Soviet of the Russian Republic from 1990 and as the elected President of Russia from June 1991, he demanded 'independence' from a union of which Russia had been the bulwark. It is unlikely that Ukraine would have switched so radically from pro-union to pro-independence sentiments in the course of 1991 but for the example set by Yeltsin and the Russian leadership from 1990. Yeltsin's determination to supplant Gorbachev, rather than share power with him, and to become master of the Kremlin, had led him to play the Russian card against the union. His entourage were more than happy with the prospect of becoming the new Russian political elite, replacing the Soviet political elite who, until the last two years of the Soviet Union's existence, had represented Russia.

If we look further back, however, we find a more surprising candidate for architect of the Soviet Union's ultimate dissolution than perestroika, the end of the Cold War, Gorbachev, or Yeltsin—none other than Josif Stalin, notwithstanding the misplaced

---

* Georgia joined the CIS in 1993, by which time Eduard Shevardnadze had become the country's leader, and left it in 2008. Ukraine withdrew its participation in the organization in 2018.

reverence in which he was held by many of those most willing to use tanks and guns to keep all fifteen republics within the USSR. In the first place, Stalin's policy of 'national in form, socialist in content', meant that the Soviet Union had republican boundaries that corresponded with the territory of various national groups, though their 'socialist' policies were determined by the highly centralized Communist Party. However far from genuine federalism this was, its modest concessions to national traditions—at any rate those deemed to be 'progressive'—and association of territory with ethnic group, helped to keep alive national consciousness. In some cases, it strengthened a sense of nationhood in places where there was very little of it before. Less obviously but importantly, as more than one scholar has pointed out, the seeds of the Soviet Union's destruction were sown by Stalin at a later stage of his dictatorial rule when, following his 1939 pact with Hitler, he proceeded to incorporate the three Baltic states into the Soviet Union and also Western Ukraine, including the city of Lwów (Lviv) which had been part of Poland. As Plokhy has emphasized, in the late 1980s it was Lviv which 'became the center of nationalist mobilization for Ukrainian independence'. He added that it was 'as difficult to imagine Ukrainian independence without Lviv as to imagine the Soviet Union without Ukraine'.[117] In the absence of the Baltic states and of Western Ukraine setting the pace of nationalist demands, a strong movement for independence in Ukraine would have been unlikely and in Russia unthinkable.

Forcibly incorporated in the Soviet Union as they were, the Balts and many Western Ukrainians harboured a desire for independence for decades before perestroika. Throughout those years, however, it remained a dream rather than a realistic aspiration. Indeed, up until the failed coup, the instruments of violent coercion remained in the hands of Soviet conservative forces, even if Gorbachev, as commander-in-chief, had a measure of control over them and prevented worse excesses. For their part, hard-line Communists were by 1991 well aware that, even if Gorbachev's position was weakening, power was slipping still faster out of the hands of the CPSU. They were acutely worried about the potential disintegration of the Soviet state. Those concerns were fully shared within the military-industrial complex. Especially from the time Leonid Brezhnev succeeded Nikita Khrushchev as party leader in 1964, the defence establishment had enjoyed a cosy relationship with party officialdom and it was by far the most privileged sector of the Soviet economy. During the second half of the 1980s, in contrast, the military had reason to be anxious about a loss of influence, loss of resources and, for many, the prospect of loss of their livelihood. In that context, the August coup should scarcely have been a surprise.

What was less predictable was that it should have turned out to be so counterproductive in terms of the aims of those who launched it. It brought forward the demise of the Soviet Union and though it hastened the fall of Gorbachev, as the hard-liners had wished, it handed power to separatists rather than to resolute defenders of the pre-existing Soviet state. Given the strength of the forces on both sides ranged against him, the wonder is that Gorbachev survived for as long as he did.[118]

Gorbachev announced his resignation from the presidency of the Soviet Union—a country ceasing to exist—on 25 December 1991. He made clear that, notwithstanding his support for republican autonomy, he deplored 'the dismemberment of the country and the breakup of the state'. He spoke, however, of some of the remarkable achievements of the perestroika years. 'We are living in a new world', he said, having put an end to the Cold War, the arms race, 'the mad militarization of our country', and the threat of world war.[119] He also stressed the huge gains in freedom and democracy that had been made—and it was fundamentally important 'to preserve the democratic achievements of recent years'. They must not be given up under any circumstance or pretext, for should that happen, he warned, 'all hopes for a better future will be buried'.[120]

16

POLITICAL LEADERSHIP AND THE END OF THE COLD WAR

Concluding Reflections

The significance for the Cold War's ending of Gorbachev, Reagan, and Thatcher has already been considered in relation to other explanations, such as economic pressures and comparative military strength.[1] It is time to return to questions raised in the book's introduction and to summarize and assess the evidence relating to them. What were the mindsets these three leaders brought to East–West relations when they came to power? How did their views evolve? To what extent were they in accord with domestic political opinion? Would any of the realistically alternative leaders of their countries in the 1980s have pursued roughly the same policies, leading to similar outcomes? And how large a part did their interaction with each other influence Gorbachev, Reagan, and Thatcher?

That the basic political beliefs of Reagan and Thatcher had much in common, and that both of them recognized this, has been made abundantly clear. When he became president, Reagan told the prime minister that they would draw strength from each other, and so it turned out. He was readier to listen to Thatcher than to any other foreign leader. Her forceful manner and certainty of tone, which her European counterparts found off-putting, were welcomed by the president as exemplary statements of their common political beliefs and goals. Thatcher, for her part, although conscious of Reagan's intellectual shortcomings, liked and respected him and admired his attachment to principles on domestic and foreign policy which she shared. The bond was strong enough to survive their periodic sharp disagreements which, at the time, would discomfit Reagan more than they did Thatcher. Though she was more diplomatic with Reagan than she was with less consequential leaders, or with her own Cabinet colleagues, Thatcher was never supine. If she strongly disagreed with what the Reagan administration was doing, she said so.

For better *and* for worse, she was a 'supreme conviction politician' who, as Malcolm Rifkind, who had served in her Cabinet, put it, was 'contemptuous' of 'any search for consensus'.[2] On one occasion the prime minister said she did believe in consensus but spoiled the surprise by adding that it should be 'a consensus behind my convictions'.[3]

She had signalled in advance what kind of prime minister she wished to be in a lengthy newspaper interview in early 1979 while she was still Leader of the Opposition, telling Kenneth Harris of *The Observer* that she intended to have in her government 'only the people who want to go in the direction in which the Prime Minister wishes to go' and that 'as Prime Minister I could not waste time having any internal arguments'.[4] The attempt to achieve this (which could never be wholly successful) was part of her eventual undoing at the hands of her own colleagues. It was also misguided since neither Margaret Thatcher nor any other prime minister was ever chosen because she was deemed to have a monopoly of wisdom.[5]

The views of both Reagan and Thatcher were well established by the time they came to power, although it is worth reiterating that they were not identical to those they held when they were younger. In his youth, Reagan had been a Democrat, but his clashes with the left in Hollywood and his resentment at paying high taxes had propelled him towards political conservatism and a neoliberal economic outlook. Thatcher had been a Conservative from her youth and, on arriving as an undergraduate at Somerville College, Oxford, she lost no time in joining the Oxford University Conservative Association. In the 1940s, she did not, however, espouse the anti-statist views with which she became associated as prime minister, for she indignantly rejected the suggestion that the Conservatives would remove all the wartime controls which had made the British economy highly centralized and state-directed.[6] But under the influence especially of her later mentor Sir Keith Joseph as well as of her reading of Friedrich von Hayek and like-minded thinkers, she came to embrace an anti-statist, pro-privatization, low tax economy and to prefer a US-style economic model to that more prevalent in western and especially northern Europe. As prime minister, she forcefully supported the neoliberal strand of thought within the Conservative Party and fought against the influence of more traditional Tories who were, in spite of what she said in early 1979, well represented in her first Cabinet. Those ministers, however, who did not share her belief that a freer, less regulated market would produce so much more prosperity that there was no need to worry about growing inequality fell by the wayside.

The views of Reagan and Thatcher had converged well before they came to hold the highest governmental office in their countries, and that applied both to domestic and to foreign policy. They agreed on broad economic issues, and their thinking was in line with fashionable economic nostrums of the late 1970s, 1980s, and 1990s. They also both believed in strong defence and an increased military budget, although they had very different views on nuclear weapons. Naturally, each regarded any prospect of nuclear war with abhorrence, but Reagan was closer to Gorbachev in believing that this meant working to rid the world of such weapons, whereas Thatcher was a strong believer in retaining them as a deterrent. But the president and prime minister were at one in the early 1980s in wishing to step up an ideological offensive against the Soviet Union (and against Communism more generally) which they regarded as still expansionist and a growing threat to the West. They believed in the replacement of Communist regimes by democratic governments, not simply in accepting an indefinite management of the East–West relationship. Reagan's view of the Cold War during the earliest years of his presidency was clearly expressed in his speech to the British Parliament on 8 June 1982. He emphasized, on the one hand, the importance of arms reduction talks and the fact that global nuclear war would mean 'the end of civilization as we know it' and, on the other, his readiness to engage in the competition of values and ideas.[7]

Making an argument which Thatcher had often deployed, the president noted that democracies 'refused to use the threat of their nuclear monopoly' in the 1940s and early 1950s 'for territorial or imperial gain' and asserted that if the nuclear monopoly had been 'in the hands of the communist world, the map of Europe—indeed, the world—would look very different today'.[8] He argued that any regime, the Soviet Union included, was 'inherently unstable' if it had 'no peaceful means to legitimize its leaders'. Therefore, while the West should be 'cautious about forcing the pace of change', they should not hesitate to do what they could to foster 'the infrastructure of democracy'.[9] Looking to 'the long term', Reagan said that 'the march of freedom and democracy' would leave 'Marxism-Leninism on the ash heap of history'.[10]

This was a call for regime change—for the democratization of the Soviet Union, albeit 'in the long term'—but not for the break-up of the Soviet state. The American president could not have imagined that, in the very same decade, democratization would be launched and then expanded by none other than the General Secretary of the Central Committee of the Communist Party of the Soviet Union. Nevertheless, by the time he made his first-ever visit to the USSR in 1988, Reagan recognized the scale of the change that had occurred when he told Moscow University students that they were living in 'one of the most exciting, hopeful times in Soviet history'.[11]

The Importance of Engagement

Reagan could well have argued that there was no inconsistency between his rhetoric of 1982 in London and the emollient tone he adopted in Moscow in 1988, for in the meantime the Soviet Union had taken substantial steps towards greater freedom (and Gorbachev, though Reagan didn't yet know it, was about to announce competitive elections for a new legislature to be held the following year). That does not mean that the change in Moscow was caused by an ideological offensive led by Washington or by American military pressure. Certainly, neither Reagan nor Thatcher renounced their previous hard line, and March 1983 was the month in which Reagan raised international tension with his 'evil empire' rhetoric about the USSR and his SDI announcement which threatened an acceleration of the arms race and endangered the 1972 ABM Treaty. Yet, 1983 was also a year when the president and prime minister became more attracted to a renewal of East–West dialogue which, so far as the US and UK were concerned, had been conspicuous by its absence ever since the Soviet invasion of Afghanistan in 1979.

We have seen that Reagan was subjected to conflicting pulls and pushes from different parts of his administration. The intransigence of Weinberger's Defense Department and the State Department's support for dialogue were hard to reconcile. Personnel change, however, favoured the Washington voices calling for engagement with the Communist world in an attempt to reduce the heightened tensions. Like Gorbachev, Reagan made both bad and good appointments, but none more significant for positive East–West dialogue than that of George Shultz. He replaced Alexander Haig as Secretary of State in mid-1982 and, once he had mastered his foreign policy brief, he exercised more influence over the president than did Haig, for Reagan liked and respected Shultz (as, by no means inconsequentially, did Nancy Reagan who was no fan of Haig). Of great importance also for a shift in the administration's Soviet policy was the replacement of the highly conservative William Clark by the more pragmatic Bud McFarlane as National Security Adviser and, no less vitally, the arrival in 1983 of Jack Matlock as the Soviet specialist within the NSC, in succession to Richard Pipes who had returned to his Harvard professorship in late 1982. Pipes had been vehemently against Reagan meeting Soviet leaders, whereas Matlock was strongly supportive of Reagan's growing desire to do so.

At a time when Clark was National Security Adviser, Reagan confided to his diary on 6 April 1983 that Shultz was 'upset', for the Secretary of State believed that the NSC was undermining him and opposing the plans for 'quiet diplomacy' with the Soviet Union which he and Reagan had agreed on. In that same diary entry Reagan wrote that 'I think I'm hard line and will never appease', but some of the NSC staff were 'too hard line' for him and were against any approach to the Soviet leadership. He, in contrast, wanted to let them see there was 'a better world' and to encourage them to show by their deeds that they were willing to get along with it.[12] There was no shortage of conservative columnists who could be relied upon to take a position closer to that of Weinberger or Perle than to Shultz, as well as conservative think-tanks, such as the Heritage Foundation, which remained sceptical of any good coming from talking to Soviet leaders. The Democrats in Congress were, however, favourably disposed towards dialogue—and in the persons of House Speaker 'Tip' O'Neill and Senators Gary Hart and Edward Kennedy—engaged in some diplomacy of their own, having separate, amicable meetings with Gorbachev in the Kremlin.[13]

During their first terms (for Thatcher the period between the Conservative Party's victories in the 1979 and 1983 general elections, for Reagan the years 1981–4), criticism of their policies came from left and mainstream liberal opinion. Reagan was attacked as a warmonger by Democrats, while Thatcher was under fire from the Labour Party and liberal opinion for her total identification with the Reagan administration at a time of rising tension with the Soviet Union. The British Foreign Office wanted to see a resumption of East–West diplomacy, as did successive Foreign Secretaries Francis

Pym and Geoffrey Howe. The FCO and Pym (who was dismissed and replaced by Howe in the summer of 1983) had been in favour of Thatcher attending Brezhnev's funeral, at which event she would have met with Andropov, but she refused to do so. She did, however, attend Andropov's obsequies and had quite a lengthy conversation with Chernenko. Reagan resolutely refused to go to either of those funerals or even to that of Chernenko which would have provided the opportunity of conversation with his successor, Gorbachev.

When the president gave that June 1982 speech to the British Parliament, the National Security Adviser was still William Clark, the Soviet expert in the NSC still Pipes, and the Secretary of State still Haig. By the time Haig's successor, Shultz, launched and chaired a series of Saturday-morning breakfast discussions on foreign policy, especially vis-à-vis the Soviet Union, McFarlane had succeeded Clark, and Matlock was the Soviet expert on the NSC (and the notetaker at those meetings). The entire breakfast-discussion group, which included Vice-President George Bush, recognized, said Matlock, that the Soviet leadership faced growing problems, but believed that American attempts to exploit them would be counterproductive. They agreed to seek Soviet compliance with past undertakings, and to lower levels of armaments through new agreements which would be 'equitable and verifiable'. They aimed to reduce tensions, but without glossing over real problems. They further agreed at a meeting on 19 November 1983 that they were *not* challenging the legitimacy of the Soviet system, or seeking military superiority, or forcing the collapse of the Soviet system, but they were prepared to exert pressure to change Soviet behaviour.[14]

Although Reagan's rhetoric was not always in accord with that cautiously pragmatic statement of what his administration was and was not trying to do, his policy of constructive engagement—from the time he had a Soviet leader he could interact with—was generally along those lines. The change of tone and of emphasis owed much to the objectives and strong personality of Secretary of State Shultz. For Western democratic politicians to seek greater freedom and democracy in the Soviet Union was both natural and proper. Shultz and his new allies in the NSC did not, however, believe that the best way of moving towards that goal was through aggressive ideological confrontation. That would have made it more, rather than less, difficult for Gorbachev to introduce democratizing change of his own.

Similar political movement, and one which picked up speed faster, was underway in Britain. In turning towards a policy of engagement with the Soviet Union and Eastern Europe, as she did from the time of her September 1983 Chequers seminar, Thatcher was coming into line with a body of opinion already well represented in her own government and across a wide section of the British political spectrum. There was nothing remotely comparable to the split between the US Defense and State departments in the UK. As was made clear in Chapter 7, the Defence Secretary Michael Heseltine was just as much an advocate of talking to the Soviet leadership as was Foreign Secretary Geoffrey Howe.[15] Their problem was that Thatcher distrusted

Heseltine (as distinct from his department) and that she distrusted the Foreign Office (and to a lesser extent, at that stage, Howe). The fact, therefore, that a policy of engagement was strongly and independently supported by academic specialists she had summoned to Chequers added force to the Foreign Office arguments and helped it to get its way.

To the extent that she did engage with the Soviet Union and Eastern Europe, Thatcher also had an easier time in Parliament than she had on domestic policy. Most MPs in her own party were in favour of East–West dialogue, and on the Opposition benches she had been criticized for being too much of a Cold Warrior and for following too closely in the footsteps of the Reagan administration at a time when it was associated with an unremitting obduracy. The intransigents within the Reagan administration were, however, supported by a section of the British press and by a significant proportion of those who participated in Thatcher's party-political seminars (convened by Hugh Thomas), as distinct from governmental seminars organized by 10 Downing Street officials and involving the Foreign Office. The hard-line informal advisers, who had tried to reinforce Thatcher's earlier scepticism about any possibility of change for the better coming from within the Soviet establishment, were increasingly disconcerted in the second half of the 1980s by the prime minister's support for Gorbachev. This was, however, a popular policy with the electorate as a whole (contrasting with bitter divisions over the Thatcher government's social and economic policies).

Having in the early 1980s regarded the Foreign Office as too accommodating with the Soviet Union, the prime minister finished up even more enthusiastically in favour of engagement with the Communist world than were the diplomats and still more pro-Gorbachev than the FCO she had scorned for being too soft. Her 10 Downing Street adviser Sir Percy Cradock (himself a former UK ambassador to China) was among those who thought she had gone too far. Following Thatcher's highly successful visit to the Soviet Union in March 1987, Cradock was worried about what he took to be her excessive enthusiasm for Gorbachev and his domestic reforms. And within the Foreign Office, as the British ambassador to Moscow noted, there was unhappiness by 1989 about Gorbachev making his third official visit to Britain. They were worried by just how popular he had become and about the defence implications of European public opinion being 'carried away by Gorbymania'.[16]

Back in 1983, when she was planning a major reassessment of British policy towards the Soviet Union and Eastern Europe, Thatcher, as her private secretary John Coles informed the FCO, was 'inclined to see our objective in the long term as the replacement of Communist by democratic regimes' and was looking for some analysis of how that objective might be achieved.[17] There was a tension, though, between her wish at that time to conduct a persistent ideological offensive against Communism and to engage in constructive dialogue with the Communist world, and especially with the Soviet Union. What, above all, led Thatcher not to abandon the first of these aims but to tone it down and give a higher priority to the latter was her personal encounters with Gorbachev. Her perceptions and approach to dealing with the USSR were different after her meetings with Gorbachev in December 1984 and March 1985 from before. Whereas in 1983 she had asked rhetorically why the Soviet Union's security should be taken into account in any arms control agreement rather than just 'that of our side',[18] by October 1985 (as noted in Chapter 8), she was writing to Reagan, offering advice on how to reassure Gorbachev at their forthcoming Geneva summit meeting. He should tell him that 'you are entitled as we are to feel secure' and that the world must be safe for both sides if it was going to be safe for either one of them.[19] After Reagan met Gorbachev the following month, he, too, concluded that this was a Soviet leader cut from a different cloth to that of his predecessors, and he was strengthened in his belief in dialogue. In a sense, Reagan and Thatcher had made essentially tactical rather than strategic adjustments, but their perceptions of how change could be brought about had shifted.

Paradoxically, it was the leader who had made his career through climbing the promotion ladder of the Communist Party of the Soviet Union who not only changed policy most fundamentally but who also had the most open mind of the three. Gorbachev's beliefs evolved over the years before he became the top leader in the Soviet Union and, still more, during the time of his general secretaryship. He was a reflective politician attracted by ideas and concepts (in a way in which George Bush clearly was not) but attentive also to policy detail (in a way in which Reagan was not). Of his foreign interlocutors who have been the principal subjects of this book, Thatcher's mindset in these respects came somewhat closer to Gorbachev's inasmuch as she, too, was interested in ideas (only some of which intersected with the Soviet leader's) but combined that with a ferocious attention to detail. What made Gorbachev very different from any of these Western leaders was not only the extent to which his ideas changed over time but also his awareness and acknowledgement of this process.

One of the sillier Western misunderstandings of the last Soviet leader, of which some of the hard-liners in the Reagan administration were guilty, was that he 'never changed' because he continued to profess his attachment to socialism. What they missed was that Gorbachev had redefined socialism radically to accommodate his new beliefs and that this was also his way of dealing with cognitive dissonance. In contrast with the orthodox Communism of his youth, or even with the reformist Communism he espoused on the eve of becoming Soviet leader, he came to believe that there was no socialism worthy of the name that did not incorporate freedom and democracy.[20] Latterly, he regarded the market, too, as an intrinsic element of socialism, since consumer sovereignty removed power from bureaucrats and handed it to citizens. The market, however, had to be regulated, subject to a rule of law, and accountable to democratic institutions. While attracted to the kind of 'social market economy' embraced by the major parties in the Federal Republic of Germany,

Gorbachev was highly critical of the irresponsible economic and political power exemplified by the oligarchical capitalism of post-Soviet Russia in the 1990s.[21]

The evolution of Gorbachev's thinking to embrace socialism of a social democratic type was, unsurprisingly, better understood in Europe (where democratic socialist governments have held power in many countries) than in the United States where no such government, or seriously contending mass party, has been formed. In this aspect of his intellectual journey, Gorbachev could find common ground with Felipe González, Willy Brandt, and François Mitterrand, but none with Reagan or Thatcher, who both embraced a form of neoliberalism and a doctrine of 'the less state, the better', even though their practice did not always cohere with that precept. Distinctly unsympathetic, as she was, even to social democratic variants of socialism, Thatcher remained, nevertheless, loyal to Gorbachev as a 'reformer' and as a friend. In a lengthy 1990 off-the-record interview about Ronald Reagan, in which she commends the policy towards the Communist world of Reagan and herself, with its mixture of toughness and engagement, she added, 'But do not forget equally, none of this could have happened without Mr. Gorbachev. Do not let us take credit without also giving the massive amount of visionary credit and courage to him.'[22] When, in her memoirs, she writes that 'Gorbachev remained a communist to the end', she is explicitly referring to his continuing membership of the Communist Party (until its post-coup dissolution).[23] Otherwise that remark would not only be remote from the reality but radically at odds with Thatcher's high regard for the last Soviet leader. She noted that doubts had been raised in her last year in office about 'the wisdom of supporting Mr Gorbachev and his reforms', but she had no regrets about continuing to do so, for 'I am not by instinct someone who throws over those I like and have shown themselves my friends simply because their fortunes change.'[24]

Thatcher's important role notwithstanding, Reagan, along with George H. W. Bush, George Shultz, and, to a lesser extent, James Baker, were, nonetheless, Gorbachev's most essential interlocutors, such was the centrality of the US–Soviet relationship for the conduct and ending of the Cold War. To the extent that there was a convergence of their views, it was Gorbachev who moved furthest—and *very* far from previous Soviet positions. With his embrace of human rights, personal freedoms, and democracy, he contributed greatly to the new atmosphere in which a series of important agreements on arms control and arms reductions could be reached. Most crucial of all for the Cold War's ending had been Gorbachev's endorsement of the rights of citizens of different countries to choose what kind of political system they wished to live under and his acceptance of the outcome, even when it led to the East European countries becoming fully independent and cutting off their organizational ties with Moscow.

Whilst Reagan and, in the last years of Gorbachev's leadership, Bush were the Soviet leader's most vital partners simply because the United States was the country with which he had to engage on major international issues, Thatcher's importance is clear. That was not merely because she was Reagan's favourite foreign leader and the one to whom he felt closest politically and ideologically, but, no less, on account of the surprisingly strong bond she formed with Gorbachev. Having established a rapport with him even before he became general secretary, she went on to develop an admiration for his political courage, resilience, and commitment to change. Moreover, Gorbachev possessed a lot of charm as, in a different way, did Reagan and the British prime minister was not immune to this.* Such was her closeness to Reagan and rapport with Gorbachev that Cradock, her official foreign policy adviser, described her as 'an agent of influence in both directions'.[25] It was, though, not only because he saw her as a conduit to Reagan that Gorbachev found his meetings with Thatcher stimulating and useful. The vigour with which she presented her arguments helped him to appreciate more fully how past Soviet actions had been perceived in the West and in Europe in particular.

Leaders, Alternatives, and Outcomes

I have partly addressed (especially in Chapter 13) the question whether the same policies would have been pursued and whether the Cold War would have ended in broadly the same way and at roughly the same time if any of the realistically alternative leaders to Gorbachev and Reagan had been chosen, although not in relation to Thatcher. The central significance, however, of what Gorbachev often called 'the human factor' for the Cold War's ending needs to be set out still more explicitly. In the case of the last Soviet leader, we know the political outlook and many of the concrete views (both at the time and subsequently) of the handful of possible alternative leaders to Gorbachev in 1985. It is inconceivable that any one of them would have embraced political pluralism and endangered, still less consciously dismantled, the institutional and ideological pillars of a Communist system. None of them would have allowed expectations to rise in Eastern Europe to the point at which one country after another seized the opportunity to escape from Soviet tutelage. With East Europe still under ultimate Soviet control, a modus vivendi with the West of the kind achieved in the 1970s might, with great difficulty, have been re-established, but that would not have meant the end of the Cold War.

Gorbachev acquired the most powerful post in the CPSU not because, faced by increased American pressures, he had signified that he would take a 'softer' line than his predecessors on relations with the West, for he had given no such signals. He became general secretary through his skill in intra-party manoeuvring, his energy,

---

* In Geoffrey Howe's view, the charm was embellished by their power. In one of the conversations I had with him, he said he thought there must be something in the remark attributed to Henry Kissinger that power is an aphrodisiac. He had observed that Mrs Thatcher, in the presence of Reagan and Gorbachev, leaders who were manifestly more powerful than she was, behaved quite differently from the way she did with other politicians.

and his abilities which had impressed important colleagues, especially Andropov, who played an important part in extending Gorbachev's powers within the Central Committee building, while his relative youth, which earlier had counted against him, became an advantage after the Soviet Union had suffered the embarrassment of state funerals for three supreme leaders within a period of less than three years. The extension of Gorbachev's powers over parts of the Central Committee apparatus had become such that it was difficult, following Andropov's death, to prevent him becoming the de facto second secretary to Chernenko and the man best placed to claim the succession to the top post when Chernenko died.

Since Gorbachev's accession to the Soviet leadership had nothing to do with Reagan's presidency and policies, the issue of whether or not Reagan was indispensable for the ending of the Cold War boils down to another question: was the American political system so dysfunctional in the 1980s that it could not produce a president other than Reagan capable of responding to the opportunities offered by a Soviet leader intent on reforming the system he inherited and in pursuing qualitatively better relations with the outside world? To believe that such was the case is to take a truly dismal view of American politicians as incorrigibly pusillanimous in the face of influential domestic lobbies. Any American president worthy of the office should have had the elementary political imagination, and the modest level of political courage, required to respond to a Soviet leader who sought to reduce the disproportionate influence within the USSR of the military-industrial complex (to some extent mirrored, as Eisenhower had warned, in the United States) and to join him in giving a new impetus to Soviet-American talks on the achievement of verifiable arms reductions. All the more so, when that Soviet leader embarked on domestic liberalization and democratization. These developments were in the interests of Americans as well as of Soviet citizens.

For Gorbachev and those of his colleagues who helped formulate the 'New Thinking', Reagan was a mixed blessing. His arms build-up, and his obsessive attachment to the idea of comprehensive missile defence, made it harder for the radically new approach of Gorbachev and his foreign policy team to prevail over Soviet military-industrial opposition and its backers within the party and government structures. But Reagan had major pluses for Gorbachev as well as those minuses. On the positive side was the fact that this was a president who was prepared to 'think big', who shared his vision of a world free from the nuclear threat, and who (to the horror of many in Washington and of Margaret Thatcher and François Mitterrand) was prepared to seek the complete outlawing of the possession of nuclear weapons. For Thatcher and for Foreign Secretary Howe (in contradistinction to Shultz) the only good thing about the 1986 Reykjavik summit meeting (and, at that time, about Reagan's Strategic Defense Initiative) was that the zero nuclear weapons option foundered on the rock of SDI. Speaking with the Spanish Foreign Minister, Fernández Ordóñez on 3 March 1989, Gorbachev said, 'Even such a conservative as Reagan was able instinctively to feel that something had to change', contrasting that with how slow the Bush administration had been up to that point in reconciling itself to new realities.[26] Less than a fortnight later, addressing Soviet ambassadors, Gorbachev referred to Reagan's 'inborn intuition' and 'political flair'.[27]

Reagan had the additional advantage for the Soviet side that he was a negotiating partner who could deliver, bolstered by his well-established conservative record and long-standing anti-Soviet credentials. He had less trouble than a liberal Republican or, still more, a liberal Democrat might have encountered in getting agreements accepted in Washington and treaties ratified. Bush's knowledge that he was not similarly trusted by the American right was one of the inhibitors on his taking up the dialogue with Gorbachev where Reagan had left off. Nevertheless, after an unnecessarily slow start, Bush and Baker pursued a policy not dissimilar to that of Reagan and Shultz. The idea that the Cold War would not have ended had there been any president other than Reagan in the White House is far-fetched. In contrast, accepting (as we must) that the choice of General Secretary of the Communist Party of the Soviet Union was limited to the small handful of men who were members of the Politburo in March 1985, there is ample evidence that no other contender would have pursued policies remotely similar to those of Gorbachev.

The case of Thatcher is different. There were many people in British politics who would have been even readier to engage with a Soviet leader than she was. As we have seen, Howe, who was Foreign Secretary during the most important years for the ending of the Cold War, had fundamental disagreements with Thatcher on some aspects of foreign policy—particularly on relations with the European Economic Community—but there was no appreciable difference between them on attitudes to either the Soviet Union or the United States. Howe enjoyed excellent personal relations with both Shevardnadze and Shultz. Nevertheless, Thatcher's role was distinctively important, for no alternative Conservative leader, and still less a Labour leader, would have enjoyed such a close and influential relationship with Reagan.

It is also highly doubtful if any other British prime minister would have made such an impact on Gorbachev. They would almost certainly have been more tactful and more restrained. But Thatcher's willingness to argue vigorously with Gorbachev, far from doing her any harm in his eyes, strengthened their mutual esteem, as close observers of their meetings perceived.[28] And Gorbachev appreciated the fact that she spoke positively about him and his domestic reforms when she was addressing Soviet audiences and in conversation with American presidents and European heads of government. No previous British prime minister had as many meetings with a Soviet leader as Thatcher had with Gorbachev or more frequent meetings with an American president. When Thatcher was forced to resign her office in 1990, Gorbachev, in his personal letter to her, as well as praising her 'enormous contribution' internationally, expressed the hope that their 'friendly meetings' would continue— which they did.[29] Reagan published an article in which he said he and Thatcher had been 'soulmates' who 'were always comfortable with each other'. He noted that the first state dinner he held in the White House was for her, and that so was the last. Most pertinently, he added: 'Before I met with Mikhail Gorbachev...I talked with Mrs. Thatcher. She told me that Gorbachev was different from any of the other Kremlin leaders. She believed that there was a chance for a great opening. Of course, she was proven exactly right.'[30]

Achievements and Failures

Ending the Cold War was in the long-term interest of Russians, as well as of the people of other countries, for the vast resources spent on the means of mass destruction could have been used more productively to raise living and environmental standards, while avoiding the real risk in times of high tension of stumbling into nuclear war through human error, technical malfunction, or political miscalculation. That is *not* to say that continuation of the Cold War was contrary to the immediate interests of the Soviet leadership. There was a reason no Soviet leaders before Gorbachev took the kind of steps that were needed to end it. If their primary aim was to sustain their power and authority within the USSR, and in relation to their subordinate allies in Eastern Europe—and that seems a fair summary of the top priorities of the Brezhnev leadership—then the Cold War, albeit one mitigated by the establishment of some rules of the game, had a lot to be said for it.

Gorbachev, however, regarded the state of international relations he inherited as extremely dangerous and from the outset of his leadership he wished to embark on the process of ending the Cold War. No doubt, he underestimated the risks this would entail for Soviet stability and, eventually, for his own authority, although for the first several years of his party leadership, removal of the threat of war enhanced his standing at home as well as abroad. But even after his domestic popularity was in steep decline, he remained committed to maintaining the relations of trust and cooperation he had established with Western leaders, just as he did not reverse the pluralization of Soviet politics which had produced unintended as well as intended consequences.

For many in Russia today, and for some in the West, Gorbachev is seen as a failure—guilty, above all, for the disintegration of the Soviet Union. At the end of the period of less than seven years in which he occupied the highest post in Soviet politics, the state over which he presided became fifteen separate countries; the economy was still performing dismally; and the United States was emerging from the Cold War as (for the time being) the one superpower. Yet, during the first five years of perestroika, Gorbachev was the most popular politician in both Russia and in the USSR as a whole (as we know from the most professional survey research at that time). The new freedoms were widely welcomed by Russians as well as by the titular national groups in those other republics who sought greater autonomy or, in some (although far from all) cases, separate statehood.

In the last two years of the USSR's existence, the problems facing Gorbachev and the Soviet leadership mounted exponentially and his popularity correspondingly declined.[31] But do the failures outweigh what he accomplished? It is worth summarizing twelve remarkable achievements which owed more to Gorbachev than to anyone else in the Soviet Union (and far more to him than to any foreign leader) which were appreciated at the time, even if increasingly forgotten, not least in Russia, thereafter.

First, the introduction of glasnost and its development into freedom of speech and publication; second, the release of dissidents from prison and exile and the resumption of rehabilitations of those unjustly repressed in the past; third, freedom of religious observation and the ending of persecution of the churches; fourth, freedom of communication across frontiers, including an end to the jamming of foreign broadcasts and a developing freedom to travel or to emigrate; fifth, the introduction of genuinely competitive elections for new federal and republican legislatures endowed with real powers; sixth, the development of civil society which was a result of perestroika and not (as some have imagined) a precursor of it; seventh, progress towards a rule of law, with the Communist Party no longer above the law and supreme power moving from party to state institutions; eighth, the replacement of Lenin and dogma with a commitment to pluralism and free intellectual inquiry; ninth, the ending of Soviet military intervention in Afghanistan and the withdrawal of the last Soviet troops from that country by February 1989; tenth, granting the right of the East European countries to become independent and non-Communist—a decisively important component of the end of the Cold War; eleventh, consent to, and negotiation of, the peaceful reunification of Germany; and twelfth, underpinning the last three foreign policy decisions, a fundamental reappraisal of world politics in which East–West relations were no longer seen as a zero-sum game but as one in which both sides could win. That last point was linked to Gorbachev's acceptance of democratic norms and values, with the principles of democracy understood in the same way as in long-established Western democratic states, and his embrace of universal interests—what was in the interest of all humanity rather than of any one class, group, or nation. All that amounted to a demolition of the ideological foundations of the Cold War, leaving zealots and irreconcilables on both sides of the old divide deprived of a role.[32]

For citizens of Western democracies, the political transformation of a country which had hitherto been, but had now ceased to be, a political, ideological, and military adversary was more important than one state becoming fifteen. But the breakup of the Soviet Union became a clear blessing for only some of the newly independent republics—the Baltic states, in the first instance. For several of the others, it has meant descent into a form of rule more authoritarian than that of the last years of the Soviet era when there was backing for political pluralism throughout the USSR from the highest political echelons in Moscow.

Disintegration of the Soviet state has led to territorial disputes and inter-ethnic tensions, some of which have resulted in violent conflict. Gorbachev's projected voluntary federation envisaged in the Union Treaty was designed to prevent the break-up of the Soviet state and to do so without resort to violent coercion. From one side, Yeltsin and his associates and, from another, the putschists played the major part in ensuring that the Union Treaty was ultimately aborted. Yet, the existence of the talks had themselves played a part in keeping the dissolution of the Soviet state in 1991 largely peaceful—remarkably so if it is compared with the deadly conflicts which accompanied the break-up of Yugoslavia.

In post-Soviet Russia, perhaps not surprisingly since it had been the dominant republic in the Union, a majority of citizens still regret the break-up of the USSR. For a significant minority of Russians, however, the gains in freedom and democracy of the perestroika years counted for more than the disappearance of the Soviet state. Whether, after all, people live in a free society and under government accountable to the public in free elections or, on the contrary, under dictatorial rule, with its accompanying censorship and self-censorship, makes a bigger difference to the quality of their lives than the size of the country. And it is not as if Russia has been left small and unviable. Even minus the fourteen other Soviet republics, it remains the world's largest state, and one rich in natural resources.

By no means all of the dozen achievements of the perestroika era I have outlined have been preserved in post-Soviet Russia. But at the time they made a major contribution to ending a Cold War which was becoming increasingly anachronistic, given the extent to which the Soviet Union had been liberalized by 1989 and the progress it was making in democratization. Gorbachev bequeathed to his successors a Russia that was freer than at any time in its previous history as well as relations of trust between Moscow, on the one hand, and Washington and West European capitals, on the other. Writing in 1989, one of the most knowledgeable of European politicians on international affairs and defence matters, Denis Healey, conveyed the optimism of the time in a highly positive assessment of the scale of Gorbachev's accomplishment and goals. In the light of what he called the 'appalling relations between Washington and Moscow during Reagan's first term', this former long-serving UK Defence Secretary wrote that 'Gorbachev's achievement was stupendous.' He had gone 'far beyond simply ending the Cold War' and had even raised the prospect of 'the sort of cooperation between the world's governments which the United Nations had been set up to achieve'. Gorbachev had shown 'extraordinary sensitivity' to the personalities of Reagan and Thatcher who had learned to trust him to a degree 'inconceivable in the light of their earlier rhetoric'.[33]

Healey was writing at the high point of Gorbachev's leadership. Up until then, while Western politicians' readiness to engage with the Soviet Union was very important, it was the Gorbachev-led breakthrough in Moscow, both in domestic and foreign policy, that was the main driver of international change. From the second half of 1989, when events moved faster in Eastern Europe than Gorbachev (or, for that matter, Western leaders) had expected, and especially in 1990–1 when separatist movements and growing economic difficulties undermined his authority, Gorbachev was a leader reacting to events rather than setting the agenda, although *how* he reacted still mattered greatly.

The Turn to Triumphalism

Although the Cold War ended primarily due to Gorbachev's transformation of Soviet foreign policy and of the Soviet political system, American politicians lost little time in allocating the credit to themselves. For Bush, with a presidential election to fight in 1992, this was somewhat understandable, but it fed into a post-Soviet Russian nationalist narrative that the break-up of the Soviet Union had been planned and orchestrated from Washington. Yet the collapse of the Soviet Union had never been an outcome Bush wanted. On the contrary, he had hoped that the Soviet republics, with the exception of the Baltic states, would remain in a Gorbachev-led union. At the beginning of August 1991, he had been sharply criticized for offering no support for Ukrainian independent statehood. But, in a Christmas address to the American people that year, the very day Gorbachev stepped down as president of a state which was ceasing to be, Bush declared that the US had led the struggle against Communism. That confrontation was now over, he noted unexceptionably, and Eastern Europe was free. As if, however, it had been an American policy goal, he added: 'The Soviet Union is no more' (italics added). The outcome was 'a victory for the moral force of our values' and 'every American' could 'take pride in this victory'.[34] That morning Gorbachev had called Bush to say goodbye. It was a warm and friendly conversation and, immediately after it, Bush recorded his thoughts on tape. He said of Gorbachev's call, 'It was the voice of a good friend; it was the voice of a man to whom history will give enormous credit.'[35]

Yet, by the late summer of 1992, when the opinion polls were not looking good for Bush's prospects for re-election, he began, in the words of Strobe Talbott (an old friend of Bill Clinton who became Deputy Secretary of State in the Clinton administration) 'to play the Russia card more aggressively'. As Talbott saw it, Bush was appealing to voters to remember that 'he had personally "won the cold War"'. Clinton's response was to say that Bush 'reminds me of the rooster who took credit for the dawn'. He, too, spoke of 'America's victory in the cold war', but gave the credit to the bipartisan approach of a succession of presidents, starting with a Democrat, Harry Truman. Talbott, who had long been a student of Russian affairs, was pained to hear Clinton use that line. He knew that 'American triumphalism', whether in Bush's version or Clinton's, 'set teeth on edge in Moscow'.[36]

In certain vital respects, the end of the Cold War *was* a victory for the West—just not the kind of victory claimed in so many Western triumphalist accounts which emphasized a supposed American military superiority and deliberate economic coercion, suggesting that these had led the Soviet leadership metaphorically to run up the white flag. What undoubtedly contributed to the Cold War ending in the way it did was pursuit of the combination of policies which George Kennan outlined in his 'Long Telegram' of 1946, and even these, though necessary, were far from sufficient conditions. The US and its allies had maintained sufficient military strength to ensure that no Soviet leadership could be seriously tempted to try extending their hegemony any further in Europe, and in the meantime Western governments and societies had, on the whole, remained true to democratic values. Force of example turned out to be even more important than military force. The Soviet Union had much less difficulty in matching the armed might of the Western alliance than it had in persuading more than a small minority of people in the developed world that the kind of society and system they had created in the USSR and imposed on Eastern Europe was better or more advanced than what was to be found in the West. Increasingly, they had great trouble in persuading even their own citizens of the superiority of the Soviet system.

The perestroika era was the peak period of Russian admiration for most things Western, including their political and economic systems. But the process had been underway earlier than that. What mattered greatly was the increased contact between highly educated Soviet citizens and their Western counterparts in the 1970s and the 1980s, and the impact of first-hand acquaintanceship with democratic institutions and unfettered societies. Such contacts became much more extensive during perestroika. The highest-level examples of how seeing for themselves influenced the way they looked at the world were, of course, those of Gorbachev, Yakovlev, and Shevardnadze (in the Foreign Minister's case only from the time he assumed that office) and, a rung or two down the hierarchy, such highly influential advisers as Chernyaev and Shakhnazarov. This occurred only because Western governments and even the pre-perestroika Soviet leadership accepted a certain amount of interaction, a development which was regarded with great suspicion by counter-intelligence services on both sides of the Cold War divide.[37]

In contrast, what has happened since Communist rule in Europe passed into history has been a sad story of missed opportunities and dissipation of the mutual trust which existed when Reagan's second term concluded and the Cold War ended a year later. That trust between Gorbachev and his Western counterparts still existed in the first two post-Cold War years of 1990–1 (at any rate after the Bush team recovered from their slow and sceptical start). Boris Yeltsin, in the afterglow of his prominent role in defying the August 1991 putschists, went on to have a good relationship with Bush, who had earlier regarded him as boorish, and he established a still stronger rapport with Bill Clinton. Nevertheless, the low priority Yeltsin gave to democratic institution-building and a rule of law, combined with successive American administrations' insensitivity to Russian interests, undermined that trust in the post-Soviet era. This was already happening in the 1990s and the trend became more marked within a few years of Vladimir Putin, Yeltsin's hand-picked successor, becoming president in 2000.*

Some of the most notable achievements of the Cold War years have been lost. The ABM Treaty, signed as long ago as 1972, was unilaterally abrogated by the George W. Bush administration thirty years later. As one of the most perceptive and well-informed of Western specialists on US–Russian relations (both in the Soviet period and after it) Robert Legvold has observed, although there were genuine concerns about new nuclear threats, 'by acting alone and over Russian objection, rather than first attempting to fashion a joint US–Russian response to third-party nuclear threats', the American government 'opened the way to what became a highly corrosive source of tension'.[38]

Much more recently, on successive days in early February 2019, the United States and Russia announced that they were suspending their participation in the Intermediate-Range Nuclear Forces Treaty—the INF Treaty signed by Reagan and Gorbachev in Washington in 1987. It had already become clear that this exceptionally important US–Soviet agreement was under threat. In a throwback to the cooperation characteristic of the later years of the Reagan presidency, Gorbachev and Shultz published a joint article in the *Washington Post* in early December 2018, warning of the danger that 'the gains achieved in the process of ending the Cold War could be wiped out'. If the INF Treaty were to be abandoned, they wrote, this would be 'a step toward a new arms race, undermining strategic stability and increasing the threat of miscalculation or technical failure leading to an immensely destructive war'. What followed two months later was less than a total abandonment of the treaty, but it was a fateful step in that direction, raising the possibility of the reintroduction by both sides of short-range and medium-range nuclear missiles in Europe.[39] The further step was taken on 2 August 2019 when the United States formally withdrew from the INF Treaty. The United States, with the backing of NATO allies, argued that Russia had been developing a new type of cruise missile which was in violation of the treaty. However, the UN Secretary General Antonio Guterres warned that what was being lost, with the abandonment of the INF Treaty, was 'an invaluable brake on nuclear

* Strobe Talbott describes an occasion when he accompanied President Clinton to a meeting with Yeltsin shortly after the latter retired from his presidency. Yeltsin, he writes, 'launched into a self-congratulatory account of how he had maneuvered Putin from obscurity into the presidency over fierce resistance', whereupon his younger daughter, Tatiana Dyachenko, whispered to Talbott, 'It really was very hard, getting Putin into the job—one of the hardest things we ever pulled off.' The 'we', he observes, was deliberate. Now that Yeltsin's presidency was over, she wanted him to realize that she had been just as influential as many commentators had said she was (Talbott, *The Russia Hand: A Memoir of Presidential Diplomacy*, Random House, New York, 2002, p. 7).

war' and that the demise of the treaty was likely to 'heighten, not reduce, the threat posed by ballistic missiles'.[40]

The repudiation of the INF Treaty did not come out of the blue. The revival of antagonism between Moscow and Washington, and a deteriorating relationship between Russia and much of Europe, had been developing over the post-Soviet period, and especially during the first two decades of the twenty-first century. No-one appeared to be paying attention to the 1990 Charter of Paris, but a contradiction in that well-intentioned and generally sensible document (already noted in Chapter 14) pinpoints a central problem at the heart of the growing discord between Russia and the West after the end of Communism in Europe. One article of the charter declared that 'the security of every participating State is inseparably linked to that of all the others' and was 'indivisible', while another article recognized 'the freedom of States to choose their own security arrangements'. In accordance with the latter stipulation, the governments of the formerly Communist states of central and eastern Europe and of several former republics of the Soviet Union—in the first instance, the three Baltic states—clamoured for admission to NATO, and in a process that began during the Clinton administration and continued in the George W. Bush presidency, a majority of them were admitted.*

From a Russian standpoint, this was setting up a new cold war frontier at their border. Countries that had been allies (however involuntarily on the part of their populations) or even components of the same Soviet state were becoming members of what had always been a hostile military alliance. When NATO exercises began to be held on the territory of neighbouring countries of Russia which had earlier been members of the Warsaw Pact, it was easy to see which potential adversary they had in mind. It was correspondingly hard to discern how such developments could be 'inseparably linked' to the security of Russia. The continuation, and especially the expansion, of NATO was anomalous, for although its founding treaty, signed in April 1949, did not mention either Communism or the Soviet Union, what provided the impetus to the creation of the organization was the fact that the Soviet Union had become a formidable military power and that it had over the previous few years taken over eastern and much of central Europe. This was accompanied by Western fears of further Communist expansion in Europe through the threat or use of force and by anxiety about the ambitions and spread of the international Communist movement. By 1992, however, there was no Soviet Union, no Communist rule in

---

* Some attempts to allay Moscow's concerns and to foster cooperative East–West relations were made by the United States and its allies, especially during the Clinton–Yeltsin years. Thus, from 1994 Russia participated in a NATO initiative called Partnership for Peace. That, however, was seen by Russian nationalists as no more than a sop and it did little to allay the suspicions of Western intentions on the part of growing numbers within Moscow's political elite. Following its military intervention in Ukraine in 2014, Russia's membership of Partnership for Peace was suspended.

Europe, no Warsaw Pact (though this counterpart of NATO was founded six years after NATO), and no international Communist movement.

Noting that Czech President Václav Havel had called as early as 1991 for Czechoslovakia, Poland, and Hungary to enter NATO, Rodric Braithwaite* said that 'the British Prime Minister and Foreign Secretary privately assured Soviet ministers that there was no such intention', while 'Manfred Woerner, NATO's secretary general, added publicly that enlargement would damage relations with the Soviet Union'. As Braithwaite observes, however much one argues that oral assurances are not binding or that what was said in 1991 was 'overtaken by events', it is hardly surprising that 'Russians took seriously these statements by apparently responsible Western officials, or that they now [he was writing in 2015] believe they were misled'.[41]

When NATO enlargement was first mooted with Yeltsin by Clinton, the Russian president was accommodating in private, so long as the process would be 'gradual and lengthy' and Russian eventual membership was not, in principle, excluded.[42] The first post-Communist countries to join were the Czech Republic, Poland, and Hungary in 1999, and among the new members added in 2004 were three former republics of the Soviet Union: Estonia, Latvia, and Lithuania. This was certainly not what was envisaged by either side when East–West negotiations over the unification of Germany were taking place in 1990—or a year later in response to Havel. Gorbachev was much criticized in retrospect in post-Soviet Russia for not getting written guarantees that there would be no NATO expansion beyond that of the GDR when it became part of a united Germany. Perhaps he should have emulated Reagan's constant refrain to him and said to Bush, *Doverai no proverai* (trust but verify) and called for incorporation of the informal promises into a formal treaty. As the later repudiation of the ABM and INF Treaties has illustrated, not even formal treaty status is a guarantee of continuity of policy, but it would have given existing NATO members good grounds for not expanding their organization eastwards and have made such enlargement more improbable. However, in the last two years of the Soviet Union's existence, not only had fissiparous tendencies and economic difficulties at home weakened Gorbachev's negotiating position, but the very notion of further NATO expansion appeared unlikely (because unnecessary) and so was far from the top of his agenda. It was not, indeed, in the minds at that time of his Western inter-locutors who gave their assurances in good faith.

NATO enlargement, though, became an increasingly sore point over time for the Russian military and for many Russian politicians. Among those in the United States who warned of this danger were William Perry, Secretary of Defense in the Clinton administration, and none other than George Kennan. At the time when NATO

---

* Immediately after serving from 1988 to 1992 as British ambassador to Moscow, Braithwaite in the latter year became foreign policy adviser to Prime Minister John Major and chair of the UK's Joint Intelligence Committee.

enlargement was being considered in Washington in the mid-1990s, 'Bill Perry', noted Deputy Secretary of State Strobe Talbott, 'would have preferred to postpone enlargement for a decade, or perhaps forever.'[43] When Thomas Friedman in 1998 asked Kennan (by then aged 94) for his reaction to Senate ratification of NATO expansion (the Czech Republic, Poland, and Hungary officially joined NATO the following year), Kennan replied that he thought it was 'the beginning of a new cold war'.

Calling it 'a tragic mistake', Kennan said that it would lead to an adverse reaction in Russia and affect their policies, and there was absolutely no reason for it.[44] Interviewed a little over a year later by the Princeton historian Richard Ullman, Kennan said that he had never seen any evidence that the recent NATO enlargement was either necessary or desirable. Some advocates of NATO expansion were now pushing for admission of the Baltic countries. This, said Kennan, 'would be highly unfortunate'. While 'NATO, as we know it, has no intention of attacking Russia', it remained, nevertheless, a military alliance. If there was any country against which it had been conceived and was still directed, that was Russia—and this, he added, 'surely is the way the Poles and others in that part of the world would perceive it'.[45]

Although too much was on Gorbachev's agenda in 1990–1 for discussion of the architecture of a new security structure to proceed beyond generalities, there was an expectation that it would involve building on the foundations of the Conference on Security and Cooperation in Europe (CSCE), created in 1975, for this embraced the United States and Canada as well as the European countries, thus preserving the organizational link between North America and Europe that the North Atlantic Treaty had earlier created and subsequently consolidated. It would have been a more inclusive organization than NATO was to become in the post-Soviet era, for it would have included all the former Communist states of Europe, including Russia and Ukraine. Western leaders with more political imagination and vision than those in office in the 1990s would have realized that there was a unique opportunity to build a post-Cold War order on new foundations. An organization that brought together all the CSCE (subsequently OSCE) signatories would have offered the best chance of avoiding the development of an antagonistic relationship between Russia and the West and between Russia and Ukraine.

Drawing Lessons

It is no part of my argument that heads of government invariably provide the key to understanding political change—often they do not—but it makes little sense to deny that *some* such leaders make a huge difference, whether domestically or internationally, and occasionally both. In the case of the Cold War's ending, any interpretation that excludes the mindsets, values, and character of particular leaders is likely to be of limited use. Reagan's and Thatcher's large contribution, and their commitment to engagement with the Soviet Union, mattered all the more because of their conservative background and hard-line credentials. Although Reagan duly received some criticism from American politicians and commentators whose default position was to blame even a greatly changing Moscow for the ills of the world, and who suggested that Reagan had been charmed into gullibility by Gorbachev, this had little resonance with a broader American public and even less in Europe where every meeting between Reagan and Gorbachev was welcomed.

As should by now be clear, however, the difference Gorbachev made was qualitatively greater than that of Reagan and Thatcher. While Reagan had become more of a partner than an adversary of his Soviet counterpart by the time he left office, and while Thatcher was the second most influential Western leader, so far as Soviet policy was concerned, during the period Reagan occupied the White House, it was Gorbachev who played by far the most decisive role in making the end of the Cold War possible. By turning Marxism-Leninism on its head, replacing Communist 'democratic centralism' (which in practice meant unquestioning obedience within a strictly disciplined and hierarchical party) by an openness to criticism and fresh thinking, and by removing the ruling party's monopoly of power (de facto already in 1988–9 and de jure, with a constitutional change, in March 1990), Gorbachev transformed the Soviet political system to the point where it was no longer meaningful to call it Communist. And if the Soviet Union as well as the countries of Eastern Europe no longer had a Communist system, what purpose could there be for a Cold War?

Yet of the three major political figures who have been the special focus of this book, only Ronald Reagan finished his political career on his own terms. By that time, he had served eight years as president and played a big part in the achievement of dramatically improved relations with the Soviet Union. In many respects he was a malleable leader, even going along with senior office-holders when they themselves agreed to exchange jobs. Reagan did not immerse himself in policy detail and so, even more than most presidents, was heavily dependent on the political and intellectual abilities of those who served in his administration and on their willingness to cooperate with each other (that last feature conspicuously lacking until well into his second term). He was able, though, to set the general guidelines of policy in domestic and foreign policy and he took a special interest in relations with the Soviet Union. He had several big, and very general, foreign policy ideas—a belief in the pursuit of peace through strength, a firm anti-Communism, and a commitment to freedom in various manifestations, including religious freedom (on which, in an echo perhaps of his upbringing, he laid particular stress). He could also become fixated on a few more specific policies, of which his Strategic Defense Initiative was the prime example.

If, however, a Secretary of State and National Security Adviser stayed within the broad parameters of Reagan's policy towards Communist countries—and the Soviet Union most specifically—these senior officials had a lot of scope to persuade the president that one approach rather than another would advance his goals. George Shultz was particularly successful in doing this. Because Reagan reposed great trust in him, his role in the peaceful ending of the Cold War was scarcely less important than the president's. By the time Gorbachev was in the Kremlin, Reagan also had more open-minded National Security Advisers than in the earliest years of his presidency and a principal adviser on the Soviet Union in the NSC, Matlock, who was far readier to recognize change in Moscow and to respond to it than his predecessor Pipes had been.

Because Reagan trusted Thatcher's judgement above that of any other foreign leader, and because her hard-line credentials were well established even in the eyes of the Pentagon (she had excellent relations with Weinberger as well as with Shultz), the fact that on engagement with the Soviet Union she came down strongly on the same side as Shultz made an impression on the debate inside Washington. Her political style was very different from both Gorbachev's and Reagan's. Of the three, she was the only 'strong leader' in a domineering and power-hoarding sense.* Gorbachev, more often than not, eventually got his way in Soviet internal debates, but he was a collegial leader who allowed free discussion in the Politburo and in his consultative groups. Especially in the earliest years of his general secretaryship, when he could have been speedily deposed if the Politburo united against him, he used persuasion rather than fiat to cajole often dubious colleagues into accepting collective responsibility for bold changes of policy about which they harboured grave doubts. And whereas Reagan had not batted an eyelid when Donald Regan and James Baker swapped their Treasury Secretary and White House Chief of Staff posts, no British minister or official would have dared come to Thatcher with a comparable proposal. Had they done so, they would have been at the receiving end of what the popular press in Britain called 'a handbagging'. Nevertheless, Thatcher, too, was heavily dependent on others. The British Foreign Office was a source of well-informed advice which came filtered by her highly capable private secretary Charles Powell who was also an influential de facto foreign policy adviser, even though Percy Cradock held that official title. Indeed, Powell on occasion introduced himself to Soviet officials as 'Mrs Thatcher's Chernyaev'.

In the view of Geoffrey Howe, who spent six years as Foreign Secretary in the Thatcher government, it was of special importance that Thatcher was persuaded both that deliberate destabilization of the Soviet Union would be dangerous and counterproductive and that a resumption of dialogue was necessary. That made possible her successful relationship with the Soviet leader and, what was 'no less crucial', her role in 'turning President Reagan away from the "evil empire" rhetoric and encouraging him towards a similar relationship with Gorbachev'. This, Howe adds,

---

* I am aware that 'strong leader' is often used as if it were a synonym for 'good leader', but I find that meaningless. Hitler and Stalin were strong leaders who imposed their will on all and sundry, but it would be indecent to call them 'good' leaders. The detailed arguments concerning overmighty individual leaders, and discussion of different types and categories of political leadership more broadly, are to be found in my book, *The Myth of the Strong Leader: Political Leadership in the Modern Age* (with updating new Foreword, Vintage, London, 2018).

'may be seen by historians as her greatest achievement in foreign affairs'.[46] Whereas in her domestic policy, Thatcher was deeply divisive and reacting against a more consensual and paternalistic Toryism in her own party, as well as antagonizing the opposition parties, in her relationship with Gorbachev's Soviet Union she was more in step with a broad swath of opinion in the country than in any other policy area. The significance of her contribution to the ending of the Cold War did not arise, therefore, from the distinctiveness in the British context of her policy but from the bond she formed with Reagan and, to a lesser but still remarkable extent, with Gorbachev and the vigour with which she pressed her views.

Thatcher's policy towards the Soviet Union from the autumn of 1983 onwards was, in fact, close to that of the Foreign Office, however much she disdained it. Writing in his diary in September 1989, when the prime minister was having yet another meeting with Gorbachev in the Kremlin (on her way back from a visit to Tokyo), British Ambassador Braithwaite observed that 'the magic of their relationship is undimmed' and Gorbachev was 'full of beans'. The ambassador added: 'I suspect he finds his exchanges with Mrs Thatcher a welcome relief from the cares of office, a sort of therapy.'[47] More emphasis than it generally receives should be given to the fact that Thatcher was well served in foreign policy not only by the FCO in London and those who worked most closely with her in 10 Downing Street, and notably Powell, but also by Britain's two perestroika-era ambassadors to Moscow, Sir Bryan Cartledge and his successor from 1988, Braithwaite.

One thing Gorbachev and Thatcher had in common—and it was unusual for leading politicians of their time—was that both (and especially Gorbachev) took seriously threats to the environment and to the very future of the planet. Gorbachev had raised 'green' issues with Bush without getting much response, but Thatcher, with her scientific background, was attentive to the issues before most of her ministers and officials were. When Braithwaite went to Vnukovo airport (near Moscow) to greet the prime minister when she was on her way to Tokyo in mid-September 1989, and took part in a supper presided over by Evgeny Primakov in an airport VIP building, they discussed her forthcoming talks with Gorbachev, for she was to make a lengthier stop in Russia on the way back from Japan. As the conversation began to flag, Braithwaite recorded in his diary, 'the indefatigable Mrs T treats us all to a lecture on the ozone layer and other threats to the world's environment'.[48]

Whereas George Bush referred dismissively to 'the vision thing' in 1987 as something he didn't do (and the absence of which he was not allowed to forget by his political opponents), Gorbachev clearly did have a vision of a future that would be unlike the past but very different also from the communist dreams of Marx, Engels and Lenin. To this, of course, his conservative critics at home and some 'realists' abroad could retort: 'And much good it did him and his country!' For others—in Russia and outside it—there was a great deal of good for his country to be discerned, important examples of which have already been summarized in this chapter.

Gorbachev, like Thatcher, had the support of a talented and well-informed foreign policy team, including—in addition to Foreign Minister Shevardnadze—Yakovlev, Primakov, Chernyaev, and Shakhnazarov. He relied particularly, as we have seen, on Chernyaev, his principal and closest foreign policy adviser, and for the day-to-day conduct of international relations on Shevardnadze. Both of them, it is fair to say, reposed even more trust in Western leaders and their good intentions than Gorbachev did, since he had to listen to many very different viewpoints, including warnings, from other parts of the foreign and security establishment, among them the International Department of the Central Committee under Valentin Falin, the Ministry of Defence, and the KGB. From those quarters the message was that the Soviet Union was conceding too much in negotiations on arms reductions and on Germany.

That the multinational Soviet state unravelled in 1990–1, and that post-Soviet international developments have turned out to be very different from what Gorbachev worked for and envisaged, are evidence enough in the eyes of unreconstructed Communists of the folly of changing the fundamentals of Soviet foreign policy and of the country's political system. For less dogmatic observers, these unintended consequences leave open the question whether the gap between aspiration and outcome, the failure to recreate the Soviet state as a voluntary federal union, and the continuing absence of a European house with a room large enough to accommodate Russia, was a result of Gorbachev's lack of realism or of others' lack of imagination and of their pursuit of short-term and narrow self-interest.

Writing in the eighteenth century, Adam Smith noted that a person responsible for the conduct of foreign policy pays scant regard to the way that policy is perceived in the other countries affected by it. The 'whole ambition is to obtain the approbation of his fellow-citizens', and since they are 'animated by the same hostile passions', he can please them most 'by enraging and offending their enemies'.[49] In the second half of the twentieth century, following two world wars, public opinion (and a much wider and enfranchised public than in Smith's time) could be more pacific in its sentiments than he suggests. Nevertheless, the general point about foreign policy being made to please domestic publics often has much truth in it. Indeed, foreign policy in the United States—where it is of exceptional importance for other countries—appears to be especially beholden to domestic constituencies. Reagan explained this to Gorbachev in terms of the US being a 'nation of immigrants' with people continuing to take a close interest in the country from which their parents or grandparents arrived. Although he still had a second election to face, Bush did not bow to domestic pressures and make Gorbachev's political life more difficult by exploiting the national-separatist problem in the USSR, but, as already noted, his regard for how his pronouncements would be received in Russia did not survive by even a day Gorbachev's departure from the Kremlin. Thatcher was particularly restrained in her desire not to destabilize Gorbachev more than he was already by exploiting the dilemmas he faced within a multinational state. But inattention to how Western foreign and security policy is perceived in Russia has been very evident in the post-Soviet era, beginning with Bush's own 1992 electoral campaign and continuing to the present day.

The idea that it was superior military strength and tough talking that forced the Soviet Union to end the Cold War, and on American terms, has had a baleful effect in subsequent years. It was never the case that isolation, or heightened East–West tension, promoted liberalizing change in Russia. On the contrary, closer contacts at all levels and the improvement in the international atmosphere strengthened liberal and democratic tendencies in Moscow and provided a context in which a negotiated end to the Cold War became possible. In that process, the advent of a Soviet leader with a very different way of looking at the world from his predecessors, the possessor of a remarkably open mind, and the courage to pursue radically different policies was of greater import than the shift in American foreign and defence policy of the Reagan administration. The latter was a relatively modest change compared with the policies of previous post-war US governments and extremely modest in comparison with the transformation of Soviet domestic and foreign policy.

In 1990, Secretary of State Baker told Shevardnadze that the United States was 'committed to building the pan-European security institutions desired by the Soviet Union', while President Bush at the end of the same year informed Gorbachev that the US did not want 'winners and losers' but a Soviet Union 'integrated…into the new Europe'.[50] Had Gorbachev succeeded in preserving a 'union state', as had been his aim—and which he sought to achieve by persuasion and negotiation—the chances of building on the relationship of trust which existed at that time between Moscow and Washington, and other Western capitals, would have been greater. But the pledged commitment to pan-European security had been proffered to the former leader of a former state. What has followed, in the years since, is a Russia so far from being integrated into the new Europe that it has eventually reacted in ways that Kennan predicted.

Mutual trust painstakingly gained, and then lost, is especially difficult to re-establish. Its rebuilding on sure foundations will require leadership no less enlightened than that of the late 1980s. One of the building-blocks should be a realization that the popular Western triumphalist interpretation of the Cold War's ending is mistaken, as is its no less popular contemporary Russian counterpart that, far from being a negotiated settlement of the conflict, it was all an American conspiracy to do down Russia. A generation after the Cold War ended, relations between Russia and the West are incomparably worse than they were at the end of the 1980s, and we are a far cry from Gorbachev's 'common European home' or Bush's Europe 'whole and free'. Understanding what went right during the years in which Soviet domestic and foreign policy were transformed—and how and why it went right—may provide useful insight into what has gone wrong since. It may even suggest ways of halting and reversing the downward spiral towards confrontation and catastrophe.

NOTES

Introduction

1. Ronald Reagan, 'Address at Moscow State University' (31 May 1988), https://www.reaganlibrary.gov/sspeeches/053188.
2. Jack F. Matlock, Jr, *Reagan and Gorbachev: How the Cold War Ended* (Random House, New York, 2004), p. 302.
3. Charles Moore, *Margaret Thatcher: The Authorized Biography, Volume One: Not for Turning* (Allen Lane, London, 2013), pp. 332–3.
4. Margaret Thatcher, 'Speech at Soviet Official Banquet, St George's Hall, the Kremlin, 30 March 1987, http://www.margaretthatcher.org/document/106776.
5. 'Leninizm—zhivoe tvorcheskoe uchenie, vernoe rukovodstvo k deystviyu', 22 April 1983, in M. S. Gorbachev, *Izbrannye rechi i stat'i*, Vol. I (Politizdat, Moscow, 1987), pp. 382–401, at 401.
6. 'Vystuplenie v organizatsii ob"edinennykh natsiy', 7 December 1988, in Gorbachev, *Izbrannye rechi i stat'i*, Vol. VII (Politizdat, Moscow, 1990), pp. 184–202, at 189.
7. Some authors regard the 1990 unification of Germany as the point at which the Cold War ended. See, for example, the perceptive, concise history of the entire Cold War by Robert J. McMahon, *The Cold War: A Very Short Introduction* (Oxford University Press, Oxford, 2003).
8. I have in mind public opinion, most notably in the United States, and that to be found in the mass media rather than the specialist literature which contains a variety of explanations of the end of the Cold War. See, for the latter, Robert D. English, *Russia and the Idea of the West: Gorbachev, Intellectuals, and the End of the Cold War* (Columbia University Press, New York, 2000); Matthew Evangelista, *Unarmed Forces: The Transnational Movement to End the Cold War* (Cornell University Press, Ithaca, 1999); Frances Fitzgerald, *Way Out There in the Blue: Reagan, Star Wars and the End of the Cold War* (Touchstone, New York, 2001); John Lewis Gaddis, *We Know Now: Rethinking Cold War History* (Clarendon Press, Oxford, 1997); Gaddis, *The Cold War: A New History* (Penguin, New York, 2005); Jonathan Haslam, *Russia's Cold War: From the October Revolution to the Fall of the Wall* (Yale University Press, New Haven, 2011); Richard K. Herrmann and Richard Ned Lebow (eds.), *Ending the Cold War: Interpretations, Causation and the Study of International Relations* (Palgrave Macmillan, New York, 2004); Melvyn P. Leffler, *For the Soul of Mankind: The United States, the Soviet Union, and the Cold War* (Hill and Wang, New York, 2007); Melvyn P. Leffler and Odd Arne Westad (eds.), *The Cambridge History of the Cold War, Volume III: Endings* (Cambridge University Press, Cambridge, 2010); Matlock, *Reagan and Gorbachev*; Olav Nolstad (ed.), *The Last Decade of the Cold War: From Conflict Escalation to Conflict Transformation* (Frank Cass, London, 2004); Robert Service, *The End of the Cold War 1985–1991* (Macmillan, London, 2015); William C. Wolforth (ed.), *Cold War Endgame: Oral History, Analyses, Debates* (Pennsylvania State University Press, University Park, PA, 2003); James Graham Wilson, *The Triumph of Improvisation: Gorbachev's Adaptability, Reagan's Engagement, and the End of the Cold War* (Cornell University Press, Ithaca, 2014); and Vladislav M. Zubok, *A Failed Empire: The Soviet Union in the Cold War from Stalin to Gorbachev* (University of North Carolina Press, Chapel Hill, 2007).

9. For very useful analyses, see Robert Legvold, *Return to Cold War* (Polity, Cambridge, 2016); and Samuel Charap and Timothy J. Colton, *Everyone Loses: The Ukraine Crisis and the Ruinous Contest for Post-Soviet Eurasia* (Routledge, London & New York, 2016).

10. Percy Cradock, *In Pursuit of British Interests: Reflections on Foreign Policy under Margaret Thatcher and John Major* (John Murray, London, 1997), p. 201.

11. John O'Sullivan, *The President, the Pope, and the Prime Minister: Three Who Changed the World* (Regnery, Washington, DC, 2006), p. 301.

12. Archie Brown, *Seven Years that Changed the World: Perestroika in Perspective* (Oxford University Press, Oxford, 2007); Brown, *The Rise and Fall of Communism* (Bodley Head, London, and Ecco, New York, 2009); and Brown, *The Gorbachev Factor* (Oxford University Press, Oxford, 1996).

13. There are, for example, multiple entries for *chelovecheskiy faktor* ('the human factor') in the indexes of Vols. VI and VII of Gorbachev's collected works published during the perestroika era (not all of which, in fact, use the precise phrase, but which have in common a stress on the importance of the individual, usually with reference to Soviet society). See Gorbachev, *Izbrannye rechi i stat'i* (Vol. VI, Politizdat, Moscow 1989; Vol. VII, 1990).

1 The Cold War and its Dangers

1. Adam Roberts, 'An "Incredibly Swift Transition": Reflections on the End of the Cold War', in Melvyn P. Leffler and Odd Arne Westad (eds.), *The Cambridge History of the Cold War, Volume III: Endings* (Cambridge University Press, Cambridge, 2010), pp. 513–34, at p. 514. Roberts cites the examples of Cuba in 1961 (when 1,300 CIA-trained Cuban exiles stormed a Cuban beach and surrendered three days later in what became known as 'the Bay of Pigs fiasco') and Czechoslovakia in 1968 (when half a million Soviet-led troops brought about a change of leadership and of policy in Czechoslovakia and secured Prague's compliance with Moscow for the next two decades).

2. Sidney and Beatrice Webb, *Soviet Communism: A New Civilization* (Longman & Green, London, 2nd edn, 1937). The first edition of this book, published in 1935, had a question-mark after 'A New Civilization', but, in the second and subsequent editions, that was removed. For the Webbs, the Soviet Union really had become a new civilization. As they put it, 'What we have learnt of the developments during 1936–1937 has persuaded us to withdraw the interrogation mark' (p. 971). It was strange timing, for 1937 was the year in which arrests and executions reached their grotesque peak, accompanied by extravagant glorification of Stalin. The Webbs, notable social reformers in their prime, were more right than they realized when they attributed this massive book, a monument of gullibility, 'to the recklessness of old age'. They were, alas, wrong in assuming that 'we had nothing to lose by the venture, not even our reputation' (p. xi).

3. Antony Beevor, *Stalingrad* (Penguin, London, 2007), p. 428.

4. Ibid., and Robert J. McMahon, *The Cold War: A Very Short Introduction* (Oxford University Press, Oxford, 2003), p. 6.

5. Winston S. Churchill, *The Second World War, Volume V: Closing the Ring* (Cassell, London, 1952), p. 320. See also pp. 356–9.

6. Churchill, *The Second World War, Volume VI: Triumph and Tragedy* (Cassell, London, 1954), p. 198.

7. Ibid. While still in Moscow, Churchill wrote a letter to Stalin on 11 October 1944, in which he said: 'These percentages which I have put down are no more than a method by which in our thoughts we can see how near we are together, and then decide upon the necessary steps to

bring us into full agreement. As I said, they would be considered crude, and even callous, if they were exposed to the scrutiny of the Foreign Offices and diplomats all over the world. Therefore they could not be the basis of any public document, certainly not at the present time. They might however be a good guide for the conduct of our affairs' (ibid., p. 202).

8. Geoffrey Best, *Churchill: A Study in Greatness* (Penguin, London, 2001), p. 259. Best writes that Churchill 'did not want to accept Stalin's axiom that the political system of a liberated country should as a matter of course be determined by its liberator. This point was embarrassing to argue about, however, in as much as Britain and the United States accepted the axiom as the guide for their own liberating conduct.' What they believed was that their system was good and the Soviet regime bad which was not a contention that would have cut much ice with Stalin.

9. Churchill, *The Second World War*, Vol. VI, p. 203.

10. In a letter to Stalin of 23 June 1945, Churchill complained, 'Our joint idea at the Kremlin in October was that the Yugoslav business should work out around 50–50 Russian and the British influence. In fact it is at present more like 90–10, and even in that poor 10 we have been subjected to violent pressure by Marshal Tito' (ibid., p. 488). On Yugoslavia's subsequent break with the Soviet Union, see Dennison Rusinow, *The Yugoslav Experiment 1948–1974* (University of California Press, Berkeley and Los Angeles, 1978), pp. 22–80.

11. Milovan Djilas, *Conversations with Stalin* (Rupert Hart-Davis, London, 1962), p. 164.

12. Churchill, *The Second World War*, Vol. VI, p. 321.

13. A letter from the head of the Soviet security forces, the NKVD, Lavrenti Beria to Stalin of 5 March 1940, proposed that some 25,700 Polish prisoners be shot. Stalin approved and his signature on the document was followed by that of Politburo members Klement Voroshilov, Vyacheslav Molotov, and Anastas Mikoyan. The letter is in Fond 89 of the Russian state archive, RGANI, in Moscow. It is available in microfilm in a number of Western libraries, including that of the Hoover Institution at Stanford (HIA, Fond 89, Reel 1.1993, opis 14).

14. Churchill, *The Second World War*, Vol. VI, pp. 290–1.

15. Ibid., pp. 319 and 370–1.

16. Harry S. Truman, *Off the Record: The Private Papers of Harry S. Truman*, ed. Robert H. Ferrell (Harper & Row, New York, 1980), pp. 21–2.

17. Ibid., pp. 53 and 58.

18. David Reynolds and Vladimir Pechatnov (eds.), *The Kremlin Letters: Stalin's Wartime Correspondence with Churchill and Roosevelt* (Yale University Press, New York, 2018), p. 549.

19. Churchill letter to Stalin, 17 February 1945, ibid.

20. Churchill, *The Second World War*, Vol. VI, pp. 498–9.

21. Ibid., p. 549.

22. William J. Perry, *My Journey at the Nuclear Brink* (Stanford University Press, Stanford, 2015), p. 10.

23. Ibid.

24. Truman, *Off the Record*, p. 132.

25. Ibid., p. 349.

26. David McCullough, *Truman* (Simon & Schuster, New York, 1992), p. 423.

27. George Kennan, *Memoirs 1925–1950* (Pantheon, New York, 1967), p. 286.

28. Ibid., p. 551.

29. Ibid., pp. 557–8.

30. McCullough, *Truman*, pp. 547–54.

31. Ibid., p. 554.

32. Ibid., pp. 768–9.

33. William J. Duiker, *Ho Chi Minh* (Hyperion, New York, 2000), pp. 321–32.

34. Patrick J. Hearden, *The Tragedy of Vietnam* (Pearson Longman, New York, 3rd edn, 2008), p. 181.

35. Ibid., p. 180.

36. Ibid., p. 181; and Jean-Louis Margolin, 'Cambodia: The Country of Disconcerting Crimes', in Stéphane Courtois et al., *The Black Book of Communism: Crimes, Terror, Repression* (Harvard University Press, Cambridge, MA, 1999), pp. 589–90 and 635.

37. Margaret MacMillan, *Seize the Hour: When Nixon Met Mao* (John Murray, London, 2007), p. 123.

38. Anatoly Dobrynin, *In Confidence: Moscow's Ambassador to America's Six Cold War Presidents (1962–1986)* (Random House, New York, 1995), p. 346. For an excellent account of the Helsinki Agreement, and of misunderstandings surrounding it, see Richard Davy, 'Helsinki Myths: Setting the Record Straight on the Final Act of the CSCE, 1975', *Cold War History*, Vol. 9, No. 1, February 2009, pp. 1–22.

39. Zbigniew Brzezinski, *Power and Principle: Memoirs of the National Security Adviser 1977–1981* (Weidenfeld & Nicolson, London, 1983), p. 404.

40. Mark Kramer, 'New Evidence on Soviet Decision-Making and the 1956 Polish and Hungarian Crises', *Cold War International History Project Bulletin (CWIHPB)*, Nos. 8–9, 1996–7, p. 361.

41. *Khrushchev Remembers: The Last Testament*, ed. and trans. Strobe Talbott (André Deutsch, London, 1974), p. 205.

42. Velko Mićunović, *Moscow Diary* (Chatto & Windus, London, 1980), p. 134.

43. Jim Newton, *Eisenhower: The White House Years* (Doubleday, New York, 2011), pp. 223–33; Charles Gati, *Failed Illusions: Moscow, Washington, Budapest, and the 1956 Hungarian Revolt* (Woodrow Wilson Center Press, Washington, DC, 2006), p. 200; D. R. Thorpe, *Supermac: The Life of Harold Macmillan* (Pimlico, London, 2011), p. 350; and Diane B. Kunz, 'The Importance of Having Money: The Economic Diplomacy of the Suez Crisis', in Wm. Roger Louis and Roger Owen (eds.), *Suez 1956: The Crisis and its Consequences* (Clarendon Press, Oxford, 1989), pp. 215–32.

44. John Lewis Gaddis, *Strategies of Containment: A Critical Appraisal of American National Security Policy during the Cold War* (Oxford University Press, New York, revised and expanded edn, 2005), pp. 146–54.

45. Gati, *Failed Illusions*, p. 2. Even the Soviet Union, as Charles Gati, a prominent specialist on East European politics, has argued, regarded military intervention within the bloc as very much a last resort. 'The Kremlin', writes Gati, 'was never particularly trigger-happy' and at times 'made prudent if tactical adjustments to new realities' (ibid. p. 210).

46. Georgy Arbatov, *The System: An Insider's Life in Soviet Politics* (Random House, New York, 1992), p. 200.

47. Contingency plans were set out in a document so secret that the number of troops and tanks that would be involved was information that not even a Central Committee typist was trusted with. A space was left in the document for the numbers that were added in ink. Headed simply 'TsK KPSS' (Central Committee of the CPSU), the document was dated 18 August 1980, and signed by the most senior members of the Politburo (apart from General Secretary Brezhnev) who constituted a Politburo committee on the Polish crisis under the chairmanship of Mikhail Suslov. A photocopy of the document is available in the Volkogonov Collection, R 9659, National Security Archive (NSA, GWU), Washington, DC.

48. Aleksandr Fursenko and Timothy Naftali, *Khrushchev's Cold War: The Inside Story of an American Adversary* (Norton, New York, 2006), pp. 436–7.

49. Perry, *My Journey at the Nuclear Brink*, p. 2.
50. Lawrence Freedman, *Kennedy's Wars: Berlin, Cuba, Laos, and Vietnam* (Oxford University Press, New York, 2000), p. 186.
51. Ibid.
52. Ibid., p. 192.
53. Thorpe, *Supermac*, pp. 528–31; and Freedman, *Kennedy's Wars*, p. 196.
54. On Robert Kennedy's role, see Arthur M. Schlesinger, Jr, *Robert Kennedy and His Times* (Ballantine Books, New York, 1978), esp. pp. 572–3.
55. Paul H. Nitze (with Ann M. Smith and Steven L. Rearden), *From Hiroshima to Glasnost: At the Center of Decision, A Memoir* (Weidenfeld & Nicolson, London, 1989), p. 237. When the Cuban missile crisis was over, General LeMay 'felt not relief but regret', for 'To his dying day, he maintained that an air strike would have removed both the missiles and the Communists from Cuba' (Gerard DeGroot, *The Bomb: A History of Hell on Earth* (Pimlico, London, 2005), p. 264). President Kennedy himself was anxious to avoid a reputation for being conciliatory. As Lawrence Freedman puts it, 'Kennedy's instincts during the crisis had been dovish, but he did not want too dovish a public image' (*Kennedy's Wars*, p. 220).
56. Fidel Castro, *My Life*, ed. Ignacio Ramonet (Allen Lane, London, 2007), pp. 277–8. Castro noted: 'We learned from news reports that the Soviets were making the proposal to withdraw the missiles. And it had never been discussed with us in any way!...Our relations with the Soviets deteriorated. For years, all this had an influence on Cuban-Soviet relations' (ibid., p. 278).
57. Fursenko and Naftali, *Khrushchev's Cold War*, p. 490.
58. Perry, *My Journey at the Nuclear Brink*, p. 3.
59. Ibid.
60. Anastas Mikoyan, *Tak bylo: Razmyshleniya o minuvshem* (Vagrius, Moscow, 1999), p. 606.
61. Perry, *My Journey at the Nuclear Brink*, pp. 3–4.
62. DeGroot, *The Bomb*, p. 262.
63. Ibid.
64. Ibid., p. 264.
65. Perry, *My Journey at the Nuclear Brink*, p. 52.
66. For an excellent concise account of the KAL 007 downing, based on access to Soviet documentation, see David E. Hoffman, *The Dead Hand: The Untold Story of the Cold War Arms Race and Its Dangerous Legacy* (Doubleday, New York, 2009), pp. 72–89.
67. Ibid., pp. 6–11 (from which my account is drawn). Petrov died at his home in Moscow as recently as May 2017, aged 77 (http://www.bbc.co.uk/news/world-europe-41314948).
68. Daniel Kahneman, *Thinking Fast and Slow* (Allen Lane, London, 2011), p. 411.
69. Vladislav Zubok, 'Cold War Strategies/Power and Culture—East', in Richard H. Immerman and Petra Goedde (eds.), *The Oxford Handbook of the Cold War* (Oxford University Press, Oxford, 2013), p. 307.
70. On the wars in the Third World, see Odd Arne Westad, *The Global Cold War: Third World Interventions and the Making of Our Times* (Cambridge University Press, Cambridge, 2005).
71. Jonathan Glover, *Humanity: A Moral History of the Twentieth Century* (Pimlico, London, 2001), p. 220.

2 The Making of Mikhail Gorbachev

1. Mikhail Gorbachev, *Zhizn' i reformy*, Vol. I (Novosti, Moscow, 1995), p. 38.
2. Mikhail Gorbachev, *Naedine s soboy* (Grin Strit, Moscow, 2012), p. 34.

3. The principal sources for this brief account of Gorbachev's family background and child-hood years are Gorbachev, *Zhizn' i reformy*, Vol. I, pp. 37–42; and Gorbachev, *Naedine s soboy*, pp. 21–36. See also the major biography by William Taubman which provides an illuminating account of Gorbachev's earlier years: Taubman, *Gorbachev: His Life and Times* (Norton, New York, 2017), esp. ch. 1, pp. 7–39.

4. Gorbachev, *Naedine s soboy*, pp. 36–52.

5. Gorbachev, *Zhizn' i reformy*, Vol. I, p. 50.

6. Gorbachev, *Naedine s soboy*, p. 52.

7. Molotov was later an opponent of Khrushchev's de-Stalinization and was expelled from the Communist Party. When already aged over 90, he was readmitted to the party during the leadership of Gorbachev's immediate predecessor, Konstantin Chernenko.

8. Taubman, *Gorbachev*, p. 32.

9. Ibid.

10. Ibid., pp. 34–5.

11. Gorbachev, *Zhizn' i reformy*, Vol. I, pp. 56–7.

12. For more detail on points made in this and the preceding paragraph, see Archie Brown, *The Gorbachev Factor* (Oxford University Press, Oxford, 1996), pp. 26–9.

13. The post-war Stalin years were not a time of intensive affirmative action to admit more students of worker and peasant origin such as had occurred earlier in the Soviet period and as was to be revived under Khrushchev. It was in a period of slower social mobility that Gorbachev began his upward ascent.

14. Gorbachev, *Naedine s soboy*, p. 55. Of this writer, who was born in 1811 and died in 1848, Isaiah Berlin noted: 'All serious questions to Belinsky were always, in the end, moral questions: about what it is that is wholly valuable and worth pursuing for its own sake' (Berlin, *Russian Thinkers*, ed. Henry Hardy and Aileen Kelly (The Hogarth Press, London, 1978), p. 156).

15. Gorbachev, *Naedine s soboy*, p. 56.

16. Zdeněk Mlynář, 'Il mio compagno di studi Mikhail Gorbaciov', *L'Unità* (Rome), 9 April, 1985.

17. Mlynář's 1985 article for the Italian Communist Party newspaper (n. 16) is one such important source, as are the reminiscences and reflections of the two men in Mikhail Gorbachev and Zdeněk Mlynář, *Conversations with Gorbachev: On Perestroika, the Prague Spring, and the Crossroads of Socialism*, trans. George Shriver (Columbia University Press, New York, 2002). In an interview with Olga Kuchkina for the newspaper, *Komsomol'skaya Pravda*, in 1994, reprinted in Valentin Tolstykh, *A Millennium Salute to Mikhail Gorbachev on his 70th Birthday* (Valent, Moscow, 2001), pp. 253–9, Gorbachev said: 'Zdenek was here recently to take part in our debate on the prospects for social democracy. He's probably the person I'm closest to. He always has been' (pp. 255–6). Mlynář was born in 1930 (one year before Gorbachev) and died in 1997.

18. Mlynář, 'Il mio compagno di studi'.

19. By the time he wrote the article for *L'Unità*, Mlynář had spent eight years in exile in Vienna, having been one of the main organizers and original signatories of the dissident Czech protest document, Charter 77. Earlier he had been expelled from the Communist Party of Czechoslovakia for his role in the Prague Spring. He was a strong critic both of the Soviet-supported post-invasion regime and of Soviet-style Communism.

20. Mlynář, 'Il mio compagno di studi'.

21. Ibid.

22. Gorbachev and Mlynář, *Conversations with Gorbachev*, pp. 22–3.

23. Zdeněk Mlynář, *Nightfrost in Prague: The End of Humane Socialism* (Hurst, London, 1980), pp. 27–9; see also Ludmilla Alexeyeva and Paul Goldberg, *The Thaw Generation: Coming of Age in the Post-Stalin Era* (Little, Brown, Boston, 1990).

24. Andrey Grachev, *Gorbachev* (Vagrius, Moscow, 2001), p. 26.
25. For the book of the thesis, see Raisa Maksimovna Gorbacheva, *Byt kolkhoznogo krest'yantsva: sotsiologicheskiy ocherk* (Knizhnoe izdatel'stvo, Stavropol, 1969).
26. A notable Western study of the role in the Soviet economy of regional party secretaries was Jerry F. Hough's *The Soviet Prefects: The Local Party Organs in Industrial Decision-Making* (Harvard University Press, Cambridge, MA, 1969).
27. Gorbachev, *Zhizn' i reformy*, Vol. I, pp. 77–85.
28. Ibid.
29. Gorbachev and Mlynář, *Conversations with Gorbachev*, pp. 25 and 27.
30. The term, 'children of the Twentieth Congress' (*deti dvadtsatogo s"ezda*) was used virtually interchangeably with *shestidesyatniki* (people of the sixties). The latter term had first been applied to reformers of the 1860s and, in its revival in the 1960s, referred to those who wished to carry on where Khrushchev had left off—i.e. in the spirit of Khrushchev's attacks on Stalin at the Twentieth Party Congress of 1956 and of the Twenty-Second Congress in 1961. The *shestidesyatniki* sincerely believed in the possibility of a more humane socialist society and were often, as a generational group, contrasted with a more cynical and conformist generation which reached adulthood during the Brezhnev era. Gorbachev was happy to be identified as a *shestidesyatnik* (interview with Yuriy Shchekochikin, *Literaturnaya gazeta*, 4 December 1991).
31. Gorbachev and Mlynář, *Conversations with Gorbachev*, p. 27.
32. Georgiy Shakhnazarov, *S vozhdyami i bez nikh* (Vagrius, Mosow, 2001), p. 277.
33. Archie Brown, *Seven Years that Changed the World: Perestroika in Perspective* (Oxford University Press, Oxford, 2007), pp. 46–7. The book by Parkinson he had read more than twenty years earlier made a big impression on Gorbachev. 'Printsip Parkinsona znaete?' ('Do you know Parkinson's Law?') he asked the Politburo in early March 1989, 'Iz vystupleniy na zasedanii Politbyuro TsK KPSS, 2 marta 1989 goda', in Mikhail Sergeevich Gorbachev, *Sobranie sochineniy*, Vol. XIII (Ves' mir, Moscow, 2009), p. 316.
34. As Aleksandr Nikonov told me when I interviewed him in Moscow on 20 April 1994. For further information on Nikonov, see Brown, *The Gorbachev Factor*, pp. 43–4.
35. Nikonov, in the 1994 interview cited above.
36. Gorbachev, *Zhizn' i reformy*, pp. 159–69.
37. Ibid., p. 169.

3 Gorbachev's Widening Horizons

1. William Taubman, *Gorbachev: His Life and Times* (Norton, New York, 2017), p. 118.
2. For the details of Andropov's failed attempt, from his sickbed, to put Gorbachev at the head of the Politburo during his enforced absence, see Archie Brown, *The Gorbachev Factor* (Oxford University Press, Oxford, 1996), pp. 67–8.
3. Zbigniew Brzezinski, *Power and Principle: Memoirs of the National Security Adviser 1977–81* (Weidenfeld & Nicolson, London, 1983), p. 567.
4. Rodric Braithwaite, *Afgantsy: The Russians in Afghanistan 1979–1989* (Profile Books, London, 2011), p. 38.
5. 'Zapis' besedy A. N. Kosygina, A. A. Gromyko, D. F. Ustinova, B. N. Ponomareva s N. M. Taraki 20 marta 1979 goda', HIA, Fond 89, 1.1003, opis 42, file 3, p. 3.
6. Braithwaite, *Afgansty*, pp. 60–72.
7. Odd Arne Westad, *The Global Cold War* (Cambridge University Press, Cambridge, 2005), p. 313.
8. Ibid., pp. 316–22.
9. Ibid., p. 321.

10. Eduard Shevardnadze, *The Future Belongs to Freedom* (Sinclair-Stevenson, London, 1991), p. 26.

11. Andropov, in spite of his declining physical strength, had injected some vitality into the Soviet system, and it was probably to Gorbachev's advantage that he did not succeed him directly, but followed on after thirteen months of Chernenko's lacklustre leadership. His dynamism made a refreshing contrast with his immediate predecessor and won him early popularity.

12. Gorbachev, *Zhizn' i reformy*, Vol. II (Novosti, Moscow, 1995), p. 237.

13. Ibid.

14. 'Zasedanie sekretariata TsK KPSS, 20 noyabrya 1972 goda', Volkogonov Papers, R 10325, NSA (GWU), p. 6. The director of the Institute of the USA and Canada at that time, Georgy Arbatov, was later to write that the conservative Communists who dominated the Soviet leadership welcomed the convenient opportunity to remove Yakovlev who, though he did not have the title of Head of the Department of Propaganda, had been in charge of it de facto. Yakovlev had been, observed Arbatov, one of the few people left in high positions in the party apparatus who still adhered to the ideas of the Twentieth Party Congress. His article, moreover, was 'the first serious public utterance in defence of internationalism and against the activization of Great Russian chauvinism'. See Georgiy Arbatov, *Chelovek sistemy* (Vagrius, Moscow, 2002), p. 224.

15. Vadim Medvedev, *V komande Gorbacheva: Vzglyad iznutri* (Bylina, Moscow, 1994), pp. 19–20.

16. Aleksandr Yakovlev, *Sumerki* (Materik, Moscow, 2003), pp. 353–4.

17. Ibid., p. 354.

18. Ibid., p. 355.

19. A fascinating account of Yakovlev's IMEMO directorship is given by the Institute's historian, Petr Cherkasov, in *IMEMO: Ocherk istorii* (Ves' mir, Moscow, 2016), pp. 513–57.

20. Mikhail Gorbachev, *Naedine s soboy* (Grin Strit, Moscow, 2012), p. 368.

21. When foreign politicians came to Moscow for Konstantin Chernenko's funeral in 1985, many of them in the hope of meeting the new leader of the Soviet Union, Gorbachev found the time to meet only one European Communist leader—the secretary general of the PCI, Alessandro Natto. For Ponomarev this was incomprehensible. How could it be, he asked a group of his subordinates in the International Department, that when the leaders of tens of 'good' Communist parties had arrived in Moscow, the only one Gorbachev chose to receive was the leader of the 'bad' Italians (A. S. Chernyaev, *Shest' let s Gorbachevym* (Progress, Moscow, 1993), p. 33).

22. Gorbachev, *Naedine s soboy*, pp. 369–70.

23. Ibid.

24. Anatoliy Adamishin, *V raznye gody: Vneshnepoliticheskie ocherki* (Ves' Mir, Moscow, 2016), p. 111. Adamishin was at the time head of the First European Department of the Ministry of Foreign Affairs (within whose purview the UK came). He notes that Gromyko was sufficiently displeased with Kovalev (who was aged 61 at that time) to propose pensioning him off, but Kovalev survived, and a year after the change of leadership in the CPSU and the ministry he became First Deputy Foreign Minister. Adamishin himself, who was very much a 'new thinker' within the Soviet diplomatic corps, became a deputy foreign minister in the same year (1986).

25. Telegram of UK ambassador to the Soviet Union, Sir Iain Sutherland, to Foreign Secretary, Sir Geoffrey Howe, 4 December 1984 (copied by FCO to prime minister's private secretary), PREM 19/1394, https://www.margaretthatcher.org/document/134714. Sutherland had met with Gorbachev in the Central Committee of the CPSU that day.

26. As Malcolm Rifkind, Minister of State at the Foreign Office at that time with responsibility for UK relations with the Soviet Union and Eastern Europe, noted in his private account of

the Gorbachev visit, written in December 1984 and quoted in his autobiography, *Power and Pragmatism: The Memoirs of Malcolm Rifkind* (Biteback, London, 2016), p. 182.

27. 'Record of Private Lunchtime Conversation between the Prime Minister and Mr Gorbachev at Chequers on Sunday 16 December, 1984', by K. A. (Tony) Bishop, who interpreted Gorbachev's Russian for Thatcher and for his other British interlocutors throughout the week, https://www.margaretthatcher.org/document/134729.

28. 'Record of the Meeting Between the Prime Minister and Mr M. S. Gorbachev, Member of the Politburo and Secretary of the Central Committee of the CPSU, at Chequers on Sunday 16 December at 3.00 PM', by C. D. P., i.e. Charles Powell, p. 7, PREM 19/1394, https://www.margaretthatcher.org/document/134730.

29. Ibid., p. 7.

30. Ibid., p. 10.

31. Ibid. p. 4. Lord Palmerston served as Foreign Secretary in three governments and was prime minister for a total of nine years (in two periods of office) in the middle decades of the nineteenth century.

32. 'Vystuplenie pered chlenam parlamenta Velikobritanii', in M. S. Gorbachev, *Izbrannye rechi i stat'i*, Vol. II (Politizdat, Moscow, 1987), pp. 109–16, at p. 111.

33. Ibid., p. 112.

34. Ibid., p. 110.

35. Gorbachev, *Naedine s soboy*, p. 371.

36. Rifkind, *Power and Pragmatism*, p. 197.

37. Denis Healey, 'Gorbachev Face to Face', *Newsweek*, 25 March 1985, p. 15.

38. 'Mikhail Sergeevich Gorbachev: A Personal Assessment of the Man during his visit to the United Kingdom, 15–21 December 1984', K. A. Bishop, 3 January 1985, PREM 19/1394, https://www.margaretthatcher.org/document/134739. Prominent British politicians who met Gorbachev during his 1984 visit came to conclusions similar to that of Bishop. Shirley Williams, a former Labour minister who by this time was one of the leaders of the Social Democratic Party, even recorded another wink. In her memoirs, Williams wrote: 'Gorbachev was an amazing man to come out of the stifling Soviet system. He had a brightness about him, an endemic optimism, a driving vision. I had met him briefly when he visited Britain in December 1984 ... The SDP was a party represented in Parliament, so David Owen as its leader, and I as its President, met with Gorbachev and his small entourage of Russian officials, one of them a general almost overwhelmed by his rows of medals and his stiff military collar. It was a sunny afternoon, the Russian delegation had enjoyed a good lunch, and the elderly general began to sway within the confines of his collar. I caught Gorbachev's eye. He winked.' See Shirley Williams, *Climbing the Bookshelves* (Virago, London, 2009), p. 341. (The only senior military man in Gorbachev's delegation was General Nikolay Chervov. Aged 62 at the time, he was presumably the 'elderly general' referred to.)

39. 'Mikhail Sergeevich Gorbachev: A Personal Assessment', p. 4.

40. Ibid. Bishop added: 'I saw no signs of vanity in him (though several in his wife).'

41. Ibid., p. 4. In a more speculative comment, which perhaps owed more to his preconceptions of a Soviet politician than to his observation of Gorbachev, Bishop added: 'I am sure he could be utterly ruthless if necessary.'

42. One cold warrior by profession, Brian Crozier, who ascribed to himself an important role in making both Margaret Thatcher and Ronald Reagan more aware of the dangers of Soviet subversion and disinformation, wrote: 'It was not by happy accident that Gorbachev's first target in his prolonged public relations exercise was Mrs Margaret Thatcher, the "Iron

Lady" of Soviet propaganda as a result of an early speech drafted for her by my "disciple" Robert Moss. If he could win over the Iron Lady, there would surely be no limit to his proselytising.' Well before the Soviet Union ceased to exist, Gorbachev had abandoned the central tenets of Leninism, but even in the post-Soviet era Crozier remained utterly oblivious to the abundant evidence for this both in Gorbachev's words and deeds. Reflecting the absence of any comparable evolution in his own thinking, Crozier wrote: 'Everything Gorbachev said and did, in fact, was in line with the teaching of Lenin, his earthly god' (Crozier, *Free Agent: The Unseen War 1941–1991* (HarperCollins, London, 1993), pp. 289–90).

43. Gorbachev, *Naedine s soboy*, p. 374. Dobrynin himself cites another example of Gromyko's displeasure at the attention being devoted to Gorbachev while Chernenko was still in the Kremlin and Gromyko himself was in the twenty-eighth year of his tenure as Minister of Foreign Affairs. Observing the growing interest in Gorbachev on the part of the American administration, following his successful visit to the UK, Dobrynin wrote: 'At their meeting in Geneva in January 1985 to negotiate the resumption of disarmament talks, Shultz told Gromyko in private (with Reagan's approval) that even though Gorbachev was not General Secretary if he wanted to pay a working visit to the United States he would be received by Reagan and Shultz. Gromyko, jealous, did not bother to disguise his displeasure. The old guard in the Politburo regarded Gorbachev with suspicion' (Anatoly Dobrynin, *In Confidence: Moscow's Ambassador to America's Six Cold War Presidents (1962–1986)* (Times Books, New York, 1995), p. 565).

44. In a private conversation I had with Ambassador Popov and Mrs Popova at St Antony's College, Oxford, on 1 February 1985.

45. Dobrynin, *In Confidence*, p. 561.

46. Interview with G. A. Arbatov, 'The Second Russian Revolution Transcripts', British Library of Political and Economic Science, London School of Economics.

47. 'Zhivoe tvorchestvo naroda', speech delivered, 10 December 1984, in M. S. Gorbachev, *Izbrannye rechi i stat'i*, Vol. II, pp. 75–108, at 80–2.

48. Ibid., p. 95.

49. Medvedev, *V komande Gorbacheva*, p. 21.

50. G. A. Arbatov, *Zatyanuvsheesya vyzdorovlenie (1953–1985 gg.): Svidetel'stvo sovremennika* (Mezhdunarodnye otnosheniya, Moscow, 1991), pp. 336–7.

51. Yakovlev, *Sumerki*, pp. 269–70. See also Gorbachev, *Zhizn' i reformy*, Vol. I, p. 254; and Medvedev, *V komande Gorbacheva*, p. 22.

52. See Brown, *The Gorbachev Factor*, pp. 77 and 335. Former Politburo member Vadim Medvedev as well as Gorbachev's two closest and most influential aides, Anatoly Chernyaev and Georgy Shakhnazarov, were among those to make that point to me in interviews and conversations in the early 1990s.

4 The Rise of Ronald Reagan

1. Lou Cannon, *President Reagan: The Role of a Lifetime* (Public Affairs, New York, 2000), p. 178.

2. Nancy Reagan, with William Novak, *My Turn: The Memoirs of Nancy Reagan* (Bantam Doubleday Dell, New York, 1989), p. 108.

3. Ibid.

4. Peter Hannaford, *Reagan's Roots: The People and Places that Shaped His Character* (Images from the Past, Bennington, VT, 2012), p. 51.

5. Nancy Reagan, *My Turn*, pp. 108–9.

6. Hannaford, *Reagan's Roots*, pp. 21–2.

7. Ronald Reagan, *An American Life* (Simon & Schuster, New York, 1990), p. 23.

8. Iwan Morgan, *Reagan: American Icon* (Tauris, London, 2016), pp. 1–2.
9. Hannaford, *Reagan's Roots*, pp. 53–4.
10. Reagan, *An American Life*, p. 22.
11. Ibid.
12. Ibid.
13. Hannaford, *Reagan's Roots*, pp. 34–5.
14. Colin Powell had a high regard for Reagan and was one of the most successful of his National Security Advisers (a post he held from 1987 to 1989), but he would roll his eyes when Reagan referred to invasions from outer space and say to his staff, 'Here come the little green men again.' See Cannon, *President Reagan*, pp. 42 and 178–9.
15. Hannaford, *Reagan's Roots*, pp. 60–6.
16. Ibid., p. 77.
17. Cannon, *President Reagan*, p. 185.
18. https://millercenter.org/the-presidency/presidential-speeches/may-31-1988-address-moscow-state-university.
19. Morgan, *Reagan*, pp. 14–15.
20. Hannaford, *Reagan's Roots*, pp. 114–16.
21. Michael Schaller, *Ronald Reagan* (Oxford University Press, Oxford and New York, 2011), p. 5. See also Chris Matthews, *Tip and the Gipper: When Politics Worked* (Simon & Schuster, New York, 2013).
22. Reagan, *An American Life*, p. 96.
23. Jacob Weisberg, *Ronald Reagan* (Times Books, New York, 2016), p. 27.
24. Larry Ceplair and Steven Englund, *The Inquisition in Hollywood: Politics in the Film Community, 1930–1960* (University of Illinois Press paperback, Urbana and Chicago, 2003), pp. 280–2.
25. Weisberg, *Ronald Reagan*, p. 26.
26. Morgan, *Reagan*, p. 59.
27. Weisberg, *Ronald Reagan*, p. 30.
28. Morgan, *Reagan*, p. 55.
29. Ibid.
30. Cory Franklin, 'The Other Man in Nancy Reagan's Life', *Chicago Tribune*, 8 March 2016: http://www.chicagotribune.com/news/opinion/commentary/ct-nancy-reagan-loyal-davis-stepfather-perspec-0309-20160308-story.html.
31. Weisberg, *Ronald Reagan*, pp. 34–5.
32. Ibid., p. 36.
33. Ibid.
34. Ibid., p. 37.
35. Gil Troy, *The Reagan Revolution: A Very Short Introduction* (Oxford University Press, Oxford and New York, 2009), p. 14; and Schaller, *Ronald Reagan*, p. 12.
36. Weisberg, *Ronald Reagan*, p. 32.
37. Ibid., p. 38.
38. Cannon, *President Reagan*, pp. 111–12.
39. For an elaboration of this general point, see Drew Westen, *The Political Brain: The Role of Emotion in Deciding the Fate of the Nation* (Public Affairs, New York, 2007), at e.g. pp. 62–3 and 146–7.
40. Morgan, *Reagan*, pp. 77–8.
41. Schaller, *Ronald Reagan*, pp. 13–14.
42. Ibid., pp. 15–16; and Morgan, *Reagan*, pp. 80–1.
43. Steven J. Ross, *Hollywood Left and Right: How Movie Stars Shaped American Politics* (Oxford University Press, New York, 2011), p. 177; and Schaller, *Ronald Reagan*, pp. 16–18.

44. Morgan, *Reagan*, p. 92.

45. Schaller, *Ronald Reagan*, p. 19.

46. Morgan, *Reagan*, p. 90.

47. Ross, *Hollywood Left and Right*, p. 173.

48. Schaller, *Ronald Reagan*, p. 20.

49. Weisberg, *Ronald Reagan*, p. 49. Iwan Morgan notes that Reagan's conservationist achievements in California owed much to the person chosen for (rather than by) Reagan as the state's natural-resource administrator, Norman ('Ike') Livermore. Morgan adds: 'Whether Reagan truly grasped the fragility of the environment must be a matter of doubt in light of his later record as president, but he was more exposed to people aware of it in the governor's office than in the Oval Office' (Morgan, *Reagan*, p. 103).

50. Morgan, *Reagan*, p. 99.

51. Ibid., pp. 110–11.

52. Cannon, *President Reagan*, p. 113.

53. https://millercenter.org/the-presidency/presidential-speeches/may-31-1988-address-moscow-state-university.

54. Reagan, *An American Life*, p. 178.

55. Morgan, *Reagan*, p. 125.

56. Frances Fitzgerald, *Way Out There in the Blue: Reagan, Star Wars and the End of the Cold War* (Touchstone, New York, 2001), pp. 82–4.

57. Morgan, *Reagan*, p. 134.

58. Jimmy Carter, *Keeping Faith: Memoirs of a President* (Bantam, New York, 1982), pp. 561–2; and, on the SALT discussions, pp. 212–72.

59. Morgan, *Reagan*, p. 142.

60. Carter, *Keeping Faith*, p. 565.

61. Morgan, *Reagan*, p. 142.

62. Margaret Thatcher, *The Path to Power* (HarperCollins, London, 1995), p. 372.

63. Reagan, *An American Life*, p. 204.

5 Reagan's First Term

1. Margaret Thatcher, *The Downing Street Years* (HarperCollins, London, 1993), p. 157.

2. Ibid., pp. 157–8.

3. Charles Moore, *Margaret Thatcher, Volume One: Not for Turning* (Allen Lane, London, 2013), p. 540.

4. Ibid., p. 541.

5. Rodric Braithwaite, 'End of the Affair', *Prospect*, Issue 86, May 2003, pp. 20–3, at p. 22.

6. Ronald Reagan, *The Reagan Diaries Unabridged, Volume I: January 1981–October 1985*, ed. Douglas Brinkley (HarperCollins, New York, 2009), p. 58.

7. Jack F. Matlock, Jr, *Reagan and Gorbachev: How the Cold War Ended* (Random House, New York, 2004), pp. 50–1; and Beth A. Fischer, *The Reagan Reversal: Foreign Policy and the End of the Cold War* (University of Missouri Press, Columbia, 1997), pp. 16–29.

8. Jacob Weisberg, *Ronald Reagan* (Times Books, New York, 2016), p. 72.

9. Chris Matthews, *Tip and the Gipper: When Politics Worked* (Simon & Schuster, New York, 2013), pp. 69–75; and Iwan Morgan, *Reagan: American Icon* (Tauris, London, 2016), pp. 148–50.

10. Matlock, *Reagan and Gorbachev*, p. 38.

11. Ibid., pp. 39–40.

12. Alexander M. Haig, Jr, *Caveat: Realism, Reagan, and Foreign Policy* (Weidenfeld & Nicolson, London, 1984), p. 229.

13. Reagan, *The Reagan Diaries Unabridged*, Vol. I, p. 139.

14. Haig, *Caveat*, p. 306–7.

15. Ibid., p. 307.

16. Memorandum for the President from Richard V. Allen: Your Meeting with John Louis: A Few Key Points for the Record (Monday, November 9, 1981), 18 November 1981, United Kingdom 9/11/81–3/31/82, Box 20, Exec. Secret. NSC: Records Country File, Reagan Presidential Library Archives.

17. Frances Fitzgerald, *Way Out There in the Blue: Reagan, Star Wars and the End of the Cold War* (Simon & Schuster, New York, 2000), p. 179.

18. Interview in *Newsweek*, 18 February 1983, cited by Raymond L. Garthoff, *The Great Transition: American–Soviet Relations and the End of the Cold War* (Brookings Institution, Washington, DC, 1994), p. 504.

19. https://www.nytimes.com/1981/10/21/us/security-adviser-ousted-for-a-talk-hinting-at-war.html.

20. Lou Cannon, *President Reagan: The Role of a Lifetime* (Public Affairs, New York, 2000), p. 155.

21. Ibid., p. 163. Cannon's account of this episode is based on his 15 November 1988, interview with Deaver.

22. The remark which so alarmed Deaver was not a one-off. Robert (Bud) McFarlane, who held the rank of Counsellor of the State Department at the beginning of Reagan's first term, was taken aback when Secretary of State Haig told him, 'I want to go after Cuba, Bud. I want you to get everyone together and give me a plan for doing it.' See Robert C. McFarlane (with Zofia Smardz), *Special Trust* (Cadell & Davies, New York, 1994), p. 177.

23. Nancy Reagan (with William Novak), *My Turn: The Memoirs of Nancy Reagan* (Dell, New York, 1989), p. 247.

24. I have set out this argument at length in Archie Brown, *The Myth of the Strong Leader: Political Leadership in the Modern Age* (Bodley Head, London, and Basic Books, New York, 2014). See also Archie Brown, 'Against the *Führerprinzip*: For Collective Leadership' and Anthony King, 'In Favour of "Leader-Proofing"', in *Daedalus*, special issue on Political Leadership, Vol. 145, No. 3, Summer 2016, pp. 109–37.

25. McFarlane, *Special Trust*, p. 323.

26. George P. Shultz, *Turmoil and Triumph: My Years as Secretary of State* (Scribner's, New York, 1993), p. 269.

27. McFarlane, *Special Trust*, p. 328.

28. Donald Regan, *For The Record: From Wall Street to Washington* (Hutchinson, London, 1988), pp. xi–xii.

29. President Reagan wrote in his diary on 7 January 1985: 'Biggest event of day was a meeting with Don Regan & then with Jim Baker. They want to trade jobs. I've agreed. As soon as Jim is confirmed by Sen. he'll be Sec. of Treasury & Don will come to the W.H. as Chief of Staff. I think it will resolve a lot of problems', Reagan, *The Reagan Diaries Unabridged*, Vol. I, p. 414; and for a fuller account, Regan, *For the Record*, pp. 220–31.

30. Haig, *Caveat*, p. 314.

31. Nancy Reagan, *My Turn*, pp. 251–2.

32. Fitzgerald, *Way Out There in the Blue*, p. 177.

33. Colin L. Powell (with Joseph E. Persic), *My American Journey* (Random House, New York, 1995), p. 292.

34. Margaret Thatcher qualified her belief that 'a summit meeting with Brezhnev could be very useful' by adding 'if there were good prospects for a suitable outcome and after we made the necessary detailed preparations'. Weinberger's Memorandum for the President

of 11 December 1981, is in the Reagan Presidential Library Archives, United Kingdom 9/11/81–3/31/82, Box 20, Exec. Secret. NSC: Records Country File.

35. Powell, *My American Journey*, pp. 258–9. On Weinberger's extreme intransigence on the defence budget, see Fitzgerald, *Way Out There in the Blue*, p. 167.

36. Matlock, *Reagan and Gorbachev*, p. 52.

37. Ibid., p. 53.

38. Ibid., p. 54.

39. Ronald Reagan, *The Quest for Peace, the Cause of Freedom: Selected Speeches on the United States and the World* (United States Information Agency, Washington, DC, 1988), pp. 49–57, at p. 56.

40. Ibid.

41. Ibid., p. 57.

42. Reagan 'was convinced', said former National Security Adviser McFarlane, 'that we were in fact heading toward Armageddon, the final battle between good and evil. "I'm telling you, it's coming", he would say. "Go read your Scripture"', McFarlane, *Special Trust*, p. 228.

43. Cannon, *President Reagan*, p. 248.

44. McFarlane, interviewed by Cannon in 1989, said that Reagan saw himself as 'a romantic, heroic figure who believes in the power of a hero to overcome even Armageddon', a notion he thought might have come from Hollywood, and that this was 'one of the intellectual contradictions in Reagan's thinking'. Ibid., p. 249.

45. Cannon, *President Reagan*, p. 249.

46. William Steding, *Presidential Faith and Foreign Policy: Jimmy Carter the Disciple and Ronald Reagan the Alchemist* (Palgrave Macmillan, New York, 2014), pp. 135–6.

47. Ibid., pp. 136–7.

48. Fitzgerald, *Way Out There in the Blue*, p. 195.

49. Ibid., p. 198.

50. Shultz, *Turmoil and Triumph*, pp. 246–64.

51. Ibid., pp. 255–6.

52. Ibid., p. 258.

53. *The Reagan Diaries Unabridged*, Vol. I, p. 209.

54. Ibid.

55. Adam Roberts, 'International Relations after the Cold War', *International Affairs*, Vol. 84, No. 2, 2008, pp. 335–50, at p. 342.

56. 'Zasedanie Politbyuro TsK KPSS, 31 maya 1983 goda', HIA, Fond 89, Reel.1.1003, opis 42, file 3, p. 7.

57. Ibid., pp. 1–14.

58. Anatoly Dobrynin, *In Confidence: Moscow's Ambassador to America's Six Cold War Presidents (1962–1986)* (Times Books, New York, 1995), p. 482.

59. As Cannon put it, 'The best that can be said about Watt's hostility to the environment is that he never disguised it. "We will mine more, drill more, cut more timber", he said, and he meant it' (Cannon, *President Reagan*, p. 469). Reagan's instincts were closer to support for making the environment a business free-for-all than with conservation, as his diary entry on his meeting with Watt on the latter's resignation makes clear: 'He knew that in carrying out my policies his days would be numbered...He gave me a report on his stewardship and it reveals the hypocrisy of the Environmental Lynch mob. I dont [sic] think the Dept. of Interior or our Nat. Parks & wild lands have ever been in better shape' (*The Reagan Diaries Unabridged*, Vol. I, p. 277), entry for 19 October 1983.

60. Cannon, *President Reagan*, pp. 374–80.

61. Ibid.

62. Jeane Kirkpatrick, 'Dictatorship and Double Standards', *Commentary*, November 1979, pp. 34–45. Although he cited the article approvingly at the time, Reagan was far from unambiguously accepting that Communist regimes were as resilient and immune to change as Kirkpatrick made out. For Reagan, 'Communist regimes were indeed the worst' but 'they were doomed as a violation of human nature' (Weisberg, *Ronald Reagan*, p. 60).

63. Kirkpatrick, 'Dictatorship and Double Standards', pp. 34–45. Kirkpatrick wrote: 'Although there is no instance of a revolutionary "socialist" or Communist society being democratized, right-wing autocracies do sometimes evolve into democracies—given time, propitious economic, social, and political circumstances, talented leaders, and a strong indigenous demand for representative government' (p. 37). This generalization became a prediction when she observed that the 'history of this century provides no grounds for expecting that radical totalitarian regimes will transform themselves' (p. 41). In reality, Communist Czechoslovakia had been well on the way to being transformed from within in 1968 before Soviet invasion put a stop to radical reform initiated by the ruling Communist Party. Kirkpatrick was writing on the eve of the flourishing of the Solidarity movement which in 1980–1 transformed Polish society until the Polish Communist authorities, under pressure from Moscow, imposed martial law and forced Solidarity into a much reduced, underground resistance. Of course, the most dramatic falsification of the Kirkpatrick thesis was the fundamental change that occurred in the Soviet Union itself in the second half of the 1980s, a pluralization of the Soviet political system initiated and protected by Gorbachev and the reformist wing of the Communist Party of the Soviet Union. If all Communist states were classified as totalitarian and it was equally contended that totalitarian states could not be transformed from within, the second statement had to be wrong and even the first was a great oversimplification. Kirkpatrick made a partial retraction of her earlier argument a decade later, by which time transformative change in Communist countries was obvious. See Jeane Kirkpatrick, *The Withering Away of the Totalitarian State…and Other Surprises* (American Enterprise Institute, Washington, DC, 1990), p. 24.

64. See Reagan diary entries of 14 and 17 October (*The Reagan Diaries Unabridged*, Vol. I, pp. 275–6).

65. Cannon, *President Reagan*, p. 380.

66. Matlock, *Reagan and Gorbachev*, p. 74.

67. Cannon, *President Reagan*, p. 380.

68. Matlock, *Reagan and Gorbachev*, pp. 74–5.

69. Ibid., p. 61.

70. Ibid., pp. 62–3.

71. David E. Hoffman, *The Dead Hand: The Untold Story of the Cold War Arms Race and Its Dangerous Legacy* (Doubleday, New York, 2009), pp. 72–87.

72. Oleg Gordievsky, *Next Stop Execution* (Macmillan, London, 1995), pp. 272–3; Christopher Andrew and Oleg Gordievsky, *KGB: The Inside Story of its Operations from Lenin to Gorbachev* (Hodder & Stoughton, 1990), pp. 502–4; and Ben Macintyre, *The Spy and the Traitor: The Greatest Espionage Story of the Cold War* (Viking, London, 2018), pp. 181–6.

73. There is continuing controversy over how seriously concerned the Soviet leadership was in 1983 about the threat of nuclear attack, but not in doubt is Gordievsky's belief that the worries were genuine. It is equally clear that it was the information he provided on that score to British intelligence which led to the modification of the NATO exercise. For an overview of the currently available evidence on Moscow's concerns on Able Archer at the time, see the article by Gordon Barrass, former Chief of the Assessments Staff in the UK Cabinet Office and member of the Joint Intelligence Committee in the last years of the

Cold War, 'Able Archer 83: What Were the Soviets Thinking?', *Survival*, Vol. 58, No. 6, December 2016–January 2017, pp. 7–29. See also Barrass, *The Great Cold War: A Journey Through the Hall of Mirrors* (Stanford University Press, Stanford, 2009), pp. 298–303; Hoffman, *The Dead Hand*, pp. 94–100; Geoffrey Howe, *Conflict of Loyalty* (Macmillan, London, 1994), pp. 349–50; and Vojtech Mastny, 'How Able was "Able Archer"?', *Journal of Cold War Studies*, Vol. 11, No. 1, 2009, pp. 108–23.

74. https://nsarchive2.gwu.edu//dc.html?doc=5754460-National-Security-Archive-Doc-6-The-Soviet-War, p. xii; and Barrass, 'Able Archer 83', p. 7.

75. Barrass, 'Able Archer 83', p. 22. See also Macintyre, *The Spy and the Traitor*, pp. 144–62.

76. Barrass, 'Able Archer 83', p. 18.

77. Matlock, *Reagan and Gorbachev*, p. 75.

78. Ibid., pp. 75–6.

79. Jack Matlock, in an email to the author, 9 May 2017.

80. *The Reagan Diaries Unabridged*, Vol. I, p. 273.

81. Matlock, *Reagan and Gorbachev*, pp. 79–83.

82. Ibid., pp. 83–5.

83. Regan, *For the Record*; and Matlock, *Reagan and Gorbachev*, p. 80.

84. Matlock, *Reagan and Gorbachev*, p. 86.

85. Ronald Reagan, *An American Life: The Autobiography* (Simon & Schuster, New York, 1990), p. 589.

86. Matlock, *Reagan and Gorbachev*, p. 89.

87. James Mann, *The Rebellion of Ronald Reagan: A History of the End of the Cold War* (Viking, New York, 2009), p. 65.

88. Suzanne Massie, *Trust but Verify: Reagan, Russia and Me: A Personal Memoir* (Maine Authors Publishing, Rockland, Maine, 2013), esp. p. 19.

89. Matlock, *Reagan and Gorbachev*, pp. 93–6.

90. Ibid., p. 99.

91. Ibid., pp. 99–100; and Reagan, *An American Life*, pp. 602–3.

92. Fiona Hill and Clifford G. Gaddy, *Mr Putin: Operative in the Kremlin* (Brookings Institution, new and expanded edn, Washington, DC, 2015), p. 289.

93. Reagan, *An American Life*, p. 604.

94. Ibid., p. 605.

95. *The Reagan Diaries Unabridged*, Vol. I, p. 396.

96. Quoted in James Graham Wilson, *The Triumph of Improvisation: Gorbachev's Adaptability, Reagan's Engagement, and the End of the Cold War* (Cornell University Press, Ithaca and London, 2014), p. 94.

97. Ibid., pp. 94–5.

98. 'Cold War: Thatcher–Reagan meeting at Camp David (record of conversation)' (declassified 2000), http://www.margaretthatcher.org/archive/displaydocument.asp?docid=109185.

99. Ibid.

6 Margaret Thatcher: The Moulding of the 'Iron Lady'

1. Margaret Thatcher, *The Path to Power* (HarperCollins, London, 1995), p. 36.

2. That may not have been the case originally with Alfred Roberts. His elder daughter, Muriel, was insistent that her father had initially been a Liberal. However, he was a strong supporter of the Conservative-dominated coalition, the National Government, formed by the former Labour prime minister, Ramsay MacDonald, and thereafter a supporter of the party his younger daughter went on to lead. See Charles Moore, *Margaret Thatcher, Volume One: Not for Turning* (Allen Lane, London, 2013), pp. 15–16.

3. For these and other details of Margaret Thatcher's early life, I am indebted to Moore's exceptionally thorough biography, ibid., pp. 3–20.

4. Ibid., pp. 80–3 and 88–94, esp. p. 93.

5. Among them, one of her earliest biographers, Hugo Young, *One of Us* (Macmillan, London, 1989), who added: 'Numerous interviews after she became famous managed to exclude all references to Beatrice Roberts. There was almost an obsessive reluctance to refer to her' (p. 9). On the day she first became prime minister, she said, 'I owe almost everything to my father' (ibid.).

6. Moore, *Margaret Thatcher*, Vol. I, p. 9. Early in her working career, and on a tight budget, Margaret Roberts (as she still was) wrote to her sister, 'I shan't be able to afford a birthday present for Mummy so shall just send a card' (ibid., p. 67).

7. Thatcher, *The Path to Power*, pp. 5–6.

8. Ibid., p. 6.

9. Moore, *Margaret Thatcher*, Vol. I, pp. 27–8, 38–9 and 46–8.

10. Thatcher, *The Path to Power*, p. 42.

11. Moore, *Margaret Thatcher*, Vol. I, p. 51.

12. Ibid., p. 87.

13. Ibid., p. 41.

14. Ibid., pp. 56–7.

15. Ibid., p. 53.

16. Ibid., p. 106.

17. Sir Terence Garvey, who was British High Commissioner in India, 1971–3, before becoming ambassador in Moscow, was host to the Thatchers when they visited New Delhi at a time when Mrs Thatcher was Education Secretary in the government led by Edward Heath. He told me how glad he was to see the back of them, and of Denis in particular, whose views (especially on South Africa) he regarded as unambiguously racist.

18. Thatcher, *The Path to Power*, p. 130.

19. Ibid., pp. 56–9 and 471–2.

20. Robin Harris, *Not for Turning: The Life of Margaret Thatcher* (Corgi, London, 2014), pp. 100–1; and Moore, *Margaret Thatcher*, Vol. I, p. 289.

21. George R. Urban, *Diplomacy and Disillusion at the Court of Margaret Thatcher: An Insider's View* (Tauris, London, 1996), at e.g. pp. 168–9 and 190–1.

22. Brian Crozier, *Free Agent: The Unseen War 1941–1991* (HarperCollins, London, 1993), p. 127.

23. Harris, *Not for Turning*, pp. 104–16.

24. For a particularly insightful analysis of the Helsinki Final Act, see Richard Davy, 'Helsinki Myths: Setting the Record Straight on the Final Act of the CSCE, 1975', *Cold War History*, Vol. 9, No. 1, February 2009, pp. 1–22. See also Svetlana Savranskaya, 'Unintended Consequences: Soviet Interests, Expectations and Reactions to the Helsinki Final Act', in O. Bange and G. Niehart (eds.), *Helsinki 1975 and the Transformation of Europe* (Berghahn, Oxford, 2008), pp. 175–90.

25. Cited by Moore, *Margaret Thatcher*, Vol. I, pp. 310–11.

26. Ibid., pp. 317–22.

27. Crozier, *Free Agent*, p. 290.

28. Moore, *Margaret Thatcher*, Vol. I, pp. 331–2. See also Harris, *Not for Turning*, pp. 133–6, esp. p. 134.

29. This was conveyed to the outside world by the Reuters correspondent in Moscow, Robert Evans, who notes that his report 'won wide play in the British media—without credit as is so often the fate of news agency reports'. See 'Witness: "The Iron Lady"—My Part in Her Ascent', https://www.reuters.com/article/us-britain-thatcher-soubriquet/witness-the-iron-lady-my-part-in-her-ascent-idUSBRE9370NY20130408. Evans, a fluent Russian speaker, was Reuters correspondent in Moscow from 1975 until 1981 and again, 1986–91.

30. Moore, *Margaret Thatcher*, Vol. I, pp. 332–3.
31. Nelson Mandela, *Conversations with Myself* (Macmillan, London, 2010), p. 385.
32. Moore, *Margaret Thatcher*, Vol. I, p. 212.
33. Callaghan's major biographer, Kenneth O. Morgan, notes that while Labour consistently lagged behind the Conservatives in the opinion polls throughout the 1979 general election campaign, 'Callaghan led Mrs Thatcher by around 20 points in polls on the party leaders and who would make the better prime minister.' See Morgan, *Callaghan: A Life* (Oxford University Press, Oxford, 1997), p. 692.
34. Moore, *Margaret Thatcher*, Vol. I, p. 429.
35. The Prime Minister's Speech at the Pilgrims' Dinner January 29, 1981 at the Savoy Hotel, London, United Kingdom: Prime Minister Thatcher—Cables. Executive Secretariat, National Security Council: Head of State File, Records, Box 35, Reagan Presidential Library Archives.
36. Moore, *Margaret Thatcher*, Vol. I, p. 541.
37. Ibid., p. 566.
38. Ibid., p. 571.
39. Ibid., p. 547.
40. Margaret Thatcher Foundation, 1990 Jan 8, Archive (Thatcher MSS), 'Cold War: Margaret Thatcher interviewed about Ronald Reagan [released 2002]', http://www.margaretthatcher.org/document/109324.
41. Harris, *Not for Turning*, p. 254,
42. John Hoskyns, *Just in Time: Inside the Thatcher Revolution* (Aurum Press, London, 2000), esp. pp. 323–36.
43. Ibid., p. 326.
44. Ibid., p. 327.
45. Ibid. Hoskyns notes that several factors made the warning irrelevant for 'the next few years'. He includes among them 'good luck', 'the Reagan factor', victory in the Falklands war, 'the growing evidence of economic success', and 'Gorbachev and the gradual collapse of the Soviet Union' (ibid., p. 328).
46. See G. Bennett and K.A. Hamilton (eds.), *Documents on British Policy Overseas, Series III, Volume I: Britain and the Soviet Union, 1968–1972* (HMSO, London, 1997), pp. 48, 87, 160, and 304.
47. Ibid., p. 308.
48. Moore, *Margaret Thatcher*, Vol. I, p. 567.
49. Percy Cradock, *In Pursuit of British Interests: Reflections on Foreign Policy under Margaret Thatcher and John Major* (John Murray, London, 1997), p. 24.
50. Rodric Braithwaite, *Across the Moscow River: The World Turned Upside Down* (Yale University Press, London, 2002), p. 51.
51. Moore, *Margaret Thatcher*, Vol. I, p. 572.
52. Ibid., pp. 572–3.
53. Ibid., p. 573.
54. Morgan, *Callaghan: A Life*, pp. 461–2.
55. In the words of Hugo Young, *One of Us*, p. 266.
56. Moore, *Margaret Thatcher*, Vol. I, esp. pp. 666–7.
57. Ibid., p. 737.
58. Ibid., pp. 752–3.
59. Ibid., p. 738.
60. Ibid., pp. 743–4.
61. Alexander M. Haig, Jr, *Caveat: Realism, Reagan, and Foreign Policy* (Weidenfeld & Nicolson, London, 1984), p. 298.

62. Caspar Weinberger, *Fighting for Peace: Seven Critical Years in the Pentagon* (Warner Books, New York, 1991), pp. 203–17, esp. 212–15.
63. Moore, *Margaret Thatcher*, Vol. I, p. 745.
64. Ibid.
65. United Kingdom 4/1/82–7/31/82 [5 of 6], Box 20, Exec. Secretariat NSC, Records Country File, Reagan Presidential Library Archives.
66. George P. Shultz, *Turmoil and Triumph: My Years as Secretary of State* (Scribner's, New York, 1993), pp. 152–4.
67. In an interesting account of the Thatcher–Reagan relationship, Richard Aldous, as the title of his book indicates, focuses heavily on the quite numerous occasions when they disagreed on policy, somewhat downplaying the underlying strength of their mutually supportive relations. See Aldous, *Reagan and Thatcher: The Difficult Relationship* (Hutchinson, London, 2012).
68. The rise of Solidarity, and Soviet reaction to it (as evidenced in Politburo transcripts and other documents), is summarized in Archie Brown, *The Rise and Fall of Communism* (Bodley Head, London, 2009), pp. 426–37.
69. United Kingdom: Prime Minister Thatcher—Cables. Executive Secretariat, National Security Council: Head of State File: Records, Box 35, Reagan Presidential Library Archives.
70. Ibid.
71. Moore, *Margaret Thatcher*, Vol. I, p. 577.
72. Aldous, *Reagan and Thatcher*, p. 121.
73. Moore, *Margaret Thatcher*, Vol. I, pp. 578–9.
74. Ibid., p. 585.
75. Ibid.
76. Aldous, *Reagan and Thatcher*, p. 123.
77. Moore, *Margaret Thatcher*, Vol. I, p. 581.
78. Ronald Reagan, *The Reagan Diaries Unabridged*, Vol. I, ed. Douglas Brinkley (HarperCollins, New York, 2009), p. 136.
79. Moore, *Margaret Thatcher*, Vol. I, p. 581.
80. Thatcher, *The Downing Street Years*, p. 258.
81. Ibid.
82. Robert Blackwell to Laurence S. Eaglebruger, United Kingdom (01/31/1983–02/051983), Box 20, Executive Secretariat, NSC, Country File, Reagan Presidential Library Archives.
83. Lawrence S. Eagleburger to Sir Robert Armstrong, United Kingdom (01/31/1983–02/05/1983), Box 20, Executive Secetariat, NSC, Country File, Reagan Presidential Library Archives.
84. Moore, *Margaret Thatcher, Volume Two: Everything She Wants* (Allen Lane, London, 2015), p. 25.
85. Ibid., pp. 29–31; and Cradock, *In Pursuit of British Interests*, p. 9.
86. Cradock, *In Pursuit of British Interests*, p. 10.
87. Francis Pym, *The Politics of Consent* (Hamish Hamilton, London, 1984), p. ix.

7 Thatcher and the Turn to Engagement with Communist Europe

1. Francis Pym, *The Politics of Consent* (Hamish Hamilton, London, 1984), pp. 55–62.
2. For a much fuller account of the Chequers seminar, for which I was able to get the relevant government papers declassified through the Freedom of Information (FOI) Act, see Archie Brown, 'The Change to Engagement in Britain's Cold War Policy: The Origins of the Thatcher–Gorbachev Relationship', *Journal of Cold War Studies*, Vol. 10, No. 3, 2008, pp. 3–47. See also Brown, 'Margaret Thatcher and Perceptions of Change in the Soviet Union',

Journal of European Integration History, Vol. 16, No. 1, 2010, pp. 17–30. Although these articles, especially the first, contain much more information on the 1983 Chequers seminar, as well as on a 1987 Chequers seminar on the Soviet Union, than does this book, I mention some details here for the first time.

3. John Coles, Private Secretary to the Prime Minister, to Brian Fall, Private Secretary to the Foreign Secretary, 27 June 1983, Foreign Office Papers, RS013/1.

4. Memorandum from John Coles to Brian Fall, 30 June 1983, Foreign Office Papers, RS013/1.

5. Ibid.

6. There are interesting accounts of this seminar, with somewhat conflicting interpretations of its genesis, in Margaret Thatcher, *The Downing Street Years* (HarperCollins, London, 1993), pp. 451–3; and Geoffrey Howe, *Conflict of Loyalty* (Macmillan, London, 1994), pp. 315–17. In his authorized biography of Thatcher, Charles Moore devotes almost five pages to the September 1983 seminar. See Moore, *Margaret Thatcher, Volume Two: Everything She Wants* (Penguin Random House, London, 2015), pp. 108–12.

7. Thatcher, *The Downing Street Years*, p. 451.

8. Foreign and Commonwealth Office, 'East–West Relations' (prepared for Chequers Seminar, 8–9 September 1983), pp. 1 and 24. (I have used the Cabinet Office copy of this document, obtained as a result of an FOI request, for, unlike the copy in the FCO files, it contains the prime minister's annotations.)

9. Thatcher, *The Downing Street Years*, p. 451. In my own contemporaneous note about the seminar, I wrote that '[Mrs Thatcher] said that a second term of office gave her an opportunity to think about long-term strategy which was much more difficult to do in the first term. She said that the papers we had produced were the best they had had (by implication at such meetings, though how many had already been held was not mentioned; but Michael Kaser was told by John Coles that a whole series of such meetings on long-term strategy in different areas of policy is underway).'

10. Anatoly Dobrynin, *In Confidence: Moscow's Ambassador to America's Six Cold War Presidents (1962–1986)* (Times Books, New York, 1995), pp. 535–9.

11. Howe, *Conflict of Loyalty*, p. 350.

12. Dobrynin, *In Confidence*, p. 537. Dobrynin adds that Georgy Kornienko, the senior deputy Foreign Minister to Gromyko, told him that Andropov had been ready to admit publicly the mistake of the Soviet military, but that he was talked out of doing so by Defence Minister Dmitry Ustinov (ibid.). In a pre-lunch conversation with Defence Secretary Michael Heseltine at the 8 September Chequers seminar, I said that I did not think that Ustinov would be woken up before the plane was brought down, to which Heseltine responded: 'I hope to God they'll wake *me* up before doing anything of that kind here' (from my notes of the Chequers 1983 meeting).

13. 'Strategy Meetings on Foreign Affairs and Defence', Memorandum from Geoffrey Howe to Prime Minister, 5 September 1983, Cabinet Office Papers, PM/83/65, p. 5.

14. 'Britain and Arms Control', Memorandum from Michael Heseltine to the Prime Minister, 1 September 1983, p. 3, Cabinet Office Papers, MO 11/9/4.

15. Ibid.

16. The Foreign Office paper prepared for the seminar, which none of the academic participants in the seminar had access to until it was declassified a quarter of a century later, included an Annex A on 'Broadcasting: The Current Effort, and Possible Future Developments', and noted the introduction of new equipment that would 'enable the BBC to penetrate Soviet jamming more effectively'. In the main body of the FCO paper for the

seminar, 'East–West Relations' (p. 27), it was pointed out that jamming of the BBC's Russian-language broadcasts was 'fairly effective in the major cities but patchy elsewhere' and that the BBC's World Service broadcasts in English were not jammed. These points were underlined by the prime minister.

17. Howe, *Conflict of Loyalty*, p. 315.
18. A. J. Colquhoun to Miss Neville-Jones, 'The Chequers' Strategy Meetings', 12 September 1983, Foreign Office Papers, RS013/1.
19. Archie Brown, 'The Political System, Policy-Making and Leadership' (The Soviet Union: Background papers for the meeting on 8 September 1983). For a fuller account, see Brown, 'The Change to Engagement in Britain's Cold War Policy'. See also Moore, *Margaret Thatcher*, Vol. II, pp. 108–12.
20. Brown, 'The Political System, Policy-Making and Leadership'. Although bolder than the much longer FCO document, my paper also did not predict the imminence or the scale of the transformation of the Soviet system that was to occur, since it observed that 'no General Secretary will have a free hand' and 'what is at issue is the style and nature of Soviet authoritarianism...rather than a transition to political pluralism'. By the end of the same decade a transition to political pluralism in the Soviet Union had occurred.
21. Ronald Amann, 'Technological Inertia and its Consequences' (The Soviet Union: Background papers for the meeting on 8 September 1983).
22. Rev. Michael Bourdeaux, 'Religion' (The Soviet Union: Background papers for the meeting on 8 September 1983). Various senior officials in the FCO, including the head of the Soviet Department within the Foreign Office, Nigel Broomfield, read all of the papers of the academics in advance of the seminar and commented on them in internal memoranda. Sir Julian Bullard was especially impressed by Bourdeaux's paper, highlighting his 'conclusion that we may one day see the collapse of the Soviet system from within with religion playing a decisive role'. He added: 'I think he exaggerates the importance of the religious factor, but I am quite prepared to believe that we ourselves often underrate it' (Memorandum from Bullard to Broomfield, 7 September 1983, Foreign Office Papers, RS 013/1). Broomfield agreed much more with Amann's emphasis on Soviet technological inertia. He wrote that 'the Soviet system will change from within' and 'whether it will collapse or evolve is perhaps the key question'. In that change 'religion will play an important but not decisive role'. What would be decisive, in all probability, was 'economic failure and the inability to understand and control the technological and communications revolution which is now sweeping the developed world' ('East–West Relations: Papers by Academics', Memorandum from N. H. R. A. Broomfield, 7 September 1983, Foreign Office Papers, RS 013/1). Officials tended to highlight points in the papers by the academics that accorded with their pre-existing views. This generally meant noting the obstacles to change and screening out the more radical alternatives that had been mooted. Thus, David Manning summarized my paper as 'a lucid description of the Soviet political system as well as the factors militating against reform and change' ('Prime Minister's Strategy Meeting: East–West Relations', Memorandum from D. G. Manning to Pauline Neville-Jones, 7 September 1983, Foreign Office Papers, RS 0131/1). On the tenth anniversary of the 8 September 1983 seminar, a meeting was held at Birmingham University to consider its significance (and to take a look at possible future developments in the former Soviet Union). Both the 1983 and 1993 meetings are discussed by one of the participants in that Birmingham seminar, Sir Julian Bullard, in Bullard, 'Judges of History in the Making', *The Independent*, 20 October 1993.
23. 'East–West Relations', p. 10.
24. John Coles to Brian Fall, 'Policy on East/West Relations', 12 September 1983, RS 013/2, Foreign Office Papers.

25. Ibid.
26. Ibid.
27. Ibid.
28. John Coles to Brian Fall, 'Chequers: Discussions of foreign and defence policy', 13 September 1983, RS 013/2, Foreign Office Papers.
29. On her Hungarian visit, see Thatcher, *The Downing Street Years*, pp. 454–8.
30. Howe, *Conflict of Loyalty*, pp. 352–3,
31. Ibid., pp. 428–35.
32. Ibid., pp. 316–17.
33. Percy Cradock, *In Pursuit of British Interests* (John Murray, London, 1997), pp. 17–18. In contrast with the secrecy that was maintained about the September 1983 Chequers seminar, 'the content of another, on Germany in March 1990, was leaked, to general embarrassment' (ibid., p. 18). After he retired (as Head of the Diplomatic Service and Permanent Under-Secretary at the Foreign Office), John Coles, like Cradock, published a book of reflections, *Making Foreign Policy: A Certain Idea of Britain* (John Murray, London, 2000). He notes, at p. 99: 'The academic input into policy-making is at its most effective in direct discussion with the policy-makers. The latter will normally have little time for extensive reading of academic work.' Coles adds: 'I fear that the resources devoted in academic circles to international relations theory are unlikely to have much influence on the practitioner, largely because the products seem rather remote from the practical business of conducting foreign policy, though that of course may not be the principal objective of these studies' (ibid., pp. 99–100).
34. Ibid., p. 18.
35. Thatcher, *The Downing Street Years*, pp. 451–3, esp. 453.
36. Ibid., p. 453.
37. Moore, *Margaret Thatcher*, Vol. II, pp. 113–14.
38. Ibid., p. 114.
39. Howe, *Conflict of Loyalty*, pp. 350–1.
40. Robert McFarlane, in his memoirs, argues that the Cuban connection was significant and that a 'Soviet plan to create a second Soviet-backed base in the Caribbean was well under way' (McFarlane (with Zofia Smardz), *Special Trust* (Cadell & Davies, New York, 1994), p. 266).
41. There is a good overview of the Grenada episode and the temporary rift it caused in US–UK relations in Moore, *Margaret Thatcher*, Vol. II, pp. 117–35. See also Geoffrey Howe's chapter entitled 'Humiliation in Grenada', in Howe, *Conflict of Loyalty*, pp. 325–37; Thatcher, *The Downing Street Years*, pp. 328–35; Richard Aldous, *Reagan and Thatcher: The Difficult Relationship* (Hutchinson, London, 2012), pp. 143–56; and James Cooper, 'For Better and for Worse: Ronald Reagan's Relationship with Margaret Thatcher, 1981–1983', in Bradley Lynn Coleman and Kyle Longley (eds.), *Reagan and the World: Leadership and National Security, 1981–1989* (University Press of Kentucky, Lexington, 2017), pp. 127–46.
42. Quoted in Howe, *Conflict of Loyalty*, p. 332.
43. Draft message of Robert C. McFarlane to Sir Robert Armstrong, 7 November 1983, Reagan Presidential Library Archives: United Kingdom, 11/1/83-6/30/84, Box 20, Executive Secretariat, NSC, Records Country File. In his memoirs, McFarlane says that Thatcher had been 'livid' when she spoke with Reagan by telephone. 'Earlier press speculation about our intention to invade', he wrote, 'had led her to ask our Ambassador, Charlie Price, about our plans. After checking, he told her no invasion was planned…She was clearly not happy at having been kept in the dark. Grenada was a member of the British Commonwealth, she reminded Reagan…Despite her arguments that the invasion would hurt Reagan politically in Europe, I'm convinced that she was chiefly piqued at not having been informed earlier, and at how this would play to her disadvantage in Parliament' (McFarlane, *Special Trust*, p. 265).

44. Howe, *Conflict of Loyalty*, p. 331.
45. Cooper, 'For Better and for Worse', p. 141.
46. Thatcher, *The Downing Street Years*, p. 458.
47. Howe, *Conflict of Loyalty*, p. 354. Howe added, 'Since half the time was needed for interpretation, each meeting was clearly too short—and Chernenko too short-lived—for it to have any real content. The significance of the occasion was that the Iron Lady had come—as she had not done for Brezhnev's last rites, hardly eighteen months before.'
48. Zamyatin produced this tale when he was interviewed in *Komersant vlast'*, 4 May 2005. He had not yet invented it when he published an entire book on the Gorbachev–Thatcher relationship a decade earlier—A. M. Zamyatin, *Gorbi i Megi: Zapiski posla o dvukh izvestnykh politikakh—Mikhaile Gorbacheve i Margaret Tetcher* (Viniti, Moscow, 1995). The story is given credence by Jonathan Aitken in his unreliable biography, *Margaret Thatcher: Power and Personality* (Bloomsbury, London, 2013), pp. 478–9, and it appears also in Aldous, *Reagan and Thatcher: The Difficult Relationship*, p. 160. It was perfectly obvious from the conversation at 10 Downing Street the night before Gorbachev arrived in the UK in December 1984, to which I had been invited specifically to speak about Gorbachev, that the prime minister had never met him. Neither (until much later) had I, but I had been following his career since he first entered the Soviet top leadership team in 1978 and, with particular interest, since June 1979 when his friend from Moscow University Law Faculty days, Zdeněk Mlynář, described him to me as 'open-minded, intelligent and anti-Stalinist'. See Archie Brown, 'Introduction to Mikhail Gorbachev and Zdeněk Mlynář', in *Conversations with Gorbachev: On Perestroika, the Prague Spring, and the Crossroads of Socialism* (Columbia University Press, New York, 2002), pp. xii–xv.
49. The letter was sent on the stationery of the Inter-Parliamentary Union, signed by Lord Hailsham (Lord Chancellor) and Bernard Weatherill (Speaker of the House of Commons), and dated 2 February 1984 (Foreign Office Papers, ESB 020/2).
50. Some accounts have been published that erroneously suggest that Romanov and Grishin as well as Gorbachev were invited and that, in the words of Charles Powell, it was 'our great good fortune' that only Gorbachev accepted' (see Brown, 'The Change to Engagement in Britain's Cold War Policy', p. 18 (fn. 50)). However, Heydar Aliev, the former Azerbaijan party boss (who had earlier served in the NKVD and KGB) and Foreign Minister Andrei Gromyko were, indeed, selected to be on the invitee list after Gorbachev. When Charles Powell took over from John Coles as private secretary to the prime minister, he wrote to Thatcher on 28 June that 'it is obviously a good idea to invite Gorbachev and Aliev', for 'there is a chance they will come and it would do them good' (though why the FCO, supported by Powell, should think there was anything to be said for doing Aliev good is unclear). In the same memorandum, Powell advised against endorsing Sir Geoffrey Howe's suggestion that, during his visit to Moscow, he issue an invitation to Chernenko to come to the UK. Thatcher wrote on the memo, 'Do not invite Mr Chernenko—it is much too soon.'
51. In a letter to Sir Anthony Kershaw, Anthony Cary, private secretary to Malcolm Rifkind, said, 'Mr Rifkind wrote to you on 8 June to confirm the arrangements for inviting Mr Gorbachev to this country. I subsequently read over to your secretary the suggested text of an invitation that you might issue' (letter of 14 June 1983, Foreign Office Papers, ESB 020/7).
52. Howe to British Embassy, Moscow, Telegram No. 535, 14 June 1984, Foreign Office Papers, ESB 020/7.
53. Sir Anthony Kershaw was a case in point, as was Peter Temple-Morris, at that time a Conservative MP (much later—in November 1997—he crossed the floor of the House of Commons and became a Labour MP) who was Chair of the British branch of the Inter-Parliamentary Union. They became the joint official hosts of Gorbachev and the Supreme

Soviet delegation when they arrived in the UK in December. See Peter Temple-Morris, *Across the Floor: A Life in Dissenting Politics* (Tauris, London, 2015), esp. pp. 127–35.

54. K. A. Bishop [Gorbachev's UK interpreter at Chequers and throughout his December 1984 visit], 'Mikhail Sergeevich Gorbachev: A Personal Assessment of the Man during his Visit to the United Kingdom, 15–22 December 1984', 3 January 1985, https://www.margaretthatcher.org/document/134739, p. 1.

55. Charles Powell, writing on 16 December 1984 to his FCO counterpart, Leonard Appleyard, who in the same year as Powell succeeded Coles had become private secretary to the Foreign Secretary. Cited in Moore, *Margaret Thatcher*, Vol. II, p. 238.

56. 'Cold War: Margaret Thatcher interviewed about Ronald Reagan [released 2002]', https://www.margaretthatcher.org/document/109324, p. 15. This lengthy interview (the text runs to 8,765 words) by Geoffrey Smith on 8 January 1990 was off-the-record at the time. It included Thatcher's reflections on her first meeting with Gorbachev and on his subsequent role at a time when both she and Gorbachev were still in office.

57. Moore, *Margaret Thatcher*, Vol. II, p. 238.

58. Ibid., pp. 234–5 and 241–2; and Ben Macintyre, *The Spy and the Traitor: The Greatest Espionage Story of the Cold War* (Viking, London, 2018), pp. 177–201.

59. No notes of the meeting appear to exist in the government archives, and the gathering was much more informal than a Chequers seminar. I first referred to it in print (and also to the 1983 Chequers seminar) only after the August 1991 coup, by which time the Soviet Union was well on the way to disintegration. See Archie Brown, 'The Leader of the Prologue', *Times Literary Supplement*, 30 August 1991, republished in Ferdinand Mount (ed.), *Communism* (Harvill, London, 1992), pp. 293–300. The December 1984 meeting is briefly referred to by Thatcher in *The Downing Street Years* (p. 459) as 'a further seminar with Soviet experts to cover the issues and work out the approach I would take' at the Chequers meeting with Gorbachev.

60. Cited in *Financial Times*, 22 December 1984.

61. Anatoliy Adamishin, *V raznye gody: Vneshnepoliticheskie ocherki* (Ves' mir, Moscow, 2016), p. 111.

62. Moore, *Margaret Thatcher*, Vol. II, p. 240.

63. Ibid., p. 243.

64. Cold War: Thatcher–Reagan meeting at Camp David (record of conversation), Reagan Presidential Library Archive; available online from Margaret Thatcher Foundation: https://www.margaretthatcher.org/document/109185 (p. 3).

65. Ibid., p. 5.

66. Ibid., pp. 3–4.

67. Ibid., p. 3.

68. Ibid., p. 8

69. Ibid., p. 9.

70. Moore, *Margaret Thatcher*, Vol. II, p. 246.

71. Ibid., pp. 247–8.

72. Ibid., pp. 309–15.

73. Ibid., pp. 313–14.

8 Breaking the Ice (1985)

1. Warren Zimmermann, interviewed by Charles Stuart Kennedy, Library of Congress: http://www.loc.gov/item/mfdipbib001307.

2. Ibid. Zimmermann said in the same interview that when he was negotiating he didn't know that the American tests had been faked 'and the Soviets didn't know we were faking tests', but they had been. For an account of the sharp practice of those who were

committed to SDI, and beneficiaries of the research and development munificence it provided, see Frances Fitzgerald, *Way Out There in the Blue: Reagan, Star Wars and the End of the Cold War* (Touchstone, New York, 2000), pp. 373–6.

3. Zimmermann interview.

4. Ibid.

5. Fitzgerald, *Way Out There in the Blue*, pp. 257–8.

6. Jim Newton, *Eisenhower: The White House Years* (Doubleday, New York, 2011), p. 344.

7. Ibid., pp. 342–3.

8. Roald Z. Sagdeev. *The Making of a Soviet Scientist: My Adventures in Nuclear Fusion and Space from Stalin to Star Wars* (Wiley, New York, 1993), p. 186.

9. *Zasedanie Politbyuro TsK KPSS, 11 marta 1985 goda*, HIA, Fond 89, Reel 1.1001, opis 36, file 16.

10. Ibid., p. 13.

11. Richard Pipes, Jack Matlock's predecessor as Soviet specialist on the National Security Council, was prominent among those arguing that the Politburo chose a 'soft-liner' in Gorbachev, 'a man committed to perestroika and disarmament' in response to the hardline policies of President Reagan. See Pipes, 'Misinterpreting the Cold War: The Hard-Liners Had it Right', *Foreign Affairs*, Vol. 71, No. 1, 1995, pp. 154–60, at 158.

12. Ronald Reagan, *The Reagan Diaries Unabridged, Volume I: January 1981–October 1985*, ed. Douglas Brinkley (HarperCollins, New York, 2009), p. 434.

13. The French president, François Mitterrand, had a very brief encounter with Gorbachev when he was in Moscow in the summer of 1984, but no substantial conversation comparable to that of Thatcher—or, indeed, of Trudeau—with the future Soviet leader.

14. Geoffrey Howe, *Conflict of Loyalty* (Macmillan, London, 1994), p. 430.

15. George P. Shultz, *Turmoil and Triumph: My Years as Secretary of State* (Scribner's, New York, 1993), pp. 530 and 532–3.

16. The figures are from *Ezhegodnik bol'shoy sovetskoy entsiklopedii 1985* (Sovetskaya entsiklopediya, Moscow, 1985), pp. 9 and 13.

17. Archie Brown, 'Did Gorbachev as General Secretary Become a Social Democrat?', *Europe-Asia Studies*, Vol. 65, No. 2, 2013, pp. 198–220; and Brown, 'The Gorbachev Factor Revisited', *Problems of Post-Communism*, Vol. 58, Nos. 4–5, 2011, pp. 56–65.

18. For much more detail on the variety of heterodox thinking that went on prior to perestroika within official institutions and institutes, as well as on the development and radicalization of the ideas during Gorbachev's years in power, see Robert D. English, *Russia and the Idea of the West: Gorbachev, Intellectuals, and the End of the Cold War* (Columbia University, New York, 2000); and Archie Brown, *Seven Years that Changed the World: Perestroika in Perspective* (Oxford University Press, Oxford, 2007), esp. 'Institutional Amphibiousness or Civil Society? The Origins and Development of Perestroika', pp. 157–89.

19. Ronald Reagan letter to Mikhail Gorbachev, 11 March 1985, USSR General Secretary Gorbachev (8590272, 8590336), Executive Secretariat, NSC Head of State File, Box 39, Reagan Presidential Library Archives.

20. Shultz memorandum to the president of 25 March, 1985, 'Letter from Gorbachev', USSR General Secretary Gorbachev (8590272, 8590336), Executive Secretariat, NSC Head of State File, Box 39, Reagan Presidential Library Archives.

21. Mikhail Gorbachev letter to Ronald Reagan, 24 March 1985, ibid.

22. Aleksandr Yakovlev, 'Zapiska A.N. Yakovleva M.S. Gorbachevu o vsreche na vysshem urovne s prezidentom SShA R. Reyganom, 12 marta 1985 g.', in Yakovlev, *Perestroyka: 1985–1991: neizdannoe, maloizvestnoe, zabytoe* (Mezhdunarodnyy fond 'Demokratiya', Moscow, 2008), pp. 11–13.

23. Cf. Jack F. Matlock, Jr, *Reagan and Gorbachev: How the Cold War Ended* (Random House, New York, 2004), pp. 52–3 and 318–19; and Richard Perle, quoted by Charles Moore, *Margaret Thatcher, Volume Two: Everything She Wants* (Allen Lane, London, 2015), p. 248.

24. Colin Powell, cited in Moore, *Margaret Thatcher*, Vol. II, p. 249. Powell probably would not have formulated that thought in quite those terms in the mid-1980s. The same caveat applies to the quotation from Richard Perle, cited in note 23. These were recollections of Powell and Perle some thirty years later in interviews for Moore's 2015 book.

25. Ibid., pp. 248–9.

26. An interesting volume of recollections of Gromyko by Russian foreign relations specialists who worked with him, mainly as senior officials in the Soviet Ministry of Foreign Affairs, was compiled to mark the centenary of his birth by the long-serving minister's grandson, Aleksey Gromyko, who is now the director of the Institute of Europe in Moscow. See Al. A. Gromyko (ed.), '*Luchshe desyat' let peregovorov, chem odin den' voyny': Vospominaniya ob Andree Andreeviche Gromyko. K 100-letiyu so dnya rozhdeniya* (Ves' mir, Moscow, 2009).

27. Mikhail Gorbachev, *Zhizn' i reformy*, Vol. I (Novosti, Moscow, 1995), p. 288.

28. 'Zasedanie Politbyuro TsK KPSS 29 iyunya 1985 goda', NSA (GWU), Volkogonov Collection, R 5276, p. 3.

29. Andrei Grachev, *Gorbachev's Gamble: Soviet Foreign Policy and the End of the Cold War* (Polity, Cambridge, 2008), p. 59.

30. Eduard Shevardnadze, *The Future Belongs to Freedom* (Sinclair-Stevenson, London, 1991), p. 39.

31. Ibid., pp. 26 and 37. In Gorbachev's version, Shevardnadze said, 'Everything's gone rotten from top to bottom' and Gorbachev replied, 'I agree with you.' Cf. Mikhail Gorbachev, *Naedine s soboy* (Grin Strit, Moscow, 2012), p. 277. There is no disagreement in the two men's recollection of the substance of what was said, but they place it in different years. In Gorbachev's account, this conversation, in the Abkhazian resort of Pitsunda, occurred in December 1979, the same time as the two men agreed that the Soviet invasion of Afghanistan had been a big mistake. The broader statement about the degeneration in the Soviet system is, however, more likely to have been made at the later date named by Shevardnadze. He recalled the conversation taking place in Pitsunda, the same place where they had exchanged their opinions on Afghanistan in late December 1979, but at the end of 1984. Shevardnadze was writing just seven years on from 1984 and his memory of the year in which the conversation occurred was fresher.

32. Author's interview with Anatoly Chernyaev, 30 March 1992.

33. This was a spontaneous remark by Howe in a conversation I had with him in Oxford on 27 October 1988. See Archie Brown, *The Gorbachev Factor* (Oxford University Press, 1996), pp. 212–20 and 365–8, for more on the choice of Shevardnadze and on Gorbachev's other key foreign policy appointments.

34. Shultz, *Turmoil and Triumph*, pp. 702 and 744–5.

35. Moore, *Margaret Thatcher*, Vol. II, p. 252.

36. Shultz, commenting on the way Thatcher treated Howe, said that 'in Geoffrey's shoes I simply wouldn't have stood for it' (Moore, ibid.). A senior Foreign Office diplomat, David Goodall, observed of Thatcher, 'Often outspokenly rude to Ministers (especially, as time went on, to Geoffrey Howe) and invariably acerbic in argument, she was never, in my experience, actually rude to officials' (ibid., p. 5).

37. Howe, *Conflict of Loyalty*, p. 392.

38. Ibid., p. 393.

39. Moore, *Margaret Thatcher*, Vol. II, p. 259.

40. Robert C. McFarlane (with Zofia Smardz), *Special Trust* (Cadell & Davies, New York, 1994), p. 306.

41. Ibid.

42. Ibid.

43. Ibid., pp. 306–7.

44. My source for this is a UK Ministry of Defence official, Oliver Barton, who has made a special study of British defence policy during the Thatcher era (conversation in Oxford, 26 April 2016).

45. McFarlane, *Special Trust*, pp. 306–7.

46. Ibid., p. 307.

47. Moore, *Margaret Thatcher*, Vol. II, p. 258.

48. Ibid., p. 259.

49. Chris Matthews, *Tip and the Gipper: When Politics Worked* (Simon & Schuster, New York, 2013), pp. 321–2. O'Neill was surely mistaken, however, in saying that Gorbachev began the conversation by saying to him in English, 'You are the leader of the opposition', since Gorbachev—unlike his wife, Raisa, who had learned a little English and his daughter, Irina, who acquired good English—did not know the language.

50. Fitzgerald, *Way Out There in the Blue*, pp. 287–8.

51. David Korn letter to President Reagan, 27 October 1985, To Geneva (11/16–21/85), File 1 (3), Box 10, Coordination Office, NSC: Records, Reagan Presidential Library Archives. (Korn had made the same point to Reagan in a conversation in the White House the previous week and the president asked him to put it in writing.)

52. Gorbachev letter to Reagan of 10 June, 1985, USSR General Secretary Gorbachev (8590683, 8590713), Box 40, Executive Secretariat, NSC, Head of State File, Reagan Presidential Library Archives.

53. 'Letter from Reagan to Gorbachev, April 30, 1985', in Svetlana Savranskaya and Thomas Blanton (eds.), *The Last Superpower Summits: Gorbachev, Reagan, and Bush. Conversations that Ended the Cold War* (Central European Press, Budapest and New York, 2016), pp. 29–33, at p. 29.

54. M. S. Gorbachev, *Izbrannye rechi i stat'i*, Vol. III (Politizdat, Moscow, 1987), p. 251. This reference to Afghanistan came in the foreign policy section of Gorbachev's main speech on 25 February 1987 to the Twenty-Seventh Congress of the Communist Party of the Soviet Union. Aleksandr Yakovlev had a large part in the drafting of that section.

55. Anatoly S. Chernyaev Diary 1985, National Security Archive (Washington, DC) website, http://www.gwu.edu/~nsarchiv, entry for 17 October 1985.

56. Grachev, *Gorbachev's Gamble*, p. 60.

57. Ibid., pp. 62–3.

58. On this, see Marie-Pierre Rey, '"Europe is our Common Home": A Study of Gorbachev's Diplomatic Concept', *Cold War History*, Vol. 4, No. 2, 2004 (published online 9 August 2006: https://ezproxy-prd.bodleian.ox.ac.uk:4563/10.1080/1468274041233139180s).

59. Ibid., p. 16; and Julie M. Newton, *Russia, France, and the Idea of Europe* (Basingstoke and New York, 2003), p. 134.

60. Gorbachev letter to Thatcher of 26 August 1985, PREM 19/1693 f382, https://www.margaretthatcher.org/document/200512.

61. Thatcher to Reagan, 12 September 1985, PREM 19/1660 f277, https://www.margaretthatcher.org/document/143042.

62. Ibid.

63. Ibid.
64. Ibid. The italicized word here was underlined by Thatcher in her letter to Reagan.
65. Ibid. Again the word which is italicized here was underlined in the Thatcher letter.
66. Ibid.
67. 'Cold War: MT briefing cards (meeting with Reagan)', 23 October 1985, PREM 19/1660 f36: https://www.margaretthatcher.org/document/150912.
68. Moore, *Margaret Thatcher*, Vol. II, p. 264.
69. Ibid., p. 268.
70. Gorbachev letter to Reagan of 12 September 1985, USSR General Secretary Gorbachev (8591009), Executive Secretariat, NSC, Head of State File, Reagan Presidential Library Archives.
71. Ibid.
72. Gorbachev letter to Thatcher, 12 October 1985, PREM 19/1693 f307 (T188(i)a185), https://www.margaretthatcher.org/document/200497.
73. Ibid.
74. Shultz, *Turmoil and Triumph*, p. 577. For a more detailed account of the argument within the administration and of congressional reaction, see Fitzgerald, *Way Out There in the Blue*, pp. 289–94.
75. Reagan letter to Gorbachev, 31 October 1985, USSR General Secretary Gorbachev (8591135), Box 40, Executive Secretariat (NSC), Head of State File, Reagan Presidential Library Archives.
76. Matlock, *Reagan and Gorbachev*, pp. 133–5.
77. Suzanne Massie, *Trust but Verify: Reagan, Russia and Me* (Maine Authors Publishing, Rockland, 2013), pp. 164–73.
78. McFarlane, *Special Trust*, p. 313; and Ronald Reagan, *An American Life* (Simon and Schuster, New York, 1990), pp. 635–41, esp. p. 635.
79. 'Points which the President might make to Mr. Gorbachev arising from the effect of S.D.I. on the Soviet approach', Archive (TNA), PREM 19/1660 f32, https://www.margaretthatcher.org/document/143014. The document was written on 24 October 1985. A copy was sent by Charles Powell to the Foreign Office with a covering letter the following day.
80. Ibid.
81. Reagan letter to Thatcher, 28 October 1985, PREM 19/1693 f289 (T200/85), https://www.margaretthatcher.org/document/200491.
82. Robert C. McFarlane letter to Sir Robert Armstrong of 4 November 1985, PREM 19/1963 f271, https://www.margaretthatcher.org/document/200484.
83. Ibid.
84. Thatcher letter to Gorbachev, 7 November 1985, PREM 19/1963 f264 (T208/85), https://www.margaretthatcher.org/document/200483.
85. Shultz, *Turmoil and Triumph*, pp. 600–1.
86. 'Memorandum of Conversation, Reagan–Gorbachev, Second Plenary Meeting, Geneva, November 19, 1985', in Savranskaya and Blanton (eds.), *The Last Superpower Summits*, pp. 69–74, at p. 70.
87. 'Memorandum of Conversation, Reagan–Gorbachev, First Plenary Meeting, Geneva, November 19, 1985', in Savranskaya and Blanton (eds.), *The Last Superpower Summits*, pp. 62–8, at p. 64.
88. Ibid., p. 66.
89. 'Memorandum of Conversation, Reagan–Gorbachev, Third Private Meeting, Geneva, November 20, 1985', in Savranskaya and Blanton (eds.), *The Last Superpower Summits*, pp. 86–92, at p. 91.

90. 'Memorandum of Conversation, Reagan–Gorbachev, Third Plenary Meeting, Geneva, November 20, 1985', in Savranskaya and Blanton (eds.), *The Last Superpower Summits*, pp. 93–101, at p. 99.

91. 'Memorandum of Conversation, Reagan–Gorbachev, Dinner Hosted by President and Mrs Reagan, Geneva, November 20, 1985', in Savranskaya and Blanton (eds.), *The Last Superpower Summits*, pp. 108–12, at p. 108.

92. Shultz, *Turmoil and Triumph*, pp. 601–2.

93. 'Joint Soviet–United States Statement on the Summit Meeting in Geneva, November 21, 1985', https://www.reaganlibrary.gov/research/speeches/112185.

94. Ibid.

95. 'Draft Private Letter from Reagan to Gorbachev, November 28, 1985', in Savranskaya and Blanton (eds.), *The Last Superpower Summits*, pp. 113–15.

96. 'Letter from Gorbachev to Reagan, December 24, 1985', in Savranskaya and Blanton (eds.), *The Last Superpower Summits*, pp. 116–19, at p. 117.

97. Ibid., p. 118.

98. Ibid., p. 119.

99. Ronald Reagan letter to Mikhail Gorbachev, 26 December 1985, USSR General Secretary Gorbachev (8591241, 8591243), Executive Secretariat, National Security Council, Head of State File, Box 40, Reagan Presidential Library Archives.

100. Moore, *Margaret Thatcher*, Vol. II, p. 586.

101. 'No. 10 record of conversation (MT, Howe, Shultz)', 10 December 1985, PREM 19/1655 f6, https://www.margaretthatcher.org/document/149938.

102. McFarlane, *Special Trust*, p. 51. McFarlane's account of the Iran–Contra Affair occupies pp. 8–108 of that book. On Iran–Contra, see also *The Tower Commission Report: The Full Text of the President's Special Review Board* (Times & Bantam Books, New York, 1987); Lou Cannon, *President Reagan: The Role of a Lifetime* (Public Affairs, New York, 2000), pp. 521–79; and especially Malcolm Byrne, *Iran–Contra: Reagan's Scandal and the Unchecked Abuse of Presidential Power* (University Press of Kansas, Lawrence, Kansas, 2014).

103. 'No. 10 record of conversation (MT, Howe, Shultz)', 10 December 1985, PREM 19/1655f6, https://www.margaretthatcher.org/document/149938.

104. Ibid.

105. Ibid.

9 Nuclear Fallout: Chernobyl and Reykjavik (1986)

1. 'Letter from Gorbachev to Reagan, January 14, 1986', in Svetlana Savranskaya and Thomas Blanton, *The Last Superpower Summits: Gorbachev, Reagan and Bush Conversations that Ended the Cold War* (Central European University Press, Budapest and New York, 2016), pp. 138–42.

2. Ibid., pp. 139–40.

3. 'Zayavlenie general'nogo sekretarya TsK KPSS M. S. Gorbacheva, 15 yanvarya 1986 goda', in M. S. Gorbachev, *Izbrannye rechi i stat'i*, Vol. III (Politizdat, Moscow, 1987), pp. 133–44.

4. Jack F. Matlock, Jr, *Reagan and Gorbachev: How the Cold War Ended* (Random House, New York, 2004), pp. 177–8.

5. Ronald Reagan, *The Reagan Diaries Unabridged, Volume II: November 1985–January 1989*, ed. Douglas Brinkley (HarperCollins, New York, 2009), p. 568.

6. George P. Shultz, *Turmoil and Triumph: My Years as Secretary of State* (Scribner's, New York, 1993), p. 700.

7. Ibid.

8. Ibid.

9. Ibid., p. 701.

10. Andrei Grachev, *Gorbachev's Gamble: Soviet Foreign Policy and the End of the Cold War* (Polity, Cambridge, 2008), pp. 68–9.

11. James Graham Wilson, *The Triumph of Improvisation: Gorbachev's Adaptability, Reagan's Engagement, and the End of the Cold War* (Cornell University Press, Ithaca and London, 2014), pp. 101–2. Cf. Grachev, *Gorbachev's Gamble*, pp. 66–70.

12. Matlock, *Reagan and Gorbachev*, p. 178.

13. Charles Moore, *Margaret Thatcher, Volume Two: Everything She Wants* (Allen Lane, London, 2015), p. 588.

14. Shultz, *Turmoil and Triumph*, pp. 703 and 705.

15. Matlock, *Reagan and Gorbachev*, p. 178.

16. Shultz, *Turmoil and Triumph*, p. 707.

17. Ibid., p. 706.

18. Ibid., pp. 706–7.

19. Gorbachev to Thatcher letter, 14 January 1986, PREM 19/1693 f237 (T9A/86), https://www.margaretthatcher.org/document/200477.

20. Thatcher to Reagan letter, 11 February 1986, PREM 19/1693 f89 (T30A/86), https://www.margaretthatcher.org/document/200455.

21. Ibid.

22. PREM 19/1693 f172, https://www.margaretthatcher.org/document/200470.

23. Draft Reply to Handwritten Letter from Gorbachev 2/12/86, USSR General Secretary Gorbachev, Box 40, Executive Secretariat (NSC), Head of State File, Reagan Presidential Library Archives.

24. Ibid.

25. Javier Gil Guerrero, 'Propaganda Broadcasts and Cold War Politics: The Carter Administration's Outreach to Islam', *Journal of Cold War Studies*, Vol. 19, No. 1, 2017, pp. 4–37, at p. 36.

26. Ibid., pp. 36–7.

27. Shultz, *Turmoil and Triumph*, p. 704.

28. Mikhail Gorbachev, *Zhizn' i reformy*, Vol. II (Novosti, Moscow, 1995), pp. 7–8.

29. 'Politicheskiy doklad tsentral'nogo komiteta KPSS XXVII s"ezdu Kommunisticheskoy Partii Sovetskogo Soyuza', 25 February 1986, in Mikhail Sergeevich Gorbachev, *Sobranie sochineniy*, Vol. III (Ves' mir, Moscow, 2008), pp. 286–392, at p. 361.

30. See Grachev, *Gorbachev's Gamble*, pp. 89–91.

31. Ibid., p. 90.

32. A. S. Chernyaev, *Moya zhizn' i moya vremya* (Mezhdunarodnaya otnosheniya, Moscow, 1995), p. 13.

33. On the Prague group, see Chernyaev, ibid., pp. 225–36; Archie Brown, *The Gorbachev Factor* (Oxford University Press, Oxford, 1996), pp. 98–101; and Brown, *Seven Years that Changed the World: Perestroika in Perspective* (Oxford University Press, Oxford, 2007), pp. 161–3.

34. Chernyaev, *Moya zhizn' i moe vremya*, p. 236.

35. 'Intrastructural dissenters' was the terminology used by Alexander Shtromas in a little-known book (partly, no doubt, because it was published in English in Germany), *Political Change and Social Development: The Case of the Soviet Union* (Peter Lang, Frankfurt am Main, 1981), esp. pp. 67–87. 'Intrasystemic dissidents' is the term employed by Evgeniy Primakov, an influential international relations specialist in the later Soviet years who in the post-Soviet 1990s was at different times Minister of Foreign Affairs and prime minister. See his

'Dissidenty v sisteme', in Primakov, *Gody v bol'shoy politike* (Sovershenno sekretno, Moscow, 1999), pp. 9–98. Former Deputy Foreign Minister during the perestroika period, Anatoly Adamishin, used the term 'apparatchiki-dissidents', a category in which he included, among others, Evgeny Velikhov, Roald Sagdeev, Georgy Arbatov, Andrei Grachev, and Fedor Burlatsky. See Adamishin, *V raznye gody: Vneshnopoliticheskie ocherki* (Ves' mir, Moscow, 2016), p. 120.

36. For example, by Leonard Schapiro, 'The International Department of the CPSU: Key to Soviet Policy', *International Journal*, Vol. 32, No. 1, 1976–77, pp. 41–55. Scholars in the 1970s, it is only fair to add, possessed much less information on the inner workings of Soviet institutions than became available in the second half of the 1980s.

37. Svetlana Savranskaya, Thomas Blanton, and Vladislav Zubov (eds.), *Masterpieces of History: The Peaceful End of the Cold War 1989* (Central European University Press, Budapest and New York, 2010), pp. 200–1.

38. Many of them have been translated at the National Security Archive in Washington, DC, and are available on the NSA (GWU) website.

39. Chernyaev, *Moya zhizn' i moya vremya*, pp. 237–80. The fullest account of Chernyaev's role is to be found in Dmitriy Belanovskiy (ed.), *'My nazyvali ego Grafom': Pamyati Anatoliya Sergeevicha Chernyaeva* (Lyubimaya Rossiya, Moscow, 2019).

40. The constraints on Gorbachev's power to make economic policy are a central theme of the book by Chris Miller, *The Struggle to Save the Soviet Economy: Mikhail Gorbachev and the Collapse of the USSR* (University of North Carolina Press, Chapel Hill, 2016), although Miller underestimates the extent to which Gorbachev pursued political liberalization and democratization for their own sake, not merely as a way of overcoming the institutional resistance to economic reform.

41. Grachev, *Gorbachev's Gamble*, p. 72.

42. I have written about this in much greater detail elsewhere. See esp. Brown, *The Gorbachev Factor*, pp. 111–15; and Brown, *Seven Years that Changed the World*, esp. pp. 161–7 and 172–87.

43. For elaboration of the point, see, for example, Robert D. English, *Russia and the Idea of the West: Gorbachev, Intellectuals, and the End of the Cold War* (Columbia University Press, New York, 2000); and Brown, *Seven Years that Changed the World*, esp. chs. 6 and 9. Of the institutes, none has had its evolution and role documented so thoroughly as has the international relations institute, IMEMO. See, in particular, Petr Cherkasov's 870-page volume, *IMEMO: Ocherk istorii* (Ves' mir, Moscow, 2016) which pays great attention to the institute's relationship with policy-makers.

44. 'Politicheskiy doklad', in Gorbachev, *Sobranie sochineniy*, Vol. III, p. 355.

45. Ibid., p. 367.

46. General Albert Makashov, 'Doktrina predatel'stva', *Den'*, 7–13 June 1992.

47. 'Politicheskiy doklad', in Gorbachev, *Sobranie sochineniy*, Vol. III, p. 304.

48. 'Zasedanie Politbyuro TsK KPSS 14 oktyabrya 1986 goda', Volkogonov Collection, NSA (GWU), Washington, DC, R9744.

49. Ronald Reagan, *An American Life* (Simon & Schuster, New York, 1990), p. 710.

50. Andrei Grachev, Chiara Blengino, and Rossella Stievano, *1985–2005: Twenty Years that Changed the World* (World Political Forum and Editori Laterza, Rome, 2005), p. 149.

51. Interview with M. S. Gorbachev, 22 March 1999, Hoover Institution and Gorbachev Interview Project on the Cold War, p. 7. (I am grateful to Viktor Kuvaldin, one of the interviewers, for supplying me with the full text of this lengthy interview.)

52. Roald Z. Sagdeev, *The Making of a Soviet Scientist: My Adventures in Nuclear Fusion and Space from Stalin to Star Wars* (Wiley & Sons, New York, 1994), pp. 268, 272–3, and 320.

53. Ibid., p. 273.

54. Ibid., pp. 273 and 320.

55. Ibid., p. 273.

56. Chernyaev notes of Politburo meeting of 24 March 1986, in Anatoliy Chernyaev, Vadim Medvedev and Georgiy Shakhnazarov (eds.), *V Politbyuro TsK KPSS…Po zapisyam Anatoliya Chernyaeva, Vadima Medvedeva, Georgiya Shakhnazarova (1985–1991)* (Gorbachev Foundation and Al'pina, Moscow, 2006), pp. 33–4.

57. William J. Perry, *My Journey at the Nuclear Brink* (Stanford University Press, Stanford, 2015), p. 68.

58. It was published in M. S. Gorbachev, *Gody trudnykh resheniy* (Al'fa-Print, Moscow, 1993), pp. 46–55; and reprinted in the fullest collection of Gorbachev's writings and speeches: Mikhail Sergeyevich Gorbachev, *Sobranie sochineniy*, Vol. IV (Ves' mir, Moscow, 2008), pp. 124–34.

59. Gorbachev, *Sobranie sochineniy*, Vol. IV, p. 125.

60. Ibid., p. 126.

61. Ibid., pp. 126–7.

62. Ibid., pp. 127–8.

63. Ibid., pp. 128–9.

64. Ibid., p. 129.

65. Ibid., p. 131.

66. Ibid., p. 133. That term was applied to Vyacheslav Molotov when he was Soviet Foreign Minister and inherited by Andrei Gromyko, who headed the Ministry from 1957 to 1985. An endnote to the fourth volume of Gorbachev's collected speeches and writings refers only to the latter. It reads: 'In diplomatic circles A. A. Gromyko was called "Mister Nyet"' (ibid., p. 544).

67. Minutes of an Extraordinary Session of the CC CPSU Politburo, 28 April 1986, Document 4. This is part of a substantial selection of Soviet contemporary documents relating to the Chernobyl crisis, made available by NSA (GWU) as recently as August 2019. See 'Top Secret Chernobyl: The Nuclear Disaster through the Eyes of the Soviet Politburo, KGB, and US Intelligence', https://nsarchive.gwu.edu/briefing-book/nunn-lugar-russia-programs/2019-08-15/top-secret-chernobyl-nuclear-disaster-through-eyes-soviet-politburo-kgb-us-intelligence.

68. Serhii Plokhy, *Chernobyl: History of a Tragedy* (Allen Lane, London, 2018), pp. 175–6.

69. Chernyaev et al. (eds.), *V Politbyuro TsK KPSS*, pp. 61–6, esp. p. 65. Plokhy (*Chernobyl*, p. 186) appears to give some credence to the unreliable accounts of Gorbachev's political enemies, the old Brezhnevite Volodymyr Shcherbytsky and his wife Rada Shcherbytska, who implied that May Day celebratory parades went ahead within the most acute danger zone of the Chernobyl explosion on the instructions of Gorbachev. Given what Gorbachev said in the Politburo on 3 July about how iniquitous it was that weddings took place and children were allowed to play on the streets at that time, this seems highly unlikely. If any telephone instruction to hold the parades did come from a senior Politburo member in Moscow, and it remains highly questionable, it would have been issued by Ligachev, who, as CC CPSU second secretary, was the person who supervised the party organization. At the emergency Politburo meeting on 28 April, Ligachev mentioned that he had already spoken by phone to the Ukrainian party first secretary Shcherbytsky and the Kiev first secretary Hryhorii Revenko (Minutes of an Extraordinary Session of the CC CPSU Politburo, 28 April 1986, Document 4).

70. S. F. Akhromeev and G. M. Kornienko, *Glazami marshala i diplomata: kriticheskiy vzglyad na vneshnyuyu politiku SSSR do i posle 1985 goda* (Mezhdunarodnye otnosheniya, Moscow, 1992),

p. 105. Among the scientists, an especially important contribution was made by the first deputy director of the Kurchatov Institute of Atomic Energy, Valeriy Legasov.

71. Plokhy, *Chernobyl*, pp. 190–4.

72. Matlock, *Reagan and Gorbachev*, p. 188.

73. Shultz, *Turmoil and Triumph*, pp. 714–15.

74. Memorandum for the President, From George P. Shultz, 19 May 1986, USSR General Secretary Gorbachev (8591241, 8591243), Executive Secretariat, National Security Council, Head of State File, Box 40, Reagan Presidential Library Archives.

75. Reagan letter to Gorbachev, 23 May 1986, USSR General Secretary Gorbachev (8690389, 8690420), Executive Secretariat, National Security Council, Head of State File, Box 40, Reagan Presidential Library Archives.

76. Shultz, *Turmoil and Triumph*, pp. 690–1.

77. Ibid., p. 691.

78. Ibid., pp. 703 and 710.

79. Ibid., pp. 710–11.

80. Anatoly Chernyaev, *My Six Years with Gorbachev* (Pennsylvania State University Press, University Park, PA, 2000), pp. 75–6.

81. Ibid., p. 76.

82. Ibid., pp. 76–7.

83. Meeting w/Private Sector Supporters of SDI, 08/05/86, RAC Box 12, Coordination Office, NSC: Records, Reagan Presidential Library Archives.

84. Ibid.

85. Ibid.

86. Ibid.

87. Quoted from personal communication—Jack Matlock letter of 2 July 2004 to the author.

88. Matlock, *Reagan and Gorbachev*, p. 195.

89. Frances Fitzgerald, *Way Out There in the Blue: Reagan, Star Wars and the End of the Cold War* (Touchstone, New York, 2000), pp. 282–3.

90. Shultz, *Turmoil and Triumph*, pp. 719–20.

91. Fitzgerald, *Way Out There in the Blue*, pp. 338–9.

92. Ibid.

93. Shultz, *Turmoil and Triumph*, p. 719.

94. Ibid., pp. 725–6; and Fitzgerald, *Way Out There in the Blue*, p. 339.

95. Matlock, *Reagan and Gorbachev*, pp. 198–9.

96. Shultz, *Turmoil and Triumph*, p. 738.

97. Cf. Shultz, ibid., pp. 728–50, and Matlock, *Reagan and Gorbachev*, pp. 197–211, esp. p. 210.

98. Shultz, *Turmoil and Triumph*, p. 744.

99. Chernyaev, *My Six Years with Gorbachev*, p. 78.

100. Gorbachev letter to Reagan, 15 September 1986, USSR General Secretary Gorbachev (8690616, 8690659), Box 40, Executive Secretariat, NSC, Head of State File, Reagan Presidential Library Archives.

101. Shultz, *Turmoil and Triumph*, p. 752.

102. Chernyaev, *My Six Years with Gorbachev*, p. 78.

103. Ibid., pp. 78–9.

104. Adamishin, *V raznye gody*, p. 131.

105. Chernyaev, *My Six Years with Gorbachev*, p. 79.

106. Ibid., pp. 79–80.

107. Ibid., p. 79.

108. Ibid., p. 80.
109. Ibid., pp. 81–2.
110. Ibid., p. 82.
111. Ibid., p. 83.
112. Chernyaev et al. (eds.), *V Politbyuro TsK KPSS*, pp. 78–9.
113. Dale R. Herspring, *The Soviet High Command, 1967–1989: Personalities and Politics* (Princeton University Press, Princeton, NJ, 1990), p. 209.
114. Akhromeev and Kornienko, *Glazami marshala i diplomata*, p. 109.
115. Ibid., p. 110.
116. Savranskaya and Blanton, *The Last Superpower Summits*, p. 162.
117. Ibid., p. 163.
118. Ibid., p. 164.
119. Ibid., pp. 164 and 168.
120. Ibid., p. 164.
121. Akhromev and Kornienko, *Glazami marshala i diplomata*, p. 110.
122. Ibid., p. 111.
123. Matlock, *Reagan and Gorbachev*, p. 213.
124. Shultz, *Turmoil and Triumph*, pp. 779–80. See also Ken Adelman, *Reagan at Reykjavik: Forty-Eight Hours that Ended the Cold War* (Broadside, New York, 2014), pp. 114–17, 120–7, and 137.
125. Adelman, *Reagan at Reykjavik*, pp. 124 and 126.
126. Akhromeev and Kornienko, *Glazami marshala i diplomata*, pp. 117–18.
127. Ibid., pp. 125–7.
128. Ibid., p. 126.
129. Shultz, *Turmoil and Triumph*, p. 755.
130. Donald Regan, *For the Record: From Wall Street to Washington* (Hutchinson, London, 1988), p. 344.
131. Matlock, *Reagan and Gorbachev*, pp. 213–14 and 232.
132. Adelman, *Reagan at Reykjavik*, p. 164.
133. Matlock, *Reagan and Gorbachev*, pp. 237–8.
134. Personal communications from Jack Matlock.
135. Savranskaya and Blanton, *The Last Superpower Summits*, p. 191.
136. Ibid., p. 192.
137. Ibid., pp. 222–35.
138. Ibid., p. 209.
139. Ibid., pp. 209–10.
140. Ibid., pp. 231–2.
141. Ibid., p. 231.
142. Ibid., p. 237.
143. William Taubman, *Gorbachev: His Life and Times* (Norton, New York, 2017), p. 302.
144. 'Zasedanie Politbyuro TsK KPSS, 14 oktyabrya 1986 goda', p. 1.
145. The word he used was *protivnik*, meaning 'opponent' or 'adversary', rather than *vrag* (enemy).
146. 'Zasedanie Politbyuro TsK KPSS, 14 oktyabrya 1986 goda', p. 2.
147. Ibid., p. 6.
148. Ibid., p. 8.
149. Ibid., p. 9.
150. Fitzgerald, *Way Out There in the Blue*, p. 350.
151. Ibid.

152. Ibid.

153. Ibid., p. 348.

154. Ibid., p. 353.

155. 'Memorandum from Poindexter for the President: "Why We Can't Commit to Eliminating All Nuclear Weapons within 10 Years", October 16, 1986', in Savranskaya and Blanton, *The Last Superpower Summits*, pp. 240–5, at p. 240.

156. Ibid., p. 245.

157. Fitzgerald, *Way Out There in the Blue*, pp. 366–7.

158. Shultz, *Turmoil and Triumph*, p. 780.

159. 'Shultz message to Howe (announcement of US–USSR Summit in Reykjavik)', 30 September 1986, https://www.margaretthatcher.org/document/143849.

160. Moore, *Margaret Thatcher*, Vol. II, p. 598.

161. Ibid., p. 599.

162. Margaret Thatcher, *The Downing Street Years* (HarperCollins, London, 1993), pp. 471–2.

163. Geoffrey Howe, *Conflict of Loyalty* (Macmillan, London, 1994), p. 523.

164. Meeting with Prime Minister Margaret Thatcher, 15 November 1986, Poindexter memo to Reagan, Thatcher Visit, 11/15/86, Box 13, Coord Office, NSC: Records, Reagan Presidential Library Archives.

165. Ibid.

166. Moore, *Margaret Thatcher*, Vol. II, p. 603.

167. 'Cold War: Lavin & Sommer memo for Poindexter' ('Thatcher visit'), 10 November 1986, Reagan Library document in https://www.margaretthatcher.org/document/143810.

168. From Archive (US State Department), 'Defence: Charles Thomas briefing for Shultz (meeting with MT)', 13 November 1986, https://www.margaretthatcher.org/document/143733.

169. Moore, *Margaret Thatcher*, Vol. II, pp. 607 and 764.

170. Malcolm Byrne, *Iran–Contra: Reagan's Scandal and the Unchecked Abuse of Presidential Power* (University Press of Kansas, Lawrence, Kansas, 2014), p. 262.

171. Moore, *Margaret Thatcher*, Vol. II, pp. 609–10.

172. Ibid., pp. 610–11 (citing interview with Carlucci).

10 Building Trust (1987)

1. Andrei Sakharov, *Memoirs* (Knopf, New York, 1990), pp. 614–18. Gorbachev had secured the agreement of the Politburo on 1 December 1986 to rescind the Supreme Soviet decree of 1980 exiling the Sakharovs and for them to be informed that they were free to return to their Moscow apartment and their dacha. See *V Politbyuro TsK KPSS…Po zapisyam Anatoliya Chernyaeva, Vadima Medvedeva, Georgiya Shakhnazarova (1985–1991)* (Al'pina, Moscow, 2006), p. 114.

2. Sakharov, *Memoirs*, p. 615.

3. Andrei Sakharov, *Moscow and Beyond: 1986 to 1989* (Knopf, New York, 1991), pp. 22 and 70.

4. 'O perestroyke i kadrovoy politike partii: doklad na Plenume TsK KPSS 27 yanvarya 1987 goda', in Mikhail Sergeevich Gorbachev, *Sobranie sochineniy*, Vol. V (Ves' mir, Moscow, 2008), pp. 391–451, esp. p. 450.

5. 'Za bez'yadernyy mir, za gumanizm mezhdunarodnykh otnosheniy', in M. S. Gorbachev, *Izbrannye rechi i stat'*, Vol. IV (Politizdat, Moscow, 1997), pp. 376–92. The speech was prepared under the supervision of the liberal deputy foreign minister, Anatoly Adamishin (promoted to that post in 1986 by Shevardnadze), who delegated the drafting to four

younger colleagues, of whom the main author became Andrei Kovalev, the son of First Deputy Minister of Foreign Affairs Anatoly Kovalev. See Andrei A. Kovalev, *Russia's Dead End: An Insider's Testimony from Gorbachev to Putin* (Potomac Books and University of Nebraska Press, Lincoln, NE, 2017), p. 68.

6. Matthew Evangelista, *Unarmed Forces: The Transnational Movement to End the Cold War* (Cornell University Press, Ithaca, 1999), p. 287.

7. An excellent analysis of Gorbachev's speech, putting it in the context of his earlier proclamations and those of his predecessors, was provided at the time by a young American researcher, Joel Hellman, who a generation later is the Dean of the Walsh School of Foreign Service at Georgetown University in Washington, DC. See 'Textual Analysis of General Secretary Mikhail Gorbachev's Speech to the Forum "For a Nuclear-Free World, For the Survival of Mankind", Moscow, February 26, 1987' (American Committee on US–Soviet Relations, 1987).

8. Sakharov, *Moscow and Beyond*, p. 15.

9. Ibid., p. 21,

10. Ibid., p. 22.

11. Ibid., p. 23.

12. 'Zayavlenie general'nogo sekretarya TsK KPSS M. S. Gorbacheva, 1 marta 1987 goda', in Gorbachev, *Sobranie sochineniy*, Vol. VI (Ves' mir, Moscow, 2008), pp. 136–8.

13. 'Zapiska A. N. Yakovleva M. S. Gorbachevu...25 fevralya 1987', in Aleksandr Yakovlev, *Perestroyka: 1985–1991: Dokumenty* (Mezhdunarodnyy Fond, 'Demokratiya', Moscow, 2008), pp. 77–89.

14. Ibid., p. 84.

15. 'Politbyuro 26 fevralya 1987 goda', in *V Politbyuro TsK KPSS*, pp. 149–2, at 151–2. See also Svetlana Savranskaya and Thomas Blanton, *The Last Superpower Summits. Gorbachev, Reagan, and Bush: Conversations that Ended the Cold War* (Central European University Press, Budapest and New York, 2016), pp. 258–9.

16. *V Politbyuro TsK KPSS*, p. 152.

17. For fuller information on Thatcher's preparation for her March 1987 visit to the Soviet Union, see Archie Brown, 'The Change to Engagement in Britain's Cold War Policy: The Origins of the Thatcher–Gorbachev Relationship', *Journal of Cold War Studies*, Vol. 10, No. 3, 2008, pp. 3–47, esp. 36–41; Brown, 'Margaret Thatcher and Perceptions of Change in the Soviet Union', *Journal of European Integration History*, Vol. 16, No. 1, 2010, pp. 17–30, esp. 26–8; and Charles Moore, *Margaret Thatcher, Volume Two: Everything She Wants* (Allen Lane, London, 2015), pp. 614–22.

18. Margaret Thatcher, *The Downing Street Years* (HarperCollins, London, 1993), p. 474.

19. Ibid.

20. The prime minister, ably abetted by Powell, had been determined to keep the number of participants at the seminar small. Even the Cabinet Secretary, Sir Robert Armstrong, and his deputy, Christopher Mallaby (who had both Soviet and arms control experience) were, to their chagrin, excluded. For the arguments about which senior officials would be allowed to attend the seminar, see Brown, 'The Change to Engagement in Britain's Cold War Policy', esp. p.37.

21. 'Cold War: Charles Powell conversation record ("Seminar on the Soviet Union") [MT meets academics at Chequers: enthusiasts vs sceptics]', 27 February 1987, https://www.margaretthatcher.org/document/205300.

22. Thatcher, *The Downing Street Years*, p. 474.

23. Percy Cradock, *In Pursuit of British Interests: Reflections on Foreign Policy under Margaret Thatcher and John Major* (John Murray, London, 1997), p. 14.

24. Ibid.

25. In the covering letter to Geoffrey Howe's private secretary, Powell wrote: 'Everyone retains his own overall impression of a discussion of this length and complexity. Mine may err slightly on the side of conveying too negative a view of what is happening in the Soviet Union' (Powell to A. C. Galsworthy, Foreign and Commonwealth Office, 1 March 1987, Cabinet Office, A2162). This is among the numerous documents of which I received declassified copies between 2006 and 2009, using the Freedom of Information Act.

26. 'Cold War: Charles Powell conversation record' ('Seminar on the Soviet Union'), 27 February 1987, p. 4.

27. Martin Nicholson, formerly of the FCO Research Department, had succeeded Malcolm Mackintosh as the Cabinet Office Sovietologist and, in that capacity, took part in the seminar. The head of the FCO Soviet Department, Michael Llewellyn Smith, successfully argued for the inclusion of Nicholson, for he wanted 'me to be his eyes and ears at the seminar'. Martin Nicholson (to whom I am grateful for sharing these recollections in an email of 19 October 2015) added that he 'felt somewhat out of my league' at the seminar, having only recently moved to the Cabinet Office and being 'still very much in Research Department mode, engrossed in detail'.

28. From my own contemporary notes, 'Meeting at Chequers on Friday 27 February, 1987'.

29. Ibid.

30. Charles Powell to A. C. Galsworthy (private secretary to Geoffrey Howe), 25 February 1987 (Cabinet Office document declassified in response to my FOI request).

31. Robert Conquest, in a symposium, 'What's Happening in Moscow?', in *The National Interest*, Summer 1987, pp. 3–30, at pp. 5 and 6. While greatly underestimating the seriousness of the political transformation Gorbachev was willing to undertake, Conquest more pertinently observed that reforms were liable to 'exacerbate the political and social crisis' and release forces which could 'transform or destroy this brutal and primitive polity' (p. 6).

32. Alec Nove, in the symposium, 'What's Happening in Moscow?', p. 18. In addition to Conquest and Nove, the other authors were: Hannes Adomeit, Archie Brown, Peter Reddaway, Alain Besançon and Françoise Thom (in a joint article), and Adam Ulam.

33. Thatcher, *The Downing Street Years*, p. 476.

34. Charles Powell letter to A. C. Galsworthy of FCO, 23 March 1987, 'ISSR: No. 10 record of conversation (MT-Mitterrand)', PREM19/2182 f67, https://www.margaretthatcher.org/document/205881, p. 2.

35. Ibid., p. 4.

36. Thatcher, *The Downing Street Years*, p. 477.

37. Gerd Ruge, *Gorbachev: A Biography* (Chatto & Windus, London, 1991), p. 216; and Andrei Grachev, *Gorbachev's Gamble: Soviet Foreign Policy and the End of the Cold War* (Polity, Cambridge, 2008), p. 132.

38. 'USSR: MT notes (conversation with Kohl on Gorbachev)', 23 March 1987, THCR 1/10/113 f3, https://www.margaretthatcher.org/document/201168.

39. Moore, *Margaret Thatcher*, Vol. II, p. 623.

40. Ibid.

41. Ibid., p. 619.

42. Ibid.

43. Thatcher's misgivings about SDI had already been attenuated by the related American investment in the British defence sector. Caspar Weinberger noted that between October 1985 and December 1988 UK companies and research establishments received $55.8 millions in contracts and subcontracts (a drop in the ocean compared with US defence spending

of $577,395 millions in 1988). See Weinberger, *Fighting for Peace: Seven Critical Years in the Pentagon* (Warner, New York, 1991), p. 316; and Patterson Clark, 'Spending on the Military, 1988–2012', *Washington Post*, 26 March 2014.

44. Margaret Thatcher, 'Speech at Soviet Official Banquet', 30 March 1987, https://www. margaretthatcher.org/document/106776.

45. Thatcher, *The Downing Street Years*, p. 482.

46. Cradock, *In Pursuit of British Interests*, p. 100.

47. 'Zapis' peregovorov M. S. Gorbacheva s prem'er-ministrom Velikobritanii M. Tetcher, 30 marta 1987 goda', Gorbachev Foundation Archives. This account of the meeting, written by Chernyaev and dated 1 April 1987, runs to sixty-four pages. The passages quoted are from pp. 50–4.

48. Anatoly Chernyaev, *My Six Years with Gorbachev* (Pennsylvania State University Press, University Park, PA, 2000), p. 99.

49. Ibid., p. 103.

50. When the meeting was still only between the two principals, Gorbachev said something which, noted the British interpreter present Richard Pollock, went untranslated by his Soviet counterpart Nikolai Uspensky. Gorbachev remarked to Thatcher, 'Peace will be good for you, it will be good for me, it will be good for mankind.' The use of 'me' in this context, noted Pollock, was unusual and perhaps a frank reference to the Soviet domestic political context. See Richard Pollock record of conversations ('Prime Minister's Talks in USSR: 28 March/1 April 1987'), THCR 1/10/117 f49, https://www.margaretthatcher.org/ document/201191, p. 4.

51. Ibid., p. 6.

52. Ibid., p. 7.

53. 'USSR: UKE Moscow telegram to FCO ("The Prime Minister's visit to Moscow 28 March–1 April")', THCR 1/10/117 f13, https://www.margaretthatcher.org/document/201155, p. 2.

54. Ibid., p. 3.

55. Ibid., p. 4.

56. Ibid., p. 6.

57. Thatcher, *The Downing Street Years*, p. 485.

58. R. F. Cornish, British Embassy, Washington, to P. J. Fowler, FCO, 6 April 1987, 'USSR: Washington to FCO ("Prime Minister's visit to Moscow")', THCR 1/10/117 f39, https://www.margaretthatcher.org/document/201156.

59. Thatcher letter to Gorbachev, 2 April 1987, Thatcher MSS. Churchill Archive Centre: THCR 3/2/214 f170, https://www.margaretthatcher.org/document/205282.

60. 'Ob itogakh visita Tetcher v Moskvu', 1 April 1987, in *V Politbyuro TsK KPSS*, p. 162.

61. Ibid., pp. 162–3.

62. Chernyaev, *My Six Years with Gorbachev*, p. 104.

63. Ibid.

64. Ibid., pp. 104–5.

65. George P. Shultz, *Turmoil and Triumph: My Years as Secretary of State* (Scribner's, New York, 1993), p. 864.

66. Ibid.

67. Frances Fitzgerald, *Way Out There in the Blue: Reagan, Star Wars and the End of the Cold War* (Touchstone, New York, 2001), p. 388.

68. Shultz, *Turmoil and Triumph*, p. 876.

69. Fitzgerald, *Way Out There in the Blue*, p. 405.

70. Ibid., pp. 406–7.

71. Shultz, *Turmoil and Triumph*, p. 868.

72. Ibid., p. 869.

73. Ibid., pp. 869–70.

74. Ibid., p. 870.

75. Massie letter to Reagan, 6 February 1987, The President (02/12/1987–04/28/1987), Box 92462, Carlucci, Frank: Files, Reagan Presidential Library Archives.

76. Memorandum to the File (by Carlucci), ibid.

77. Shultz, *Turmoil and Triumph*, pp. 880–1.

78. Jack F. Matlock, Jr, *Reagan and Gorbachev: How the Cold War Ended* (Random House, New York, 2004), p. 256. See also Shultz, *Turmoil and Triumph*, pp. 881–2.

79. Matlock, *Reagan and Gorbachev*, p. 256.

80. Ibid.

81. Ibid.

82. Ibid.

83. Shultz, *Turmoil and Triumph*, p. 881.

84. Matlock, *Reagan and Gorbachev*, p. 257; and Shultz, *Turmoil and Triumph*, p. 885.

85. Matlock, *Reagan and Gorbachev*, pp. 264–5; and Shultz, *Turmoil and Triumph*, p. 886.

86. Reagan letter to Gorbachev, 10 April 1987, USSR General Secretary Gorbachev (8790364), Box 41, Executive Secretariat, NSC, Head of State File, Reagan Presidential Library Archives.

87. Meeting w/Private Sector Supporters of SDI, 08/05/86, RAC Box 12, Coordination Office, NSC: Records, Reagan Presidential Library Archives.

88. Matlock, *Reagan and Gorbachev*, p. 258.

89. Shultz, *Turmoil and Triumph*, p. 890; and Matlock, *Reagan and Gorbachev*, p. 258.

90. Matlock, *Reagan and Gorbachev*, p. 258.

91. 'Memorandum of Conversation between Gorbachev and Shultz', 14 April 1987, in Savranskaya and Blanton, *The Last Superpower Summits*, pp. 278–84, at p. 283.

92. Ibid. General Colin Powell was impressed by Gorbachev's mastery of military detail at the Washington summit meeting later in 1987. 'Gorbachev', he wrote, 'was tossing off terms like "MIRV" and "depressed trajectories" and the throw weights of SS-12s, -13s, -18s, and -24s, like one of Ken Adelman's wonks in the Arms Control and Disarmament Agency.' See Colin L. Powell (with Joseph E. Persico), *My American Journey* (Random House, New York, 1995), p. 362.

93. 'Memorandum of Conversation between Gorbachev and Shultz', p. 283.

94. Shultz, *Turmoil and Triumph*, p. 890.

95. Ibid., p. 896.

96. Ibid., pp. 891–3, esp. 893.

97. Ibid., p. 897.

98. Ibid., p. 900.

99. 'Zasedanie Politbyuro TsK KPSS 30 maya 1987 goda', Volkogonov Papers, NSA (GWU), p. 485.

100. On the break-up of the Soviet state, see Archie Brown, *The Rise and Fall of Communism* (Bodley Head, London, and Ecco, New York, 2009), pp. 549–73.

101. Anatoly Dobrynin, *In Confidence: Moscow's Ambassador to America's Six Cold War Presidents (1962–1986)* (Times Books, New York, 1995), pp. 625–6.

102. Ibid., p. 626.

103. Grachev, *Gorbachev's Gamble*, p. 89.

104. Ibid.

105. Iwan Morgan, *Reagan: American Icon* (Tauris, London, 2016), p. 304.
106. Reagan meeting with former President Richard Nixon, 28 April 1987, The President (02/12/1987–04/28/1987), Box 992462, Carlucci, Frank: Files, Reagan Presidential Library Archives, pp. 2–3.
107. Ibid., p. 3.
108. Morgan, *Reagan*, p. 305.
109. Ibid.
110. Powell, *My American Journey*, p. 359.
111. Morgan, *Reagan*, p. 306; and Lou Cannon, *President Reagan: The Role of a Lifetime* (Public Affairs, New York, 1991), pp. 694–5.
112. Vladislav Zubok, 'With his Back against the Wall: Gorbachev, Soviet Demise, and German Reunification', in *Cold War History*, Vol. 14, No. 4, 2014, pp. 619–45, at pp. 621–2.
113. Shultz Guidance on Summit, 5 May 1987, 0930 Meetings, Box 92462, Carlucci, Frank C.: Files, Reagan Presidential Library Archives.
114. 'Zasedanie Politbyuro TsK KPSS, 15 oktyabrya 1987 goda', R 10012, Vokogonov Papers, p.137, NSA (GWU).
115. Mikhail Gorbachev, *Perestroika: New Thinking for Our Country and the World* (Collins, London, 1987).
116. 'The Diary of Anatoly S. Chernyaev, 1987', http://www.nasarchive.org, p. 24.
117. Savranskaya and Blanton, *The Last Superpower Summits*, p. 289.
118. (Soviet) 'Memorandum of Conversation between Gorbachev and Shultz, October 23, 1987', ibid., pp. 290–300.
119. Shultz, *Turmoil and Triumph*, p. 991.
120. Matlock, *Reagan and Gorbachev*, pp. 266–7.
121. Pavel Palazchenko, *My Years with Gorbachev and Shevardnadze: The Memoir of a Soviet Interpreter* (Pennsylvania State University Press, University Park, PA, 1997), p. 74.
122. Gorbachev's letter, Shultz memorandum to Reagan, 30 October 1987, USSR General Secretary Gorbachev (8790986, 9791196), Box 41, Executive Secretariat, NSC, Head of State File, Reagan Presidential Library Archives.
123. Gorbachev letter to Reagan, ibid.
124. Ibid.
125. Palazchenko, *My Years with Gorbachev and Shevardnadze*, pp. 74–6.
126. 'Zapis' peregovorov M. S. Gorbacheva s prem'er-ministrom Velikobritanii M. Tetcher, 7 dekabrya 1987 goda', pp. 1–2, Gorbachev Foundation Archives, Moscow. This eighteen-page document is the Soviet transcript of the Thatcher–Gorbachev discussions at Brize Norton in Oxfordshire.
127. Ibid., p. 3.
128. Ibid.
129. Ibid., p. 4.
130. Ibid., p. 8.
131. Ibid., pp. 11–14.
132. Ibid., p. 17.
133. Ibid., p. 18.
134. Mikhail Gorbachev, *Zhizn' i reformy*, Vol. II (Novosti, Moscow, 1955), pp. 59–60.
135. S. F. Akhromeyev and G. M. Kornienko, *Glazami marshala i diplomata: kriticheskiy vzglyad na vneshnyuyu politiku SSSR do i posle 1985 goda* (Mezhdunarodnye otnosheniya, Mosow, 1992), pp. 130–1.
136. Savranskaya and Blanton, *The Last Superpower Summits*, pp. 262–3.

137. Matlock, *Reagan and Gorbachev*, pp. 274–5.
138. Grachev, *Gorbachev's Gamble*, pp. 95–100.
139. Kornienko and Akhromeyev, *Glazami marshala i diplomata*, p. 129.
140. Matlock, *Reagan and Gorbachev*, p. 275.
141. Ibid.
142. Shultz, *Turmoil and Triumph*, p. 1014.
143. Ibid., pp. 1010–11.
144. Ibid., p. 1011.
145. Powell, *My American Journey*, pp. 362–3.
146. Shultz, *Turmoil and Triumph*, p. 1015.
147. Ibid. p. 1011; and Powell, *My American* Journey, pp. 362–3.
148. Shultz, *Turmoil and Triumph*, p. 1011.
149. Ibid., p. 1014.
150. 'Notes of a CC CPSU Politburo Session, December 17, 1987', in Savranskaya and Blanton, *The Last Superpower Summits*, p. 362.
151. Ibid., p. 361.
152. Ibid.
153. Ibid., p. 363.
154. 'The Diary of Anatoly S. Chernyaev, 1987', http://www.nsarchive.org, p. 30.

11 The End of the Ideological Divide (1988)

1. Svetlana Savranskaya and Thomas Blanton, *The Last Superpower Summits. Gorbachev, Reagan, and Bush: Conversations that Ended the Cold War* (Central European University Press, Budapest and New York, 2016), p. 455.
2. Nina Andreeva, 'Ne mogu postupat'sya printsipami', *Sovetskaya Rossiya*, 13 March 1988, p. 3.
3. Ivan Laptev, who was at that time chief editor of the newspaper, *Izvestiya*, described the meeting when interviewed at length for a major oral history project on perestroika. See 'The Second Russian Revolution Transcripts', 1991, British Library of Political and Economic Science, London School of Economics, Roll A9, p. 35.
4. Gorbachev noted this in the manuscript of a book he wrote in 1988 but did not, in the end, publish because the speed of change in the Soviet Union was so great that the text was being overtaken by events (M. S. Gorbachev, 'Perestroyka—ispytanie zhizn'yu', pp. 46–7). For access to this manuscript in the Gorbachev Foundation, I am especially grateful to the late Anatoly Chernyaev who assisted Gorbachev in the work's composition.
5. Georgy Shakhnazarov interview, 'The Second Russian Revolution Transcripts' (Shakhnazarov, Tape 62D, p. 13).
6. *V Politbyuro TsK KPSS…Po zapisyam Anatoliya Chernyaeva, Vadima Medvedeva, Georgiya Shakhnazarova (1985–1991)* (Al'pina, Moscow, 2006), p. 307.
7. Ibid.
8. 'Tezisy k vystupleniyu A. N. Yakovleva na Politbyuro TsK KPSS po povodu stat'i N. A. Andreevoy v gazete "Sovetskaya Rossiya", 25 marta 1988 g.', in Aleksandr Yakovlev, *Perestroyka: 1985–1991. Neizdannoe, maloizvestnoe, zabytoe* (Mezhdunarodnyy fond 'Demokratiya', Moscow, 2008), pp. 192–200, at p. 192.
9. 'Printsipy perestroyki: revolyutsionnost' myshleniya i deystviy', *Pravda*, 5 April 1988, p. 2.
10. *V Politbyuro TsK KPSS*, p. 309.
11. 'Politbyuro, 18 aprelya 1988 goda, Ob Afganistane', Chernyaev notes, Gorbachev Foundation archives.

12. George P. Shultz, *Turmoil and Triumph: My Years as Secretary of State* (Scribner's, New York, 1993), p. 1080.
13. Ibid., pp. 1080–1.
14. Ibid., p. 1138.
15. Ibid., p. 1081.
16. Ibid., p. 1082.
17. Julie M. Newton, *Russia, France, and the Idea of Europe* (Palgrave Macmillan, Basingstoke, 2003), p. 147.
18. Ibid., pp. 130–1.
19. Pavel Palazchenko, *My Years with Gorbachev and Shevardnadze: The Memoir of a Soviet Interpreter* (Pennsylvania State University Press, University Park, PA, 1997), pp. 84–5.
20. Margaret Thatcher, *The Downing Street Years* (HarperCollins, London, 1993), p. 775.
21. Ibid.
22. Ibid.
23. Ibid.
24. Richard Aldous, *Reagan and Thatcher: The Difficult Relationship* (Hutchinson, London, 2012), p. 251.
25. Ibid., p. 252.
26. Ibid.
27. Caspar Weinberger, *Fighting for Peace: Seven Critical Years in the Pentagon* (Warner, New York, 1990; paperback 1991), p. 331.
28. Ibid.
29. Interview with Caspar Weinberger, 20 October 1998, Oral History of the Cold War, HIA, p. 7.
30. Denis Healey, *The Time of My Life* (Michael Joseph, London, 1989), p. 519.
31. Jack F. Matlock, Jr, *Reagan and Gorbachev: How the Cold War Ended* (Random House, New York, 2004), p. 284.
32. 'Vstrecha Gorbacheva s tret'ey gruppoy sekretarey obkomov, 18 aprelya 1988 goda', Gorbachev Foundation Archives.
33. Jack F. Matlock, Jr, *Autopsy on an Empire: The American Ambassador's Account of the Collapse of the Soviet Union* (Random House, New York, 1995), p. 122.
34. Ibid.
35. Ronald Reagan, *The Reagan Diaries Unabridged, Volume II: November 1985–January 1989*, ed. Douglas Brinkley (HarperCollins, New York, 2009), p. 892.
36. Savranskaya and Blanton, *The Last Superpower Summits*, p. 400.
37. Ibid., p. 399.
38. Ibid., p. 370.
39. Ibid.
40. Ibid., p. 411.
41. Ibid., p. 404.
42. Ibid., pp. 409–11.
43. Ibid., p. 435.
44. Ibid., p. 438.
45. Palazchenko, *My Six Years with Gorbachev and Shevardnadze*, p. 92.
46. Shultz, *Turmoil and Triumph*, p. 1105.
47. Savranskaya and Blanton, *The Last Superpower Summits*, pp. 436–7.
48. Matlock, *Reagan and Gorbachev*, p. 299.
49. Anatoly S. Chernyaev Diary 1985, p. 156, National Security Archive website: http://www.gwu.edu/~nsarchiv.

50. Matlock, *Reagan and Gorbachev*, p. 300; and Shultz, *Turmoil and Triumph*, p. 1102.

51. Matlock, *Reagan and Gorbachev*, p. 301.

52. Ibid.

53. Frances Fitzgerald, *Way Out There in the Blue: Reagan, Star Wars and the End of the Cold War* (Touchstone, New York, 2001), p. 452.

54. Shultz, *Turmoil and Triumph*, p. 1104.

55. Ronald Reagan, Address at Moscow State University (31 May 1988): https://www.reaganlibrary.gov/speeches/053188b

56. Ibid.

57. Ibid.

58. Ibid.

59. Ibid.

60. Ibid.

61. Ibid.

62. Matlock, *Reagan and Gorbachev*, pp. 301–2.

63. Ronald Reagan, *An American Life* (Simon and Schuster, New York, 1990), p. 713.

64. William Taubman, *Gorbachev: His Life and Times* (Norton, New York, 2017), p. 416.

65. Michael R. Beschloss and Strobe Talbott, *At the Highest Levels: The Inside Story of the End of the Cold War* (Little, Brown, London, 1993), p. 9.

66. *The Reagan Diaries Unabridged*, Vol. II, p. 894.

67. Reagan letter to Gorbachev [undated draft, but alongside a Powell memorandum of 9 June 1988], CHRON OFFICIAL 1988 (I) (JAN–JUN) [9], Box 2, Powell, Colin L.: Files, Reagan Presidential Library Archives.

68. Ibid.

69. 'O vizite Reygana v Moskvu', Politburo, 6 June 1998, *V Politbyuro TsK KPSS*, p. 373.

70. Ibid.

71. Ibid.

72. 'Memorandum from Arbatov to Gorbachev, June 1988'. in Savranskaya and Blanton, *The Last Superpower Summits*, pp. 445–9, at p. 446.

73. *V Politbyuro TsK KPSS*, pp. 378–9.

74. Ibid.

75. M. S. Gorbachev, *Ponyat' perestroyku* (Al'pina, Moscow, 2006), p. 39.

76. James Graham Wilson, *The Triumph of Improvisation: Gorbachev's Adaptability, Reagan's Engagement, and the End of the Cold War* (Cornell University Press, Ithaca, 2014), p. 149.

77. Scowcroft in George Bush and Brent Scowcroft, *A World Transformed* (Knopf, New York, 1998), p. 13. Scowcroft was, however, a moderate sceptic on the extent of change in the Soviet Union, once he was in office, compared with other senior members of the Bush administration such as Defense Secretary Dick Cheney, deputy director of Central Intelligence Robert Gates who moved in March 1989 to become number two to Scowcroft within the NSC, and Vice-President Dan Quayle, all of whom had still deeper doubts about Gorbachev. See Bartholomew Sparrow, *The Strategist: Brent Scowcroft and the Call of National Security* (Public Affairs, New York, 2015), esp. pp. 292–3.

78. Ivan Laptev interview, 'The Second Russian Revolution Transcripts', A10, p. 9.

79. Ligachev speech in *XX Vsesoyuznaya konferentsiya kommunisticheskoy partii Sovetskogo Soyuza 28 iyunya – 1 iulya 1988 goda: Stenograficheskiy otchet*, Vol. II (Politizdat, Moscow, 1988), pp. 82–8, at p. 82.

80. Taubman, *Gorbachev*, pp. 159–365, esp. p. 163; and Archie Brown, *The Rise and Fall of Communism* (Bodley Head, London, 2009), pp. 514–18.

81. All the quotations are from the translations of the texts of the conference resolutions in BBC SWB, SU/0196, pp. C19-C34, 6 July 1988.

82. Laptev interview, A11, pp. 53–5. The official transcript of the conference provides the text of the resolution but does not convey the drama of the moment. See *XX Vsesoyuznaya konferentsiya kommunisticheskoy partii Sovetskogo Soyuza*, Vol. II, pp. 185–6.

83. Ibid., Vol. I, pp. 44–5.

84. Ibid., p. 41.

85. Ibid., p. 42.

86. Ibid., p. 43.

87. Ibid.

88. Mikhail Gorbachev, *Zhizn' i reformy*, Vol. II (Novosti, Moscow, 1995), pp. 390–404.

89. Thatcher, *The Downing Street Years*, p. 777.

90. Ibid., p. 780.

91. Ibid., p. 781.

92. Ibid.

93. Ibid., p. 782.

94. Jeffrey A. Engel, *When the World Seemed New: George H. W. Bush and the End of the Cold War* (Houghton Mifflin Harcourt, Boston and New York, 2017), p. 19.

95. Ibid., p. 20.

96. Ibid., p. 21. Thatcher's readiness to support Gorbachev surpassed not only that of Bush but also of Reagan. In a passage of Charles Hill's draft of George Shultz's memoirs which did not make it into the printed version, Shultz is cited as saying of Thatcher, 'Gradually, she came to believe that it was important not only to engage with Gorbachev but to help Gorbachev. She was more the advocate of this view than Ronald Reagan ever was' (Charles Moore, *Margaret Thatcher, Volume Three: Herself Alone*, Allen Lane, London, 2019, pp. 166 and 878).

97. Thatcher, *The Downing Street Years*, p. 783.

98. Ibid.

99. Ibid.

100. Scowcroft in Bush and Scowcroft, *A World Transformed*, pp. 13–14.

101. Ibid., p. 14.

102. Robin Harris, *Not for Turning: The Life of Margaret Thatcher* (Corgi, London, 2014), p. 305; and Moore, *Margaret Thatcher*, Vol. III, pp. 144–6.

103. Ibid., pp. 385–6.

104. Thatcher, *The Downing Street Years*, p. 783.

105. Matlock, *Reagan and Gorbachev*, p. 306.

106. Akhromeyev in S. F. Akhromeyev and G. M. Kornienko, *Glazami marshala i diplomata: kriticheskiy vzglyad na vneshnyuyu politiku SSSR do i posle 1985 goda* (Mezhdunarodnye otnosheniya, Moscow, 1992), p. 203.

107. Ibid., p. 204.

108. Matlock, *Reagan and Gorbachev*, p. 306.

109. Ibid.

110. Ibid., p. 314.

111. On this issue in broader context, see George W. Breslauer and Philip E. Tetlock (eds.), *Learning in U.S. and Soviet Foreign Policy* (Westview, Boulder, 1991), esp. Robert Legvold's chapter, 'Soviet Learning in the 1980s', pp. 684–732.

112. 'Vystuplenie v organizatsii ob"edinennykh natsiy', in M. S. Gorbachev, *Izbrannye rechi i stat'i*, Vol. VII (Politizdat, Moscow, 1990), pp. 184–202, at 198–9.

113. Palazchenko, *My Six Years with Gorbachev and Shevardnadze*, p. 370.

114. Ibid., p. 104.

115. Gorbachev, 'Vystuplenie v organizatsii ob"edinennykh natsiy', p. 187.

116. Ibid., p. 193.

117. Ibid.

118. Ibid., p. 188.

119. Ibid.

120. Ibid., p. 189.

121. Ibid., p. 190.

122. Andrei Grachev, *Gorbachev's Gamble: Soviet Foreign Policy and the End of the Cold War* (Polity, Cambridge, 2008), p. 166.

123. Ibid.

124. Akhromeyev and Kornienko, *Glazami marshala i diplomata*, p. 213.

125. Ibid.

126. Ibid., p. 214; and *V Politbyuro TsK KPSS*, pp. 419–20.

127. Rodric Braithwaite, Diary 1988–1992 (manuscript), entry for 9 December 1988.

128. Shultz, *Turmoil and Triumph*, p. 1108.

129. Ibid., p. 1138.

130. Scowcroft in Bush and Scowcroft, *A World Transformed*, p. 46.

131. Beschloss and Talbott, *At the Highest Levels*, pp. 17–18.

132. Savranskaya and Blanton, *The Last Superpower Summits*, p. 461.

133. Braithwaite diary, entry for 13 September 1988.

12 The End of the Cold War (1989)

1. Frances Fitzgerald, *Way Out There in the Blue: Reagan, Star Wars and the End of the Cold War* (Touchstone, New York, 2001), p. 466.

2. Jeffrey A. Engel, *When the World Seemed New: George H. W. Bush and the End of the Cold War* (Houghton Mifflin Harcourt, Boston & New York, 2017), p. 84.

3. Ibid., p. 85.

4. Jon Meacham, *Destiny and Power: The American Odyssey of George Herbert Walker Bush* (Random House, New York, 2015), p. 369.

5. James A. Baker, III, with Thomas M. DeFrank, *The Politics of Diplomacy: Revolution, War and Peace 1989–1992* (Putnam's, New York, 1995), p. 45.

6. Robert M. Gates, 'Gorbachev's Gameplan: The Long View', memorandum of 24 November 1987, in Svetlana Savranskaya, Thomas Blanton, and Vladislav Zubok (eds.), *Masterpieces of History: The Peaceful End of the Cold War in Europe, 1989* (Central European Press, Budapest and New York, 2010), pp. 261–3, at 263.

7. Savranskaya, Blanton, and Zubok, comment, ibid., p. 261.

8. 'National Intelligence Estimate 11-4-89, "Soviet Policy toward the West: The Gorbachev Challenge"', in Savranskaya et al. (eds.), *Masterpieces of History*, pp. 442–5, at 444–5.

9. See, for example, MacEachin's contribution to a 1998 conference in Savranskaya et al. (eds.), *Masterpieces of History*, esp. p. 187.

10. On this point, see the testimony of MacEachin and of Jack Matlock, ibid., pp. 186–7.

11. Ibid., p. 68.

12. Condoleezza Rice, *No Higher Honor: A Memoir of My Years in Washington* (Simon & Schuster, London, 2011), p. 23.

13. Ibid.

14. Ibid.
15. Baker, *The Politics of Diplomacy*, pp. 68–9.
16. Ibid., p. 69.
17. Ibid.
18. Ibid., p. 70.
19. Ibid., p. 74.
20. Ibid.
21. Colin L. Powell, with Joseph E. Persico, *My American Journey* (Random House, New York, 1995), p. 362.
22. Jack F. Matlock, Jr, *Autopsy on an Empire: The American Ambassador's Account of the Collapse of the Soviet Union* (Random House, New York, 1995), p. 183.
23. Ibid., p. 185.
24. Engel, *When the World Seemed New*, p. 88. Nevertheless, that Matlock remained US ambassador to Moscow throughout the greater part of Bush's presidency indicated respect for the expertise of this Reagan-era appointee. In the book he co-authored with Scowcroft, Bush refers approvingly to Matlock's 'long, detailed and helpful cables' from Moscow. See George Bush and Brent Scowcroft, *A World Transformed* (Knopf, New York, 1998), pp. 39–40.
25. The significance of this was stressed by Valentin Karasev (a Gorbachev aide who became a deputy in the Soviet legislature) at the June 1999 roundtable Moscow conference referenced in the first *footnote* of this chapter, p. 253 (Moscow Cold War Conference transcript, Tape 6, p. 16).
26. 'Otchet o rabote Komiteta gosudarstevnnoy bezopasnosti SSSR za 1988 god, 17.02.89', HIA, Fond 89, Reel 1006, Opis 51, file 15, pp. 1–2.
27. Ibid., p. 7.
28. In his diary entry of 8 March 1989, Chernyaev wrote that the manuscript was already 400 pages and he expected it to be completed the following day. Provided Gorbachev did not 'clean up' the 'most bracing and striking parts', it would 'make an even greater impression' than his 1987 book. See Chernyaev diary, 1989 (in Russian), 8 March 1989, p. 7, NSA (GWU), https://nsarchive2gwu.edu//rus/Chernyaev.html.
29. Unpublished manuscript of M. S. Gorbachev, *Perestroyka—ispitanie zhizn'yu* (Perestroika—tested by life). The phrase in quotation marks is from p. 25.
30. Ibid., p. 15.
31. Matlock, *Autopsy on an Empire*, p. 210.
32. For a fuller account of the 1989 Soviet election, see Archie Brown, *The Gorbachev Factor* (Oxford University Press, 1996), pp. 179–84 and 188–93; and Stephen White, Richard Rose, and Ian McAllister, *How Russia Votes* (Chatham House, Chatham, NJ, 1997), pp. 21–9.
33. Stephen White, *Gorbachev and After* (Cambridge University Press, Cambridge, 1991), pp. 246–7.
34. *Reytingi Borisa El'tsina i Mikhaila Gorbacheva po 10-bal'noy shkale* (VtsIOM, Moscow, 1993).
35. *V Politbyuro TsK KPSS...po zapisyam Anatoliya Chernyaeva, Vadima Medvedeva, Georgiya Shakhnazarova (1985–1991)* (Al'pina, Moscow, 2006), p. 460.
36. Ibid., p. 463.
37. Ibid., pp. 464–5.
38. M. S. Gorbachev, *Ponyat' perestroyku...pochemu eto vazhno seychas* (Al'pina, Moscow, 2006), p. 374.
39. Ibid., pp. 373–4.
40. Georgiy Shakhnazarov, *S vozhdyami i bez nikh* (Vagrius, Moscow, 2001), pp. 331–2.
41. Ibid., p. 332.
42. Ibid., pp. 332–3.

43. Archie Brown, *The Myth of the Strong Leader: Political Leadership in the Modern Age* (Bodley Head, London, and Basic Books, New York, 2014).

44. Anatoly Chernyaev diary (in Russian), entry for 11 March 1989, National Security Archive, Washington DC, https://nsarchive2.gwu.edu//rus/Chernyaev.html.

45. Ibid.

46. Ibid. See also Artemy M. Kalinovsky, *A Long Goodbye: The Soviet Withdrawal from Afghanistan* (Harvard University Press, 2011), pp. 178–87.

47. 'Cold War: MT letter to Reagan', 19 January 1989, Reagan Library Archives, https://www.margaretthatcher.org/document/110359.

48. 'Cold War: Reagan letter to MT', 19 January 1989, Reagan Library Archives, https://www.margaretthatcher.org/document/110358.

49. Rodric Braithwaite, Diary 1988–1992 (manuscript), entry for 3 April 1989, p. 37.

50. Ibid.

51. Ibid., entries for 31 March and 3 April 1989, pp. 37–8. See also Alec Nove, *Glasnost' in Action: Cultural Renaissance in Russia* (Unwin Hyman, London, 1989).

52. Mikhail Gorbachev, *Zhizn' i reformy*, Vol. II (Novosti, Moscow, 1995), p. 82.

53. Ibid., pp. 81–6.

54. 'Vizit M. S. Gorbacheva v Velikobritaniyu 5–7 Aprelya 1989 goda', in Mikhail Sergeevich Gorbachev, *Sobranie sochineniy*, Vol. XIV (Ves' mir, Moscow, 2010), pp. 42–74, at 44–5.

55. Gorbachev, *Zhizn' i reformy*, Vol. II, pp. 82–3.

56. 'Vizit M. S. Gorbacheva v Velikobritaniyu', p. 45.

57. Anatoly Chernyaev, *My Six Years with Gorbachev and Shevardnadze* (Pennsylvania University Press, University Park, 2000), p. 221.

58. Rodric Braithwaite, 'Gorbachev and Thatcher: Witness Remarks', *Journal of European Integration History*, Vol. 16, No. 1, 2010, pp. 31–44, at p. 38.

59. Chernyaev, *My Six Years with Gorbachev*, p. 221.

60. 'Vizit M. S. Gorbacheva v Velikobritaniyu', p. 45.

61. Geoffrey Howe, *Conflict of Loyalty* (Macmillan, London, 1994), p. 563.

62. Ibid., pp. 586–92.

63. Ibid., pp. 645–76

64. Braithwaite diary, entry for 6 April 1989.

65. 'Vizit M. S. Gorbacheva v Velikobritaniyu', p. 62.

66. Ibid.

67. Ibid., pp. 64–5.

68. Ibid., p. 66.

69. Ibid., p. 64.

70. Ibid., p. 67.

71. Ibid.

72. Ibid., p. 68.

73. Ibid., pp. 68–9.

74. Ibid., pp. 72–3.

75. Ibid., p. 73.

76. 'Cabinet: Minutes of full Cabinet', 13 April 1989, CAB 128 f93, p. 5, https://www.margaretthatcher.org/document/149512.

77. Ibid., pp. 5–6.

78. Chernyaev, *My Six Years with Gorbachev*, p. 222.

79. Ibid.

80. 'Iz vystupleniy na zasedanii Politbyuro TsK KPSS, 13 aprelya 1989 goda', in Gorbachev, *Sobranie sochineniy*, Vol. XIV, p. 93.

81. Eduard Shevardnadze, *The Future Belongs to Freedom* (Sinclair-Stevenson, London, 1991), p. 193.

82. Anatoliy Sobchak, *Khozhdenie v vlast': Rasskaz o rozhdenii parlamenta* (Novosti, Moscow, 1991), p. 97. For a fuller account of the Tbilisi brutality of April 1989, including a summary of the Sobchak report, see Brown, *The Gorbachev Factor*, pp. 264–7.

83. *Izvestiya TsK KPSS*, No. 5, 1989, pp. 45–6.

84. Although the general secretary was always more than a first among equals within the Soviet leadership, throughout most of the Soviet Union's existence, the country was more of an oligarchy than a personal dictatorship. The last two decades or so of Stalin's rule are the main exception to that generalization. On this, see Graeme Gill, *Collective Leadership in Soviet Politics* (Palgrave Macmillan, London, 2018).

85. Gorbachev, *Sobranie sochineniy*, Vol. XIV, p. 163.

86. Ibid., pp. 165 and 167.

87. Gorbachev, *Sobranie sochineniy*, Vol. XIII (Ves' mir, Moscow 2009), pp. 295 and 330–1.

88. Gorbachev, *Sobranie sochineniy*, Vol. XIV, p. 94.

89. Ibid.

90. Gorbachev, *Zhizn' i reformy*, Vol. II, p. 444.

91. Ibid., pp. 435–6.

92. Zhao Ziyang, *Prisoner of the State* (Simon & Schuster, London, 2009); see also Richard McGregor, *The Party: The Secret World of China's Communist Rulers* (Penguin, London, 2011).

93. Pavel Palazchenko, *My Years with Gorbachev and Shevardnadze: The Memoirs of a Soviet Interpreter* (Pennsylvania State University Press, University Park, PA, 1997), p. 127.

94. Ibid.

95. Ibid.

96. Baker, *The Politics of Diplomacy*, p. 63.

97. Ibid., pp. 64–5.

98. Ibid., p. 67; and Palazchenko, *My Years with Gorbachev and Shevardnadze*, p. 129.

99. Palazchenko, *My Years with Gorbachev and Shevardnadze*, p. 128.

100. Baker, *The Politics of Diplomacy*, p. 70.

101. Ibid., p. 75.

102. Ibid.

103. Ibid., p. 79.

104. 'Iz besedy s gosudadarstennym sekretarem SshA Dzh. Beykerom, 11 maya 1989 goda', in Gorbachev, *Sobranie sochineniy*, Vol. XIV, pp. 181–93, at p. 183.

105. Baker, *The Politics of Diplomacy*, pp. 79–80.

106. Ibid., p. 82.

107. Ibid.

108. Svetlana Savranskaya and Thomas Blanton, *The Last Superpower Summits. Gorbachev, Reagan, and Bush: Conversations that Ended the Cold War* (Central European University Press, Budapest and New York, 2016), p. 507; and Palazchenko, *My Years with Gorbachev and Shevardnadze*, p. 132.

109. Baker, *The Politics of Diplomacy*, pp. 82–3.

110. Bush speech in Mainz, 31 May 1989, cited in Philip Zelikow and Condoleezza Rice, *Germany Unified and Europe Transformed: A Study in Statecraft* (Harvard University Press, Cambridge, MA, 1995), p. 31. The coiner of the phrase, 'Europe whole and free' appears to

have been Harvey Sicherman. This wording was in the original State Department draft of the speech which he wrote (ibid., p. 381).

111. 'Cold War, China: White House memcon (Bush–Mitterrand)', 13 July 1989, Bush Library memcons, https://www.margaretthatcher.org/document/149392, pp. 2–3.

112. Savranskaya et al. (eds.), *Masterpieces of History*, p. 491.

113. Letter from Bush to Gorbachev, 21 July 1989, in Savranskaya and Blanton, *The Last Superpower Summits*, pp. 513–14, at p. 513.

114. The transcripts of Gorbachev's meetings with Kohl are published in Aleksandr Galkin and Anatoliy Chernyaev (eds.), *Mikhail Gorbachev i Germanskiy vopros: sbornik dokumentov* (Ves' mir, Moscow, 2006), pp. 156–70 and 176–9.

115. Ibid., pp. 180–7; and 'Cold War: Soviet–German statement', 13 June 1989, PREM 19/3554 f44, https://www.margaretthatcher.org/document/205904.

116. https://www.margaretthatcher.org/document/205904.

117. 'Cold War: White house telcon (Bush–Kohl), 15 June 1989, Bush Library (FOIA 1999-0393-F), https://www.margaretthatcher.org/document/109448.

118. 'Cold War: UKE Bonn telegram to FCO (Gorbachev's visit to the FRG: assessment)', 16 June 1989, PREM 19/3554 f39, https://www.margaretthatcher.org/document/205907, pp. 1–2.

119. Ibid., p. 2.

120. Ibid., pp. 2–3.

121. Ibid., p. 3.

122. Ibid., p. 1.

123. 'Cold War: UKE Paris telegram to FCO (Gorbachev's visit to France: comment)', 7 July 1989, PREM 19/3554 f23, https://www.margaretthatcher.org/document/205910, p. 4.

124. Ibid, pp. 2 and 4.

125. Ibid., p. 4.

126. 'Rech' pered deputatami parlamentskoy assambley Soveta Evropy v Strasburge', 6 July 1989, in Gorbachev, *Sobranie sochineniy*, Vol. XV (Ves' mir, Moscow, 2010), pp. 156–69, at p. 157.

127. Ibid., pp. 159–60.

128. Ibid., pp. 163–4.

129. Ibid., p. 169.

130. Mikhail Gorbachev and Zdeněk Mlynář, *Conversations with Gorbachev: On Perestroika, the Prague Spring, and the Crossroads of Socialism* (Columbia University Press, New York, 2002), pp. 82–91.

131. Gorbachev–Brandt conversation of 17 October 1989 in Gorbachev, *Sobranie sochineniy*, Vol. XVI (Ves' mir, Moscow, 2010), pp. 251–8, at p. 253.

132. 'Beseda s predsedatelem pravitel'stva Ispanii F. Gonzalesom sostoyalas v Madrid 26 oktyabrya 1990 g', in M. S. Gorbachev, *Gody trudnykh resheniy* (Al'fa-print, Moscow, 1993), pp. 234–53, at p. 239.

133. Jacques Lévesque, *The Enigma of 1989: The USSR and the Liberation of Eastern Europe* (University of California Press, Berkeley, 1997), p. 253.

134. Margaret Thatcher, Press Conference in Moscow, COI transcript, 23 September 1989, https://www.margaretthatcher.org/document/107776, pp. 1–12, at 1–3. Gorbachev's side of the conversation is available in detail in the relevant volume of his collected works, *Sobranie sochineniy*, Vol. XVI, pp. 98–109. Gorbachev told Thatcher that political reform had to precede economic reform for otherwise it would end in failure (p. 104).

135. Rodric Braithwaite, *Across the Moscow River: The World Turned Upside Down* (Yale University Press, London, 2002), p. 62.
136. Braithwaite diary, entry for 24 May 1989, p. 55; and Howe, *Conflict of Loyalty*, pp. 562–3.
137. Braithwaite diary, entry for 27 May 1989, p. 58.
138. Ibid., entry for 23 September 1989, p. 86.
139. This is one of several quotations from Tocqueville used as an epigraph to Mary Elise Sarotte's excellent study, *The Collapse: The Accidental Opening of the Berlin Wall* (Basic Books paperback, New York, 2015), p. vii.
140. Andrey Grachev, *Kremlevskaya khronika* (Eksmo, Moscow, 1994), p. 247.
141. There is a large literature on the political transformation of Eastern Europe in 1989. The documents collected and edited by Savranskaya, Blanton and Zubok, *Masterpieces of History* (already cited) are a particularly valuable contribution. Lévesque's *The Enigma of 1968* is an insightful single-author book. A substantial and particularly well-informed three-part article by Mark Kramer, 'The Collapse of East European Communism and the Repercussions within the Soviet Union' was published in *Journal of Cold War Studies*, Part 1 in Vol. 5, No. 4, 2003, pp. 178–256; Part 2 in Vol. 6, No. 4, 2004, pp. 3–64; and Part 3 in Vol. 7, No. 1, 2005, pp. 3–96. For a concise overview and interpretation, see Archie Brown, *The Rise and Fall of Communism* (Bodley Head, London, and Ecco, New York, 2009) on 'The End of Communism in Europe', pp. 522–48.
142. 'Record of Conversation between Mikhail Gorbachev and Members of the CC SED Politburo', 7 October 1989, in Savranskaya et al. (eds), *Masterpieces of History*, pp. 544–6, at p. 545.
143. Hans-Hermann Hertle, 'The Fall of the Wall: The Unintended Self-Dissolution of East Germany's Ruling Regime', *Cold War International History Project Bulletin*, No. 12/13, 2009, pp. 131–40, at pp. 136–7.
144. For a well-informed and detailed account of what happened that night, see Sarotte, *The Collapse*.
145. Hertle, 'The Fall of the Wall', p. 138.
146. Sarotte, *The Collapse*, esp. pp. 136–7 and p. 150.
147. Ibid., p. 121.
148. Bush and Scowcroft, *A World Transformed*, pp. 149–50.
149. Ibid., p. 149.
150. Brown, *The Rise and Fall of Communism*, pp. 538–41.
151. 'Record of Conversation between Mikhail Gorbachev and François Mitterrand', 5 July 1989, in Savranskaya et al. (eds), *Masterpieces of History*, pp. 490–1, at p. 490.
152. 'Memorandum of Conversation, Bush–Shevardnadze, Washington', 21 September 1989, in Savranskaya and Blanton, *The Last Superpower Summits*, pp. 515–20, at pp. 516–17.
153. Ibid., pp. 519–20.
154. 'Letter from Bush to Gorbachev', 22 November 1989, in Savranskaya and Blanton, *The Last Superpower Summits*, pp. 521–2, at p. 521. The Rowny letter is discussed in Savranskaya and Blanton's commentary on the Bush letter (ibid.).
155. Ibid.
156. Brent Scowcroft in Bush and Scowcroft, *A World Transformed*, pp. 154–5.
157. Bush, ibid., p. 154.
158. Ibid., p. 155.
159. Ibid., p. 159.
160. Margaret Thatcher, 'Press Conference visiting Washington', 24 November 1989, COI transcript, https://www.margaretthatcher.org/document/107827, pp. 1–9, at p. 2.

161. 'Memorandum from Baker for the President, "Your December Meeting with Gorbachev"', 29 November 1989, in Savranskaya and Blanton, *The Last Superpower Summits*, pp. 523–7, at p. 523.

162. Ibid., p. 525.

163. Ibid.

164. Ibid.

165. Ibid.

166. Ibid., p. 527.

167. 'Memorandum of Conversation, Bush–Gorbachev', 2 December 1989, in Savranskaya and Blanton, *The Last Superpower Summits*, pp. 531–64, at 531–2. The quotation here is from the American transcript of the Malta summit meeting, declassified in 2008. The Russian text was translated and published as 'Soviet Transcript of the Malta Summit', 2–3 December 1989, in Savranskaya et al. (eds.), *Masterpieces of History*, pp. 619–46.

168. Savranskaya and Blanton, *The Last Superpower Summits*, p. 541.

169. Engel, *When the World Seemed New*, p. 297.

170. Savranskaya and Blanton, *The Last Superpower Summits*, p. 539.

171. Ibid., pp. 543–4.

172. Ibid., pp. 537–8.

173. Ibid., p. 557.

174. Ibid., pp. 559–60.

175. Bush and Scowcroft, *A World Transformed*, p. 190.

176. Ibid., pp. 192–3.

177. Andrey Grachev, *Gibel' Sovetskogo 'Titanika': Sydovoy zhurnal* (Prozaik, Moscow, 2015), pp. 180–3.

178. Zelikow and Rice, *Germany Unified and Europe Transformed*, p. 123.

179. 'Soviet Transcript of the Malta Summit', 2–3 December 1989, in Savranskaya et al. (eds.), *Masterpieces of History*, pp. 619–46, at pp. 634–5.

180. Ibid.

181. Jack F. Matlock, Jr, *Reagan and Gorbachev: How the Cold War Ended* (Random House, New York, 2004), p. 315.

182. Chernyaev, *My Six Years with Gorbachev*, p. 233.

13 Why the Cold War Ended When It Did

1. As Alexander Dallin wrote, 'To claim that the Soviet system was bound to crash amounts to committing what Reinhard Bendix…called "the fallacy of retrospective determinism"—denying the choices (however constrained) that the actors had available before acting', 'Causes of the Collapse of the USSR', *Post-Soviet Affairs*, Vol. 8, No. 4, 1992, pp. 279–302, at p. 297.

2. The retrospective views of members of the Reagan administration are available in the Oral History of the Cold War transcripts (a joint enterprise between the Hoover Institution at Stanford and the Gorbachev Foundation) in the Hoover Institution Archives. The predominant view among those who served under Reagan is that his hard line ideologically, economically and militarily forced the Soviet Union to admit defeat. Academic interpretations are generally more nuanced, although some accounts are tinged with American triumphalism.

3. Robert G. Patman, 'Reagan, Gorbachev and the emergence of "New Political Thinking"', *Review of International Studies*, Vol. 25, No. 4, 1999, pp. 577–601, at p. 598.

4. On the many different strands of heterodox and 'new' thinking in the Soviet Union pre-Gorbachev (and pre-Reagan), see Robert D. English, *Russia and the Idea of the West: Gorbachev, Intellectuals, and the End of the Cold War* (Columbia University Press, New York, 2000), esp. pp. 81–157; Archie Brown, 'Institutional Amphibiousness or Civil Society? The Origins and Development of Perestroika', in Brown, *Seven Years that Changed the World: Perestroika in Perspective* (Oxford University Press, Oxford, 2007), pp. 157–89; Ronald J. Hill, *Soviet Politics, Political Science and Reform* (M. E. Sharpe, New York, 1980); Neil Malcolm, *Soviet Political Scientists and American Politics* (Macmillan, London, 1984); and Vladislav Zubok, *Zhivago's Children: The Last Russian Intelligentsia* (Belknap Press, Cambridge, MA, 2009).

5. Robert G. Patman, 'Some Reflections on Archie Brown and the End of the Cold War', *Cold War History*, Vol. 7, No. 3, 2007, pp. 439–45. Patman compounds the misconception by writing that Gorbachev was elected general secretary by a 'slim Politburo majority' (ibid., p. 441), whereas he was elected unopposed. He had seized the initiative by convening a Politburo meeting on the evening Chernenko died. Colleagues who joined in the chorus of support for him did so in the hope of keeping their positions of authority and privilege and not because they sought radical change.

6. Stephen G. Brooks and William C. Wohlforth, 'Economic Constraints and the End of the Cold War', in Wohlforth (ed.), *Cold War Endgame: Oral History, Analysis, Debates* (Pennsylvania State University Press, University Park, PA, 2003), pp. 273–309, at p. 308; and Brooks and Wohlforth, 'Clarifying the End of Cold War Debate', *Cold War History*, Vol. 7, No. 3, 2007, pp. 447–54, esp. p. 450.

7. François Mitterrand was very ready to engage with Russia, and Gorbachev's first visit to a Western country as Soviet leader was to France. However, Mitterrand was, if anything, even more intransigent than Thatcher when it came to defending nuclear weapons. Neither Mitterrand nor, still less, premier Jacques Chirac were happy about the INF talks and they were eager to modernize their own '*force de frappe*'. The French were unhappy about the 'double zero' of the INF talks, involving the removal of both Soviet and NATO intermediate-range missiles from Europe. In contrast, the West Germans favoured a 'triple zero' that would have added the elimination of battlefield nuclear weapons. See Julie M. Newton, *Russia, France, and the Idea of Europe* (Palgrave Macmillan, Houndmills, Basingstoke, and New York, 2003), p. 148.

8. The French model of semi-presidentialism—whereby there is both a president with executive power who is the principal foreign policy-maker and a prime minister in day-to-day charge of the government's domestic policy—was, however, an influence on the political structures adopted in the Soviet Union in 1990. (It was not totally dissimilar from the division of labour between the General Secretary of the Central Committee of the CPSU and the Chairman of the Council of Ministers in the Soviet Union.) Semi-presidentialism carried over into post-Soviet Russia and was adopted by many other post-Communist states.

9. Robert D. English, in his study of the changing ideas of a significant segment of the Soviet intelligentsia who analysed international relations and other countries (especially in Moscow research institutes), aptly calls his chapter about their greatly enhanced influence after 1985, 'The New Thinking Comes to Power': English, *Russia and the Idea of the West*, esp. pp. 193–228. See also Petr Cherkasov, *IMEMO: Ocherk istorii* (Ves' mir, Moscow, 2016), esp. pp. 338–428; and Brown, *Seven Years that Changed the World*, pp. 157–89 and 213–76.

10. Stephen Shenfield, *The Nuclear Predicament: Explorations in Soviet Ideology* (Routledge & Kegan Paul, London, 1987), pp. 88–9; and S. F. Akhromeyev and G. M. Kornienko, *Glazami marshala i diplomata: kriticheskiy vzglyad na vneshnyuyu politiku SSSR do i posle 1985 goda* (Mezhdunarodnye otnosheniya, Moscow, 1992), pp. 121–7.

11. Alexander Wendt, a notable representative of the 'constructivist' tendency and influential critic of 'realist' explanations among international relations theorists, stresses the importance of ideas and perceptions in international politics. He touches briefly, and appositely, on the case of Soviet 'New Thinking'. See Wendt, *Social Theory of International Relations* (Cambridge University Press, Cambridge, 1999), esp. p. 129.

12. 'Zasedanie Politbyuro TsK KPSS, 31 maya 1983 goda', HIA, Fond 89, Reel 1.1003, opis 42, file 3, p. 7.

13. Anatoly Dobrynin, *In Confidence: Moscow's Ambassador to America's Six Cold War Presidents (1962–1986)* (Times Books, New York, 1995), p. 482.

14. Robert M. Gates, *Duty: Memoirs of a Secretary at War* (Knopf, New York, 2014), p. 159.

15. William J. Perry, *My Journey at the Nuclear Brink* (Stanford University Press, Stanford, 2015), p. 68.

16. Andrei Sakharov, *Moscow and Beyond 1986 to 1989* (Knopf, New York, 1991), p. 22.

17. Ibid., pp. 22–3.

18. Ibid., p. 22.

19. Interview with A.L. Adamishin (in Russian), 5 August 1999, Hoover Institution and Gorbachev Foundation (Moscow) Collection, Acc. No. 98067–16.305, Box 1, HIA, p.5.

20. 'Zasedanie Politbyuro TsK KPSS, 14 oktyabrya 1986 goda', Volkogonov Papers, R 9744, NSA (GW), p. 9.

21. Anatoliy Adamishin, *V raznye gody: Vneshneopliticheskie ocherki* (Ves' mir, Moscow, 2016), p. 131.

22. Anatoly Gromyko was at this point speaking specifically about Gorbachev's unwillingness to use 'even minimal force' in order 'to preserve the Soviet Union'. He continued: 'And with all due respect to Mikhail Sergeyevich, from the time of his coming to power we gradually achieved political freedom, but in general in his soul he was not only a social democrat, but a pacifist, and therefore was unable, in my view, to direct events' (Transcript of Moscow Cold War Conference, June 1989, under the auspices of Institute of General History of the Russian Academy of Sciences and the Mershon Institute of Ohio State University. Tape 7, pp. 15–16).

23. Perry, *My Journey at the Nuclear Brink*, p. 68.

24. Georgiy Shakhnazarov, *Tsena svobody: Reformatsiya Gorbacheva glazami ego pomoshchnika* (Rossika Zevs, Moscow, 1993), p. 36.

25. Alec Nove, *The Soviet System in Retrospect: An Obituary Notice*, Fourth Annual W. Averell Harriman Lecture, February 17, 1993 (Harriman Institute, Columbia University, New York, 1993), pp. 30–1.

26. Akhromeyev and Kornienko, *Glazami marshala i diplomata*, pp. 132–3.

27. Matthew Evangelista, 'Turning Points in Arms Control', in Richard K. Herrmann and Richard Ned Lebow (eds.), *Ending the Cold War: Interpretations, Causation, and the Study of International Relations* (Palgrave Macmillan, New York, 2004), pp. 83–105, at p. 92.

28. John W. Kingdon, *Agendas, Alternatives, and Public Policies* (HarperCollins, New York, 1984). Kingdon, who opens his book with the Hugo quotation, calls his first chapter (pp. 1–22) 'How Does an Idea's Time Come?' The author provides an insightful analysis of agenda-setting in a democracy—the USA first and foremost—which is relevant in certain respects to agenda-change in the Soviet Union later in the same decade.

29. Vladislav M. Zubok, 'Gorbachev and the End of the Cold War: Different Perspectives on the Historical Personality', in William C. Wohlforth (ed.), *Cold War Endgame: Oral History, Analysis, Debates* (Pennsylvania State University Press, University Park, PA, 2003), pp. 207–41, at p. 214.

30. Ibid., pp. 215, 230, and 239.

31. Evangelista, 'Turning Points in Arms Control', p. 93.

32. Transcript of Moscow Cold War Conference, June 1999, Tape 2, p. 31.
33. Peter Schweitzer, *Victory: The Reagan Administration's Secret Strategy that Hastened the Collapse of the Soviet Union* (Atlantic Monthly Press, New York, 1994) suggests that a deliberate Reagan administration policy of ruining the Soviet Union economically led to American victory. Contradictory aims were to be found in different parts of the Reagan administration. Trying to bankrupt the Soviet Union was not a policy pursued by Shultz's State Department. Shultz's desire, increasingly, became that the Soviet Union should reform and succeed. Jonathan Haslam (*Russia's Cold War: From the October Revolution to the Fall of the Wall* (Yale University Press, New Haven, 2011)) holds that the Soviet Union's concessions to the West 'were impelled by pressure from outside', including 'the anticommunist zeal within Reagan's administration', SDI and, very curiously (given that her own Foreign Policy Adviser, Sir Percy Cradock, worried that Gorbachev had become an 'icon' for Thatcher), he includes what he calls 'Thatcher's endless berating of Gorbachev' (pp. 399–400). A further weakness of Haslam's account lies in its interpretation of the domestic context in which Gorbachev operated.
34. Transcript of Moscow Cold War Conference, June 1999, Tape 3, p. 15.
35. Ibid., p. 14.
36. Ibid., p. 26.
37. As Chris Miller correctly noted: 'When Gorbachev became general secretary in 1985, the Soviet economy was wasteful and poorly managed, but it was not in crisis…Gorbachev saw his task not as rescuing a country on the brink of bankruptcy, but as reinvigorating an economy that needed new energy and a new direction.' See Miller, *The Struggle to Save the Soviet Economy: Mikhail Gorbachev and the Collapse of the USSR* (University of North Carolina Press, Chapel Hill, NC, 2016), p. 60.
38. Marshall I. Goldman, *U.S.S.R. in Crisis: The Failure of an Economic System* (Norton, New York, 1983), p. 182.
39. At the beginning of 1990, Gorbachev invited the deputy director of the Central Economic-Mathematical Institute (TsEMI), Nikolay Petrakov, to become one of his aides and his adviser on economic reform. 'The very fact that he offered me the job of his economic adviser in itself demonstrates that Gorbachev had realised the need to go over to the market economy, because everyone knows me as an economist who believes in the market', said Petrakov (Petrakov interview, 'The Second Russian Revolution Transcripts', British Library of Political and Economic Science, London School of Economics). This shift in Gorbachev's view of the economy was reinforced in conversations with Petrakov throughout 1990. (Petrakov departed from Gorbachev's team at the beginning of 1991.) Gorbachev, said Petrakov, had come to the conclusion that there was 'no alternative to the market economy', but 'the big question is how to go over to the market' (ibid.). Petrakov found it easier to discuss the problems of transition with Gorbachev than with any member of Ryzhkov's government. When I interviewed him on 18 June 1991, Petrakov told me that Gorbachev had confidence in Ryzhkov during the first several years of his leadership, but by late 1989 he realized that more drastic economic change was needed and that Ryzhkov would be opposed to it. In that same interview, Petrakov recalled a conversation with Ryzhkov in which he had told the Chairman of the Council of Ministers that there was no need for a State Committee on Prices and that it should be abolished. Ryzhkov said that was right, 'but in a few years' time', to which Petrakov responded, 'Nikolay Ivanovich, you talk about the market as we used to talk about communism—it's always sometime later!' On Gorbachev's preference for a market economy of a social-democratic type, see Archie Brown, 'Did Gorbachev as General Secretary Become a Social Democrat?', *Europe-Asia Studies*, Vol. 65, No. 2, 2013, pp. 198–220.

40. Referring to criticism that perestroika had opened up too many fronts at once, Gorbachev said to Thatcher, 'But how can you reform the economy without a reform of the political system? It will not work. And we already have the sad experiences with Khrushchev, and Kosygin with Brezhnev', Gorbachev–Thatcher conversation of 23 September 1989, READD/RADD Collection, Box 23, R 2896, NSA (GWU).

41. Mikhail Gorbachev, 'Perestroika Lost', *New York Times*, 13 March 2010, https://www.nytimes.com/2010/03/14/opinion/14gorbachev.html.

42. Schweitzer, *Victory*. As already remarked in note 33, that was not, however, the policy of Shultz's State Department, and Shultz himself was hugely influential in the making of the Reagan administration's Soviet policy.

43. Miller, *The Struggle to Save the Soviet Economy*, p. 62.

44. Ibid., p. 64.

45. Ibid.

46. Ibid., p. 66.

47. George F. Kennan, *Memoirs 1925–1950* (Pantheon, New York, 1967), Annex C, p. 550.

48. Brown, *Seven Years that Changed the World*, esp. pp. 213–330; Robert D. English, 'The Road(s) Not Taken: Causality and Contingency in Analysis of the Cold War's End', in Wohlforth (ed.), *Cold War Endgame*, pp. 243–72; Zubok, 'Gorbachev and the End of the Cold War', ibid., pp. 207–41; and Zubok, Alex Pravda, Sergey Radchenko, Ronald Grigor Suny, James Graham Wilson, and William Taubman in Roundtable Review, Vol. XX, No. 1 (2018), *H-Diplo*, http://www.tiny.cc/Roundtable-XX-1.

49. Kennan, *Memoirs 1925–1950*, Annex C, p. 559.

50. Cf. Drew Westen, *The Political Brain: The Role of Emotion in Deciding the Fate of the Nation* (Public Affairs, New York, 2007); and Daniel Kahneman, *Thinking Fast and Slow* (Allen Lane, London, 2011).

51. Mikhail Gorbachev, *Zhizn' i reformy*, Vol. I (Novosti, Moscow, 1995), pp. 168–70.

52. Aleksandr Yakovlev, *Sumerki* (Materik, Moscow, 2003), pp. 353–5 (as noted at greater length in Chapter 3 of this book).

53. John Lewis Gaddis, *The Cold War: A New History* (Penguin, New York, 2005), p. 222.

54. Ibid. The other two leaders who rejected the idea of the Cold War's permanence, according to Gaddis, were Lech Wałęsa and Deng Xiaoping.

55. Ibid., p. 257.

56. Adam Smith, *The Theory of Moral Sentiments*, ed. D. D. Raphael and A. L. Macfie (Clarendon Press, Oxford, 1976), pp. 233–4. The book was first published in 1759.

57. That is not merely a post-hoc observation. In my paper for Margaret Thatcher's 8 September 1983 Chequers seminar, I wrote that Soviet leaders saw political pluralism 'as but a short step to disintegration and anarchy' and added that this was 'a view which has much more plausibility in the case of the vast and multi-national Soviet state than it had in 1968 in Czechoslovakia' (Archie Brown, 'The Change to Engagement in Britain's Cold War Policy: The Origins of the Thatcher–Gorbachev Relationship', *Journal of Cold War Studies*, Vol. 10, No. 3, 2008, pp. 3–47, at 12–13).

58. James Mann observes that Reagan was not much interested in 'the nuances of formal communication', much more in the concrete entity of the wall (Mann, *The Rebellion of Ronald Reagan: A History of the End of the Cold War*, Viking, New York, 2009, pp. 300–1).

59. Ibid., p. 320.

60. Richard E. Neustadt, *Presidential Power: The Politics of Leadership* (Wiley, New York, 1960), p. 10.

14 Unintended Consequences (1990)

1. Mary Elise Sarotte, *The Collapse: The Accidental Opening of the Berlin Wall* (Basic Books, New York, 2015), p. 8. The author notes that in West Germany at that time there were almost three times as many NATO troops—some 900,000.
2. Ibid., p. 150.
3. Bartholomew Sparrow, *The Strategist: Brent Scowcroft and the Call of National Security* (Public Affairs, New York, 2015), p. 295.
4. Shultz 1999 Oral History of the Cold War interview, HIA, Acc. No. 98067–16.305.
5. Valuable sources on German unification include Aleksandr Galkin and Anatoliy Chernyaev (eds.), *Mikhail Gorbachev i Germanskiy vopros: Sbornik dokumentov* (Ves' mir, Moscow, 2006), an exceptionally important collection of documents; Helga Haftendorn, 'The Unification of Germany, 1985–1991', in Melvin P. Leffler and Odd Arne Westad (eds.), *The Cambridge History of the Cold War, Volume III: Endings* (Cambridge University Press, Cambridge, 2010), pp. 333–55; Jeffrey A. Engel, *When the World Seemed New: George H. W. Bush and the End of the Cold War* (Houghton Mifflin Harcourt, Boston & New York, 2017), esp. pp. 231–375; George Bush and Brent Scowcroft, *A World Transformed* (Knopf, New York, 1998); James A. Baker III, *The Politics of Diplomacy: Revolution, War and Peace 1989–1991* (Putnam, New York, 1995); Timothy Garton Ash, *In Europe's Name: Germany and the Divided Continent* (Jonathan Cape, London, 1993); Philip Zelikow and Condoleezza Rice, *Germany Unified and Europe Transformed: A Study in Statecraft* (Harvard University Press, Cambridge, MA, 1995); Svetlana Savranskaya and Thomas Blanton, *The Last Superpower Summits: Gorbachev, Reagan, and Bush* (Central European University Press, Budapest and New York, 2016), esp. pp. 653–76 and 700–3; Valentin Falin, *Konflikt v kremle: sumerki bogov po-russki* (Tsentropoligraf, Moscow, 2000); Andrei Grachev, *Gorbachev's Gamble: Soviet Foreign Policy and the End of the Cold War* (Polity, Cambridge, 2008); Pavel Palazchenko, *My Years with Gorbachev and Shevardnadze: The Memoir of a Soviet Interpreter* (Pennsylvania State University Press, University Park, PA, 1997), pp. 167–204; and Patrick Salmon, Keith Hamilton, and Stephen Twigge (eds.), *Documents on British Policy Overseas, Series III, Volume VII, German Unification 1989–1990* (Routledge, London, 2010).
6. When the Congress of People's Deputies of the Russian republic elected Yeltsin as Chairman of their Supreme Soviet on 29 May, he used his televised acceptance speech to call for Russian law to take precedence over Union law. Two weeks later, responding to Yeltsin's urging, the Congress of People's Deputies of the Russian Republic declared Russian 'sovereignty' on 12 June 1990 and said that its laws would have supremacy over federal legislation. See Timothy J. Colton, *Yeltsin: A Life* (Basic Books, New York, 2008), p. 185.
7. Archie Brown, *The Gorbachev Factor* (Oxford University Press, Oxford, 1996), pp. 252–305; Colton, *Yeltsin*, pp. 177–210; Andrei S. Grachev, *Final Days: The Inside Story of the Collapse of the Soviet Union* (Westview, Boulder, 1995), pp. 113–52; and Serhii Plokhy, *The Last Empire: The Final Days of the Soviet Union* (Basic Books, New York, 2014), pp. 255–343.
8. Rodric Braithwaite, Diary 1988–1992 (manuscript), entry for Friday 14 September 1990, pp. 197–8.
9. For more detailed discussion of these changes, see Brown, *The Gorbachev Factor*, pp. 200–11; and William Taubman, *Gorbachev: A Life* (Basic Books, New York, 2017), pp. 503–13.
10. *Izvestiya*, 4 June 1989.
11. The Soviet ministries mattered more than is suggested by the scant attention accorded them by Western Sovietologists. When the very real state power that the Communist Party had wielded was gradually removed by Gorbachev during the perestroika era, the

ministries were left as the main repositories of executive power in most areas of policy. For a valuable corrective to the underestimation of the Soviet economic ministries, in particular, see Stephen Whitefield, *Industrial Power and the Soviet State* (Clarendon Press, Oxford, 1993).

12. Brown, *The Gorbachev Factor*, p. 205.

13. George R. Urban, *Diplomacy and Disillusion at the Court of Margaret Thatcher: An Insider's View* (Tauris, London, 1996), pp. 146–7. Urban regarded Thatcher's answer on Gorbachev's presidential powers as unsatisfactory because it was the same as Gorbachev's own response, and he found her 'attitude to the world's politicians' now 'highly personalized' and permeated by a 'subjectivism' dangerous for a prime minister (ibid., p. 147).

14. Anatoliy Sobchak, *Khozhdenie vo vlast': rasskaz o rozhdenii parlamenta* (Novosti, Moscow, 1991), pp. 199–200.

15. Ibid., p. 182; and Brown, *The Gorbachev Factor*, pp. 204–5.

16. Mikhail Gorbachev, *Ponyat' perestroyku…pochemu eto vazhno seychas* (Al'pina, Moscow, 2006), p. 374.

17. *Reytingi Borisa Yel'tsina i Mikhaila Gorbacheva po 10-bal'noy shkale* (VTsIOM, Moscow, 1993).

18. By the standards of the Soviet past, there had already been a remarkable degree of devolution of power to the republics, with each having leeway to decide on the institutional forms their legislature would take. Only the Russian republic followed the federal example of direct election of a larger outer body, the Congress of People's Deputies, that went on to choose an inner legislative assembly, the Supreme Soviet, which met for longer periods of the year than the Congress. The other republics elected their Supreme Soviet directly by popular vote.

19. Stephen White, Richard Rose, and Ian McAllister, *How Russia Votes* (Chatham House, Chatham, NJ, 1997), pp. 29–35.

20. *Perekhod k rynku: Chast' 1. Kontseptsiya i programma* (Arkhangel'skoe, Moscow, 1990).

21. Michael Ellman and Vladimir Kontorovich (eds.), *The Destruction of the Soviet Economic System: An Insiders' History* (M. E. Sharpe, Armonk, 1998), p. 236; and Colton, *Yeltsin*, pp. 219–20. Colton, the principal biographer of Yeltsin, was told by Grigory Yavlinsky that Yeltsin did not read a single page of the bulky report of the '500-days team'. This reflected his lack of interest in policy detail, but he 'homed in on the political facets—the zippy title and the taut timetable' (Colton, *Yeltsin*, pp. 219–20 and 524).

22. Leonid Abalkin interview, 'The Second Russian Revolution Transcripts', British Library of Political and Economic Science, London School of Economics.

23. Yasin in Ellman and Kontorovich (eds.), *The Destruction of the Soviet Economic System*, p. 237.

24. Interview of G. Kh. Shakhnazarov by E. I. Kuznetsov, *Demokratizatsiya*, Vol. 2, No. 2, 1994, pp. 228–33, esp. p. 230.

25. Taubman, *Gorbachev*, pp. 519–21.

26. Archie Brown, 'Did Gorbachev as General Secretary Become a Social Democrat?', *Europe-Asia Studies*, Vol. 65, No. 2, 2013, pp. 198–220.

27. The report of Akhromeyev's views is contained in Matlock's cable to Washington about the Crowe–Akhromeyev meeting in Moscow, quoted at length by Brent Scowcroft in Bush and Scowcroft, *A World Transformed*, pp. 217–18.

28. Ibid.

29. Valentin Falin, *Bez skidok na obstoyatel'stva* (Respublika, Moscow, 1999), p. 434.

30. 'Zasedanie Politbyuro TsK KPSS ot 16 noyabrya 1900 goda', HIA, Fond 89, 1.003, opis 42, file 30, p. 6.

31. Ibid., p. 8.

32. Ibid., p. 11.
33. Ibid., p. 25. Writing in 1992, Gorbachev noted that with the decision to drop the old Article 6 of the Soviet Constitution which guaranteed the 'leading role' of the party, together with the creation of an executive presidency and legislature with real powers, the Politburo lost its state functions. They could discuss problems, but they had been 'relieved of executive power', even though 'earlier decisions of the Politburo formed the decisions of the government and were even issued as joint decisions'. See Mikhail Gorbachev, 'Novaya politika v novoy Rossii', *Svobodnaya mysl'*, No. 13, 1992, pp. 3–19, at p. 15.
34. Mikhail Gorbachev, *Zhizn' i reformy*, Vol. I (Novosti, Moscow, 1995), p. 585.
35. For further detail on the membership of the Security Council, see Archie Brown, *Seven Years that Changed the World: Perestroika in Perspective* (Oxford University Press, Oxford, 2007), p. 303.
36. Galkin and Chernyaev (eds.), *Mikhail Gorbachev i Germanskiy vopros*, p. 309.
37. Ibid., p. 308.
38. Baker, *The Politics of Diplomacy*, p. 197.
39. Ibid., pp. 196–9.
40. The editors of the transcripts of all the Reagan and Bush summit meetings with Gorbachev (and authors of illuminating commentary on them), Svetlana Savranskaya and Thomas Blanton, believe that historians took their eyes off 'the main event of German unification— the West German negotiations with Gorbachev', mainly because leading figures in the Bush administration got their story out first. See Savranskaya and Blanton, *The Last Superpower Summits*, p. 574.
41. 'NATO Expansion: What Gorbachev Heard', https://nsarchive.gwu.edu/briefing-book/russia-programs/2017-12-12/nato-expansion-what-gorbachev-heard-western-leaders-early, pp. 1–46. Published on 12 December 2017, this account from the National Security Archive in Washington, DC, includes important recently declassified American, British, and German documents. For other views on this question, see Joshua R. Itzkowitz Shifrinson, 'Deal or No Deal? The End of the Cold War and the U.S. Offer to Limit NATO Expansion', *International Security*, Vol. 42, No. 1, 2017, pp. 7–44; Mark Kramer, 'The Myth of a No-NATO-Enlargement Pledge to Russia', *Washington Quarterly*, Vol. 32, No. 2, 2009, pp. 39–61; and Hannes Adomeit, 'NATO's Eastern Enlargement: What Western Leaders Said', *Security Policy Working Paper*, No. 3, 2018 (Federal Academy for Security Policy, FRG).
42. 'NATO Expansion: What Gorbachev Heard', p. 3.
43. 'Iz besedy M. S. Gorbacheva s Dzh. Baykerom, 9 fevralya 1990 goda', in Galkin and Chernyaev (eds.), *Mikhail Gorbachev i Germanskiy vopros*, pp. 332–8, at p. 338.
44. Memorandum of Baker–Gorbachev discussion, Kremlin, 9 February 1990, US Department of State, FOIA 199504567 (National Security Archive Flashpoints Collection, Box 38), p. 6.
45. Memorandum of Baker–Shevardnadze discussion, 9 February 1990, US Department of State, FOIA 199504567, NSA (GWU) Archive Flashpoints Collection, Box 38, p. 3.
46. 'Iz besedy M. S. Gorbacheva s G. Kolem odin na odin, 10 fevralya 1990 goda', in Galkin and Chernyaev (eds.), *Mikhail Gorbachev i Germanskiy vopros*, pp. 339–55, at p. 345.
47. 'Record of Conversation between Gorbachev and Baker (with Delegations), Moscow', 18 May 1990, in Savranskaya and Blanton, *The Last Superpower Summits*, pp. 626–52, at p. 628.
48. 'Record of Conversation between Gorbachev and Baker', 18 May 1990, p. 637.
49. Ibid., p. 638.
50. Savranskaya and Blanton, *The Last Superpower Summits*, p. 577.
51. Gorbachev–Bush conversation at Washington summit, 31 May 1990, ibid., p. 671.

52. Ibid., p. 573; and Bush in Bush and Scowcroft, *A World Transformed*, pp. 282–3.

53. 'Zapiska V. M. Falina M. S. Gorbachevu', in Galkin and Chernyaev (eds.), *Mikhail Gorbachev i Germanskiy vopros*, pp. 398–408, at p. 406.

54. Falin, *Konflikty v kremle*, p. 180.

55. Ibid., p. 163.

56. Ibid., p. 172.

57. Falin, *Bez skidok na obstoyatel'stva*, pp. 450–1; and Grachev, *Gorbachev's Gamble*, p. 144.

58. Grachev, *Gorbachev's Gamble*, p. 147.

59. Palazchenko, *My Years with Gorbachev and Shevardnadze*, p. 182.

60. Rodric Braithwaite, 'The Uses and Abuses of History', 8 June 2015, https://www.opendemocracy.net/od-russia/rodric-braithwaite/uses-and-abuses-of-history.

61. Transcript of Bush–Kohl telephone conversation, 30 May 1990, in Savranskaya and Blanton, *The Last Superpower Summits*, pp. 656–7.

62. Palazchenko, *My Years with Gorbachev and Shevardnadze*, p. 192.

63. Ibid., p. 193.

64. 'Cable from U.S. Embassy Moscow to Department of State: "Gorbachev Confronts Crisis of Power"', in Savranskaya and Blanton, *The Last Superpower Summits*, pp. 619–25.

65. Ibid., p. 623.

66. Falin, *Konflikty v Kremle*, pp. 185–7.

67. Hans-Hermann Hertle, 'Germany in the Last Decade of the Cold War', in Olav Nølstad (ed.), *The Last Decade of the Cold War: From Conflict Escalation to Conflict Transformation* (Cass, London, 2004), pp. 265–87, at pp. 281–2. The transcripts of the Gorbachev–Kohl meetings and the press conference, given by two leaders which followed their breakthrough discussions, are in Galkin and Chernyaev (eds.), *Mikhail Gorbachev i Germanskiy vopros*, pp. 495–541. Bush spoke by telephone with Kohl and Gorbachev the day after they had reached their historic agreement and congratulated them both on the outcome. There was some disappointment on the part of the Bush administration that they had not been present when the deal was struck, but, as Pavel Palazchenko wrote, 'If the United States was not totally comfortable with this fact, it was a small problem compared with those Gorbachev and Shevardnadze had to face' (Palazchenko, *My Years with Gorbachev and Shevardnadze*, p. 204).

68. Douglas Hurd, *Memoirs* (Little, Brown, London, 2003), p. 384.

69. Ibid.

70. Ibid.

71. Ibid., pp. 384–5.

72. Ibid.

73. Urban, *Diplomacy and Disillusion at the Court of Margaret Thatcher*, pp. 118–59, esp. 147–9 and 157. The questions sent to the participants in advance of the seminar were, wrote Powell, 'formulated by me rather than by the prime minister' (ibid., p. 149). The seminar is discussed also in Adam Sisman, *Hugh Trevor-Roper: The Biography* (Phoenix, London, 2011), pp. 431–2.

74. These apparently included: 'their obsession with themselves, a strong inclination to self-pity, and a longing to be liked. Some even less flattering attributes were also mentioned as an abiding part of the German character: in alphabetical order, angst, aggressiveness, assertiveness, bullying, egotism, inferiority complex, sentimentality.' See 'Cold War: Chequers Seminar on Germany ("Summary Record")', 24 March 1990, https://www.margaretthatcher.org/document/111047, p. 1. The two American participants were angry about the thrust of the minute and about its leak, Gordon Craig especially so, as he felt it had damaged his reputation in Germany. Sisman notes that both Craig and Fritz Stern

wrote articles in the German press 'disowning Powell's leaked minute' (*Hugh Trevor-Roper*, p. 432). Trevor-Roper himself, who was irritated by the minutes and especially by their leaking and publication within a few months of the seminar, believed that the source must have been 'a mole in the British embassy in Bonn', for the first details to be published appeared in the *Rheinischer Merkur* (Richard Davenport-Hine and Adam Sisman (eds.), *One-Hundred Letters from Hugh Trevor-Roper* (Oxford University Press, Oxford, 2014), Letter to Max Perutz of 15 August 1990, pp. 369–72, at p. 371). The minute of the March 1990 seminar was officially declassified in 2007. The *Financial Times*, as recently as 30 December 2016, implied, when quoting from the minute, that these were the shared views of 'Mrs Thatcher and eminent historians'. Timothy Garton Ash, in a letter to the *FT* published on 4 January 2017, responded: 'As I and several of the other historians present stated clearly when the document was first leaked to the press in 1990…this Gilbert & Sullivan list of alleged German qualities came from an imaginative note by Margaret Thatcher's private secretary, Charles Powell, and in no way fairly reflected the spirit of the meeting. In fact, all the historians present urged the prime minister to recognise that the opportunity of having a peacefully united, democratic Germany, firmly anchored in the west, was one we should seize with both hands.'

75. 'Miss Neville-Jones (Bonn) to FCO, 16 July 1990, Mr Ridley's Resignation and the Germany Seminar', in Salmon et al. (eds.), *German Unification 1989–1990*, pp. 432–4, at 433. Engaging in damage-limitation, the Foreign Secretary Douglas Hurd wrote to Pauline Neville-Jones, who was UK Minister in the Bonn Embassy (i.e. number two in the embassy hierarchy after the ambassador) on 18 July, telling her not to comment in detail on 'the Chequers seminar record, an internal and confidential paper', and suggesting that she publicize a public opinion poll which found that 'a large majority, especially of younger people, are confident about a united Germany's peaceful intentions' and that only 23 per cent of respondents 'did not favour a united Germany', ibid., pp. 437–8.

76. Ivan Berend, *History in my Life: A Memoir of Three Eras* (Central European Press, Budapest, 2009), p. 225.

77. Urban, *Diplomacy and Disillusion at the Court of Margaret Thatcher*, p. 143.

78. Ibid., pp. 118–59.

79. Ibid., p. 140.

80. Ibid., pp. 140–1; and Davenport-Hine and Sisman (eds.), *One-Hundred Letters from Hugh Trevor-Roper*, Letter to Max Perutz of 15 August 1990, p. 370.

81. Urban, *Diplomacy and Disillusion at the Court of Margaret Thatcher*, p. 141.

82. Hurd, *Memoirs*, p. 385. That last statement was, however, qualified in Powell's minute, the final sentence of which read: 'But even the optimists had some unease, not for the present and the immediate future, but for what might lie further down the road than we can yet see', 'Cold War: Chequers Seminar on Germany', p. 7.

83. Ian Kershaw, *Roller-Coaster: Europe, 1950–2017* (Allen Lane, London, 2018), p. 371.

84. Bush and Scowcroft, *A World Transformed*, pp. 213–14. Scowcroft wrote, apropos German unification and related European security issues, that 'We launched Eagleburger and Gates on their missionary circuit on January 28, with London as the first—and most difficult—stop.' It became apparent that Thatcher was 'not happy', but she would 'acquiesce in what we wished to do'. He adds, 'As this staunch ally cordially bade the two emissaries goodbye, she said they would always be welcome there, "but never again on this subject"' (ibid.).

85. Ibid., p. 222.

86. 'Iz besedy M. S. Gorbacheva s M. Tetcher, 8 iyunya 1990 goda', in Galkin and Chernyaev (eds.), *Mikhail Gorbachev i Germanskiy vopros*, pp. 478–85, at p. 479.

87. 'Letter from Mr Powell (No. 10) to Mr Wall', 8 June 1990, in Salmon et al. (eds.), *German Unification 1989–90*, pp. 411–17, at p. 411.

88. 'Letter from Sir C. Mallaby (Bonn) to Mr Weston, 11 October 1990', in Salmon et al. (eds.), *German Unification, 1989–1990*, pp. 488–90.

89. Savranskaya and Blanton, *The Last Superpower Summits*, p. 713.

90. Memorandum of Conversation, Bush–Gorbachev, Private Meeting, Helsinki, 9 September 1990, ibid., pp. 732–47, at p. 734.

91. Ibid., p. 741.

92. Baker, *The Politics of Diplomacy*, p. 313.

93. Yevgeny Primakov, *Russian Crossroads: Toward the New Millennium* (Yale University Press, New Haven, 2004), pp. 44–5.

94. Ibid., p. 51. See also Savranskaya and Blanton, *The Last Superpower Summits*, pp. 707–18; and Grachev, *Gorbachev's Gamble*, pp. 191–7.

95. Engel, *When the World Seemed New*, pp. 409–14.

96. Primakov, *Russian Crossroads*, pp. 53–6.

97. https://www.nobelprize.org/prizes/peace/1990/press-release/.

98. The First Deputy Soviet Foreign Minister, Anatoly Kovalev, travelled to Oslo to accept the prize on Gorbachev's behalf ('Aide Accepts Gorbachev's Nobel Peace Prize', 11 December 1990, https://www.nytimes.com/1990/12/11/world/aide-accepts-gorbachev-s-nobel-peace-prize.html).

99. Anatoly Chernyaev, *My Six Years with Gorbachev* (Pennsylvania State University Press, University Park, PA, 2000), p. 366.

100. Ibid., pp. 366–7.

101. The resignation speech is published in full in Geoffrey Howe, *Conflict of Loyalty* (Macmillan, London, 1994), pp. 697–703.

102. Margaret Thatcher, *The Downing Street Years* (HarperCollins, London, 1993), p. 839. The final line of his speech—that it was time for others to consider their own response to the conflict of loyalties—was, she said, 'an open invitation to Michael Heseltine to stand against me' and one which 'electrified the House of Commons' (ibid.). Her bitterness about Howe comes out strongly in her memoirs when she says that 'Geoffrey Howe from this point on would be remembered not for his staunchness as Chancellor of the Exchequer, nor for his skilful diplomacy as Foreign Secretary, but for this final act of bile and treachery' (ibid., p. 840). She was scarcely less bitter about the advice that she could not win the leadership election she received from almost every member of the Cabinet and what she called 'the weasel words whereby they had transmuted their betrayal into frank advice and concern for my fate', ibid., pp. 850–5, esp. p. 855.

103. https://www.margaretthatcher.org/search?dt=5&w=gorbachev+farewell&searchtype=and&t=0&starty=&startm=&startd=&endy=&endm=&endd=&onedayy=&onedaym=&onedayd=&doctype%5B%5D=archive&theme%5B%5D=F-USSR (Thatcher Foundation Archives). In the translation of the letter provided for the prime minister, Gorbachev's reference to Thatcher's contribution 'as a politician' (*kak politik*) was changed to 'as a political leader'. In a covering note, Charles Powell drew the departing prime minister's attention to the fact that Gorbachev had addressed her as 'Dear Margaret'. See also L. M. Zamyatin, *Gorbi i Meggi: zapiski posla o dvukh izvestnykh politikakh—Mikhaile Gorbacheve i Margaret Tetcher* (Pik Viniti, Moscow, 1995), pp. 128–9. Although far from always a reliable source, Zamyatin accurately reproduced the full text of Gorbachev's letter. He was Soviet ambassador to Britain at the time and responsible for conveying communications between Moscow and London.

104. *Charter of Paris for a New Europe*, CSCE, Paris, 19–21 November 1990, https://www.osce.org/mc/39516.
105. Chernyaev, *My Six Years with Gorbachev*, pp. 299–300.
106. *Charter of Paris for a New Europe*, p. 3.
107. Ibid., p. 5.
108. Ibid., pp. 5–6.
109. Ibid., p. 8.
110. Ibid., p. 12.
111. Ibid., pp. 12–13.
112. Jack F. Matlock, Jr, *Autopsy on an Empire: The American Ambassador's Account of the Collapse of the Soviet Union* (Random House, New York, 1995), p. 422.
113. Vadim Bakatin, *Doroga v proshedshem vremeni* (Dom, Moscow, 1999), p. 219.
114. Ibid., pp. 227–8.
115. Eduard Shevardnadze, *The Future Belongs to Freedom* (Sinclair-Stevenson, 1991), p. 202. The speech is published in full as an appendix to that book.
116. Ibid., pp. 201–4.
117. Matlock, *Autopsy on an Empire*, p. 432.
118. Ibid., p. 432.
119. Bush in Bush and Scowcroft, *A World Transformed*, p. 430.
120. Baker, *The Politics of Diplomacy*, p. 474.
121. Ibid.
122. Bush, in Bush and Scowcroft, *A World Transformed*, pp. 430–1.
123. Shakhnazarov's words when I interviewed him in his large office in the Kremlin on 16 December 1991, a little over a week before he and the other members of Gorbachev's team, and Gorbachev himself, had to vacate their rooms to make way for Yeltsin and his entourage.
124. Matlock, *Autopsy on an Empire*, p. 433.
125. Ibid.

15 Final Year—of the USSR and of Gorbachev's Power (1991)

1. Vitaliy Ignatenko, 'Ot Vil'nyusa do Forosa: Samye trudnye dni Gorbacheva', *Novoe vremya*, 12 March 1992, pp. 22–6; and author's interviews and conversations with Andrei Grachev who throughout most of 1991 was Gorbachev's press secretary.
2. For more detail on the national question in the USSR, the killings in Georgia, Azerbaijan, and the Baltic states, and the August 1991 coup, see Archie Brown, *The Gorbachev Factor* (Oxford University Press, Oxford, 1996), pp. 252–305; and Brown, *Seven Years that Changed the World: Perestroika in Perspective* (Oxford University Press, Oxford, 2007), pp. 294–324. Of the various applications of coercive force in Soviet republics, the only instance where Gorbachev approved it in advance was in the capital of Azerbaijan, Baku, following the killing there by Azeris of scores of Armenians in January 1990. The indiscriminate response by Soviet troops, in which people other than the perpetrators were killed, was not what Gorbachev intended, but he had accepted the advice of Primakov, who had travelled to Baku to investigate the pogrom, that the introduction of troops to protect Armenians was essential.
3. David Remnick, *Lenin's Tomb: The Last Days of the Soviet Empire* (Viking, London, 1993), p. 387; and John Miller, *Mikhail Gorbachev and the End of Soviet Power* (Macmillan, London, 1993), pp. 172–4.

4. Ignatenko, 'Ot Vil'nyusa do Forosa', pp. 25–6.
5. William Taubman, *Gorbachev: His Life and Times* (Norton, New York, 2017), p. 577; and Mikhail Gorbachev, *Ponyat' perestroyku…Pochemu eto vazhno seychas* (Al'pina, Moscow, 2006), pp. 292–3.
6. Anatoly Chernyaev, *My Six Years with Gorbachev* (Pennsylvania State University Press, University Park, PA, 2000), pp. 317–27.
7. Jack F. Matlock, Jr, *Autopsy on an Empire: The American Ambassador's Account of the Collapse of the Soviet Union* (Random House, New York, 1995), p. 451.
8. Ibid., p. 457.
9. Ignatenko, 'Ot Vil'nyusa do Forosa', p. 26.
10. Aleksandr Yakovlev, *Sumerki* (Materik, Moscow, 2003), pp. 519–20.
11. George Bush and Brent Scowcroft, *A World Transformed* (Knopf, New York, 1998), p. 497. Replying to Bush, Gorbachev said that 'a military and civilian cabal had ordered the attack without his knowledge'. At a conference on the Cold War in 1995, Bush observed that 'I believed him at the time, and still do' (ibid., p. 496).
12. Matlock, *Autopsy on an Empire*, pp. 470–1.
13. Ibid., pp. 471–2.
14. Ibid., pp. 471–3.
15. Ibid., p. 471.
16. *Pravda*, 27 March 1991; and Mikhail Gorbachev and Zdeněk Mlynář, *Conversations with Gorbachev: On Perestroika, the Prague Spring, and the Crossroads of Socialism* (Columbia University, New York, 2002), p. 131.
17. Author's interview with Andrei Grachev in Moscow, 18 September 1992; and A. S. Chernyaev, 'Gorbachev i Yaponskaya problema', *Novaya i noveyshaya istoriya*, No. 3, 2000, pp. 141–56. Andrey Kozyrev and Vladimir Lukin made the Yeltsin position clear. In Lukin's words, 'The islands are no business of Gorbachev's. They belong to Russia!' (ibid., p. 154).
18. Michael Beschloss and Strobe Talbott, *At the Highest Levels: The Inside Story of the End of the Cold War* (Little, Brown, London, 1993), pp. 377–8.
19. Ibid., p. 378.
20. Andrei Grachev, *Gorbachev's Gamble: Soviet Foreign Policy and the End of the Cold War* (Polity, Cambridge, 2008), p. 207.
21. Ibid.
22. Bush and Scowcroft, *A World Transformed*, pp. 504–6.
23. Rodric Braithwaite, Diary 1988–1992 (manuscript), entry for 27 May 1991.
24. It was first published in Russian in 2015. See Mikhail Sergeevich Gorbachev, *Sobranie sochineniy*, Vol. XXVI (Ves' mir, Moscow, 2015), pp. 113–24 and 547–52.
25. Braithwaite diary, entry for 27 May 1991.
26. 'Iz besedy s Margaret Tetcher, 27 maya 1991 goda', in Gorbachev, *Sobranie sochineniy*, Vol. XXVI, pp. 113–24, at p. 113.
27. In a poll conducted by the most authoritative survey research team in the last years of the Soviet Union, Margaret Thatcher came top by some distance when respondents were asked in December 1989 to name their 'woman of the year'. Neither the Soviet Union nor any other country was excluded, and whereas most answers to such open-ended questions in the USSR turned out to be very russocentric, Thatcher bucked that trend (*Obshchestvennoe mnenie v tsifrakh*, VTsIOM, Moscow, 6/13 February 1990). When Gorbachev was in London, following a meeting with the G-7 leaders in 1991, he was taken to the first act of an opera at Covent Garden before a dinner hosted by Prime Minister John Major. British ambassador to Moscow Rodric Braithwaite, who was in the group, recorded:

'Gorbachev is cheered as he comes into the theatre, and again in the street outside as he leaves. A great boost to his morale, I should think: he can no longer hope for any such popular enthusiasm in his own country' (Braithwaite diary, entry for 18 July 1991).

28. 'Iz besedy s Margaret Tetcher', pp. 116–17.
29. Ibid., p. 121.
30. Braithwaite diary, entry for 27 May 1991.
31. Matlock, *Autopsy on an Empire*, p. 537. 'I was delighted at the opportunity', Matlock added, 'not least because I knew that the Braithwaites were among the keenest observers of the Soviet scene', so 'the evening would be well worthwhile quite apart from the chance to hear the former prime minister's views'.
32. Ibid.
33. Ibid., pp. 537–8.
34. Ibid., pp. 538–9.
35. Ibid., p. 539.
36. Georgiy Shakhnazarov, *S vozhdyami i bez nikh* (Vagrius, Moscow, 2001), p. 377.
37. Brown, *The Gorbachev Factor*, p. 290; Matlock, *Autopsy on an Empire*, pp. 539–40; and Taubman, *Gorbachev*, pp. 583–5.
38. Taubman, *Gorbachev*, p. 584.
39. Yakovlev, *Sumerki*, pp. 534–5.
40. Ibid., pp. 534–7.
41. Taubman, *Gorbachev*, pp. 584–5.
42. Grachev, *Gorbachev's Gamble*, pp. 207–8; and Bush and Scowcroft, *A World Transformed*, p. 506.
43. Bush and Scowcroft, *A World Transformed*, p. 507.
44. 'Memorandum of Conversation, G7 Meeting with President Gorbachev, London', 17 July 1991, in Svetlana Savranskaya and Thomas Blanton, *The Last Superpower Summits: Gorbachev, Reagan, and Bush* (Central European University Press, Budapest and New York, 2016), pp. 855–63, at p. 857.
45. Matlock, *Autopsy on an Empire*, pp. 552–4.
46. Bush–Gorbachev First Private Meeting, Moscow, 30 July 1991, in Savranskaya and Blanton, *The Last Superpower Summits*, pp. 868–82, at pp. 873–4.
47. Ibid., p. 873.
48. Ibid., p. 870.
49. Ibid., p. 876.
50. Matlock, *Autopsy on an Empire*, p. 564.
51. Pavel Palazchenko, *My Years with Gorbachev and Shevardnadze: The Memoir of a Soviet Interpreter* (Pennsylvania State University Press, University Park, PA, 1997), p. 304. In Bush's account, it is Bessmertnykh, rather than Chernyaev, who was dispatched by Gorbachev to find out what happened (Bush and Scowcroft, *A World Transformed*, p. 513).
52. Palazchenko, *My Years with Gorbachev and Shevardnadze*, p. 304.
53. Gorbachev, *Ponyat' perestroyku*, pp. 326–8; interview with Nursultan Nazarbayev, *Nezavisimaya gazeta*, 28 July 1993; and Boris Yeltsin, *The View from the Kremlin* (HarperCollins, London, 1994), pp. 38–9.
54. 'Record of the Main Content of Conversation between Bush and Gorbachev, Novo-Ogarevo, July 31, 1991' in Savranskaya and Blanton, *The Last Superpower Summits*, pp. 889–902, at p. 890.
55. Ibid., p. 892.
56. Ibid.
57. Ibid., p. 896.

58. Ibid., p. 891.
59. Serhii Plokhy, *The Last Empire: The Final Days of the Soviet Union* (Basic Books, New York, 2014), p. 58.
60. George H. W. Bush speech in Kiev, 1 August 1991, https://en.wikisource.org/wiki/Chicken_Kiev_speech.
61. Plokhy, *The Last Empire*, p. 56.
62. 'Memorandum of Conversation, Bush–Yeltsin', 30 July 1991, in Savranskaya and Blanton, *The Last Superpower Summits*, pp. 886–8, at p. 887.
63. Bush Kiev speech.
64. Ibid.
65. Yu. V. Bondarev speech, *XIX Vsesoyuznaya konferentsiya kommunisticheskoy partii Sovetskogo Soyuza, 28 iyunya—1 iyulya 1988 goda, Stenograficheskiy otchet*, Vol. I (Politizdat, Moscow, 1988), pp. 223–8, at p. 224.
66. *Sovetskaya Rossiya*, 23 July 1991.
67. 'Sotsializm, demokratiya, progres', *Nezavisimya gazeta*, 23 July 1991, translated in BBC SWB, 26 July 1991, Draft Party Programme, SU/1134.
68. Georgiy Shakhnazarov, *Tsena svobody: Reformatsiya Gorbacheva glazami ego pomoshchnika* (Rossika Zevs, Moscow, 1993), pp. 253–4; and Archie Brown, 'Did Gorbachev as General Secretary Become a Social Democrat?', *Europe-Asia Studies*, Vol. 65, No. 2, 2013, pp. 198–220, esp. pp. 215–16.
69. Draft Party Programme', 23 July 1991 (see above, n. 67).
70. M. S. Gorbachev, 'O proekte novoy Programmy KPSS. Doklad M. S. Gorbacheva na Plenume TsK KPSS 24 iyulya 1991', *Pravda*, 26 July 1991.
71. Alexander Lukin, *The Political Culture of the Russian 'Democrats'* (Oxford University Press, Oxford, 2000), esp. p. 298; see also Juan Linz and Alfred Stepan, *Problems of Democratic Transition and Consolidation: Southern Europe, South America, and Post-Communist Europe* (Johns Hopkins University Press, Baltimore, 1996), esp. pp. 16–37, '"Stateness", Nationalism, and Democratization'.
72. Author's interview with Andrei Grachev, 25 January 1992, and *Pravda*, 29 July 1991.
73. The draft was first published in a weekly newspaper sympathetic to it, *Moskovskie novosti*, on 14 August 1991, and in a very hostile daily paper, *Sovetskaya Rossiya*, on 15 August.
74. That lengthy article was published in Moscow in September 1991, 'Stat'ya napisannaya v Forose', in M. S. Gorbachev, *Avgustovskiy putch: prichiny i sledstviya* (Novosti, Moscow, 1991), pp. 64–90. It is available in English, with the note that it was written a few days before the coup, as Appendix C of Mikhail Gorbachev, *The August Coup: The Truth and the Lessons* (HarperCollins, London, 1991), pp. 97–127. Gorbachev wrote: 'The introduction of a state of emergency, in which even some supporters of *perestroika*, not to mention those who preach the ideology of dictatorship, see a way out of the crisis, would be a fatal move and the way to civil war.' Those who appealed for emergency rule were, he added, in reality seeking a return to the pre-perestroika political system (ibid., p. 111).
75. Chernyaev, *My Six Years with Gorbachev*, p. 372.
76. Mikhail Gorbachev, 'Novaya politika i novaya Rossiya', *Svobodnaya mysl'*, No. 13, 1992, pp. 3–19, at p. 3; and Vladimir Kryuchkov, *Lichnoe delo*, Vol. II (Olimp, Moscow, 1996), pp. 126–42.
77. Chernyaev, *My Six Years with Gorbachev*, p. 371.
78. Ibid., pp. 371–423; and Gorbachev, *Avgustovskiy putch*.
79. Gorbachev, *Avgustovskiy putch*, pp. 9–13, esp. p. 13; and Gorbachev, *Zhizn' i reformy*, Vol. II (Novosti, Moscow, 1995), p. 559.

80. V. G. Stepankov and E. K. Lisov, *Kremlevskiy zagovor* (Ogonek, Moscow, 1992), p. 14.
81. Ibid., pp. 149–50; and Plokhy, *The Last Empire*, pp. 99–100.
82. Palazchenko, *My Years with Gorbachev and Shevardnadze*, pp. 314–15.
83. Gorbachev told Andrei Grachev that he was convinced that his wife's fatal illness, from which she died (aged 67) in September 1999, had its origins in their three-day incarceration at Foros (Grachev, *Gibel' Sovetskogo 'Titanika': Sudovoy zhurnal* (Prozaik, Moscow, 2015), p. 119); see also Taubman, *Gorbachev*, p. 620.
84. Palazchenko, *My Years with Gorbachev and Shevardnadze*, p. 340.
85. Andrei S. Grachev, *Final Days: The Inside Story of the Collapse of the Soviet Union* (Westview, Boulder, 1995), p. 75.
86. Jeffrey A. Engel, *When the World Seemed New: George H. W. Bush and the End of the Cold War* (Houghton Mifflin Harcourt, Boston and New York, 2017), p. 462.
87. Scowcroft in Bush and Scowcroft, *A World Transformed*, p. 520.
88. *New York Times*, 31 October 1991, https://www.nytimes.com/1991/10/31/world/gorbachev-and-mitterrand-meet-for-a-little-embarrassment.html. Mitterrand went out of his way to recreate his good relationship with Gorbachev in the final months of the latter's presidency, especially when Gorbachev took up the French president's invitation to visit him at his country home near the Spanish border at the beginning of November 1991, following a conference on the Middle East, attended by Bush and Gorbachev, in Madrid. See Grachev, *Final Days*, pp. 75–83.
89. Margaret Thatcher, *The Path to Power* (HarperCollins, London, 1995), pp. 512–13.
90. Ibid., p. 513.
91. Ibid.
92. Palazchenko, *My Years with Gorbachev and Shevardnadze*, p. 314.
93. One of Gorbachev's most loyal supporters within the Politburo and Secretariat of the Central Committee of the CPSU (who remained with him in the Gorbachev Foundation in post-Soviet Russia), Vadim Medvedev, noted the exceptional speed with which Kravchuk had moved from being an orthodox Communist critic of much that was happening during perestroika to becoming a completely 'new Kravchuk' with little resemblance to the old who went on to play an important role in the break-up of the union. See V. Medvedev, *Prozrenie, mif ili predatel'stvo? K voprosu ob ideologii perestroyki* (Evraziya, Moscow, 1998), p. 142.
94. Plokhy, *The Last Empire*, p. 160.
95. Palazchenko, *My Years with Gorbachev and Shevardnadze*, p. 320.
96. Vadim Bakatin, *Izbavlenie ot KGB* (Novosti, Moscow, 1992), pp. 14–15.
97. Rodric Braithwaite, *Across the Moscow River: The World Turned Upside Down* (Yale University Press, New Haven and London, 2002), p. 147. A somewhat fuller account was provided by Braithwaite in his diary, although the precise content of the military men's ultimatum remained elusive, Braithwaite diary, entry for 18 July 1991, pp. 339–40.
98. Akhromeyev left several letters, for different recipients, explaining his decision to take his own life. His letter to Gorbachev, dated 22 August 1991, is published in full in Stepankov and Lisov, *Kremlevskiy zagovor*, pp. 240–2. In it, Akhromeyev writes: 'The thing is that, starting in 1990, I became convinced, as I am convinced also today, that our country is heading for destruction' (p. 241).
99. Ken Adelman, *Reagan at Reykjavik: Forty-Eight Hours that Ended the Cold War* (Broadside, New York, 2014), pp. 289–92.
100. Bush and Scowcroft, *A World Transformed*, p. 537.
101. Taubman, *Gorbachev*, p. 619.
102. Jack F. Matlock, Jr, *Reagan and Gorbachev: How the Cold War Ended* (Random House, New York, 2004), p. 258. Matlock writes that the copy of the plans for the installation of

listening devices in the new US embassy 'probably contained nothing that the United States did not already know from its meticulous examination of the structure, but Bakatin's action—which Gorbachev approved—was, nevertheless, a gesture of goodwill'.

103. Oleg Kalugin, *SpyMaster: My 32 Years in Intelligence and Espionage Against the West* (Smith Gryphon, London, 1994), pp. 346–60, esp. pp. 357–60.

104. Graeme Gill, *The Collapse of a Single-Party System: The Disintegration of the CPSU* (Cambridge University Press, Cambridge, 1994), pp. 174–6; and Palazchenko, *My Years with Gorbachev and Shevardnadze*, pp. 317–18.

105. Gill, *The Collapse of a Single-Party System*, pp. 175–6.

106. Plokhy, *The Last Empire*, p. 398.

107. Ibid., pp. 175–7.

108. Grachev, *Final Days*, pp. 108–9.

109. Plokhy, *The Last Empire*, pp. 401–2.

110. Grachev, *Final Days*, p. 69.

111. Savranskaya and Blanton, *The Last Superpower Summits*, p. 915.

112. Grachev, *Final Days*, p. 74.

113. Ibid., p. 75.

114. Ibid., p. 72.

115. Plokhy, *The Last Empire*, p. 292. In Crimea just over 54 per cent voted in favour (p. 293).

116. Ibid., p. 320.

117. Ibid., pp. 400–1. The general point about Stalin's culpability was made earlier by a specialist on Russian politics. See Peter Rutland, 'Stalin Caused the Soviet Collapse', *The Moscow Times*, 17 August 2011. Rutland notes that the overwhelming majority of inhabitants of these occupied states did not want to be part of the Soviet Union, and 'if Stalin had not insisted on absorbing the Baltic states but had let them go the way of Finland—independent of Russia since 1918—perhaps Gorbachev's reform efforts during the perestroika period could have succeeded'.

118. Andrey Grachev, *Dal'she bez menya…ukhod prezidenta* (Progress-Kul'tura, Moscow, 1994), p. 136.

119. Mikhail Gorbachev, *Zhizn' i reformy*, Vol. I, pp. 5 and 7.

120. Ibid., p. 8.

16 Political Leadership and the End of the Cold War: Concluding Reflections

1. See Chapter 13.

2. Malcolm Rifkind, *Power and Pragmatism: The Memoirs of Malcolm Rifkind* (Biteback, London, 2016), p. xii.

3. Ibid.

4. Margaret Thatcher interview with Kenneth Harris in *The Observer*, 18 and 25 February 1979, https://www.margaretthatcher.org/document/103816.

5. I have argued elsewhere against too much power in the hands of an individual leader and in favour of more collegial, more collective leadership—in democracies as well as in authoritarian regimes. In the latter, oligarchy is usually a lesser evil than personal dictatorship. See Brown, *The Myth of the Strong Leader: Political Leadership in the Modern Age* (with updating new Foreword, Vintage, London, 2018); Brown, 'Against the *Führerprinzip*: For Collective Leadership', *Daedalus*, Vol. 145, No. 3, 2016, pp. 109–23; and Brown, 'The Top Leader Fixation in British Politics', in Ivor Crewe and David Sanders (eds.), *Liberal Democracy*

and Authoritarian Populism: Essays in Memory of Anthony King (Macmillan, London, 2019), pp. 227–39.

6. Charles Moore, *Margaret Thatcher, Volume One: Not for Turning* (Allen Lane, London, 2013), pp. 51 and 87.

7. Ronald Reagan, *The Quest for Peace, the Cause of Freedom: Selected Speeches on the United States and the World* (United States Information Agency, Washington, DC, 1988), 'To Foster the Infrastructure of Democracy: Address to the British Parliament, London, June 8, 1982', pp. 198–207, at pp. 200–1.

8. Ibid.

9. Ibid., p. 204.

10. Ibid., p. 206.

11. Ronald Reagan, 'Address at Moscow State University', 31 May 1988, https://www.reaganlibrary.gov/sspeeches/053188b.

12. Ronald Reagan, *The Reagan Diaries Unabridged: Volume I, January 1981–October 1985*, ed. Douglas Brinkley (HarperCollins, 2007), entry for 6 April 1983, p. 212.

13. At a time when he looked likely to be a strong contender for the Democratic nomination for the presidency, Senator Gary Hart had a three-hour meeting with Gorbachev in Moscow in December 1986. A critic of SDI, Hart took a strong interest in change in the USSR and was given wide access in the perestroika period to leading Soviet reformers. See Hart, *The Second Russian Revolution: Despatches from the Front* (Hodder & Stoughton, London, 1991). See also Chris Matthews, *Tip and the Gipper: When Politics Worked* (Simon & Schuster, New York, 2013), esp. pp. 309–27; and Philip Taubman, 'Gorbachev Wants Results at the Summit' (Edward Kennedy meeting with Gorbachev), *New York Times*, 7 February 1986, https://www.nytimes.com/1986/02/07world/gorbachev-wants-results-at-the-summit-html.

14. Jack F. Matlock, Jr, *Reagan and Gorbachev: How the Cold War Ended* (Random House, New York, 2004), pp. 75–7.

15. The evidence was presented in Chapter 7.

16. Percy Cradock, *In Defence of British Interests: Reflections on Foreign Policy under Margaret Thatcher and John Major* (John Murray, London, 1997), pp. 99–101; and Rodric Braithwaite, 'Gorbachev and Thatcher' in *Journal of European Integration History*, Vol. 16, No. 1, 2010, pp. 31–44, at p. 38.

17. Memorandum from John Coles to Brian Fall, 30 June 1983, Foreign Office Papers, RSO13/1. The fuller discussion of this is in Chapter 7.

18. From my contemporaneous notes of the 8 September 1983 Chequers seminar (already discussed in Chapter 7). The prime minister was responding to Alec Nove who had made the point about the Soviet side's entitlement also to feel secure. The Defence Secretary Michael Heseltine intervened to agree with Nove.

19. Thatcher's 'Points which the President might make to Mr. Gorbachev...', 24 October 1985, cited more fully in Chapter 8.

20. In the course of a long and interesting interview Gorbachev gave to the weekly newspaper of the Soviet Writers' Union not long before the USSR and his presidency came to an end, he was asked why he still defended socialism. He replied that 'I associate socialism with political and spiritual freedom, with respect for culture, humanization and democracy' (*Literaturnaya gazeta*, 4 December 1991). Writing fifteen years later, Gorbachev said that he came to the realization that what had existed hitherto in the Soviet system should not be regarded as socialism—'Slogans, yes! Elements of socialism, indeed, but not more' (Mikhail Gorbachev, *Ponyat' perestroyku...Pochemu eto vazhno seychas* (Al'pina, Moscow, 2006), p. 25).

21. M. S. Gorbachev, *Posle kremlya* (Ves' mir, Moscow, 2014); and *Nekonchennaya istoriya: Besedy Mikhaila Gorbacheva s politologom Borisom Slavinym* (Olma-Press, Moscow, 2001).

22. 'Cold War: Margaret Thatcher interviewed about Ronald Reagan [released 2002]', https://www.margaretthatcher.org/document/109324.

23. Margaret Thatcher, *The Downing Street Years* (HarperCollins, London, 1993), p. 803.

24. Ibid., pp. 800–1 and 803.

25. Cradock, *In Defence of British Interests*, p. 201.

26. 'Iz besedy s ministrom inostrannykh del Ispanii F. Fernadesom Ordon'esom, 3 marta 1989 goda', in Mikhail Sergeevich Gorbachev, *Sobranie sochineniy*, Vol. XIII (Ves' mir, Moscow, 2009), pp. 328–34, at p. 333.

27. 'Iz vystupleniy na vstreche s Sovetskimi poslami, uchastvovavshimi v rabote plenuma, 15 marta 1989 goda', in Gorbachev, *Sobranie sochineniy*, Vol. XIII, pp. 391–6, at p. 395. Gorbachev immediately followed his remarks about Reagan's positive attributes with several which were, however, less complimentary, describing the former president as 'idle' (which, by his standards or Thatcher's, he was) and 'feeble', presumably with Reagan's intellect, rather than either his physique or his political capacity, in view.

28. As noted in earlier chapters, Anatoly Chernyaev, in particular, testified to this, as at various times did Thatcher's interpreter Richard Pollock, Gorbachev's interpreter Pavel Palazchenko, and successive UK ambassadors to Moscow Sir Bryan Cartledge and Sir Rodric Braithwaite.

29. https://www.margaretthatcher.org/search?dt=5&w=gorbachev+farewell&searchtype=-and&t=0&starty=&startm=&startd=&endy=&endm=&endd=&onedayy=&onedaym=&onedayd=&doctype%5B%5D=archive&theme%5B%5D=F-USSR (Thatcher Foundation Archives). In her reply, Margaret Thatcher wrote, 'I share your hope that we can continue to meet on future occasions' (https://www.margaretthatcher.org/document/149428, Thatcher Foundation Archives).

30. Ronald Reagan, 'My Heart Was with Her', *Newsweek*, 3 December 1990, p. 37. Robert Zoellick, who was James Baker's closest aide, reported Baker as saying that 'he'd watched Margaret Thatcher wrap Ronald Reagan around her little finger'. Interviewed for the authorized biography of Thatcher, former President George H. W. Bush said that Thatcher had exercised too much influence over Reagan. He would sit and agree with her at international meetings when she said 'Ronnie and I think this. Ron and I want to do that.' Reagan was, said Bush, 'just smitten by her' (Charles Moore, *Margaret Thatcher, Volume Three: Herself Alone*, Allen Lane, London, 2019, p. 197).

31. In post-Soviet Russia, the mass media were discouraged from presenting Gorbachev in a positive light. That Stalin comes out as more highly esteemed than Gorbachev in many post-Soviet surveys reflects the fact that it has become more acceptable to publish praise of the former than of the latter in twenty-first century Russia.

32. These points draw upon Archie Brown, 'Gorbachev and Perestroika: A Twenty-Fifth Anniversary Perspective', *Baltic Worlds*, Vol. III, No. 3, 2010, pp. 22–6; and the final chapter of Brown, *Seven Years that Changed the World: Perestroika in Perspective* (Oxford University Press, Oxford, 2007).

33. Denis Healey, *The Time of My Life* (Michael Joseph, London, 1989), p. 519.

34. Jeffrey A. Engel, *When the World Seemed New: George H. W. Bush and the End of the Cold War* (Houghton, Mifflin, Harcourt, Boston and New York, 2017), p. 473.

35. George Bush and Brent Scowcroft, *A World Transformed* (Knopf, New York, 1998), p. 561.

36. Strobe Talbott, *The Russia Hand: A Memoir of Presidential Diplomacy* (Random House, New York, 2002), p. 33.

37. See Robert D. English, *Russia and the Idea of the West: Gorbachev, Intellectuals, and the End of the Cold War* (Columbia University Press, New York, 2000); Matthew Evangelista, *Unarmed Forces: The Transnational Movement to End the Cold War* (Cornell University Press, Ithaca and London, 1999); and Brown, *Seven Years that Changed the World*, especially chs. 6 and 8.

38. Robert Legvold, *Return to Cold War* (Polity, Cambridge, 2016), p. 136. See also Vasile Rotaru, 'Instrumentalizing the recent past? The new Cold War narrative in Russian public space after 2014', *Post-Soviet Affairs*, Vol. 35, No. 1, 2019, pp. 25–40.

39. Mikhail Gorbachev and George P. Shultz, 'We participated in INF negotiations. Abandoning it threatens our very existence', *Washington Post*, 4 December 2018; and 'INF Nuclear Treaty: Russia Follows US in Suspending Pact', https://www.bbc.co.uk/news/world-europe-47101429, 2 February 2019.

40. 'INF nuclear treaty: US pulls out of Cold War-era pact with Russia', 2 August 2019, https://www.bbc.co.uk/news/world-us-canada-49198565.

41. Rodric Braithwaite, 'The Uses and Abuses of History', 8 June 2015, https://www.opendemocracy.net/od-russia/rodric-braithwaite/uses-and-abuses-of-history.

42. Talbott, *The Russia Hand*, p. 136.

43. Ibid., p. 145.

44. Thomas L. Friedman, 'Foreign Affairs; Now a Word from X', *New York Times*, 2 May 1998, http://www.nytimes.com/1998/05/02/opinion/foreign-affairs-now-a-word-from-x.html.

45. Richard Ullman, 'The US and the World: An Interview with George Kennan', *New York Review of Books*, 12 August 1999. The warnings came from many other experienced participants in the foreign policy community. An open letter sent to President Clinton on 26 June 1997, and signed by more than forty former senators, cabinet secretaries, ambassadors, and leading analysts, argued that 'Russia does not now pose a threat to its western neighbors and the nations of Central and Eastern Europe are not in danger' and 'NATO expansion is neither necessary nor desirable.' The signatories included former Senators Bill Bradley, Gary Hart, and Sam Nunn, former Secretary of Defense Robert McNamara, Reagan's chief arms control negotiator Paul Nitze, Susan Eisenhower (granddaughter of the president), Jack Matlock and even Richard Pipes (https://www.bu.edu/globalbeat/nato/postpone062697.html).

46. Geoffrey Howe, *Conflict of Loyalty* (Macmillan, London, 1994), pp. 316–17.

47. Rodric Braithwaite, Diary 1988–1992 (manuscript), entry for 23 September 1989, p. 87.

48. Ibid., 18 September 1989, p. 84. Thatcher took global warming and climate change seriously at a time when very few heads of government worldwide did so. As a science graduate, she had respect for the relevant evidence. Martin Nicholson, who had become Cabinet Office Sovietologist in 1983, was invited to Chequers for Mikhail Gorbachev's December 1984 visit to act as interpreter for Raisa Gorbachev. Ahead of the arrival of the Russian delegation, he found himself alone with Mrs Thatcher. 'You know, Prime Minister,' he said, 'my brother [Robin Nicholson] is your Chief Scientific Adviser.' The prime minister, who had been tense up to that point, was surprised by the information, but 'her features softened' and she said, 'Robin, what *would* I do without Robin? He's the *only* one who will tell me the truth!' (Martin Nicholson, *Twitching the Iron Curtain in Central Europe and London: Memoirs 1972–1984*, Lulu, London, 2017, p. 158). Charles Moore devotes a whole chapter of the final volume of his biography to Thatcher's ecological concern ('From blue to green', Moore, *Margaret Thatcher, Vol. III*, pp. 399–430). Thatcher's advocacy of car travel and relative disdain for public transport was somewhat at odds with her concern about global warming, and in old age she appeared to retreat from the ecological worries she expressed when prime minister. In office, however, she had the benefit of expert advice, and out of office

her views were much influenced by the political milieu in which she moved. Moreover, by the time the book, *Statecraft*, in which she appeared to be recanting her stand on global warming, was written for her and completed in 2001 (published 2002), her mental deterioration was such that she was giving her imprimatur to passages where, by the time she got to the bottom of a page, she could no longer remember what was written a paragraph or two earlier (ibid., pp. 429–30 and 824–5).

49. Adam Smith, *The Theory of Moral Sentiments*, ed. D. D. Raphael and A. L. Macfie (Clarendon Press, Oxford, 1976 [1759]), p. 154.

50. Joshua R. Itzkowitz Shifrinson, 'Deal or No Deal? The End of the Cold War and the U.S. Offer to Limit NATO Expansion', *International Security*, Vol. 40, No. 4, 2016, pp. 30–1.

ACKNOWLEDGEMENTS

While my most concentrated work on this book has been over the past five years, some of the conversations and interviews which have fed into it go back a long way—to the Cold War era and shortly thereafter. This means that quite a few people I wish to acknowledge have died in the meantime. I include them in my thanks without repetitive use of 'the late'.

For both Russian and American documentation on the Cold War, the National Security Archive at George Washington University has been invaluable. That applies equally to the materials I was able to access during study visits there and to what the NSA (GWU) has made available online and in their printed volumes of documents. I am particularly grateful to Svetlana Savranskaya, a senior researcher at that institution and Cold War specialist, for facilitating my access to relevant information. In the United States I have gathered much material also at the Reagan Presidential Library Archives in Simi Valley, California, where archivist Jennifer Mandel was an invaluable guide. I have benefited from work in the Hoover Institution Archives at Stanford which house, inter alia, many Politburo minutes and an interesting collection of interviews with significant players in the ending of the Cold War. I have drawn also upon the especially useful interviews conducted for an excellent television series, The Second Russian Revolution, made by Brian Lapping and Norma Percy (with specialist input from Angus Roxburgh) during the last two years of Gorbachev's time in power. The leading figures on the Soviet side were questioned in depth when their memories of recent events were still fresh and detailed. The transcripts are in the British Library of Political and Economic Science at LSE. For a contemporary document of a different kind, I am very grateful to Sir Rodric Braithwaite for giving me access to the fascinating manuscript diary of his years as British ambassador to the Soviet Union and early post-Soviet Russia, 1988–92. In Oxford, I have greatly benefited from the electronic resources of the Bodleian Library and from the bibliographical expertise and helpfulness of the librarian of the Russian and Eurasian Studies Centre at St Antony's College, Richard Ramage.

In Russia many of the relevant sources are available in the archives of the Gorbachev Foundation where I hugely appreciated the generosity of Anatoly Chernyaev who, from the early 1990s onwards, let me see documents that were only later made generally available, and from whom I learned a lot in interviews and conversations. I am also greatly indebted to Mikhail Sergeyevich Gorbachev for invitations to take part in several conferences he chaired in Moscow (and also in Turin) on the Cold War and perestroika.

A unique roundtable conference held in Moscow in 1999, to which I was invited by Ned Lebow (then of the Mershon Center of Ohio State University, now of King's College London) and Richard Herrmann (Mershon Center), brought together some influential perestroika-era foreign and defence policy specialists, among them Andrei Grachev, Sergey Tarasenko, Vitaly Kataev, and Oleg Grinevsky, with the leading 'putschists'—Soviet government members and party officials (including Oleg Baklanov, Vladimir Kryuchkov, Oleg Shenin, Gennady Yanaev, and Dmitry Yazov) who mounted the coup against Gorbachev in August 1991. That conference was a remarkable joint venture between the Mershon Center and the Institute of General History of the Russian Academy of Sciences under the auspices of Aleksandr Chubaryan and Natalia Yegorova.

Many documents relating to Margaret Thatcher's relations with Gorbachev and with Ronald Reagan are available in the Gorbachev Foundation archives and at the Reagan Presidential Library. I have also used the UK Freedom of Information Act to get Cabinet Office and Foreign Office materials declassified. Government documents, once declassified, find their way on to the Thatcher Foundation website which, thanks to Chris Collins, provides online access to a treasure trove of archival materials from the Thatcher premiership. For resuscitating a number of UK government electronic links which had become inaccessible, I am enormously grateful to Daniel Collings, an expert on Thatcher source material, for helping out at short notice. (As of November 2019, when this book went to press, the URLs were accessible.) Taking part in three UK-government seminars on the Soviet Union and on British–Soviet relations convened and chaired by Margaret Thatcher in the mid-1980s offered an interesting opportunity to observe at first hand her leadership style as well as the pains she took to become well-informed.

On US policy and Ronald Reagan's role, I've benefited from conversations with people who were active during his presidency in American politics, especially the American foreign policy establishment, among them Max Kampelman, Warren Zimmerman, Marshall Shulman, Senator Gary Hart, Charles Price (a Reagan appointee as US ambassador to the UK), and, above all, Jack F. Matlock, Jr., the Soviet specialist on Reagan's National Security Council before he became from 1987 to 1991 a particularly influential American ambassador to Moscow. Numerous conversations with Jack, both on conference panels in Washington and elsewhere, and informally (especially when we were both conducting research in the Reagan Presidential Library Archives in 2016) have been immensely useful.

On the Soviet and Russian side, I am grateful for interviews and conversations with a wide range of political practitioners and diplomats. In addition to Chernyaev, Andrei Grachev has been a particularly helpful interlocutor, and I have had very useful meetings with, among others, Aleksandr Nikolaevich Yakovlev, Georgy

Shakhnazarov, Vadim Medvedev, Pavel Palazchenko, Anatoly Adamishin, Oleg Bogomolov, Fedor Burlatsky, Yegor Gaidar, Grigory Karasin, Vladimir Lukin, Eduard Malayan, Aleksandr Nikonov, Nikolay Petrakov, and Yegor Yakovlev.

I have had illuminating conversations over the years with British ministers and officials (some of whom played centrally important foreign policy roles during the Thatcher era) and with leading figures in the Labour Party. They have included, most notably, Sir Geoffrey (later Lord) Howe, Sir Malcolm Rifkind, Charles (Lord) Powell, James (Lord) Callaghan, Denis (Lord) Healey, Peter (Lord) Temple-Morris, Sir Anthony Parsons, Sir Rodric Braithwaite, Sir Bryan Cartledge, Sir David Logan, Geoffrey Murrell, Sir Michael Llewellyn Smith, David Gowan, and successive Cabinet Office Sovietologists Malcolm Mackintosh and Martin Nicholson.

Friends and academic colleagues in different countries with whom I have had valuable discussion on end-of-the-Cold-War themes include Roy Allison, Vladimir Baranovsky, George Breslauer, Samuel Charap, Aleksandr Chubaryan, Timothy Colton, Sergey Chugrov, Anne Deighton, Robert English, Rosemary Foot, Alexey Gromyko, Joel Hellman, David E. Hoffman, David Holloway, Eugene Huskey, Mikhail Ilyin, Charles King, Nikolay Kosolapov, Mark Kramer, Viktor Kuvaldin, Melvyn Leffler, Robert Legvold, Yury Levada, Aleksandr Lukin, Andrei Melville, John Miller, Julie Newton, Aleksandr Obolonsky, Vladimir Pechatnov, Sergey Peregudov, Ilaria Poggiolini, Silvio Pons, Alex Pravda, Sir Adam Roberts, Viktor Sergeyev, Robert Service, Lilia Shevtsova, Nodari Simonia, Rair Simonyan, William Smirnov, William Taubman, Odd Arne Westad, Natalia Yegorova, Olga Zdravomyslova, and Vladislav Zubok.

For their generous hospitality in Moscow, I owe huge thanks to several great friends—in particular, to Rair and Tatiana Simonyan, Sasha Obolonsky and Olya Obolonskaya, and David and Marna Gowan.

Of most immediate relevance to this book has been the willingness of friends to read and comment on the draft chapters. I am especially grateful to Julie Newton and William Taubman, the only two scholars on whom I inflicted the entire manuscript. It is probably longer than they expected, for it became significantly longer than I expected. So, I am lastingly indebted to Julie and Bill for the time they have devoted to a careful reading of the entire text and for their helpful suggestions. Nobly, given how busy they are, Roy Allison, Anne Deighton, and Adam Roberts each read several chapters and provided very useful comments on them. At a late stage in the making of the book, my student granddaughter Isobel Hollingsworth found several electronic sources that were proving elusive, and did so in a fraction of the time it would have taken me. Younger members of the family are not only a delight, but they come in awfully handy, I've discovered, for authors who grew up long before the arrival of personal computers.

It goes without saying that no one mentioned above should be blamed for any of the judgements and interpretations in my book. For these, and for any errors, I alone am responsible. Some of those whose names appear in these acknowledgements will doubtless find plenty to disagree with in what I have written; few, if any, will agree with every word.

Penultimately, it is a special pleasure to thank my literary agents and publishers. Writing a book is a solitary activity, but to publish it well is a collective enterprise. I am enormously grateful to Felicity Bryan and the outstanding team at Felicity Bryan Associates in Oxford (among whom I am especially obliged to Michele Topham). I am similarly indebted to George Lucas of the US agency, Inkwell, in New York. Both Felicity and George offered wise guidance at the book's earliest stage, heroic patience subsequently, and great support at the end. I have benefited a lot from the close reading of the manuscript by two editors: the American commissioning editor of the book, Tim Bent, for his many helpful suggestions (including those I appreciated more in retrospect than at first glance) and for his stimulating questions; and my British copy-editor, Jeremy Langworthy who, like Tim, has been a pleasure to work with and a true professional in his meticulous scrutiny of the text. In the Oxford building which houses OUP, major contributions have been made by Luciana O'Flaherty, my UK commissioning editor; Matthew Cotton, who has been in overall charge of the book at its British end; Kizzy Taylor-Richelieu who coordinated much of the work; Senior Production Editor Emma Slaughter; Senior Picture Researcher Deborah Protheroe; Marketing Manager Kate Roche; and Senior Publicist Kate Shepherd. I am also very grateful to Andrew Hawkey for his careful checking of the proofs and to Mike Parkin for compiling the thorough index.

Lastly, my biggest debt is to my wife Pat, not only for reading each chapter as soon as I produced it but, still more, for her encouragement, unfailing support in every possible way, and for putting up with the countless hundreds of hours I have spent immersed in research and writing. She is, I'm aware, even more relieved than I am that the end has been reached.

ARCHIE BROWN
Oxford

PICTURE CREDITS

INDEX

Abalkin, Leonid 319, 320
'Able Archer' NATO exercise (1983) 83–4,
    417–18 n. 73
Abrahamson, General James 201
Academy of Sciences, Soviet Union 252
Achalov, General Viktor 344
Acland, Anthony 114*, 117, 185
Adamishin, Anatoly 125, 175, 293, 410 n. 24,
    433 n. 35, 437–8 n. 5
Adelman, Ken 178, 179, 369
Afghanistan, Soviet invasion (1979) and
    occupation 24, 45–6, 49, 107, 140, 143–4,
    143*, 157–8, 206, 213, 381, 428 n. 31
  political settlement 152
  withdrawal from 221, 228, 236, 247, 257
African National Congress (ANC) 357, 358
Aganbegyan, Abel 56, 320
agriculture, Soviet Union 31, 41, 43, 47
Aitmatov, Chingiz 317
Akhromeyev, Marshal Sergey 175, 204, 207, 241,
    259, 268f, 270, 321, 324, 328, 333
  Chernobyl disaster 168
  conventional forces reduction 245
  German reunification and NATO
    membership 326
  INF Treaty 214, 215, 217, 297
  Reykjavik Summit (1986) 176, 177, 178–9,
    180, 181
  SDI 165
  suicide (1991) 369, 468 n. 98
Albania 20, 237
Aldous, Richard 421 n. 67
Alexandrov-Agentov, Andrey 49, 160
Alexandrova, Tamara 345
Aliev, Heidar 182, 123, 425 n. 50
Alksnis, Colonel Viktor 340
Allen, Richard 73, 74, 83
Allende, Salvador 218
Amann, Ronald 114*, 117–18, 192*, 423 n. 22
American Medical Association 65
Ames, Aldridge 203
Amin, Hafizullah 46
Anderson, John 68
Andreyeva, Nina, *Sovetskaya Rossiya* article
    (1988) 219–21, 225
Andropov, Yury 2, 39, 83, 86, 116, 117, 118, 123, 387,
    410 n. 11
  Afghanistan intervention 45, 46
  death and funeral (1984) 44, 122, 81, 81*
  expands Gorbachev's responsibilities 43–4,
    47, 387
Antiballistic Missile (ABM) Treaty (1972) 80,
    124–5, 132, 148, 181, 201, 216, 217, 228, 293–4,
    380, 394, 396
Arbatov, Georgy 55, 233, 410 n. 14
Armacost, Mike 202
Armageddon, Reagan's belief in 79, 416 n. 42,
    426 n. 44
Armenia 347, 358, 464 n. 2
  independence 372
Armenian earthquake (1988) 246
Armstrong, Robert 110, 121, 148, 438 n. 20
Attlee, Clement 13, 15, 63, 224
August coup (1991), Soviet Union 360, 361, 362–8,
    467 n. 74
  collapse and aftermath 368–9

Bacall, Lauren 62
Bahr, Egon 327
Bakatin, Vadim 339–40, 352, 366, 369
  appointed chairman of KGB 371
Baker, Howard 201, 222, 224
Baker, James 75, 76, 82, 83, 240, 254f, 307–8, 333,
    349, 354, 356, 358, 367, 385, 399, 415 n. 29
  contrasting views of 'hawks' and 'doves' on
    Soviet reforms 249
  criticism of strategic review of US foreign
    policy (1989) 249
  de-emphasizing arms negations with Soviet
    Union 251
  early views on Gorbachev and his intentions
    248, 249, 250–1
  German reunification and NATO membership
    280, 285, 324, 325–8, 472 n. 44
  Gorbachev meetings 249, 308
  Gorbachev's reforms 267–8, 282
  Gulf War 333
  Malta Summit (1989) 283–4
  Moscow visit (1989) 260, 267–70
  Shevardnadze meetings and relationship 251,
    268–9, 275, 308, 341, 402
  Thatcher relationship 239, 471 n. 30
Baklanov, Oleg 165, 296*, 297, 299, 344, 364, 366
Baltic republics 234, 254–5, 283, 464 n. 2; *see also*
    Estonia; Latvia; Lithuania
Barrass, Gordon 417–18 n. 73

Bay of Pigs attempted US invasion of Cuba
  (1961) 27*, 404 n. 1
BBC broadcasts to Soviet Union and Eastern
  Europe 116, 118, 423 n. 16
Beirut bombing (1983) 121
Belarus 154, 164, 167, 344
Belinsky, Vissarion 36, 408 n. 14
Bendix, Reinhard 435 n. 1
Beneš, Eduard 17
Berend, Ivan 331
Beria, Lavrenti 405 n. 13
Beriut, Boleslaw 13
Berlin, Isaiah 408 n. 14
Berlin blockade (1948–49) 17
Berlin Wall 209, 272
  fall of (1989) 2, 209–10, 279–81,279*f*, 313–14
Berlinguer, Enrico 49, 50
Bessmertnykh, Aleksandr 164–5, 212, 217, 229, 341,
  356, 358, 369, 466 n. 51
  becomes Foreign Minister 342
Best, Geoffrey 405 n. 8
Bethell, Nicholas 368
Bevin, Ernest 15, 63
Bialer, Seweryn 192, 193
Bishop, Maurice 121
Bishop, Tony 51, 53–4, 125
Blackwill, Robert 110
Blanton, Thomas 227, 452 n. 141, 460 n. 40
Bogart, Humphrey 62
Boldin, Valeriy 344
Bolshevik Revolution (1917) 10, 210
Bondarev, Yury 234–5, 360
Bonner, Elena 187, 197
Bourdeaux, Michael 114*, 118, 423–4 n. 22
Boyle, Edward 92
Bradley, Senator Bill 472 n. 45
Brady, Nicholas 349
Braithwaite, Rodric 45, 70, 260, 276, 304, 327, 358*f*,
  396, 396*, 465–6 n. 27, 466 n. 31
  Gorbachev's UN speech (1988) 245
  Shevardnadze-Howe relationship 261
  Thatcher-Gorbachev relationship 246, 258–9,
    350, 351, 400, 471 n. 28
  Thatcher's distrust of the Foreign Office 102
  and Yeltsin 316
Brandt, Willy 40, 142, 275, 327, 349, 385
  Ostpolitik 101
Breslauer, George 250
Brezhnev, Leonid 2, 39, 48, 71, 136, 159, 213, 214,
  238, 335, 376, 389
  Carter meeting (1979) 137
  death and funeral (1982) 43, 44, 288, 382
  Soviet invasion of Afghanistan 45
Brezhnev doctrine 200, 200*, 273, 274
Britain, *see* UK
Broomfield, Nigel 423 n. 22
Brown, Archie 114*, 192*, 425 n. 48, 457 n. 57
Brown, Edmond G. (Pat) 66
Brussels NATO Summit (1988) 223

Brzezinski, Zbigniew 20, 45, 158, 163
Buchanan, Pat 169
Buckley, William F. 64, 208
Bullard, Julian 423 n. 22
Bulgaria 10, 281
Bush, President George H. W. 68, 84, 122, 126, 133,
  158, 203, 213, 233, 247, 248–51, 269, 275, 307,
  334*f*, 335, 385
  4+2 (2+4) formula on German reunification
    323, 324, 330
  administration's Soviet policy, uncertain
    start 248–51
  August coup response (1991) 367
  Berlin Wall, fall of 280–1
  'Chicken Kiev' speech, (1991), Ukraine 359–60
  claim that the US 'won' the Cold War 392
  Cold War viewed as 'permanent' 305
  elected President 239
  'Europe whole and free' 270, 402
  European diplomacy (1989) 270–1
  European leaders urge meeting with Gorbachev
    (1989) 271, 272
  G7 summit (1991), London 353–4
  Gorbachev correspondence 271, 346
  Gorbachev meetings
    1985: Moscow 134
    1991: London 354
    1991: Novo-Ogarevo 355*f*, 356–8
    see also New York (1988), Malta
    (1989), Washington (1990, and Helsinki
    (1990) summits
  Gorbachev relationship 308, 309, 324, 354–9,
    401, 465 n. 11
  Gorbachev's support for Mandela 357–8
  Helsinki Summit with Gorbachev (1990) 333
  Kohl relationship 286, 286*, 313
  Malta Summit with Gorbachev (1989) 282, 284–7
  Mitterrand relationship 271, 286*
  Moscow summit with Gorbachev (1991) 356
  NSC meetings on Soviet Union and Eastern
    Europe (1989) 249
  refuses Gorbachev's loan request (1991) 349
  Shevardnadze meeting (1989) 282
  START agreement (1991) 356
  Thatcher meeting (1989), Camp David 283
  Thatcher relationship 239, 286*, 332, 471 n. 30
  Treaty on Conventional Armed Forces in
    Europe (CFE) 338
  Ukraine visit (1991) 354–6, 359–60
  wartime experience 34
  Washington and Camp David Summit with
    Gorbachev (1990) 326, 327–8
  Yeltsin meeting (1991) 349
Bush, President George W. 394, 395
Butler, Robin 14*, 99*f*, 125
Byrnes, James F. 15

Cadogan, Alexander 14
Callaghan, James 96, 98, 103–4, 420 n. 33

Cambodia, Communist regime 19
Canadian agriculture 47
Cannon, Lou 74, 83, 416 n. 59
Carlucci, Frank 186, 202, 210, 211, 222, 228, 241, 268f
    appointed Defense Secretary (1987) 208
    tussle with Shultz 200–1
Carrington, Lord (Peter) 98, 100, 102, 103
    resignation 104
Carter, President Jimmy 45, 68
    administration 108, 158
    Brezhnev meeting (1979) 137
    US-China relations 20
Cartledge, Bryan 114*, 146, 192–3, 192*, 196f, 198,
    400, 471 n. 28
Casey, William (Bill) 82, 84, 86, 156, 169, 208
Castro, Fidel 26, 27, 28, 142, 218, 262, 284, 357, 358,
    407 n. 56
Catholic Church 49 (and PCI, Italy), 278 (Poland)
Ceaușescu, Nicolae 237, 281
Central Committee (CC), Communist Party of the
    Soviet Union 31, 40, 43, 44, 47–8, 49, 54,
    159–60, 210, 225, 255, 350
    approval of draft party programme 361
    compulsory 'retirements' (1989) 265
    dissolution (1991) 372
    Gorbachev becomes General Secretary
       (1985) 133
    International Department 160, 162, 163, 175, 302
    Propaganda Department 163
    resistance to perestroika and reform 219–20
Central Economic-Mathematical Institute (TsEMI),
    Moscow 136
Central Europe, see Eastern and Central Europe
Centre for Policy Studies (CPS), UK 95
Chamberlain, Neville 13
Chambers, Whittaker 64
Channon, Paul 89f
Charter of Paris for a New Europe (1990)
    337–8, 395
Chayanov, Aleksandr 41
Chebrikov, Viktor 165, 176, 182, 293
chemical weapons 151, 157, 197, 212, 223, 228, 261, 262
    finding locations for destruction 358
Cheney, Dick 251, 269, 282, 445 n. 77
Chernenko, Konstantin 1, 2, 31, 43, 44, 49, 50,
    56–7, 81, 81*, 86, 117, 122, 131, 289, 300,
    425 n. 47, 425 n. 50
    illness, death and funeral 47, 132, 133–4, 382
Chernobyl nuclear power station accident
    (1986) 154, 164–5, 167–9, 434 n. 69
Chernyaev, Anatoly 170, 199, 199f, 225, 229, 276,
    285, 292, 302, 324, 335, 338, 393, 401,
    412 n. 52, 448 n. 28, 466 n. 51
    appointed foreign policy advisor to
       Gorbachev 160–1, 163, 265
    August 1991 coup 363–4, 365
    Gorbachev-Thatcher relationship 197, 200,
       259–60, 263, 471 n. 28
    Gorbachev's UN speech (1988) 244

International Department, Central
    Committee 162
Malta Summit (1989) 284, 286–7
Moscow Summit (1988) 219
perestroika and New Thinking 211, 253
Reykjavik Summit (1986) 173–82
SDI development 165
trust 217
undelivered letter of resignation (1991) 345
vacations with Gorbachev 173
Chervov, General Nikolay 411 n. 38
Chiang Kai-shek 17, 18
China:
    civil war (1945–49) 17–18
    Communists 11, 18
    Cultural Revolution 20
    Gorbachev's visit (1989) 266–7
    interest in Soviet perestroika 266, 266*
    marketizing reforms and opening to the
       world 298
    nuclear missiles 172
    Sino-Soviet split 19
    US relations (1970s) 19–20
Chiraq, Jacques 454 n. 7
Churchill, Winston 10, 14, 92, 109, 404–5 n. 7,
    405 n. 8, 405 n. 10
    Comintern dissolution 11
    election defeat (1945) 13
    iron curtain speech, Fulton, Missouri
       (1946) 109, 244
    iron curtain term 13, 15
    Poland's post-war frontiers 10, 11–12, 13
    spheres of influence in post-war Europe
       10–11
    and Stalin 3, 13, 14
    Yalta conference (1945) 12, 13
CIA (Central Intelligence Agency), US 73, 156, 187,
    201, 203
    disputes over Gorbachev's reforms 249
    intelligence before Reykjavik Summit 177–8
    perception of Soviet Union 169–70
    spy scandal (1986) 172–3
    see also Casey, William; Gates, Robert M.
Clark, William 67, 73, 74, 79, 80, 82, 83, 105, 106,
    381, 382
Cleaver, Margaret 60
Clinton, President Bill 392, 393, 394*
    NATO enlargement 396, 472 n. 45
COCOM (Co-ordinating Committee for
    Multilateral Export Controls) 356, 356*
Cold War:
    Bush, contribution to ending 400, 401–2
    claims that the US 'won' 290–1, 392, 454 n. 2
    dangers of 9–31, 57
    'democratic values' and East-West convergence
       290–1
    economic and technological arguments for
       ending 4, 290
    end-date 1–2, 286–7, 313, 313*

engagement, significance of 380–6
Gorbachev, contribution to ending 306–7,
398–402
Gorbachev's views on (1984) 52–3
leadership and ideas in Cold War's ending
291–9, 378–402
missile attack false alarms and computer
malfunctions 28–9
origins 9–10, 10–14
Reagan administration's increased military
spending 288–9
Reagan, contribution to ending 290, 306–7,
397–402
Thatcher, contribution to ending 290, 308,
397–402
why it ended when it did 288–309
Coles, John 111, 113–14, 113*, 114*, 118–19, 120, 383,
422 n. 9, 424 n. 33
Colton, Timothy J. 459 n. 21
Comecon (Council for Mutual Economic
Assistance) 21
disbanding (1991) 348
Cominform (Communist Information
Bureau) 20–1
Comintern, dissolution 11
Commission on Military-Industrial Issues,
Soviet Union 132
Committee on the Present Danger, US 67
'common European home,' Gorbachev's concept
of 145, 270, 273, 282, 298, 349, 402
Commonwealth of Independent States (CIS)
creation (1991) 374–5
Communism:
in Asia 17–20
compromise with Catholicism in
Italy 49
Czechoslovakian 15, 17, 36, 55, 281
ending in Hungary 281
ending in Poland 267
takeover of Eastern Europe 15–17
transformation of 4, 88, 134, 163, 219*, 261, 265,
276–81, 287, 288, 295, 318, 343, 392, 417 n. 63,
452 n. 41
Communist Party of Great Britain 262
Communist Party of the Soviet Union (CPSU) 31,
33–4, 36, 37, 38, 49, 160, 249, 252, 266,
290, 352
beginnings of reform 136
bypassed in 9+1 talks 348
ceases to exist (1991) 372
conservative Communism's lowest point 370,
370*
declining status (1990) 316
democratizing reforms 117, 266, 362
differing views within 135, 136, 252, 290, 291,
316, 328, 339
establishing a Communist world order
not a policy goal, post-Khrushchev
135

Gorbachev, growing opposition to (1989) 293,
339, 364–5
'leading role' of 265, 316, 460 n. 293
Nineteenth Party Conference (1988):
decision on contested elections 236
glasnost resolution 235–6
ideological change 219, 225–6, 234–5,
236, 252
'theses' for 224–5
nomenklatura system 235
power transferred to Soviet state 265, 460 n. 33
Party Congresses:
Twentieth (1956) 21, 33, 39–40
Twenty-Second (1961) 39
Twenty-Seventh (1986) 144, 158, 159, 163, 164
Twenty-Eighth (1990) 320–1
see also August coup (1991), Soviet
Union; Central Committee (CC),
Communist Party of the Soviet
Union; Politburo, Soviet Union
Conference on Security and Co-operation in
Europe (CSCE) 299, 337–8, 337*, 397
Conflict Prevention Centre, Vienna 338
Congress of People's Deputies, Soviet Union 316
elections (1989) 252, 254–5, 277
parliamentary debate 256
Politburo views on elections 255–6
reserved seats 255
Conquest, Robert 95, 96, 102, 192*, 193, 439 n. 31
Conservative Party, UK 1, 13, 92, 93, 96, 98, 100,
104, 109
election success 96, 98, 111, 113
Brighton bombing (1984) 127
Euroscepticism 95
women prime ministers 92*, 96
Conventional Forces in Europe (CFE) talks (1989),
Vienna 268
Council of Ministers, Soviet Union 39, 44, 45, 123,
132, 163, 167, 265, 322, 329; see also Ryzhkov,
Nikolay
Cradock, Percy 3, 111, 119–20, 157, 185, 191–2, 192*,
197, 330*, 383, 386, 399, 424 n. 33
Craig, Gordon 330*, 461–2 n. 24
Craxi, Bettino 142
Crimea, viewed as Russian territory 373
Crowe, Admiral William (Bill) 178, 183, 201, 241,
321, 369
Crozier, Brian 95–6, 412 n. 42
cruise missiles 72, 171, 189, 241
deployment in Western Europe 73, 198
Cuba 21, 75, 282, 284
Bay of Pigs invasion (1961) 27*, 404 n. 1
Cuban missile crisis (1962) 24–8, 30, 84, 407 n. 55
Cuban Revolution 289
Cultural Revolution, China 20
Czechoslovakia 4, 101*
Communist Party 15, 17, 36, 55, 200*, 281
Communist takeover (1948) 15, 17
Marshall Plan 17

Czechoslovakia (*Contd.*)
  Prague Spring and Soviet invasion (1968) 15, 23,
    41–2, 49, 107, 274
  'velvet revolution' (1989) 281

Dallin, Alexander 453 n. 1
Daniloff, Nicholas 172
Davis, Loyal 63
de Gaulle, Charles 272
de Klerk, F. W. 358
de Tocqueville, Alexis 276
Deas, Malcolm 103*
Deaver, Michael (Mike) 67, 75, 77, 82, 83
Defense Department, US 138, 169, 187
  deployment of Pershing and Cruise missiles 74
  differences with State Department 73, 77, 76, 81,
    201, 381
  reaction to Gorbachev's aim to eliminate
    nuclear weapons by 2000 155–6
  SDI 141, 148, 150, 294
  UK Trident deal 103
  see also Carlucci, Frank; Cheney,
    Dick; Weinberger, Caspar
DeGroot, Gerard 28
Delors, Jacques 240
'democratic centralism', Soviet Union 252, 398
Democratic Party, US 22, 66, 82, 183, 224, 381
  Democrats in Congress favouring dialogue 381
'Democratic Russia' demonstration (1991) 345–6
Deng Xiaoping 266–7, 298, 366
Directive No. 75 (NSDD-75), National Security
  Council, US 78
Disciples of Christ Church, US 60
Dobrynin, Anatoly 86, 147–8, 165, 174f, 190, 199,
  202, 204, 293, 302, 422 n. 12
  appointed head of International
    Department 160, 161–2, 162*
  early attitudes to Gorbachev 54–5, 207, 412 n. 43
  Reagan's policies and Soviet reaction 81, 292
  SDI 80
  secret negotiations with Robert Kennedy 26
Dodds, Norman 93
Dole, Robert (Bob) 216
Dolgikh, Vladimir 167, 265
Donnelly, Christopher 114*, 192*
Douglas-Home, Alec 94, 94*, 96
Dubček, Alexander 23, 281
Dubinin, Yury 204
Dukakis, Michael 246
Dulles, John Foster 22
Dunaev, Aleksandr 165
Dyachenko, Tatiana 394*

Eagleburger, Lawrence 110, 282, 283, 332
East Germany, *see* German Democratic Republic
  (GDR)
Eastern and Central Europe:
  change and unrest (1947–56) 20–4
  communist takeovers 15–17

'creeping stagnation' (early 1980s) 117–18
dismantling of Communist regimes 4, 287
Gorbachev's hope for evolutionary change 274
Malta Summit understanding 285
Thatcher's diplomacy (1988) 237–40
transformation of (1989) 247–8, 276–81
see also individual states
economy and economic reform (Soviet
  Union) 55–6, 57, 177, 213*, 301–2, 373–4
Eden, Anthony 14
Eisenhower, President Dwight D. 67, 132
  Suez crisis (1956) 22
Eisenhower, Susan 472 n. 45
Elizabeth II, Queen 121
  Gorbachev meeting (1989) 262, 263
  Reagan meeting (1982) 109
Engels, Friedrich 400
English, Robert D. 427 n. 18, 454 n. 9
Ermath, Fritz 73, 208, 249
Estonia 344, 345, 347, 354
  independence 372
Eureka College, Illinois 60–1
'Eurocommunists' 40, 49
'Europe whole and free,' Bush formulation 270,
  402, 450–1 n. 110
European Environment Agency (EFA) 338
European Union (formerly European Economic
  Community) 94, 273
Evans, Robert 419 n. 29

Falin, Valentin 163, 259, 285, 302, 321, 324, 326–7,
  327*, 328–9, 401
Falklands War (1982) 98, 103–6, 110, 111, 121, 197
Federal Bureau of Investigation (FBI), US 62, 83,
  172, 203
Federation Council (created 1990), Soviet
  Union 316, 317
Fedorov, Rafael 324
Fergusson, Ewen 273
First Motion Picture Unit, US 62
Fitzgerald, Frances 131
Fogel, Hans-Jochen 266
Foot, Michael 104, 109
Ford, President Gerald 67, 68, 97
Foreign and Commonwealth Office (FCO/FO),
  UK 95, 101–2, 104, 111, 113, 120, 123, 260
  Chequers seminar (1983) 114–15, 117, 423 n. 22
  new policy on the Soviet Union and East
    Europe (1983) 113*, 118, 119
  Thatcher's distrust of 101, 102–3, 114, 120, 195
  see also Howe, Geoffrey; Hurd, Douglas
Foros, Black Sea coast 363
France:
  French nuclear weapons excluded from INF
    negotiations 297
  Gorbachev, engagement with 145, 147, 273
  INF fears before Moscow Summit
    (1988) 223
  Suez crisis (1956) 22

and Vietnam 18
see also Mitterrand, President François
Frank, Peter 192*
Freedman, Lawrence 125*
Friedman, Thomas 397
Frolov, Ivan 225, 226, 226*, 259, 361

G7 economic summits:
London (1991) 351, 353–4
Versailles (1982) 105, 106, 109
Gaddafi, Muammar 357, 358, 367
Gaddis, John Lewis 305
Gaidar, Yegor 295, 319
Gale, Robert 169
Galtieri, General Leopoldo 106
Garton Ash, Timothy 330*, 462 n. 74
Garvey, Terence 419 n. 17
Gates, Robert 73, 76, 152*, 156, 169, 208, 245, 292, 332, 462 n. 84
scepticism about change in the Soviet
Union 249, 282, 445 n. 77
Gati, Charles 406 n. 45
General Agreement on Tariffs and Trade (GATT)
talks 284
General Electric Theater 63–4
General Secretaryship of CC of CPSU 159*, 179, 190, 221, 283, 291–2, 371, 450 n. 84
Geneva arms control discussions (restarted 1985) 131
Geneva chemical weapons talks (1986) 157
Geneva Protocol on Chemical Weapons 148
Geneva Summit (1985) 5, 149–53
joint declaration 151
Genscher, Hans-Dietrich 223, 286, 329f
ruling out NATO expanding eastwards 325–8
Georgia 343, 347, 375*
independence 372
German Democratic Republic (GDR) 278–81, 281*, 314, 348
and Berlin Wall fall 314
Soviet troops stationed in 313
workers strike (1953) 23
German reunification (1990) 21, 313, 322–33, 458 n. 5, 460 n. 41, 461 n. 67, 462 n. 84
Gorbachev and 4+2 (2+4) formula on talks 323, 324, 330
Kohl's Bundestag speech 285–6
and Malta Summit (1989) 285–6
NATO membership 325–8, 328–9
Thatcher and 240, 285, 323, 330–3
Germany, Federal Republic of (FRG) 150, 240, 247, 348, 349
Gorbachev's popularity 271, 272, 290
NATO membership (1955) 21, 325–8, 328–9
US nuclear missile deployment 73
Giraud, André 223
Giscard d'Estaing, Valery 267
glasnost (transparency) 4, 56, 136, 168, 188, 198, 199, 220, 230, 232, 235–6, 275, 282, 390
Goldman, Marshall 300

Goldwater, Barry 65, 67
Gomułka, Władysław 21–2
González, Felipe 224, 274f, 275, 278, 331, 374, 385
response to August coup (1991) 367
Goodall, David 428 n. 36
Gopkalo, Panteley (Gorbachev's maternal
grandfather) 31, 34
arrest 32, 35
Gopkalo, Vasilisa (Gorbachev's maternal
grandmother) 33, 34
Gorbachev, Aleksandr (Mikhail's brother) 32
Gorbachev, Andrey (Mikhail's paternal
grandfather) 31
arrest 32, 35
Gorbachev, Mikhail 1, 31–57, 60, 71, 90, 108, 120, 122, 164, 199f, 204, 217, 255, 274f, 277, 277f, 288, 347, 350, 358f, 387, 393, 428–9 n. 31, 466 n. 27
4+2 (2+4) formula on German reunification
323, 324, 330
9+1 talks (1991) 348
achievements 390, 391–2, 398
Afghanistan 143–4, 150, 221, 228, 257, 428 n. 31
amateur dramatics 35
appointment of hard-liners (1990) 339–40, 371
appointment of vice-president (1990) 342
armed forces cuts 241–2, 245, 251
assassination attempt during November parade
(1990) 339
August coup (1991) 344, 362–8, 371
Baker meeting (1989), Moscow 249
Baku killings 464 n. 2
becoming CPSU general secretary and Soviet
leader (1985) 1, 31, 57, 58, 132–4
becoming President of Soviet Union 316–18
Berlin Wall 209–10, 272, 280–1
belief change 57, 303–4, 305–6, 319, 384
break-up of Soviet Union and creation of the
CIS 375
Bush, administration's scepticism of 248–9
Bush meetings:
1985: Moscow 134
1991: London 354
1991: Novo-Ogarevo 355f, 356–8
Bush relationship 308, 309, 324
Bush, Soviet loan request to (1991) 349
and Bush's Ukraine visit (1991) 354–6, 359–60
Canada visit (1983) 47–9
CC meetings with provincial leaders (1988) 225
character 36, 53–4, 204, 217, 305, 411 n. 38
Chernobyl accident, impact on 164–5, 434 n. 69
childhood and family background 31–3
China visit (1989) 266–7
Cold War, contribution to ending 291–9, 398–402
'common European home' 145, 270, 273, 282, 298, 349, 402
compulsory 'retirements' from Central
Committee (1989) 265
Conference on Security and Co-operation in
Europe (CSCE, Paris (1990) 338

Gorbachev, Mikhail (*Contd.*)
Congress of People's Deputies, criticism from 256
Czechoslovakia visits (1969/87) 41–2, 274–5
December innovative speech (1984) 55–7
democratization 187, 188–90, 218–19, 225, 261
draft party programme (1991) 361–2
early attitude to Soviet system 36–7
Eastern Europe, proposes withdrawal of tactical nuclear weapons 370
'ecological/green' concerns 243, 358–9, 400
economic policy and reforms 55–6, 162–3, 192, 213*, 229–30, 259, 265–6, 295–6, 300–2, 319–20, 433 n. 40, 452 n. 134, 456 n. 37, 456–7 n. 39
European diplomacy (1989) 264–7, 271–6
'freedom of choice' 1, 236–7, 243, 247–8, 267–8, 274, 287, 291, 385
G7, meetings with leaders (1991), London 353–4, 354*
Geneva Summit with Reagan (1985) 5, 144, 149–53, 384
German reunification and NATO membership 324, 325–8, 328–9, 458 n. 5
Gromyko replaced by Shevardnadze 138–40
Guildhall speech (1989), London 261–2
Helsinki Final Act (1975), support for 243–4
Helsinki Summit with Bush (1990) 333
independence movements and nationalism in Soviet republics 54, 315, 318, 343–8, 372, 373, 459 n. 18
institutchiki, influence of 163–4
International Forum speech, Moscow (1987) 188–9
Italy visit (1984) 49–50
Japan visit (1991) 349
John Paul II meeting (1989) 271
Kohl meetings 271–3, 328–9, 329f*
Kohl relationship 290, 286, 313, 461 n. 67
Komsomol and Communist Party promotions 37, 38–40
leadership, power and ideas 291–9
literature, reading of 40–1
Lithuania customs attack (1991) 357
Malta Summit with Bush (1989) 282, 284–7
Mandela, support for 357–8
MFA speech on evils of arms race (1986) 166
Middle East conference (1991), Madrid 373–4
military and party opposition to Gorbachev's defence policies 293, 299–300
Mitterrand relationship 144–5, 170, 273, 323f, 468 n. 88
Moscow Summit with Reagan (1988) 219, 222, 225, 226–33, 227f
Moscow summit with Bush (1991) 356
Moscow University 35, 36–8, 57
NATO expansion eastwards 325–8, 396–7, 472 n. 44

Nineteenth Party Conference (1988) 224–5
Nixon meeting (1986) 170
Nobel Peace Prize (1990) 305, 335, 463 n. 98
Novo-Ogarevo process 373
nuclear weapon elimination by year 2000 aspiration 154–5, 175, 260, 261–2
opinion on 216, 290, 307, 315, 350, 389–90, 465–6 n. 27, 471 n. 31
Order of Red Banner of Labour 35
Pavlov's attempt to curb powers 352, 353
'peaceful coexistence' 229, 307
Perestroika: New Thinking for Our Country and the World 211, 212, 253
Politburo, promotion to and within 43–4
Politburo relationship 232–3, 255–6, 322, 339
political thinking, evolution of 31, 37–8, 42, 55–7, 247, 252–7
Primakov's mission to Saddam Hussein 334–5
Reagan correspondence 136–7, 146–7, 151–2, 153, 211–12
Reagan relationship 134–5, 182, 217, 269, 387–8
referendum on future of the union (1991) 347–8
reforming agenda 1, 4, 48, 158–67, 159*, 206–7, 234–7
resignation (1991) 372, 376–7
resignation threat (1991) 350
Reykjavik Summit with Reagan (1986) 173–82, 174f, 182–3, 294
Russian parliament appearance after failed coup 370–1
Sakharov relationship 187–8
and SDI 150, 151–2, 153, 180–1, 189–90, 293–4
Shevardnadze, attempt to dissuade him from resigning 341
short-range missiles in Europe 270
Shultz relationship 204–6, 211, 394
social democracy 226, 266, 275, 298, 300, 361, 408 n. 17, 471 n. 20
socialism radically re-defined 275, 384–5
Soviet relations with other Communist states 166–7
SS-20 missiles, halting deployment in Europe 142
and Stalin's crimes 40*
START signing (1991) 356
Stavropol years 38–42
Strasbourg speech to the Council of Europe (1989) 273
Tbilsi killings, Georgia (1989) 264
Thatcher correspondence 145, 147, 149, 463 n. 103
Thatcher meetings
1984: Chequers 5, 50–2, 53, 88, 89f, 124–5, 126, 191
1985 Moscow 133–4
1987: Brize Norton 212–13, 440 n. 50
1987: Moscow 195–200
1989: London 259–60

1989: Moscow 275–6, 451–2 n. 134
  1991: Moscow 350–1
Thatcher relationship 95, 125, 191, 195*, 197, 198,
  199–200, 258–63, 388–9, 463 n. 103
Tiananmen Square massacre 267, 273
Treaty on Conventional Armed Forces in
  Europe (CFE) 338
Trilateral Commission discussion (1989) 267
Twentieth Congress of CPSU, impact on 39–40
UK and French nuclear weapons excluded from
  INF negotiations 176, 297
UK visit (1984) 5, 47, 50–5, 57, 88, 89f, 123–5,
  126, 191
UK visit (1989) 259–63
Ukrainian independence 372
UN speech (1988) 1, 219, 241–5, 242f, 247
Union Treaty 301, 343, 348, 353, 356–7, 359,
  362–3, 374, 391
unpublished book manuscript 253–4, 443 n. 4,
  448 n. 28
US, reluctance on verification 228
'use of force ... has become historically
  obsolete' 237
wartime experiences 33–4, 58, 124
Washington Summit with Bush (1990) 326, 327–8
Washington Summit with Reagan (1987) 210,
  213–17, 215f
West European visits (1970s) 42
Western influence and power 40–1, 200, 302–9
Yakovlev, relationship 48–9, 137
and Yeltsin 210, 211, 319–20, 352
zero options and nuclear disarmament 11, 72–3,
  74, 155, 178, 184, 211, 215–16, 223, 337
see also glasnost, New Thinking; perestroika;
  political pluralism
Gorbachev, (née Titarenko) Raisa 32, 34*, 36, 38,
  41, 89f, 151, 164, 259, 260, 277f, 366
  death of 468 n. 83
  marriage to Mikhail 37
  Reykjavik Summit (1986) 179
  UK visit (1984) 53
Gorbachev, Sergey (Mikhail's father) 32, 33, 35
Gorbachev Foundation 284, 475–6
Gorbacheva, Maria (née Gopkalo) (Mikhail's
  mother) 32, 34
Gordievsky, Oleg 83–4, 116, 124, 190, 417–18 n. 73
  defection 146
Gosplan (State Planning Committee), Soviet
  Union 162, 295
Grachev, Andrei 139, 207, 363, 374
Graham, Billy 73
Granada, US intervention (1983) 120–1, 424 n. 41,
  425 n. 43
Greece 10, 11
Grinevsky, Oleg 299
Grishin, Viktor 123, 133, 294
Gromov, General Boris 360, 361
Gromyko, Aleksey 428 n. 26
Gromyko, Anatoly 293, 455 n. 22

Gromyko, Andrei 2, 44, 45, 46–7, 50, 54–5, 80,
  81*, 86, 117, 123, 144–5, 160, 161, 167, 220,
  256, 265, 299, 304, 410 n. 24, 412 n. 43,
  428 n. 26, 434 n. 66, 455 n. 22
  Geneva arms control discussion restarted
    (1985) 131
  meeting with Reagan (1984) 87
  replaced by Shevardnadze (1985) 138–9
  and SDI 182, 190
GRU (Soviet military intelligence), RYAN
  operation 84
Guantánamo Bay naval base, US 26
Guerrero, Gil 158
Gulag Archipelago, The (Solzhenitsyn) 135
Gulf War 314–15, 335, 347, 349, 353–4
Gurenko, Stanislav 322
Guterres, Antonio 394–5

Haig, Alexander 52f, 70, 73, 105, 106*, 215, 381, 382
  bombing Cuba threat 75, 415 n. 22
  Communist subversion in Latin America 75
  resignation 76, 106
  zero option policy, opposition to 72–3, 74
Hanssen, Robert 203
Harriman, Averell 15
Harris, Kenneth 379
Harris, Robin 95, 100, 240
Hart, Senator Gary 183, 381, 470 n. 13, 472 n. 45
Hartman, Arthur 203
Haslam, Jonathan 456 n. 33
Havel, Václav 281, 396
Hayek, Friedrich von 64, 94, 379
Healey, Denis 53, 122, 224
  on Gorbachev's achievements 391
Heath, Edward 94, 96
Hegel, Georg Wilhelm Friedrich 36–7
Hellman, Joel 438 n. 7
Helsinki Final Act (1975) 20, 96–7, 148, 150, 196,
  243–4, 285, 326, 406 n. 38
Heritage Foundation, US 381
Hesburgh, Theodore 73
Heseltine, Michael 89f, 99f, 110, 114*, 116, 336,
  337, 382–3
  Thatcher relationship 115, 115*
Heston, Charlton 208
Hill, Charles 446 n. 96
Hinckley, John, assassination attempt on
  Reagan 71
Hirohito, Emperor 14
Hiroshima nuclear attack (1945) 14
Hitler, Adolf 16, 30
Hmong people, Laos 19
Ho Chi Minh 18
Hodges, Joy 61
Hodgkin, Dorothy 91
Hoffman, David E. 262
'Hollywood Ten' 63
Honecker, Erich 209, 278–9, 314
Hong Kong 125

Horowitz, Lawrence 87, 202
Hoskyns, John 100, 110, 420 n. 45
House of Representatives Un-American Activities
    Committee 62
Howard, Edward Lee 203
Howard, Michael 192*
Howe, Geoffrey 96, 99f, 111, 113, 122, 123–4, 125, 133,
    138, 157, 185, 276, 386*, 387, 399–400
  Chequers seminar on East-West relations
    (1983) 114*, 115*, 117, 119, 191
  demotion to Leader of the House of
    Commons 261
  East-West dialogue 113, 115, 115*, 119, 157, 382
  Gorbachev's UK visit (1984) 50, 51, 53, 89f
  INF 'zero option', view on 184
  KAL 007 destruction 116, 422–3 n. 12
  report on Gorbachev's 1989 London visit 262–3
  resignation and speech to Parliament
    (1990) 140, 261, 336
  RUSI speech on SDI (1985) 140–1
  Shevardnadze relationship 140, 260–1
  Thatcher relationship 105, 240, 388, 429 n. 36,
    463 n. 102
  Thatcher's Soviet visit (1987) 194–5
  visits to Warsaw Pact countries (1984–85) 119
Hryniov, Volodymyr 368
Hugo, Victor 273, 298
human rights 20, 85, 204, 213, 238
  Geneva Summit (1985) 150
  Helsinki Final Act (1975) 20, 97, 146, 150, 244
  Moscow Summit (1988) 227
  Reykjavik Summit (1986) 180
Hungary 10, 56, 119, 125*, 255, 271
  Communization 11
  fall of Communist regime 281
  following Stalin's death 21, 22
  radical change (1989) 278
  Revolution and Soviet invasion (1956) 22, 23, 39,
    107, 276
  Thatcher's visit (1984) 119, 122
Hunt, John 98
Hurd, Douglas 316, 337, 462 n. 75
  Chequers seminar on German reunification
    (1990) 330–2
  Kohl relationship 330
Husák, Gustáv 101*

Ignatenko, Vitaly 346
IMEMO 48, 50, 136, 137, 163, 433 n. 43
Institute of Economics and Organization of
    Industrial Production of Siberian
    Academy of
    Sciences 136
Institute of Economics of the World Socialist
    System ('Bogomolov institute'), Soviet 136
Institute of Europe, Soviet Academy of
    Sciences 200
inter-continental ballistic missiles (ICBMs) 171–2,
    176, 177, 181

Intermediate-Range Nuclear Force (INF) Treaty
    (1987) 87, 205, 210, 211, 214, 270, 294, 396
  European government fears of US denucleari-
    zation 222
  ratification by US Senate 222, 225
  signing 215*, 215–16, 217
  UK and French nuclear weapons excluded from
    INF negotiations 297
  US withdrawal from (2019) 394–5
International Department of the Central
    Committee, CPSU 160, 161–2, 162*
International Monetary Fund (IMF) 346
Iran-Contra Affair 152, 185–6, 202
Iranian government of Mossadeq overthrown
    (1953) 218
Iraq, invasion of Kuwait 333–5; see also Gulf War
Irish Republican Army (IRA), Brighton bombing
    (1984) 127
Israel, war with Egypt (1956) 22
Italian Communist Party (PCI) 49–50
Izvestiya 258, 259

Jackling, Roger 110–11
Japan 14, 349
Jaruzelski, Barbara 277f
Jaruzelski, General Wojciech 24, 107, 238, 267, 271,
    272, 277f, 278
Jenkins, Roy 111
John Brown Engineering, Glasgow 107–8, 109
John Paul II, Pope 4, 188, 271, 297
Johnson, President Lyndon B. 19, 23, 65
Joint Chiefs of Staff, US, reaction to Reykjavik
    Summit (1986) 183
Jopling, Michael 89f
Joseph, Keith 92, 94, 95, 379
Juan Carlos, King 374

Kádár, János 21
Kahneman, Daniel 29–30
KAL 007, destruction of (1983) 28, 83, 115–16,
    422 n. 12
Kalugin, General Oleg 371
Kampelman, Max 131, 202
Karagodina, Yulia 35
Karasev, Valentin 448 n. 25
Karmal, Babrak 46, 144
Karpov, Viktor 175, 212
Kaser, Michael 114*, 125*, 422 n. 9
Kataev, Vitaly 214
Katyn forest massacre, Smolensk (1940) 12
Kaye, Danny 62
Kazakhstan 357
Kechekyan, Stepan 37, 37*
Kennan, George 15, 302–3, 396–7, 402
  'Long Telegram' (1946) 16, 393
Kennedy, Senator Edward (Ted) 202, 381
Kennedy, President John F. 30, 64, 272
  Cuban missile crisis (1962) 25–7, 30, 407 n. 55
  support for South Vietnamese regime 19

Kennedy, Robert 26
Kershaw, Anthony 123, 425 n. 53
KGB, Soviet Union 39, 44, 45, 46, 135, 146, 159, 160,
    204–5, 206, 346, 353
  Bakatin succeeds Kryuchkov as Chairman 371
  and the new political environment (1989) 252–3
  Novo-Ogarevo bugging 357
  RYAN operation 84
  spy scandal (August 1986) 172–3
  support for August 1991 coup against
    Gorbachev 344, 370
  see also Chebrikov, Viktor; Kryuchkov,
    Vladimir; NKVD, Soviet Union
Khmer Rouge 19
Khrushchev, Nikita 21, 24, 29, 33, 53, 65, 213, 255,
    267, 373, 376
  Cuban missile crisis (1962) 24–7, 407 n. 55
  and Gomułka 21–2
  and the Hungarian uprising (1956) 22
  'Secret Speech' with Stalin revelations (1956)
    21, 39
  U-2 spy plane 28
Kim Il-sung 18
Kingdon, John W. 455 n. 28
Kings Row (1942 film) 62
Kinnock, Neil 122, 202*, 262
Kirkpatrick, Jeane 82–3, 105, 106, 106*, 178,
    417 n. 62, 417 n. 63
Kissinger, Henry 97, 163, 208, 215, 222, 228,
    267, 307
  US-China policy 18–20
Knute Rockne, All American (1940 film) 62
Kohl, Helmut 3, 187, 260
  Berlin Wall fall (1989) 280
  Bundestag speech on German reunification
    284–5
  Bush relationship 272, 286, 313
  German reunification and membership of
    NATO 324–5, 326–7
  German reunification and vulnerability of
    Gorbachev's position 323, 324, 328–9
  Gorbachev meetings
    1989: West Germany 271–3
    1990: Arkhyz 328–9, 329f
  Gorbachev relationship 286, 290, 313, 461 n. 67
  Hurd relationship 330
  ruling out NATO expanding eastwards
    325–8
  Thatcher relationship 194, 330, 332
  wartime experience 34
Koldunov, Aleksandr 207
Komsomol (Young Communist League), Soviet
    Union 35, 37, 38
Kondratev, Nikolay 41
Korean War (1950–53) 18
  death toll 18
Korn, David 429 n. 51
Kornienko, Georgy 149, 162*, 422 n. 12
Kosolapov, Richard 56, 163

Kosygin, Aleksey 39, 45, 46
Kovalev, Anatoly 50, 174, 176, 196f, 410 n. 24,
    464 n. 98
Kovalev, Andrei 437–8 n. 5
Kozyrev, Andrey 349
Kramer, Mark 452 n. 141
Krasnoyarsk radar facility 171, 228
Kravchuk, Leonid 359, 368, 374, 468 n. 93
  9+1 talks (1991) 348
Krenz, Egon 279, 280
Kruchina, Oleg 364, 364*
Kryuchkov, Vladimir 257, 299–300, 320, 324, 339,
    344, 352, 357
  attack on Yakovlev 353
  August coup (1991) 253*, 362, 366, 370*
  becomes head of KGB (1988) 221, 244f, 252–3
  Gorbachev 'treasonous' 253*, 296*
  KGB Novo-Ogarevo bugging 357
  letter of apology vs. real feelings about
    Gorbachev 253*
Kulakov, Fedor 43
Kurile Islands 349

Labour Party, UK 13, 53, 95, 98, 100, 104, 109, 112
  and nuclear disarmament 185
  SDP split 111–12
Lance II missiles, US 214
Landsbergis, Vytautas 318, 344
Laos Communist regime 19
Laptev, Ivan 234, 236, 258, 443 n. 3
Lardner, Jr, Ring 63
Latsis, Otto 363
Latvia 41, 255, 344, 345, 347, 354
  independence (1991) 372
Lawson, Nigel 330*
Leach, Admiral Henry 104
Lebanon terrorist bombing (1983) 84
Legasov, Valeriy 434–5 n. 70
Legvold, Robert 394
LeMay, General Curtis E. 25, 407 n. 55
Lenczowski, John 88
Lenin, Vladimir 31, 36, 253–4
Levada, Yury 38
Lévesque, Jacques 275, 452 n. 141
Liberal Democrats, UK 95
Liberal Party, UK 112
Ligachev, Yegor 160, 168, 190, 210, 219–21, 220*,
    235, 236, 255, 434 n. 69
Likhachev, Dmitry 318
Limited Test Ban Treaty 148
Lithuania 118, 255, 344, 347, 354
  customs attack (1991) 356–7
  demand for sovereignty 321
  independence (1991) 372
  Sajudis nationalist movement 318
  Soviet security forces attack (1991),
    Vilnius 344–5, 346
Llewellyn Smith, Michael 192, 439 n. 27
Los Angeles Olympic Games, Soviet boycott 87

Lukin, Vladimir 465 n. 17
Lukyanov, Anatoly 352, 366
Lwów (Lviv) 376

MacEachin, Douglas 249
Mackintosh, Malcolm 114*, 439 n. 27
Macmillan, Harold 92, 94, 209
    and Cuban missile crisis (1962) 26
Maisky, Ivan 13
Major, John 330*, 337, 353, 354*
    response to August coup (1991) 367
Makashov, General Albert 164
Mallaby, Christopher 272, 332–3, 438 n. 20
Malta Summit (1989) 271, 282–7
Mamardashvili, Merab 38
Mandela, Nelson 98, 357–8
Manhattan Project, US 14
Mann, James 457 n. 58
Mann, Thomas 330
Manning, David 423 n. 22
Mao Zedong 17–18, 19–20
Marshall, General George 16
Marshall Plan 16–17
Marx, Karl 36, 64–5, 400
Marxism-Leninism 1, 36, 49, 109, 243, 249
Masaryk, Jan 17
Massie, Suzanne 86–7, 147, 202
Matlock, Jack F. 83, 85, 147, 155, 168, 172, 204–5,
        208, 211, 229, 234, 254, 254f, 304, 328, 354,
        381, 399, 448 n. 24
    Bessmertnykh, view of 342
    Gorbachev's conversation with (1991) 346–7
    Gorbachev's 'theses' (1988) 226
    INF Treaty 216
    Reagan's Moscow University speech (1988) 232
    Saturday breakfast meetings (1983) 84
    SDI and the Reykjavik Summit 179–80
    Soviet specialist on NSC 81–2
    Soviet withdrawal from Afghanistan 152*
    spoof memoranda 172
    support for East-West dialogue 86, 138
    and Thatcher's plea to support Gorbachev 351
    urges Bush to engage with Soviet Union
        (1989) 251
    US ambassador to the Soviet Union 202, 203,
        448 n. 24, 468–9 n. 102
Maudling, Reginald 96
Maxim Gorky (cruise ship) 284
McCarthy, Senator Joseph 16, 22
McFarlane, Robert (Bud) 76, 79, 86, 87, 88, 121,
        137–8, 144f, 146, 148–9, 381, 415 n. 22,
        416 n. 42, 416 n. 44
    National Security Advisor appointment
        82, 83
    resignation 152
    Saturday breakfast meetings (1983) 84
    and SDI 80, 126–7, 141, 142, 150, 180
McLennan, Gordon 262

Medvedev, Vadim 56, 160, 163–4, 165, 199, 220*,
        221, 225, 267, 412 n. 52, 448 n. 93
Meese III, Edwin 67, 74, 75, 82, 84, 85
Meshkov, Aleksandr 168
Methodist Church, US 90, 91
Meyer, Stephen 250
MI6, UK 84, 116, 146
Middle East conference (1991), Madrid 373–4
Mikoyan, Anastas 24, 27, 405 n. 13
military-industrial complex, Soviet Union 47, 49,
        57, 132, 136, 160, 175, 290, 376
    'Big Five' meetings 160
    drain on the economy 177, 302
    influential power within the system 292
    'Little Five' (1986) 160
    opposition to losing any part of Soviet
        Union 344
    unwillingness to give up power and
        resources 296
military industrial complex, US 132, 170
    and SDI 80
    UK and SDI research contracts 141–2
Miller, Chris 433 n. 40
Miller, Ronald 100
ministerial network (Soviet) 317, 433 n. 40,
        458–9 n. 11
Ministry of Defence, Soviet Union 160
    Rust's landing in Red Square 207
    see also Sokolov, Marshal Sergey; Ustinov,
        Dmitry; Yazov, General Dmitry
Ministry of Defence, UK 104, 114, 115, 120
Ministry of Foreign Affairs, Soviet Union 159, 160,
        161, 162, 344; see also Bessmertnykh,
        Aleksandr; Gromyko,
        Andrei; Shevardnadze, Eduard
Mitterrand, President François 2, 106, 145, 223,
        224, 281, 385
    Bush meeting (1989) 271
    German reunification doubts 332
    Gorbachev meetings 144–5, 170, 273, 323f,
        427 n. 13
    Gorbachev relationship 273, 468 n. 88
    reaction to Gorbachev's elimination of nuclear
        arsenals by 2000 156
    response to August coup (1991) 367
    Thatcher meeting (1987) 194
    view on the INF 'zero option' 184, 454 n. 7
Mlynář, Zdeněk 36, 37, 274, 408 n. 17, 408 n. 19,
        425 n. 48
Moldova 347, 372
Molotov, Vyacheslav 13, 15, 35, 405 n. 13, 408 n. 7,
        434 n. 66
Mondale, Walter 79, 88
Mongolia 21
Moore, Charles 91, 103, 104–5, 472–3 n. 48
Moos, Malcolm 132
Morgan, Iwan 414 n. 49
Morgan, Kenneth O. 420 n. 33

Moscow Olympics, US boycott 87
Moscow State University 67
    Gorbachev and 35, 36–8, 57, 231
    Reagan speech (1988) 1, 230–2, 379
Moscow Summit (1988) 222, 225, 226–9, 227f
    final communiqué 228–9
Moscow and Novo-Ogarevo Gorbachev-Bush
    Summit (1991) 355f, 356–8
Moskovskie novosti 345
Moss, Robert 97, 412 n. 42
Mossadeq, Mohammad 218
Mount, Ferdinand 110
Mulcahy, Catherine (Reagan's paternal great-
    grandmother) 59
Mutual Balanced Force Reduction (MBFR)
    talks 268
Mutually Assured Destruction (MAD) strategy 79

Nagasaki nuclear attack (1945) 14
Nagy, Imre 21, 22
Najibullah, Mohammad 221, 257
Nakasone, Yasuhiro 267
Nasser, Gamal Abdel 22
National Guard, California 66–7
National Review 64
National Security Council (NSC), US 73, 99, 105,
    106, 138, 200, 201, 208, 209, 249
    conflict with Shultz 381
    Matlock replaces Pipes as Soviet specialist
        181–2
    Reagan advocates waging economic war on
        Soviets (1982) 108
    Reykjavik Summit (1986) 173, 183
    splits 88, 250
    zero option nuclear arms reduction
        proposals 74
    see also Carlucci, Frank; Clark, William; Matlock,
        Jack F.; Powell, General Colin; Poindexter,
        Admiral John; Scowcroft, Brent
NATO (North Atlantic Treaty Organization) 72,
    97, 98, 108, 197, 218, 293, 338, 349
    'Able Archer' exercise (1983) 83–4, 120
    Brussels summit (1988) 223
    'double zero' atomic weapons reductions 211
    establishment of (1949) 21
    exercises in former Warsaw Pact countries 395
    expanding eastwards 325–8, 395, 396–7,
        460 n. 41, 472 n. 45
    'flexible response' strategy 216
    and former Soviet republics 395
    military parity with Warsaw Pact
        (1970s–1980s) 289
    missiles removed from Turkey (1962) 27
    and Soviet SS-20 deployment 176
    summit (1989) 270
Natto, Alessandro 410 n. 21
Nazarbayev, Nursultan 322, 342, 373
Nazis 34

Neave, Airey 96
Németh, Miklós 271
Neustadt, Richard 308
Neville-Jones, Pauline 462 n. 75
New Thinking, Soviet Union 52–3, 164, 170, 209,
    211, 241–6, 261, 263, 291, 298, 293, 297, 343,
    387, 389–90
    'all-human values' 233, 298
    emergence 289
    'the human factor' 56, 204, 217, 404 n. 13
    new freedoms 236–7, 248, 267–8, 287, 385, 389–90
    'new world order' 243
    'reasonable sufficiency' in defence 164, 291
    universal interests 233, 298, 390
New York Times 199, 359
Nicaragua 282, 284
Nicholson, Martin 192, 439 n. 27, 472 n. 48
Nicholson, Robin 472 n. 48
NIE (1989) notes disagreements among US
        intelligence specialists on Soviet
        change 249
Nikonov, Aleksandr 41, 409 n. 34
Nitze, Paul 26, 67, 171–2, 178, 180, 204, 211
Nixon, Richard 64, 67, 75, 170, 222, 307
    China policy and Mao Zedong meeting 19–20
    Reagan meeting (1987) 208
NKVD, Soviet Union 33
    Katyn forest massacre, Smolensk (1940) 12,
        405 n. 13
Non-Proliferation of Nuclear Weapons Treaty 151
Nott, John 103, 104
Nove, Alec 114*, 115*, 125*, 193–4, 193*, 259, 296
Novo-Ogarevo meeting of Gorbachev, Yeltsin and
    Nazarbayev (1991) 357
Novo-Ogarevo process (9+1 talks, 1991) 348, 373, 374
Novotný, Antonín 23
Novy mir 41
nuclear weapons, *see* individual weapon systems
    and arms control agreements
Nunn, Senator Sam 183, 201, 472 n. 45

Obama, Barack 27*
Obolensky, Aleksandr 256
Odom, General William 203
Ogarkov, Marshal Nikolai 176
Ogonek 259, 259*
O'Neill, 'Tip' 142–3, 381, 429 n. 49
Ordonez, Fernández 387
O'Regan, Michael (Ronald Reagan's
    great-grandfather) 59
Orlov, Yuri 172
Ormsby-Gore, David 26
Orwell, George 94, 94*, 304
OSCE 337*, 397; *see also* Conference on Security
    and Co-Operation in Europe (CSCE)
O'Sullivan, John 4, 293
otkrytost (openness) 188
Owen, David 111–12, 411 n. 38

Oxford University 90, 91, 93
Oxford University Conservative Association
    (OUCA) 92
ozone layer 400

Palazchenko, Pavel 139f, 211, 212, 223, 229, 242–3,
    267, 268–9, 327, 328, 355f, 357, 461 n. 67
Palmerston, Lord 52, 411 n. 31
Pankin, Boris 369, 371
Parada, Petr (Raisa Gorbachev's maternal
    grandfather), arrest 32
Parkinson's Law (C. Northcote Parkinson) 41
Parsons, Anthony 110, 111, 113, 113*, 114*, 120
Patman, Robert G. 454 n. 5
Pavlov, Valentin 317, 340, 344, 351, 357, 365, 366
    attempt to curb Gorbachev's powers 352, 353
Pell, Senator Claiborne 183
Pelshe, Arvid 41
People's Democratic Party of Afghanistan
    (Afghan Communists) 45–6
perestroika 4, 71, 47, 48–9, 101, 136, 161, 163, 210,
    218–19, 234–5, 244, 249, 252, 253, 255, 261,
    263, 274, 282, 288, 298, 300, 301, 303, 341,
    345, 354, 393, 457 n. 40,
    impact in Eastern Europe 237
    meaning of 219*
    media and TV during 304
    new freedoms 234–5, 295–6, 304, 389–90
    resistance to reform 219–21
    Thatcher and 190–5, 263, 275
Perle, Richard 52, 74, 77, 99, 103, 131, 138, 141, 155,
    156, 178, 428 n. 24
Perry, William J. (Bill) 14, 25, 27, 28, 166, 292,
    293, 396
Pershing II ballistic missiles 72, 214
    deployment in Western Europe 73, 198
Pertini, Alessandro 50
Petrakov, Nikolay 319, 345, 456 n. 39
Petrov, Stanislav 28–9
Petrushenko, Colonel Nikolay 340
Piatashvili, Dzhumber 264
Pierce, Samuel 71
Pilgrims' Society 98
Pipes, Richard 67, 74, 81–2, 381, 382, 399, 427 n. 11,
    472 n. 45
Plekhanov, Yury 363–4
Plokhy, Serhii 373, 376
Poindexter, Admiral John 152, 155, 168, 183, 184,
    185, 186, 200
Poland 4, 271, 297–8
    Committee of National Liberation 12
    Communism, end of 267
    Communization 11, 24
    introduction of martial law 107
    legislative elections (1989) 277–8
    NKVD execution of Polish prisoners 12,
        405 n. 13
    political crisis (1980) 24, 406 n. 47
    post-war borders 10, 11–12, 13,

Solidarity movement 23–4, 107, 135
Thatcher's visit (1988) 238–9
unrest after Khrushchev denunciation of
    Stalin 21–2, 39
Politburo, Soviet Union 23, 24, 31, 39, 43, 44, 44,
    45, 46, 53, 54, 55, 56, 57, 122, 210, 263, 274
    Afghanistan withdrawal agreement 221
    Andreyeva article 220–1
    approves broad lines of Gorbachev's UN
        speech 245
    Chernobyl, reaction to 167–8, 435 n. 69
    concern over elections (1989) 255–6
    diminished power (1990) 316, 460 n. 33
    Gorbachev suggests a 'democratic coalition'
        (1990) 322, 339
    Gorbachev's report of Thatcher's visit (1987) 200
    Helsinki Final Act (1975) 20
    post-Moscow Summit meeting (1988) 233
    radical overhaul (1990) 320
    relations with US 81, 182
    Reykjavik Summit (1986), reaction to 182
    selecting Gorbachev 57, 132–3, 294
    support for uncoupling of Soviet missile cuts
        from SDI restriction 190
political culture 50, 256–7, 346
political pluralism 1, 163, 210, 238, 254, 285, 294,
    386, 390, 391, 423 n. 20, 457 n. 57
    China, absence of 298
Pollock, Richard 196f, 197–8, 350, 358f, 440 n. 50,
    471 n. 28
Polozkov, Ivan 322
Ponomarev, Boris 44, 49, 50, 160, 161, 265
Popov, Gavriil 352, 373
Popov, Viktor 51*, 55, 89f
Porton Down, UK 262, 262*
Portugalov, Nikolay 285
Poseidon submarines, US 176
Post, Manning 66
Potsdam conference (1945) 13, 14
Powell, Charles 125, 141, 157, 185, 190, 196f, 259, 272,
    273, 276, 334f, 399, 400, 425 n. 50, 428 n. 24,
    439 n. 25, 463 n. 103
    Chequers discussions with Gorbachev
        (1984) 51, 52
    Chequers seminar on Germany (1990) 330–2,
        461 n. 73, 461 n. 74
    Chequers seminar on Soviet Union (1987) 190–3
    closeness to Thatcher 191–2
    Howe's RUSI speech (1985) 140
Powell, General Colin 77, 78, 138, 208, 209, 216,
    222, 225, 230, 251, 282, 369, 413 n. 14,
    428 n. 24, 441 n. 92
Power, General Tommy 28
Prague Spring (1968) 15, 36, 55, 101*, 117, 161, 276
Pravda 56, 221
Pravda, Alex 114*
Presidential Council, Soviet Union:
    created (1990) 316–17
    disbanded (1990) 322, 339

Price, Charles (Charlie) 152, 232
Primakov, Evgeny 163, 259, 333, 364, 366, 369, 400,
    432–3 n. 35, 464 n. 2
  Gulf War 334, 335
Privolnoe, Stavropol region, Russia 31, 32, 33–4, 35
Prokhanov, Aleksandr 360
Pugo, Boris 339, 340, 340*, 353, 357
Putin, Vladimir 394, 394*
pyaterka system, Soviet Union 160
Pym, Francis 104, 110, 111, 113, 381–2

Quayle, Dan 282–3, 445 n. 77

Rakowski, Mieczyslaw 238
Rasputin, Valentin 317, 360
Ratford, David 192*
Razumovsky, Georgy 264
Reagan, Jack (Ronald's father) 58–9
Reagan (Davis), Nancy 59, 63, 75, 77, 82, 85–6, 109,
    179, 180, 226, 232, 381
Reagan, Neil (Ronald's brother) 59
Reagan (née Wilson), Nelle (Ronald's mother)
    59–60
Reagan, Ronald 1, 2, 4, 19, 20, 34, 50, 52f, 58–89,
    77f, 90, 91, 98, 103, 139f, 144f, 187, 247, 277,
    323, 385, 415 n. 29
  administration internal disagreements 76, 108,
      169–73, 200–2, 206, 377–8
  Afghanistan discussions with Gorbachev 143,
      152, 152*, 157–8, 228
  anti-Communist views and conservative
      credentials 62–3, 64–5, 67–8, 388
  Armageddon, belief in 79, 416 n. 42, 416 n. 44
  arms control and arms reduction 170–7
  assassination attempt (1981) 71, 305
  astrological advice 85–6
  becomes President (1981) 9, 68
  California governorship 66–7
  and Chernenko's funeral 133
  Chernobyl accident 168–9
  childhood and family background 58–60
  Cold War, contribution to ending 290, 306–7,
      397–402
  Communism and CPSU, view of 71–2, 135
  The Day After, reaction to seeing 85
  domestic opposition to improved US-Soviet
      relations (1987) 207–10, 207*
  'dual track' approach 72
  environmental record 82*, 414 n. 49,
      416 n. 59
  Eureka College 60–1
  'evil empire' rhetoric 1, 78–9, 111, 380, 399
  Falklands War 105
  Father Gleb Yakunin meeting (1988),
      Moscow 230
  first term 70–89
  General Electric Theater host 63–4
  Geneva Summit with Gorbachev (1985) 5, 144,
      147–53, 384
  Gorbachev correspondence 136–7, 146–7, 151–2,
      153, 204, 211–12
  Gorbachev relationship 134–5, 182, 217, 269,
      387–8
  Gorbachev's elimination of nuclear arsenals by
      2000 proposal 155
  Gorbachev's 'theses' discussions 226
  Gromyko meeting (1984) 87
  Haig relationship 75
  Hollywood career 61–3
  intellectual limitations 100
  Iran-Contra affair 185–6, 202
  Joint Chiefs of Staff objections to elimination of
      ballistic missiles 183
  KAL 007 destruction 115–16, 422–3 n. 12
  leadership and policy detail 75–6
  'march of freedom and democracy' speech, UK
      Parliament (1982) 379
  marriage to Nancy 63, 180
  Massie, Suzanne, rapport with 86–7, 202
  Moscow State University speech (1988) 1,
      230–2, 379
  Moscow Summit (1988) 219, 222, 225, 226–33,
      227f
  Nixon meeting (1987) 208
  nuclear-free world vision 387–8
  'peace through strength' policy 71, 72, 85, 86,
      258
  political career before presidency 63–9
  Presidential Library Archives, Simi Valley,
      California 59
  relationship with senior aides 74–6
  Reykjavik Summit with Gorbachev (1986)
      173–82, 174f, 182–3, 294
  SDI 51–2, 78, 79–81, 150, 157, 170, 180, 189, 292,
      294, 380
    offer to share with Soviet Union 180–1, 356
    suggestion it not be tested for 10
      years 180
    Thatcher's misgivings on 141–2
    see also Strategic Defense Initiative (SDI)
  Shultz appointment as Secretary of
      State 76–8
  Soviet grain embargo lifted 108
  Soviet human rights arguments 227
  Soviet treaty violation accusations 148
  Soviet Union, commitment to engagement
      77–8, 83, 382
  Soviet-US relations speech (1984) 85–6
  Springfield, Massachusetts speech (1988) 230
  spy scandal (1986) 172–3
  'tear down this wall' speech (1987), Berlin 209,
      313–14
  Thatcher correspondence 145–6, 148–9, 384
  Thatcher meetings
    1975: London 68–9, 97
    1984: Camp David 55, 88, 125–7, 141,
      153, 157
    1986: Camp David 184, 185–6

Reagan, Ronald (*Contd.*)
  Thatcher relationship 70–1, 99–100, 105,
    106–10, 120–1, 124, 126–7, 194, 240, 258,
    378–80, 388–9, 421 n. 67, 424 n. 43,
    471 n. 30
  Thatcher's advocacy of dialogue with
    Moscow 119
  Thatcher's nuclear deterrent stance 184–6
  use of stories and anecdotes 64–5
  Vietnam War support 66
  Washington Summit (1987) 210, 213–17, 215f
  Writers' Club address (1988), Moscow 229–30
  'zero option' nuclear weapons disarmament in
    Europe (1981) 11, 72–3, 74, 99, 155–6, 178,
    184, 215–16, 223, 387
Red Army, Soviet Union 10
Regan, Donald 76, 86, 144f, 152, 399, 415 n. 29
Rentschler, Jim 105
'retrospective determinism' 288, 453 n. 1,
    453 n. 2
Reykjavik Summit (1986) 154, 173–82, 174f, 201,
    205, 387
  'double zero'/'triple zero' proposals 178
  reaction in Moscow, Washington and
    London 182–5
  SDI wrecking agreement 178, 179, 180–1
Rice, Condoleezza, and strategic review of US
    foreign policy (1989) 250
Ridgway, Rozanne (Roz) 152, 158, 204, 211, 229,
    307–8
Ridley, Nicholas 331, 331*
Rifkind, Malcolm 53, 89f, 114*, 123, 378,
    410–11 n. 26, 425 n. 51
Road to Serfdom, The (Hayek) 64, 94
Roberts, Adam 80, 404 n. 1
Roberts, Alfred (Margaret Thatcher's father) 90,
    91, 92, 419 n. 2
Roberts, Beatrice (Margaret's mother) 90, 91
Roberts, Muriel (Margaret's sister) 90–1, 92, 418 n. 2
Robinson, Peter 209, 308
Rockefeller, Nelson 65, 67
Rodgers, Bill 112
Romania 10, 237
  execution of Ceaușescus (1989) 281
Romanov, Grigory 123, 133
Roosevelt, Eleanor 12
Roosevelt, President Franklin D. 3, 10, 12, 62
  spheres of influence in post-war Europe 10–11
  Yalta conference (1945) 12, 13
Ross, Dennis 268, 324, 335
Rowny, General Ed 282
Royal United Services Institute (RUSI),
    London 140
Rukh separatist movement, Ukraine 359, 360
Rusakov, Konstantin 160
Russian Federation, relations with the West
    395–7, 395*
Russian White House 365
Rust, Mathias 206–7, 299

Rutland, Peter 469 n. 117
Rutskoy, Aleksandr 366
  demanding the arrest of Yeltsin, Kravchuk and
    Shushkevich 375
Ryder, Richard 97
Ryzhkov, Nikolay 163, 167, 213*, 220*, 221, 259,
    265, 316, 317, 320, 324, 352, 456 n. 39
  and Chernobyl 168

Sadat, Anwar 46
Saddam Hussein 314, 332, 333, 367
Safire, William 208, 360
  'Chicken Kiev' article 359, 360
Sagdeev, Roald 132, 165
Sakharov, Andrei 135, 189, 196, 252
  return to Moscow 187–8, 437 n. 1
  SDI impeding progress on disarmament 187,
    189, 292–3
Salinger, Pierre 30
SALT II Treaty, *see* Strategic Arms Limitation
    Treaty
Savranskaya, Svetlana 227, 452 n. 141, 460 n. 40
Schapiro, Leonard 95, 108, 433 n. 36
Scharansky, Anatoly (Natan Sharansky) 156
Schlesinger, James 97
Schmidt, Helmut 70
Schöpflin, George 114*
Schweitzer, Peter 456 n. 33
Schweitzer, Major-General Robert L. 74
Scowcroft, Brent 222, 233, 234, 251, 269, 284, 285,
    314, 332, 334f, 349, 355f, 356, 367, 445 n. 77
  differences within administration over
    Gorbachev 239–40, 282–3, 248
  dismisses Gorbachev's UN speech 245–6
  scepticism of Gorbachev's reforms 267–8
Screen Actors Guild, US 62
Security Council (created 1990), Soviet Union 322,
    339, 340
semi-presidentialism 454 n. 8
Seton-Watson, Hugh 95
Shakhnazarov, Georgy 40–1, 161, 199f, 225, 226*,
    259, 294, 324, 342, 361, 393, 412 n. 52,
    464 n. 123
  August coup (1991) 364
  and criticism of Gorbachev in Congress of
    People's Deputies 256
  'dual power' concerns 320
  Eastern Europe memorandum 281*
  German reunification and NATO
    membership 326
  Sovetskaya Rossiya article 220
Shalamov, Varlam 304
Shatalin, Stanislav 319
Shatrov, Mikhail 259
Shcherbakov, Vladimir 354*
Shcherbytsky, Volodymyr 359, 434 n. 69
Shenin, Oleg 296*, 322, 340, 340*, 344
Sherman, Alfred 95
Shestanovich, Stephen 250

shestidesyatniki 409 n. 30

Shevardnadze, Eduard 50, 139f, 160, 195, 199, 247, 259, 265, 292, 302, 308, 320, 324, 327, 328, 371, 393, 401, 428 n. 31
  Afghanistan, Soviet occupation 46, 221, 257
  Baker meetings 249, 251, 254f, 268–9, 275
  becomes leader of Georgia 375*
  Berlin Wall dismantling suggestion 209
  Bush meeting (1989) 282
  clash with Primakov over Gulf War 333, 334
  Congress of People's Deputies elections 255
  Foreign Minster appointment 138, 139–40, 143
  Gorbachev relationship 46, 140, 143, 161–2, 339, 339*
  Howe talks 260–1
  objection to Cheney's 'ultimately fail' remark 269
  Politburo membership 161–2
  resignation 336, 339, 339*, 340–2
  Reykjavik Summit (1986) 173, 180
  SDI, countering and compromise on 165, 190
  Shultz meetings 204, 212, 214
  spy scandal (1986) 172–3
  SS-23s as concession in INF negotiations 296
  START talks 222
  and Tbilsi tragedy (1989) 264

Shikhany facility, Soviet Union 262*

Shtromas, Alexander 432 n. 35

Shultz, George 83, 86, 115, 126, 133, 137, 139f, 153, 156, 163, 210, 229, 239, 241, 247, 258, 296
  battles in Washington 76, 82, 88, 200–2
  CIA's hidebound view of the Soviet Union 169–70
  Chernobyl accident 169
  Cold War, contribution to ending 385, 398–9
  cuts to conventional forces 228
  'double zero' aspiration on nuclear arms reduction 211
  Falklands War 106
  frankness with Reagan and Gorbachev 216–17
  Geneva Summit (1985) 149, 151
  Gorbachev, arms reduction discussions (1987) 205
  Gorbachev ending the Cold War in his UN speech (1988) 242–3, 245
  Gorbachev relationship 206. 228, 245, 381
    1985: Moscow 134
    1987: Moscow 204–6
    1987: pre-Washington summit 211–12
    joint letter in defence of INF Treaty 394
  Gorbachev's reforms 158
  Howe, opinion of 140, 428 n. 36
  INF Treaty, Republican 'Hawks' opposition to 207–8
  INF Treaty and Senate ratification 222, 225
  as key figure in East-West dialogue 291, 306–7, 381
  nuclear weapons, position on 155
  resignation threat 172

Reykjavik Summit (1986) 173, 183–4, 177–8

Saturday breakfast meetings (1983) 84–5, 150, 180, 382

SDI 80, 131, 150, 180, 201
  Shevardnadze relationship 140, 203–4
  spy scandal (1986) 172–3
  and Thatcher 185, 446 n. 96
  US verification reluctance 227–8

Shushkevich, Stanislaŭ 374

Sicherman, Harvey 450–1 n. 110

Silayev, Ivan 366, 371

Simon, Bill 97

Slavsky, Efim 168

Smith, Adam 306, 401

Sobchak, Anatoly 264, 317, 352

Social Democratic Party (SDP), UK 111–12

socialism 135, 200*, 275
  democratic socialism/social democracy 298, 361–2, 470 n. 20
  'socialist democracy' 225
  socialist idea 275

Sokolov, Marshal Sergey 190, 207, 214–15, 299, 361

Solidarity movement, Poland 23–4, 238, 276, 417 n. 20
  inspiration of Wotyła's elevation to papacy (1978) 297–8
  legalization of (1989) 278

Solovev, Yury 254

Solzhenitsyn, Aleksandr 41, 135, 230, 304

South Africa 357–8, 419 n. 17

Soviet Union (Union of the Soviet Socialist Republics, USSR)
  acquisition of nuclear weapons 14
  Afghanistan invasion and withdrawal 24, 45–6, 49, 107, 140, 143–4, 143*, 152, 157–8, 206, 213, 221, 236, 247, 381
  alternatives to Gorbachev 386, 388
  anti-alcohol campaign (launched 1985) 301
  'Children of the Twentieth Congress' 40, 409 n. 30
  Comecon 21
  Constitution (1990) 316
  Council of Minsters replaced by Cabinet of Minsters 322
  'creeping stagnation' (early 1980s) 117–18
  Cuban missile crisis (1962) 24–8, 30, 84, 407 n. 55
  Cultural Agreement with Britain (1981) 102
  cuts of armed forces proposed by Gorbachev 241–2, 245
  Czechoslovakia invasion (1968) 15, 23, 41–2, 49, 107, 197, 200*
  disintegration of Soviet state 318–19, 372–7, 390–1
  dissidents and opposition to the ruling party 135–6

Soviet Union (Union of the Soviet Socialist
    Republics, USSR) (*Contd.*)
  domestic policy ruling group (late 1970s and
    early 1980s) 44–5
  economic problems and projected reforms
    56–7, 162–3, 192, 213*, 269–70, 295–6,
    300–2, 319–20, 343, 351–2, 433 n. 40,
    451–2, n. 134, 456 n. 37, 456 n. 39
  famine, southern Russia (1933) 32
  foreign and defence policy (late 1970s and early
    1980s) 44, 45–7, 57
  grain embargo lifted 108
  Hungary invasion (1956) 107, 197
  ideological change 218–19
  intrastructural dissenters 433 n. 35
  KAL 007 destruction (1983) 28, 422–3 n. 12
  media during perestroika 304
  national question 343–8
  nationalism in Soviet republics 315, 318,
    459 n. 18
  oil and gas revenue decline 301
  pipeline sanctions (1982) 107–8
  political pluralism 254, 285, 386, 390–1,
    457 n. 57
  post-war expansion into Central and Eastern
    Europe 289, 289*
  propaganda/reality gap 36, 37
  religion 118, 423 n. 22
  semi-presidential political reform 454 n. 8
  Sino-Soviet split 19
  spy scandal (1986) 172–3
  Stalinist repression 37
  State Committee for the State of Emergency
    (1991) 363
  state subsidies on food prices 301
  superpower perception 207–8*
  support for UN resolution demanding Iraqi
    withdrawal from Kuwait 335
  'Transition to the Market Conception and
    Programme' report (1990) 319
  Union Treaty 301, 343, 348, 353, 356–7, 359,
    362–3, 374, 391
  US missile false alarms (1983) 28–9
  World War II 10, 33
  see also glasnost; New Thinking; perestroika
'Special Relationship' (UK/US) 70, 122, 124,
    258, 259
Spiljak, Mika 86
SS–18 missiles, Soviet 177
SS–20 missiles, Soviet 72, 73, 175, 198, 214
  deployment 176
SS–23('Oka') missiles, Soviet 211, 214–15,
    270, 295
Stalin, Josif 31, 35, 469 n. 117, 471 n. 31
  and Churchill 3
  Czechoslovakia and the Marshall Plan 17
  death 18, 21, 38, 39
  exposure of crimes 33, 39, 40
  and Greek civil war 11

incorporating Baltic states and Western
    Ukraine into USSR 375, 469 n. 117
  inevitability of war with the West 29, 30
  knowledge of the Manhattan Project 14
  'national in form, socialist in content'
    policy 376
  Poland's post-war frontiers 10, 11–12, 13
  Potsdam Conference (1945) 12–13
  purges 32–3, 41
  renewed repression (early 1950s) 37
  Soviet-style systems in post-war Eastern
    Europe 13
  spheres of influence in post-war Europe 10–11
  support for Chinese Communists 18
  support for Kim Il-sung 18
  Yalta conference (1945) 3, 12, 13, 17
Staravoitova, Galina 368, 368*
Starodubov, General Viktor 156
START talks 87, 205, 211, 214, 217, 222, 241
  signing of START (1991) 356
State Department, US 16–17, 73, 99, 106, 110, 209
  tensions with Defense Department and CIA 76,
    82, 88, 169–70, 201
  see also Armacost, Mike; Baker,
    James; Eagleburger, Lawrence; Shultz,
    George
Stepanov-Mamaladze, Teimuraz 209
Stern, Fritz 330*, 461–2 n. 74
Stone, Norman 330*
Strategic Arms Limitation Treaty (SALT 2)
    (1979) 68, 156, 171, 205, 282
  US ceasing to observe 172, 185
Strategic Defense Initiative (SDI), 'Star Wars' 51–2,
    78, 79–81, 87, 111, 147, 148, 155, 170, 288–9
  and the ABM Treaty 148, 165
  as bargaining chip in negotiations
    131–2, 201
  disagreements with US military establish-
    ment 201
  Geneva Summit (1985) discussions 150
  Gorbachev and 131–2, 150, 151–2, 153, 165–6,
    180–1, 189–90, 293–4
  Howe's speech (1985) 140–1
  limitations 292–3
  Sakharov's condemnation of 187, 189
  Soviet reaction to 51–2, 126, 165, 179, 180, 181,
    189, 223, 228, 292–3
  Thatcher and 126–7, 196, 197, 439–40 n. 43
  wrecking agreement at Reykjavik Summit
    (1986) 178, 179, 180–1
  UK contracts 439–40 n. 43
submarine-launched ballistic missiles
    (SLBMs) 171–2, 181
Suez crisis (1956) 22
summit meetings, *see* Geneva (1985); Reykjavik
    (1986); Washington (1987); Moscow (1988)
  Malta (1989); Helsinki (1990); Washington
    (1990); Moscow (1991)
Supreme Soviet 252, 352–3

Suslov, Mikhail 39, 43, 44
Sutherland, Iain 50, 89f, 123–4

Taft, Robert A. 16
Taiwan 18
Talbott, Strobe 392, 394*, 397
Taraki, Nur Mohammad 45, 46
Tarasenko, Sergey 162, 212, 268, 341
Taubman, William 35
Tbilsi tragedy, Georgia (1989) 264
Teheran conference (1943) 3, 10
Teller, Edward 79–80
Teltschik, Horst 285
Temple-Morris, Peter 425–6 n. 53
Tereshkova, Valentina 259
Thatcher, Carol 98
Thatcher, Denis 53, 69, 89f, 90, 259, 260
    marriage to Margaret 93
    racism 419 n. 17
Thatcher, Margaret 1, 4, 20, 34, 77–8, 77f, 90–112,
        99f, 113–27, 187, 251, 256, 273, 277, 334f, 358f,
        387, 415–16 n. 34
    Andropov's funeral 122
    anti-Communism 53, 94, 95, 96–7, 120, 121, 135
    anti-Soviet speeches 96–7, 97–8, 98–9
    Armenian earthquake aid (1988) 246
    arms control progress (1985) 145–6
    August coup (1991) response 367–8
    avoiding defence cuts (1989) 293
    Baker relationship 239
    belief in Britain as great power 92–3
    Brighton bombing (1984) 127
    Bruges speech attacking the 'Euro-federalist
        project' (1988) 240
    Bush meeting (1989), Camp David 283
    Bush relationship 239, 286, 286*, 332
    Cabinet agreement on East-West engagement
        382–3
    Canada visit (1983) 120
    Chequers seminar on Soviet Union and Eastern
        Europe (1983) 113–18, 113*, 114*, 119–20,
        191*, 382
    Chequers seminar on Soviet Union (1987)
        191–3
    Chequers seminar on Germany (1990) 330–2,
        424 n. 33, 462 n. 74, 462 n. 75, 462 n. 82
    Cold War, contribution to ending 290, 308,
        397–402
    Cold Warrior image 383, 412 n. 42
    commitment to nuclear weapons as deterrent
        99, 108, 145, 149, 155, 157, 184–5, 186, 196,
        202*, 213, 379
    'conviction politician' 91–2, 378–9
    denuclearization fears 222–3
    early life and family background 90–2
    early years of premiership 98–103
    East-West diplomacy (1988) 3–4, 237–40
    ecological/'green' concerns 400, 472–3 n. 48
    elected for second term (1983) 113

    engagement with Soviet Union and Eastern
        Europe 108–20
    Falklands War (1982) 98, 103–6, 110, 111, 121, 197
    Foreign and Commonwealth Office (FCO),
        distrust of 101, 102–3, 114, 120, 195
    foreign policy and defence/intelligence, adviser
        posts created 110–11
    foreign policy influences 94–8
    free market commitment 94–5
    Gdansk shipyard visit (1988) 238
    Geneva Summit (1985), memorandum to
        Reagan 148
    German reunification and NATO membership
        240, 285, 323, 330, 332, 339–3
    Gorbachev, admiration for 126, 133–4,
        385–6, 386*
    Gorbachev correspondence 145–7, 149,
        463 n. 103
    Gorbachev, early assessment of 124–6, 138
    Gorbachev meetings:
        1984: Chequers 5, 50–2, 53, 88, 89f, 124–5,
            126, 191
        1985: Moscow 133–4
        1987: Brize Norton 212–13, 440 n. 50
        1987: Moscow 195–200
        1989: London 259–63
        1989: Moscow 275–6, 451–2 n. 134
        1991: Moscow 350–1
    Gorbachev relationship 3–4, 95, 195 , 125,
        146, 191, 195*, 198, 199–200, 263, 388–9,
        463 n. 103
    Gorbachev's proposal to eliminate all nuclear
        arsenals by 2000 156
    Gorbachev's reforms, support for 275–6, 383–4
    as 'guided missile' 113*
    Heseltine relationship 115, 115*
    Hong Kong agreement 125
    Howe relationship 105, 240, 388, 428 n. 36,
        463 n. 102
    Howe's RUSI speech on SDI (1985), reaction
        to 141, 189
    Hungary visit (1984) 119, 122
    Iron Lady, origin of name (zheleznya dama) 97–8
    Izvestiya interview before Gorbachev's 1989
        visit 258–9
    Jaruzelski meeting (1988) 238
    Kohl meeting (1987) 194
    Labour Party critical of her identification with
        Reagan's policies 381
    leadership style 100, 388
    Mitterrand meeting (1987) 194
    neoliberal, anti-statist views 379, 385
    opinion on 98, 111, 332, 350, 430 n. 33, 465 n. 27
    Oxford University 90, 91, 92, 93
    Poland visit (1988) 238–9
    Primakov meeting before Gulf War 335
    Reagan correspondence 145–6, 148–9
    Reagan meetings:
        1975: London 68–9, 97

Thatcher, Margaret (*Contd.*)
1984: Camp David 55, 88, 125–7, 141, 153, 157
1986: Camp David 184, 185–6
1988: after Moscow Summit 222, 232
1988: Washington 239
Reagan relationship 70–1, 99–100, 105, 106–10, 120–2, 124, 126–7, 194, 240, 258, 378–80, 388–9, 421 n. 67, 424 n. 43, 471 n. 30
resignation (1990) 315, 336–7, 463 n. 102
SDI misgivings and reservations 126–7, 141–2, 148, 153, 197, 439–40 n. 43
Soviet television interview (1987) 198, 200, 304
Soviet visit (1987) 195–200, 196f, 383
START agreement, urging caution 223–4
UK-Soviet relations, domestic support for improving 201–2
UK's nuclear deterrent 145, 149, 153, 157
US Granada intervention, anger over 121–2, 424 n. 41, 425 n. 43
US visit (1975) 97
US visit (1981) 99–100
US visit (1983) 120
as US/Soviet go-between 258
waning influence on East-West relations 314
'zero option' nuclear disarmament 184–5, 189, 223–4
Thomas, Hugh 95, 103*, 108, 114*, 183, 192*
Tiananmen Square, Beijing:
demonstrations 266
massacre (1989) 267, 271, 273, 366
Tikhonov, Nikolay 44–5, 133, 265
Tito, Josip Broz 22
Tomahawk cruise missiles, US 72
'Transition to the Market Conception and Programme' report (1990), Soviet Union 319
Treaty on Conventional Armed Forces in Europe (CFE) 338
Trevor-Roper, Hugh 330*, 331, 462 n. 74
Trident programme, UK 103, 184, 185, 186
Trilateral Commission delegation (1989), Moscow 267
Trotsky, Leon 263
Trudeau, Justin 48
Trudeau, Pierre 47, 120
Truman, President Harry 15, 109, 308
Churchill, suspicion of 12
French colonialism in Vietnam 18
Potsdam conference (1945) 12–13, 14
Stalin relationship 12–13, 14
'Truman Doctrine' 16–17
Trumbo, Dalton 63
'trust but verify' (*doverai no proverai*) proverb 87, 396

Ukraine 254, 343, 348, 354–6, 359–60
December referendum (1991) result 374
independence movement 368, 372, 376
Union of Sovereign States (USS) proposed 373, 374

Union Treaty, Soviet Union 348, 353, 356, 357, 359, 361, 362, 374, 391
published draft (August 1991) 363
United Kingdom (UK):
Cultural Agreements with Soviet Union 102, 102*
expulsion of Soviet officials (1989) 276
nuclear weapons and US/UK 'dual key' 109–10
public protests against missile deployment 73
Reagan's policies, opposition to 381
Soviet pipeline sanctions 107–8, 108–9
UK nuclear weapons excluded from INF negotiations 297
view of US Grenada intervention 121–2
women in government 92
United Nations (UN) 82, 105, 110
Dumbarton Oaks conference (1944) 138
Gorbachev speech (1988) 219, 241–5, 242f
invasion of South Korea 18
resolution demanding Iraqi withdrawal from Kuwait 335
Security Council debate on Falklands ceasefire 105, 106
Suez crisis (1956) 22
United States of America (US):
aid for Chiang Kai-shek 18
atomic bomb test (1945) 14
backing Islamist fighters in Afghanistan 158
Chile, military coup (1973) 218
China policy 19–20
Communist witch hunt 16
Cuban missile crisis (1962) 24–8, 30, 84, 407 n. 55
Europe, US nuclear missile installation 73, 99, 108
Falklands War (1982) 105
Granada intervention (1983) 120–2, 424 n. 41, 425 n. 43
Gulf War (1990–91) 335
Iran-Contra Affair 152, 185–6, 202
Korean War (1950–53) 18
NATO enlargement debate 396–7
opposition to INF Treaty signing 215–16
Soviet missile false alarms (1979) 28
Soviet pipeline sanctions 107–8, 108–9
spy scandal (1986) 172–3
Thatcher's Soviet visit (1987), media coverage 198–9
Trident deal with UK 103
triumphalism after end of Cold War 382–3, 402, 454 n. 2
UK nuclear weapons 'dual key' 109–10
Vietnam War (1965–75) 18, 19, 65
Urban, George R. 95, 317, 330*, 331–2, 459 n. 13
US embassy, Moscow marine spy scandal (1987) 203, 204–5, 206
US-Soviet trade treaty (1990) 328
Uspensky, Nikolay 51, 89f, 369, 440 n. 50

Ustinov, Dmitry 2, 44, 45, 46, 47, 80–1, 81*, 86, 117,
    132, 160, 214, 292
  death 2, 53
  KAL 007 422 n. 12

Vance, Cyrus 20
Varennikov, General Valentin 344, 360, 361, 364,
    365, 368
Velikhov, Yevgeny 50
Vietnam 18–19, 21
Vietnam War (1965–75) 18, 19
  growing opposition to 65
  Reagan's support for 66
Virganskaya, Irina (daughter of Mikhail and Raisa
    Gorbachev) 364, 429 n. 49
Virgansky, Anatoly 364, 367*
Vorontsov, Yuly 175, 202
Voroshilov, Klement 405 n. 13
Vyshinsky, Andrei 13

Wałęsa, Lech 238, 278
Warner Brothers 61
Warsaw Pact 97, 1–2, 98, 209, 218, 237, 276, 395
  dissolution (1991) 295, 348
  establishment (1955) 21
  military parity with NATO 289
  Soviet SS–20 deployment 176
  superiority in conventional forces 241
Washington Summit (1987) 210, 213–17, 215f
Watt, James G. 82, 416 n. 59
Weatherill, Bernard ('Jack') 124
Webb, Sydney and Beatrice 404 n. 2
Webster, William 208
Weinberger, Caspar 52, 52f, 67, 74, 77–8, 82, 83, 86,
    99, 105, 156, 381
  clashes with Shultz 76, 88, 169, 202
  Gorbachev's proposal to eliminate all ballistic
    missiles 171–2
  resignation (1987) 208, 211
  Saturday breakfast meetings (1983) 84
  SDI 126, 127, 201, 228, 439 n. 43
  views on Gorbachev's reforms 224
  'zero option' policy 72–3, 74
Weizsäcker, Richard von 272
Wendt, Alexander 455 n. 11
West Germany, see Germany, Federal Republic
  of (FRG)
Western literature in Russian translation
    40–1, 304
Whelan, Eugene 47
Whitefield, Stephen 458–9 n. 11
Whitelaw, William 96
Williams, Shirley 111, 411 n. 38
Wilson, Duncan 101
Wilson, Harold 104
Witness (Chambers) 64
Woerner, Manfred 396
Wolfson, David 100
Wooding, Norman 125*

'Word to the People' article Sovetskaya Rossiya
    360, 363
World Bank 346
World Marxist Review 161
World War II 10, 33–4, 90, 92, 124
Wotyła, Cardinal Karol, elevation to the papacy
    (1978) 297; see also under John Paul II
Wyman, Jane 62, 63

Yakovlev, Aleksandr 50, 51, 56–7, 89f, 165, 199, 225,
    244f, 253, 259, 265, 266, 292, 302, 320, 324,
    339, 346, 371, 393, 410 n. 14
  Afghanistan 257
  Andreyeva's Sovetskaya Rossiya article 220, 221
  August coup (1991) 366
  Chernobyl accident 167
  election to the Congress of People's Deputies
    (1989) 255
  head of Department of Propaganda appoint-
    ment (1985) 137, 304
  IMEMO director 48–9
  Kryuchkov's attack 353
  out of favour with Brezhnev 47–8
  perestroika 298–9
  Twenty-Seventh Party Congress (1986)
    159–60, 163
  uncoupling Soviet missile cuts from SDI 189–90
Yakunin, Father Gleb 230
Yalta conference (1945) 3, 12, 13, 17
Yanaev, Gennadiy 340, 340*, 342, 357, 365
Yasin, Yevgeniy 319, 320
Yavlinsky, Grigory 319, 371
Yazov, General Dmitry 207, 241, 257, 268f, 299,
    352, 353, 357, 365, 366
Yeltsin, Boris 235, 270, 340, 343, 347, 349, 359, 370,
    391, 393–4, 394*
  9+1 talks (1991) 348
  August coup (1991) 365–8, 393
  banning CPSU and Russian Communist
    Party 372
  Bush meeting (1991) 349
  clash with Central Committee (1987) 210, 211
  condemns use of force in Lithuania 345
  cuts in Soviet budget and economic
    reform 373–4
  'détente' with Gorbachev (1990) 319–20
  elected President of Russia (1991) 352
  Gorbachev and Nazarbayev meeting (1991),
    Novo-Ogarevo 357
  NATO enlargement 396
  political comeback (1989) 254
  popular appeal (1990) 255, 318
  prime aim to replace Gorbachev 315–16
  role in break-up of the USSR 319, 374–5
  supremacy of Russian law over Soviet law 315,
    458 n. 6
  undermines Gorbachev's Japan diplomacy 349
  Twenty-Eighth Party Conference (1990),
    walking out 321

Yugoslav Communists 11
Yugoslavia 10, 237
  break-up 391

Zagladin, Vadim 49, 50, 87
Zaikov, Lev 176
Zakharov, Gennady 172
Zalygin, Sergey 230
Zamyatin, Leonid 50, 51, 122, 260,
  354*, 368
Zarechnak, Dimitry 254f, 355f

Zaslavskaya, Tatiana 56
Zaykov, Lev 160
zero option nuclear arms reduction proposals
  11, 72–3, 74, 211, 155–6, 178, 184, 215–16,
  223, 387
Zhao Ziyang 266, 267
Zhirinovsky, Vladimir 352
Zhivkov, Todor 281
Zimmermann, Warren 131
Zoellick, Robert 324
Zubok, Vladislav 298